THE COMPLETE BOOK OF GAMES

Other Books by the Same Authors:

GAMES FOR TWO

LET'S HAVE A GOOD TIME TONIGHT: AN OMNIBUS OF PARTY GAMES

PARTY GAMES FOR GROWN-UPS

CONTRACT BRIDGE FOR BEGINNERS

THE COMPLETE BOOK OF GAMES

BY

CLEMENT WOOD & GLORIA GODDARD

ILLUSTRATED WITH OVER ONE HUNDRED DIAGRAMS

GARDEN CITY BOOKS
GARDEN CITY, NEW YORK

The authors wish to express their indebtedness to Bernard S. Mason and Elmer D. Mitchell for the use of material from ACTIVE GAMES AND CONTESTS published by A. S. Barnes and Company in the section on outdoor games in this book.

Printed in the United States
At the Country Life Press, Garden City, N.Y.

CONTENTS

The Euchre Group

Miscellaneous

The All Fours Group

The Hearts Group

Two-Ten-Jack

The Rummy Group

Cassino

The Stops Group

Miscellaneous Play-Off Games

The Patience or Solitaire Group

The Cribbage Group

B.—SHOWDOWN GAMES

LIFT SMOK	E	•		•	•	•											304
Faro . Stuss,				•		•	•		•	·	•	•	•	•	•	1	305
LANSQUENE	T										•						309
MONTE BA	NK,	, 01	RS	SPA	NIS	н	Mo)N]	ſΕ		•	•	•			•	310
THREE-CAR	DI	Mo	N	ГE													310
Commerce												•		•			311
My Bird S	ING	s;	01	R, I	Иv	SI	HIP	SA	ILS			•		•			312
Speculatio	N											•		•			312
BLIND HOO	KE	¥, (OR	Du	JTC	н	BA	NK				•					313
RED DOG, O	R F	HIG	H	-CA	RD	Pe	DOL										313
HAVANA																	314
PUT AND T	AK	Е															316

BOOK II

OTHER SPECIAL EQUIPMENT INDOOR GAMES

DICE AND MILITARY GAMES	•	•	•		319
Васксаммон					322
How to Score Backgammon Plays,					328a
Playbackgammon, Duplicate Backgammon, Russian Backgammon, 329 Tabard Backgammon, 329 Parcheesi, 330	7.7 (38) (38)	(†) (†) (†)			328a
CHESS	•	•	•1 •1 •1	11 • •	330
CHECKERS, DRAUGHTS	•			•	337
German Draughts, Damenspiel, Minor Polish	D	rai	lgh	ts.	341

BOOK III

PARTY GAMES FOR ADULTS AND JUNIORS

II. *Alphabet Games*

INITIALS	•	•	•	•		(/ *	•	•	440
Grab on Behind, Alpha and Omega							3.51		441
Alphabetical Adverbs Mary Jones Came to Town, 442	•	•	•	•	•	•			441
INITIAL ANSWERS	•	•	10 14 10 10 10 10	•		•	·		442
INITIAL QUESTIONNAIRE			•						443
NEVER SAY IT		6.			1.2				443
Mrs. Pettigrew's Tea Our Cook Doesn't Like Peas, 444 The G Man Never Takes His Eas		• 444	•				í. 		443
Rнумінс Том		ей (Со	•	•	•		•	•41) •	444
Zoo	uni S	14 . 1	•	•	•	•	·	·	445
Sing and Skip	•	na) Dil	•	•	our de	•	•	•	445

III. Games for the Clever

HIDDEN TREASURES									446
TREASURE HUNT			•	•	•				447
BIG GAME HUNT				•					447
HUNTSMEN AND HOUNDS Hens and Chickens, 448									
Cobweb Treasure Hunt Cobweb, 448	- 10A	0	•	•	•	•	•	÷	448
Blind Pig	•	•				•			448

IV. Guessing Games

V. Stunts and Gags

Reading Sentences, 511 Reading the Globe, 512

VI. Hilarious Games

SARDINES	•	•	•	•	•	•	•	•	•	•	•			•	•	•	512
Balloon Footh Balloon Pu Balloon Vo Egg Footb	shb	all, 7 B	all		13	•	•	•	•	•	•	•	•	•	•	•	513
Getting Your	Nu	ME	BER														513
Wнo's Got тни Catch the						•	·	·	·	·	·	•	•	•	•		514
NAME ME												•		•			514
ORCHESTRA .																	514
WHO, SIR, I, Si The Prince														•		•	515
DUTCH BAND																	515
KAZOO ORCHES	TRA																515
THE CAT AND	THE	c D)og								•	•	•				516
Don't Laugh																	516
JACK'S ALIVE .																	517
Fizz Buzz, 517 Fizz-Buzz,			•	•	•	·	•	•	•	•	•	÷	•	•	·	·	517
Gossip																	517
VENTRILOQUISM																	517
POISON PENNY																	518
Нот Ротато .																	518
DUCKS FLY .																	518

UNCLE JOSHUA	•	•	•	•	•	•	•									3	519
Do and Add .					•					•					•		519
Fox, Gun, Man			•	•	•	•	•	•			•						520
I WENT TO THE	Cr	TY	•														520
Том Тнимв.			•		•							•					521
Proverbs			•					•		•	•	•	•			•	521
SHOUTED PROVER Singing Prov	RBS ver	bs	, 5	22	•	•	•	•	•	•	4	•	•	•	•	•	521

VII. Indoor Athletics

BLIND TOM OBSTACLE RACE								537
WALKING THE PLANK						•		537
BLINDFOLD BOXING MATCH Blindfold Swat, 537	•	 •		•				537
SCRAMBLED SHOES	•	 •					n o	538
BUTTON YOUR COAT			•			•	•	538
STANDING BROAD GRIN								538
"Do This" Race					•			538
MECHANICAL DOLL RACE					•	•		539
Legs Crossed Race								539
Скав Race								539
Freeze								539
RABBIT RACE								539
MUSH RACE, WHIPPET RACE					ei.	9		539
Ротато Race							1	539
HOP HURDLE								540

VIII. *Mixers*

IX. Dances

X. Children's Games: Indoors

XI. Holiday Games

II. The Tennis Group

III. The Football Group

IV.	The	Hockey	Grout

HISTO	DRY												,		•	•			711
FIELD	Носк	EY						0					•	•		•			712
ICE 1	Hockey										•		•				•	•	716
	osse . Lacrosse Box Lac					72-	4	·	•	•	•	•	1.0	•	•	•	•	•	720
Polo	 Wheelba	arro	• w :	Pol			7	•	•	•	•	•	•	•	•	•	·		725
	tev Kei Hockey				ses	, 7:	27	•	•	•	•	•	•	•	•	•	•	•	727
(NY . Roller S Charley- Shinny 2	Ho	rse	P	olo	, 7		•	•	•	•	•	•	•		•	•	•	728
STICE	k Polo							•									•		729
FLOO	R Hock	EY										۰					•		729
Broo	м Носи	KEY																	730
Roll	ER-SKAT	re F	Io	CKI	EY			•											731
HANI	носки	EY									•			•					732
Mass	FIELD	Ho	ск	EY															733
Kon	ANO .	•	•	•		•	•	0	•	•	11. 1. 1. 1. 1. 1. 1. 1. 1. 1. 1. 1. 1.	•		•	•	•	•	i	733

V. The Basketball Group

BASKETBALL					135
Basketball for Women, 738					
Bucketball, 738					
Hobble Bucketball, 739					
Keep-Ball, Keep-Away, Pig, 739					
Ten Catches, 739					
Guard Ball, 739

VI. Other Outdoor Games

VII. Track and Field Events

VIII. Personal Combats

IX. Miscellaneous Games and Contests

X. Water Sports

XI. Horseback Games

XII. Winter Activities

XIII. Children's Games: Outdoor

FOREWORD

A GAME means any amusement or sport, any frolic or play. Man, like all the higher animals, is a gaming animal; witness the gambolings of monkeys, cats, dogs, lambs, horses, and many more. All work and no play makes Jack a dull boy, and Jill a perfect dud; and the human race, as a whole, is made up of neither dullards nor duds. Animals play without formal rules, in rough and tumble boisterousness. Human play began so, continues so, and only slowly were strict and solemn rules evolved for such earth-shattering contests as a Masters' Tournament in Bridge or Skat, a World Series in Baseball, a Rose Bowl game of Football, a Heavyweight Boxing Championship, a Derby or the Olympic Games. The same admirable solemnity presides today over a Horseshoe Pitch for the championship of Jukes Center, a Pie-Eating contest in Kankakee, or a Seidel-Downing meet in Milwaukee.

Any trial of one's ability is a test. When more than one person is tested, and the results are matched and compared, this is a contest. A physical or mental contest, with set rules, for amusement, recreation, or to win a stake, is called a game; games include, as well, contests without set rules. There are three great groups of games:

I. Showdown Games, in which each contestant exhibits his best, whether physical, mental, or determined by chance, without interference from any other contestant. Examples are:

Card Games: Poker, Black Jack, Faro, Havana, Red Dog.
Indoor Special Equipment: Craps, Keno, Bagatelle, Crag.
Party Games: Hidden Words, Treasure Hunt, Card Toss, Identifications, Pun Questionaires.
Athletics: Track and Field Events, Bowling, Golf.

II. Playing Games, in which one or more opponents interfere with the trial of ability. These call also for more strategy and deception, and provide more opportunities calling for choice between several lines of action. Examples are:

Card Games: Whist, Bridge, Euchre, Skat, Pope Joan.
Indoor Special Equipment: Backgammon, Chess, Checkers.
Party Games: Word Squares, Ghosts.
Athletics: Tag, Boxing, Wrestling, Tennis, Baseball, Croquet, etc.

III. A group combining both preliminary playing and subsequent showdown:

Card Games: Bezique, Pinochle.
Special Equipment: Mah Jongg.
Party Games: Stagecoach, Categories, Rhyming Tom.
Athletics: Horseshoe Pitching, Quoits.

Games may be primarily games of skill, or primarily games of chance. Many games combine both elements, in varying degrees. Chess and Checkers are games of skill; Craps, of chance; Backgammon, most card games, of both. Games may be between individuals or groups, the latter being teams, competing together or in relays, in successive individual competition.

It is uncertain which came first, the playing games or the showdown games. Certainly the play of most animals is of the playing type, although the solemn strut of the peacock or turkey cock to win the female's favor is showdown, and not playing. What is more certain is that games commenced as youthful efforts to imitate adult life's business: as in a girl's playing with dolls, or a boy's trials and contests with weapons. We shall find that the two great sources of card and indoor special equipment games are an invocation to the god of chance, and a symbolized military struggle. Party games add to this imitation of life's other businesses, from wooing and marriage to the affairs of daily life; and athletic games range from simple physical showdown contests to the most complicated military games. In games, we may relive the career of an Alexander, a Napoleon, or the finder of Captain Kidd's treasure, with a small stake or a prize replacing the guerdons of life or death. Life can never be dull when we are equipped with the ancient and recent lore of this book, and spread it to the game-hungry world.

Special thanks are due to Eugene Reynal, Freeman Lewis, Robert de Graff, Hubert S. Juergens, Charles H. Stringer, Albert E. Richardson, Winifred Walsh, Belle R. Harrison, Leonard Thomas, Andrew Edson, Harvey Roberts, and Roger Young; to the editorial staff of A. G. Spalding and Brothers; as well as to many more, for their assistance in compiling this omnibus of games. It is dedicated to

EDMOND HOYLE

our greatest predecessor in the same fascinating field.

GLORIA GODDARD.
CLEMENT WOOD.

Bozenkill, N. Y.

PREFACE TO THE THIRD EDITION

THE healthy American desire for fun and amusement, coupled with the educational value of many indoor and outdoor games, is shown by the fact that the first edition of this omnibus of all man's games was snapped up like the proverbial hot cakes.

Meanwhile, in these few months games history has been made. The history of chess was pushed back a thousand years, when a set of terra cotta chess men, 6,000 years old, was discovered by the Pennsylvania Museum Expedition at Tepe Gawra, Northern Iraq, Mesopotamia. The present year has been marked by the sudden emergence of Five-Suit Contract Bridge, and the invention of Playbackgammon or Duplicate Backgammon. Six-Man Football is sweeping the country. The danger of party games was illustrated when the Mayor of Portland, Oregon, on January 2nd, sat balanced on a milk bottle, feet outstretched, and tried to write his name on a piece of paper. When the bottle broke, three stitches were taken in the Mayor's side. Rubber or unbreakable milk bottles are recommended for this stunt in the future.

If you do not find your favorite game here under the name you know it by, search further, and it will be found under some other name. Most important of all, to all readers of this book: the editors will thank you for sending in at least one new or omitted game, to keep this the world's standard game book.

For this enlarged and improved edition additional thanks are due to Eric Almquist, Bert Lippincott, Sarah Biddle, Willard L. Kauth, Dixie Russell, Wister Bennett, Fred Lape, Henry Abel, Anna Herrick, Max Daum, Wallace Hudgins, and Louis Stoddard. Especial thanks are due to A. S. Barnes & Co., and to Bernard S Mason and Elmer D. Mitchell, for permitting the use of material from their *Active Games and Contests*.

GLORIA GODDARD.
CLEMENT WOOD.

Bozenkill, N. Y.

BOOK ONE

CARD GAMES

THE ORIGIN OF PLAYING CARDS

PLAYING CARDS originated in the Orient, in remote antiquity. They were designed to teach military strategy to young nobles. Instead of the single warfare between a Red and a Black army, as represented in chess, checkers, and backgammon, cards have two differing red armies and two differing black ones, permitting intricate military maneuvers and conflicts. Red and black were the colors chosen, because these were the first two colors recognized by man.

In India, cards have been traditional from time immemorial. The legend there is that they were invented by the Brahmans. The invention of the game is also attributed to the ancient Egyptians. A Chinese dictionary of 1678 says that they were originated in China in the reign of Sèun-ho, about A.D. 1120, to amuse the emperor's concubines; which would indicate that they spread eastward into China long after their origin in India or Egypt. Their unequalled popularity as a game of chance is due to their superiority over other game symbols, chess, checker and backgammon men, dominoes, dice, and so on, when it comes to handling, shuffling, dealing, and playing. Chess, checkers and backgammon remain games for two players; cards, with their four armies, are fitted for larger groups.

Playing cards probably reached Europe through the Moorish invasion of Spain, or through the return of the Crusaders from their sojourn in the Near East. A 1328 French romance inveighs against the folly of such games as "Dice, Checkers and Cards," indicating a use of cards for many years before then. Cards were well known in Italy in 1379, a manuscript of that year indicating that they came from the land of the Saracens and were called

Naib. A 1392 entry in the registers of the *Chambres des Comptes*, providing for the payment of fifty-six sols of Paris to the painter Jacquemin Gringonneur for three packs of cards in gold and various colors, and ornamented with several devices, to carry before King Charles VI of France for his amusement, indicates the growing popularity of cards. A Parisian edict of 1397 prohibited people from playing "tennis, bowls, dice, cards on working days." In 1404, the Synod of Langres forbade card-playing to the clergy. In 1415, the Duke of Milan had a deck of cards painted on pieces of ivory. In 1423, St. Bernard of Sienna preached against cards with such effect that the people "brought their cards, dice and games of hazard" and burnt them. The National Library of Paris has fifteen Venetian tarot cards dating back to 1425. Saints were used as the designs on cards early in the 15th century. By 1441, Venice laid a high tax on the importation of foreign playing-cards, to encourage the Venetian manufacture of them.

The Morgan Library possesses thirty-five tarocco (modern, tarot) cards painted late in the 15th century for Cardinal Ascanio Maria Sforza, probably painted by Antonio Cicognara of Cremona. There were seventy-eight tarocco cards in the deck, comprising four suits of fourteen cards each (the numeral cards, numbered from one through ten, and four coat or court cards, King, Queen, Chevalier, and Valet) and twenty-two trump (corrupted from *triumph*) cards, numbered from one through twenty-one, with the last one unnumbered. The trumps represented such personifications as Force and The Priestess, while the numeral suits represented such occupations as Herding (symbolized by shepherds' staves), Agriculture, and so on.

Modern playing cards developed directly out of tarots. The twenty-two trump cards were eliminated, but many card games preserved the trump idea by having some suit selected as trumps. One of the four court cards of each suit was also eliminated, perhaps to provide an odd number of tricks. At first this was the Queen, the remaining court cards being King, Chevalier and Knave (or Jack). Italy restored the Queen and discarded the Chevalier; and this is now universal. A fifty-third card, the Joker or Mistigris (F. *mistigri*) came in as a blank or special card which could be used as any other card. It represented the court jester, who could assume without rebuke any rôle he chose. Originally the cards were all one-way full-length cards. Some unknown genius recently invented the double-headed card.

On early German cards, the suits were Hearts, Bells, Leaves, and Acorns. These were soon replaced by Swords, Batons, Cups and Money, representing the military forces, the officials, the clergy, and the merchants. In the 16th century in France, the suits were *Cœur* (hearts), *Tréfle* (a three-lobed object, such as a clover-leaf, misinterpreted as our Clubs), *Pique* (akin to our word "pike," now Spades), and *Carreau* (a tile, misunderstood as our Diamonds). The French suit-name for clerics (*gens de chœur*) had already been corrupted to *Cœur,* or hearts; the Spanish *Espada* (swords) became mistranslated as Spades.

The court cards all differ slightly from each other. The face of jovial Henry VIII of England is preserved on all four Kings. The four suit symbols are to the right of the Kings. The Diamond King has a battle-axe to his left, and is in profile. The other three Kings are full-faced, the Heart and Club facing right, the Spade facing left. The Heart King has a sword held in his left hand behind his head; the black Kings, both left-handed, hold swords vertically. Only the Heart Queen has her symbol to her right. Two Queens face right, and two left. Each holds a flower above her left shoulder; but their robes differ. Only the Spade Jack has his suit symbol to his right. The Heart and Spade Jacks are profiles looking left, the other two full-faced, the Diamond looking left, the Club right; the four tokens of office that they hold differ. All of the court cards differ markedly from deck to deck.

PRELIMINARIES TO ACTUAL PLAY

The Preliminaries to each card game are approximately the same. The general rules given here apply to all card games, unless the description of the particular game points out divergences.

The Draw or Cut for Deal.—One shuffled deck is spread face downward on the table, and each player draws one card. A player must draw again if he exposes more than one card, or draws one of the four cards at either end of the deck. A drawn card must not be exposed until all have drawn.

Low as a rule wins choice of decks and seats, and the right to deal first. Ace usually ranks low in cutting—the ace standing historically as the lowest pip card in the suit. In case of a tie, the cut is repeated until the tie is broken. In many games, the suits are equal in rank; in other games, as in the bridge group, Spades today rank highest, Hearts next, Diamonds third, and Clubs lowest.

In certain games, the cards are dealt one at a time face upward, and the first Ace, or first Jack, etc., wins choice of decks and seats, and the deal or right to play first.

Drawing for Partners and Precedence.—Where more than the proper number of players offer, a preliminary draw is made from a shuffled pack, and the four highest (or, in some games, the four lowest) become the first table. Where partners are to be selected by the draw, the two highest of those selected become partners, and also the two lowest. It is customary to repeat the draw for partners before each rubber or group of games.

In the bridge group, high and not low wins the cut for deal, Ace ranking highest of all.

The Shuffle.—As a rule, each player has the right to shuffle the deck, the player to the left of the Dealer first, then in rotation left to right, and the Dealer last of all. In many games, only the player to the right of the Dealer shuffles. While he is shuffling, the Dealer's partner shuffles the still deck, and places it on his right for the next hand.

The Cut.—Cards are cut by the player to the Dealer's right. In cutting, at least four cards should be left in each pile. As a rule, the cards should be cut once only, the top pile being placed toward the Dealer, the bottom pile toward the player cutting. The Dealer then brings the bottom pile toward him, to place it on the top pile.

New Shuffle and Cut.—Any player, before the deal commences, may demand a new shuffle and cut if the cut is not made by the proper player; if less than four cards are left in either portion; if the face of a card is shown in cutting; if any other player than the Dealer completes the cut; if there is doubt as to the exact place of the cut or which was the top portion; if any player shuffles the cards after the cut; or if the cut is made before the play of the preceding hand is completed.

The Deal.—The cards as a rule are dealt in rotation, one or more to each player, from left around to the Dealer, with or without additional stop hands between the player to Dealer's right and the Dealer.

Misdeals.—The rules covering misdeals are approximately the same for all card games. In general, a misdeal does not lose the deal; the cards are collected, shuffled, cut and dealt again by the same player.

It is a misdeal if the cards are not dealt in regular order, as each game requires, giving to each player the proper number of cards in the hand, in rotation left to right, the Dealer last. It is a misdeal if any card is found faced up in the deck, or is dropped and exposed during the deal. It is a misdeal if the wrong person deals; in that case the cards are shuffled and cut and the right person deals. It is a misdeal if the wrong deck is used. It is a misdeal if the deck is found to be incomplete or imperfect, before the play of the hand is finished. It is a misdeal if the cards are not offered for a shuffle or cut, or if the cut portions of the deck are not properly reunited.

If, after the deal has been completed, one hand is found to have too few or too many cards, it is not a misdeal if the missing cards are located in the room in which the playing takes place; unless they are found in such a place as to make it probable that they were not dealt, in which case it is a misdeal. If one or more hands are more than normal in number and one or more under normal, the custom is for those lacking cards to draw the requisite number from the hands with more than the proper number, sight unseen.

Where less than all the cards are dealt out, an insufficiency in any hand may be corrected by adding the necessary number from the balance of the deck, called the stock.

CLASSIFICATION OF CARD GAMES

Card games may be divided into Playing Games, in which hands are dealt and played; and Showdown Games, in which hands are dealt and shown, and not played. Major sub-classifications are:

A.—Playing Games

I. To win tricks, bonuses, premiums, penalties, etc.

1. Hand of thirteen cards.
   Whist and Bridge, all varieties; Boston; Vint, etc.
2. Hand of five cards.
   Euchre, all varieties; Five Hundred; Hasenpfeffer; Skat; Spoil Fives; Napoleon, all varieties; Écarté.
3. Other games.
   Preference; Grand.

II. To gain or avoid counting cards in play, including melding.

1. To gain counting cards.
   Solo or Sluff, all varieties; Sheepshead; Cassino.
2. To hold or win counting cards.
   All Fours or Seven Up, all varieties; Cinch, all varieties, including Sixty-three.
3. To win counting cards, and meld others.
   Bezique, all varieties; Pinochle, all varieties, including Gaigel; Piquet; Evansville Clabber; Sixty-six, all varieties.
4. To avoid taking losing cards.
   Hearts, all varieties; the Four Jacks.
5. To take counting cards and avoid taking losing cards
   Two-ten-Jack.
6. To meld the most cards.
   Authors.

III To get rid of cards, primarily.

1. By melding or assembling, etc.
   Rum, all varieties; Coon-can or Conquian; Panguingue.
2. By playing off in sequence.
   Pope Joan; Michigan; Fan Tan; Go Boom; Desperation; I Doubt It; Stung.
3. By pairing until odd card is left.
   Old Maid.

IV. Solitaire Games: by playing or rearranging to go out, in some way.

1. Solitaire for two or more players: Russian Bank; Double Klondike, etc.
2. Other Solitaire games.

B.—Showdown Games

I. Showdown of five cards.
   Poker, all varieties.

II. Showdown of less than five cards.
   Red Dog or High Card Pool; Havana; Monte Bank; Faro; Stuss.

III. Showdown for color, red against black; and matching pips.
   Put and Take.

IV. Successive showdown to arrive at a definite number of pips.
   Cribbage; Black Jack or Twenty-One, including Farmer, Macaa, Baccarat, Chemin de Fer, Seven and One-Half.

A.—PLAYING GAMES

THE WHIST GROUP

History

Whist, a card game for four players, was developed from a 16th century game called *Trump,* which in England was elaborated into *Ruffs and Honors,* the immediate parent of Whist. After being popular for almost a century, it was described fully in the 1734 *Compleat Gamester, for the Use of Young Princesses,* by Richard Seymour, Esq. Each player was dealt 12 cards of a 52-card deck. The 49th card was faced up on the remaining 3 of the stock for the trump. Whoever held the Ace of trumps could "ruff," or take in these 4 cards, discarding in their place any four he chose. Honors were the Ace, King, Queen and Jack of trumps. Seymour recommends methods of stealing a glance at your opponents' hands, and of signaling your partner, by finger or eye, what honors you have. He explains further how an on-looker can signal, by fingers placed against the pipe he is smoking, and by comments. Such methods permitted a player to describe to his partner, by a spoken or gestured code, his entire hand. This explains the altered name of Whist; "the very name implies, Hold your tongue," says Seymour.

Whisk, first mentioned in the 1674 *Compleat Gamester* of Cotton, was played with a deck of 48 cards, the 4 deuces being discarded. The 48th card was turned up for the trump. The name came from the swift whisking up of the tricks. It was replaced by *Whist,* meaning "Silence!"

Swabbers, a variation, was played as early as 1680. The Swabbers were the heart Ace, club Jack, and the Ace and deuce of trumps

The persons to whom these were dealt received a certain share of the stake, independent of the play for tricks and honors.

Whist had the deuces restored to the deck in the 18th century, permitting the odd trick. The *Short Treatise on the Game of Whist,* attributed to Edmond Hoyle, appeared in 1742. This emphasized the probabilities at various stages of the rubber. *Boston,* an American variation, is said to have been introduced into Paris by Benjamin Franklin about 1767. By 1810, *Long Whist,* which required 10 points to win, was replaced by *Short Whist,* requiring 5 points. In America, honors were disregarded, and the play was for the tricks alone. Turning the trump from the still deck is still known in Europe as *Prussian Whist. Dummy Whist* came in, when only three players were available; and *Double Dummy,* when only two. The French game of *Mort* is merely Dummy Whist, with improved scoring.

In *Cayenne,* the Dealer and his partner had the privilege of changing the trump from the suit turned up. In *Bridge,* they named the trump suit without any facing of a trump card, and played the hands as at Dummy. In *Boston* and *Boston de Fontainebleau,* the trump is made instead of being turned, and the number of tricks to be played for is announced; a call of No Trumps is permitted; and certain hands may be "spread," without allowing the adversaries to call the exposed cards. *French* and *Russian Whist* are simply variations of this. *Solo Whist* simplifies Boston, and eliminates the spreads.

Scotch Whist added the objective of catching the ten of trumps, it and the 4 former honors having especial values attached to them. This can be played by two to eight players, a small number of players having several hands apiece, which are played in rotation. *Humbug Whist* is Double Dummy with certain privileges of exchanging hands dealt to players for their dummies; and in which Dealer may make the trump sometimes to suit himself.

German Whist is played by two players, permitting the refilling of the hand after each trick is played by drawing from the stock, until it is exhausted. *Chinese Whist* is complicated Double Dummy for two, three or four players, with half of each player's cards exposed, and the concealed cards faced up one at a time as the exposed cards are played. As early as 1897, R. F. Foster predicted that Mort or Bridge was destined to supplant old-fashioned Whist. The world followed the prophet.

By 1905, Bridge was the dominant Whist type game in England; by 1914, *Auction Bridge* was coming in. Bridge scoring (Spades, 2; Clubs, 4; Diamonds, 6; Hearts, 8; and No Trumps, 12) was used in Auction Bridge. But already *Royal Auction Bridge* had brought in the "new count," with Spades, 2; Clubs, 6; Diamonds, 7; Hearts, 8; Royal Spades or Lilies, 9; and No Trumps, 10, the honors being multiples of these values. Meanwhile *Nullos* had been introduced, permitting players to contract to lose tricks at No Trumps, scoring 10 for each overtrick so lost. By 1926, *Contract Bridge* came in as an innovation, and within a few years it had become the leading world game in the Whist group. Already *Contract Whist* is being suggested to replace it.

CONTRACT BRIDGE

Equipment: Two full decks of 52 cards each, preferably with backs of different colors.

Rank of Suits: Major suits, Spades (highest), Hearts; minor suits, Diamonds, Clubs (lowest).

Rank of Cards: Ace (highest), King, Queen, Jack, 10, 9, down to 2. Ace is also high in the cutting.

Object: To win the highest score, by taking tricks constituting the contract, and by scoring for overtricks, bonuses, and penalties.

Preliminaries.—The chapter on Card Games describes the cut or draw for partners, the shuffle, and the cut. The two highest play against the two lowest, high having choice of seats and decks, and becoming Dealer. At times, a second draw for Dealer is made. Dealer deals the entire deck in rotation, left to right, starting at his left, one card at a time, until each player has a hand of 13 cards. These are usually then arranged in suits by the players.

THE BIDDING OR AUCTION.—The bidding for the right to declare the trump suit then commences, passing in rotation from the Dealer to the left. The four players compete as partners in the bidding. Each player must bid or pass up his right to do so. Four passes before any bid is made results in the deal passing to the left. A bid indicates how many tricks the bidder contracts to take, above the first 6 tricks (called the book). Bids may be from 1 to 7, the denominations ranking No Trumps, Spades, Hearts, Diamonds, and Clubs, the lowest.

When a bid is made, the next player must pass, overbid, or double. An overbid must consist of the same number of tricks in a higher ranking denomination, or more tricks in the same or a lower ranking denomination. A double affects trick and other values and penalties. The succeeding player must then pass, overbid, double, or redouble the opponent's double. Any bid can be doubled only once, and any double redoubled only once. Whenever three players in rotation have passed any bid, double, or redouble, that becomes the contract; and the first namer of the trump suit for the winning side becomes the Declarer.

THE PLAY.—In the play, the Declarer, playing both his and his partner's hand, plays to make his contract against the defense of the two opponents, called Defenders. The Defender to the left of the Declarer leads any card of any suit. The Declarer's partner then exposes his hand (formerly termed the Dummy), usually arranged in suits, and the Declarer then plays from this hand. It is always required to follow suit if possible. If impossible, a player may trump, or throw off (discard). Each four cards played in rotation constitute a trick. A trick is won by the highest card in the suit led; unless it is trumped, in which case the highest trump wins. The winner of each trick leads to the next trick.

When a trick is ended, it is quitted, that is, turned over and faced down on the table. Quitted tricks must be so placed that the players may see at a glance how many tricks have been taken by each side. It is usual for the Declarer to rack together his first six tricks, constituting his book. The round ends when the 13th trick has been quitted; and it is then scored.

The player to the Dealer's left deals the next round: and so on in rotation.

THE SCORING.—

New International Code (Effective March 31, 1935)

	Suits			
	♣	♦	♥	♠
Each trick over 6: If doubled, multiply by 2; if redoubled, multiply by 4	20	20	30	30
	No trump			
	1st trick	each subsequent trick		
	40	30		

Overtricks:	Not Vulnerable	Vulnerable
Undoubled, each	Trick Value	Trick Value
Doubled, each	100	200
Redoubled, each . . .	200	400
Slams:		
Little Slam	500	750
Grand Slam	1000	1500

A Little Slam means taking 12 out of 13 tricks; a Grand Slam, taking all 13 tricks.

Vulnerable means having won one game toward rubber, which is the first two games won by either side.

Honors consist of the Ace, King, Queen, Jack and Ten, in a suit bid; or the 4 Aces, in No Trumps.

Honors: if held in one hand { Four honors 100, Five honors 150, Four Aces, at no trump . . 150

Penalties:	Not Vulnerable Undoubled	Not Vulnerable Doubled	Vulnerable Undoubled	Vulnerable Doubled
1 Down . . .	50	100	100	200
2 Down . . .	100	300	200	500
3 Down . . .	150	500	300	800
4 Down . . .	200	700	400	1100
5 Down . . .	250	900	500	1400
6 Down . . .	300	1100	600	1700
7 Down . . .	350	1300	700	2000

If redoubled, multiply the doubled values by 2.

GAME.—Only the value of tricks above the book of 6 actually contracted for and made, or this value doubled, or doubled and redoubled, counts toward game, and is scored *below* the line. All other scores, bonuses and penalties are scored *above* the line. Score for tricks over the book is called score below the line; any other score, bonus or penalty is called score above the line. A score of 100 points below the line constitutes game. All tricks made over the contract count as overtricks, and are scored above the line. No partial score below the line toward game can be carried over to the next game. A rubber is two out of three games; that is, the first two games won, whether opponents win any game or not.

Rubber Premium: If made in 2 games, 700; if made in 3 games, 500. If unfinished, winner of one game, 300. Revoke: 2 tricks for the first revoke, 1 trick for each subsequent revoke. No tricks made before revoke can be claimed for penalties. No penalty for revoke made on 12th trick.

How to Bid

The experienced player will develop his own system of bidding, or will rely upon the Culbertson, Sims, Four Aces, Official, or some other system. The beginner can start much more simply. Bids are based upon the expectation of taking so many tricks above the book, that is, above the first 6 tricks. For an opening bid of the first or second hand, when the side is non-vulnerable, a 2½ quick trick value is needed; in the third or fourth hand, 3. When vulnerable, add ½ quick trick value to each of these. Quick trick values are computed thus:

	Quick tricks
Any A-K	2
Any A-Q, A-J-10, or K-Q-10	1½
Any A, K-Q, K-J-x, or K-x and Q-x in different suits .	1
Any K-x, Q-J-x, or Q-x and J-x in different suits . . .	½

x represents any card below the 10. A minimum biddable suit is a 4-card suit with at least 1½ honor tricks, or slightly less in minor suits; or a 5-card suit with at least ½ quick trick value; or a 6-card or longer suit. Each additional quick trick value of 1 justifies one additional later bid.

The responding hand, to raise once in the suit bid, should have at least Queen-x-x or 4 small trumps in the trump suit, and a total quick trick value of 1½. With a quick trick value of 1½ and inadequate trump support, he should bid his longest biddable suit. Lacking a biddable suit, he should bid No Trumps. Each additional quick trick value of 1 justifies an additional raise. In general, the lowest response to a bid of 1 is a bid of 2 in the same suit; the next lowest (as showing no biddable suit), a bid in No Trumps; the best raise at a non-jump level, a bid of another suit. It is important to keep the bidding open, even when the quick trick value is slightly shaded under the requirement; for a partial contract toward game is of small value, since most games are made in one contract. It is more valuable, however, to make a safe partial contract than to fail to secure one of higher value and incur penalties.

Where the side has a partial score toward game, any bid by either partner above the needed level to win game is an invitation to arrive at a Slam contract.

Bids which conventionally force partner to bid include:

An opening bid of 2, which requires 5½ tricks.
If responding player has 1½ quick tricks, he raises or bids in another suit; if he has less, he bids 2 No Trumps, a complete denial. Some require the bidding in this case to be kept open until a game contract is reached. Others accept the 2 No Trump response as a sign off, and are content to try for a contract below game.

A jump bid of 1 more than necessary by responding hand; or a jump bid of a second suit by first bidder.

An overcall in an opponent's suit. This usually means that the overcaller guarantees to take the first trick only in the opponent's suit: either by holding the Ace, or by having a failure, which can be trumped.

An opening bid of 1 No Trump usually calls for 4 to 4½ quick tricks. The adage is, Anything can happen to a No Trumper.

Suit bids are usually much safer. A No Trump bid should preferably have protection in at least three suits. Single protection consists of Ace, King-x, Queen-x-x, etc. In a suit bid by opponents, there should be at least double protection, or No Trump should not be bid.

An opening bid of 3 in any suit indicates that the hand is suitable only to be played in that suit; and it should not be raised unless the responding hand sees a prospect of game.

An unforced bid or jump to game (3 No Trumps, 4 in a major suit, 5 in a minor suit) is a shutout, and should not be raised by the partner unless he sees possibility of a slam—6 being a Little Slam, 7 being a Grand Slam. A forced bid to game is the same as any other bid, and is not a shutout.

After the opening bid, an opponent's bid need not guarantee quite as much strength as an opening bid. In general, the best defense to a No Trump bid is to play it, since it may result in large penalties. Doubles are wise only when they will not tend to drive the opponents into a better contract.

A double of 1 No Trump or up to 3 in a suit forces a bid from partner, if he has not bid. This is called an informatory double, and calls on partner to name his longest suit, preferably a biddable one; the responsibility being on the doubler. A double above that level is regarded as a business or serious double, and should be left alone unless responding partner is assured of going game or slam.

A 4 No Trump bid, where either partner has opened the bidding, is forcing, requiring partner to respond. It guarantees 3 Aces; or 2 Aces and a King. A jump to 5 No Trumps, not preceded by a 4 No Trump, is similarly forcing, guaranteeing 3 Aces and a King in a suit bid by one of the partners. It indicates a Little Slam probability, and a Grand Slam possibility.

How to Lead

The opening lead, where partner has indicated by bidding a suit, usually should be the highest card in that suit, to avoid blocking: however, the player who opens may lead a suit which he desires to establish. Later leads in partner's suit should be of the highest card held at the time. Where No Trumps is the contract, and no suit has been named by partner, open with the fourth from the top of your longest suit; unless it is headed by three touching honors, in which case lead the highest. In a suit bid, if you hold Ace-King and other cards in a suit, it is well to lead the King before leading your partner's suit, to show him your possession of the Ace for a reentry. From a bare Ace-King, lead Ace and then King, showing your partner you can ruff (trump) the third round. Otherwise, lead King from Ace-King-x etc., and also from King-Queen-x etc.; and Queen from Queen-Jack-x etc. A lead of a singleton is sometimes wise, to indicate you wish the suit returned, to ruff it; even a lead of a doubleton is proper, when it does not include an honor.

It is usually wise for the Declarer to lead out his trumps first, and then establish his longest suit in the two hands, protected by the remaining trump length. In No Trumps, his effort is to establish the suit of which he has the most cards in the combined hands; a 6-3 distribution being preferred to a 5-4 one. Be sure to arrange for reentries in the hand which holds the largest number. When the contract can only be won by double ruffing, trumps should not be led out by the Declarer.

After the first lead, the Declarer's partner's hand goes down on the table face upward, and this alters the knowledge of all three players as to where 13 cards are. The third hand should usually play his highest card on the opening lead, unless it is a discouragement card (9, 8, 10 etc.) which denies possession of any of the high cards in the suit; or a King, clearly led from an Ace-King or King-Queen; or unless the card is clearly a taker, all higher cards being in the exposed hand. Third hand should then usually return his partner's lead, unless the play indicates that this is unwise. If, however, he can lead his own takers and thus set (defeat) the contract, it is often wisest to do this before returning partner's lead.

How to Play

The object of Declarer is to make the contract, with such overtricks as he can; of the Defenders, to set the contract. It is better to make a contract than to gamble on overtricks and go down one or more.

A lead to a finesse may be made when the Declarer has in his or his partner's hand a tenace (as, Ace-Queen, King-Jack, Queen-10, etc.), with one of the Defenders holding the missing honor. The Declarer leads low to the lower of these, uncertain where the intervening card is. If it lies to his left, he takes 2 tricks; if to his right, 1; averaging 1½ by taking the finesse. If he leads immediately to the higher card, he usually takes only 1 trick. Of course, if the intervening honor is played by the player on his left, he at once takes with his ranking card, and is assured of 2 tricks.

A force is made, for instance, when the Ace is in his partner's hand, and the Queen in his own. It is always incorrect to lead the Queen toward the Ace. In this case, if the King falls, the leader makes only 1 trick; if the King does not fall and the leader lets the Queen ride, the King on the right takes it, and thus the leader takes only 1 trick. Let him lead low from the Ace toward the Queen, and, as in a finesse, he takes on the average 1½ tricks from the combination. If the leader has the Jack as well as the Ace and Queen, he should force—that is, lead Queen or Jack toward the Ace or Ace combination; and then he makes 2½ tricks on the average.

Additional Contract Bridge Laws

Information as to Calls Made.—During the bidding any player, when it is his turn to bid, may have the entire bidding reviewed.

Claiming a Penalty During Bidding.—Any player may call attention to an irregularity in bidding, when made. He may ask his partner if he knows his rights, and give or obtain information as to the law covering the irregularity. Such questions must be settled before further proceeding. A penalty paid or an action taken stands, though later discovered to be in error.

Slips of the Tongue.—A player may correct a slip of the tongue without penalty. He may not correct a mistake or change his mind.

Improper Call Overcalled by Opponent.—When an improper call is overcalled by the player next in rotation, and before the non-offending side calls attention to it, the bidding proceeds as though the improper call had been properly made.

Insufficient Bid.—Unless overcalled as above, an insufficient bid must be made sufficient in the same or another suit or No Trumps. If the offender makes the lowest sufficient bid in the same suit, his partner must pass on his next turn; if some other bid is made, his partner must pass throughout the entire bidding

Incorrect Double.—Unless overcalled as above, doubling a bid not as made is considered a double of the bid made, and the offender's partner must pass in his next turn. Double or redouble of a bid which a partner has already doubled or redoubled forces the offender and his partner to pass during the remainder of the bidding.

Call Out of Turn.—Unless overcalled as above, a proper call out of turn is cancelled, and the player whose turn it should have been to call has the next call. If this is before the first bid, the offender must pass, at his first turn; if at any other time, his partner must pass during the rest of the bidding.

Cards Faced, Seen or Disclosed.—During the bidding, if a player faces (exposes) a card on the table, or sees the face of one of his partner's cards, or reveals by a remark a card in his hand, such cards must be left faced up during the bidding. If the owner becomes Defender, the Declarer may forbid the opening of such suit or suits, or may treat them as penalty cards. If the card is of honor rank, or there are at least two of them, the owner's partner must pass during the rest of the bidding.

New Deal During Bidding.—If a player picks up another's hand and looks at it, or holds more than the proper number of cards while another player has less, or if the deck has the wrong number of cards or any duplication, there must be a new deal by the same dealer.

REVIEWING THE BIDDING.—Before the opening lead, any player may ask to have the bidding reviewed. After the opening lead, a player may only ask what the contract is, and whether doubled or redoubled.

CALL DURING PLAY.—If a Defender makes a call other than a pass after the bidding is closed, the Declarer may call a lead from the other Defender, when it is his turn next to lead.

PLAYED CARD.—A card is played by the Declarer from his own hand when it touches the table; and from the faced hand when he touches it, unless for purpose other than play. A card is played by a Defender when his partner sees its face after it has been detached from his hand with the apparent intent to play. A card is played by either Defender or Declarer when he names it as the card he intends to play.

WITHDRAWING A PLAYED CARD.—A player may not withdraw his played card except to correct a revoke (see below), or when directed by the application of a penalty.

PLAYER UNABLE TO PLAY AS REQUIRED.—When unable to play as required to comply with a penalty, a player may play any card, subject to the requirement to follow suit, and the penalty lapses; in the case of a penalty card, for the current trick only, the penalty card remaining still exposed as a penalty card, subject to the rule concerning penalty cards.

LEAD OUT OF TURN.—A lead out of turn may be treated as a correct lead, if, before it is withdrawn, the other side plays to it. In all other cases, a Declarer's lead out of turn may be required to be corrected, by leading a card of the same suit from the correct hand. If by a Defender, the Declarer may treat the card as a penalty card, call the lead from the other Defender if he won the previous trick, or from the Defender who next wins a trick, if it was the Declarer's lead. If both Defenders lead at the same time, the correct lead stands, and the other card becomes a penalty card.

PREMATURE PLAY BY DEFENDER.—When a Defender plays to a trick when it is his partner's turn to play, the Declarer, if he has not played both cards, may require the other Defender to play to the trick his highest or lowest card in the suit led; and, if he cannot follow suit, may specify the suit he is to play.

Premature Lead by Defender.—If a Defender leads to the next trick before his partner has played to the preceding one, the same penalty applies. If the offender does not win the current trick, he has led out of turn to the next trick.

Playing Before Penalty Named.—In this case, the penalty may still be exacted; the card so played being regarded as a penalty card. If the non-offending side plays after the offender, before the penalty is named, the right to enforce the penalty is lost.

Corrected Revoke.—If a player revokes—that is, fails to follow suit when he has a card of the proper suit in his hand—and corrects his error by withdrawing the revoke card before the revoke is established, he must substitute a correct card. If the revoke card belongs to a Defender, the Declarer may treat it as a penalty card, or require him to play his highest or lowest correct card; if it belongs to the Declarer, it may be taken up and, if the Defender to the Declarer's left has played, he may require the Declarer to play his highest or lowest correct card. A revoke from the Declarer's partner is put back without penalty. A card played by the non-offending side after the revoke and before its correction may be taken back.

Establishing a Revoke.—A revoke becomes established when the offending side leads or plays to the next trick. The trick then stands as played. A revoke cannot be made from a hand legally faced; or if it is claimed or attention called to it after the cut for the next deal; or, if made in the last hand of a rubber, after the rubber score is agreed. A trick so transferred, as penalty for an established revoke, is regarded in scoring as a trick won in play.

Settling a Revoke Claim.—Tricks and unplayed cards may be examined at the end of play to settle a revoke claim. If, after such claim, an opponent mixes the cards so that the claim cannot be established, it must be allowed.

Information as to Cards Played.—Until a trick has been quitted, a player may require the players to indicate which cards have been played from their respective hands.

Inspecting Quitted Trick.—A quitted trick may be inspected without penalty before the end of the hand only if there is a difference of opinion as to which hand won it; if it is found to have an incorrect number of cards; or if it is necessary to turn it to substitute a correct card. The penalty for inspection other than above is 50 points for the opponents, scored above the line.

Directing Partner's Attention to Trick.—If a player directs his partner's attention in any way to a trick, without request, the Declarer or the Defender on the left of the Declarer's partner, as the case may be, may require the offender's partner to play his highest or lowest card of the suit led; and, should he be unable to follow suit, to play a specified suit.

Claim or Concession of Tricks by Declarer.—If the Declarer claims or concedes one or more of the remaining tricks, or implies such claim or concession, he must leave his hand face up on the table, and state specifically how he will play each card in his two hands, and play them so. He may not take any finesse not announced at the time of the claim. Cards exposed as a result of his declaration do not become penalty cards. If both defenders abandon their hands, this allows the claim or concession; but an exposure of cards does not constitute abandonment.

Claim or Concession by a Defender.—A claim or concession by a Defender is only valid if the other Defender agrees.

Tricks Conceded in Error.—If a side concedes a trick which it could not lose by any play of the cards, this concession is void.

Declarer's Partner.—Declarer's partner forfeits all his rights by looking at the face of a card in a player's hand. Otherwise, he may reply to a player's proper question; discuss questions of fact and law, when requested; and draw the Declarer's attention to a Defender's irregularity, and ask the Declarer whether he knows his rights. These are all his rights; he does not rank as a player. If he suggests, by touching or otherwise, the play of a card, the Defender on his right may require the Declarer to play it or not, unless it would constitute a revoke. If he, without request, informs the Declarer which hand has the lead, the Defender on his left may choose the hand from which the Declarer must lead.

Claiming a Penalty During Play.—Same rule as for a penalty during bidding.

Penalty Card of a Defender.—If a Defender drops a card face up on the table, sees the face of his partner's card, or discloses a card by a remark, this becomes a penalty card, and as such it must be left faced up until played. Subject only to the requirement to follow suit, the Defender who owns it must play it at his first opportunity. If he has two or more penalty cards, the Declarer may specify which should be played at any time it may properly be played.

New Deal During Play.—During the play, if the deck is found to be imperfect, or the deal has been imperfect, there must be a new deal by the same dealer with a perfect deck or the same deck properly dealt. When the surplus card is due to failure to play to a trick, this must be played to, preferably with a correct card. If the player has played to a later trick, his side forfeits one trick. If the missing card is found and was apparently not dealt, there must be a new deal. If properly dealt and it has caused a revoke, the penalty cannot be more than two tricks. If a quitted trick contains more than four cards, and there is uncertainty as to source, the Declarer or the Defender on offender's left, as the case may be, may direct which card is to be restored to the deficient hand of the other side.

Scoring.—A side which fails to make its contract can score only for honors held in one hand.

Correction of Score.—Established errors in trick points, including errors in counting the number of tricks taken, may be corrected before a call is made in the next hand; or, if in the final hand of a rubber, before the rubber score is agreed upon. Established errors in premium points or in addition or subtraction may be corrected before the rubber score has been made up and agreed. Scores made with an imperfect deck stand, if the discovery is not made until after the cut for the next deal is completed, or the rubber score agreed upon.

CONTRACT WHIST

Contract Whist is a combination of Contract Bridge and Whist. Down to the actual play of the hand, the game is identical with Contract Bridge. Thereafter, it differs. There is no Dummy, the Declarer's partner playing his hand in the same manner as the other players. All laws concerning the Declarer's partner as Dummy are automatically cancelled. Scoring and rules are the same as in Contract Bridge.

MAYONNAISE, GOULASH

In both Contract and Auction Bridge, when all four hands pass a deal, certain players at once insert a hand of Mayonnaise. The sorted hands are piled in rotation, the Dealer's last. The deck is cut once. The cards are then dealt 5, 5, and 3. Bidding and play proceed as usual. Mayonnaise produces extraordinary hands, and frequently results in Slam bids.

Goulash is the same game, played without the cut. This permits more knowledge of what cards you have given your partner and your opponents.

Passing Goulash is the most thrilling variation. The deal is as in Mayonnaise, the piled deck being cut. Each player then passes four cards to the player on his left. The effort is primarily to build up length and strength in some one suit, while holding on to Aces and other tops. Each player then passes four cards to the player on his left a second time. The third time, each player passes four cards to his partner, at the same time receiving four from him. Unless a hand has slam possibilities, it is sometimes wisest to pass your four highest to your partner. Bidding and play now proceed as in Contract Bridge. Slam bids are almost inevitable.

THREE-HANDED CONTRACT, or CUTTHROAT

This is Contract Bridge played by three players, two playing as partners against the one who becomes the Declarer. The highest in the draw becomes the Dealer; the next highest sits at his left, and the lowest at his right. The player to the left of the Dealer shuffles, while the player to the right shuffles the still deck for the next hand. The player to the Dealer's right cuts.

Twelve cards each are dealt in rotation, left to right, to four hands: Dealer's left hand opponent, Dummy, Dealer's right hand opponent, and Dealer. A widow of 4 cards is left faced down in the center,—the purpose of the widow being to equalize the tendency to overbid slightly. The 12 cards in Dummy are exposed, and the bidding takes place as in Contract, each player seeing 24 of the cards he will control if he becomes Declarer. The successful Declarer takes the seat opposite Dummy. He takes the widow, and distributes these 4 cards, face down, one each to the four hands. After the hand is played, the Declarer resumes the seat he won on the draw. A rubber is the first two games won by any player, and may therefore require two, three or even four games.

Bidding and play are as in Contract Bridge. Each game won scores 250, with a 500 bonus for rubber. Both opponents score for their joint undertricks, penalties, honors, etc. Honors are scored as in regular Contract. The only penalty for an insufficient bid is that it must be made sufficient. An out-of-turn call, if one player calls attention to it before his call, scores 100 for him; if both players call attention to it, 50 for each. Any call, except a pass, after the bidding is closed, scores 100 for the Declarer. The laws concerning exposed cards, revoke, and so on, are the same as in regular Contract.

HONEYMOON BRIDGE

The best two-handed Contract Bridge is Honeymoon Bridge. In this, after the draw, shuffle, and cut, four hands of 12 cards each are dealt as in Cutthroat, and a widow of 4 is left in the center. One dummy is exposed, and one kept face down. Bidding may be based on a player's hand in combination with either the faced dummy or the concealed one, the player stating which as he bids. The first bid from each player must be the lowest bid possible in the suit named; on the second round, the bid can go as high as the combined hands justify. When the contract is arrived at, the Declarer takes the widow and distributes the 4 cards, one to each of the four hands, as in Cutthroat.

An important difference in the scoring is that the penalty for undertricks is a double penalty: the regular Contract Bridge penalty for undertricks, plus the trick value for the undertricks, scored below the line for the Defender. This is a brake on reckless bidding; for a persistent overbidder thus often pushes the Defender into game and then rubber. When played for stakes sufficiently high, this double penalty feature may be eliminated, the penalty for undertricks being scored as in regular Contract.

One Dummy Exposed.—Honeymoon Bridge may also be played without the widow, the Declarer dealing four hands of 13 cards each. Otherwise, it is the same as Honeymoon Bridge.

STRIP HONEYMOON BRIDGE

The first object in Strip Honeymoon Bridge is to build up a powerful hand of 13 cards, by taking or failing to take the first 13 tricks, which do not count toward the score. After the draw, shuffle, and cut, 13 cards are dealt face down, one at a time, to each player. The next card on the stock (the half of the deck remaining undealt) is faced. Without bidding, the non-dealer leads any card. If the faced card is high, or fits into his hand, he leads to take it; if undesirable, he leads low, hoping to lose it and get the card concealed beneath. This stage of the game is played at No Trump, and following suit is not required. The highest card in the suit led takes the trick. The winner of each trick takes the exposed card, and leads to the next trick; the loser takes the card beneath. As each preliminary trick is quitted on a trash pile, the Dealer then faces the top card on what is left of the stock, and the play continues until the stock is exhausted, each player now having a final hand of thirteen cards.

Bidding, play and scoring thereafter proceed as in Honeymoon Bridge, except that there are no widow and dummies. Each trick consists of only 2 cards.

SIX-FACED BRIDGE

In this two-handed Contract, four hands of 13 cards each are dealt. In each dummy, 6 cards are exposed, and 7 concealed. Bidding and play then continue as in regular Honeymoon Bridge, each player specifying which dummy he bids on, at each bid.

Six-Faced Bridge with a Widow.—This game may also be played with a widow of 4 cards, distributed after the contract is arrived at by the Declarer, as in Honeymoon Bridge.

SOLITAIRE BRIDGE

One of the best methods for a player to improve his game is to deal and play all four hands, bidding and playing each as if no other hand but the dummy were exposed. This should be scored by naming the hands South (the player), West, North, East, in rotation; or 1, 2, 3, 4; the deal, etc. passing as in regular Contract.

DUPLICATE CONTRACT BRIDGE

In Duplicate Contract Bridge, each deal is played over at a later period by the same players, with the hands played by the Declarer and his partner played by the Defenders, and vice versa; or by the other two couples of two teams of four players, with the hands shifted as above; or by other competing couples. Each deal is played as a unit; there is no play for rubbers. The scoring is the same, except that there is a premium of 50 for making a contract less than game; one of 300, for game when the side is non-vulnerable; and one of 500, for game when the side is vulnerable.

The cards are shuffled, cut and dealt as in regular Contract. Bidding is the same. The cards are not played to the center, but are played before each player, with cards faced down vertically or horizontally, to indicate which side took each trick. At the end each hand is collected separately. The hands are then placed in envelopes marking precisely where they lay on the table—usually marked arbitrarily South, West, North, and East, South and North being partners, and East and West; or are slipped into trays especially prepared for the purpose, marked with these designations. One-fourth of the trays are marked Neither side vulnerable; one-fourth, North and South vulnerable, East and West not vulnerable; one-fourth, East and West vulnerable, North and South not vulnerable; and one-fourth, both sides vulnerable.

For a social evening, 16, 24 or 32 deals or trays may be played. After an interval, the trays may be shuffled, and the same deals played back in a different order, with the former North-South pair playing the East-West hands, and vice versa, and the final scores totalled to ascertain the winners. One pair plays all the North-South hands the first half of the evening, and all the East-West hands the second half of the evening. Or the play-off may occur on some later evening.

Contract Bridge tournaments are often conducted with Duplicate Contract, the rules and scoring being much more intricate. Match points are awarded, based on the North-South scores only; and on the East-West scores only. A pair which betters any score on a deal in its direction is scored one; one which ties, one-half. Individuals score the match points awarded to the pair. Teams ordinarily score similarly. In Howell pair play, the pair having the greatest number of match points wins. In Mitchell pair play, separate winners are declared from the North-South group, and from the East-West group.

PROGRESSIVE CONTRACT BRIDGE

In Progressive Contract Bridge, popular for bridge parties, the tables are numbered, and two couples are assigned to each. Four deals are played at each table, and each is scored separately. Thus there can be no rubber score. The scoring is the same as in Duplicate Bridge. At the end of each round of four deals, the winning pair at Table 1 remain, and the losers move to the lowest table. At all other tables, the losers remain, and the winners move up one table. At each progression, the visiting lady at each table becomes the partner of the gentleman who remains.

Sometimes the first deal is played as if neither side were vulnerable; the second, as if the Dealer's side were vulnerable alone; the third, as if the other side were vulnerable alone; and the fourth, as if both sides were vulnerable. In any case, the player with the largest plus for the evening wins. Usually six or seven rounds are played.

PROGRESSIVE RUBBER BRIDGE

Progressive Rubber Bridge is an interesting variation of Progressive Bridge. Usually 30 minutes or eight deals is allowed for a round. The scoring is the same as in ordinary Contract Bridge, except that 300 points is allowed for a game won by one side toward rubber, when the other side has not won a game.

PIVOT CONTRACT BRIDGE

Four or five players at a table may use the pivot method. The players draw, and from highest to lowest may be called A, B, C, D, and E. With four playing, the partners would be: A and B against C and D; A and C against B and D; A and D against B and C. With five playing, A and B against C and D; A and C against B and E; A and D against B and E; A and E against C and D; B and C against E and D. Each round may consist of four deals, in which case it is scored as in Progressive Bridge; or of a rubber, in which case it is scored as in Rubber Bridge.

FIVE-SUIT BRIDGE, EAGLE BRIDGE, ROYAL BRIDGE or QUINTRACT

EQUIPMENT: Two full Five-Suit decks of 65 cards each. The fifth suit, usually green, is called Eagles or Castles in the United States, and Royals in England.

Rank of Suits: No Trumps, Eagles, Spades, Hearts, Diamonds, Clubs (lowest.)

Rank of Cards, and Object: the same as in Contract Bridge.

History.—Five-Suit Contract Bridge was invented during 1937 in Vienna by a scientist, Dr. Marculin, and reached the United States from England, with the fifth suit copyrighted as Royals. The Eagle suit, originally blue, not green, was derived from an eccentric eight-suit deck invented during the American Civil War, the three other suits being Shields, Stars and Flags.

Preliminaries.—The deal is as in Contract Bridge, except that 16 cards are dealt to each player. The 65th card is dealt face up on the table, as a Widow or Kitty card, to be awarded to the successful bidder. When the contract has been arrived at and the opening lead made, the Widow card must be placed by Declarer in his own hand, his partner's exposed hand, or must be rejected. If placed in Declarer's partner's hand, one card is discarded from this, and is placed with the cards in the first trick, when it is quitted. If the Widow card is placed in Declarer's hand, he must make a similar discard, which must be exposed to all the players, before being similarly quitted. Such a discard can neither be played, nor aid in the scoring.

Bidding and Play.—Eight tricks (not six) constitute the book. Bids may be from 1 to 8. Play continues until all sixteen tricks have been quitted. Three slams may be bid and made: Little Slam, 14 out of the 16 tricks; Grand Slam, 15 out of the 16 tricks; and Super Slam, all 16 tricks. With these exceptions, Contract Bridge rules apply.

The Scoring.—Each trick over the book of 8, bid and made:

♣	♢	♡
20	20	25
♠	*(Eagle")*	*No Trumps*
25	30	40

If doubled, multiply by 2; if redoubled, by 4. Each overtrick:

	Not Vulnerable	*Vulnerable*
Undoubled	Trick Value	Trick Value
Doubled	100	200
Redoubled	200	400
Little Slam (14 out of 16) .	500	750
Grand Slam (15 out of 16) .	1000	1500
Super Slam (all 16 tricks) .	1500	2000

Slam premiums are not increased by doubling or redoubling. As in Contract Bridge, Vulnerable means having won one game toward rubber, which is the first two games won by either side. Honors: 4 suit honors in one hand, 100; 5 in one hand, 150. Four Aces in No Trumps in one hand, 150; five Aces in one hand, 300. Penalties:

If undoubled, Not Vulnerable, 50 for each undertrick; Vulnerable, 100 for each undertrick.

If doubled, Not Vulnerable, 100 for the first undertrick, and 200 additional for each additional undertrick; Vulnerable, 200 for the first undertrick, and 300 additional for each additional undertrick.

If redoubled, multiply the doubled penalty by 2.

Game consists of 120 points (not 100), scored below the line. Rubber premium, if made in 2 games, 700; if in 3 games, 500. If the rubber is unfinished, for each game won, 300. In non-rubber and duplicate games, game in hand, Not Vulnerable, 300; Vulnerable, 500. The side with the higher score at the end of a rubber, regardless of the number of games won, is the winner of the rubber.

The Widow Card.—The Widow card was devised, because 65 cards did not divide evenly among four players. It became an unexpectedly important factor in the bidding. In bidding, the first bidder on each side should consider the Widow card in his hand, for quick trick or honor purposes. If he bids the suit of the Widow card, he is using it also to increase the length of his trump suit. A responding bidder should not include it in his calculations, unless the original bid was not in the suit of the Widow card, and he responds in the suit of the Widow card. In this case its high card value is not included by him, but merely its aid in lengthening his suit.

The Widow card should be placed where it will do the most good, in Declarer's or his partner's hand; and the discarding should be done as shrewdly. In a suit bid, discarding may be used to shorten a suit or create a failure, for ruffing. In No Trumps, the Widow card may be used to create or strengthen a stopper. It may be used to create an entry or reentry in either hand, to give or increase an honor score, and so on.

How to Bid.—Bidding is generally similar to that in Contract Bridge. With 4 suits, the quick trick value ranges from 8 to 10; with 5 suits, from 10 to 12½. This increase of 25% requires a corresponding increase in the quick trick requirements for all bids. An opening bid of 1 in any suit calls for slightly more than 3 quick tricks, instead of the 2½ required in Contract Bridge; and the minimum response should be based on a count of slightly less than 2 quick tricks, instead of 1½. The Widow card is an additional advantage to Declarer's side, due to discard possibilities. An opening 1 No Trump should have 5 quick tricks, instead of 4 as in Contract Bridge; any opening bid of 2 should have 6½ quick tricks, instead of 5½.

The Four Aces vary from this in their recommendations. They consider a count of slightly under 4 quick tricks as always worth an opening bid; and permit such a bid with a count as low as 2½, when the hand holds a 7-card suit, or a 6-card and a 5-card suit; or with a count of three, when the hand contains a 6-card suit or two 5-card suits; or with a count of 3½, when there is a 5-card suit. Their figures for opening 1 No Trump and opening bids of 2 are approximately the same as those given above. They place the minimum response at 1½, instead of slightly less than 2.

Opening bids of 3 or more are more unusual in Five-Suit Contract than in the regular game. The Four Aces have turned the Blackwood Four No Trump conventional bid into an accurate method of ascertaining how many of the six vital cards—the five Aces and the King of trumps—the bidder's partner has. When 4 No Trumps is bid, the suit to be played ultimately as trumps is any suit bid by both partners, or bid and rebid by either partner, or bid first by the bidder of 4 No Trumps. Their conventional responses to this are: 5 Clubs—none of the six vital cards; 5 Diamonds—1 of them; 5 Hearts—2; 5 Spades—3; 5 Eagles—4; 5 No Trumps—5. If partner has not responded with 5 No Trumps, and bidder of 4 No Trumps wishes to learn which of the other four Kings his partner holds, he may now bid 5 No Trumps. Their conventional responses to this are: 6 Clubs—none of these kings; 6 Diamonds—1; 6 Hearts—2; 6 Spades—3; 6 Eagles—4.

The Four Aces conclude that slams may be bid and made in Five-Suit Contract three times as often as in simple Contract Bridge. With 120 required for game, a game bid in Clubs or Diamonds (6 odd, or 14 tricks out of 16) also means a Little Slam, and earns its premium. Five-Suit Contract, especially with the addition of the Widow card, shows a far higher percentage than regular Contract Bridge of suits of 5 cards or better. It is advisable to bid first your longest suit held in your hand, and not created artificially by the addition of the Widow card; but between a 6-card suit with the Widow card and a 5-card suit without it, bid the 6-card suit first. Doubling is riskier in Five-Suit Contract than in the regular game, because of the advantage of the Widow card and the discard in shortening suits and creating failures for ruffing.

How to Play.—The rules for leading and play are the same as in regular Contract Bridge. The advantage of leading trumps as the opening lead is greater than in the regular game, in view of the probability of the discard's having been used to shorten suits or create a failure for ruffing. At any stage during the play, any player may inquire which card was discarded.

AUCTION BRIDGE

The Equipment, Rank of Suits, Rank of Cards, and Object in Auction Bridge are the same as in Contract Bridge (which see), except that all tricks taken, once the contract is made, count as scoring tricks, and there are no overtricks. The cut or draw for partners, the shuffle, the cut, and the deal are identical.

The bidding or auction is identical, until the contract is reached.

The difference in the two games is in the scoring. If the Declarer fails to make his contract, his side scores nothing for tricks. If he makes his contract, his side scores for all odd tricks, that is, all tricks above the book of 6, including any won in excess of the contract. It is thus to the advantage of a bidder to become Declarer as cheaply as possible, since, once the contract is made, all odd tricks score. (The only advantage in bidding high, where the bid can be made, is to secure a double by opponents, or secure a double and redouble it, and thus increase the total score.)

The Scoring.—

Each odd trick, or trick over 6: No Trumps, 10; Spades, 9; Hearts, 8; Diamonds, 7; Clubs, 6.

Doubling doubles these values; redoubling multiplies them by four.

Bonus for doubling: for making contract, 50; for each trick beyond contract, 50. Bonus for redoubling: for making contract, 100; for each trick beyond contract, 100. All scored in the honor score.

Undertricks: Defenders score in their honor score, not their game score, 50 for each undertrick, when contract is not doubled; 100, when it is doubled; 200, when it is redoubled.

Honors: Suit Bid

3 honors in one or both hands	30
4 honors in both hands	40
5 honors in both hands, divided 3 and 2	50
4 honors in one hand	80
4 honors in one hand, 5th in partners	90
5 honors in one hand	100

No Trumps

3 honors (Aces) in one or both hands	30
4 honors in both hands	40
4 honors in one hand	100

Little Slam, where Declarer takes 12 tricks: a bonus of 50, added to the honor score. This is scored even when contract is Grand Slam, and Declarer fails to make it by one.

Grand Slam, where Declarer takes 13 tricks: a bonus of 100.

Only the score for the odd tricks (or this doubled, or doubled and redoubled) is scored toward game, that is, below the line. All other scores go to the honor score, that is, above the line.

Game: a score of 30 or more, made by the score for odd tricks, or these doubled, or doubled and redoubled. No partial game score is carried over to the next game.

Rubber: a score of 250 is added for the rubber—that is, for the first side scoring two games, whether or not their opponents have scored a game.

Rubber Score: The scores are totalled, and the smaller subtracted from the larger. The difference is the value of the rubber. Whichever score is larger wins the rubber.

Partial Rubber Score: When an appointed time limit is reached, and one or both sides have one game toward rubber, there is an honor score of 125 for this partial rubber score.

How To Bid, Lead and Play: and Rules

There are no elaborate systems of bidding, as in Contract Bridge; since, once the contract is made, all odd tricks score, and the object is to secure the contract as cheaply as possible, as a rule. The general principles of bidding in Contract are applicable to Auction, although such conventions as bids forcing the partner to respond are unknown. The general principles of leading and playing in Contract are equally applicable to Auction. In general, all of the Additional Contract Bridge Rules are equally applicable to Auction.

OH HELL

This variation of bridge was invented by Geoffrey Mott-Smith. It is best with 4 or 5 players; any number, from 2 up, may play. On the 1st hand, 1 card is dealt to each player; on the second, 2; and so on upward, to the largest possible number for each player. Thus, with 4 players, the last hand is of 13 cards each. This hand is played at No Trumps. In all other hands, the next card is faced up, for a trump. The deal passes to the left. Except where stated otherwise, the rules of Contract Bridge apply.

Each player, commencing *left* of the dealer, bids how many tricks he will take, with the trump established as above. First lead is made by the player to the left of the dealer. Play and count as in bridge.

For bidding none and making none, a player scores 5. For bidding 1 or more and making it, he scores 10 plus the number bid (that is, a total of 11, 12, 13, etc.). With a hand of 5 or more cards, Little Slam, 25 bonus; Grand Slam, 50. For failure to make bid, no score. The highest score at the end wins.

Alternate Scoring.—The above, with a minus 10 for failing to make a bid.

BRIDGE

EQUIPMENT: Same as in Contract and Auction Bridge.

RANK OF SUITS: Hearts, (highest,) Diamonds, Clubs, Spades, (lowest.)

RANK OF CARDS: Same as in Contract and Auction Bridge; except that Ace is low in the cut.

OBJECT: To win tricks above the book of 6, toward game and rubber.

Four players cut or draw for partners, the two lowest being partners against the two highest. The lowest cut has choice of seats and cards, and the first deal. The Dealer deals four hands of 13 cards each, one at a time, in rotation left to right. He then examines his cards, and announces what suit the hands will be played in as trumps, or No Trump if he prefers that. He is required to name the trump, or bridge (pass). If his hand does not permit a No Trump or red suit declaration, usually he bridges (passes) the declaration to his partner, who must name a trump suit without consultation.

A game consists of 30 points or more. The value of the suits as trumps and No Trumps is, for each trick over the book of 6: No Trumps, 12; Hearts, 8; Diamonds, 6; Clubs, 4; Spades, 2. Thus 3 odd (that is, over the book) at No Trumps is 36, a game; 3 odd at Hearts is 32, a game; 5 odd at Diamonds is 30, or a game. But even 7 odd at either Clubs or Spades is less than 30, and hence it is impossible to go game on a black suit as trumps, without doubling in the case of Clubs, or doubling and redoubling in the case of Spades.

The opponents cannot make the trump; but they can double, which the player left of the Dealer does by saying "I double" or "I go over." This doubles the value of each trick, according to the scale above. If he does not wish to double, he asks his partner, "Shall I play?" His partner either answers, "If you please," if he wishes the contract to stand undoubled, or "I double" or "I go over" if he wishes to double it. If the contract is doubled, the maker of the trump may either redouble, or say "Enough" or "Content"; in which case his partner has the right to redouble, or announce that he is content. In the case of a redouble, both opponents in rotation have the right to redouble this redouble; and so alternately, provided only that the value of the trick never exceeds 100.

If the declaration is Spades, undoubled, the hands are not played, unless the Dealer's side has a score of 24 or more. The honors are shown and scored, and the Dealer's side scores 2 for the odd trick, without play.

When the declaration and the doubling are settled, the player to left of the Dealer leads, and the Dealer's partner's hand goes down on the table faced upward, arranged in suits; the partner becoming Dummy for that hand. Players must follow suit if possible; if not, they must trump or discard, that is, play a card of one of the remaining suits. The highest card of the suit led wins the trick, unless it is trumped, in which case the highest trump wins. The winner of each trick leads to the next. Game must be made up by trick points only; and no points above 30 can be carried over to the next game, or constitute more than one game.

Three honors in one or both hands count twice the value of a trick, in the honor score above the line; 4 honors in both hands, four times the value of a trick; 5 honors, divided 3 and 2, five times the value of a trick; 4 in one hand, eight times the value of a trick; 4 in one hand, 5th in partner's, nine times the value of a trick; 5 in one hand, ten times the value of a trick. At No Trumps, 3 Aces in both hands count 30; 4 Aces in both hands, 40; 4 Aces in one hand, 100. Little Slam (taking 12 tricks) counts 20; Grand Slam (taking 13 tricks) 40.

Any player who has no trumps in his hand should claim Chicane after the hand is played. This counts the same as 3 honors—that is, twice the value of the trick. (Chicane is credited as an honor score above the line, similarly to other honors.) There is no Chicane in No Trumps.

Rubber, or winning two out of three games, adds 100 to the side of the winners. If one side wins two games in succession, the third is not played.

The suits have no rank in the cutting. A tie in cutting is ignored if the cards are the two highest. If the cards are the two lowest, however, players cut again until the tie is broken, the lowest becoming Dealer, etc., as above. If the two intermediate cards tie, another cut is necessary to decide which plays with the original low; the latter's right to be the Dealer is not affected by this recut. Three players who cut equal cards must cut again, to see which plays with the fourth. If the odd card was high, the lowest two of the new cut are partners, and the lower becomes Dealer. If the odd card was low, the cutter becomes the Dealer, even if one of the other players gets a lower one in the recut.

REVERSI BRIDGE

In this variation of bridge, the object of the declaration is to lose tricks, not to win them. At the end of the hand, each side scores what the other hand makes. The adversaries can double, if they think they will not win the odd trick.

WHIST

Equipment: Two full decks of 52 cards each, preferably with backs of different colors.

Rank of Suits: All equal.

Rank of Cards: Ace (highest), King, etc., down to 2. In cutting, however, Ace ranks as the lowest.

Object: To win tricks above the first six, called the book, and reach the game score, which may be 5, or 7, or 10.

Preliminaries.—The players cut or draw for partners, the two lowest playing against the two highest. The lowest cut has the choice of seats and cards, and is Dealer for the first hand. After shuffle and cut, he deals in rotation 13 cards to each player, left to right, one at a time, the last card being turned up for trumps This belongs to the Dealer, and it must be left exposed until the Dealer has played to the first trick. If it is still exposed after the second trick has been turned and quitted, it is liable to be called. Thereafter players may ask what the trump suit is, but may not ask what the trump card was, on penalty of having the offending player's highest or lowest trump card called for by either opponent.

The Play.—The player to the left of the Dealer leads to the first trick, and is called Leader for that trick. The players in rotation to his left are called respectively Second Hand, Third Hand and Fourth Hand for that trick; these titles thereafter shifting, depending upon which player is Leader. It is required to follow suit if possible; otherwise, a player may either trump or discard. The highest card of the suit led wins the trick, unless the trick is trumped; in which case the highest trump played wins. Four cards constitute a trick. The winner of each trick becomes Leader for the next trick.

The first 6 tricks won by either side constitute the book, and do not count in the scoring. All tricks above the book count 1 each. The 7th trick is called the odd trick; the seventh and eighth score "two by cards," and so on. All 13 tricks constitute a Slam. In Long Whist, 10 points constitute a game; in Short Whist, 5 points. As played usually in America, 7 points constitute a game—the maximum number that can be won on one hand. When the 7-point game is played, it is usual to play the hand out, the winners scoring all they make. When the winners' total has been arrived at, the losers' score is deducted, and this constitutes the value of the game.

Sometimes a rubber is played, consisting of the best two out of three games, of 7 or 5 points each. If one side wins two games before the opponents have won one, that constitutes rubber, and the third is not played.

The purpose of the play is to take the largest number of tricks; and all leads and plays conducive to this end are proper. With a powerful trump hand, it is wise to lead out trumps before seeking to establish your long suit, which will then be protected by the remaining trumps. To a lead of a low card, Second Hand usually plays low, Third Hand high, and Fourth Hand takes the trick if possible. Never finesse against your partner: that is, respond to his low card lead with an intermediate card, when you hold a higher one. A partner's lead should be returned at the first opportunity, unless the player has some suit of his own which must be established, or the return of partner's suit is clearly unwise. An ancient axiom of the game is, When in doubt, lead trumps.

Rules for misdeals, revokes and so on are the same as in Contract and Auction Bridge.

ENGLISH WHIST

English Whist differs from the game as commonly played in America only in the scoring. The game is for 5 points, and rubbers are always played. Honors score, as well as tricks; the games are valued differently, according to the score of the opponents; and winning a rubber adds 2 points to the score.

A revoke made and established, and discovered before the cut for the ensuing deal, costs the offending side one of these three penalties: 3 tricks from the revoking side, added to the non-offending side's tricks; a deduction of 3 points from the offending side's game score; or an addition of 3 points to the non-offending side's game score. Revoke points are scored first; trick points second, and Honors last.

The Honors are the Ace, King, Queen and Jack of Trumps. With 4 Honors in one side's hands, the score is 4; 3 Honors, 2; Honors divided 2 to each side, nothing. If the Honors are not claimed before the trump is turned for the next deal, they do not score. Partners who have a score of 4 at the beginning of a deal cannot win the game by an Honor score; they must win the odd trick to go out. If one side goes out by tricks, and the other by Honors, the tricks win the game, the Honors scoring nothing.

In the English game, rubber points are scored at the end of each game: game with a blank score to the opponents counts a treble, scoring 3 rubber points; game with not more than 2 points to opponents counts a double, scoring 2 rubber points; game with more than 2 points to opponents counts a single, scoring 1 rubber point. Winning the rubber adds 2 additional rubber points. The value of the rubber is determined by deducting the score of the losers from that of the winners. The highest possible rubber score is called a bumper, consisting of 2 triples and a rubber score of 2, to their opponents' nothing. The lowest possible rubber score is 1—the winners having scored 2 singles and the rubber score of 2 points, or 4 in all, from which a triple won by their opponents is deducted. It is important to remember the order of scoring. If one side go out by Honors, the score for tricks won by their opponents may reduce the victory from a triple to a double or a single. If the side go out by tricks, even an Honor score of 4 made by opponents is not counted, and a double or triple victory may result.

DUPLICATE, PROGRESSIVE, PROGRESSIVE RUBBER, and PIVOT WHIST

These are all played the same as in Contract or Auction Bridge, except that Whist scoring and play is used. Each deal is a unit in Duplicate and Progressive Whist, and a bonus of 2 is added for game on a deal.

PRUSSIAN WHIST

Prussian Whist is the same as 5-, 7- or 10-point Whist, with or without Honors; except that, instead of turning up the last card for trump, the player to the Dealer's left cuts a trump from the still pack, which is presented to him by the Dealer's partner.

FAVORITE WHIST

Favorite Whist is regular 5-, 7- or 10-point Whist, with or without Honors, with this variation: whenever the suit first cut for trumps reappears as trumps during the rubber, tricks and Honors count double. A favorite suit must be cut for afresh at the beginning of each rubber.

SUIT VALUE WHIST

In Suit Value Whist, tricks are worth 1 when Spades are trumps; 2, when Clubs; 3, when Diamonds; and 4, when Hearts. Honors do not count, and game is 10 points. Winners and losers score all tricks taken, by the suit values above; and there is a bonus of 10 points for winning the rubber. The difference between the score of the winners and that of the losers is the value of the rubber.

DUMMY WHIST

In Dummy Whist, originating in England, three players cut. Lowest wins Dummy for the first rubber; next to lowest, for the second; highest, for the third. It is regarded as compulsory to play three rubbers. The Dummy's hand is faced up, arranged in suits, after the opening lead, and thereafter Dummy's partner plays Dummy's cards one by one. Dummy is not allowed to revoke.

DOUBLE DUMMY WHIST

Double Dummy Whist is played by two players. Lowest in the cut deals for his Dummy first, and has the privilege of sitting to the right or the left of the other player. The seat to the right is regarded as preferable, for the reason that it permits leading through the concealed hand.

HUMBUG WHIST

In this variation of Double Dummy, the two players sit opposite each other. Deal and seats are cut for in the usual manner. Four hands of 13 cards each are dealt, and the last card is faced for the trump. Either or both players, after examining the hands dealt to them, have the privilege of exchanging the hands dealt to them for the hands respectively to their right, facing down the hand they have examined. If the Dealer exchanges his, the trump suit remains the same, but he loses the faced trump card. Dealer's opponent has the first lead. Only 2 cards are played to each trick, the two hands faced down not being played. Scoring counts as in English whist, Honors being reckoned.

Naming the Trump Humbug Whist.—In this variation, the Dealer examines his hand, and names a trump suit. His opponent then has the privilege of playing the hand dealt to him, or exchanging it for the hand to his right. Otherwise the game is played as Humbug Whist.

BID WHIST

After partners and Dealer have been selected, the latter deals four hands of 13 cards each, one at a time, in rotation left to right. No trump is named. The player to the Dealer's left bids first, naming the number of points he will win in tricks and honors if he is allowed to make the trump. The Dealer's partner then bids, and so on in rotation until no one will bid higher. The highest possible bid is 17: 13 for tricks, and 4 for Honors (Ace, King, Queen and Jack of trumps). The highest bidder leads to the first trick, and the winner of each trick leads to the next. Suit must be followed when possible; otherwise, players can trump or discard. The Honors count to the side that wins them in tricks, not to the original holders.

CHINESE WHIST

Chinese Whist is a game for four players. After selection of partners and Dealer, 6 cards are dealt, one at a time, face down, to each player. Then 6 more cards are dealt, one at a time, and faced up, covering the 6 faced down. Then one "playing card" is dealt to each player, face down. The playing cards are held in the hands of the players until the Dealer surveys the situation and names the trump. Player to Dealer's left then leads his playing card or one of the cards faced up, and the other players in rotation play to it. It is required to follow suit if possible; if not, players may trump or discard. As soon as a card faced up is played, the concealed card beneath it must be faced up. The scoring is for tricks only, above the book of the first 6 tricks. A game consists of 7 points.

NORWEGIAN WHIST

The equipment, rank of suits and rank of cards is the same as in Whist. The cut and deal are the same. No trump is turned or named; every hand must be played at No Trumps. There are two declarations which may be made: Grand, in which the object is to win tricks; and Nullo, in which the object is to lose them. The player to the left of the dealer has the first right to bid one of these declarations, or pass. If he passes, the chance passes to the player on his left, and so in rotation. Whatever declaration is named first must be played. If all pass, the hand is played at Nullo.

If the declaration is Grand, the player to the *right* of the bidder leads first; if the hand is played at Nullo, the player to the left of the bidder, or, if there has been no bid, the player to the left of the Dealer. Players must follow suit wherever possible, and may discard any card when unable to follow suit. The highest card in the suit led wins the trick. Winner of each trick leads to the next trick.

There are two ways of scoring. The game is usually 50. In a bid of Grand, each trick over the book of 6 counts 4 for the side that bid. If the bid is not made, each trick over the book of 6 taken by the opponents counts twice as much, or 8. If Nullos is bid, the side making the bid is penalized 2 for each trick taken over the book of 6; and opponents score 2 for all tricks below book they have failed to take. In Nullos, the value of tricks is always 2 points.

A simpler scoring is to score for every trick, with tricks at Grand scored at 4 when bid is made, and, when it is not made, opponents scoring 6 for each trick they took; while at Nullos, the side taking the smallest number of tricks scores 2 for each trick taken by their opponents. This permits game to be made in one hand only by Grand Slam or all 13 tricks at Grand, 13 times 4 or 52; or for opponents to go game in one hand by setting a Grand bid at least 3 tricks, in which case they would take 9, and score 9 times 6 or 54.

The revoke penalty is to give up 3 tricks in Grand or to take 3 tricks in Nullo, if the other side has that number; if not, to take what they have. A call out of turn forfeits 20 points to the other side, and loses the player's right to bid on that hand.

CAYENNE

EQUIPMENT: A full deck of 52 cards.

PLAYERS: Four, two as partners against the other two.

RANK OF CARDS: King, Queen, Jack, 10, down to 2, (low), in cut and play.

PRELIMINARIES.—No trump is turned. After the cut for deal (low winning), and the shuffle and cut, four hands of 13 cards each are dealt, 4, 4 and then 5 to each, in rotation left to right, beginning with the Dealer's left. The player left of the Dealer then cuts the still pack, and exposes the top card of the bottom part of the cut for Cayenne, which settles the order of preference and value in the suits.

After examining his hand, the Dealer names a trump suit, or says he will play Grand, without trump; or Nullo, also without trump, with Aces ranked below the deuces. If the Dealer cannot decide, he bridges it to his partner, who must select a trump suit, Grand or Nullo.

THE PLAY.—The object of the game is to win tricks; except in Nullo, where the aim is to lose them. The hand left of the Dealer leads to the first trick; the others must follow suit if they can. If not, they may trump, if possible; if they do not trump, they must discard. The winner of each trick leads to the next.

THE SCORING.—All tricks taken above the book of 6 count 1 each. In addition to the tricks, there are 5 honors when a suit is trumps, the Ace, King, Queen, Jack and 10 of trumps. For 3 honors between the partners, the count 2; 4 honors, 4; and 5 honors, 6. These points, made by tricks and honors, are multiplied at the end of the hand, according to the value of the trump suit. In a Grand or Nullo, the multiplier is always 8. Otherwise the multiplier depends on which suit is trumps, and its relation to the suit which has been cut for Cayenne on that deal. Here is the table of values:

Cayenne	*2nd Color*	*3rd Color*	*4th Color*
Hearts	Diamonds	Clubs	Spades
Diamonds	Hearts	Clubs	Spades
Clubs	Spades	Hearts	Diamonds
Spades	Clubs	Hearts	Diamonds

If the Cayenne is trumps, the multiplier is 4; if 2nd color is trumps, the points are multiplied by 3; if 3rd color, by 2; if 4th color, by 1. In Nullos, every trick over the book counts to the other side. There are no honors in Nullos and Grand.

The game is 10 points. Any points over 10 won in one game are credited toward the next game or games. Where the opponents have not reached 4, the game is worth 4; if they have not reached 7, 2; if they are 8 or 9 up, it is worth 1 only. The side that first wins four games of 10 each adds 8 points for the rubber, and then deducts all game points scored by the other side; the difference being the final value of the rubber. Tricks count before honors, and players cannot go game on honors alone, but must stop at 9 points if they have no trick score on that hand. A revoke carries with it a penalty of 3 tricks, and the side in error cannot go game on that deal; but they may play the game out, and score as high as 9, if they can.

SOLO WHIST

Solo Whist may be played by five, four or three players. When five or four play, the full deck of 52 cards is used, the cards ranking from the Ace (highest) down to the 2. When three play, either 40 cards are used, the 2's, 3's and 4's being stripped from the deck; or 39 cards, one entire suit being omitted.

In the cut, low wins the deal. In the four-handed game, each player receives 13 cards, four rounds of 3 cards each, and a final single card to each. The last card is turned for the trump, and belongs to the dealer. In five-handed Solo Whist, the player to the Dealer's right receives no cards. In three-handed, the 40th card is turned for trumps and belongs to no one; or, if only 39 cards are used, the last card, turned for trump, belongs to the Dealer. The deal passes to the left.

The object of the game is to take tricks, according to one of the following bids:

1. 8 tricks (with a partner), called Proposal. (Not used in three-handed game.)
2. 5 tricks, alone against the others, called Solo.
3. No tricks, alone against the others, at No Trumps, called Nullo or Misère.
4. 9 tricks, alone against the others, naming trump, called Abundance.
5. 9 tricks, alone against the others, with suit turned as trump, called Abundance in Trumps.

6. No tricks, alone against the others, at No Trumps, the lone player's hand being exposed on the table after the first trick, called Open Misère or Spread.
7. 13 tricks, alone against others, naming trumps, and having first lead, called Abundance Déclarée or Slam.

THE BIDDING.—The Player to the left of the Dealer has first bid, bidding any of the above (which outrank one another in the order named) or he may pass. To bid Proposal, bidder says "I propose." Any succeeding player in turn may propose to become his partner, by saying "I accept." The sitting at the table remains unaltered. The Proposer and Acceptor must take 8 tricks, if no higher bid is made. No player may bid after once passing; except that the player to the left of the Dealer, who opened the bidding, may accept a Proposal, even if he has previously passed. The bidding continues in rotation, until no one will bid higher. In the three-handed game, if all pass, a player is sometimes allowed to bid Six-trick Solo. He must then take 6 tricks alone against the two others.

THE PLAY.—The Player to the left of the Dealer leads, except in the case of a Slam bid, when the bidder leads. Each player must follow suit, if possible; if not possible, he must trump or discard. The highest card of the suit led wins a trick; unless it is trumped, in which case the highest trump wins. The winner of each trick leads for the next trick. In the case of a revoke, the revoking side cannot win the hand; and at the end of the play it must forfeit 3 tricks to their adversaries, after which the over and under tricks are computed and paid for.

SCORING.—It is usual to score with red counters, valued at 5, and white counters, valued at 1. Each player begins with an equal amount in counters. In Proposal, the bidder and his partner, if successful, win 1 red counter each from each adversary; if unsuccessful, they pay 1 red counter to each.

A bidder playing alone against the others wins from or pays to each other player, depending on whether he succeeds or not, the following:

	Red Counters
Solo	2
Nullo or Misère	3
Abundance	4
Abundance in Trumps	4
Open Misère or Spread	6
Abundance Déclarée or Slam	8

For each trick under or above the amount bid, 1 whole counter is paid by the bidder or by each adversary. In partnership play, each partner wins or loses from one opponent, according to the above table.

The first player losing all of his counters loses the game; or the first player winning an agreed number of counters wins. Misères, Spreads and Slams pay no odd tricks. The moment a Misère player takes a trick, or a Slam player loses one, the hands are abandoned, and the stakes paid.

BOSTON

EQUIPMENT: Two full decks of 52 cards each, one of which is played with at a time. Red and white counters.

RANK OF SUITS: Equal.

RANK OF CARDS: Ace (highest), King, Queen, Jack, 10, down to 2. In cutting, the Ace is low.

OBJECT: Playing alone against three adversaries, to bid to win a certain number of tricks, after naming the trump; or to lose a certain number of tricks at No Trumps.

Boston is played by four players, each playing for himself. Two decks of 52 cards each are used alternately; while one is being used for dealing, the other is used to determine the trump. The players are supplied with red and white counters, 1 red being equal to 10 whites. At the beginning, a pool is formed by each player putting up 1 red counter.

The players cut or draw for deal and choice of seats and cards, low winning. The Dealer deals 13 cards to each player, in rotation left to right, giving 4, 4 and finally 5 cards at a time to each. While the deal is going on, the player opposite the Dealer cuts the still deck, and turns up the top card of the cut for a trump. Neither pack must be shuffled after the first deal with each, but must be simply cut, so as to secure good hands on which to bid.

The trump suit is First Preference, and the suit of the same color is Second Preference, or Color. The others are Plain Suits for that deal.

THE BIDDING.—There are thirteen varieties of bids, which rank as follows, beginning with the lowest:

1. Boston—to win 5 tricks.
2. To win 6 tricks.
3. To win 7 tricks.
4. Little Misery—to lose 12 tricks, after discarding a card which is not shown.
5. To win 8 tricks.
6. To win 9 tricks.
7. Grand Misery—to lose every trick.
8. To win 10 tricks.
9. To win 11 tricks.
10. Little Spread—playing a Little Misery with the cards exposed.
11. To win 12 tricks.
12. Grand Spread—to play a Grand Misery with the cards exposed.
13. Grand Slam—to win all 13 tricks.

The player to the Dealer's left either makes a bid, or passes. If, for instance, he thinks he can make 5 tricks against the combined opposition of the other three, ignoring the faced trump and naming his own, he bids "Boston." In rotation, left to right, the others now bid or pass. The lowest raise over "Boston" would be for a player to announce, "In color" or "I keep," meaning that he will make the same number of tricks in the suit of the same color as the faced trump. The lowest raise over this is for a player to say "I keep over you" or "Preference," meaning that he will keep the faced card as trumps and make the same number of tricks. The lowest bid over Preference must be for a greater number of tricks, or one of the Miseries or Spreads. This is the order of all bids: number of tricks; same number in color; same number in First Preference.

The Play.—The hand left of the Dealer always leads. Each player in turn must follow suit if he can; if not, he must trump or discard. The winner of each trick leads to the next trick. When Little Misery is played, each player discards a card, which is not to be shown. Spreads are laid down before a card is led. It is usual to abandon the rest of the hands as soon as the successful bidder, the Caller, makes good his bid, since there are no payments for overtricks.

If no one bids, there are two ways to play: the deal may be passed, each player adding a red chip to the pool; or a General Misery may be played, at No Trumps, the object of each player being to avoid taking tricks. The player taking the most tricks pays a red counter to each other player for each difference of one between the number of his tricks and of the other player's. If two players tie for high score, each pays half of the penalty to each of the other players. If three tie for high score, each pays the fourth player a red chip.

Table of Payments

The bidder is paid by each of the others just what he bid and made, by this scale:

Tricks bid:	5	6	7	8	9	10	11	12	13
Payment:	10	15	20	25	35	45	65	105	170

When the bidder fails, he is said to be "put in for" so many tricks, and pays as follows:

Tricks bid	*Number put in for:* 1	2	3	4	5	6	7	8	9	10	11	12	13
5	10	20	30	40	50								
6	15	25	35	45	55	65							
7	20	30	40	50	60	70	80						
8	25	35	45	55	70	85	100	115					
9	35	45	55	65	80	95	110	125	140				
10	45	55	70	80	95	110	125	140	155	170			
11	70	80	95	110	125	140	155	170	185	200	220		
12	120	130	145	160	180	200	220	240	260	280	300	320	
13	180	200	220	240	260	280	300	320	340	360	390	420	450

When Miseries are bid, the Caller wins from, or loses to, each player: 20 for Little Misery; 40 for Grand Misery; 80 for Little Spread; and 160 for Grand Spread.

A player who has passed without making a bid cannot enter into the bidding again, except to offer a Misery, and then only if it outranks any previous bid.

Any player making a bid of 7 tricks or better takes the pool, if he succeeds. If he fails, he must not only pay for the tricks he is put in for, but must double the amount that was in the pool when he made his call. Bids of less than 7 tricks do not win the pool, unless the adversaries insist on playing the hand out. To save the pool from being won on a small bid, the opponents can offer to pay before playing to the second trick; but all three must agree to this. The ritual is for an opponent to say, when he wins the first trick, or for the one who is to play first to the second trick among the opponents, "I will pay." If the other opponents say "Agreed," or throw up their cards, the pool is saved. If one of the opponents says "I will play it," the others must abide by this decision. An offer to pay a bid of 7 tricks or better must be accepted by the Caller.

If the pool grows to exceed 25 red counters (as by such penalties as 1 counter for a misdeal, 4 for a revoke, and double the amount in it for a failure) it is customary to set aside all above 25 as a foundation for the next pool. If there is anything in the pool when the game ends, this is divided among the players. Another method of penalizing for revokes is to have the Caller put in for 1 trick, and have him pay as if he had failed by 1 trick to make good. If an opponent revokes, each must pay the bidder what was called, and the hands must be thrown up. The individual who made the revoke then pays 4 red counters into the pool. In a General Misery, if a player revokes, he pays 5 counters to each of the other players, puts 4 into the pool, and the hand is abandoned.

If the call is Little Misery, and one opponent leads before all the others have discarded, the Caller can abandon the hand and claim the call as won. A lead out of turn, or an exposed card by an opponent of a Misery call, loses the game at once. In all such cases, the offending player pays 4 red counters into the next pool.

In a General Misery, there is no penalty for exposing cards or for leads out of turn, since there are no partners.

BOSTON DE FONTAINEBLEAU

This game differs from Boston in the ranking of the bids, the value of the payments, and the elimination of the Preference suit. There are two additional calls, Piccolissimo, to win one trick precisely, after having discarded one card, at No Trumps; and Spread Slam. The calls rank:

1. Boston—5 tricks.
2. 6 tricks.
3. Little Misery.
4. 7 tricks.
5. Piccolissimo.
6. 8 tricks.
7. Grand Misery.
8. 9 tricks.
9. Little Spread.
10. 10 tricks.
11. Grand Spreao.
12. 11 tricks.
13. 12 tricks.
14. 13 tricks.
15. Spread Slam.

The payments are the same whether the Caller wins or loses. Overtricks and undertricks are paid for at the rate of 5 counters per trick.

TABLE OF PAYMENTS

	Clubs or Spades	*Hearts*	*Diamonds*
Boston—5 tricks . . .	10	20	30
6 tricks	30	40	50
7 tricks	50	60	70
8 tricks	70	80	90
9 tricks	90	100	110
10 tricks	110	120	130
11 tricks	130	140	150
12 tricks	150	160	170
Slam, 13 tricks	250	300	350
Spread Slam	350	400	450

In England, Slams are paid for at 400, 450 and 500 respectively; and Spread Slams at 600, 700 and 800. Little Misery is 75; Piccolissimo, 100; Grand Misery, 150; Little Spread, 200; and Grand Spread, 250.

A player who has once passed cannot bid later, nor can he increase his own bid, unless he is overcalled. The suits must be named in the bidding, spades ranking lowest, then clubs, hearts and diamonds. The successful Caller may ask for a partner, and if one accepts him, their joint score must be 3 tricks more than the call.

A General Misery gives the pool to the player who takes the least number of tricks. In case of a tie, the pool is divided. There are no other payments.

The pool is made up by 5 red counters from each dealer in turn, plus such penalties as increase it. There is no limit to its size. Any successful call wins the pool; any call that fails requires the Caller to pay into the pool the amount he pays to each opponent. Partners whose call succeeds divide the pool equally; partners whose call fails each pay one opponent, and half that amount into the pool. If opponents agree to pay before playing to the second trick, this does not save the pool, but merely possible overtricks.

Boston de Fontainebleau with Honors.—Originally Honors were counted, in trump bids only. The 4 Honors, Ace, King, Queen and Jack of Trumps, if held by Caller, scored 4 overtricks as far as payments were concerned; but bids and the tricks necessary to make them could not include any count for Honors. If Caller held 3 Honors, he scored them as 2 overtricks. A partnership call scored the honors, if divided between the partners. Honors never counted for the opponents of the call. Otherwise, the game was played as above.

FRENCH BOSTON

To select the Dealer, the cards are dealt in rotation right to left—the French custom—one at a time, faced up, until the Jack of Diamonds falls. The player who receives it becomes the first dealer. The game consists of 40 deals; and each Dealer puts 10 counters in the pool up to the last deal, when 20 are put in.

The suit turned up for trumps on the first deal is called Belle, and remains so for the entire 40 deals. The suit turned up for trumps on each deal thereafter is called Petite for that deal only. The suits have a permanent ranking:

Rank of Suits: Hearts (highest), Diamonds, Clubs, Spades (lowest).

Rank of Cards: In all trump suits except Diamonds, Diamond Jack, Ace, King, Queen, Jack, 10, down to 2 of trumps. If Diamonds are trumps, Jack of Hearts, Ace, King, Queen, Jack, 10 down to 2 of trumps.

The cards are dealt 4, 4, 5 as in Boston, but from right to left. Bidding is the same way; but the play is from left to right. If the successful bidder asks for a partner, he must do so in Belle or Petite, and the two must take 8 tricks. If he is not accepted, he must make 5 alone, or whatever his bid becomes. If he does not ask for a partner, he must make 6, 8, or 9 tricks, there being no 7, 10, 11, 12 and 13 bids. The calls rank:

1. 5 tricks; or 8 with a partner; in Petite.
2. 5 tricks; or 8 with a partner; in Belle.
3. 6 tricks solo, in any suit.
4. Little Misère.
5. 8 tricks solo in any suit.
6. Grand Misère.
7. Misère with 4 Aces.
8. 9 tricks in any suit.
9. 9 tricks in Petite.
10. 9 tricks in Belle.
11. Little Spread.
12. Grand Spread.

Table of Payments

Miseries (Misères) are paid in accordance with the trump turned on that deal. Here is the table of payments, when Spades are trumps:

5 tricks alone, or 8 with partner	4
3 honors	3
4 honors	4
Each extra trick	1
6 tricks, or Little Independence	6
3 honors	4
4 honors	6
Each extra trick	2
8 tricks, or Grand Independence	8
3 honors	6
4 honors	8
Each extra trick	4
Little Misery (Misère)	16
Grand Misery	32
Misery with 4 Aces	32
Misery on the Table (Spread)	64
Slam by Two Partners	50
Slam Solo	100
Slam on the Table (Spread)	200

To get the payments in Clubs, multiply these figures by 2; in Diamonds, by 3; in Hearts, by 4.

The holder of the Jack of Diamonds, except in Miseries, is paid 2 counters by each of the others. During the last 8 deals, he is paid double.

When Misery with 4 Aces is played, the Caller may renounce at pleasure for the first 10 tricks.

RUSSIAN BOSTON

This is a variation of Boston de Fontainebleau. After the trump suit is named, any player who has no trump in his hand may announce Carte Blanche or Chicane, and immediately receives 10 counters from each of the other players.

If a player bids 6, 7 or even 8 tricks, he must say that he is playing Solo; or another player may offer to join him, in order to make 4 tricks more than the bid.

Honors are paid for as overtricks, exactly as in Boston de Fontainebleau.

VINT

Equipment: Two full decks of 52 cards each.

Rank of Suits: No Trumps (highest), Hearts, Diamonds, Clubs, and Spades (lowest).

Rank of Cards: Ace, King, Queen, Jack, 10, down to 2.

Object: To score as highly as possible, for tricks, game, rubber, bonuses and penalties.

Preliminaries.—Vint is played by four players. If more than four offer, the players are selected by drawing or cutting, as in Contract and Auction Bridge. Of the four to play at a table, the two lowest play together, and the two highest. The lowest of all has choice of seats, and cards, and deals first. The round is not concluded until each player has had one of the other players for a partner for a complete rubber. Thus, if the four players cut in this order, A, B, C, and D, A being lowest, the three rubbers are played: A and B against C and D; A and C against B and D; A and D against B and C. In cutting, the Ace is low.

The Dealer deals 13 cards, one at a time, in rotation left to right, to each player. No trump is turned.

The Bidding.—Beginning with the Dealer, each player must bid or pass. The minimum bid is to win 7 tricks out of the 13, with Spades as trumps. There is no book of 6 tricks in Vint; every trick counts in the actual scoring. But the bidding is worded as if there were. Thus a bid of 7 in Spades is worded "Simple game, in Spades" or "One, in Spades." Each player in rotation to the left can overbid by bidding a simple game in a higher suit or No Trumps, or by a bid for a greater number of tricks: "Two, in Hearts" (meaning a bid to take eight tricks), etc. A bid of an identical number in a higher ranking suit or No Trumps overcalls a bid of the same number in a lower ranking suit. The highest possible bid is 7 No Trumps. A player cannot overcall himself after three passes. If a player is overcalled, he can bid higher, and partners can overcall each other, without an intervening bid by opponents, as in Contract Bridge.

THE PLAY.—The player on the left of the successful bidder always leads for the first trick, and each player in rotation must follow suit if he can. If not, he must trump or discard. The winner of each trick leads to the next. All four players play their own hands, there being no Dummy.

THE SCORING.—The scoring in Vint differs in principle from that of any game so far considered. Both sides score for every trick taken, whether the bid is made or not. The score per trick depends upon the number of tricks bid, not the suit rank. For every trick taken, each side scores:

If the bid is	*Points*
7 (1 over book)	10
8 (2 " ")	20
9 (3 " ")	30
10 (4 " ")	40
11 (5 " ")	50
12 (6 " ")	60
13 (7 " ")	70

These scores are entered below the line, and alone count for game. Game is 500. The first side that reaches 500 goes game, although they may score more, since the hand is played out to the end. If both sides approach 500, the first to win it goes game, regardless of which side won the bidding. This is contrary to the principle of other bidding games.

For winning a game, 1,000 is added, in honor points, above the line. For winning a rubber, the first two games, whether opponents have won a game or not, there is an honor score of 2,000. The partners then pivot, as above; for no round is complete until each player has had every other player as a partner.

Other honor score bonuses are:

Little Slam, 12 tricks, made but not bid . . .	1,000
Grand Slam, 13 tricks, made but not bid . . .	2,000
Little Slam bid and made	6,000
Little Slam Bid, Grand Slam made	7,000
Grand Slam bid and made	12,000

If the declaring side fails to make its bid, the penalty for each under-trick is 100 times the value of each trick, scored above the line. A bid of 4 No Trumps, each trick being worth 40, failing by 3 tricks, would cost a penalty of 3 times 40 times 100, or 12,000. In addition, the opponents would score 6 tricks won at 40 each, or 240, below the line, toward game. At the same time, the bidders would score for the 7 tricks they took 7 times 40, or 280. This again differs from most other bidding games, in which unsuccessful bidders do not score below the line.

All honors score above the line. The honors are the Ace, King, Queen, Jack, 10 of trumps, and also the 3 Aces. At No Trumps, the Aces are the only honors. When there is a trump suit, the Ace counts twice, as an honor and as an Ace. Each honor is worth 10 times as such as a trick; so its value varies with the final bid. Thus, if the game is 5 in Spades, the tricks are worth 50 each, and each honor is worth 10 times 50, or 500.

The side that has the majority of both Aces and honors scores for all they hold: not merely for the difference. If one side has the majority of one, the other side of the other, the one is set off against the other. If one side holds 4 Aces and 2 honors, and the other side 3 honors, the majority of honors (3) is deducted from number of Aces (4), and the former side scores 1 only—worth 10 times the value of the trick, according to the number of tricks bid. If one side has 2 honors and 3 Aces, and the other side 3 honors and 1 Ace, neither side scores, because the 3 honors offset the 3 Aces. If each side holds 2 Aces, only the side that wins the majority of the tricks can score them. If one side holds 3 honors and 2 Aces, they score 5 times 10 times the value of the tricks, if they win the majority; if the other side wins the majority of the tricks, they score only 1 times 10 times the value of the tricks, since the Aces do not count and they have a majority of 1 only in honors.

At No Trump, the value of each Ace is 25 times the value of a trick. If Aces are easy (2 for each side), neither side scores. If not, the side having the majority of Aces scores for each Ace it holds.

Sequences in the hand of a single player of 3 cards or more headed by an Ace, in any suit, are called Coronets, no matter whether the declaration be a trump or No Trumps. Also, 3 or 4 Aces in one hand rank as a Coronet. In a declared trump, the Ace, King, Queen of a plain suit, or 3 Aces, is worth 500. Each additional card in the sequence adds 500. A sequence from the Ace to the 7 in a plain suit would count 3,000. In the trump suit, or in any suit when the declaration is No Trumps, these sequences are worth double, the Ace, King, Queen being worth 1,000; so that a sequence from the Ace through the 9 in a trump suit, or in any suit in a No Trumper, is worth 4,000 points.

The laws for irregularities are the same as those for Whist and Bridge, except that, since there is no Dummy, the laws concerning them are eliminated.

THE EUCHRE GROUP

History

The Euchre group includes four games which at times have been regarded as the national card games in four different countries: *Euchre* in the United States, *Spoil Five* in Ierland, *Napoleon* in England, and *Écarté* in France.

Euchre was long regarded as descended from the old Spanish game of *Triomphe,* mentioned in the earliest works on card games as far back as 1520. In France, the game, called Triomphe or *French Ruff,* became greatly modified, and Écarté is regarded as one of its indirect descendants. The antiquity of these games can be seen from the fact that in Écarté and some versions of *Rams,* a descendant of Euchre, the King outranks the Ace. The King of course commenced at the head of the suit, with the Ace lowest; and only a subtle democratic revolution made the last first

Similarly, in our own memory, in games of the Whist group, the lowest ranking suit, Spades, has by a coup d'état or putsch established a firm dictatorship over the other suits. According to this first viewpoint, Euchre was sired in France, and was probably introduced into America by the French in Louisiana.

A more persuasive modern view is that Euchre is of more mixed ancestry, and probably originated in an effort to play the venerable Irish game of Spoil Five with a Piquet pack. The name Euchre is not French, but of unknown origin; its meaning is identical with the "spoil" in Spoil Five, that is, an effort to prevent the maker of the trump from taking 3 tricks. There are other close resemblances. In its turn, Spoil Five derived through *Five Fingers,* a game described in the *Compleat Gamester* of 1674, (the Five Fingers being the 5 of trumps, the ranking card in the trump suit), from the ancient Irish game of *Maw,* fashionable during the reign of James I (1603-1625). Since the Piquet deck had no 5, the second ranking trump, the Jack, now heads the trump suit.

Skat is more modern in origin than any of these games. It apparently originated among the farmers of Thuringia, a province of Saxony, probably as a variation of the Wendish game of Schapskopf. It was first mentioned in 1818. It has many devotees who insist that it is superior to any of the Whist group of games.

EUCHRE

Equipment: A deck of 32 cards, from Ace through 7 in each suit; or of 28 cards, the 7's being omitted; or of 24 cards, the 8's also being omitted. The Joker is sometimes used.

Players: Four, partners, two against two; or three, or two, as individuals.

Rank of Cards: Trump suit—Right Bower (Jack of trumps), Left Bower (Jack of same color), Ace, King, Queen, 10, 9, etc. Suit of same color, Ace, King, Queen, 9, etc. Suits of opposite color, Ace, King, Queen, Jack, 10, 9, etc. If the Joker is used, it is the highest trump, outranking both Bowers.

PRELIMINARIES.—In the cut or draw for deal, low deals. The Ace is low on the cut, and the Jack ranks immediately below the Queen. If the Joker is cut or drawn, the player must cut or draw again. After shuffle and cut, the Dealer deals 5 cards to each player: first 3 to each, and then 2; or first 2, and then 3; in rotation, left to right. The next card is faced for the trump. After each hand is ended, the deal passes to the left.

The deal is forfeited: if a wrong number of cards is dealt to any player; if more than one card is faced for trump; or if the same number of cards is not given each player in the same round. The other rules for misdeals given in the opening chapter on Card Games also apply.

If the Joker is turned as the trump, the Dealer may, before looking at his cards, announce what suit it represents on that deal; or this may be agreed on before the deal. Formerly, for purpose of facing as a trump, the Joker was usually regarded as a Spade.

MAKING THE TRUMP.—The player to the Dealer's left then has the privilege of ordering up the trump, or passing. By ordering it up, he makes it trump for the hand. Dealer, if it is ordered up, must at once discard a card face down from his hand, and the trump becomes a part of his hand, although he does not take the card into his hand before his turn to play to the first trick.

If the player to the left of the Dealer passes, the latter's partner may order the trump up, by saying "I assist," or he may pass. If he passes, the player to the Dealer's right has the same option. If three pass, the Dealer may take up the trump, or pass. If the Dealer passes, he faces down the card turned as trump. If all four pass, in rotation left to right each player has one chance to name the trump suit, or may pass. The suit first named becomes trump. If all four players pass the second time, the deal is void, and passes to the left.

After the trump is taken up, no player can demand its denomination; but Dealer must at any time, when asked, name the trump suit. If the new trump is of the same color as the card faced down, this is called "making it next"; if of the other color, "crossing the suit."

The Play.—The object of the game is to win tricks. If the partners who make the trump (either by ordering it up, taking it up, or naming it) win 3 tricks out of 5, they score 1 point toward game. If they win all 5 tricks, they score 2 points. If the partners who make the trump fail to get 3 tricks, they are euchred, and their opponents score 2 points. If all 5 tricks are taken by a player who has declared to play Alone, he scores 4 points.

The player to the Dealer's left leads any card; and in turn, left to right, each player plays a card, following suit if possible; if he cannot, he must trump or discard. It is not required to win the trick. If a trick is trumped, the highest trump wins. The winner of each trick leads for the next. Tricks must be gathered in by the winner of each and quitted, and cannot thereafter be re-examined until the end of the hand. After the 5 tricks have been completed, the deal passes to the left.

The player who ordered up, took up or named the trump may play alone against both opponents, his partner laying his hand face downward on the table and taking no part in the play. The partner cannot object to a player's going Alone. Decision to go Alone must be announced when trump is declared. Formerly a Dealer whose partner had assisted was allowed to go Alone; this is still played, in some localities.

If a revoke is made and established, the hands are abandoned and the opponents score 2 points. If the revoke is made against a lone hand, the lone player scores 4 points. The game is 5, 7 or 10 points, as agreed. The rules for exposed cards, insufficient hands, and so on, are the same as already given for other games.

LAPS

Laps is a variation of Euchre, in which all points scored in excess of those needed to win a game are carried over to the next game.

SLAMS

Slams is another variation, in which a side which scores 5 points before its opponents score are credited with winning 2 games.

JAMBONE

Jambone is a lone hand variation, requiring the lone hand to be exposed, face up, on the table, and played so. The player to the left of the lone player may call the first card to be played by the lone hand. Among some players, all cards may be called from the Jambone hand. For 5 tricks won by a Jambone hand the score is 8 points; otherwise the scoring is the same.

JAMBOREE

Jamboree is a Euchre variation, in which a player holding the 5 highest trumps may show them and score 16 points, without playing the hand. If the Dealer is the player, he may use the faced trump to complete the 5.

CUT-THROAT, or THREE-HANDED EUCHRE

When three players play, each is for himself. A euchre counts 2; and a march, or winning every trick, 3. The two opponents combine against the player making the trump.

TWO-HANDED EUCHRE

When only two players play, the 7's and 8's are usually eliminated from the deck. A euchre scores 2, and a march 2.

SIX-HANDED EUCHRE

When six play, three against three, the partners sit alternately around the table. A lone hand against three opponents is game. A euchre scores 2, and a march 2.

RAILROAD EUCHRE

This is a four-handed variation of Euchre. The Joker is always used. A player going alone may discard one card, and call for his partner's best card. The partner gives it up, and faces his hand down during the play of the hand. Either opponent may also call for his partner's best, and go alone against the first lone. Euchre of a lone hand by two opponents scores 2; by a second lone player, 4.

Laps, Slams, Jambone and Jamboree are often played with Railroad Euchre, in various combinations.

AUCTION EUCHRE

Equipment: For five players, regular Euchre deck of 32 or 28 cards; for six players, regular Euchre deck of 32 cards, or this with the 6's added. For seven players, a full deck of 52 cards. For eight players, a 60-card deck, with 11 and 12 spots. The Joker is sometimes added.

Number of Players: Five, six, seven or eight.

The cards rank as in regular euchre; except that, where the 60-card deck is used, the 11's rank above the 10's and the 12's above the 11's. In the five- and six-handed games, the cards are dealt as in regular Euchre; in the seven- and eight-handed game, seven cards are dealt to each player, either 4-3, or 2-3-2. No trump is turned.

There is a widow of from 2 to 5 cards, as agreed upon, dealt face down. The player who makes the trump takes the widow into his hand, and discards an equal number of cards from his hand or from the widow, or both.

The successful bidder, and his partner or partners, must take as many tricks as are bidden. The player to the Dealer's left bids first, or passes; and so in rotation from left to right, the Dealer having last bid. Each player may bid only once. Each bid must be for a greater number of tricks than the last bid, 5 being the highest bid in five- and six-handed Euchre, and 7 in seven- and eight-handed.

Lone hand bids are permitted. With the widow, a lone hand at five- and six-hand scores 8 points; without the widow, 15. At seven- and eight-handed, a lone hand with the widow scores 10 points; without the widow, 20 points. By a lone hand at five- and six-hand, 3 tricks is the lowest bid recognized, and 4 tricks at seven- and eight-hand.

In some localities, trump must be named when bid is first made; in others, only after the bid becomes final, and the widow examined, if it is to be used. If no one bids, the deal passes.

The arrangement of partners is intricate. Six-handed Euchre is a partnership game, three against three, the partners sitting alternately. In some localities, the successful bidder names his partners.

In some localities, at five-, seven- and eight-hand, the successful bidder announces that the holder of a card he designates is his partner. He may designate any card. In this case, the bidder does not know which player is his partner until the designated card falls.

In other localities, at five-hand, a bid of 3 entitles the bidder to name one partner; of 4 or 5, to name two partners. At seven- and eight-hand, a bid of 4 or 5 tricks entitles him to name one partner; of 6 or 7, two partners.

As a rule, the play is the same as in regular Euchre. In some localities, the successful bidder becomes the leader; and among some players he must lead a trump for his first lead.

Scoring.—The player making the trump and his partners, if they make their bid, score 1 point for each trick they take. If unsuccessful, they are set back the amount of their bid; or the opponents each score this amount. There is no extra score for overtricks.

Lone hand scores: five- and six-hand, all the tricks, with widow, 8; without, 15. Seven- and eight-hand, all the tricks, with widow, 10; without, 20. In some localities, when lone hand fails, opponents score 5 each on a bid of 8 or 10, and 10 on a bid of 15 or 20.

The game, in all these variations, is 21, or sometimes 25.

BUCK EUCHRE

Buck Euchre is played by four, five or six players. Four players use the 24-card deck and the Joker; five, the 28-card deck and the Joker; six, the regular 32-card Euchre deck, with the Joker.

Before the deal, each player puts one chip into a pool. The Dealer deals 5 cards to each player, in rotation left to right, one at a time, and turns up the next for trump. If the Joker is turned up, the Dealer must announce what suit it shall stand for. Each player in turn can order up the trump, or pass. The player ordering up or holding his cards must take in one trick, or put one chip in the pool. For each trick taken in, a player scores 1 point. The game is 12 points. A player taking in all 5 tricks wins the pool, no matter what his score is.

CALL-ACE EUCHRE

For four, five or six players, using the deck as in Buck Euchre, except that the Joker is not used. The Dealer turns up the trump, leaving 3 unknown cards in the four-handed game, 2 in the five-handed game, and 1 in the six-handed game. Each player in turn, left to right, may order the trump up, or pass. If all pass, the Dealer may take it up or turn it down. If it is turned down, in rotation each player may name a trump, the first trump named becoming the trump for the hand. If the trump is ordered up, the Dealer takes it up, as in regular Euchre.

The player ordering up, taking up or naming the trump has the privilege of calling on the best card of any suit but the trump; and the player holding that card becomes his partner, although this is not announced until the best card falls in play. As certain cards are not in play, the best card may turn out to be a King, Queen or even a Jack; or the caller may hold it himself, in which case he has no partner. The maker of the trump may also say "Alone," or call on a suit of which he holds the Ace.

If the maker of the trump and his partner take 3 tricks, they score 1 point apiece; for a march, 3. If they are euchred, each opponent scores 2. A lone hand scores 1 for 3 tricks; for a march, 1 for each player, including himself: [4, 5, or 6, depending on the number playing.]

PROGRESSIVE EUCHRE

In Progressive Euchre, there are a number of tables, the players changing partners at the end of each round. The tables are numbered, from No. 1, the Head Table, down to the last, the Booby Table. The hostess allots (or has drawn slips identifying) each couple at each table, as: Table I, Couple 1; Table III, Couple 2, etc. Play begins simultaneously at all the tables, and a round ends when the Head Table finishes and taps a bell.

There is a cut for first deal at each table, low dealing, the Ace being low. After the first round, the visiting lady, who is paired with the remaining gentleman, deals; except in Rapid Euchre, where the remaining lady deals, to save time. Play continues at each table until the Head Table reaches game (5, or 7), even though some tables may have gone into a second game. The losing couple at Table I go down to the Booby Table; at all other tables, the losing couples remain, and the winners go up to the table next above.

Another method is to provide each table with a bell; set a stipulated number of points for game, as 15; and let the table first reaching that number tap the bell, as a signal for play to stop at all tables. Progression as above.

Another method of progression is to have the winning ladies move up, and the winning gentlemen move down, 1 table each time. Alternatively, the winning lady may move up and the losing gentleman down, leaving the losing lady and the winning gentleman to play as partners on the next deal. This may be reversed the second half of the evening.

Another method is to retain partners all evening, and have the East-West pair move up each time, while the North-South pair remain. In this arrangement, there is a cut for deal at the beginning of each round. To provide that each pair play every other pair, let the North-South pairs move up until they reach Table I, where the North-South pair remain so designated all the evening. At Table I, the visiting North-South pair become an East-West pair, and progress as so reclassified down to the Booby Table. The East-West pairs, after each deal, move away from Table I, except at the lowest table, where they exchange for the North and South seats at the same table. Or arrange some other method of progression, which will permit the North-South pairs, after playing all the East-West pairs in turn, to play the other North-South pairs, while the East-West pairs play the other East-West pairs.

In general, the rules of regular Euchre apply.

RAPID EUCHRE

A variation of Progressive Euchre, each round ending as soon as 5 points are scored at any table. Each table has a bell, which is tapped when the first table reaches 5, ending play at all tables. Lone hands are not allowed. The winners at Table I progress to the Booby Table. Otherwise, the game is played as Progressive Euchre.

FIVE HUNDRED, or BID EUCHRE

Equipment: For two-handed, a 24-card deck, from Ace (high) to 9 (low). For three-handed, the regular Euchre deck of 32 cards. For four-handed, a 42-card deck, Ace (high) through the 5's, with two 4's added. For five-handed, a regular 52-card deck. For six-handed, a 62-card deck, the regular 52-card deck with the 11's, 12's and two 13's added. The Joker may be added to any of these.

Rank of Cards: Exactly as in Euchre.

Preliminaries.—The players cut for deal, low winning. In the cut, the Ace is low, and the Joker lowest of all. After shuffle and final cut, the cards are dealt in rotation left to right. Each player must receive 10 cards; the remainder is faced down for a widow. The order is, 3 to each, then the widow, then 4 to each, and finally 3 to each. Rules concerning misdeals are as in the first chapter on Card Games.

Making thf Trump.—Beginning with the player left of the Dealer, each player in turn, ending with the Dealer, has the right to bid once for the privilege of naming the trump, or must pass. A player who passes cannot bid thereafter. Bids are made to capture a certain number of tricks, with a named suit as trumps, or at No Trumps. The form of bid is: 6 in Hearts, 7 in Diamonds, etc. In bidding, suits rank: No Trumps (highest); Hearts; Diamonds; Clubs; Spades (lowest. No bid can be for less than 6 tricks. If no bid of 6 or better is made, the deal passes to the left.

In some localities, if there is no bid, the hands are played at No Trumps, each trick scoring 10, with no set-back. In this case, the widow is not used, but is left faced down. By agreement it may be faced up to be looked at, but not drawn from.

An overcall must be for a higher number of scoring points, or for a greater number of tricks or the same scoring value. If a player bids out of turn, the bid is void, and the offender's partner or partners may not bid during the rest of the hand. When playing each for himself, there is no penalty for a bid out of turn.

The highest bidder takes the widow, and then discards enough cards to reduce his hand to 10 cards. He may discard some or all of the cards from the widow.

THE PLAY.—The successful bidder leads to the first trick, leading any card he chooses. Each player in turn must follow suit, if possible; if impossible, he must trump or discard. The winner of each trick leads to the next trick.

In a trump bid, the Joker is the highest trump. It is always the highest card in play. In No Trump and Nullo bids, the Joker is regarded as a suit by itself, and cannot be played as long as a player can follow suit. If the holder of a Joker leads it, he can name the suit that must be played to it.

The rule for exposed cards is the same as in most card games. Exposed cards become penalty cards, liable to be called by an opponent whenever they can properly be played.

If, after the first trick is played to, the bidder or widow has the wrong number of cards, and his opponents have the right number, the player is set back. The hand is played out, however, to see how many tricks the opponents can win. The penalty for a revoke established is the abandonment of the hands. If an opponent revokes, the bidder scores the full amount of his bid, and the offending side nothing. If the bidder revokes, he is set back the full amount of his bid, while opponents score any tricks taken in up to that time.

PARTNERS.—The four-handed game is played by partners, two against two; the six-handed game, by three pairs of partners. In the five-handed game, in some localities, the successful bidder names his partner for the hand, who cannot refuse the designation. In other localities, he names one partner on a bid of 6 or 7, and two partners on a bid of 8, 9 or 10. In other places, he may name the holder of a certain card as his partner. The identity of this partner is not made known until the card falls in play. In other localities, the holder of the named card announces the fact at once.

Scoring: If bidder takes as many tricks as he bid, he scores as follows:

Trumps	6 tricks	7 tricks	8 tricks	9 tricks	10 tricks
Spades	40	80	120	160	200
Clubs	60	120	180	240	300
Diamonds	80	160	240	320	400
Hearts	100	200	300	400	500
No Trumps	120	240	360	480	600

In some localities, the value of the black suits and of the red suits is reversed. In this case, the figures given above for Spades and Clubs should be marked Clubs and Spades; and the figures given for Diamonds and Hearts should be marked Hearts and Diamonds.

There is a third table, the Avondale Schedule, preferred by some players:

Trumps	6 tricks	7 tricks	8 tricks	9 tricks	10 tricks
Spades	40	140	240	340	440
Clubs	60	160	260	360	460
Diamonds	80	180	280	380	480
Hearts	100	200	300	400	500
No Trumps	120	220	320	420	520

The one advantage of this is that no values are duplicated. The Original Schedule, first given, is generally preferred.

If the bid was for less than 250, and bidder wins all 10 tricks, he is entitled to be scored 250 instead of the exact amount bid.

Each opponent scores 10 points for each trick individually taken.

If the bidder fails to take the number of tricks he bid, he is set back: that is, the amount of his bid is deducted from his score. If he has scored nothing previously, he is "in the hole" to the amount of his bid, and his score is marked minus, usually indicated by drawing a circle around the amount. Partners are set back together the full amount of their bid.

Game is 500 points or more. If a side gets 500 in the hole, it loses the game. If more than one player reaches 500 on a hand, the bidder, if he makes his bid, wins. If neither is bidder, the one reaching 500 first wins. If a player reaches game during the play of a hand, the balance of the hand must not be played; but the hands must be exposed, to make sure there was no revoke.

FIVE HUNDRED FOR TWO

When two play Five Hundred, the deck of 32 or (with Joker) 33 cards is used, and a dead hand is dealt and faced down to the left of the Dealer, besides the usual widow in the center of the table. This hand must not be examined until the play of the hand is over.

ONE THOUSAND, and FIFTEEN HUNDRED

These are played the same as Five Hundred, except for additional scores: for each Ace taken in, 1; each King, Queen, Jack or 10, 10; each 9 and so on, the pip value. The Joker scores nothing. These additional points do not aid toward making the bid, and are thrown out if bidder fails to make his contract. Game, 1,000 or 1,500, as agreed upon in advance.

PROGRESSIVE FIVE HUNDRED

Progressive Five Hundred is managed the same as Progressive Euchre, with Five Hundred bidding, play and scoring. In three-handed, the two high scores progress; in four-handed, the winning partners; in five-handed, the two high scores; in six-handed, the winning partners.

NULLOS IN FIVE HUNDRED

Some players like the variation in which a player bids Nullo, contracting not to take a trick. If he wins, he scores 250; if he takes one trick, he is set back 250, and opponents score 10 for each trick the bidder takes. In non-partnership games, each opponent scores for each trick the bidder takes. If the bidder does not discard the Joker, providing it is in his hand or the widow, he is set, since the Joker is bound to take any trick to which it is played. In Nullo, holder of Joker cannot play it, as long as he can follow suit. The Joker is regarded as a separate suit, but takes any trick to which it is played. The leader of a Joker may specify which suit must be played to it.

RAMS

The name Rams is a corruption of the German *Ramsch,* a type of game, or method of play, once played in the game of Skat, in which the four Jacks alone were trumps, and whoever took the most points lost. By general consent this has now been generally eliminated from Skat. The game of Rams is different, and is still popular; as is *Rounce,* another game whose name is corrupted from Rams.

EQUIPMENT.—A deck of 32 cards, Ace, King, Queen, Jack, 10, 9, 8, 7, in each suit.

PLAYERS.—Three to six. If six play, the player to the Dealer's right receives no cards.

RANK OF CARDS.—King (high), Queen, Jack, Ace, 10, 9, 8, 7 (low); sometimes Ace (high), King, Queen, Jack, 10, 9, 8, 7 (low).

PRELIMINARIES.—Any player deals the cards, one at a time, face up, in rotation left to right, the first player receiving a Jack becoming Dealer. Any player may shuffle the cards, the Dealer last, and the player to Dealer's right cuts. Beginning with the player to the left, 5 cards are dealt to each player—either 3, then

2; or 2, then 3. An extra hand, the widow, is dealt face down to the table, just before the Dealer receives his cards. The next card after the hands have been dealt is faced for trumps.

THE PLAY.—The player to the left of the Dealer may play with his original hand; or discard his hand face down on the table, and take the widow; or pass. Any player may discard his hand for the widow, as long as no other preceding player has done so. Each player in turn must decide to play; or exchange for the widow, if this has not been done; or pass. The hands of those who have passed must not be discarded until every player has said whether he will play or pass. Hands, once discarded, may not be examined thereafter. If all have passed except the player to the Dealer's right, he must play with the Dealer. If all but one have passed, the Dealer must play with him. If two or more declare to play, the Dealer may play or pass, as he chooses. The Dealer is allowed to discard one card and take the turned trump into his hand in its place. Each player who plays must take at least 1 trick, or forfeit 5 counters to the next pool.

Any player may declare a General Rams. He then has the lead, and must win all 5 tricks. Each other player must play in a General Rams, even if he has already passed.

Except where a General Rams is declared, the player first left of the Dealer of those who are playing leads a card of any suit. Each player in turn must follow suit, and must play a higher card than the one led if he can,—that is, head the trick. If he cannot head the trick, he may play any card of the suit led. If he cannot followed suit, he must trump (or overtrump, if trumps have already been played). Even though he cannot overtrump, he must still play trump if he can. If he can neither follow suit nor trump, he may discard. The highest card played of the suit led wins, unless the trick is trumped; in which case the highest trump wins. The winner of the first trick leads to the second, and so until the hand is played out.

SCORING.—The players begin with an equal number of counters. Each Dealer in his turn contributes 5 counters to the pool. Any player who does not pass and who fails to take a trick puts 5 counters in the next pool. At the end of each hand, each player takes one-fifth of the pool for each trick he has taken. A pool containing only the Dealer's 5 counters is called a Simple Pool, and all players must play. If it contains more than the 5 counters, it is called a Double Pool, and players can pass or play. If a player declaring General Rams takes all 5 tricks, he takes the pool, and each other player pays him 5 counters. If he fails, he must pay each player 5 counters, and double the pool.

The first player losing all of his counters loses the game; or the player first winning an agreed number of counters wins the game.

ROUNCE

In the variation of Rams called Rounce, the full deck of 52 cards is used. The cards rank Ace, King, Queen, Jack, 10, 9 down through 2 (low). The widow is dealt 6 cards. If there are six players, the Dealer takes no cards. A player taking the widow must discard one card, to bring his hand down to 5. A player is not obliged to take a trick, but must follow suit, if possible. The winner of the first trick must lead trumps for the second trick. Thereafter, any suit may be led. There is no General Rams. Otherwise, the game is played the same as Rams.

BIERSPIEL

In the variation of Rams called Bierspiel, the 32-card deck is used, as in Rams. The cards rank as in Rams, except that the 7 of Diamonds is always the second highest trump, no matter the suit. If the 7 of Diamonds is turned for the trump, the next card must be turned up, and it indicates the trump suit. The Dealer may take both cards into his hand, discarding 2 others. If the Dealer passes, the player to his left has the privilege of taking up the trump card or cards.

Players may not look at their cards until the Dealer has turned the trump and said "Auf," the signal for them to look at their cards. If four players declare to play, the first three leads must be trumps; if three play, the first two leads; if two, the first lead. If the leader has no trump, he must play, face down, the lowest card in his hand, and the other players having trumps must play trumps upon it.

Each player starts with three crosses chalked before him, each cross counting 5. A score of 1 causes him to erase the center of the first cross, leaving it worth four; he erases one arm of the cross for each subsequent point scored. The first player cancelling all 15 of his points wins the game.

Otherwise, it is played the same as Rams.

LOO, or DIVISION LOO

This relative of Euchre was at one time the most popular of all round games at cards; today, Napoleon (or, more generally, Nap) in England and Poker in America (and frequently in England) have entirely overshadowed it. Any number of players from three to seventeen can play; but five to eight is the usual number. A full deck of 52 cards is used, ranking from Ace, King, Queen, down through the 2.

To determine the Dealer, the cards are faced up one at a time, the first player receiving a Jack becoming the Dealer. After the cards are shuffled and cut, the Dealer puts 3 counters in the pool, and deals 3 cards to each player, in rotation left to right, one at a time. No trump is turned when there are only 3 counters in the pool, which is called a Simple Pool. This deal is called a Bold Stand, since everyone must play the hand dealt him.

The player to the dealer's left leads any card he pleases. The other players must not only follow suit if they can, but must head the trick. The cards are not gathered into tricks, but are left faced up before each player. If all follow suit, the winner of the trick leads for the next, and so on. If one or more players cannot follow suit to any trick, the Dealer turns up the top card of the stock for a trump, before play to the next trick. If any trump has been played, the highest trump wins the trick. If a trump is turned, the winner of a trick must lead a trump to the next trick, if he can.

The winners of the 3 tricks take a third of the pool for each trick won. All the other players are looed, and must put up 3 counters each for the next pool, a Double Pool. In Double Pools, the Dealer adds 3 counters; deals as before; deals a hand just before his own for a widow; and turns a trump. Beginning with the player to his left, each player in turn has the choice of standing on the cards dealt him, exchanging his hand for the widow if it has not been taken up, or passing. Any player standing or exchanging will be looed, unless he wins a trick. If all pass but the player to the right of the dealer, he must play the hand, take the widow, or surrender the pool to the dealer.

If only one player stands, and has not taken the widow, Dealer must stand or defend with the widow. If he takes any tricks, his winnings are left in the pool. If he is looed, he does not pay. If the one player standing has taken the widow, the pool is his, unless the dealer will play against him on his own account.

All having declared, the player to the left of the dealer who is still in leads. He must lead a trump if he has one, and he must lead the top of 2 or more. The winner of the trick must lead a trump if he has one. Each player in turn must follow suit, and must head the trick if he can; but he need not undertrump a trick on which a higher trump than he holds has been played. The winners of the 3 tricks divide the pool proportionately. All who are looed put up 3 counters each for the next pool. If no one is looed, the next will be a Simple Pool. Deal passes to the left.

This is called Limited Loo.

Unlimited Loo.—In Unlimited Loo, every player who is looed must double the amount in the current pool, as a foundation for the next pool.

Loo with Flushes.—It is sometimes agreed to play flushes. If any player in a Double Pool holds 3 trumps, either dealt to him or found in the widow, he waits until all the players (including Dealer) have declared or passed. He then shows his flush in trumps, and takes the pool without playing for it, all who have declared being looed. If two players hold trump flushes, the one on the left of the Dealer wins the pool, regardless of the rank of the cards; but the other flush is not looed.

If a Dealer deals a wrong number of cards or hands, he loses the deal, forfeits 3 counters to the pool, and the next pool is a Double. If a player revokes, by failing to follow suit, or to head a trick, or to lead a trump when required, the pool is divided equally among the rest who hold cards; and the offender antes up 6 counters for the next pool.

IRISH LOO

All pools are alike, and there is no widow. A trump is always faced. Those who stand are asked by the Dealer if they wish to exchange any cards. If any are demanded, the faced trump is laid on the table, and the players are helped from the top of the stock.

FIVE-CARD LOO

The Dealer antes up 5 counters into the pool, and deals 5 cards to each player. A flush of 5 trumps wins the pool without playing. Everyone at the table, whether playing the hand or not, is looed if he does not take a trick, and must contribute 5 counters to the next pool.

PAM

When, at Loo, the Jack of clubs is made the best trump, no matter what suit is turned up, the game is called Pam. This card must not be played when the trump Ace is led, unless its holder has no other trump. Otherwise, Pam is played the same as Loo.

SPOIL FIVE, or FORTY-FIVE

Equipment: A full deck of 52 cards.

Players: From two to ten, as individuals. Best played as a five- or six-handed game.

Rank of Cards: In trumps, the Ace of Hearts is always the third best trump, no matter the suit. Of the trump suit, the 5 is high, the Jack second highest, the Ace of Hearts third, then the Ace, King, Queen in order. The rank of the spot or pip cards, trump or not, is expressed "highest in red, lowest in black." In plain suits (that is, suits not trumps) the King, Queen, Jack are high in that order; followed by the pip cards, as above. In plain suits, the Diamond Ace is lowest of all; the black Aces come between the Jack and the deuce. Where Hearts are trumps, 13 trumps: 5, Jack, Ace, King, Queen, 10, 9, 8, 7, 6, 4, 3, 2. Where Diamonds are trumps, there are 14, the Ace of Hearts ranking third highest and 2 lowest. Where Spades or Clubs are trumps, there are 14, ranking 5, Jack, Ace of Hearts, Ace, King, Queen, 2, 3, 4, 6, 8, 9, 10 (low).

Preliminaries.—Instead of a cut, the cards are dealt one at a time, left to right, face up, the first player receiving a Jack becoming Dealer. After the shuffle and cut, 5 cards are dealt to each player, left to right: 3, and then 2; or 2, and then 3. The next card is faced up for trumps. Rules for misdeals are the same as those given in the first chapter on Card Games.

Robbing the Trump.—The player holding the Ace of the suit turned for trumps may exchange any card in his hand for the trump faced, if he wishes. If not, he must request the Dealer to turn down the faced trump; otherwise, he loses the right to "rob the trump" and his Ace becomes the lowest trump, even if it is the Ace of Hearts. If the Ace is turned, the Dealer may discard at once, and after the first trick take the Ace into his hand. The hand left of the Dealer should ask the Dealer to do this before the first lead; but if the Dealer does not want the Ace, he may play with his original hand, announcing this intention.

The Play.—The hand to the Dealer's left leads any card. In turn, left to right, the players, if able to follow suit, must either do so, or trump. If a player cannot follow suit, he must trump or discard. The highest card of the suit led wins the trick; unless it is trumped, in which case the highest trump wins. Winner of trick leads to the next trick.

Reneging.—The 3 highest trumps are allowed to renege, in this fashion: When a trump lower than the one held is led, the player holding one of these 3 tops need not follow suit, even though a higher card than the one he holds falls on the lead. As usually played, if he holds a lower trump as well, he is required to follow suit, but not to play the higher trump unless he chooses.

Scoring.—Each player begins with an equal number of counters. Each player puts an equal number of counters into the pool; and, if the pool is not won on any deal, each Dealer in turn adds another counter. After a pool is won, each player puts up an equal number of counters for a new pool.

The player who takes 3 tricks and immediately abandons the rest of the hand, wins the pool. If he continues playing, he must "Jink it," that is, take all 5 tricks. If he does so, he wins the pool and 1 counter from each player. If he fails, he loses the pool, which then goes to the next player winning 3 or 5 tricks.

The game is lost by the first player losing all his counters; or an agreed number of counters may be fixed for game, and the first player winning this total wins.

When a hand is found to have too many or two few cards, it must be abandoned face down, and the player loses further interest in the pool, although he retains any tricks taken before the discovery that his hand was incorrect was made. If a player takes the turned trump when he does not hold the Ace; or exposes a card out of order when any player has taken 2 tricks; or throws off when he should have followed suit, he must discard his hand, face down, and forfeit his interest in that pool until it is later won. If it is not won on that hand, he must add to it as if he were eligible to play for it.

Players who have no chance to win 3 tricks and the pool play to distribute the tricks among the others, so that no one may win 3 tricks, and the play therefore be "spoiled" for that deal: hence the name of the game. When one player has won 3 tricks, if he does not abandon the rest of his hand he should say "I Jink it," meaning he intends to play to take all 5 tricks, and so collect an extra counter from each player.

FORTY-FIVE; FIVE AND TEN

This is a variation of Spoil Five, for two, four (two against two) or six (three against three) players. The game is scored by points, the side taking 3 or 4 tricks scoring 5 points; the side taking 5 tricks, 10 points. In some localities, each trick scores 5 points, and the score of the side taking the fewest tricks is deducted from the score of the winners. Thus: 3 tricks count 5; 4 tricks, 15; 5 tricks, 25. The game is 45 points.

TWENTY-FIVE

In some localities, the game is played for 25 points; otherwise it is played the same as Forty-Five.

ÉCARTÉ

EQUIPMENT: A deck of 32 cards, Ace, King, Queen, Jack, 10, 9, 8, 7 in each suit.

PLAYERS: Two. There are three players in Pool Écarté.

RANK OF CARDS: King (highest), Queen, Jack, Ace, 10, 9, 8, 7 (low).

The two players cut for deal, high winning. Both players have a right to shuffle, the Dealer last; and Dealer's Opponent cuts. Each player is dealt 5 cards, 3-2 or 2-3, beginning with the Opponent. The eleventh card is turned up for trump. If this is a King, the Dealer scores 1 point for himself immediately.

ARRIVING AT THE HANDS.—If the Opponent wishes to play his original hand, he says "I play." If he wishes to strengthen his hand by discarding and drawing to it from the stock, a privilege the Dealer then shares, he says "I propose." The Dealer may refuse this privilege, by saying "Play"; or he may accept it, dealing the Opponent as many cards from the top of the stock as he discards. The Dealer may then discard and draw to fill his own hand. This process may be repeated alternately until one of the players announces that he is ready to play. Each time, the number drawn must be the same as the number discarded.

Discards are made face down, and may not be examined thereafter. A player who violates this may be called upon to play with his cards exposed, though they are not subject to call. If a player asks for more cards than are left in the stock, he must take back enough from his last discard to fill his hand. If the Dealer finds there are not as many cards as he wishes to draw after he accepts a proposal, he has no remedy. An Opponent who proposes, and whose proposal is accepted, must discard at least one card. The Dealer, if requested, must announce how many cards he has discarded. The faced trump is laid to one side when the hands are filled, and is never taken into the hand.

THE PLAY.—The Opponent leads any card he pleases to the first trick, announcing its suit. The Dealer must follow suit, if possible; and is compelled to take the trick with a higher card, if he can. If he cannot follow suit, he must trump, if possible; if not possible, he discards. The higher card of the suit led takes the trick, unless it is trumped; in the latter case the trump or the highest trump wins. The leader of each trick leads to the next, announcing the suit of the card led. If this is announced incorrectly, the other player may demand that the card be taken back and one of the announced suit led; or that the card led remain. If the leader has no card of the suit he announced and failed to lead, the other player may name a suit for him to lead.

If a player fails to follow suit or win a trick when possible, or if he trumps when he could follow suit, it is a Renounce. The cards are taken up, the hand is played over, and if the Renouncer takes less than 5 tricks on the replay, he does not score. If he takes 5 tricks, he scores 1 point only. A player leading out of turn must take back the card, unless the opponent has played to it, in which case it stands. Tricks must be turned down and quitted as soon as taken, and may not be reexamined until the end of the hand, on penalty of playing the balance of the hand exposed, though not subject to call.

If a player abandons his hand as not worth a point, he may not score on it, though he might have won. If he abandons it claiming 1 or 2 points, he scores them, if his hand substantiates the claim. If he abandons it, granting his opponent 1 or more points, the adversary is entitled to score all he could have made, if the hand had been played out.

SCORING.—Trump King turned, 1 point for the Dealer; held in either hand, 1 point for holder, provided the holding is announced before a card is led. An Opponent who stands, or Dealer who refuses, or either player who finally elects to play, scores 1 point for 3 tricks; 2 points for Vole, or 5 tricks. If a player stands or refuses, and fails to take 3 or more tricks, the other player scores 2 points.

Misdeals.—A misdeal loses the deal. Any faced card except the eleventh causes a misdeal. If either hand has too few or too many cards, the Opponent may claim a misdeal, or may have the correct number arrived at by adding from the stock or drawing. If more than one card is faced for trump, the Opponent, if he has not examined his hand, may claim a misdeal, or select the trump; or if he has seen his hand, he may claim a misdeal, or declare the eleventh card to be the trump.

Jeux de Règle.—There are certain hands, called Jeux de Règle, on which the Opponent should play without proposing, and on which Dealer should refuse. These are:

Any hand with 3 trumps in it.

Any hand with 2 trumps and 3 cards of one suit; or 2 cards of one suit as high as Queen; or 2 cards of one suit and King of another suit; or 3 cards of different suits, as good as King and Jack.

One trump and 3 winning cards in another suit; or a 4-card suit to a King; or 3 cards of one suit, with 2 Kings in hand.

A hand without a trump should have 4 court cards, or as good as 3 Queens.

POOL ÉCARTÉ

Three players contribute equally to a pool. The three cut, the two highest playing, highest of all dealing. They play as in the regular game. The loser of the first game puts in as many counters as he originally chipped in, and drops out of the next game in favor of the odd player, called the Rentrant. This continues until one player wins two games in succession, in which case he takes the entire pool. A new pool is then made up, and played for in the same manner.

The odd player must not advise either player on the first

hand of any pool. Thereafter, as he has an interest in the pool, he may advise one player or the other, by pointing only. He may also call attention to errors in the score.

NAPOLEON, or NAP

EQUIPMENT: A full deck of 52 cards.

PLAYERS: Two to six, four being the usual number. In five- or six-hand games, the Dealer takes no cards.

RANK OF CARDS: Ace, King, Queen, Jack, 10, 9, 8, 7, 6, 5, 4, 3, 2 (low). Ace is highest in play, but lowest in cutting.

PRELIMINARIES.—In the cut for deal, low deals, Ace being the lowest. After shuffle and cut, the Dealer deals 5 cards to each player, in rotation left to right: either 3, and then 2; or 2, and then 3. Any irregularity in the deal requires a new deal by the same Dealer.

THE BIDDING.—Each player in turn, beginning on the Dealer's left, may bid the number of tricks he will take playing alone against all the others, if allowed to name the trump; or may pass. If he bids, he does not name the suit he intends to name as trumps. Each bidder is allowed only one chance to bid or pass, the Dealer last. The successful bidder then names the trump suit. Sometimes a bid of 3 No Trumps is allowed, called Misère; this ranking above 3 with trumps and below 4 with trumps. Ordinarily 5 with trumps, called Nap, is the highest possible bid. In some localities, two bids are allowed, which successively outrank Nap: Wellington, and Blucher. Each contract to take 5 tricks with trumps, these last three bids differing only in the scoring. If no one bids, the Dealer must bid at least 1.

THE PLAY.—The successful bidder leads, and must lead trumps. Each player must follow suit, if possible; if not, he must trump or discard. The winner of each trick leads to the next. Tricks taken should be quitted face down, in such arrangement that they may be easily counted; and they may not thereafter be examined. The highest card of the suit led takes the trick; unless it is trumped, in which case the highest trump wins. When the hand is ended, the deal passes to the left. It is only required to lead trumps to the first trick. As soon as the bidder gets the number of tricks he has bid, the rest of the hand is abandoned, and the players pay up the appropriate number of counters.

A claim of misdeal through an incorrect number of cards must be made before a player bids or passes; otherwise, he must play out the hand. If the bidder has the correct number of cards in this case, and another hand is defective, he must be paid, if he succeeds; if he fails, he need not pay. If the bidder has too many cards, he scores nothing for making his contract; if less, he must pay or be paid as he loses or wins. He loses any tricks upon which he has no card to play.

A bidder leading out of turn must take back the card, unless all have played to it; in the latter event it stands. An opponent leading out of turn pays 3 counters to the bidder, and is not paid if the bidder loses. In case of a revoke, the bidder pays each player the amount of his bid; an opponent must pay the amount of the bid to the bidder and also to the other players. When a revoke is detected, the hands are abandoned.

Scoring.—At the beginning of the game, the players are given an equal number of counters. Where the bidder is successful, each opponent pays him 1 counter for each trick bid; if he fails, he pays each opponent 1 counter for each trick bid. Misére is paid for as 3 tricks. Nap scores 10 from each player, if successful; if it fails, bidder pays 5 to each. Wellington scores 5 from each player, if successful; and pays 10 to each, if it fails. Blucher scores 10 from each player, if successful; and pays 20 to each, if it fails.

The first player who loses all his counters loses the game; or, the first player winning an agreed number of counters wins the game.

MISERY NAP

Misery Nap amounts to a bid of Nullos. It ranks the same as Misère, and scores 3 counters either way. When a player bids Misery, he contracts to lose every trick.

POOL NAP

Each player contributes an equal amount to a pool; and each Dealer in turn adds a stipulated sum. Revoke pays 5 to the pool, and lead out of turn 3 counters. First player winning 5 tricks on a bid of Nap, Wellington or Blucher wins the pool. Any such bid failing, the player must double the pool.

WIDOW NAP

An extra hand, the widow, is dealt just before the Dealer's. The player who takes up the widow must bid Nap or better, discard 5 cards face down, and win all 5 tricks.

PEEP NAP

This is a variety of Pool Nap. A widow of 1 card is dealt. Each player in turn may look at it, by paying 1 counter to the pool. The successful bidder gets the widow (whether he has peeped or not) and discards 1 card, to bring his hand down to 5. Even after Nap has been bid, later players in turn may pay their counter and peep at the widow.

SIR GARNET

The same as Widow Nap, except that the player who takes up the widow and bids Nap must pay 10 to each player if he fails to take all 5 tricks.

ÉCARTÉ NAP or PURCHASE NAP

This is a variation of Pool Nap. Before the bidding commences, each player in turn may discard as many cards as he pleases and buy others one at a time from the stock, paying into the pool 1 counter for each card so purchased. Otherwise it is played the same as Pool Nap.

HASENPFEFFER

Equipment: A deck of 25 cards, Ace, King, Queen, Jack, 10, 9 of each suit, and the Joker.

Players: Four, two partners against the other two.

Rank of Cards: In trumps, Joker, Jack of trumps, Jack of the other suit of the same color, Ace, King, Queen, 10, 9 of trumps. Suit of same color, Ace, King, Queen, 10, 9. Suits of other color, Ace, King, Queen, Jack, 10, 9.

In the cut for partners, the two lowest play against the two highest, lowest winning choice of seats, and becoming Dealer. In cutting, the Ace is high. Each player is dealt 6 cards, 3 and then another 3. The last card remains faced down on the table.

Each player in turn, beginning with the Dealer's left, has one bid, giving the number of tricks he will take if allowed to specify the trump but not naming the suit. The highest bidder names the trump, and leads to the first trick. If no bids are made, the holder of the Joker must bid 3, and play the hand. Players must follow suit, if possible, or trump; if both courses are impossible they must discard.

Each trick counts 1 point; and 10 points make game. If the bidder fails to make his bid, he is set back the amount of his bid.

DOUBLE-PACK HASENPFEFFER

Two, three, four or six players may play with the double Pinochle deck, 48 cards, Ace down to 9, without the Joker. If duplicate cards are played to a trick, the first of these played is ranked higher. When three players play, they play each for himself; when four, as partners, two against two; when six, three against three. Each player is dealt 4 cards at a time, until the whole deck is distributed.

In bidding, the lowest bid is 6. If the bidder thinks he can win all the tricks, he may, after naming the trump suit, discard 2 cards and ask his partner (or partners, if any) for his 2 best; thereafter he plays alone.

If the game is four-handed, his side scores 24 if he wins, but is set 12 if he fails. In six-handed, his side scores 16 if he wins, or is set 8. If all pass without a bid, the Dealer must bid 6 and play the hand. Each trick counts 1, except in lone hands; and 62 makes the game.

SKAT

Equipment: A 32-card deck, Ace, King, Queen, Jack, 10, 9, 8, 7 of each suit.

Players: Three, four, or five—of whom only three receive cards and play in any deal.

Rank of Cards, in Trump Games: The four Jacks, called Wentzels or Bowers, are always the four highest trumps, in this order: Clubs (highest), Spades, Hearts, Diamonds (lowest). After the four Jacks, the trumps rank Ace, 10, King, Queen, 9, 8, 7. Non-trump cards rank Ace (high), 10, King, Queen, 9, 8, 7. *In Nullos,* the play is at No Trumps, and each suit ranks Ace, King, Queen, Jack, 10, 9, 8, 7.

Rank of Suits: Clubs (highest), Spades, Hearts, Diamonds (lowest). This ranking only affects the score when one of these suits is named as trumps; it does not affect trick-taking value.

Matadors: The Jack of Clubs and each trump in unbroken sequence with it is called a Matador. This sequence is given above, in listing the rank of cards in trump games: Club Jack, Spade Jack, Heart Jack, Diamond Jack, trump Ace, 10, King, etc. The maximum number of Matadors a hand may hold is 10, Club Jack down through trump 8. If highest bidder has the Club Jack, he plays *with* a certain number of Matadors; if an opponent holds it, he plays *without* a certain number. The number of Matadors either with or without affects the value of the game.

Preliminaries.—The players cut for choice of seats, the lowest having choice of seats and dealing first; the next lowest sits to his left, and so in rotation. The cards rank in cutting as they do in trump play; the suits rank as above. The player to the right of the first dealer keep the score, showing when each round of deals is completed. If four play, the Dealer receives no cards, but shares in the fortunes of the two opposed to the single player. If five play, the Dealer deals to the two players next to him on the left and the player next to him on the right; players not receiving cards share in the fortunes of the two who oppose the successful bidder.

Any player may shuffle, the Dealer last. The player to the Dealer's right deals 3 cards to each active player, in rotation to the left; then 2 face down on the table (the Skat); then 4 in rotation; then 3; so that each active player has a hand of 10 cards, and the Skat has 2. Any irregularity of dealing constitutes a misdeal. The Dealer is penalized 10 points, deducted from his score, and deals again. A deal out of turn may be stopped if discovered before the last card is dealt; otherwise it stands. The next and later deals proceed correctly, the Dealer out of turn being omitted on his next turn. Thus each player deals once in each round.

Types of Games.—There are two main types of games: those in which the player contracts to take no trick; and those in which the player's object is to take enough counting cards to make 61 or more out of a possible 120 in the deck. The cards count as follows: Aces, 11; 10's, 10; Kings, 4; Queens, 3; Jacks, 2. The games are:

Tournée.—The successful bidder turns up one card of the Skat, thereby declaring the suit of this card to be the trump. If the turned card is a Jack, he may name the suit to which it belongs, or play a Grand Tournée, the 4 Jacks then being the only trumps. After declaring, the player takes the card turned up and the other Skat card into his hand and discards 2 cards. If the discarded cards are of any counting value, they score for the maker of the trump.

Solo.—The successful bidder names a trump suit from his hand, without looking at the Skat. He must play with the hand dealt to him, and cannot use the Skat in play; nevertheless the latter belongs to him, and any points and Matadors found in it when the deal is played are counted for him.

Grand.—When a Grand is played, the 4 Jacks are the only trumps. There are four varieties of Grand:

Grand Tournée, where a Jack is turned from the Skat for trump. Player then takes the other Skat card, and discards 2 cards.

Guckser or Grand Frage, in which a player takes up both Skat cards and announces the 4 Jacks will be the only trumps. He discards 2 cards from his hand, as in Tournée.

Grand Solo, announced by a player without looking at either Skat cards. These Skat cards are not seen by any player until the hand is played out, when the counting value, if any, of the Skat cards counts for the bidder.

Grand Ouvert, in which a successful bidder announces a Grand; he spreads his cards face up on the table, and plays them in that manner, though they are not subject to call. Every trick must be won in order to win game.

Bidding.—The three active players are known by these names: Player to the left of the Dealer, Leader or Vorhand; second player, Middlehand or Mittelhand; and the third, Endhand or Hinterhand. Where only three play, the Dealer is also Endhand.

The Leader has the right to name the game; but the others may bid to take this privilege from him, by naming a certain number of points, which must never be less than 10, and must represent the value of some game. He must not name the type of game at first.

The Middlehand has the first bid, and bids a number, 10 or more, representing the value of some game. If the Leader thinks he can make as many points as Middlehand has bid, he says "Yes," in which case Middlehand must bid higher, or pass. If the Leader is offered more than he thinks he can make, he passes. As soon as either the Leader or the Middlehand passes, the Endhand has the privilege of bidding with the survivor. These two bid in the same way, until one of them passes. The highest bidder then declares the type of game to be played. The bidder may play any game he chooses, providing the value equals or exceeds the amount of his bid. He is known as the Player.

Nullo—This is a bid to lose every trick.

Nullo is played at No Trumps, with no Jacks or Wentzels, no Matadors, and no trump suit. A Nullo is valued 20, if played out of hand.

Null Ouvert is a Nullo which is laid open on the table before a card is led. It counts double—40 points.

Gucki Nullo is a bid to take the Skat cards and discard 2 in their place, afterward playing a Nullo. Before touching the Skat, it must be distinctly stated that it is a Gucki Nullo, and not a Gucki Grand. If it wins, it is worth 15; if it loses, it counts double, or 30.

Gucki Nullo Ouvert is a Gucki Nullo in which the cards are faced up after taking the two from the Skat and discarding. This is worth 30, but counts double if lost, or 60.

Passt-Mir-Nicht Tournée.—When a player turns a Skat card for a Tournée, and it does not suit him, he may so declare without showing it. He must then turn up the other Skat card, which becomes the trump. If this second Skat card is a Jack, the Player may either declare that suit trump, or declare a Grand Tournée. The player must show this second Skat card before mixing it with his cards, or the opponents may determine which game shall be played, the opponent naming the highest game having the privilege. If the player playing Passt-Mir-Nicht Tournée wins, it counts as a Tournée; if he fails, it counts double against him.

Ramsch.—When both players pass without bidding, the Leader may declare Ramsch. The cards rank as in Grand, the Jacks being the only trumps. The object then is to take as few tricks as possible. If each player takes at least 1 trick, the player winning the greatest number of points loses the value of the game, 20 points; if one player has taken no trick, the value of the game is 30 points.

Values of Games.—Each of these games has a unit value; and, except in Nullos, these values may be increased by certain Multipliers. The unit values are as follows:

	If trumps are:			
	Clubs	*Spades*	*Hearts*	*Diamonds*
Tournée	8	7	6	5
Solo	12	11	10	9

	The four Jacks
Grand Tournée	12
Guckser or Grand Fraje (double if lost)	16
Grand Solo	20
Grand Ouvert	24

	No Trumps
Nullo	20
Null Ouvert	40
Gucki Nullo (double if lost)	15
Gucki Nullo Ouvert (double if lost)	30

MULTIPLIERS.—The following are the multipliers, used when suits or the 4 Jacks are Trumps:

Simple Game (61 points or more)	1
Schneider or Little Slam (91 points or better)	2
Little Slam announced in advance, or Schwarz or Grand Slam (winning every trick)	3
Grand Slam after announcing Little Slam	4
Grand Slam announced in advance	5

Grand Ouvert is always Grand Slam announced. In addition to these values, the value of each game is increased by the number of Matadors the Player is *with* or *without*. Thus, if the Player has the Jack of Clubs, but lacks the Jack of Spades, he is *with* one; if he has the Spade Jack but lacks the Club Jack, he is *without* one; and these score the same, being added to the Multipliers above. Similarly having both these Jacks, but lacking the Heart Jack; or lacking both, but having the Heart Jack, he adds 2 to the Multipliers in either case, as *with* 2 or *without* 2.

Thus: Little Slam, not announced (2) *with* or *without* 3 Matadors (adding 3 to total 5) in Clubs Tournée (8) would give five times 8, that is, 40; in Hearts Solo (10), it would give 5 times 10, or 50, providing the Little Slam is made.

If a player fails to secure 61, he loses the game. If he fails to get 31, he is made Schneider; if he fails to win a trick, he is made Schwarz. These add to the cost of the game he loses, as they would have added to the value of the game if he had won them. In Solos, the Player may announce Schneider (Little Slam) or Schwarz (Grand Slam) in advance, but his opponents cannot announce anything. Announcing adds 1 Multiplier in each case, as above.

The Play.—After the successful bidder has announced the type of game he will play and has properly disposed of the Skat cards, the Leader leads any card, and the others must follow suit, if possible, or trump or discard. The highest card of the suit led wins the trick; unless it was trumped, in which case the highest trump wins. The winner of the first trick leads to the second, and so on, until the hands are played out. In a Grand, if a Jack is led, the holder of another Jack must play it; since the 4 Jacks alone constitute the trump suit.

In a Tournée, if a successful bidder announces that he cannot win his hand, before he plays to the second trick he may abandon his hand, thus losing the value of the game, but escaping a possible Little Slam or Grand Slam. This cannot be done in a Solo game.

Irregularities in Play.—If, during the play, a player discovered to have too few cards, through having dropped a card or played 2 to a trick unintentionally, he loses; but his opponent or opponents may demand that the hand be played out, to try for a Slam. The last trick, lacking the missing card, is considered as won by the opponent of the player in error. If the player is not the single player, his partner loses with him. Should the player find the missing card, he cannot restore it to his hand if if he has played to a trick in the meantime.

If an adversary of the single player leads or plays out of turn, he loses the game. The single player may demand that the error be corrected and the hand played out, for the purpose of increasing the value of the game. If the single player leads out of turn, either opponent may demand that the card be taken back, if both have not played to the trick.

If a revoke is established, the player revoking loses the game; but his opponent or opponents may demand that the error be corrected and the hand played out, in order to increase the value of the game.

A player who examines a quitted trick (except the last) loses the game; but any one of the participants may demand that the hand be played out, to increase the player's loss.

Scoring.—The Player winning the game he has made or announced receives its value from each other player. If he loses, he must pay to each the value of the game lost. Both these include non-active players participating in the fortunes of the two opponents of the Player. Payments may be by counters; or, more usually, by scoring the amounts won and deducting the amounts lost. At the end, each player settles up with each other player, by adding what he has lost to what the other player has won from him, or vice versa.

STANDARD SKAT

As often played in America, Skat has been simplified into Standard Skat. Suits have only one value, the Solo value: Clubs 12, Spades 11, Hearts 10, Diamonds 9. The lowest possible bid is 18 (simple game 1, plus *with* or *without* 1 Matador, giving 2 times 9, or 18). The successful bidder takes the Skat into his hand, and discards any 2 cards face downward, which count for him at the end. A successful bidder can play without the Skat, which is called Handplay; and scores 1 more Multiplier for doing this. The values for Nullo are: Plain Nullo, 23; Open Nullo, 46; Handplay Open Nullo, 59. In Grand, the unit value is 20; the other Grands being eliminated. Otherwise, the game is played the same.

ORIGINAL SKAT

As originally played, there were three types of suit bids: Frage (trump declared after Skat is added to the hand), scoring 1, 2, 3, and 4 for Diamonds, Hearts, Spades and Clubs; Tournée, with the turned Skat card, scoring 5, 6, 7, and 8 respectively;

and Solo, naming the trump without Skat, scoring 9, 10, 11 and 12 respectively. Grand Tournée scores 12; Grand Solo, 18; Grand Ouvert, 24; Nullo Tournée, 10; Nullo Solo, 23; Null Ouvert, 46. Otherwise the play was the same or similar in every respect.

SOLO or SLOUGH (SLUFF)

Equipment: A 36-card deck, from Ace (high) down to 6 (low).

Players: Three to seven. Only three are active players each time, the others receiving no cards.

Rank of Cards: Ace, 10, King, Queen, Jack, 9, 8, 7, 6.

Point Value of Cards: Ace, 11; 10, 10; King, 4; Queen, 3; Jack, 2. This is the same point value as in Skat and Sheepshead (Schafkopf).

Preliminaries.—Players each draw one card from a deck spread face downward. Low gets choice of being Dealer or sitting at the Dealer's left. After shuffle and cut, the whole deck is dealt left to right one at a time. The 1st, 4th and 8th cards are dealt into a separate pile, constituting the widow, and are known as the Slough cards. Any irregularity in the deal requires the same Dealer to redeal.

Each player is provided with 21 chips, 11 worth 10 points each, and 10 of a different color worth 1 point each; the total value to each player is therefore 120 points.

A Frog (German, *Frage*). In a Frog, Hearts are trumps, other suits being plain. The maker of a Frog adds the widow to his hand, and discards an equal number of cards. These add to his point score after the hand has been played out, and are not exposed until then. In localities where Straight Solo is played, there are no Frogs, and the Simple Solo and the Heart Solo points have a value of 1 and 2, respectively.

A Simple Solo.—When a player wishes to play a Simple Solo, he merely says "I offer to Solo." He need not tell what suit he will name as trumps until the others have passed and the player to Dealer's right is about to lead. The player who Solos is given credit for the points in the widow, which must not be exposed until after the hand has been played out. Spades, Clubs or Diamonds may be named as trump in a Simple Solo.

A Heart Solo.—A Heart Solo, the highest bid, has Hearts for trump.

The Bidding.—The object of the game is to take in on tricks cards whose points total to 60 or more. The player to the Dealer's right has first bid, or may pass. The bid passes to the left. If all, including the Dealer, pass, the hands are thrown in and the deal passes to the left. A player who has bid a Frog may raise his own bid to a Heart Solo, over an intervening bid of Simple Solo.

The Play.—The player to the left of the Dealer leads any card. Each player in turn, left to right, must follow suit if possible; otherwise he must trump, or, failing that, he must discard. The highest card of the suit led wins the trick; unless it is trumped, in which case the highest trump played wins the trick. The winner of each trick leads to the next trick. The bidder plays against the combined efforts of the two other players to prevent his making game. If the bidder revokes, the hand must be played out. If he wins, he scores nothing; if he makes below 60 points, he must pay. If a player who is not the bidder revokes, the hand must be played out. He scores nothing if the bidder is set; but must pay if the bid is made.

Scoring.—After the hand is played out, the point value of the cards taken in by the bidder, plus the points in the widow, are counted, and the bidder is paid, or pays the other players, as follows:

In a Frog,	1 chip	for	each	point	above	or	below	60
In a Simple Solo,	2 chips	"	"	"	"	"	"	60
In a Heart Solo,	3 chips	"	"	"	"	"	"	60

The Dealer, where there are four players, and any other extra players, receive, but do not pay. In some localities, the Dealer and any other non-active players both receive and pay; in other places they receive only on Frogs, but both receive and pay on all Solos. The first player unable to pay his losses loses the game.

The Penalty Frog.—This variation pays the bidder, if the bid is made, the same as a regular Frog; but, if he loses, he must pay at the rate of a Heart Solo.

For bidding a Simple Solo, 3 Aces and a 10 in one of the 3 suits headed by the Ace should be held. For a Heart Solo, 4 Aces and at least 3 Hearts.

COEUR D'ALENE SOLO

In this variation, each hand constitutes a complete game, 61 points being needed to win; excess points are not considered. If a bidder makes 60 points, it is rated a tie, and the deal passes to the left. The settlements for winning and losses are computed as follows: 1 chip for a Frog; 2 chips for a Simple Solo; 3 chips for a Heart Solo.

DENVER PROGRESSIVE SOLO

In this variation, there are five standard bids, which rank upward: Frog, Spade Solo, Club Solo, Diamond Solo, Heart Solo. The bidding continues around and around, until four players finally pass. For every point under or over 60, the scoring is: Frog, 1 chip; Spade Solo, 2 chips; Club Solo, 3 chips; Diamond Solo, 4 chips; Heart Solo, 5 chips. If both sides make 60, it is rated a tie. In addition, each player contributes equally to a Frog Pot and a Solo Pot. If a bidder succeeds, he takes the appropriate pot; if he fails, he doubles the value of the pot. This is in addition to the usual payments for points.

SIX BID SOLO or SLOUGH (SLUFF)

This Salt Lake City variation eliminates the Frog bid. The widow of 3 cards is dealt after the players have received 4 and then 3 cards each, and before the final 4 to each player are dealt. There are six games which may be bid, each requiring bidder to make 60 points to win, and ranking, from low upward:

1. *Solo.* If this bid is not overcalled, the bidder names any suit but Hearts for trumps. The widow is not touched until the hand has been played out. The score for points above or below 60 is 2 chips per point.

2. *Heart Solo.* With Hearts trumps; the score is 3 chips per point.

3. *Misère.* There are no trumps, and the bidder contracts not to take in a single counting card. As soon as he takes one, the hand is abandoned. The cards in the widow are not counted. This bid wins or loses a flat 30 chips from, or to, the other players.

4. *Guarantee Solo.* If the player names Hearts for trumps, he must make at least 74 points, in play and widow; if he names any other suit, he must make 80. This bid wins or loses a flat 40 chips from, or to, the other players.

5. *Spread Misère.* This is played at No Trumps. The player to the left of the bidder leads, no matter who dealt. The other player then plays, and the bidder's cards are spread face up on the table, but cannot be called. The widow is disregarded. If the player does not take a single counting card, he wins 60 chips; if he takes one, the hand is abandoned, and he loses 60 chips to each player.

6. *Call Solo.* The bidder names a card and asks for it. Any player holding the card must surrender it to the bidder, and receive a card in exchange. If the named card is in the widow, there is no exchange. The bidder then names the trump, and undertakes to win the entire 120 counting points, being of course entitled to those in the widow. The moment the opponents take in a counting card, the game is lost. If the bidder has named Hearts, he wins or loses a flat 150 chips from, or to, each player; if he has named any other suit, 100 chips.

In the two lowest bids, Solo and Heart Solo, if each side takes in 60 points, it is rated a tie, and the bidder neither wins nor loses. After the hands are played out (except in Misère) the widow is faced up, and points in it count for the bidder. In the play, a player who cannot follow suit is required to trump, if he can; otherwise he must discard. If a bidder revokes, he makes nothing if he makes his bid; if he loses, he must pay. If an opponent revokes, neither opponent can win anything, but both must pay if they lose. In a Misère, a revoke loses the game at once.

SHEEPSHEAD, or SCHAFKOPF

Game No. 1

Equipment: A 32-card deck, Ace (high) through 7 (low) in each suit.

Players: Four.

Rank of Cards: The four Jacks are permanent trumps, and rank, Clubs (highest), Spades, Hearts, Diamonds (lowest). After the four Jacks, the other cards of the trump suit rank Ace (highest), 10, King, Queen, 9, 8, 7. Non-trump suits rank Ace, 10, King, Queen, 9, 8, 7, the same as the seven lowest trumps.

Point Value of Cards: Ace, 11; 10, 10; King, 4; Queen, 3; Jack, 2, as in Solo or Slough, and Skat.

Preliminaries.—In the cut for partners and deal, the two highest play against the two lowest, the highest of all dealing. After the shuffle and cut, the Dealer deals 8 cards to each player, 4 cards at one time in rotation left to right, beginning at the Dealer's left, twice. The deal passes to the left. Each side puts an equal number of counters into a pool before the deal.

The Bidding.—The object of the game is to win the bid, the number of points above 60 which a player undertakes to secure; the successful bidder has the privilege of naming the trump. Thus, a player who bids 10 must win 70, etc. The player to the left of the Dealer has the first bid, and the bidding passes in rotation to the left, each player having but one bid. If all pass, the player holding the Jack of Clubs must name the trump.

The Play.—The player to the left of the Dealer leads to the first trick. Each player in turn to the left must follow suit if possible; failing a suit card, he may trump or must discard. The winner of each trick leads to the next. When the hand is played out, the points are counted and settlement is made. The rule for a revoke is as in Solo or Slough.

Scoring.—If the bidding partners win their bid, they take the pool. If they secure their bid and 91 points they win double the pool. If they make 120 points, they win four times the pool. In the case of no bid, the pair holding the Jack of Clubs win the pool if they score 60 points; otherwise, the opponents win the pool. If the bidder fails to make good his bid, the opponents win the pool; if the opponents secure 91 points, they win double the pool; if all 120, they take four times the pool.

Game No. 2

The same as Game No. 1, except that there are 6 permanent trumps: Queen of Clubs (highest) and Queen of Spades, followed by the 4 Jacks as in Game No. 1. Otherwise the rules for Game No. 1 apply.

Game No. 3

Played by four players as individuals. Diamonds are always trumps. Each player forfeits 1 chip for each trick he takes less than 2, and receives 1 chip for each trick he takes more than 2. Tricks are scored, and not points. Otherwise this is played like Game No. 1.

Game No. 4

Four players, two against the other pair. There are 6 permanent trumps, as in Game No. 2. The player holding the Queen of Clubs, with his partner, must make 61 points, or pay double the forfeit. Otherwise it is the same as Game No. 1.

Game No. 5

Played by two partners against the other pair. There are 14 trumps, which rank as follows: the 4 Queens, Club (highest),

Spades, Hearts, Diamonds; the 4 Jacks in the same order; then Ace, 10, King, 9, 8, 7 of Diamonds. Usually Diamonds are trumps, but the trump suit may be announced, as in Game No. 1. The score is as in Game No. 2.

Game No. 6

For six players, three partners against the other three, partners being seated alternately. There are 14 trumps, as in Game No. 5. The rules otherwise are the same as in Game No. 5.

Game No. 7

Played with a double pack of 24 cards each, or 48 cards, the 9's being low. Diamonds are always trumps, and the trumps rank as in Game No. 5. There are 24 trumps in all. If 2 cards of the same suit and denomination fall on the same trick, the first one ranks higher. The game is 121 points.

Game No. 8

Played with the deck used in Game No. 7, by six players, three against three, the partners seated as in Game No. 6. Otherwise the same as Game No. 7.

Game No. 9

Played with a double deck of 64 cards, down through the 7's. There are eight players, four against four, the partners being seated alternately. Diamonds are always trumps. Otherwise the rules of Game No. 7 apply.

SOLO, GERMAN SOLO

Solo is a German variation of the ancient game of Ombre, which originated in Spain, and was popular throughout Europe in the 17th and 18th centuries. The Spanish origin of the game appears in the use of the word Matadors for the 3 highest trumps, as well as in the names of these trumps: the Queen of Clubs, or Spadilla, the highest trump; the 7 of the trump suit, Manilla, the second highest; and the Queen of Spades, Basta, the third highest.*

EQUIPMENT: A 32-card deck, Ace, King, Queen, Jack, 10, 9, 8, 7 of each suit.

PLAYERS: Four.

RANK OF SUITS: One suit, usually Clubs, is selected as "color" for the entire sitting. When this suit is named as trump, it is called "in color," and increases the value of the game.

RANK OF CARDS: In trumps, the Queen of Clubs (Spadilla) is highest; 7 of the trump suit (Manilla) is second; Queen of Spades (Basta) is third highest. Aside from these 3 cards, all suits rank Ace (highest), King, Queen, Jack, 10, 9, 8, 7 (low).

PRELIMINARIES.—Instead of cutting, any player deals the cards around, left to right, one at a time, face up. The first player receiving a Club deals. The deal thereafter passes to the left. After shuffle and cut, the Dealer deals 8 cards to each player, 3, 2, 3, beginning at his left, in rotation left to right.

The Dealer places an agreed number of counters in the pool before commencing to deal. This pool is won by the first player winning a Solo in Color (Clubs in the four-handed game; usually Diamonds in the three-handed game), a Solo Do (or Tout), or a Null Ouvert. A player trying any one of the 3 bids and failing to make it must double the pool.

The object of the game is to win a certain number of tricks, with or without a partner.

Frog or Simple Game.—The bidder names a suit for trumps, and calls for the Ace of another suit. The player holding this Ace becomes the bidder's partner; but his identity is not known until the called Ace is played. If the player calls for an Ace in a suit in which he is blank, he must so declare before play begins, and

* In the once popular 18th-century game of Quadrille, the Matadors were Spadille, the Ace of Spades; Manille, the deuce of Spades or Clubs; and Basto, the Ace of Clubs. In Skat, Matador is used with a different meaning: for one of the trumps in direct sequence, high to low, beginning with the Jack of Clubs, the highest trump. The word "Frog," used in Solo, is a corruption of the German *Frage,* "I ask," used in the original game of Skat.

must place a card face downward before him, which is thereafter regarded as belonging to the suit of the called Ace; and it must be played the first time that suit is led.

The bidder and his partner win the value of the game from their opponents if they win 5 tricks; if they fail to win 5 tricks, they lose the value of the game to their opponents. The holders of Spadilla and Basta must announce them, unless a holder of one of them bids Solo, or unless a Solo bid has been made by a previous bidder. If no Solo bid is made, then the holder must call for an Ace to make trump, but not in the suit of the called Ace. This is called Forcée.

Solo.—In the Solo game, the bidder names a trump suit, and plays alone against the three other players. If he wins 5 tricks, he wins the value of the game from each opponent. If he fails to win 5 tricks, he loses the value of the game, divided equally among his opponents.

Solo Do or Tout.—The bidder names the trump suit, and plays alone against the three other players. If he wins 8 tricks, he wins the value of the game; if he fails, he loses the value of the game to each opponent, and doubles the pool.

Null Ouvert.—This bid is rarely played, as it may ruin a Solo Do bid. It is a bid to lose every trick, and the player lays his cards on the table face up. There is neither a trump, nor any Matadors; the cards rank Ace, King, Queen, Jack, 10, 9, 8, 7. If the bidder loses every trick, he collects 14 counters from each opponent. If he is forced to take a trick, he pays 14 to each opponent, and doubles the pool.

The Bidding.—The bids rank, lowest to highest, in the following order:

1. Simple game in suit.
2. Simple game in Color.
3. Solo in suit.
4. Solo in Color.
5. Tout in suit.
6. Tout in Color, or Solo Do.
7. Null Ouvert, if played.

The player to the left of the Dealer bids first. If he wishes to bid a Simple Game, he says "I ask" (*Frage,* in German). The player to his left may make the next higher bid, by asking "Is it in Color?" If the first bidder is willing to make the Color trump, he says "Yes." If not, he passes; and the next player in turn takes up the bidding, or passes. This order of bidding continues until no player will bid higher.

If no player makes a bid, the player to the left of the Dealer leads any card he chooses. The player taking in the last trick pays 4 counters to each opponent. The player taking in all the tricks receives 4 counters from each other player. There are no trumps or Matadors, and the cards rank Ace (highest) down to 7 (lowest).

THE PLAY.—After the trump is named, the player to the left of the Dealer leads any card. Each player in turn to the left plays a card, and must follow suit if possible. If impossible, he must trump or discard. The highest card of the suit led wins the trick; if it is trumped, however, the highest trump played wins. The winner of each trick leads to the next.

As soon as a player or side playing Simple Game or Solo wins the first 5 tricks, the hands must be abandoned; or, if the winner leads to the sixth trick, the play must continue until all 8 are won, or the game is forfeited.

THE VALUE OF GAMES.—

Simple, with a partner	2
Color, with a partner	4
Forcée Simple, with a partner	4
Forcée in Color, with a partner	8
Solo Simple, without a partner	4
Solo in Color, without a partner	8
Tout Simple	16
Tout in Color	32
Null Ouvert (if played)	14

A revoke by any player, or a lead out of turn against a player without a partner, loses the game at once. Any player who fails to play a Forcée when he should do so, pays 16 counters to the pool.

HEART SOLO, THREE-HANDED SOLO

The pack is reduced to 24 cards, by throwing out the 8 of Hearts and all the Diamonds except the 7. Diamonds are always Color, and the 3 Matadors are the only trumps in Color. The only bids allowed are Solos, as there are no partners. If no one bids, the hand is played in Color, and the winner of the last trick loses the value of a Solo on Color.

MISCELLANEOUS

PREFERENCE

EQUIPMENT: A 32-card deck, ranking Ace (high), King, Queen, Jack, 10, 9, 8, 7 (low) in each suit.

SUIT RANK: Hearts, Diamonds, Clubs, Spades; Hearts being always Preference.

There are three active players. If four play, the Dealer takes no cards. Each player puts an equal amount into the pool.

Any one may deal the first hand; after which the deal passes to the left. The cards are dealt 3—4—3, 2 being laid off face down for the widow at the end of the first distribution of dealing, in which the first 3 cards are dealt around.

On the first round of the bidding, beginning to the left of the dealer, any player who thinks he can take 6 tricks bids by naming the suit he wishes for trumps, without mentioning the number of tricks. In rotation, the bid may be raised only by a higher ranking suit, highest of all being Hearts, the Preference. If there are no bids, each player can bid for the privilege of adding the widow to his hand, naming the number of counters he will pay for this privilege. The highest bidder takes the widow, discards 2 cards, and then names the trump suit. He leads to the first trick; the winners of each trick to the succeeding trick.

Payments are made from the pool, according to an agreed value for the tricks, varying with the suits.

GRAND

EQUIPMENT: A full deck of 52 cards.

PLAYERS: Four, two as partners against the other two.

OBJECT: For a side to make 100 points, or be closest to 100 points after the last deal, playing the cards at one of these four types of games: Whist, Euchre, Hearts or Grand.

Grand is a combination of Whist, Euchre, and Hearts—the bid Grand meaning Whist without a trump. Players must be familiar with all of these games. The cards rank as in these games, depending on the type of game the bidder announces.

PRELIMINARIES.—The two lowest on the cut play against the two highest, lowest of all having choice of seats and cards, and being the first Dealer. The Ace is low in cutting. Since the suits have no rank before being named as trumps, ties recut.

The Dealer deals 13 cards to each player, one at a time, in rotation left to right, beginning with the player on his left. No trump is turned.

THE BIDDING.—The player to the left of the Dealer has the first bid, and must either call the number of points he bids to make, 5 or more, or pass. He announces neither the type of game he intends to play, nor the trump he intends to announce, if any. Bids are usually multiples of 5, but this is not obligatory. Only one bid in turn is allowed to each player; and the highest bidder names the game. If all pass, the Dealer must bid 5 and play some game. The highest bidder leads first.

The Whist Game.—If played at Whist, each trick over the book of 6 is worth 5 points; Grand Slam is 30 extra. Honors do not score. The highest possible score at Whist is 65.

The Whist type of Grand is played without trumps. There is no exposed dummy hand. Each trick over the book of six is worth 9, and a Grand Slam is worth 40. The largest possible score is 103. A Grand Slam at Grand immediately wins the game, even if bidder is in the hole.

The Euchre Game.—When the game is Euchre, each player discards down to 5 cards, and nothing lower than the 8 may be kept in the trump suit. Any player found with a lower trump, or with more than 5 cards in his hand, has a foul hand. The hands are abandoned, and the offending side, if that of the successful bidder, is set back the amount of the bid; if that of the opponents, the bidding side scores, the amount of the bid.

The odd trick, called the Point, is worth 5; 4 tricks are worth 10; a march, or all 5 tricks, made by two players, is worth 20; by a player playing alone, 25. A player playing alone must discard one card and ask for and receive his partner's best; his opponents have the same privilege. This bid is usual when the player's hand holds both Bowers and the Ace.

The Hearts Game.—Hearts is primarily a safety bid. When the Dealer's side has a score of 70 or more, the player to his left, who leads, may declare Hearts without any bidding. He leads a card, and says "This is Hearts." At any lower score, this cannot be done; and the privilege is restricted to the player to the left of the Dealer.

If neither this player nor his partner takes in a heart card, they score 50, and the Dealer is set back 13, one for each heart. If this player or his partner takes in any Hearts, they not only score nothing, but are set back 1 point for each heart card taken in; so both sides are set. If, however, the Dealer's side takes in no hearts, they score 50, and the opponents are set back 13.

If the Dealer's score is below 70, and the player to his left passes, it is usually a sign he is willing to play Hearts, but wants to give his partner a chance to make a higher bid; when he does not want to play Hearts, he should make a bid of at least 5. The highest bidder can always make the game Hearts, unless he has bid more than 50. A Hearts bid is always scored as above.

Scoring.—Bidders who make their bids are scored as above; scoring for all tricks they take, if the bid is successful. If a bidder fails to make his bid, he is set back the amount of his bid; and his opponents score any scoring tricks they take: that is. any odd tricks (tricks above the book) in Whist or Grand, or three or more tricks in Euchre. In Euchre, the successful bidder scores what he makes. If he fails, he is penalized as if his bid had been for a march, as well as the amount of his bid. A bidder playing alone in the Euchre game is penalized only as if he were playing with his partner, if his bid was 20; if it was 25, he loses this amount plus the value of a march played alone, 25—or 50.

A time for ending the play is usually set. The side nearest 100 wins when this time is reached. The other side pays them the difference in scores, plus or minus the set-back score. A separate tally is kept of the number of times each side is set back. The lower number of set-backs is deducted from the higher, and the difference multiplied by the penaly for a set-back, 10 points.

SCOTCH WHIST, or CATCH THE TEN

This game is very unlike Whist, although named as a Whist.

EQUIPMENT: A 36-card deck, ranking Jack, Ace, King, Queen, 10, 9, 8, 7, 6 in the trump suit, and Ace down to 6 in the others.

With four or more players, the whole pack is dealt out, one card at a time, the last being turned up for trump. The player to the left of the Dealer leads any card he pleases, and the others must follow suit if they can.

The object of the game is to win tricks containing certain counting cards in the trump suit: Jack, 11; 10, 10; Ace, 4; King, 3; Queen, 2.

At the end of the hand, the players count the number of points taken in; to which they add 1 point for each card taken in more than the number originally dealt them. Individual players count their points so; and, if two play as partners against two, partnerships count their points in the same manner. Game is made with 41 points. In case of a tie for game, the points go out (that is, win) in this order: 10 of trumps; majority of the cards; Ace, King, Queen, Jack of trumps. Revoke ends the game, the non-offender winning at once.

FRENCH WHIST

In this variation of Catch the Ten, the Diamond 10 is always a counting card, worth 10, whether it is trumps or not. Otherwise the game is the same as Catch the Ten.

CALABRASELLA

Equipment.—The Spanish deck of 40 cards, Ace, King, Queen, Jack, 7, 6, 5, 4, 3, 2 in each suit.

Players: Three or four. If four play, the Dealer takes no cards.

Rank of Cards: 3, 2, Ace, King, Queen, Jack, 7, 6, 5, 4. There is no trump.

Preliminaries.—Low deals, the cards ranking as above. The Dealer deals 12 cards to each player, 4 at a time, left to right, beginning with the Dealer's left. The 4 remaining cards are faced down as a stock. The privilege of playing one hand against the two is bid for in turn, the player left of the Dealer bidding first. A player may either pass, or say "I play," in which case he becomes the single player against the other two. A player can ask for the 3 of any suit he names. Another player holding it passes it over, receiving another card in exchange. If the 3 asked for is not out, no other card can be asked for. If a player holds all the 3's, he may ask for a 2.

Object of the Game.—The object of the game is to take in the highest number of points, out of the possible 35 to be made on each hand.

Scoring Points.—Tricks (excepting the Last Trick) are only of value for the scoring cards they contain. Every Ace is worth 3; each 3, 2, King, Queen and Jack is worth 1. Thus each suit is worth 8, or 32 altogether; which, added to the 3 for Last Trick, makes 35 possible on each hand.

The Discard.—After the Ask, the Single Player must discard from 1 to 4 cards, face down. He then faces the stock, and selects from it as many cards as he has discarded. Such of the stock as he does not take are faced down and placed with the discards.

THE PLAY.—The player left of the Dealer leads to the first trick; and the others must follow suit if they can, though there is no obligation to head, or win, a trick. The opponents keep their tricks together as against the Single Player. The winner of the Last Trick takes the 4 stock cards, with such counting cards as are among them.

At the end of the hand, each side counts the points it has taken in, and the lower score is then deducted from the higher, the difference being the point value of the game. If one side makes the whole 35, it counts double, that is 70. If the Single Player loses, he pays both adversaries; if he wins, both pay him.

MISCELLANEOUS.—If there is an irregularity in the deal, the same player deals again. If no one offers to play, or at the end of any hand, the deal passes to the left.

Looking at the stock before declaring to play and discarding loses the game, and forfeits 35 to each opponent. After a player has declared to play, there is no penalty for looking at a card in the stock; moreover, the Single Player can examine it before discarding, where an opponent has been the offender. If one of the partners leads out of turn, the Single Player may abandon the rest of the hand, score 3 for Last Trick, and allow the opponents to count only points taken in before the offense. The penalty for revoke is 9 points, deducted from the side in error and added to the other side.

THE ALL FOURS GROUP

The All Fours group, which includes Seven Up and its many variations, was listed among the principal card games in Cotton's *Compleat Gamester* as early as 1674. In 1735 Daines Barrington writes that it was confined chiefly to the servants' hall, with Whist and Put. For years it vied with poker as the favorite American gambling game.

SEVEN UP, ALL FOURS, or OLD SLEDGE

EQUIPMENT: A full deck of 52 cards.

PLAYERS: Two, three, or four playing as partners (two against two).

RANK OF CARDS: Ace (high), King, Queen, Jack, 10, etc., down to 2 (low).

PRELIMINARIES.—In the cutting for choice of seats, deal, and partners (where four are playing), high wins, Ace ranking highest. After the shuffle and cut, 6 cards are dealt to each player, 3 at a time, in rotation left to right, starting at the Dealer's left; the next card is faced for trump. The deal passes to the left.

OBJECT OF THE GAME.—The object of the game is to hold in hand the highest and the lowest trumps in play; to turn the Jack for trumps, or capture it in a trick; and to take in cards which count toward game.

Making the Trump.—The player left of the Dealer has the first right to "stand" or "beg." If he is satisfied with the trump turned, he stands, and play begins at once. If he begs, the Dealer must either give him 1 point to let the trump stand, or deal 3 new cards to each player, and face up a new trump. The original trump card is left faced up on the table. If this trump is the same suit as the one first turned, the same process is repeated, until a different suit is reached. This is called "running the cards." The last card of the deck cannot be turned for trumps. If the whole deck has been run, without arriving at a different suit for trumps, the cards are collected and dealt over by the same Dealer. No player but the Dealer and the player to his left may look at his cards until the first trump turned has been decided upon. The Dealer cannot give a player enough to put him out into game.

In a three-handed game, a second beg is not allowed. In a two-handed, a player not satisfied with his cards may suggest that the cards be bunched and shuffled over. If the other player agrees, the same Dealer redeals.

In some localities, all cards more than 6 are discarded from the hand, after the cards have been run, to get rid of superfluous worthless cards.

THE PLAY.—The player to the left of the Dealer leads any card. If this is a trump, players must follow suit if possible; if not a trump, they must follow suit, but if unable to do so they may trump or discard. The highest card of the suit led wins; unless the trick is trumped, in which case the highest trump wins. The winner of each trick leads to the next.

SCORING.—The scoring points are:

High—highest trump in play; player to whom dealt . 1

Low—lowest trump in play; player to whom dealt . . 1

Jack—Jack of trumps, to Dealer turning it for trump, or player taking it in a trick 1

Game—highest total of point values of cards taken in tricks 1

Toward arriving at Game, 10's count 10; Aces, 4; Kings, 3; Queens, 2; and Jacks, 1 each. In case of a tie for Game, the non-Dealer scores it. In the three-handed game, if the two non-Dealers tie, Game is not scored. As above, when a player begs and Dealer "gives," 1 point is scored for the non-Dealer or non-Dealers, being scored for each in the three-handed game.

MISCELLANEOUS.—If Jack is not in play, and a player revokes, he cannot score for Game if he makes it, and his adversary or adversaries score 1 point penalty. If an adversary makes game, in this instance, he scores it. If Jack is in play the same applies, except that the offending player cannot score for Jack if he makes it, and the penalty is 2 points.

GAME.—The game consists of 7 or 10 points, as agreed upon in advance. If both players secure enough on which to win game in a single hand, the points are scored in this order, to determine the winner: High; Low; Jack; Game. The player who first scores out wins. If the Dealer needs but one point to go game, and turns the Jack for trumps, he wins.

CALIFORNIA JACK

In this variation of Seven Up, after the deal the stock is faced up, the top card indicating the trump suit; or the trump suit may be established by cutting before the deal. The player to the left of the Dealer leads. The winner of the first trick takes the top card from the stock, and in rotation left to right the other players each take one card from it. The winner of each trick leads to the next, and this is continued until the stock is exhausted. Low scores for the player taking it, not the player holding it. The game consists of 10 points.

SHASTA SAM

In this variation of California Jack, the stock remains faced down. The trump is determined by cutting before the deal.

AUCTION PITCH, or SET BACK

Players.—Two to seven.

In this variation of Seven Up, the players in rotation, left to right, beginning with the player left of the Dealer, may bid from 1 to 4, indicating how many points they intend to make if allowed to name the trump; or they may pass. No trump is turned. The player to the left of the Dealer may name the trump without waiting for any bidding, but in that case he must make 4 on the hand. Each player is allowed one bid only; except that the player to the left of the Dealer has the privilege of naming the trump himself, provided he contracts to make as many points as the highest bid.

The successful bidder leads for the first trick, the card he leads becoming trump, whether led in error or not. This is called "pitching the trump." If the Joker is used and led, it calls for Spades as trumps. The Joker counts 1 point to the player holding it; and, although it is the highest trump, there is the usual score for High, going to the holder of the highest trump in the actual trump suit. As in all these games, if Jack is the only trump in play, it scores 3, for High, Low and Jack; or it may score 2, for High and Jack; or 2, for Low and Jack.

If a player fails to make the amount of his bid, he is set back that amount. If he is set back more points than he has, or before scoring, he is "in the hole," and his minus score is ringed with a circle. If a player who did not make the trump revokes, there can be no set back for the bidder, each player except the offender scoring what he makes; the revoking player is set back the amount bid. If no bid was made, he is set back 2 points. If the maker of the bid revokes, he cannot score on the hand; is set back his bid; and the other players score what they make.

Otherwise the game is played as Seven Up.

Selling.—In the original game, the player to the left of the Dealer had the option of pitching the trump himself at the highest bid made, or of selling the privilege of pitching the trump. If he sold, he added to his own score the number of points bid. He was not allowed to go game, however, on such a sale. The modern game is almost entirely bidding to the board, with selling eliminated.

SMUDGE

This is a variety of Set Back, in which any player who bids and makes 4 wins the game, if he was not in the hole when the bid was made. However, making 4 without bidding it does not automatically win game.

PEDRO, or PEDRO SANCHO

This is a variety of Set Back, in which the 9 of trumps (Sancho) and the 5 of trumps (Pedro) count 9 and 5 points respectively for the players who take them in tricks. Low counts for the player taking it, instead of the player to whom it is dealt. The bidding goes around and around until no one will bid higher. Points required for game are 50. The order of scoring points: High; Low; Jack; Joker (if used); Game (merely the 10 of trumps, the other cards not being counted); Pedro; and Sancho.

DOM PEDRO, or SNOOZER

This is a variation of Pedro, in which the Joker (called Dom Pedro or Snoozer) is added. The Joker ranks below the deuce of trumps in play, and it counts 15 to the player taking the trick on which it is played. The deuce still ranks as low, or the lowest actual trump in play. The Joker will win over any card in a plain suit, but is taken by any higher trump. The game is won by 50 or 100 points.

CINCH, HIGH FIVE, DOUBLE PEDRO

EQUIPMENT: A full deck of 52 cards.

PLAYERS: Four, two against two as partners.

RANK OF CARDS: Trump suit, Ace (high), King, Queen, Jack, 10, 9, 8, 7, 6, 5, 5 of same color, 4, 3, 2 (low.) The suit of the same color as trumps ranks the same, omitting both 5's; the other suits, Ace down to 2, as in Whist.

PRELIMINARIES.—In the cut for partners, seats, and deal the higher two play against the lower two. High wins choice of seats and deal, the Ace being high in the cutting. After shuffle and cut, nine cards are dealt to each player, in rotation left to right, in three rounds of 3 cards each; the deal passes to the left. A deal of too many or too few cards to any player, if discovered before the first bid is made, forfeits the deal; otherwise it stands, if the other hands are correct. Any other irregularity in the deal calls for a redeal by the same Dealer.

OBJECTS OF THE GAME.—To hold in hand High and Low of trumps, and to take tricks in which are Jack, 10 (called Game), 5 of Trumps (Right Pedro) and 5 of same color (Left Pedro). Sometimes the Low is also played for. If not, it should not be quitted with the rest of the trick, but should be laid face up in front of the holder, after being played.

THE BIDDING.—Beginning with the player to the left of the Dealer, each player is allowed one bid in turn, naming the number of points he contracts to take if allowed to name the trump. Each bid must top previous bids, or the player must pass. The highest possible bid is 14. The highest bidder then names the trump suit.

Drawing.—Each player now discards, face downward, all cards in his hand except trumps, and may not keep more than 6 of these. Dealer deals in rotation, as before, enough cards to each to fill the hand up to 6. The Dealer may then search through the remainder of the stock to fill out his own hand; this is called "robbing the deck." If a player discards a trump by mistake, he can take it back before he has taken into his hand the card the Dealer dealt him to replace it; but not afterwards. If bidder's adversary discarded it. and it is of counting value, it scores for bidder. If discarded by bidder or his partner, it does not score for either side.

The Play.—The successful bidder now leads any card he pleases. When trumps are led, players must follow suit if possible. When a plain suit is led, a player may trump, even though able to follow suit. If he does not trump, he must follow suit if possible; if unable to follow, he must discard. The highest card of the suit led wins the trick; unless it is trumped, in which case the highest trump wins. The winner of each trick leads to the next.

If a player revokes during the play, or is found to have too many cards, the hands are played out; but neither the offending player nor his partner can score on that hand. If the offending player is the bidder's opponent, the bidder and his partner score all they make on the hand, even if they do not make their bid. If a card is played out of turn, this must be corrected, unless all have played to the trick. If it was the turn of the partner of the offending player to lead, the adversary to his right may require him to lead trumps if possible, or not to lead them. If it was the turn of the non-offending side to lead, the card led out of turn becomes a penalty card, faced up, subject to call.

Scoring: *High*—Ace of trumps—1 for the player holding it.

Low—2 of trumps—1 for the player winning it in play. In some localities, the player to whom it is dealt scores it.

Jack—Jack of trumps—1 for the player winning it in play.
Game—10 of trumps—1 for the player winning it in play.
Right Pedro—5 of trumps—5 for the player winning it in play.
Left Pedro—5 of same color as trumps—5 for the player winning it in play.

If the bidder and his opponents score out in the same deal, the bidder scores out first, and wins.

If the bidder and his partner fail to make the bid, they score nothing for what they did make, and are set back the amount of their bids. If this puts them "in the hole," a circle is drawn around the minus amount. The opponents of the bidder always score whatever they make. Another method of scoring, where the bid is made, is to deduct the opponents' score, if any, from the bidder's score, and to credit the bidder's side with the difference.

Game is 51 points; or it may be some other agreed number.

RAZZLE-DAZZLE, or AUCTION CINCH

This is a variation for five or six players. Each player is dealt 6 cards, 3 at a time. No trump is turned, the privilege of naming the trump being bid for, as in Cinch; each player is allowed only one bid. All cards that are not trumps or sure winners are discarded, and the Dealer fills out the hands from the stock. The highest bidder then names a card he needs, and the holder of that card says "I play with you," thereby becoming bidder's partner, but the players do not change seats. In all of these games, where there are partners, it is wise to play high counting cards, such as the Pedros, on a partner's sure trick, as when partner has played the Ace of trumps, or the top trump at any stage of the game.

CINCH WITH A WIDOW

Cinch is sometimes played with a widow of 4 cards dealt face down in front of each player, after the first round of 3 cards apiece has been dealt. After the bidding is over, but before the trump suit is named, each player takes up his widow. After the trump is named, the hands are stripped down to 6 cards each, and play proceeds as in Cinch.

PROGRESSIVE CINCH

The tables are made up as in a Progressive Euchre. Each table is provided with a bell. As soon as any pair of partners score 32 at any table, they ring the bell, and play stops at once at all tables. Totals are added up, as of the last hand scored, and winning couples progress, as in Progressive Euchre. In the case of a tie, each player may be credited with half a game, and progressing is decided by cutting; or both progression and score may be decided by a cut.

SIXTY-THREE

Sixty-Three is modified Cinch, and all variations applicable to Cinch may be used with it. Nine cards are dealt to each player; and, after discarding, the hands are filled out to 6 cards, as in Cinch. Game is 152 points. The trump cards count as follows: Ace (high), 1; King, 25; trey (3), 15; 9, 9; 10 (Game), 1; 5 (Right Pedro), 5; 5 of same color (Left Pedro), 5; 2 (low), 1. All of these count to the player taking them in in play. Bidding continues in rotation until no one will bid higher. The highest possible bid is 63. In Progressive Sixty-Three, four hands may be played at each table; or the method used in Progressive Cinch may be used.

THE BÉZIQUE GROUP

The Bézique group of games, including Pinochle, Cinq-Cents, and Sixty-Six, are all of comparatively recent development, but their ancestry traces back almost to the beginning of European card games. A double ancestral line, in fact.

The French game of Piquet is said to have been introduced during the reign of Charles VII (1422-1461), as the motif for a ballet of living cards given in the palace of Chinon. From Piquet, the Bézique group derived Sequence, Four of a Kind, and Last Trick, as well as the general manner of playing. Originally, all card suits were equal, as are the Red and the Black armies in Chess, Checkers and Backgammon. Man's boastfulness disposed a player to claim superiority for the suit in which he was strongest. As soon as the suits began to represent professions (militia, officials, clergy, and merchants), these personifications became reflected in superiorities of certain suits over the others, depending upon the locality, the one represented by the clergy (later corrupted to Hearts) generally being regarded as dominant. A democratic revolution, as late as our own time, elevated the lowly Spades to precedence; just as the humble Ace, lowest of the suit, rose to dictatorship over the rest—except where the Jacks or Bowers (from the German word for "peasant") climbed above him. Similarly, the merchant's 10 reached high rank in many games; as well as lowly 5's, 3's, and 2's.

Another early and inevitable personification regarded the court cards, Queen, King, and Jack, as human beings, subject to human conventions and emotions. This appeared first in the ancient showdown game of Matrimony, in which any King and Queen represented matrimony; any Queen and Knave, Intrigue; and any King and Knave (Jack), Confederacy. Again, by merchant predominance, the Diamond Ace is the highest card in this game—as a Diamond is the most powerful card in Pope Joan. For the Bézique group of games, Confederacy was eliminated. But this group borrowed from Matrimony the idea of Marriage, Royal Marriage and Bézique or Pinochle—the Queen of Spades and the Jack of Diamonds, surely an undeniable Intrigue. It is interesting that the low-born Queen and the moneyed Knave are the participants in this. Some seek to derive the name Bézique (from the French *besique,* of unknown origin) from the Spanish *besito,* or *besico,* a little kiss. In Germany, the legend is that Pinochle, a derivative of Bézique, came from Switzerland, and that the Swiss got it from the Spanish. So legends grow. Bézique itself was not introduced into England until the winter of 1868-69, which shows how recent are its wanderings.

BÉZIQUE

Equipment: A double deck, consisting of 64 cards, two each of Ace, King, Queen, Jack, 10, 9, 8, 7 of each suit.

Players: Two.

Rank of Cards: Ace (high), 10, King, Queen, Jack, 9, 8, 7 (low)—the usual ranking in German games. If 2 identical cards fall on a trick, the first played ranks higher.

Preliminaries.—In the cut for deal, high wins, the cards ranking as above. If there is a tie, there must be a recut until it is broken. After the shuffle and cut, 8 cards are dealt to each, beginning with the Dealer's opponent, 3, 2, and then 3. The next card is faced up for the trump. The stock or remainder of the deck, called talon in this game, is placed face downward on the table, and the trump card is faced up beside it. If this trump is a 7, Dealer scores 10 points (dix) for it at once. Any irregularity in the deal, which cannot be corrected by drawing from the talon, calls for a new deal by the Dealer; and the opponent may demand a new deal even for being dealt too few cards.

Object of the Game.—To score as many points as possible on each hand, toward game, which is usually 1,000 points, by these scoring combinations:

Class A

	Points
Marriage (King and Queen of any suit)	20
Royal Marriage (King and Queen of trumps) . .	40
Sequence (Ace, 10, King, Queen, Jack of trumps)	250

Class B

Bézique (Spade Queen and Diamond Jack) . .	40
Double Bézique (two Spade Queens and two Diamond Jacks)	500

Class C

4 Aces	(any suits)	100
4 Kings	"	80
4 Queens	"	60
4 Jacks	"	40

Other Scores

Brisque (any 10 or any Ace taken on tricks)	10
Dix (any 7 of trumps)	10
Last Trick	10

The Play.—The opponent leads any card, and the Dealer plays any card he pleases upon it. Neither player is obliged to follow suit or trump, at any time. The higher card played of the suit led wins the trick, unless it is trumped, when the trump wins. The winner of each trick takes the top card from the stock or talon before leading to the next trick, his opponent taking the next card. This continues until the talon is exhausted.

Either player, after winning a trick, and before drawing from the talon, may declare any one combination that he holds by laying the cards constituting it faced up on the table. He scores for such a combination at once. Only one combination may be declared after each trick; but a player having more than one combination may announce them all, score for one of them, and hold the others in abeyance, to be scored, one at a time, after each trick that he wins thereafter, and before drawing in each instance from the talon. If, before he has scored all of his declarations, the player draws a card or cards which form another combination he prefers to declare, he may announce it and score upon taking a trick, still holding in abeyance the combinations already on the table.

A card used in one combination cannot be used in another combination of less, or the same, value in the same class. Thus, cards used in a Royal Marriage may be used later for a Sequence; but cards used in a Sequence cannot thereafter be used in a Royal Marriage. If King and Queen of a suit have been announced as a Marriage, another King or Queen cannot be used to reform the Marriage; but either King or Queen can be used, with 3 other Kings or Queens, to make 4 Kings or 4 Queens.

The player holding the trump 7 may, upon taking a trick, exchange it for the turned trump, and score 10 for Dix. Should he hold both 7's, he may score 10 for each. The player holding the second 7 may show it upon taking a trick, and score 10 for it. Neither player can announce a combination and score for it, and score for the 7 at the same time.

A player exposing and scoring an erroneous combination must deduct the amount from his score; and his opponent may direct him to lead any card of that combination. If he has in his hand the card or cards to correct the error, that may be done without penalty, providing he has not meanwhile drawn a card from the talon.

When the talon is down to one card, the winner of the trick just quitted takes it, and the loser takes the trump. All declarations now end, and each player takes into his hand all cards exposed on the table. The winner of the last trick then leads any card; and thereafter each player must not only follow suit, but must win the trick if possible. If unable to follow suit, he must trump, if possible.

Miscellaneous.—There is no penalty for a lead out of turn, and it may be taken back if discovered before the opponent has played to it. If either player has too few or too many cards after the first draw, the player must be allowed to play without drawing until his hand is reduced to 8 cards, or he must draw from the talon to bring the number up to 8. If, after the talon is exhausted, a player fails to take a trick he could have taken, his opponent may demand that the cards be taken back and replayed from the trick where the error was made.

If a player fails to draw at the proper time, his opponent may declare the deal void, or may allow the player to draw 2 cards after the next trick. If a player draws 2 cards, he may restore the extra one, if he has not seen it; otherwise, he must show it to his opponent, before replacing it. If the loser of a trick, in drawing, looks at 2 cards, his opponent may do the same thing after the next trick, and choose which of them to take, without exposing it. When, through error, 2 cards remain in the talon beside the trump, the winner takes the top card, the loser the trump card, leaving one card in the talon unexposed.

Scoring.—All scores are counted as soon as made. A pad may be used for the scoring, or poker chips, each player having 9 blue chips each worth 100, 4 red chips each worth 20; and 2 whites each worth 10. These are laid out in front of the players, and are moved forward as the score is made. The game is usually 1,000 points.

BÉZIQUE WITHOUT A TRUMP

This is played in the same manner as the regular game, except that no trump is turned. The first Marriage declared and scored determines the trump suit. The 7 of trumps does not score for Dix; otherwise, the regular scorings count.

THREE-HANDED BÉZIQUE

This game requires three decks of cards, 32 of each being used. A Triple Bézique scores 1,500 points. All other combinations score the same. The game is 2,000 points.

FOUR-HANDED BÉZIQUE

This game requires four decks of cards, 32 of each being used. The play may be as partners, or as individuals. Scored as in Three-handed Bézique. On taking a trick, a player may declare all combinations he holds, or pass this privilege to his partner; but only one combination may be scored after each trick is won. Partners may combine their cards to form combinations, provided one part of any such combination is already on the table. The game is 2,000 points.

RUBICON BEZIQUE

Four decks of 32 cards each are used. There are two players. Nine cards are dealt to each, and no trump is turned. The first

Marriage declared and scored determines the trump suit. In addition to the regular combinations, the following are added:

	Points
Sequence in plain suit, not trumps	150
Triple Bézique	1,500
Quadruple Bézique	4,500
Carte Blanche (no Jack, Queen or King on original deal)	50

On every successive draw thereafter which does not give the player scoring Carte Blanche a Jack, Queen or King, he may show the card and score another 50 for Carte Blanche.

Combinations which have been scored may be broken into, a new card or cards substituted, and the combination scored again. Thus, if 4 Kings have been declared and scored, and one played, another King may be added, scoring 4 Kings again. But no card may be used in a combination of less value in the same class.

Scoring.—Each deal is a game in itself. At the end of the play, the lower score is deducted from the higher. All fractions of 100 are disregarded, the score being counted by 100's only. Brisques are counted only when the score is close enough for the Brisque score to change the result; or where, by counting Brisques, a player may save himself from being rubiconed. If the final difference between the scores is less than 100, the winner adds 100 for bonus. To this is added 500 for game, the final sum being the value of the game.

If a player scores less than 1,000 points, he is rubiconed, and all his points are added to the higher score. The winner of a Rubicon also adds 1,000 to his score, making it a double game; plus 300 for all the Brisques, no matter by whom won. If the rubiconed player has won less than 100, an additional 100 is added by the winner for bonus.

If, by adding his Brisques, a player can bring his score up to 1,000, he is not rubiconed; but in this case the other player also counts his Brisques.

CINQ-CENTS

Cinq-Cents (literally, Five Hundred) may be regarded as a one-deck variation of Bézique; however, it is probably the original form of the game. There is one additional declaration:

Sequence in a suit not the trump 120

Points in the tricks are not scored as they are taken in, but are counted up at the end of the hand. When the last trick has been scored, the value of the hands is computed by adding these Scoring Points: Ace, 11; 10, 10; King, 4; Queen, 3; Jack, 2, as in Skat, Solo or Slough, and Sheepshead. There are thus 120 points to be divided between the players. It is usual for one only to count, the other taking the difference between 120 and his score. In this game, Bézique is called Binage. It is possible that a German corruption of this word gave us the name Pinochle.

As the name implies, 500 points make the game. The players keep mental note of the points they take in, in addition to the value of the declarations scored down on a slate or pad. The first player to reach 500 knocks on the table with his knuckles or his cards, which stops the game. If he has reached 500, he wins, even if the other player's score is more. If he has not, he loses, no matter what he may have as score. If neither knocks, and at the end of the hand it is found that both have passed 500, the game must continue to 600; and then on to 700, etc. If only one reaches 500, and does not knock, he wins on his score.

PINOCHLE

TWO-HANDED PINOCHLE

Equipment: A double deck of 48 cards, Ace, King down through 9 of each suit; or of 64 cards, adding 8's and 7's.

Players: Two.

Rank of Cards: Ace (high), 10, King, Queen, Jack, 9, 8, 7. In the 48-card deck, 9 is low. Where two identical cards fall on the same trick, the first played ranks higher.

Preliminaries.—The cards are cut for deal, high winning and the Ace being highest; in the case of a tie, there is a recut. After shuffling and cut, from the 48-card deck 12 cards are dealt to each player, in three groups of 4 each, beginning with the non-Dealer. The next card is turned up for trumps. If the 64-card deck is used, 16 are dealt to each, in groups of 4, and the next card is turned up for trumps. If the trump turned is a low (9, or 7, as the case may be) the Dealer scores 10 for it at once, as Dix (pronounced "Deece.") The rest of the deck, called the talon, is faced down on the table, and the trump card, faced up, beside it.

Any irregularity committed by the Dealer calls for a new deal by him. A card faced in the talon must be faced down at its proper place. An insufficient number of cards in a hand may be remedied before the first trick is turned by the Dealer adding the proper number of cards from the talon; or the Opponent may require a new deal.

Objects of the Game.—The objects are to form, during play, certain melds or point-counting combinations of cards; and to take in point-counting cards on tricks.

Scoring Value of Melds

Class A

	Points
Common Marriage (King and Queen of one plain suit)	20
Royal Marriage (King and Queen of trump suit)	40
Royal Sequence (Ace, 10, King, Queen, Jack, of trumps)	150

Class B

Pinochle (Spade Queen and Diamond Jack)	40

Class C

4 Aces (1 each of the four suits)	100
4 Kings " " " " " "	80
4 Queens " " " " " "	60
4 Jacks " " " " " "	40

SCORING VALUE OF CARDS TAKEN IN TRICKS

Ace, 11; 10, 10; King, 4; Queen, 3; Jack, 2. This is the same scoring as that used in Skat, Solo or Slough, and Cinq Cents. Among some plaers, Ace and 10 count 10 each, King and Queen 5 each, Jack nothing. Among others, Ace, King and 10 count 10 each, Queen and Jack count nothing. These are score simplifications for convenience.

OTHER SCORES

Dix—turning the lowest card in a suit as trump, or exchanging it for the turned trump, provided no other meld is made at the same time	10
Last trick	10

THE PLAY.—The non-Dealer leads any card, and the Dealer plays any card on it. It is not required to follow suit or trump, even if trumps are led, until the talon is exhausted. The highest card of the suit led wins the trick; unless it is trumped, in which case the trump wins. If two identical cards are played on a trick, the one led wins.

The winner of a trick may meld any one combination that he holds, by laying the cards forming the combination face upward on the table. This must be done before he draws from the talon. He scores for this immediately. The player holding the low of trumps may, after winning a trick, exchange it for the turned trump; and he scores 10 for Dix for this, unless he makes any other meld at the same time, in which case he loses the 10 for Dix.

A card used in one combination cannot be used again in another combination of less or equal value in the same class. Thus King and Queen of trumps, melded as a Royal Marriage, may be used again in a Sequence; but if used in the Sequence first, they cannot thereafter be scored as a Royal Marriage. Any King and Queen used in any Marriage cannot, by the addition of another King or Queen or both, be used to form other Marriages; but they may be used, with 3 Kings or 3 Queens of the three other suits, to form 4 Kings or 4 Queens. Cards melded in one class can be used to form any scoring combination in any other class.

After melding, if a player has a meld to declare, the winner of the trick draws the top card from the talon, his opponent taking the second card. The winner then leads to the next trick, and this is continued until the talon is exhausted. Melding then ceases. After this, the second player on each trick must not only follow suit, if possible, but must win the trick, if possible. When unable to follow suit, if possible, a player must trump. Cards used in melding must be left on the table until the talon is exhausted; but they may be played at any time, as they are still part of the player's hand. After the talon is exhausted, they are taken into the hand again and played from there.

A lead out of turn may be taken back without penalty, if the opponent has not played to the trick. Thereafter, it stands. If, after the first draw, either player has too many or too few cards, the player must play without drawing until his hand reaches the right number, or, at his first draw, draw enough from the talon to bring his hand up to the right number. If, after the talon is exhausted, a player fails to win a trick, when he was able to, his opponent may demand that the cards be taken back and replayed from the trick in which the failure to win occurred.

CALLING OUT.—Each player should keep mental count of his score, as it nears 1,000. The first player who correctly announces that he has reached 1,000 wins the game, no matter what his opponent's score may be. If a player calls out incorrectly, he loses the game at once. A player may call out at any time, whether he is in the lead or not. If both have reached 1,000 or better and neither has called out, the game must be continued until 1,250 is reached. If a player makes a meld which is enough to put him out, he need not win another trick to make the meld good. If the score of 10 for Last Trick is enough to put a player out, he must call out before he picks up the trick.

MISCELLANEOUS.—If a player fails to draw at the proper time, his opponent may declare the deal void, or permit the player to draw 2 cards at his next turn to draw. If a player draws 2 cards, he may replace the second one at once, if he has not seen it. If he has seen it, he must show it to his opponent. A player drawing out of turn must replace the card incorrectly drawn. If this card belongs to the opponent, the player in error must show the card he draws to the opponent. If both players draw in error, the draw stands. If the loser of a trick in drawing looks at 2 cards, his opponent on his next draw may look at 2 cards, and select which of them he will take into his hand. If he takes the second card, he need not show it. If 2 cards remain in the talon at the end, through some error, winner of the last preceding trick takes the top card, the loser takes the faced trump, and the final card in the talon remains unexposed.

SCORING.—After the hands are played out, the scoring value of the cards taken by each player in tricks are counted, and the points added to the score for melds already scored. Points may be scored on paper; on a cribbage board; or with poker chips—9 blue chips representing 100 each; 4 red chips, 20 each; and 2 white chips, 10 each. These are laid out on the table, and chips representing the proper amounts are moved forward as points are made.

THREE- and FOUR-HANDED PINOCHLE

For the three-handed game, use the 48-card deck; for the four-handed game, the 48- or 64-card deck. In the four-handed game, the two highest are partners against the two lowest. In the three-handed game, and in the four-handed when the 64-card deck is used, deal hands of 16 cards each, as in regular Pinochle. If the 48-card deck is used in the four-handed game, deal 12 cards to each. The last card is turned for the trump.

In the four-handed game, in rotation, left to right, beginning at the Dealer's left, the holder of the low trumps may exchange this for the turned trump, and score 10 for Dix. The holder of the other low may then show it and score 10 for Dix. In the three-handed game, Dix is a meld, even if the Dealer turns it up, and it is scored with the other melds, if any, after winning a trick.

Melds are made and scored as in Auction Pinochle with a Widow. In the four-handed game, melding combinations may not be made by using faced cards in front of a partner. Beginning with the player to the left of the Dealer, each player exposes whatever melds he holds, and a note is made of their value. Melds are then taken back into the hand, and the player to the left of the Dealer leads any card. Each player in turn, left to right, must then head the trick, following suit with a higher card in the suit led, if possible. If he cannot follow suit, the player must trump; and if the trick has already been trumped, he must trump higher, if possible. A player must win his partner's trick, if possible. If a player can neither follow suit nor trump, he must discard. The winner of the first leads to the next, and so on, until the hands are played out. As soon as a player takes a trick, he is entitled to score all the melds which he exposed before the play commenced. If a player takes no trick, he cannot score his melds. When there are partners, if either partner takes a trick, both score their melds. If any player exposes a card, leads out of turn, or discloses any information, he and his partner may not score on that deal.

The game is 1,000 points. The call-outs are the same as in regular Pinochle. A partner is bound by his partner's call-out.

AUCTION PINOCHLE

Auction Pinochle is played the same as the three- and four-handed game, except that no trump is turned, and the players bid for the privilege of naming the trump. Bidding starts with the player to the left of the dealer, and rotates to the left. Each player is allowed only one bid. In bidding, the player names the number of points that he (and his partner, in the four-handed game) will score. The highest bidder names the trump.

After the trump is named, the play proceeds as in regular three- and four-handed Pinochle. If the bidder, or bidder and his partner, makes his bid, and takes at least one trick so that the melds are scored, he scores all he makes. If he fails to make his bid, he is set back, the amount of his bid being deducted from his previous score. If he had scored nothing previously, or if the set back is larger than his score, he is "in the hole," and the minus score is indicated by a circle around the score. The bidder's opponents score all they make.

The game is 1,000 points. There is no calling out, the bidder always having the first count. If the bid is made and that puts the player or his side out, they win, no matter what may be the score of the other side.

AUCTION PINOCHLE WITH A WIDOW

This is the form of Pinochle now almost universally played by three or four players. The deck contains 48 cards, as in regular Pinochle. Three players alone are active; if four form the table, the Dealer takes no cards. Each player is dealt 15 cards, 3 at a time, in rotation left to right. After the first round of 3, a widow of 3 cards is faced down.

In the bidding, the player to the left of the Dealer has the first right to bid. He must make a bid of not less than 200; and thereafter in rotation, left to right, each player may increase the bid by at least 10 points, until no one will bid any higher. The suit intended for trumps is not named during the bidding. A bid or pass once made cannot be recalled.

The Widow.—When the bidding is ended, the highest bidder must face up the 3 cards in the widow, so that all players can see them. He then takes them into his hand, announces the trump suit, and discards 3 cards in place of the widow. Any points in this discard counts for him at the end of the play. If any cards in the widow are exposed before the bidding is finished, no further bids are allowed, and the last bid made before the exposure is final. The discard must be made before the melding, since no melded card may thereafter be discarded. If a player leads before discarding, his opponents may call upon him to discard before they play to the lead. If, after playing to the first trick, the widow is found to contain more or less than 3 cards, the opponents' hands having their right number, the bidder's hand is foul, and he loses double the value of his bid.

THE MELDS.—Only the successful bidder is allowed to meld. The melds score as in regular Pinochle. There is one additional meld:

The Round Trip (4 Kings and 4 Queens) . . . 240

When combined with the trump Sequence, the two melds are worth only 350, as the trump marriage is lost. Scoring is usually one of the two latter methods in regular Pinochle: Ace and 10, 10 each; King and Queen, 5 each; Jack, 0; or Ace, 10, and King, 10; Queen and Jack, 0. Since the Last Trick is worth 10, the point value of the cards in each hand is 250. The highest bidder scores his melds, whether he has taken a trick or not.

THE PLAY.—The play is as in Three- and Four-Handed Pinochle. If either opponent leads or plays out of turn, or fails to head a trump trick, the bidder wins his game. There is no penalty if a bidder leads out of turn. Failure to follow suit or head a trick, when able to do so, is a revoke, and ends the game at once. If the bidder revokes, he pays double. The revoke is established the moment the card is played. After playing to the first trick, any player with too many cards loses the game. If the bidder is at fault, he loses double. After a successful bidder examines the widow and counts his possible melds, he may abandon his cards and pay the full value of his bid to each opponent, the deal passing to the left. When four play, the Dealer shares the fortunes of the bidder's opponents. If a bidder fails to make his bid, he loses double the value of his bid to each of the others at the table. If the bidder plays the hand, he cannot score more than his bid. If his melds cover his bid, he can score the bid without playing the hand.

SIX- and EIGHT-HANDED PINOCHLE

In the six-handed game, a double Pinochle pack of 96 cards is used, dealing 15 cards to each player, with a widow of 6. There are two sets of three partners. In the eight-handed game, a triple Pinochle deck of 144 cards is used, dealing 17 cards to each player, and 8 to the widow. There are two partnerships, of four players each. The game is played otherwise as Auction Pinochle with a Widow.

Here are additional melding scores:

Double Marriage (2 Kings and 2 Queens of same suit)	300
Triple Marriage (3 Kings and 3 Queens of same suit)	600
Quadruple Marriage (4 Kings and 4 Queens of same suit)	1,200
Double Royal Sequence	1,500
Triple Royal Sequence	3,000
Double Pinochle	300
Triple Pinochle	600
Quadruple Pinochle	1,200
8 Aces	1,000
8 Kings	800
8 Queens	600
8 Jacks	400
12 Aces	2,000
12 Kings	1,600
12 Queens	1,200
12 Jacks	800
15 of same denomination, as 15 Aces, 15 Kings, ect.	3,000

CONTRACT PINOCHLE

Contract Pinochle is played with a double 48-card Pinochle deck, or 96 cards. Four players take part, two against two, as partners. The rank of cards and cut, the shuffle, and cut, are the same as in regular Pinochle. Each player is dealt 12 cards, 3 at a time.

The Bidding.—The Dealer has the right to bid first. He must either bid at least 100, or pass. If all four players pass before a bid is made, the deal passes. In bidding, a player names the number of points he and his partner contract to make, and the suit to be named for trumps: for instance, 200 Hearts. Each player in turn may bid; double a previous bid made by an opponent; redouble an opponent's double; or pass. Each subsequent bid must be at least 10 points higher than the last previous bid. In bidding, a player may name a suit previously named by his partner or by an opponent, or any other suit. A bid, double, redouble or pass, once made, cannot be recalled. Bidding continues until there have been three successive passes. The player who first names for his side the suit of the successful bid becomes the Contractor. Doubling doubles all points bid and made; redoubling doubles the double.

The Play.—Melds may only be made by the Contractor and his partner. No meld, correct or incorrect, may be made or changed after a card is led. The meld values are the same as in regular Pinochle, with the addition of The Round Trip, 4 Kings and 4 Queens, worth 240. When combined with trump Sequence, the two melds are worth only 350, as in Auction Pinochle with a Widow. Either player on the contracting side may make melds in combination with cards melded by his partner.

After both contracting players have made all their melds, the Contractor may call for his partner to show any card that might complete a meld. If he has melded a Royal Marriage and holds the Ace and Jack of trumps, he may call for the 10, to make a trump Sequence. He may continue to call for such cards as long as his partner is able to respond. When the partner fails to hold a card called for, the privilege of calling passes to the partner. When the partner calls for a card not held by the Contractor, the privilege of calling ends. Combination melds may be made on cards called for. If a Contractor holds the Spade Queen and calls for the Spade King and receives it, his partner, holding the Diamond Jack, may meld Pinochle.

Ace and 10 score 10, King and Queen 5 each, Jack 0. Since there is 10 for Last Trick, this makes 250 points possible by cards in each deal. After the melds are made, the Contractor may concede the deal without play. This scores half the value of the bid for the opponents, if undoubled; the full value, if doubled; and twice the value, if redoubled.

In the play, a player need not head a plain suit trick. If he cannot follow suit, he must trump. If the trick has already been trumped and a player cannot follow suit, he must trump, but need not head the trump. When trumps are led, each player in turn must head the trick, if he can. Partners must win each other's trump tricks in this manner.

If an opponent of the contracting side leads or plays out of turn, or fails to head a trump trick when possible, the contracting side wins and scores the amount of the bid, whether undoubled, doubled or redoubled. If a member of the contracting side leads or plays out of turn, or fails when able to head a trump trick, the deal is lost, and the opponents score the amount of the contract. Failure to follow suit, to trump when unable to follow suit, or to head a trump trick when able to do so, constitutes a revoke, and loses the deal, the non-offending side scoring the amount of the bid. A revoke is established when a card is played

Scoring.—The opponents score only when the contracting side concedes the deal or fails to make the contract, or in case of a penalty. They cannot meld nor score for cards taken in play. The contracting side can only score the amount of their contract. If they can show this in melds, the hand need not be played out.

The game is 3,000 points.

GAIGEL

Equipment: A 48-card deck, two each of the Ace, King, Queen, Jack, 10 and 7 of each suit.

Players: Two to eight. Best as four-handed, two partners against the other two.

Rank of Cards: Ace (high), 10, King, Queen, Jack, 7 (low). If 2 identical cards are played on a trick, the first played ranks higher.

Preliminaries.—In the cut for deal, partners and seats, the highest pair play against the lowest pair, high winning choice of seats, and becoming Dealer. In the cut, the cards rank as above. After shuffle and cut, 5 cards are dealt to each player, beginning with the player to the Dealer's left, left to right in rotation—2, then 3; or 3, then 2. The next card is faced up for the trump. The rest of the cards, the talon, is faced down on the table.

OBJECT OF THE GAME.—The object of the game is to score 101 points, or game, before the opponents score it.

MELDING POINTS

	Points
Common Marriage (King and Queen of plain suit)	20
Double Common Marriage (2 Kings and 2 Queens of plain suit)	40
Royal Marriage (King and Queen of trumps) . .	40
Double Royal Marriage (2 Kings and 2 Queens of trumps)	80
Any five 7's (drawn or held by one player at one time)	101

POINTS TAKEN IN ON TRICKS

Each Ace, 11; each 10, 10; each King, 4; each Queen, 3; each Jack, 2.

THE PLAY.—The player to the left of the Dealer leads any card. In rotation, left to right, each player plays any card, not being required to follow suit or trump. The highest card of the suit led wins; unless the trick is trumped, in which case the highest trump wins. After winning a trick, and before drawing from the talon, the winner may declare one Marriage, exposing it so that all the players can see it. Two single Marriages cannot be declared in the same suit, even at different times. The second marriage, after one has been scored, counts nothing. After declaring a Marriage or not, the winner of the trick takes the top card from the talon, and each player in rotation left to right takes one. The winner of each trick leads to the next trick. Any player holding a 7 of trumps may exchange it for the faced trump, as soon as he takes a trick, and before drawing from the talon.

When the talon is exhausted, all melding ceases, and thereafter each player must not only follow suit, but must head the trick in the suit led if possible. If he cannot follow suit, the player must trump; and if the trick has been trumped, he must head the trump, if possible. Failure to do either of these forfeits the game to the opponents. If unable to follow suit or trump, a player must discard.

Scoring.—The players must keep a mental count of points made by cards taken in tricks. Points made by melds are scored as soon as they are made. When a player or side reaches 101 points, he must cease playing and knock on the table, signifying that he has won the game. If incorrect, he forfeits the game. Before game is claimed, no player is allowed to examine any trick except the last trick quitted, under penalty of forfeiting the game to the opponents. If a claim of game is questioned by an opponent, the disputed player's or side's tricks are turned over at once, and the points counted. In counting for going out, Marriages take precedence over all other scores.

A Gaigel counts two games (202 points) and consists of:

1. Scoring 101 before opponents have won a trick.
2. Holding five 7's in one hand, before opponents have won a trick.
3. When an opponent claims to be out, and is proved to be in error.
4. When the opponents play again, after reaching 101.
5. When the opponents refuse the privilege of counting the current trick again, or mix the cards before the count is settled.
6. When an error is claimed and the claim is proved to be baseless, the disputing players score a Gaigel for their opponents.

SIXTY-SIX

Sixty-six is one of the simplest forms of Bézique.

Equipment: A 24-card deck, Ace, King, Queen, Jack, 10, 9 of each suit.

Players: Two.

Rank of Cards: Ace (high), 10, King, Queen, Jack, 9 (low).

Preliminaries.—In the cut for seats and deal, high wins, the Ace being high. After the shuffle and cut, 6 cards are dealt to each, beginning with the opponent, in two rounds of 3 cards each. The next card is faced up for the trump, and laid beside the remainder of the pack, the talon, which is faced down.

Objects of the Game.—To reach 66 in points, by forming, during play, certain scoring melds, and by winning, in tricks, certain cards of counting value.

Melding Points

	Points
Marriage in trumps (King and Queen announced)	40
Marriage in plain suit (King and Queen announced)	20

Points Taken in on Tricks

Each Ace, 11; each 10, 10; each King, 4; each Queen, 3; each Jack, 2. The winner of the last Trick, after the talon is exhausted, scores 10. The player who first reaches 66 scores 1 game point. If his opponent has not reached 33, he scores 2 game points. If his opponent has not taken a trick, he scores 3 game points. If neither player scores 66 on a hand, or both have reached 66 without announcing it, neither scores in that hand, 1 point being added to the winner of the next game which is decided. If a player closing gets 66 or more, he scores the same as if the game had been played out. If he fails, his opponent scores 2. If a player closes before his opponent has taken a trick, and fails to score 66, his opponent scores 3. During the play, either player may claim to have reached 66. If his claim is correct, he scores as though the hand had been played out. If not, his opponent scores 2; unless he has not taken a trick up to the time his opponent closes, in which case he scores 3. A player must "close" before claiming 66.

The Play.—The Dealer's opponent leads any card. The other player need not follow suit or trump. The highest card of the suit led wins the trick; unless it is trumped, in which case the trump wins. The winner of the trick draws the top card from the talon, the loser taking the next card. The winner of each trick leads to the next trick. Either player holding the trump 9 may exchange it for the turned trump at any time, provided he has previously won a trick; unless it is the last card in the talon, in which case the player drawing it must keep it.

A Marriage is announced by showing the cards composing it, and leading one of them. The opponent may declare a Marriage on his first lead, but he cannot score it unless he wins the trick, or some subsequent trick. A player may show a Marriage without leading it, if it makes his score 66 or more.

The play continues as above until the talon is exhausted or the player has closed. When the talon is exhausted or closed, players must follow suit on each trick, but need not head the trick. If a player is unable to follow suit, a player may trump or discard. Marriages may still be announced and scored during the play of the last 6 cards.

CLOSING.—Either player may *close,* when he has the lead, either before or after drawing, by turning down the trump card. Thereafter no cards are drawn from the talon, and the cards in the hand are played, subject to the same rules as those governing play after the talon is exhausted, except that the last trick does not score 10. The opponent, having the lead, may close before a card has been played. If either player announces, during the play, that his score is 66 or more, the play stops for that deal, and the game is considered closed.

GAME.—The game is 7 points, scored as above.

THREE-HANDED SIXTY-SIX

This is similar to the two-handed game. The Dealer takes no cards, the other two players alone being active. The Dealer scores as many points as are won on his deal by either of the players. If neither scores 66, or both score 66 but fail to announce it, the Dealer scores 1 point, and the active players nothing. The game is 7 points. A Dealer cannot score enough to go game. His 7th point must be won when he is an active player.

FOUR-HANDED SIXTY-SIX

The 32-card deck is used—Ace down through 7 in each suit. The cards rank Ace (high), 10, King, Queen, Jack, 9, 8, and 7 (low).

Eight cards are dealt to each player—3, 2, then 3, in rotation as above. The last card is faced for trumps, and belongs to the Dealer. The player to the left of the Dealer leads; and each player thereafter must not only follow suit, but must win the trick, if possible. When unable to follow suit, a player must trump or overtrump if possible; if impossible, he must discard.

There are no Marriages. The cards score as in the two-handed game, and the Last Trick scores 10. After the hand is played out, the side counting 66 or more, but less than 100, scores 1 game point; over 100 and less than 130, 2 game points; if they take every trick (130), 3 points. If both sides have 65, neither scores, and 1 point is added to the score of the winners of the next hand.

The game is 7 points. In some localities, the 10 of trumps counts 1 game point for the side winning it, in addition to its value as a scoring card. If one side has 6 game points and wins the trump 10 on a trick, it scores game at once.

AUCTION SIXTY-SIX

The deck of 24 cards is used, as in regular Sixty-Six. The trump is not faced, but is bid for. There are four players, who cut for partners, the highest two paired against the lowest two. Partners sit opposite each other. The lowest cut deals the first hand. Each player is dealt 6 cards, 3 at a time, in rotation left to right.

The player to the left of the Dealer has the first bid, or he may pass. He may bid that he will play; that he will make 90; or 100; or 120. The next player must bid higher or pass. There is no limit to the number of bids a player may make. If the first bidder refuses, he is considered as able to make as much, and to advance his bid to that amount. The highest bidder names the trump.

The player to the left of the Dealer leads. Marriages are counted when it is a player's turn to lead, one of the Marriage cards being led, and one shown. The highest bidder's side scores

1, if they make 66, and bid less than 90. They get 2 points for reaching 90 before their opponents reach 66, if they bid 90. They get 4 points if they bid and make 100; and 5 points if they bid and make all the tricks. The game is 20 points. Failure to make the bid loses the amount of their bid.

A player may bid and play a Lone Hand, without a partner. If he succeeds, he wins double; if he loses, he loses double.

CLABBER, EVANSVILLE CLABBER, CLOBERYASH

EQUIPMENT: A 32-card deck, Ace, King, Queen, Jack, 10, 9, 8, 7 of each suit.

PLAYERS: Two, three, or four, either as individuals or partners.

RANK OF CARDS: Jack, 9, Ace, 10, King, Queen, 8, 7 in trumps; Ace, 10, King, Queen, Jack, 9, 8, 7 in plain suits.

PRELIMINARIES.—In the cut, high deals. The cards rank as in plain suits for the cut. After the shuffle and cut, the Dealer deals 8 cards to each, one card at a time, in rotation left to right, facing up the last card for a trump, when four play. When three play, remove the 7's, deal 9 to each player, facing the last card up as a trump. A player holding the 8 of trumps may substitute it for the faced trump. In the two-handed game, remove the 7's from the deck. Deal 6 cards to each player, then 3 to each player. The last 3 dealt to each player are called the Blind, and are not to be picked up until the trump is made.

OBJECT OF THE GAME.—To score 500 points, or a game, as follows:

MELDING POINTS

	Points
Belle, trump King and Queen	20
4 Jacks	200
4 9's, 4 Aces, 4 10's, 4 Kings or 4 Queens	100
5 cards of same suit in Sequence	100
4 cards of same suit in Sequence	50
Dad, 3 cards of same suit in Sequence	20

Belle must be called when played. No cards, except the trump King and Queen, may be counted in more than one meld. The players playing the trump must have higher meld than their opponents to count, only the high meld to be shown. When trump and plain suit melds are of the same rank, the trump meld counts. These cards count to the player holding them, and must be announced thus: All melds must be announced before the first play; and the commanding meld must be shown before the second play.

POINTS TAKEN IN ON TRICKS

Trump Jack, called Yass, 20; trump 9, called Menel, 14; each Ace, 11; each 10, 10; each King, 4; each Queen, 3; each Jack, 2. Last Trick, 10. Each hand is worth 162 by cards.

THE PLAY.—Commencing with the player to the left of the Dealer, and in rotation to the left, each player has the privilege of playing with the faced card as trump, or passing. If the trump is not accepted, in rotation, in the same order, the players have the privilege of naming the trump, or passing. If all the players pass on this round, the deal passes to the left.

When the trump is made, the player to the left of the Dealer leads. The others must follow suit if possible; failing that, they must trump; if that is not possible, they must discard. If a trick is trumped, or a trump led, the players in rotation must head the trick; if that is not possible, they are required to play trumps; failing in these courses, they must discard. The winner of each trick leads to the next trick. Any player who revokes does not score for melds or counts.

SCORING.—The player or side playing or making trumps must score more than any opponent; failing to do so, he or they do not score. The opponents score all that they make.

As often played, only the player or side playing or making the trumps may meld. If the player or side playing trumps gets less than the opponent, or opponents, the latter score the combined points. Otherwise, the opponents score all that they make.

PIQUET

Piquet is far older than any of the games in the strict Bézique group. Its introduction is credited to the middle of the 15th century, in the reign of Charles VII of France.

Equipment: A 32-card pack, Ace, King, Queen, Jack, 10, 9, 8, 7, in each suit.

Players: Two.

Rank of Cards: As above. Ace is high in cutting and play. There are no trumps.

Preliminaries.—In cutting, low has choice of seats, and deals. The Dealer is called the Younger Hand, his opponent the Elder Hand. Each player is dealt 12 cards, 2, or 3, at a time. The remaining 8 cards are faced down on the table, the upper 5 laid across the lower three.

Objects of the Game.—The objects of the game are to score for certain combinations of cards held in the hand, and afterwards to win tricks. The game is 100 points.

The Discarding.—Each player examines his hand. If the Dealer's opponent has no King, Queen or Jack, he announces Carte Blanche, and scores 10 points at once. If the Dealer has Carte Blanche, he does not announce it until his opponent has discarded. The opponent must discard at least 1 card, and may discard up to 5. To replace his discards, he takes from the stock as many cards as he has discarded, announcing if he has left any of the 5 to which he was entitled. The Dealer then discards, and draws to replace his discards. He may take none, or any or all of those left by the opponent; and if he takes the latter he must do so before taking the 3 cards to which he is entitled. The opponent may look at any of the first 5 that he leaves in the talon. If the Dealer looks at what he leaves, the opponent may also look at them, after he has led to the first trick.

The Scoring Points.—The object in discarding and drawing is to secure some of the counting combinations. These are:

COUNTING COMBINATIONS

	Points
The Point: the suit of the greatest pip value, counting Aces, 11; court cards, 10; 10, 9, 8, 7 at pip value; each card in the winning suit counting	1
Sequence, 3 or more cards of the same suit in sequence, for each card in the winning sequence	1
Sequence bonus, for winning sequence of 5 or more cards	10
Three of a kind, better than 9's	3
Four of a kind	4

Only the better Point value is scored. Only the longer Sequence wins. In case of Sequences of equal length, the one headed by the higher card wins. The player who has the higher Three of a kind or Four of a kind may count any inferior ones; his opponent counts none.

OTHER SCORES

Carte Blanche (no King, Queen or Jack in original hand)	10
Lead—any lead	1
Win—any winning of a trick from opponent . . .	1
Last trick	1
Cards (taking more than six tricks)	10
Capot (taking all tricks)	40
Pic (30 in points and leads by opponent before the Dealer scores anything)	30
Repic (30 in either hand before play, equalities counting for Repic scorer)	60

DECLARING.—After the discarding and drawing is finished, the opponent calls his Point, and the Dealer says "Good" or "Not good," depending on whether or not the Point called is superior or inferior to the Dealer's strength. The point is called by the number of cards, as "A point of five." If the Dealer says "Equal," the pips are counted. Sequences are called next, "Good," "Equal," or "Not good." If "Equal" is answered, the highest card is announced. In case of a tie in either, neither side scores.

The hand is always called in regular order—Point, Sequence, Threes or Fours. At the end of his opponent's counting, the Dealer announces "I lead a heart," or whatever may be the suit led. He announces the sum of his count, plus one for the lead. Before the Dealer plays to the first trick, he announces what cards he holds better than those of his opponent.

If the Dealer takes a trick before his opponent gets to Pic, the latter cannot then make it. The Dealer can never make Pic, because the opponent's lead scores 1 point for him. Either player can score Repic, by reaching 30 points without playing a card.

THE PLAY.—The opponent leads any card he pleases, and scores 1 for it. The Dealer must follow suit; if he cannot, he discards. If the leader wins the trick, he scores nothing except 1 for his next lead. If his opponent wins, he scores 1 for winning, and then 1 more for the next lead. No matter which player wins the last trick, he scores 1 for it. The 40 for Capot, or winning every trick, includes the scores for the odd trick and for the last trick.

SCORING.—The game is 100 points, and the first player to reach that total wins. If there is a tie, the order of precedence is: Carte Blanche, Point, Sequence, Threes or Fours, Pic, Repic, points for Leads and Wins, the Last Trick, and Capot.

RUBICON PIQUET

In Rubicon Piquet, six deals make a game. At the end of six deals, the lower score is deducted from the higher, and a bonus of 100 added to the difference. If either or both players fail to reach 100 in the six deals, the higher score wins, and he adds to his score the lower score, instead of deducting it.

PIQUET À ÉCRIRE

There may be any number of players from three to seven. Each plays two consecutive deals, first with the player on the right, and then with the player on the left. At the end of the round, each pays the difference between his score and that of the others.

THREE-HANDED PIQUET, or PIQUET NORMAND

Each of the three players has 10 cards dealt to him. The remaining widow of two can be taken by the Dealer in exchange for two of his own cards. The player to the left of the Dealer declares first, and scores 90 for Repic if he can count 20 that is good before he leads. He scores 60 for Pic, if he reaches 20 in hand and play combined—both before an adversary has scored. If the Point score is a tie, each player scores 5. If one player does not take a trick, the others count 20 each.

FOUR-HANDED PIQUET, or PIQUET VOLEUR

This is a game for four players, two playing as partners against the other two. The player to the left of the Dealer declares everything he has, without waiting to know if it is good, and then leads. If the player to his left admits the announcements to be good, he says nothing, but plays to the trick. If he has better, he announces it. And so on around the table. If one player has already announced anything that is good, his partner may show and score anything in the same class. If one side has scored a high Four, his partner may score all of his fours or threes, for instance. If a partnership reaches 20 that is good before leading, they score 90 for Repic. If, before the other side scores, they reach 20 that is good in hand and play, they secure 60 for Pic. In this game Carte Blanche counts toward Pic or Repic, so that a double Carte Blanche between partners would be a certain Repic.

PIQUET WITH A TRUMP, or IMPERIAL

PLAYERS: Two.

RANK OF CARDS: King, Queen, Jack, Ace, 10, 9, 8, 7, the King, Queen, Jack, Ace, 7 of the trump suit being honors.

Each player is provided with 6 white counters, altogether worth 1 red; and 4 red counters. As soon as either player has put up all his counters, he wins game. Each player is dealt 12 cards, 2 at a time, and the next is faced for trumps. If this is an honor, the Dealer puts up a white counter for it.

There is no drawing from the stock. Sequences must be confined to the 4 highest cards, King, Queen, Jack, Ace. Three of a kind does not count. The combinations known as Imperials are: Carte Blanche; any sequence of King, Queen, Jack, Ace; or a Sequence in trumps, one of the cards being the faced trump. Catching the Jack and Ace of trumps in play by leading the King and Queen is an Imperial in play. Four of a kind, except of the 8's, 9's and 10's, is an Imperial.

The opponent calls his Point first; if it is good, he puts up a white counter for it. Sequences and Fours are then called. The opponent wins all ties. After his opponent has led, the Dealer calls his Imperials, if good, and then plays to the trick. The second player in each trick must win if he can, by a higher card in the suit, or, if he cannot follow suit, by a trump; otherwise he must discard. The winner of a trick with any trump honor or honors in it puts up a white counter for each such honor, at the end of the hand. If one player wins more tricks than the other, he puts up a white counter for each trick's difference. Capot is worth two red counters.

Each time a player puts up his 6th white counter, he substitutes a red counter in their place. This compels his opponent to take down any white counters he may have up, so that these points are lost. When the end game is close, the order of precedence is: The turned trump; Carte Blanche; the Point; Imperials in hand, Sequences first; Imperials with the aid of the faced trump; Imperial catching honors in play; honors taken in tricks; odd tricks.

THE HEARTS GROUP

Hearts and the allied games, in which the object is to avoid taking certain cards and tricks, constitute an ancient answer of poor card-holders and non-trump-holders to such games as Whist and Euchre. For here the premium is on holding poor cards. A similar impulse led to the invention of Nullos, and its introduction into various forms of Whist, Euchre, Skat, etc.; for in Nullos poor cards are essential, and taking a trick is fatal. "The last shall be first. . . ." In these games and devices, too, the lucky in love capitalize their ill luck in cards, and demand a new card skill—the ability to lose strategically and overwhelmingly. Two-Ten-Jack combines this losing mood with the winning mood. Although the omnipresent martyr complex may enter into the spirit of these games, the player at Hearts has never been observed to try to lose the game.

HEARTS

Equipment: A full deck of 52 cards.

Players: Two to six; best for four players, as described below.

Rank of Cards: Ace (high), King, Queen, Jack, 10, 9 etc. down to 2 (low).

Preliminaries.—In the cut for deal, the lowest card cut deals, the Ace being high in the cut. After shuffle and cut, the Dealer deals 13 cards to each player, in rotation left to right, one at a time, beginning with the player to his left; the deal passes to the left. Any irregularity in the deal is a misdeal, causing the deal to pass; the exception is an imperfect deck, in which case the same Dealer redeals with a perfect deck.

Object of the Game.—To win, on tricks, as few hearts as possible.

The Play.—The hand to the left of the Dealer leads any card, and in rotation, to the left, each player must follow suit; if unable to do so, he must discard. The highest card played of the suit led wins the trick. The winner of each trick leads for the next. When the hands are played out, the hearts taken by each player are then counted and settled for, and the cards are shuffled for a new deal.

Irregularities.—A player is compelled to take the last trick if he fails to play to one trick and plays to the next; or if, at the end, he has too few cards, the other hands being correct. Any exposed card becomes a penalty card, subject to call, provided it may be played to the trick on which it is called. A lead out of turn must be taken back, unless all have played to it, the card becoming a penalty card subject to call; on his next turn to lead, the player on his right may, should he so desire, compel him to lead hearts. If a card is played out of turn, it must be taken back, and the player on the left may compel the player in error, when his turn comes, to play his highest or lowest of the suit led, or to refrain from discarding a heart. If a player revokes, the hands are played out, and the revoking player, if he loses, must settle for the losses of all the others; if he wins, he must put up his winnings as a jackpot. If two players revoke, each must pay the full penalty, as if each alone were in error. If the revoking player wins with another player as his partner, he must settle all losses, and put up his share of the winnings for a jackpot.

Scoring.—After the hearts are counted, each player pays one counter for each heart he has taken; and the player with the fewest hearts takes all the counters so paid. If two or more players tie for the lowest number of hearts, they divide the pool, an odd counter remaining in the pool for the next deal. In the Sweepstakes method of scoring, the pool, called the jackpot or jack, accumulates until one or more players take no hearts on a hand; in which case, the jackpot goes to that one, or is divided between those winners, an odd counter remaining in the pool for the next deal. In the Howell method of scoring, each player puts up for each heart he has taken as many counters as there are players; and takes out of the pool as many counters as the difference between 13, the total number of hearts in play, and the number of hearts he took on that hand.

Game.—Each deal is a game in itself. By agreement, each player may begin with an equal number of counters, the first player to lose all of his counters losing the game; or, the first player winning an agreed number becoming winner of the game.

DOMINO HEARTS

In Domino Hearts, the full deck of 52 cards is used. Three to seven may play; the game is best for four or five players. Each player is dealt 6 cards, in rotation left to right, one at a time. The remainder of the pack, the stock or talon, is faced down on the table.

The player to the left of the Dealer leads, and each player in turn must follow suit if possible. If a player has no card of the suit led, he must draw one card at a time from the top of the talon until he draws a card of the suit led, or until the talon is exhausted. After the talon is exhausted, a player who cannot follow suit must discard. The highest card played of the suit led wins the trick. The winner of each trick leads for the next. At the end, the hearts taken in are counted and settled for, as in regular Hearts.

A player who plays out all the cards in his hand retires from the play for the rest of the hand. If a player wins a trick with his last card, the next active player to his left leads for the next trick. If all except one player play out their hands before the talon is exhausted, the hearts remaining in his hand and in the talon are counted against him. If all of the active players play out on the same trick, any hearts remaining in the talon count against the player of the last card.

Domino Hearts may be scored as regular Hearts; or, the first player reaching a stipulated score for hearts taken, such as 31, may be regarded as the loser. The player with the fewest hearts scored against him at this time becomes the winner.

AUCTION HEARTS

In this variation, the players bid for the privilege of naming the suit to be avoided. In bidding, each player, commencing with the one to the left of the Dealer, names the number of counters he will put up as a pool, if allowed to name the suit. Each player is allowed one bid only; and each player must bid higher than the highest preceding bid, or pass. The highest bidder puts up the pool and names the suit; he leads first, and thereafter the play is the same as in regular Hearts.

When the hands are played out, each bidder pays into the pool one counter for each card he has taken in of the suit to be avoided. The player who has taken no card of this suit wins the pool; if two players have taken none, they divide the pool, leaving any odd counter as the basis for a new pool, which is a jack, as at Sweepstakes scoring in regular Hearts. If more than two players take none, or one player takes all 13, or each player takes at least one, no player wins. The deal passes, and the successful bidder on the preceding deal names the suit to be avoided, without bidding. At the end of the play, each player puts up one counter for each card of the suit not to be taken in, as before; this continues until some player wins the pool.

HEARTSETTE

When three or four play, omit the Spade 2; when more than four, use the entire deck. Dealing as in regular Hearts, in three-handed, each player receives 16 cards; four-handed, 12; five-handed, 10; six-handed, 8. The remaining cards are faced down for a widow. The winner of the first trick must gather in the widow with the trick, and all hearts in it count against him. No other player is allowed to examine the widow. Otherwise, the play is as in regular Hearts.

JOKER HEARTS

In this variation, the Heart 2 is omitted from the deck, and the Joker added. It ranks between the Heart 10 and Jack, and wins any trick unless a Heart Jack or higher is played, in which case the higher heart wins, regardless of the suit led. The holder of the Joker must follow suit to Hearts. In scoring, the Joker counts as 5 Hearts.

BLACK JACK HEARTS

This is a variation of Hearts, in which the Spade Jack counts as 10 Hearts against the player taking it, but retains its rank as a

Spade. The holder must follow suit to Spades with it, unless he has some other Spade he prefers to play. Otherwise, he may discard Black Jack.

RED JACK HEARTS

This is a variation of Hearts, in which the Diamond Jack (called Red Jack) counts ten plus points for the player taking it, but retains its rank as a Diamond. The holder of it must follow suit to Diamonds with it, unless he has some other Diamond he prefers to play. This variation may be used with any of the variations of Hearts.

BLACK LADY

The same as Black Jack, except that the Spade Queen, called Black Lady, fills the rôle of the Spade Jack. The Queen retains its rank as a Spade, and counts as 13 Hearts.

SPOT HEARTS

In this variation of Hearts, the Hearts are settled for according to their denominations, Ace being worth 14; King, 13; Queen, 12; Jack, 11; 10, 10; and so on.

PROGRESSIVE HEARTS

The players are seated as in Progressive Euchre. One deal only is played at each table. The lady and the gentleman with the fewest Hearts in their combined hands progress from all tables except No. I, where those with the most move down to the Booby Table. One method of scoring is by gold stars pasted on the score cards for each winning at Table No. I; red stars, at any other table; and green stars, for those losing at the Booby Table. Prizes may be given for each group, no player being awarded more than one prize. If there is a tie in any group, the number of other stars breaks it.

FOUR JACKS, QUATRE-VALETS, or POLIGNAC

EQUIPMENT: A 32-card deck, Ace, King, down through 7, in each suit.

PLAYERS: Four to seven. When five or six play, the black 7's are thrown out. When seven play, the Dealer takes no cards.

RANK OF CARDS: Ace (high), King, Queen, Jack, 10, 9, 8 ,7 (low). In France, the cards rank as at Écarté, King, Queen, Jack, Ace, 10, 9, 8, 7. There is no trump suit.

The preliminaries are settled as at Hearts. When four play, 8 cards are dealt to each, 3, 2, 3; when five, 6 cards, 3 at a time; when six or seven, 5 to each, the Dealer taking no cards in the seven-handed game.

The object of the players is to avoid taking in any tricks containing a Jack. The Spade Jack, called Polignac, requires a loss of 2 points; any other Jack, of 1 point. The first player to lose 10 points is out, and pays the stakes on the result; it is usual for him to pay each player the difference between 10 and the player's score.

THE PLAY.—The player to the left of the Dealer leads any card he wishes. The others must follow suit if possible, but need not head the trick. The highest card played of the suit led wins the trick; and the winner of each trick leads to the next. Any player unable to follow suit may discard a Jack, if he has one, or any other high card, as in Hearts.

SLOBBERHANNES

The 32-card deck is used, as in Four Jacks. The cards rank Ace, King, down to 7, Ace being high both in cutting and play. Four to seven can play, the omission of the black 7's, and the deal, being the same as in Four Jacks. There is no trump suit.

The object of the game is to avoid taking the first trick; the last trick; and the trick containing the Queen of Clubs. The player or players winning any of these tricks has 1 point scored against him or them for each trick; for taking all 3, 4 points. The first player to have a score of 10 against him pays to the other players the difference between 10 and their score. The penalty for a revoke is 1 counter; if it occurs on the first or last trick, however, the penalty becomes 2 counters.

The player to the left of the Dealer leads any card he pleases, and in rotation, left to right, the others play, following suit if possible. If a player cannot follow suit, he may discard the Queen of Clubs or, lacking that, any card he pleases.

TWO-TEN-JACK

EQUIPMENT: A full 52-card deck.

PLAYERS: Two, three or four; best as a two-handed game. See the three- and four-handed games below.

RANK OF CARDS: Hearts are always trumps. The Ace of Spades, called Speculation, is the highest trump, ranking above the others in this order: Spade Ace, Heart Ace, King, Queen, Jack, 10, 9, 8, 7, 6, 5, 4, 3, 2 (low). In plain suits, the ranking is Ace (high) down to 2 (low), Spades, of course, ranking downward from the King.

PRELIMINARIES.—In the cut, low deals, Ace being low in the cutting. After shuffle and cut, the Dealer deals 6 cards to each player, one at a time, beginning with his opponent. The remainder of the deck, the talon, is faced upward on the table.

OBJECTS OF THE GAME.—To win in tricks certain cards of counting value, and to avoid winning cards which count against the winner.

THE PLAY.—The opponent leads any card, and the Dealer then plays to the lead. A player is required to follow suit, except in one instance: when trumps are led, it is optional with the holder of Speculation whether to play it or not. If the holder of Speculation holds no other Spade, Speculation must be played to a Spade lead. The highest card of the suit led wins a trick; unless it is trumped, in which case the trump wins.

The winner of the first trick takes the top card of the talon into his hand and the loser takes the second. The winner of each trick leads to the next. This continues until the talon and the hands are exhausted. Points made are then recorded, and the deal passes.

SCORING POINTS

		Points
Plus Points:	Heart 2, 10, Jack, each	10
	Heart Ace, King, Queen, each . .	5
	Diamond and Club, Ace, King, Queen, Jack, each	1
Minus Points:	Spade 2, 10, Jack, each	10
	Spade Ace, King, Queen, each . .	5

At the end of each hand, each player totals his plus points, then his minus points, and deducts the lesser total from the greater. If the greater score is plus, it is scored plus; if minus, as minus.

The game is an agreed number of points, ranging from 30 to 100. A 30-point game may be long; a 100-point game may be overlong.

THREE-HANDED TWO-TEN-JACK

Omit the Club 3 from the deck and deal 6 cards to each player, beginning to the Dealer's left. The deal passes to the left. In rotation, left to right, the winner of a trick and the two other players take cards from the talon.

FOUR-HANDED TWO-TEN-JACK

Two players play as partners against the other two, determining partners by the cut. Each player receives 4 cards, dealt in rotation left to right, beginning with the player left of the Dealer. The play is the same as three-handed Two-Ten-Jack, the winner of each trick drawing the top card from the talon, and the others drawing a card apiece in rotation, left to right.

THE RUMMY GROUP

CONQUIAN, or COONCAN

Conquian, named from the Spanish *con quien?* (with whom?) is popular throughout Mexico and the border States across the Rio Grande. It is the parent of the popular game of Rummy or Rum, in all its varieties.

EQUIPMENT: A 40-card deck, omitting the 8's, 9's and 10's of each suit. In the United States, it is more usual to omit the Kings, Queens and Jacks, leaving an unbroken sequence from Ace (low) up to 10 (high).

PLAYERS: Two or three. When three play, two only take cards, each player in turn remaining out for one deal.

RANK OF CARDS: King, Queen, Jack, 7, 6, 5, 4, 3, 2, Ace (low); or 10 (high), 9, 8, etc., down to 2, Ace (low).

PRELIMINARIES.—In the cut for deal, low deals, Ace being low. After the shuffle and cut, 10 cards are dealt to each player, two at a time. The balance of the deck, the talon, is faced down on the table. The deal passes at the end of each hand.

OBJECT OF THE GAME.—The object of the game is to show on the table 11 cards, made up of any of these combinations:

A Triplet—3 cards of the same denomination.
Fours—4 cards of the same denomination.
Sequence—3 or more cards of one suit in numerical rotation.
The Ace is in sequence with the 2, not with the King.

The player first combining 11 cards in this manner wins the game.

THE PLAY.—The opponent starts the play, by turning up the top card of the talon. If he can use this card to form a combination with others in his hand, he may place it faced upward in front of him, adding at least 2 cards from his hand to form the combination. The player must show how he uses the turned card, and is never allowed to put it in his hand. If he cannot or does not wish to use it, the Dealer has the privilege.

If either player uses a card from the talon, he must discard one card from his hand in its place. His opponent may then use this discard, or turn it face downward. Each player must discard in this manner after using a card faced upward from the talon, or a discard from his opponent's hand. If a player uses his opponent's discard, he must discard to fill its place, and the other player may in turn use this discard.

If neither player uses the card faced up on the talon, the second player to pass faces it downward and turns up the next card on the talon; uses it in a combination; or passes this privilege to his opponent. This continues until the talon is exhausted, or until one of the players has 11 cards on the table in combinations.

Any card of a Fours combination, or either end card of a sequence of 4 or more cards, may be borrowed to form other combinations. No card may be borrowed which leaves less than a combination of three remaining in the combination from which it was taken.

A player may pass a turned up card which he can use in a combination he has exposed on the board, unless the opponent objects; in which case, the card must be added to the combination. A player forces an opponent to use a card which he has discarded, by placing it with the opponent's combination. If the player faces it up on the table, the opponent may pass it, and the player has no right to object. If either player examines a card or cards faced down, his opponent may examine all the cards faced down. If either player examines any card in the talon, his opponent may examine all of them, leaving them in their proper order. If a player turns up a card out of turn, his opponent has prior claim to it.

Scoring.—Each player begins with an equal number of counters. Each deal is a game, and as soon as one player succeeds in combining his 11 cards, the opponent pays him 1 counter. If neither side scores 11, it is a tie, and each puts 1 counter in the pool. The first player making an 11 takes all the chips in the pool, and is paid 1 additional counter by his opponent.

PANGUINGUE

EQUIPMENT: Eight Conquian decks, or full decks with the 8's, 9's and 10's omitted. In some localities, as few as five decks are used.

PLAYERS: Any number.

PRELIMINARIES.—A portion of the pack is spread, and the players draw. Low sits to the right of the Dealer, the play in this game going from right to left, not, as is usual, from left to right. The cards rank as in Conquian, the Ace being low. After the shuffle and cut, each player is dealt 10 cards, 5 at a time. Each shuffle consists of all the discards, and a group of cards from the bottom of the pack. The shuffling is done by the player to the left of the previous Dealer, the deal passing to the right. If a player discovers that he has too few or too many cards before he has drawn a card, he may abandon the hand and have a new one dealt to him. If, at any other time, his hand shows too few or too many cards, he must abandon the hand. This player may make no further collections on his hand, but must pay all other players making combinations of value. One foul hand does not affect the valid hands.

OBJECTS OF THE GAME.—(a) To form certain combinations of value:

Three cards or more of the same denomination, but of different suits. Aces or Kings may be combined, separately, regardless of suit.

Three cards or more of the same suit and denomination.

Three cards or more of the same suit, in Sequence. The Ace is in Sequence with the 2, not with the King.

(b) To form in combination 11 cards, the first player forming such combination winning the game.

VALUE OF THE HANDS.—Cards are divided into two classes: valle or value cards, the 3's, 5's and 7's; and non-valle cards, all the others. Combinations of values are known as Conditions, which are:

a. Any 3 valle cards of the same denomination, all of different suits, or all of the same suit.
b. Any 3 non-valle cards, of the same suit and denomination.
c. Ace, 2 and 3 of the same suit.
d. King, Queen and Jack of the same suit.

Each condition is worth 1 counter from each other player, if in Hearts, Clubs or Diamonds. If in Spades, it is worth 2 counters.

THE PLAY.—After the deal is completed, the Dealer turns the top card or Deck Head face up. The player to his right may either use this card in some combination, or draw another card. No other player may use the Deck Head except in a two-handed game; but any other card turned by any other player and not used by him may be used by the player immediately to his right, but by no other player.

If the player to Dealer's right forms from the cards in his hand, and with the card drawn by him, any acceptable combination, he lays these cards faced up on the table in front of him. If the combination forms a Condition, he announces the fact, and collects from the players the counters due on the Condition. If he has another combination he may expose it at the same time, if he so decides; and at the same time he may make another collection from the other players, if this, too, is a Condition. After he has exposed such combinations as he desires, he discards any card remaining in his hand, leaving a total of 10 cards in his hand and exposed on the table in front of him.

The next player to his right may either use this discard, or may turn a new card from the talon. The play proceeds in this manner until the hand is out.

At the request of any other player, a player must use a card discarded or passed to him or drawn by him, if it applies to any combination which he has already exposed. If not so requested he may use the card or not, as he decides.

No player may show on the table any combinations other than those named above; except that when he has a Condition in his hand, as 3 Spade 5's, he may combine them with any other 5 which he may draw, or which may be discarded or passed to him, and thus form a combination. This applies to any other pay combination—that is, one held in the player's hand. In addition, a player may, should he hold Ace, 2 and 3, add a 4 which he has received; or should he hold King, Queen and Jack, add a 7 of the same suit, as provided above, and collect on the hand.

A player may remove a card from either end of a Sequence or Stringer, provided he leaves 3 cards in the Stringer: or he may cut off from a combination of more than 3 cards of the same denomination, provided the combination is valid after this card is removed. Thus, if to a Spade, Heart and Club 3 another Club 3 is added as a Stringer, a Club 3 could be removed, but not the Spade or the Heart, since the remaining spread would not be valid: only three 3's of the same suit, or of three different suits, scoring.

Aces and Kings are called non-Comoquers; that is, any three Aces or three Kings, irrespective of suit, may be spread. An Ace or a King accordingly may be cut off at any time, provided 3 cards remain in the spread. A player may cut off from any combination, and at the same time add another card from his hand to make the original combination valid.

After a valid combination has been exposed, if it was of 3 cards, another card of the same denomination may be added; or, if it was a Stringer, cards may be added to either end of it. If desired, a Stringer may be split, so long as at least 3 cards remain in either portion of it. Where cards are added to a Condition, a new Condition must be made before any added collections can take place. For example, a player exposes the Heart, Diamond and Club 7, and collects 1 counter. Later, he draws 2 more Diamond 7's. The new Condition is worth 2 counters; but as the player has already used one Diamond 7 in a previous Condition, he is paid but 1 counter. If another 7 is added, as a Spade 7, he would again collect 1 counter. A player who has exposed 3 cards of the same suit and denomination collects the original value of the Condition on adding any additional identical card or cards. These rules apply generally to all Conditions. Cards used in one Condition can be cut off and used in another Condition; but no collection can be made on the new Condition, unless the former Condition is first made good again by drawing the necessary additional cards.

When a player has 10 cards exposed on the table, the player to his left cannot discard from his hand a card that will give this player game; unless he should be forced,—that is, draw such cards that he has no discard that will not give the player the right to go game.

When a player wins the game by showing 11 cards in combination, as described above, he collects 1 counter from each player for the game, and, in addition, the value of all Conditions shown by him at the end of the game.

Counters of an agreed value are used. At any stage of the game, a player may declare that he will pay no losses greater than the amount of his counters. If, afterwards, he makes a Collection, he receives from each player only counters to the extent of those he possessed at the time. If, on any subsequent round during the same hand, the player exposes another combination, whether a Condition or not, he collects the remaining chips due him, again up to the number of counters he possessed when he made his declaration.

An understanding of the far simpler Conquian will aid in comprehending the intricacies of Panguingue.

Penalties.—Any inaccurate spread claimed as a Condition constitutes a Foul Play, and any player may call attention to it at any time before the end of the game. The offending player then forfeits his hand, but pays to all Conditions to the end of the game. If a player plays with an erroneous number of cards, called a Foul Hand, he must repay to each player all Collections made from him; discard his own hand; and continue to pay until the end of the deal. If he makes a foul spread, he must do the same as if he had a foul hand, unless he has the correct card in his hand, or draws it before the foul spread is discovered.

RUMMY, or RUM

Equipment: A full 52-card deck.

Players: From two to six, four to six making the best game.

Preliminaries.—Choice of seats and the first deal are determined by a cut, low winning, and Ace being low. In counting, Ace counts 1; 2, 2; etc., up to Jack, 11; Queen, 12; and King, 13. After the shuffle and cut, the Dealer deals. In two-handed Rummy, 10 cards are given to each; in three-handed, 7; when four or more play, 6. The cards are dealt one at a time, left to right in rotation. The next card is faced up and placed beside the stock, which is faced down near the center of the table.

Object of the Game.—To get rid of all the cards in a player's hand, by laying them out in Threes or Fours, or in a Sequence of 3 or more in the same suit.

The Play.—The player to the left of the Dealer must either draw a card from the top of the stock, without showing it, or must take the card that is faced up beside the stock. Before he has added the card to his hand, he must discard a card in its place. If he holds a Three of any denomination, a Four of any denomination, or a Sequence of 3 or more cards in any suit, he may lay them on the table in front of him. After the first player has played, each player in rotation to his left has the same right to play in his turn. Only one combination may be laid down at a time.

In some localities, the game is rendered more difficult by having only one card faced up, each discard being placed on the top of the original faced card or where it lay. This gives 2 piles from which to draw, one faced and the stock faced down. Only the top card may be taken from either. This makes the game longer, and requires a keen memory of the cards in the faced up pile.

After drawing and discarding, any player may get rid of one card from his hand by placing it on some combination already laid down by another player. Thus, if a player holds the Club 10 and 6, and a player has faced the Club 7, 8, and 9, the player may add either the 10 or the 6, after draw and discard, to the faced Sequence. Only one card at a time may be played in this way.

The first player to get rid of all his cards, either faced in front of him or played to some other player's combination, wins the game. After his last draw, he has of course made his customary discard, before facing up his final cards or card. The other players settle by paying him according to the number of pips on the cards they still hold, the cards counting up from Ace, 1; 2, 2, to Jack, 11; Queen, 12; King, 13.

After the game is over, no more cards may be faced up. If a player cannot use any of the cards faced up, or the top of the faced pile if these cards are piled, it is usually wiser to draw from the stock, to try and get something to fit the cards in the hand. It is wiser to play for smaller than larger combinations, since the value of cards faced up is equal, and the higher the cards remaining in the hand, the larger the amount that the player has to pay at the end of the game.

If the stock is exhausted before any player wins, there are two ways to proceed: 1. All the hands are faced, and that of the lowest pip value wins. After the last card is drawn, no further discarding is allowed. 2. The discards are all gathered up, shuffled, and cut, and the top card faced up, the remainder constituting a stock faced down, as at the beginning of the game.

SHOWDOWN RUMMY

In this variation, a player at any time holding combinations which include every card in his hand may lay the entire hand down at once, scoring double the pip value of all cards left in the opposing hands.

DISCARD RUMMY

In this variation, the order of procedure for each player is Draw; Play; Discard, instead of Draw; Discard; Play, as in regular Rummy.

BOAT HOUSE RUMMY

In this variation, a player's hand is not shown until he is able to show a completed hand, and declare Rummy. In settling up, the King, Queen, Jack and 10 count 10 each; the others their pip value, down to 1 for the Ace. In some localities, the points are not counted, each player paying 1 or more counters for each card remaining in his hand that cannot be matched in Three, Four or Sequence. The Round-the-Corner Sequence is allowed, permitting an Ace to be used in sequence with a King as well as with a 2. Thus these would be proper Sequences: 2, Ace, King; Ace, King, Queen.

After the first deal, the winner of each hand deals the next. The number of cards dealt to each player is computed thus: 9 cards, minus the number of players. Thus, in two-handed, there would be 7 cards to each; in three-handed, 6; in four-handed, 5; in five-handed, 4; in six-handed, 3. Each player in turn, beginning to Dealer's left, may draw the 2 top cards of the exposed cards if available; or the top exposed card and one from the top of the stock; or only one from the stock. He cannot draw a card from the exposed cards after he has drawn from the stock. When all the cards have been faced up, the top card is left faced up, and the balance are reshuffled and cut and faced downward, constituting a stock, as at the beginning of the game; and the play continues.

As soon as any player declares Rummy, he must face up all his cards. A penalty should be agreed upon for an incorrect declaration. The other hands are then faced up, and the players settle as above; either for pip value, or for each unmatching card. When only one card is left unmatched, it is a draw, each player putting into a pool the amount of counters his unmatched cards call for, the winner of the next game taking the pool.

MICHIGAN RUMMY

In Michigan Rummy, in melding and settling, the Ace scores 15 points, except when used in Sequence with the 2 and 3, in which case it scores only 1 point. The Kings, Queens, Jacks and 10's score 10 each; the other cards, 9 down to 2, their pip value.

In the cut for deal, Ace ranks as low. Subsequent hands are dealt by the winner. In the two-handed game, 9 cards are dealt to each player; in three- or four-handed, 7; when more play, 6. The object is to get rid of cards by melding Threes, Fours, and Sequences of 3 or more cards.

THE PLAY.—Each player in turn, beginning at the Dealer's left, draws one card from the stock, or from the row of cards faced up, which must be so placed that the denomination of each is visible. If he draws from the row of faced cards, he must take up the card he wishes and also all cards above it—that is, exposed since it was exposed—in the row. After the draw, and before discarding, the player may lay down all possible melds; and may also face up, in front of him, any cards that can be added to melds made by any opponent. He must then discard one card, face up, to the row of exposed cards. If a player discards a card which could be used in any meld, any player can call "Stop!" and then play the card and take credit for the meld. One player must be delegated to keep score of the melds as made, and see that they are correct.

The player first getting rid of all his cards, by laying down his melds and discarding one card on the row of exposed cards, declares "Rummy." If the declaration is incorrect, each opponent scores 20 points. If it is correct, each opponent pays the winner the pip value of his hand, scored as above. After Rummy is declared, no more melds may be made.

The game is usually 500. If two or more exceed a score of 500 on one hand, the higher score wins.

BOZENKILL RUMMY

This variation of Michigan Rummy has 7 cards dealt in the two-, three-, and four-handed game; and 6 cards, when more play. When a player melds a card or cards in front of him to some meld of his opponents, he must announce to which meld it or they are played. A card once melded may not be used again in another combination.

If a player takes a card from the exposed row (together with any cards that are above it, that is, that have been exposed subsequent to it), he must at once use this card in forming a new meld, or by adding it to some existing meld of his own or to an opponent's meld. There is no "Stop!" in the game, a player having the right, if he pleases, to discard a card which could be melded.

The winner's score consists of the combined point score of all cards melded in front of him, plus the pip value of all cards left unplayed in each opponent's hand. An opponent's score is only the cards actually melded by him. The score for game is as in Michigan Rummy.

WILD CAT RUMMY

In this variation of Rummy, the deuces are wild—that is, any 2 can be called and played as any card the player melding it wishes. It then scores as of the value of the card it is called. The Joker may also be used, counting as a fifth deuce, and scoring as of the value of the card it is called. Deuces or Joker held in hand when Rummy is declared count 15 each.

If more than six play, a double deck of 104 cards should be used. To select the first dealer, the cards are dealt face upward one at a time in rotation left to right; and the first player receiving a Jack deals. The winner of each hand deals the next one. When four or less play, 7 cards are dealt to each; when more, 6. When a double pack is used, 7 are dealt to each.

Round-the-Corner Sequences are permitted, as in Boat House Rummy. The draw and discard are the same as in Michigan and Bozenkill Rummy. In melding, all possible melds may be made when it is a player's turn to play. A card in a Sequence or in a Three or Four combination may also be used in the other combination. Thus, these 5 cards, King, King, King, Queen, Jack, may be melded together, and score at once 30 for the three Kings, and 30 more for the King, Queen, Jack Sequence. Or cards may be added subsequently to make such combination melds. The Ace always count as 1 only. No melds may be made after Rummy is declared. The Showdown is as in Michigan Rummy.

In some localities, if a player can declare Rummy on the hand dealt to him without drawing or discarding a single card, the other players pay three times the pip value of their hands. If a player can declare Rummy after drawing the first card, he is paid double. The game is 300 or 500, as agreed.

FIVE HUNDRED RUMMY

In this variation, the Ace counts 15, except when played in an Ace, 2, 3 Sequence, in which case it counts only 1. If more than four play, a double deck of 104 cards is used. The first Dealer is selected as in Wild Cat Rummy. He deals to each player 11 cards minus the number of players: 9 each when two play, 8 when three, 7 when four. If the double deck is used, 9 cards are dealt to each.

As in Bozenkill Rummy, a player drawing from the row of exposed cards must not only draw all cards above the one he wishes, but must use that card in a meld at once. If a card is exposed on the row of exposed cards which could have been used in a meld, the opponent first discovering this may claim it and add it to his own melds.

When the stock is exhausted, the play continues. Each player in turn plays from the row of exposed cards if he can; if not, he knocks on the table. If a player draws cards from the row of exposed cards and cannot play the lowest one, he must keep the cards, and each other player adds 25 to his score. If this 25 gives a score of 500 to any player, the value of the game to be reached at once becomes 525. Rummy is declared as in Michigan Rummy In settling, Aces left in the hand are scored as 15. The game is 500; if more than one player scores 500 on a hand, the highest score wins.

RUM POKER

In this variation of Rummy, each player continues to draw and meld after the deal until he has 15 points or less in his Deadwood, that is, in his unmelded hand. When all have finished drawing and melding, the Deadwoods are exposed; and the one with the lowest number of pips in his Deadwood collects 1 chip from each other player for every pip point the other player has more than the Deadwood of the winner. Game is 500, or an amount agreed upon.

GIN RUMMY

EQUIPMENT: A full deck of 52 cards.

PLAYERS: Two.

PRELIMINARIES.—Deal is selected by a cut, low dealing. Ten

cards are dealt each player, one at a time. The next card, called the up-card, is faced up beside the undealt cards, or stock.

Object of the Game.—To score 100. The difference between the scores of the unmatched cards in a hand is scored in favor of the lesser score.

The Play.—Dealer's opponent may take the upcard, and discard, if he desires. If not, dealer may. If neither desires it, opponent draws the top card of the stock, and discards. The discard pile must show only the top card. By previous agreement, players may look through the discard pile.

The Down.—In order to go down, a player must be able to meld or match his cards into groups of 3 or 4 of a kind, or sequences of 3 or more in the same suit, or both; while his unmatched cards total 10 or less. Ace always counts 1; face cards, 10 each; the rest, their pip value. Aces may not be used in sequence with face cards.

To declare a down, a player, after any draw, exposes his cards. and announces the points he has remaining, at the same time making his final discard. Going down is usually indicated by knocking on the table, and the game is sometimes called Knock Rummy. Opponent then melds his own combinations, and in addition may play or lay off on the melds of the player who has gone down. He then announces his remaining score. The difference between these scores is credited to the player with the lower score.

If the player who does not go down has the lower score, he receives a bonus of 10 additional points. For "going gin," or knocking with all 10 cards matched, a player receives a bonus of 20 points. Even if the opponent can lay down all his cards, the player who goes gin wins, receiving the bonus. The winner of a hand always deals the next hand.

The player first scoring 100 wins the game, and receives an additional bonus of 100. For a shut-out game, the bonus is 200. An additional bonus of 20 points for each hand won is computed at the end of the game. This is called the line or box bonus, winning scores being underlined.

Three- and Four-Handed Games.—When 3 players play, one sits out each hand, playing the winner of the hand. The game ends when any player reaches 100. Each player then pays the difference between his score and the high score.

When 4 or more play, they divide into partnerships, and play separate 2-handed games, alternating opponents after each hand. Game ends at 125, not 100.

Multiple Games, or Hollywood Gin.—It is common for 2 players to score 3 or more games at once. First hand counts only on the 1st game; second, on the 1st and 2nd; subsequent hands on all three, until each game ends. (Some play that a player cannot score on the second game until he has scored on the first, nor on the third until he has scored on the second, etc.)

FOUR HAND RUMMY

Equipment: Two full 52-card decks, with 4 jokers. The extra jokers are the score cards or extra cards found in all decks.

Players: Four or more. If more than eight, add another deck, with two more jokers. Six makes the best game.

Preliminaries.—The deal is determined by a cut, low winning, Ace being low. In scoring, joker counts 25; Ace, 15; face cards, 10; all others according to their pip value. 10 cards are dealt to each, one at a time, left to right. The next card is faced up in the center of the table, beside the stock, which is faced down.

Object of the Game.—To get rid of all the cards in a player's hand by melding them according to the requirements for each hand. Low score wins; the score being determined by the value of the cards in each player's hand after one player has melded his hand.

First Hand: A sequence of four or more, one group of three or more, and a final discard.

Second Hand: Three groups of three or more each, and a final discard.

Third Hand: Two sequences of four or more each, and a final discard.

Fourth Hand: One sequence of four or more, and two groups of three or more each. No final discard.

The Play.—The player to the left of the dealer draws either the exposed card or a card from the stock. He then discards a card from his hand, facing it up beside the stock. Each player plays in turn, facing up his discard on top of the exposed pile, so that only the top card is visible. Each player may draw either the top card of the exposed pile or the top card of the stock.

The jokers are wild, and may be used as the player wishes in forming sequences or groups. A player may not meld any part of his hand until he has all the required groupings for each, as above. In the first three hands, he may meld as required, and still retain cards in his hand. These cards may be played, in subsequent plays, either on his own melds or those of any other player. A player may not play his extra cards until he has melded his own required groupings. In all but the final hand, the player draws, makes his plays or melds, then discards. In the final hand, the last card drawn must fit into the hand and be melded with it. Thus a player's meld in the final hand must contain a minimum of 11 cards. Only one player may meld in this hand.

Buying: If a player does not wish the exposed card, when it is his turn to draw, any other player may say "I buy," and take that card, and one from the stock, thus adding two cards to his hand. A buyer does not discard. This privilege passes from left to right of the immediate player, the one at his left having first choice, and so on around the table. If the one who is playing draws from the stock, and then decides to buy the exposed card, he may do so, providing no one else at the table wishes that card. Buying is desirable in the first three hands, but should be done sparingly in the fourth hand.

Jokers: If a player melds a joker, any other player may take that joker for his own hand, provided he can replace it with the card it has been used for. Thus, if a player melds a sequence using the joker as a 4 of spades, any other player having a 4 of spades may take the joker and put the 4 of spades in its place. This privilege passes from left to right as above.

If the stock is exhausted before the play is completed, the discard pile is reshuffled and cut, the top card faced, and the remainder placed face down as the stock, and the play continues.

If a player discards a card that can be played on any meld, any other player who has melded may call "rummy," take the card and play it, and discard a card from his hand.

As soon as a player has got rid of all his cards, the play of that hand is ended. The remaining players score according to the value of the cards left in their hands, each getting the score of his hand. The melded cards are not counted.

Players may buy, or take an exposed joker, as above, whether or not they have melded.

JAVA RUMMY

In this variation, the Ace counts 1; the deuce and the joker, 25; the face cards 10 each; and the others according to their pip value. Cut for deal as in Rummy, the deal passing from left to right. A full deck of 52 cards is used, plus 2 jokers. Seven cards are dealt to each player. The next card is faced up in the center of the table, beside the stock, which is faced down.

Object of the Game.—To get rid of all the cards in a player's hand by melding in sequences of three or more, or groups of three or more. Low score wins.

The Play.—Deuces are wild. In some localities, one or two jokers are also added, and are wild. The player to the left of the dealer draws a card from the stock, or draws the exposed card, and discards a card from his hand, face up beside the stock. All subsequent discards are placed on top, so that only the top card is visible. If a player wishes to meld, when his turn comes, he must do so before he draws, and cannot discard. He must meld all seven cards at once. He may meld one or more sequences of three or more, groups of three or more, or a sequence and a group. If he can meld six cards, and the seventh is a five or less, he may meld the six and face the seventh, saying "I take four," or whatever the value of the card is. This quantity is added to his score. As soon as one player has melded his cards, the play ends, and the others score. Any melding combinations a player holds are not scored against him. The remaining cards are counted as above. Deuces and jokers, if used, only count against a player if they cannot be used in a combination with other cards in his hand.

As soon as a player's score reaches 100, he is eliminated from the game, until all but one player are eliminated. If, in the final play between the last two players, both scores go over 100, the one having the lower score wins.

If a player forms a sequence of seven cards, this is counted minus 25. That is, it takes 25 from his score, or if he has no score, he is scored —25. It is possible to win the game by obtaining a score of —100. In some localities, this score is only permitted if the player has melded his sequence of seven, merely holding it not being sufficient.

CHICAGO RUMMY

This is a variation of Java Rummy, with 2 decks of 104 cards used, and hands of 10 cards each. Ace always counts 10. A hand may go down with all 10 cards; or with 9, the 10th being a 3, scored as a string of 3.

A straight of ten cards, including jokers and wild deuces, if any, gives a bonus of minus 25. So does a flush, or any 10 cards in the same suit. A straight flush scores a bonus of minus 50. Players are eliminated at plus 100. At minus 100, a player wins at once.

CASSINO

EQUIPMENT: A full deck of 52 cards.

PLAYERS: Two, three or four (as partners, two against two).

THE DEAL.—In the cut for deal, low deals, Ace ranking as lowest. After shuffle and cut, the Dealer deals 4 cards to each player, face down, and 4 to the table, face up, dealing them 2 at a time, in rotation, left to right, commencing to his own left. The stock, the remainder of the deck, is left faced down on the table. After each player's first 4 cards have been played, 4 more are dealt to each player as before; but none to the table. This continues until all of the cards have been dealt and played. The deal passes to the left.

An irregularity in the deal forfeits it, except that a card exposed by the Dealer during the first round calls for a new deal by the same Dealer. If a card is exposed after the first round, the player to whom it falls may replace it face down in the stock, and have a new card dealt to him. Should the exposure occur on the last round of the deal, the Dealer must take the exposed card, and the player must draw from the Dealer's hand. If the wrong number of cards is given to any player after the first round, the error must be corrected by drawing from the hand or replacing the deficiency from the stock; and the Dealer cannot count on that hand of four cards.

SCORING POINTS.—The object of the game is to score points by taking in certain cards and card combinations with point value:

	Points
Cards (greatest number taken in)	3
Spades (greatest number taken in)	1
Big Cassino (Diamond 10)	2
Little Cassino (Spade 2)	1
Each Ace	1
Sweep (taking in all cards on the table)	1

If the count of Spades or cards is a tie, neither side scores them.

THE PLAY.—There are four possible taking plays:

1. Taking in a combination. If the player holds in his hand a card of the same denomination as one faced on the table, he may play his card and take in the 2. If several such cards are on the table, he may take them all in on this play. He may also take in any cards, the sum of which equals the pip value of the one he plays. An Ace may always be counted as 1 toward such a combination. It is also common to count Jack as 11, Queen as 12, King as 13, and give the Ace an alternate value of 14.

2. Building a combination. The player may play a card from his hand by adding it to one or more cards faced up on the table, provided he has in his hand a card of the pip value needed to take this combination in on the next play, if meanwhile no other player has taken it in or built it higher.

3. Calling a combination. If a player holds, for instance, 2 or more 4's, and another 4, or a group of cards whose pip value equals a 4, is on the table, he may play one 4 from his hand to the card or group of cards on the table, calling it "Fours"; and may take them on his next play, provided no other player has taken them in with a 4. Unlike a Build, which may be built higher, a Call cannot be altered.

4. Making a sweep. When a player plays a card which takes in every card on the table, this is called making a sweep. Sweeps

are marked by facing up one card of the combination in which the sweep was made.

If a player cannot make any of these four plays, he simply plays a card face up to the table. After the last card in the deck has been dealt and the final hands played, the player who took in the last combination takes in all the cards remaining on the board This is not scored as a sweep.

MISCELLANEOUS.—A player may raise his own build only if he holds in his hand the card to take both the first and the second build. A player is entitled to make a second build or call, or take in another combination, or capture another's build or call, before taking in his first build. If he can do none of these, he must take it in on his next play.

Cards once taken in cannot be reexamined, except the last combination won; neither points nor cards may be counted until all the cards have been played. A mistake cannot be corrected after another combination has been taken in.

A card played out of turn must be faced to one side and played to the table when it becomes the player's turn to play; it cannot be used in any other way. Any cards taken in with it by the offending player must be restored to the table.

Builds may be raised with cards from the hand only—never with cards from the board. The builder or caller must name the denomination of his build or call; otherwise, any player may separate the cards and use them in any other way possible for him. If a player makes a build or call lacking the necessary taking card in his hand, he must separate the cards on the table; and, if the opponents so choose, any opponent's cards played after the offense may be taken back and different cards played. If another player has already taken in the erroneous build or call, there is no remedy.

Each deal may be regarded as a complete game, a majority of the 11 points played winning. Sweeps might make this a tie; or 21 may be game. If both players reach 21 on the same deal, the points count out in this order: Cards, Spades, Big Cassino, Little Cassino, Spade Ace, Club, Heart, Diamond, then sweeps.

ROYAL CASSINO

In Royal Cassino, each Jack is an 11, each Queen a 12, each King a 13, and each Ace a 1 or 14, as player decides. As sometimes played, Royal Cassino is played with a deck containing 11's and 12's, which make the Jack worth 13, the Queen 14, the King 15, and the Ace 1 or 16. Otherwise, it is played as regular Cassino.

ROYAL DRAW CASSINO

Royal Draw Cassino is played in the same way as Royal Cassino, except that each player, after playing a card in any way, draws one card from the top of the stock, which is faced down; his hand is thus kept always at 4, until the end of the game. If a player fails to draw in proper turn, he must wait until his next turn, and draw two cards then.

SPADE CASSINO

It is played like any of the above three games, except that each Spade counts 1 point for game, with the exception of the Spade Ace, Jack and 2, which count 2 each: 1 for their Spade value, plus 1 for their value as an Ace, Jack and Little Cassino. The game is 61 points.

SCAPA, ITALIAN CASSINO

EQUIPMENT: The Spanish or Continental deck of 40 cards, King, Queen, Jack, 7, 6, 5, 4, 3, 2, and Ace (which counts as 1.)

PLAYERS: Two or more.

In this variation of Cassino, 3 cards are dealt to each player, and 4 exposed. After the cards in hand have been played, using any of the methods used in regular Cassino, 3 more cards are dealt to each player; and so until all of the cards have been dealt and played. Combinations may be taken in, built, or called, as in regular Cassino. The points are scored as follows:

	Points
Cards (greatest number taken in)	1
Diamonds (greatest number taken in)	1
The 7 of Diamonds	1

	Points
Four 7's, four 6's, or 4 Aces, each	1
Sweep (taking in all cards on the table)	1

Game consists of 11 points.

THE STOPS GROUP

The first card game to use cards faced down as Stops (to prevent playing out a suit in sequence) was invented, according to Tenac, in 1682, during the world-wide apprehension over the appearance of Halley's comet. It was called in France Comète, the comet; and the English corrupted the name into Commit. The suits were played out in upward sequence, a string of cards forming a tail to the first one played, like a comet. In popular belief, the comet threatened the end of the world, a stoppage to everything; and the Stops in the game poked gentle fun at this belief.

There was an old showdown game called Matrimony, in which 2 cards only were dealt to each player, one faced down, and one up. The layout provided for counters paid into five compartments: Matrimony, Intrigue, Confederacy, Pair, and Best. Best was always the Ace of Diamonds; if a faced up card, its holder won all the counters on the whole layout. Matrimony meant any King and Queen; Intrigue, any Queen and Jack; and Confederacy, any King and Jack. Here was a sudden reversion to the original idea that the court cards should be regarded as persons, with a delicate satire perhaps directed toward some particular queen. The underlying combination idea in Matrimony was added to Commit, to form the popular round game Pope Joan. The Pope, the 7 or 9 of Diamonds, was eliminated, to form the game of Newmarket or Stops, renamed, in America, Boodle, Chicago, or Michigan. And there are many other variations of the old game

COMMIT

Equipment: A deck of 51 cards, the Diamond 8 being omitted.

Players: Any number.

Rank of Cards: Ace (low), 2, 3, etc. up to Jack, Queen, King (high).

Preliminaries.—The players cut for choice of seats and deal, low winning. The Ace is always low. The cards are dealt, left to right in rotation, beginning with the Dealer's left, one at a time, until all are dealt. Any odd cards left over are faced down as the Stops hand. It is desirable to have a number of Stops; thus when there are two players, hands may be of 20 cards each, leaving 11 stops; if three, of 14 each, leaving 9; if four, of 11 each, leaving 7; if five, of 9 each, leaving 6; if six, of 7 each, leaving 9, etc. A better way is to follow the method of dealing in Pope Joan: that is, deal an extra hand for Stops to the right of Dealer.

The Play.—The player left of the Dealer leads any card he pleases, facing it upward in the center of the table, and placing on it any other cards in sequence above it in the same suit. When he can no longer continue, he announces "Without the ten," or whatever card he lacks. In rotation, left to right, the players must continue the sequence upward, or announce "without" whatever card they lack. This continues until a King is reached, a natural stop; or the Diamond 7; or some card concealed in the Stops hand. Each player playing a King receives 1 counter from each other player.

The player who has played the Stop card (a King, the Diamond 7, or the card next below a card in the Stops hand) then leads, and the play proceeds until a player gets rid of all his cards. If any player holds the Diamond 9, he may play that card whenever it is his turn to play. The play then passes to his left, and the next player may either continue the original sequence, or continue with the 10, Jack, etc. of Diamonds. When the 9 of Diamonds is played, the player playing it receives 2 counters from each other player.

The first player getting rid of all his cards wins. Any player holding a King at the end of play pays 1 counter for it to each other player; any player holding the 9 of Diamonds, 2 counters.

POPE JOAN

Equipment: A deck of 51 cards, the Diamond 8 being omitted

Players: Any number. Four and up are best.

Rank of Cards: The Diamond 9 is Pope Joan. The other cards rank Ace (low), 2. 3, etc., up to 10, Jack, Queen, King (high).

PRELIMINARIES.—In the cut for choice of seats and deal, low wins, the cards ranking as above. There is a layout prepared on the card table, consisting of eight compartments, marked Ace, Jack, Queen, King, Pope Joan, Matrimony, Intrigue, and Game. Each player contributes a counter to each compartment. In some localities, 4 counters are put into Pope Joan; 2 into Matrimony and Intrigue; and 1 into each of the others.

THE DEAL.—The whole deck is dealt out, one card at a time, left to right in rotation, beginning left of the Dealer. A card to the Stops hand is dealt just before the Dealer deals his own card each time. When there are less than enough cards undealt to go around, all except the last may be dealt to the Stops hand; or the Dealer, at such a time, may skip his own hand, and deal on around to the left, until the last card is reached. This last card is always faced up for the trump, and belongs to the Dealer; it is usually placed upon the Stops hand, which must not be examined until the end of the play.

If King, Queen, Jack or Ace is turned up for the trump, the Dealer takes the counters in the appropriate compartment. If Pope Joan is turned up, he takes all the counters on the board, and the deal passes to the left. In some localities, turning Pope Joan only entitles the Dealer to the counters in that compartment.

THE PLAY.—The player to the left of the Dealer opens by leading any card, and naming it. If he has one or more cards in upward sequence in the same suit, he immediately plays these on the played card, naming them. Any player at the table who has the next one or more cards in upward sequence in the suit led plays these, naming them. This is continued until a Stop is reached—that is, a card of which no one holds the next highest in the same suit.

All Kings are stops, and so is the Diamond 7, the Diamond 8 being deleted from the deck. All cards one in denomination below a card in the Stops hand are stops. All cards one pip below cards already led are stops. When a stop is reached, all cards played are faced downward, and the player of the Stop card leads next. This continues until one player has gotten rid of all of his cards; he then wins the game. and collects.

THE SETTLING.—The winner is entitled at once to all the counters in Game. He receives from each player 1 counter for each card remaining in the player's hand; except that the player who still holds Pope Joan is not required to pay anything.

Any player who plays the King, Queen, Jack or Ace of trumps, or Pope Joan, is entitled to all the counters in these respective compartments immediately. If any player plays the trump King and Queen, he takes all the counters in King, in Queen, and also in Matrimony; if Queen and Jack, all in Queen, in Jack, and also in Intrigue. These cards must be actually played, to win Matrimony and Intrigue; except that a Dealer's faced King, Queen, or Jack is regarded as already played by the Dealer, and his play of the other honor entitles him to Matrimony or Intrigue. All counters not collected are allowed to accumulate for the next or subsequent deals.

In some localities, the playing of Pope Joan is regarded as a universal stop, immediately winning Game and calling for a new deal. It is more usual to regard Pope Joan as a universal stop, only when faced up as trump. In some localities, when King and Jack of trumps, or Confederacy, are played, a penance of 1 counter must be paid by the player and added to the Pope Joan compartment.

THE POPE JOAN HAND.—When the agreed time for ending the session has come, the counters are heaped in the center of the board; and at times each player antes up to increase the pile. Then the cards are dealt slowly, one at a time, left to right, face up. The player to whom Pope Joan falls takes the pool.

MICHIGAN, BOODLE, CHICAGO, NEWMARKET, or STOPS

Michigan, the old English game of Newmarket or Stops, is a simplified Pope Joan. The full deck of 52 cards is used. The layout consists of 4 Boodle Cards from another deck: the Ace of Hearts, the King of Diamonds, the Queen of Spades, and the Jack of Clubs. Ace ranks low in the cut, but high in the play. The Ace is thus an automatic Stop, instead of the King.

The cut, shuffle and cut, and deal, are as in Pope Joan. The Dealer has previously placed 4 or more counters on any or all of the Boodle Cards; and each other player has done the same thing, either on any one Boodle Card or distributed on them as he pleases.

In Michigan, the leader must lead each time his lowest card of whatever suit he selects. The next leader must lead a different suit, if possible. In some localities, the play is as in Commit, each player to the left in rotation playing higher cards in sequence in the suit led, or announcing "Without the eight," etc.; in others, the play is continuous, until a Stop is reached, as in Pope Joan. The play continues until one player has gotten rid of all of his cards.

When a player plays one of the 4 Boodle Cards (Heart Ace, Diamond King, Spade Queen or Club Jack) he takes all the counters on the like layout card. When a player goes game, each other player pays him 1 counter for each card still left in his hand. The deal then passes to the left, any chips remaining on the Boodle Cards accumulating for the next deal. Any irregularity causes a player to pay 1 counter to each player. If the irregularity consists in not playing a card just under a Boodle Card, the offender must pay the holder of the Boodle Card the number of counters on it; or, if it is in the Stops hand, he must double the number of counters on it.

SPIN, or SPINADO

In this variation of Michigan or Boodle, the holder of the Diamond Ace is allowed to stop any sequence with it; but this must take place only when it is his turn to play. The Diamond Ace thus once during the game terminates the play as a Stop, as if it were a Joker in Poker. When he plays the Diamond Ace so, he calls "Spin." He may then start another sequence of his own, it being necessary to begin always with the lowest in the suit led.

SARATOGA

Saratoga is Michigan played with the requirement that each player must ante up an equal number of counters on each Boodle Card.

MISCELLANEOUS PLAY-OFF GAMES

FAN TAN

EQUIPMENT: A full deck of 52 cards.

PLAYERS: Any number; six or seven best.

Rank of Cards: Ace (low), 2, 3, etc., to Jack, Queen, King (high).

Preliminaries.—In the cut for deal, low deals, Ace being lowest. After the shuffle and cut, the cards are dealt one at a time in rotation left to right, beginning at the Dealer's left. The deal passes to the left.

Object of the Game.—To get rid of all the cards in one's hand before the other players have done so.

The Play.—In this game, a Tableau of 12 piles is built up in the center of the table, 4 rows of 3 piles each. The central vertical row consists of the four 7's, in any order. A 7 must be played before a card is played left or right of it. On one side of the 7's, the matching 6's are played; and, on these, players build down in descending sequence in the same suit from 6 through Ace. On the other side, the matching 8's are played; and, on these, players build up in ascending sequence in the same suit from 8 through King.

On each 6, build down in suit 5, 4, 3, 2, Ace; to the right. On each 8, build up in suit 9, 10, Jack, Queen, King.

♡	6	7	8
♠	6	7	8
◇	6	7	8
♣	6	7	8

Each player is provided with an equal number of counters. The player to the left of the Dealer must face up a 7 on the table, as a foundation 7 in the central row of the Tableau. If he has no 7, he pays 1 chip into the pool. The next player must then either play a card to the Tableau, or pay a chip into the pool. He may play a second 7, if he has one; or, if a 7 has already been played, he may play a 6 or 8 to it, as above. Each player in turn then plays a card, if he is able to, or pays a counter into the pool. 6's and 8's cannot be played until the matching 7 is played; 5's and 9's cannot be played until the matching 6's and 8's are played, and so on.

The player getting rid of all his cards first wins the pool. Each player with cards remaining in his hand then pays to the winner 1 counter for each card he holds.

If a player fails to play when he is able to, he forfeits 3 chips to the pool. If he fails to play a 7 when he could have played it, he forfeits 5 chips each to the holder of the matching 6 and 8; but he is not required to play the 7, until there is no other card he prefers to play and can play.

Decks of 60 cards, containing the 11 and 12 spots, are often used for Fan Tan, since they divide equally among a larger number of players than the 52-card deck. When this pack is used, 8's start the Tableau, flanked by 7's and 9's.

TWO-HANDED FAN TAN

With only two players, the hands are dealt for three players, the third hand constituting a stock faced down on the table. Whenever a player is unable to play he must draw the top card from the stock; if he then cannot play, he forfeits 1 counter and draws again. This continues until he reaches a card that he can play.

ORIGINAL FAN TAN

In this simple variation of Stops, there is no Tableau. The preliminaries are as in regular Fan Tan. The player to the left of the Dealer then leads any card he chooses. In rotation, left to right, each player must either play the next card above it in that suit, or pay 1 chip into the pool. After the King is reached, the sequence continues with the Ace, 2, etc., until the suit is ended. The player of the last card of a suit then leads any card he pleases of another suit, and so on. The first player to play out his hand wins, collecting 1 counter from each other player for each card still remaining in the player's hand.

To gain the privilege of leading to the second and subsequent suits, the leader should lead the highest of 2 touching cards in that suit. Thus, holding a Queen, Jack in any suit, he should lead the Queen, which will make the Jack the last card played, and so let him lead to the next suit; or holding a 2, 3, he should lead the 3.

ENFLÉ, or SCHWELLEN

Equipment: A 32-card deck, Ace, King down through 7 in each suit. If more than four players play, add eight cards (two of each suit) to the deck for each additional player.

Rank of Cards and Preliminaries: Same as in Hearts.

Each player is dealt 8 cards, 3, 2, 3 at a time. There is no trump. The player to the left of the Dealer leads any card he pleases, and in rotation, left to right, each player must follow suit. If all follow, the trick belongs to nobody, and is turned down as dead. The player of the highest card in the suit led then leads to the next trick.

If a player cannot follow suit, he is not allowed to discard. Instead, he must at once gather up the cards already played to the trick, and add them to his hand. Players following the one who renounces to a trick do not play on it at all. The player who renounced and picked up the cards now leads to the next trick. The play is continued in this manner, until a player gets rid of all his cards, and so wins the game.

Enflé is usually played for a pool, to which all contribute equally, the winner taking the pool.

GO BOOM

Equipment: A full deck of 52 cards. If more than six play, use a Five Hundred deck of 64 cards, including the 11's, 12's and 13's; or two full decks, of 104 cards.

Players: Two to twelve.

Preliminaries.—In the cut for deal, low deals, Ace being low in both cut and play. After shuffle and cut, the Dealer deals 7 cards to each player, one at a time, left to right in rotation, beginning with the player to his right. The balance of the deck is faced down in the center of the table as a stock. Any irregularity in dealing calls for a new deal by the same Dealer.

Object of the Game.—To get rid of the cards in hand. The player first getting rid of all his cards calls "Boom," and wins.

THE PLAY.—The player to the left of the Dealer leads any card he chooses. Each player in rotation, left to right, must then either follow suit, or play a card of the same denomination. Thus if the Heart 9 were led, the other players in turn would have to play a heart, or any other 9. The same denomination cards are in effect compulsory discards, and cannot take the trick. If a player can neither follow suit nor play a card of the same denomination, he must draw from the stock until he can do so. When the stock is exhausted, if a player cannot play, he knocks on the table, and the next player in rotation plays to the trick.

The highest card of the suit led wins the trick. The winner of each trick leads to the next. The play continues until a player gets rid of all his cards, calls "Boom," and wins. All cards still held are faced up.

SCORING.—In settling up the score, the winner scores the value of the cards remaining in the hands of the players: the pip value of the cards from Ace (1 point) through 10, and 10 points each for the King, Queen, and Jack. The game is for some agreed score, as 100, or 250; or each deal may be regarded as a game in itself, and settled for before continuing the play.

I DOUBT IT

This is one of the fastest and most hilarious of round games, the premium being on shrewd bluffing, as well as on ingenuity.

EQUIPMENT: The full deck of 52 cards.

PLAYERS: Any number, but best with four or more.

RANK OF CARDS: Ace (low), 2, 3, etc., on up to 10, Jack, Queen, King and then continuing with Ace, 2, 2, etc. Suit distinctions are ignored; cards function by denomination only.

PRELIMINARIES.—In the cut for seats and deal, the drawer of the highest card deals. After the shuffle and cut, the cards are dealt around, one at a time, left to right, beginning at the Dealer's left, until the entire deck is dealt out.

OBJECT OF THE GAME.—To get rid of all the cards in one's hand, by playing 1, 2, 3 or 4 of any denomination face downward at the regular time in rotating sequence; or by playing cards purporting to be these.

THE PLAY.—The player to the left of the Dealer opens the play by playing 1, 2, 3 or 4 cards of any denomination, face down, on the table, announcing "One 7," "Two 10's," "Three 5's," "Four Kings," and so on. Without any delay the player to his left must play down 1, 2, 3, or 4 cards of the next higher denomination, similarly announcing them. This continues until all the cards are played out, the first player to play out his cards winning.

The cards played and announced by the Leader or any subsequent player need not correspond to his announcement in any way. Any player, at any time, may say "I doubt it." The cards just played and announced, and no others, must then be faced up. If the announcement was correct, the player doing the doubting must pick up all the cards on the table and add them to his hand. If the announcement was incorrect, wholly or in part, the player who played and announced the cards must pick up all the cards on the table and add them to his hand. In this case, the player who did the doubting gets the next lead, and leads as the original Leader did, playing and announcing any 1, 2, 3 or 4 cards to the table. The play continues until one player gets rid of all his cards, in which case the others settle up at the rate of 1 counter for each card still held.

It is permissible to doubt in order to secure cards played and announced, in order to build up a set of 3 or 4 in that denomination, which equips the player holding them with an almost or entirely safe doubt. On securing the lead, a player holding 4 Jacks, for instance, might lead and announce a 10, and then doubt the player to his left, who could not possibly hold a Jack; or lead one or more 9's, and doubt the player second to his left, whose turn it would be to play Jacks, again being without Jacks. No delay is permitted in the play at any time. It is not permitted to say "I haven't any"; in this case, however, the player so stating picks up all the cards on the table, and the player to his left leads. The game grows fast and furious toward the end; and a player with only a few cards remaining is usually ganged against by the other players, in the endeavor to enlarge his hand by inevitable doubts.

If one player shows uncanny ability at the game, it is well to have him merely watch every other game, while the less able players struggle to get rid of their cards more on an equal footing.

THREE-CARD I DOUBT IT

As sometimes played, an equal number of cards is dealt around, and the remainder is faced down, as the first play. Each play must consist of the play and announcement of exactly 3 cards, which are announced as of the same denomination. Only the player to the left has the privilege of doubting. If doubted, the doubt is settled at once, as in regular I Doubt It. If not, this player then plays and announces any 3 cards; but these need not be in sequence with the former player's announcement.

When a player does not have 3 cards to play and announce, he must draw from the cards on the table until he holds 3; and then play and announce them. If there are not enough cards on the table, he must pass his turn until there are cards from which to draw, when his turn to play comes around again. Otherwise, the game is played and settled for as in regular I Doubt It.

EARL OF COVENTRY, or SNIP-SNAP-SNOREM

Equipment: A full deck of 52 cards.

Players: Any number.

Rank of Cards: None, play being by denominations only.

The object of the game is to get rid of one's cards before another player can do so. In the cut for deal, low wins, Ace being low. After shuffle and cut, the cards are dealt in rotation, left to right, beginning at the Dealer's left, until all have been dealt out. It makes no difference if some players have more cards than others.

The player to the left of the Dealer leads any card, face upward on the table, saying "There's as good a King (or, Jack, or Eight, etc.) as can be." If the player to his left has another card of the same denomination, he lays it down, and says, "There is one as good as he." The holder of the third card plays it, saying "There's the best of all the three," and the fourth holder, "And there's the Earl of Coventry." The leader of each fourth card leads to the next trick. In some localities, the shorter announcements for the second, third and fourth card are "Snip," "Snap," "Snorem." The first one to get rid of his cards collects one counter from each other player for every card they still hold. The play must always be in proper order from the Leader to the left. A player plays only 1 card of a denomination, until each other player has had one chance to play his card of the same denomination.

JIG

In this variation, instead of playing a card of the same denomination, each player to the left must play one of the next higher denomination, until 4 are played, constituting a trick. The winner of each trick leads to the next. Otherwise it is the same as the foregoing.

OLD MAID

EQUIPMENT: A deck of 51 cards, the Queen of Hearts being removed.

PLAYERS: Any number playing as individuals.

OBJECT OF THE GAME: To get rid of the cards in one's hands, by pairing; and not to be caught at the end with the odd queen.

PRELIMINARIES.—In the cut for deal, low deals, Ace being low, the other cards ranking up 2, 3, etc., to 10, Jack, Queen, King. In case of a tie, since the suits rank equally, there is a recut. The cards are shuffled and cut, and the Dealer then deals the cards out in rotation, left to right, beginning at his left, one at a time, until the whole deck is dealt out.

THE PLAY.—Beginning with the player to the left of the Dealer, each player sorts his cards into pairs of the same denomination, irrespective of suit: as, 2 Aces, 2 Kings, 2 7's, etc. All paired cards are faced down, without showing them to the other players. All pairs are faced down in front of the players, to permit examination for misplays, if any, at the end of the game. Neither 3 of a kind can be laid down, nor 2 cards not of the same denomination.

After all the players have melded their pairs in this manner, the player to the left of the Dealer draws any card from the Dealer's hand. If this forms a pair, the pair is at once melded, face down, in front of the player. The next player to the left draws one card from the player to his right, melding a pair if any is formed. The play continues so until only one player has a single card, which is the odd queen. He becomes Old Maid for that deal only. If at any time a player commits an irregularity in play, he at once becomes Old Maid for that deal, and the deal passes to the left.

SLAP-JACK

EQUIPMENT: A full deck of 52 cards.

PLAYERS: Three or more, playing as individuals.

OBJECT OF THE GAME: To capture all of the cards, by being the first to touch each Jack as it is played.

PRELIMINARIES.—In the cut for deal, a shuffled deck is dealt around, in rotation left to right, one at a time; the player receiving the first Jack dealing. The cards are shuffled and cut, and the Dealer deals out the entire deck, one at a time, in rotation left to right, beginning with the player to his left. Each hand must be left faced down at an equal distance from the center of the table. No hand may be examined before being faced down.

THE PLAY.—Beginning at the Dealer's left, each player in rotation plays one card face up to the center of the table, by a quick turn of it toward the other players. Whenever a Jack is thus played, the first player to slap or lay his hand on it wins it and all other cards faced up in the center of the table. Where several hands have touched it, the one touching it first, or the one beneath, wins; in case of a dispute, the other players must decide.

The penalty for slapping at the wrong time is the loss of a card to the player who has just played.

As soon as a Jack has been slapped, the player winning the cards shuffles them with his own hand, cuts them, and places his now enlarged hand faced down on the table as at the beginning of the game. The player to his left now leads, as at the outset. Each player who plays out all of his cards drops out of the game; except that he is given one chance to slap the next Jack to be restored to the game. If he fails to win this slap, he is out until the next game. The player staying in longest and thus capturing all the cards wins.

SNAP, or SNAP JACK

This game is similar to Slap-Jack, except that each player faces up his cards one at a time on a pile in front of his faced-down hand; the cards being faced up one at a time in rotation When a card is faced up which corresponds in denomination to a card already faced on another pile, the first player among those in the game to call out "Snap!" wins both piles, and adds them to his pack. The player staying in longest and winning all the cards wins.

ANIMALS

EQUIPMENT: A full deck of 52 cards.

PLAYERS: Three or more, playing as individuals.

OBJECT OF THE GAME: To capture all of the cards, by being the first to make the proper call, when matching cards are faced up.

PRELIMINARIES.—In the cut for deal, low deals, Ace being low for the cut. The cards are then dealt and placed in hands faced down, as in Slap-Jack. Each player chooses the name of an animal, whose call he must imitate before play commences, to let the other players know how to call him. The animals chosen might include a cat, a dog, a goat, a sheep, a cow, a lion, a snake, a mouse, and so on.

THE PLAY.—Beginning at the Dealer's left, each player in rotation plays one card face up to an exposed trash pile in front of his hand. Whenever a card so faced up matches a card faced up on the trash pile of any other player, each endeavors to give the proper call of the other. The one who does this first correctly wins the other's trash pile, and places it below his own trash pile. If both give the calls correctly, the one starting it first wins. An incorrect call, or a call given at the wrong time, costs a penalty of the gift of the top card of the trash pile (or of the hand, if there is no trash pile) to the other player. After each call, the player who loses leads. When a hand has been played out, the trash pile is reversed, and becomes a hand, as at the beginning of the game. When a player loses all of his cards, he drops out of the game. The player who captures all of the cards in the deck wins.

As thus played, the end of the game often becomes a long-continued duel between two players, the others losing interest in the game. One way to lessen this is, when only two players are left, to have each build two trash piles, playing from his hand alternately to them. Another way is to provide for a set number of final plays, as 25 to 50, the player with the most cards at the end of this number of plays being declared the winner.

In a simpler variation of this hilarious game, the names of the animals are called out, instead of their calls.

THE PATIENCE OR SOLITAIRE GROUP

Patience is any game played with playing cards or small numbered cards, in which the object is to arrange the cards, taken as they come from the shuffled deck, in some systematic order. There are excellent games of Patience for two or more players; but most of them are designed for one player, and the whole group is hence often called Solitaire, which properly applies to any game that one person can play alone. Many of the games of Patience, for one or more players, are favorite gambling games.

Thousands of games of Patience have been invented. One ingenious author has published more than seven separate books of her own inventions in Patience, totalling almost 400 different games. Most of these never become popular. Only the most popular games are included here.

RUSSIAN BANK or CRAPETTE

This Double Patience or Double Solitaire is often regarded today as the most enjoyable game for two players ever invented.

EQUIPMENT: Two full decks of 52 cards each, with backs of different colors.

PLAYERS: Two. Either or both of these may, by agreement, have a consulting partner, who may give advice; the latter may take no part in the actual play, nor is he allowed to point out or call Stops on the opponent.

RANK OF CARDS: From A (low), 2, 3, etc., up to the 10, Jack, Queen, King, when played on the Foundation Piles. Suits are of equal rank.

PRELIMINARIES.—In the cut, low has choice of packs and seats, and makes the first play. Ace is low in the cut. In case of a tie, there is a recut. Each player shuffles and cuts his opponent's pack. As usually played, each player shuffles and cuts his own deck.

THE DEAL.—*The Misery Pile.*—Each player now deals from the top of his own pack 13 cards (in some localities, 12), one at a time, face down, in a pile to his right. This constitutes his Misery Pile. When it is a player's turn to play, after all possible plays from the Tableau to the Foundation Aces have been made, the player next faces up the top card on his Misery Pile. *The Tableau.*—He then deals 4 cards, face up, 1 at a time, and places them in a row to his right, between his opponent and himself. The two rows of 4 cards each form the Tableau. Space must be left between the two rows for the two rows of Foundation Aces. *The Stock.*—The remaining 35 (or 36) cards are faced down to the player's left, and form his Stock—sometimes called his Hand.

The Play.—*The Foundation Aces.*—As the 8 Aces appear, in the Tableau, or from a player's Misery Pile or Stock, in that order, they are faced up, the two of each suit side by side, in any order of suits, between the two rows of the Tableau. *The Trash Pile.*—When a player whose turn it is to play reaches a card from his Stock that he cannot play to the Foundation, and does not desire to play elsewhere, he places it faced up on a pile between his Stock and his Misery Pile. This is called his Trash Pile. When the Stock becomes exhausted, the player, when it is his turn to play, reverses the Trash Pile, and makes it a Stock as at the beginning of the game, and continues to play to a new Trash Pile from it.

Object of the Game.—To get rid of all the cards in one's Misery Pile, Stock and Trash Pile, before the other player has done so, by:

1. Building up on Foundation Aces, in ascending sequence in the same suit.
2. Building down on the Tableau, in descending sequence with alternating colors.
3. Playing to an opponent's Trash Pile, or the faced-up top card on his Misery Pile, in ascending or descending sequence, or both, in the same suit, on one or both piles. Thus on an exposed spade 6 on either pile the play might be spade 5, 6, 5, 4, 3, etc.; or 7, 6, 5; or 7, 6, 7, 8, etc.

Order of Plays.—Plays must be made in the following exact order:

1. From Tableau, Misery Pile or Trash Pile to the Foundation. This includes every possible shifting of the Tableau to release a card playable to the Foundation.
2. Filling Tableau spaces from the Misery Pile.
3. (Optional). Shifting Tableau, whether to make a space or not; playing from your own Misery or Trash Pile to opponent's Misery or Trash Pile, or to the Tableau.
4. Playing a card from your Stock to the Foundation; or, (optional) to an opponent's pile or the Tableau; or, if played nowhere else, to your own Trash Pile.

The Play.—The player who won the cut has the first play and may play off as many cards as he can, in the above order. If a player at any time fails to play to the Foundation, his opponent may call "Stop!" This terminates the play, and it becomes the opponent's turn to play. Any card touched, unless the player previously states that the touch was not for purposes of play, constitutes a Stop, only if there is a possible play to the Foundation. "Stop!" can only be called for failure to play to the Foundation. If any other failure takes place, the opponent has the option to call attention to it or not. If he calls attention to it, it must be played. A card once played to the Foundation cannot thereafter be moved under any circumstances.

Only the top card of a Tableau row may be moved at any time; so that, if it were desired to move 2 Tableau cards, to make a space, this could only be done if there were already a space, or if there was another card of the same color and denomination as the lower card of the 2, to which the top card could be temporarily removed. After making all the Foundation plays possible, and such other plays as the player is able to and desires, he must take the top card from his Misery Pile, and play it, as in the Order of Plays. When any card is exposed, by playing from the Trash Pile (which exposes the card beneath) or from the Misery Pile, (in which case the card beneath must be faced at once) this must be played to the Foundation, if possible; or it may be played according to the Order of Plays. When all possible cards from the Misery Pile have been played (the one that cannot be played being faced up), the player exposes the top card from his Stock, and plays this, as in the Order of Plays. His last play must be to play a card from his Stock on to his Trash Pile, unless he has been Stopped.

The play now passes to his opponent, who plays his cards in the same way, as long as he can or so desires, his last play being to play a card from his Stock to his Trash Pile, as above. A player can continue to play from Misery Pile, Stock and Tableau, as long as playable cards are exposed. It is important to get rid of the Misery Pile first of all. A player playing to his opponent's exposed Misery or Trash piles may play in upward or downward sequence in the same suit; or, using cards from the Tableau, in both, if he so desires. A player is not allowed to play on his own Misery or Trash Pile, except the final card taken during each play from the Stock, which must be played to the Trash Pile.

When a player's Misery Pile is exhausted, he plays from his Stock and Trash Piles alone, with or without the aid of cards in the Tableau. If a player's Stock and Trash piles are exhausted, but he still has cards on his Misery Pile, when it comes his turn to play he must pass, unless he can play the exposed card from his Misery Pile.

Any irregularity in play must be corrected when attention is called to it by either player unless this has caused a Stop.

GAME.—The player who gets rid of his Misery, Stock and Trash piles first wins the game. In some localities, he scores 30 for this, and in addition 2 points for each card remaining in his opponent's Misery Pile, and 1 for each card remaining in his opponent's Stock and Trash Piles. When neither player can play further, and there are cards remaining, the remaining cards are counted, and score 2 for those in the Misery Pile, 1 for those in the Stock and Trash Pile; and the difference between the sums of the player's points is scored to the player with the lesser sum.

VARIATIONS.—In some localities, a player is allowed to use his opponent's exposed cards in his Misery and Trash piles, if he so desires. Where this is done, the player is required to play to the Foundation from these piles as if they were his own.

STUNG

Stung is a multiple Patience or Solitaire game, closely related to Russian Bank. It is an excellent game, especially for two.

EQUIPMENT: A full deck of 52 cards.

PLAYERS: Two to eight.

RANK OF CARDS: Ace (low), 2, 3, etc., to 10, Jack, Queen, King (high.)

PRELIMINARIES.—For the choice of seats and deal, the cards are cut, and low wins, Ace being low. After the shuffle and cut, the cards are dealt one at a time left to right, beginning to the

Dealer's left, until the deck has been dealt. If the cards do not divide equally, the remaining ones are faced up in a row in the center of the table, as the Tableau. In the two- and four-handed games, none are left for the Tableau; in the three-handed game, 1; in the five-handed, 2; in the seven-handed, 3; in the six- and eight-handed, 4, constituting the entire Tableau.

Each player's hand, constituting his stock, may not be sorted or examined but must be laid faced down in front of the player. At the end of each hand the deal passes to the left.

Object of the Game.—To get rid of all the cards in one's hand before the other players have done so, by:

1. Building up on Foundation Aces, in ascending sequence in the same suit.
2. Building down on the Tableau, in descending sequence with alternating colors.
3. Playing from a player's stock to an opponent's exposed Misery Pile.
4. Giving cards to other players, who are penalized for misplays during the game.

Building the Tableau.—If there are any cards missing from the Tableau, which is a vertical row of 4 cards of any denomination faced up on the table, the player to the left of the Dealer faces the first card from his stock, which must be at once exposed so that all players can see it. If it is an Ace, he plays it to another vertical row, which will hold the 4 Foundation Aces and the piles built on them, parallel to the Tableau. If it is not an Ace, he faces it up on the Tableau. If, however, an Ace from the deal is already exposed on the Tableau, it must be played to the Foundation row before the player faces a card from his own stock; the player must also play any other cards on the Tableau which are exposed from the deal, these cards playing upwards in ascending sequence in the same suit on any Foundation Ace. Until the Tableau is complete, players make no other play.

The player next to the left plays similarly, and so in rotation left to right until the Tableau contains its quota of 4 cards.

ORDER OF PLAYS.—Plays must be made in the following exact order:

1. From the Tableau to the Foundation.
2. From one Tableau row to another.
3. From one Tableau row to a space in the Tableau, to permit a card to be played to the Foundation.
4. From the Misery Pile to the Foundation.
5. From the Misery Pile to a space, if any, in the Tableau.
6. From the Misery Pile to the Tableau.
7. From the Misery Pile to another's Misery Pile.

THE PLAY.—Each player in turn, left to right, plays as above. Plays from the Tableau come first, in the order given above. If the player has as yet no Misery Pile, he exposes the first card from his stock,—this card being regarded as the first card in his Misery Pile—and plays it as above, if possible. If it will not play, he faces it up, as his Misery Pile. As soon as a player has played through his stock, and it is his turn to play, he turns the Misery Pile over, and it becomes his stock, as at the beginning of the game, and play continues from it, as above.

After the first player has completed his first play after the Tableau has been completed, he will have one card exposed on his Misery Pile in front of him. Thereafter, any player may play to this Misery Pile any card in upward or downward sequence in the same suit, provided that he is unable to play it, as set out in the Order of Plays, to the Foundation or the Tableau. If his card may be played to two or more Misery Piles, it must be played on the first one to his life.

The play continues in this manner, the players dropping out as their hands and Misery Piles become exhausted, until only one player has cards remaining in his hand. This last player loses the game: or the first player getting rid of his cards may be regarded as the winner.

In playing from the Tableau, only one card may be moved at a time. The top card of one row may always be moved to become the top card of another; and, by moving one card at a time only, the rows must be combined, where possible. When there is a space, it is possible to move a sequence of two cards in the

Tableau to another row ending in a card of the opposite color and the next highest denomination; and this must be done. Shiftings of cards in the Tableau are always compulsory, moving only one at a time, when this will release a Tableau card to play to the Foundation.

When a card from the Misery Pile is played, the exposed card beneath it comes at once into possible play, and must be played, according to the Order of Plays, before another card is played from the pack.

When a player commits an irregularity of any kind, by failing to make a possible play in the right order, by exposing a card from his pack when a play could be made, by examining cards in his hand, by exposing a card out of turn, or by any other irregularity, the player discovering the misplay calls out "Stung!" Each player then gives the player in error the top exposed card from his Misery Pile, or, if none is exposed, from his stock, these cards being delivered in rotation left to right. These cards are faced up in the order in which they are given on the offending player's Misery Pile. If the player has played a card or cards in error, the misplayed card or cards must be taken back. The play then passes to the left.

SINGLE DECK RUSSIAN BANK

The best single deck game of Russian Bank when played by two players is Stung. This has an even stricter Order of Plays than regular Russian Bank, and uses the Foundation as in Russian Bank.

Another variation is sometimes played, however, quite differently from these two games. The preliminaries are the same as in Stung, with 26 cards dealt to each player. The non-dealer faces his first 4 cards up, 1 at a time, as his half of the Tableau. He may build on this Tableau, as follows: only in cards of the same suit, and in either upward or downward sequence, or both; but each sequence, once started in a direction, must continue in that direction. Since the builds are in sequence in suit, an entire pile may be moved to another pile without a space, provided it continues the sequence; or, if there is a space, the sequence may be entirely reversed, card by card; and may then be moved entire to another pile, provided it continues the sequence.

When the first player has finished, the second player faces up his 4 cards similarly for his half of the Tableau. He may now build on these 8 Tableau piles as above.

The non-Dealer now exposes a card from his Hand, and makes such builds with it on the Tableau (as above) as he can. When he turns a card with which he cannot build, he faces it up for his Trash Pile. There are no Stops in this variation of the game. As soon as there are no cards left in a player's Hand, when it is his turn to play he reverses his Trash Pile and makes it a Hand again, as at the beginning, and continues to play. Cards exposed from the Hand which fit the exposed card on opponent's Trash Pile in sequence and suit may be played to it; but cards cannot be taken from the foundation for this purpose. The game is scored as regular Russian Bank.

DOUBLE KLONDIKE, or SCRIMBLE-SCRAMBLE

This is the liveliest and most exciting of all double games of Patience. It may be played by any number of players, each using a separate deck of distinguishing design or color. It is thrilling enough, even when only two play. The description of the two-handed game below needs no elaboration if three or more play.

Equipment: Two full decks of 52 cards each, with differing backs.

Players: Two. Three or more may play, as above.

Rank of Cards: In sequence, from Ace (low), 2, 3, etc., to 10, Jack, Queen, King. The suits rank equally.

Preliminaries.—The cut is as in Russian Bank. Each opponent shuffles and cuts the other player's deck. Usually each player shuffles and cuts his own. Each player then deals his own Layout. The first card is faced up on the player's right, and 6 cards are faced down in a row with this card in front of the player, thus making a total of 7 cards in a row. On the 6 cards faced down, a second row is dealt, the first of these faced up and the rest faced down. Then 5 cards, one faced up and 4 faced down; and so on until there are 7 piles, each topped by a faced card, containing respectively 1, 2, 3, 4, 5, 6, and 7 cards, or 28 cards altogether. The remaining 24 cards constitute a player's Stock.

Object of the Game.—For a player to build his Stock and Layout cards on the Foundation Aces before his opponent does so; or, if neither does, to play out more cards than his opponent.

Foundation Aces.—Play starts the moment the second player completes his Layout. Any misplay must be corrected, when attention is called to it. There is no other penalty, except that the swiftest player usually wins the game. A player cannot be required to play a card to the Foundation Aces, except at the end of the game; and then he may play them in any proper order he elects. Only one card may be lifted for play and played in each hand at any time.

Any Aces in a player's Layout must be played out to the center as Foundation Aces; but a player can complete all proper plays in his Layout before playing an Ace. The Aces are usually arranged in pairs of the same suit. A player may play to any Foundation Ace, but only in upward sequence in the same suit. On the Layout, cards are played in descending sequence and alternate color. Any or all of the cards on any Layout pile may be shifted to an appropriate other place on the Layout, so long as the descending sequence in alternating color is preserved. This permits cards buried in a Layout pile to be obtained and played to Foundation piles. Only a King, or a Layout pile with a King beneath it, may be shifted to a space in the Layout.

Once the preliminary Layout shifts are completed, each player runs through his Stock, 3 cards at a time, not reversing the orders of the threes, but facing them up so that each third card is exposed. This card may then, if desired and if it is playable, be played to the Foundation piles or the Layout; and playing a card exposes the card beneath it, which may also be played similarly. Similarly, the moment a faced down Layout card is bared by playing the card above it to the Foundation piles or by removing it to some other pile on the Layout, the card beneath is faced, and may be played, if there is a place to which it is playable.

When the last group of 3 or less cards in the Stock has been faced and plays completed from it and cards exposed beneath it, the Trash Pile is reversed and becomes a Stock or Hand again, to be played through in groups of 3 again.

THE GAME.—The game ends when either player first exhausts his Stock and Layout, by playing them to the Foundation piles. If neither is able to go out, the game ends when no card from those faced on the Trash Pile or in running through the Stock in three, is playable to the Foundation piles or to the Layout; and when no card from the Layout is playable to the Foundation piles. The cards played to the Foundation piles are then divided into decks according to their backs and counted, the player playing out the most winning the game. These may be a stake of from 1 to 5 counters per card.

MULTIPLE PATIENCE, or MULTIPLE SOLITAIRE

This is a variation of Double Canfield, played by four players. Each has his own full deck, of distinguishing design or color. The objection is to be the first player to get rid of all his cards on the Foundation Aces, which are common property.

Each player shuffles and cuts a deck, and passes it to his right hand opponent, receiving for himself a deck from the opponent on his left. Each player deals 13 cards one by one from the top of the deck, facing them down to his left, for a Boneyard; the topmost card is then faced up. Next, 4 cards in a row are faced up, to constitute the Layout. The 35 remaining card of a player's deck constitute his Stock. Each player looks at the top and bottom cards on his Boneyard, and if either is an Ace it must be played out to the center immediately, as a Foundation Ace. An Ace must be played to the center immediately, whenever it is properly exposed. No other card need be played out to the Foundation piles. The top and bottom cards on the Boneyard, or any cards exposed after playing an Ace or any other card to the Foundaton piles from the top or bottom of the Boneyard, may be played to the Foundation piles at any time. The top card of the Boneyard must be faced up; and, whenever it is played out to the Foundation piles or used to fill a space in the Layout, the card beneath must be exposed.

Foundaton Aces are built on in upward sequence, Ace to King, in suit. Cards on the Layout are built in downward sequence, in alternating colors. Spaces on the Layout must be filled by using the top card or succeeding cards of the Boneyard. When the Boneyard is exhausted, the spaces may only be filled by Kings.

The stock is then run off as in Double Klondike or Canfield, 3 cards at a time, faced upward so that the third is exposed. The play to the Foundation piles or the Layout is the same as in Double Klondike. When the Stock has been gone through in this fashion, as in Double Klondike, it is reversed, and the process continues, until no further cards can be played from Layout, Boneyard or Stock; or until a player has played out to the Foundation piles all of his cards, in which case he wins the game.

A player is not obliged to play to the Foundation piles or to the Layout until the end of the game unless he so desires; and even then he may play playable cards in any order he pleases. At the end, if no player has played out all his cards, the cards played out are separated by their differing backs into 4 piles, and each player counts his cards played out. The largest number wins from the others the difference in each case. Speed is of the essence of this game, as it is of Double Klondike.

DESPERATION

This is a swift-moving complicated game of the multiple Patience or Solitaire type.

Equipment: Six full decks of 52 cards each.

Players: Two to six. There are only two sides; when more than two play, either they are divided into equal partnerships, or 1 against 2 or 2 against 3. In this latter case, 3 cards from the talon of the smaller number of players are removed to the talon of the larger side.

Rank of Cards: King (high), Queen, Jack, 10, 9, etc., down to Ace (low).

Preliminaries.—After the cut for partners (those drawing highest playing against those drawing lowest, and sitting alternately as far as possible) any player, after shuffle and cut, deals the two talons of 21 cards each, one for each side, faced downward. The remainder of the cards are dealt into 54 hands of 5 cards each, arranged one above the other alternately sideways and lengthwise, in one pile, and faced downward.

Object of the Game.—For one side to be first in ridding itself of its talon, by playing the cards to Foundation Aces, in upward sequence, regardless of suit.

The Play.—The player to the left of the Dealer, the Leader, takes the top hand of 5 cards from the stock of hands, and, if possible, plays an Ace to the center of the table, which then becomes a Foundation Ace. If the Leader does not get an Ace in the first hand, he passes, and in rotation the players to his left, one at a time, take a hand from the stock of hands, and either play an Ace or pass. When no player secures an Ace from the first round of hands, the Leader plays one card face upward, as the beginning of one of his Reserve piles. In rotation the other players play each one card faced upward, until all 5 have been played out. There are 4 Reserve piles to each player, and a card which may be played to a Reserve pile may be played to any of the 4. Only the top card of any Reserve pile may remain visible, and it alone is available for play from these piles.

When all the cards in the first round of hands have been played, the Leader takes another hand, and the play continues as before, until the first Ace is played out as a Foundation Ace. Up to this time, the talons must remain untouched.

As soon as the first Ace appears, the top card of each talon is faced up. The player of the Ace continues to play from his hand, talon, or Reserve, building in upward sequence from the Ace by playing the 2, 3, 4, etc., regardless of suit, until a King is reached, and the Foundation pile is faced down and eliminated. The player may also begin another Foundation, by playing another Ace. If he plays out his hand, he takes another hand from the stock, and continues playing as long as possible. No player may take a hand until it is his turn to play.

When a card from either talon is played out to a Foundation pile, the card next beneath it is faced upward and becomes available for play. Each player continues to play as long as he can play upward in sequence to the Foundation piles, from talon, hand or Reserve. When a player can no longer play in this manner, he must either play one card from his hand to any one of his Reserve piles, or must transfer the top card of one Reserve pile to another. The play then passes to the left.

The double objective is to play off the cards of the talon, and to block the opponents' play from their talon. If a player fails to play a card exposed on Reserve pile or talon, any opponent, in his turn to play, may call for the immediate play of this card, the opponent then continuing his play. The player may prevent this, in his turn to play, by covering the exposed card with a card he has played, in his turn, to his Reserve piles. No one is allowed to call attention to a possible play. A proper play, when made, must stand; and if a player overlooks a playable talon card and plays another, it must stand.

Whenever a player exhausts his hand by playing to the Foundation piles, he draws another hand and continues playing. If the last card in his hand is played to his Reserve, he may not draw another hand until it is again his turn to play. All Aces must be played to the center of the table; but a player may hold an Ace in his hand until it is the last card in his hand, before playing it.

GAME.—The game is won by the side first exhausting its talon.

INDIVIDUAL PATIENCE

FIRING-SQUAD

EQUIPMENT: A full deck of 52 cards. Ranking of cards, Ace (high), King, Queen, down to 2 (low).

There is no Tableau or Layout. A row of four faced cards is laid out in the center of the table; subject to the eliminations described hereafter, these 4 cards are the top cards in 4 vertical rows which will be laid out from them toward the player. The object of the game is to strip these rows, by eliminations as below, until each consists of one Ace and no other card.

When the first 4 cards are rowed up, the eliminations begin if 2 or more of them are of the same suit or suits. Before more cards are played out, remove to a Trash Pile all cards of less denominations in each suit exposed, leaving only the highest card of each suit exposed. If the 4 cards played out on the first or any subsequent row are one each of the 4 suits, there can be no elimination until another row is dealt upon them.

Now play out another row upon the first 4, or such of them as remain, filling in spaces as if the cards from the first row had not been eliminated. When there is a space, any card may be removed to it from the top of any row; this permits the elimination of buried cards. Only the bottom card of any vertical row may be eliminated at any time.

Cards are always played out in groups of 4, until the end of the deck is reached. Winning consists of stripping each vertical row down by these eliminations, until only one Ace remains upon it.

It is difficult to go out in this game. It is best to play it by scoring several competitive attempts, the low winning; or by playing it competitively with two or more players, the player having the fewest cards left after the deck has been gone through once winning.

TOWER OF BABEL

Equipment: A full deck of 52 cards.

There is no Tableau or Layout. The player faces up the cards in one long row, one at a time. Any card may be piled upon either the card next left of it or the card to the left third from it, if it corresponds either in suit or in denomination. Cards and the piles beneath them are always moved toward the left; and a card of the same suit or denomination may be piled on the card next to it, or may skip over two and be piled on the third card. Where there is a choice, the player may decide on which card to place the card in play.

Any play may open up other possible piling combinations, which should all be piled before another card is exposed from the deck. Thus, if a portion of the row is—

Club 7, Heart 8, Spade 7, Diamond 5

none of these can be combined. If the next card turned is a Heart 7, this can skip over the last two cards and be piled on the Heart 8. This gives 3 7's in a row, which can be piled all to the left on the Club 7, as being of the same denomination.

The object of the game is to end up with all the cards piled in one pile on the left. It is difficult to go out in this game. It may be played by scoring several attempts, the lowest number of piles winning; or competitively with two or more players, the lowest number of piles winning.

When the row becomes too long for the table, double it back upon itself. This may have to be done more than once. All plays must always be made toward the first card played.

AULD LANG SYNE

Equipment: A full deck of 52 cards.

Place the 4 Aces as Foundation Aces in a horizontal row. Then deal out the cards, one at a time, face up, in 4 Trash Piles, building on the Foundation Aces in upward sequence, regardless of suit and color. Exposed cards on top of the Trash Piles may be played to the Foundation Piles at any time. No redeal is permitted.

The game is won when all the cards have been built up on the Foundation Aces; if this proves impossible, it is lost.

HIDDEN ACES

A variation is to leave the Aces in the deck, and play them out as Foundation Aces only when they are reached in turning over the deck one card at a time. Otherwise, the same as Auld Lang Syne.

Following Suit

Another variation is to start with the Foundation Aces, and follow suit in upward sequence in building on them. Two redeals are permitted in this game; otherwise, it is the same at Auld Lang Syne. This game can also be played with the Aces left in the deck.

Variations in Patience Games

Any of the above may be played by the player's selecting which of his 4 Trash Piles he plays each successive card on; or by permitting redeals, or any other device to render the game more playable. This applies to all of the games of Patience. Moreover, any of them may be played in competition by two or more players; and, where Foundation Aces are played to, all players participating may be permitted to play to any Foundation Aces played out.

THE PYRAMID

Equipment: A full deck of 52 cards.

One card is faced up in the center of the table, as the first row of the Layout. A second row of 2 cards is played upon the lower half of the first card, the cards in the second row touching each other. The first row card cannot be played until the 2 cards of the second row have been played. A third row of 3 cards is now dealt, similarly overlapping; then a fourth, fifth, sixth, and seventh row, the last row having 7 cards. This gives a Layout in the shape of a pyramid, requiring 28 cards, and a stock of the remaining 24 cards. Since the cards all overlap, only the 7 cards in the bottom row of the pyramid can be played first. When the first 2 of these are played, the card above them in the sixth row is freed for play; and so on. The cards have pip value, Ace being worth 1, and Jack, Queen, King, 11, 12 and 13 respectively.

Object of the Game.—To play off (remove) Kings, and all pairs of cards whose pip value is 13 (Queen-Ace, Jack-2, 10-3, 9-4, 8-5, 7-6) from the Layout, and so get rid of all the cards on it.

The Play.—Begin by playing off from the bottom row, or this and the rows above (if not overlapped), all Kings or pairs of cards whose value totals 13. Such eliminated cards are faced up on a Trash Pile; and in eliminating, any 2 of one denomination and 1 of the matching denomination, or 3 and 2 as below, may be eliminated at a time. Thus two 8's and one 5 may be played off, 8, 5, 8, the central 5 combining with each of the 8's. But these could not be eliminated in the order 5, 8, 8, or 8, 8, 5; the 5 must be free to be eliminated between the 8's, or the 3 cards cannot be eliminated. Nor could 3 8's be eliminated with one 5.

When cards have been eliminated from the Layout as above, the cards in the Stock are faced up, one at a time, and may be used in combination with cards still remaining in the Layout, to aid in eliminating these. They are faced up on a pile, and only the top one may be used in eliminating Layout cards; but if one is so used, the card beneath becomes exposed, and may be used then. This continues until the Layout has been eliminated, which wins the game; or until all the Stock has been played out, one by one.

THREE'S IN THE CORNER

Equipment: A full deck of 52 cards.

The Layout consists of 5 cards arranged in the form of a Greek cross—a central horizontal row of 3 cards, and top and bottom rows of 1 card each above and below the central card in the central row. On this Layout, cards are built from high (the 2) in downward sequence, Ace, King, Queen, Jack, 10, 9, 8, 7, 6, 5, to 4 (low), irrespective of suits and colors. To fill spaces in the Layout, cards are faced from the top of the stock.

Whenever a 3 is reached, in Layout or stock, it is placed in one of the corners of the cross. On these 3's, cards are built in upward sequence, 4, 5, 6, 7, 8, 9, 10, Jack, Queen, King, Ace, 2, in the suit of the 3. One by one the cards from the stock are faced up, and played to the Layout or the Foundation Threes if possible. If not, they are faced up for a Trash Pile. If a space occurs in the Layout after the Trash Pile is started, it must be filled by the top card of the Trash Pile. Cards can only be moved one at a time.

The game is won when all 4 suits have been built up from the Foundation 3's to the respective 2's. This game can be won about once out of every three attempts.

GOOD MEASURE

EQUIPMENT: A full deck of 52 cards.

Lay out 2 Aces as the first 2 Foundation Aces. The other 2 will be placed beside them, when they appear in the play.

Deal out ten packets of 5 cards each, faced down, the top card of each being faced up. When the 2 other Aces appear, place them in the Foundation Row. As the Kings appear, place them just above the ten packets.

In the play, cards are built on the Foundation Aces in ascending sequence in suit, Ace, 2, 3, etc., to 10, Jack, Queen, King. On the ten packets, cards may be built in descending sequence, without regard to suit or color. The same applies to cards built on the Kings. Only the top card on each of the ten packets is available for play. A vacated space among the ten packets may not be filled.

The play continues until all the cards are built up on the Foundation Aces; or until it is impossible to play further, in which case the game is lost.

A more difficult variation is to make the play on the Kings in alternate colors.

KLONDIKE, also called CANFIELD

This is the most famous of all Patience games. It is commonly known as Canfield, although that name properly applies to another game; and Klondike is the original name.

EQUIPMENT: A full deck of 52 cards.

THE LAYOUT.—After shuffle and cut, the Tableau is laid out thus: A card is faced to the player's left, and 6 cards are laid faced down in a horizontal row with it. A card is faced up on the faced-down card furthest to the left, and 5 cards are faced down on the remaining faced-down cards. This is repeated with a row of 5, 4, 3, 2, and 1 cards. The Tableau then contains 28 cards, the piles from left to right containing respectively 1, 2, 3, 4, 5, 6, and 7 cards, each being topped by 1 card faced up. The remaining 24 cards of the deck constitute the player's Stock.

THE PLAY.—Any Ace faced up on the Tableau (or exposed when a Tableau card is removed or played and the card beneath it is faced up) is played out beyond the Tableau as a Foundation Ace. On the faced cards on the Tableau, cards are built down in descending sequence in alternate colors. Spaces in the Tableau are filled only with Kings or with sequences headed by a King; and the Kings may come from other piles of the Tableau or from the Stock, when its cards are faced. If one card of a sequence is moved to another pile on the Tableau, all must be moved. (In many localities, the rule is more liberal: any part of a sequence may be moved, so long as the bottom card moved is of alternating color and 1 lower in denomination than the card to which it is moved.)

When the Tableau rearrangements are concluded, the cards in the Stock are faced, one at a time, and either played as Foundation Aces, on Foundation Piles, or on the Tableau. If a card cannot be played, it is placed faced up on a Misery Pile. The top card on the Misery Pile may always be played; and playing it makes the card exposed beneath it available for play.

After the Stock is run through only once, the game is over. In settling, a player usually pays 52 counters for the deck, and is paid back 5 counters for each card played out on the Foundation Piles. A complete winning, where all the cards are played out to the Foundation Piles, repays the winner five times his stake.

FIVE-DEAL KLONDIKE

An interesting variation is to play the game as above, as the first deal. Then all Foundation Aces and Foundation Piles are left as they are, and the balance of the pack is shuffled, cut, and dealt to a new Tableau, containing only 21 cards—6 on the bottom row, then 5, 4, 3, 2, 1, the top card of each pile faced as in regular Klondike. This is played through as above.

In the third deal, the Tableau contains only 15 cards—5 on the bottom row, then 4, 3, 2, and 1. In the fourth deal, the Tableau contains only 10 cards, 4 on the bottom row, then 3, 2, and 1. In the fifth and last deal, the Tableau contains only 6 cards, 3, 2, and finally 1. In all deals, the play is to the original Foundation Piles. In this variation, when it comes to settling, the player receives only 1 counter for each card, at the end of the 5th deal; 2 for each card, if he goes out on the 4th deal; 3, if on the 3rd; 4, if on the 2nd; and 5, if he goes out on the first deal.

CANFIELD

This game of Patience was invented by Richard A. Canfield of New York.

EQUIPMENT: A full deck of 52 cards.

A Misery Pile of 13 cards is counted off, face down, and is laid to the left, face up. The next card turned up is the first Foundation Card: and, whatever its denomination, all other Foundation Piles must begin with a card of the same denomination. This Foundation Card is placed beyond the Misery Pile. A Tableau of 4 cards is now faced up on a line horizontal with the Misery Pile.

Holding the Stock, face down, in your left hand, take 3 cards at a time from the top, and face them. Cards on the Foundation Piles are built in upward suit sequence: thus, Ace, 2, 3, etc., to

10, Jack, Queen, King; or, if a Jack, for instance, is your Foundation Card, Jack, Queen, King, Ace, 2, 3, 4, etc., up to 9, 10 (high). Cards on the Tableau are built in downward sequence, in alternating colors. No cards may be built on the Misery Pile, but the top card on it may be played to a Foundation Pile or the Tableau rows. If there is a space in the Tableau, it is filled from the top of the Misery Pile. When a card is played from the Misery Pile, the card exposed beneath it is available for play.

After running through the Stock in threes, it may be taken up and run through again in threes, without reshuffling. If a Tableau pile contains only 2 cards, the top card may be transferred to another pile, if it may be used there.

The object is to play off all the deck on the Foundation Piles. In settling, players usually pay 52 counters for the deck, and are repaid 5 counters for every card played off to the Foundation Piles.

In some localities, the Stock may be run through, in threes, as above, until no exposed card in it will play. Settling is the same as above.

WHITEHEAD

This variety of Patience is a combination of Klondike and Canfield, with added elements of its own.

EQUIPMENT: A full deck of 52 cards.

The Tableau is as in Klondike, except that all 28 cards are dealt faced up, in 7 piles containing, left to right, 1, 2, 3, 4, 5, 6, and 7 cards, as in Klondike. The 29th card is turned up for a Foundation card; and the Foundation Piles all start with this denomination, as in Canfield.

On the Tableau, cards are built in descending sequence in color, but not necessarily in suit. Such groups as are in both color and suit sequence may be moved bodily, where the card to which they are moved is of the same suit, and one higher in denomination than the bottom card of the group being moved. Any top card of a Tableau pile may be moved to fill a space in the Tableau. The Stock is played through by being faced one card at a time, as in Klondike. The Foundation Piles are built up in ascending suit sequence, as in Canfield.

Settling is on the same basis as Klondike.

THE RAINBOW

This is a variation of Canfield.

EQUIPMENT: A full deck of 52 cards.

After thorough shuffling, 13 cards are dealt face up to form a Misery Pile. A Tableau is formed of 4 cards faced up; the 35 remaining cards constitute the Stock. The first of the Tableau cards is then moved up as the first Foundation Card, and thereafter cards of the same denomination are placed beside it as Foundation Cards; and on these cards are built up the entire deck, in ascending sequence in suit, as in Canfield.

The top card of the Misery Pile is immediately moved, to replace the first card of the Tableau. Cards are built down on the Tableau in descending sequence, in alternating colors, using the faced card on the Misery Pile whenever possible. Vacancies in the Tableau must always be filled from the Misery Pile.

The Stock, faced down, is then exposed, card by card, and each card is played to Foundation Piles or Tableau if possible, and if not it is faced up for a Trash Pile. When the whole Stock has been run through, one card at a time, the Trash Pile, without shuffling, may be run through twice again. The object is to play out all the cards in ascending suit sequence on the Foundation Cards.

In some localities, when the Misery Pile is exhausted, vacancies in the Tableau may be filled from the top of the Trash Pile. The Misery Pile space cannot again be filled.

THE MASKED TWELVE

EQUIPMENT: A full deck of 52 cards.

The Tableau consists of 7 rows of 32 cards: 8 faced up; 6 faced down upon the central 6 of the first row, and 6 faced up upon these; similarly, faced down and then faced up rows of 4;

and finally, faced down and faced up rows of 2 cards. The cards do not overlap to the sides. The Tableau now has 8 cards exposed and free to be played on; 12 cards faced up not free to be played on; and contains 12 cards faced down, the Masked Twelve. The 20 remaining cards of the deck constitute the Stock.

Any Aces among these 8 exposed Tableau cards may be played in front of the player, as Foundation Aces. On exposed free cards in the Tableau, cards are played as below in downward sequence in alternating colors. A group of such cards may be removed together, provided they are placed on an exposed free Tableau card of the denomination next higher than the bottom card of the group, and of the other color. On the Foundation Aces, cards are played in upward sequence in suit. When there is a space in the Tableau—that is, less than 8 vertical rows—a King, or any sequence in alternating colors with a King as its highest card, must be used as below to fill it.

When all rearrangements of the Tableau have been completed, one by one the cards in the Stock are faced; played out as Foundation Aces or combined on the Tableau as above; or faced up for a Trash Pile. Only the top card from the Trash Pile at any time may be played, the play of one card exposing the card beneath for play. The object of the game is to play out all the cards on the Foundation Aces, in upward suit sequence. The cards in the Stock can be gone through only once.

THE LUCKY THIRTEEN

Equipment: A full deck of 52 cards.

For a layout, deal 13 piles of 3 cards each, faced down; and then 13 piles faced up on these piles. On these exposed Layout cards, cards are played as below from the 13 faced-up cards in downward sequence in alternating colors. The Aces are at once removed and placed face up before the player, as Foundation Aces. On Foundation Aces, cards are played in upward sequence, in suit. Either a single card or a group of cards in proper sequence may be moved from one Layout pile to another, provided its bottom card is 1 lower and of the opposite color from the top card on the pile to which it is removed. Where there is a space in the Layout, Kings, or sequences with a King as the bottom card, may be moved to fill it. When the exposed card or sequence on a Layout pile is moved to another pile, the top card faced down beneath it is then exposed, and may be played if possible.

The object is to play off all the cards on the 4 Foundation Aces, in upward suit sequence. Where no Ace is faced up on the original Layout, or revealed by rearrangements of it, the game is automatically lost.

ALEXANDER THE GREAT

EQUIPMENT: A full deck of 52 cards.

This is one of the most fascinating of all games of Patience. The whole deck is spread for a layout, in 17 piles of 3 cards each, and 1 pile of 1—all faced up, and all visible by overlapping. Only the top card of any 3 can be moved at a time; and only 1 card may be moved at a time.

As Aces become exposed they are played down in front of the player to constitute the Foundation Aces. On Foundation Aces, cards are played in upward suit sequence; on exposed cards on top of any Layout pile, in downward suit sequence. It is wise to go after Aces first, then 2's, etc. Every card in the deck being visible, its position should be carefully studied. A King on any Layout pile automatically locks up the cards beneath it, unless a space can be made in the Layout to which the King can be moved; or unless the King can be played off at the top of a suit from Foundation Ace. Suits often become interlocked. If a Club Jack is beneath a Diamond 10, and a Diamond 9 on top of a Club 10, the Diamond 9 could be played on its 10; but this would lock up the Club Jack, so that the Club 10 could not be played on it, and a card below the Club 10 would be locked. There are often more intricate interlocks of several suits.

The play is continued until there can be no more plays on the Layout or to the Foundation Aces. But Alexander required three battles in which to conquer the world; and the player is given a second, and then a third, shuffle and deal, of all cards not played on Foundation Aces, to aid him in going out. The game is won when all the cards have been played on the Foundation Ace piles in upward suit sequence. If a player does not win in three attempts, he may see how many battles he requires, by continuing the shuffles and deals until he goes out.

SHAM BATTLE

EQUIPMENT: A full deck of 52 cards.

For the Layout, the 4 Foundation Aces are placed in a vertical row in the center of the table. On each side of each Ace, 6 cards are dealt, face upward, from the Ace outward, so that they overlap. Thus all 52 cards are exposed, and their positions known.

On the Foundation Aces, cards are played in upward suit sequence. On the outer ends of the eight Layout rows, cards are played from the appropriate place in the layout in downward sequence, irrespective of suit or color. Only one card may be moved at a time. When a row is cleared and a space made to the left or right of a Foundation Ace, any card may be played from the outer end of any other Layout row. The play continues until all the cards have been played on the Foundation Aces, which wins the game; or until no further plays are possible, and cards remain on the Layout rows, which loses the game.

If one space is cleared, a win is possible; if two spaces are cleared, it is probable.

STREETS AND ALLEYS

In this variation of Sham Battle, a space is left for the Foundation Aces in the center of the table. All 52 cards are dealt out in vertical rows of 4 cards each, 7 rows to the left and 6 to the right of the space left for the Aces; and the cards overlapping, as in Sham Battle. As Aces are exposed in play they are immediately transferred to the Alley, the central space. Other cards may be built on the Aces in upward sequence, but this need not be done at once. Otherwise the game is played like Sham Battle

THE IDIOT'S DELIGHT

EQUIPMENT: A full deck of 52 cards.

In this intricate Patience, the player who goes out oftener than once in four attempts is lucky or uncannily skilled. To form the Tableau, 9 cards are faced up; then 8 more are faced up on the right 8 of these; then 7, 6, 5, 4, 3, 2, and 1. The final 7 cards are faced up below the Tableau, as a Playing Row. Thus, all the cards are now faced up.

Only the card at the bottom of a vertical pile may be moved. As Aces appear they are played out to constitute Foundation Aces. On Foundation Aces, cards are built up in ascending suit sequence. On the bottom cards of vertical Tableau piles, cards are built down in descending sequence, in alternating colors. Spaces in the vertical Tableau rows may be filled by any available card from Tableau or Playing Row. A player is not forced to play to the Foundation Piles unless he wishes; but a card once played there cannot be withdrawn to be used elsewhere. A card played from the Playing Row to the Tableau cannot be restored to the Playing Row.

The game is won when all 52 cards have been built up on the Foundation Aces.

UPSIDE-DOWN PYRAMID

EQUIPMENT: Two full decks of 52 cards each, or 104 cards.

Lay out a Tableau of 55 cards, all faced up, as follows: 10 for the top row, left to right; then, starting on the extreme right card, 9 right to left, overlapping underneath slightly; then, starting on the extreme left card of this row, 8 left to right, overlapping as before; and so on until 7, 6, 5, 4, 3, 2, and 1 have been dealt. The Tableau now has 10 horizontal rows. The number of cards in the 10 vertical rows, left to right, is 1, 3, 5, 7, 9, 10, 8, 6, 4, 2. The remaining 49 cards constitute a Stock.

Object of the Game.—To play out the 8 Aces as Foundation Aces in front of the player, and to build up all of the cards on these, in upward suit sequence.

The Play.—Only the 10 bottom cards of the 10 vertical rows are in play. All Aces on these should be played out as Foundation Aces. Bottom cards can be played to other bottom cards, in downward sequence and alternating colors. Groups of cards from the bottom of any vertical pile may be moved to another, if the top card of the group is 1 in denomination below the bottom card of the pile it is being moved to, and of opposite color.

After all possible plays from the Tableau have been made, the player faces one by one the cards in the Stock, and plays them as above, as Foundation Aces, on Foundation Piles, or on the bottom cards of the vertical rows of the Tableau. If there is a space in the Tableau, that is, a missing vertical row, only a King or a sequence with a King as its bottom card may be moved to fill it.

The game is won when all the cards have been built up on the Foundation Aces.

FINANCIER

This masterful game of Patience was a favorite of J. P. Morgan, Sr., and Junius Morgan. It ranks among the greatest games of the group ever invented.

Equipment: Two decks of 48 cards each, or 96 cards, the Aces being eliminated; they should be thoroughly shuffled.

Preliminaries: A Tableau of 3 rows of 8 cards each is dealt. The theoretical and desired cards in each position on these three rows, plus the cards playable on them in upward skip suit sequence, are:

The 2 Row. 2, (5, 8, Jack)
The 3 Row. 3, (6, 9, Queen)
The 4 Row. 4, (7, 10, King)

A Playing Row of 8 additional cards is laid out below the three rows. All these cards are faced upward. The remaining 64 cards constitute the Stock.

On any 2 in the 2 Row, a 5, then an 8, then a Jack, in the same suit, may be played, from another Tableau Row, or from the Playing Row. On any 3 in the 3 Row, similarly a 6, 9, and Queen; on any 4 in the 4 Row, a 7, 10, and King. But no space can be left in the Tableau at any time, the spaces being filled immediately by a card shifted from another Tableau Row, or from the Playing Row. Only a 2 can fill a space in the 2 Row; only a 3 in the 3 Row; only a 4 in the 4 Row.

OBJECT OF THE GAME.—To build up all of the cards on the 8 2's on the 2 Row, the 8 3's on the 3 Row, and the 8 4's on the 4 Row. Game is won when each of these rows holds in skip suit sequence, as above, all the cards in the two decks, headed by 8 Jacks, 8 Queens and 8 Kings.

THE PLAY.—If any 2's, 3's or 4's are in the Playing Row, dealt out to start the game, cards may be played from the appropriate rows to the same or different rows, creating a space on the proper row into which the 2, 3, or 4, or more than one of them, may be played from the Playing Row. Any card in its appropriate skip suit sequence may be played from the Playing Row to any Tableau Row 2, 3, or 4, or to these with the next higher skip sequence cards built upon them.

When no more cards can be played from the Tableau Row or Rows, or are desired to be played from the Playing Row to the Tableau Rows, 8 cards from the Stock are faced up on top of the Playing Row cards and spaces, each revealing the numerals of the card, if any, beneath it. Cards may not be shifted from one pile to another on the Playing Row, even to fill spaces. As before, no space can be left on a Tableau Row unless there is a 2, 3, or 4 to fill it in the appropriate row from the Playing Row. When this second round of Playing Row cards has been played off as before, a third Playing Row round of 8 cards is dealt; and this continues until the entire Stock has been dealt out.

Game is won by having all 24 Tableau Rows filled as above, headed by the 8 Jacks, the 8 Queens and the 8 Kings.

It is dangerous to place a higher card in any of the three skip sequences on a lower one, in the Playing Row. If 2 such are so placed in the Playing Row, the game is lost, since the 2 higher cards can never be played to the Tableau Row.

NAPOLEON AT ST. HELENA, BIG FORTY, or FORTY THIEVES

EQUIPMENT: 2 full decks of 52 cards each, or 104 cards.

Deal, face up, 4 rows of 10 cards each, from left to right— 40 cards in all—for a Tableau. Only the bottom card of each row can be moved. All Aces on this bottom row, or exposed when a bottom row card (or this with cards above it) has been moved, are played out in front of the player as Foundation Aces. The remaining 64 cards constitute the Stock.

Cards are built up on the Foundation Aces in ascending suit sequence, Ace, 2, etc. to Jack, Queen, King. Cards are built on the bottom cards of the vertical Tableau Rows in descending suit sequence. This is called Marriage. A Married group may be moved to another bottom card of a vertical Tableau Row, providing its highest card is one denomination lower in the same suit than the bottom card of the Tableau Row.

Spaces or vacancies in the vertical rows of the Tableau may be filled with any available card, either from the bottom card of a Tableau Row, or from the exposed Trash Pile, when that has been started. When all the Tableau rearrangements have been made, face up one at a time the cards in the Stock. Any cards that can be played as Foundation Aces, on Foundation Ace piles, or on the bottom cards of the vertical Tableau Rows, may be played. A card that will not play to any of these is faced up on a Misery Pile. At any time the top card on the Misery Pile may be played; and playing it exposes the card beneath, which is the subject to play.

The game is won when all the cards are so played up in ascending suit sequence on the Foundation Aces; otherwise it is lost. There is no redeal of the Trash Pile.

THIRTY-SIX CARD TABLEAU

The Tableau consists of 4 rows of 9 cards each. On Foundation Aces build up in ascending suit sequence; on the bottom cards of vertical Tableau Rows, in descending sequence, in alternate colors. In all other respects, the game is played like Forty Thieves.

THIRTY-TWO CARD TABLEAU

The Tableau consists of 4 rows of 8 cards each. Any Aces or suitable cards to play on Aces may be played directly to the Foundation Piles, while dealing the Tableau. Build on Foundation Aces in ascending suit sequence; on the available Tableau cards, in descending sequence, in alternate colors. There is no redeal. In all other respects, the game is played like Forty Thieves.

TWENTY-EIGHT CARD TABLEAU

The Tableau consists of 4 rows of 7 cards each. On Foundation Aces, build in ascending sequence, in alternate colors, regardless of suits. Available cards in the Tableau may be built on in descending sequence in alternate colors, regardless of suit. In all other respects, the game is played like Forty Thieves.

TWENTY-FOUR CARD TABLEAU

The Tableau consists of 4 rows of 6 cards each. Foundation Aces are built on in ascending sequence in suits. Available Tableau cards are built on in descending sequence, in alternate colors. The player is entitled to redeal the Misery Pile once. In all other respects, the game is played like Forty Thieves.

CRIBBAGE

THE SIX-CARD GAME

EQUIPMENT: A full deck of 52 cards.

PLAYERS: Two or three; or four, as partners; best two-handed.

RANK OF CARDS: King (high), Queen, Jack, 10, 9, etc., down to 2, Ace (low).

Preliminaries.—In the cut for deal, low deals, Ace being low. After shuffle and cut, the Dealer deals 6 cards to each player, one at a time, alternately, beginning with his opponent. The loser of the game deals the next hand. Any irregularity in the deal scores 2 at once for the opponent. The Dealer's opponent also has the right to demand a new deal by the same Dealer, if he wishes; but he must decide this before looking at his cards. If either hand has too few or too many cards, the opponent has the same alternative—if the deal stands, having superfluous cards restored to the stock, and a deficiency completed from the stock by the Dealer; but if the wrong number is in his own hand, he must decide before looking at the cards.

The Crib.—Each player discards from his hand 2 cards, face down. These cards constitute the Crib, and belong to the Dealer. They are not touched until the hands are played out; the Dealer then scores any points contained in them, combined with the Starter.

The Starter.—After the Crib is formed, the opponent cuts the stock. The Dealer reunites the pack, and faces up the top card of the reunited stock as the Starter. The Starter is not used during the play of the hands, but is counted with each hand and the Crib on the final count. If the starter is a Jack, called His Heels, the Dealer scores 2 points immediately. If the points are not scored before the Dealer plays a card, this score is lost.

Object.—To form counting combinations in play, or held in the hands and Crib combined with the Starter, toward game, which is 61 or 121 points.

The Play.—Cards are played without regard to suit, by denomination only. Moreover, each player plays his cards in front of himself, so as to keep them separate from his opponent's.

The opponent first plays any card from his hand face up on the table immediately in front of him, announcing its pip value. King, Queen, Jack and 10 are announced as 10 pips each. The Dealer then plays any card from his hand face up immediately in front of him, and announces the sum of his card and the one already played. The play continues alternately in this manner, in each case the pip value of the card played being added to the sum last announced; however, the sum of the cards played must not exceed 31.

If, on his turn to play, either player has no card to play which will bring the sum up to 31 or below, he announces "Go"—that is, "Go on and play, as I cannot play further." The other player, if he is able to, plays card after card, announcing the sums as before, until he has reached 31, or can play no further. If he cannot play, he states this.

When 31 has been reached, or a Go declared by both and pegged on the cribbage score-board, each player faces down the played cards immediately in front of him, and the player whose turn it is to play begins to play again exactly as before, from the cards remaining in his hand. The count is commenced again, and the cards played as above, until the hands are played out. The players must always play alternately, except when one player has announced a Go, and the other can still play one or more cards.

Scoring Points.—All points must be scored when made, or are lost.

His Heels—any Jack turned as Starter 2
His Nobs—Jack of Starter's Suit, in hand or crib 1
31, reached exactly in play 2
Nearest to 31, in play 1
15, reached exactly in play 2
15 reached on last card played: counts for 15 and Nearest to 31, or 3
Pair—a card which makes a pair with the last card played 2
Triplet, Three or Pair Royal—a third card of the same denomination played immediately after a pair, with no 31 or pegged Go intervening, each card pairing with each other, or 6
Four, Double Pair or Double Pair Royal—a fourth card of the same denomination played immediately following a Triplet as above, scores for 6 pairs, or 12

Sequence or Run—3 or more cards in numerical rotation, [though not necessarily in the sequence order]—with no 31 or pegged Go intervening; for each card of the sequence 1

An intervening card or duplicate of the same denomination breaks the Sequence. Pairs, Triplets, Fours and Sequences must be formed by the opponents playing alternately, or by this in combination with a player's playing after a Go is declared, or by a player's playing after a Go is declared, provided 31 has not been exceeded.

After the cards are played out, each player takes up his hand and counts all the points that it contains, in combination with the Starter. The Dealer's opponent counts first, and then the Dealer. Last of all, the Dealer counts and scores all the points in his Crib, combined with the Starter. All points must be scored as soon as counted.

Further Scoring.—

Double Run of Three—a 3-card sequence with a pair to any one of the 3 cards 8

Double Run of Four—a 4-card sequence with a pair to any one of the 4 cards 10

Triple Run—a Triplet, with 2 other cards in sequence with it 15

Quadruple Run—2 Pairs and a card in sequence with both 16

In any such combination, each card constituting it is counted and scored once with each other card in the combination. High scores can thus be made. Thus 4 5's and a 10 score 28—6 pairs, 12; and 8 possible 15 combinations, worth 2 each, or 16.

Four-Card Flush—4 cards of 1 suit in hand only, not Crib 4

Five-Card Flush—4 cards in hand or Crib, of same suit as the Starter 5

Scoring the Points.—Scoring is usually done on a Cribbage Board, with 4 rows of holes, 30 to a row; and 1 extra hole at each end between the 4 rows. Each player is equipped with 2 pegs and keeps his score on one pair of rows. Scoring starts from the same end for both players, down the outside row of holes first, then back up the inside row, until 61 is reached. The first count is scored with the first peg; the second, with the second peg placed appropriately beyond it; and so with the pegs alternately.

Lacking a Cribbage Board, one can be made out of paper or cardboard for each player, perhaps in this model:

Units:	1	2	3	4	5	6	7	8	9	10
Tens:	1		2		3		4		5	6

Two small markers should be used by each player, to score on this. Or the score may merely be written down on paper.

GAME.—Game consists of 61 or 121 points. If the winner reaches 61 before his opponent reaches 31; or 121 before his opponent reaches 91, it is a Lurch, and scores as 2 games won.

MUGGINS.—In some localities, if a player fails to peg the full value of his hand, Crib or any play, the opponent who discovers it may call out Muggins and add the neglected points to his own score, pointing out the omission.

THREE-HANDED CRIBBAGE

The deal is decided by a cut, and thereafter passes to the left. Each player is dealt 5 cards, and 1 to the Crib. Each player contributes 1 more card to the Crib, thus making 4 cards in each hand, and in the Crib. The game is scored in a board having three sets of 61 holes, each player having 2 pegs. Otherwise the game is the same as two-handed.

FOUR-HANDED CRIBBAGE

In the cut, the two lowest play as partners against the two highest, low becoming the Dealer. One player from each side is selected to score, and the board is placed between these two players. The other players may not touch the board or pegs, although they may advise the scorers. The deal passes to the left.

Each player is dealt 5 cards. Each discards 1 toward the Crib. The player left of the Dealer cuts for the Starter. Game, 121 points.

FIVE-CARD CRIBBAGE

In this variation, for two players, only 5 cards are dealt to each player, one at a time. Each player lays out 2 of these for the Crib, so that only 3 are left for play in the hands. The Dealer's opponent pegs 3 points for Last, on the first hand in each game, to compensate for the advantage of the deal. Otherwise, the game is played as in Six-card Cribbage.

SOLITAIRE CRIBBAGE

This is a game for one player, to see how many points he can score. The cards are dealt, 3 to hand, 2 to Crib, 3 to hand; and then 2 are discarded from the hand to complete the Crib. He then turns up the Starter. There is no play, the hand being scored first, and then the Crib, on a regular Cribbage Board.

The Starter is then placed at the bottom of the pack, and new hands, Crib and Starter arrived at, as before. This is continued until there are only 4 cards in the stock; which are faced up and scored as a hand.

Two or more may play this in competition, each with his own individual deck; the successive deals taking place at the same time.

B.—SHOWDOWN GAMES

BLACK JACK, VINGT-ET-UN or TWENTY-ONE

EQUIPMENT: A full deck of 52 cards.

PLAYERS: Any number.

RANK OF CARDS: No rank, except a counting pip value: Ace, 11 or 1; King, Queen, Jack, 10, 10 each; 9, 9; etc.

PRELIMINARIES.—Each player begins with an equal number of counters. A limit to the betting is usually decided upon before play. To decide who is to deal, the cards are dealt face up around the table, left to right; the first player receiving an Ace becomes the first Dealer and banker, and the deal thereafter passes to the left. In some localities, the first Dealer continues to deal and act as banker until another player turns up a Natural which the Dealer has none to offset; in which case this player becomes Dealer. In other localities, the change of Dealer is after a certain number of hands; or when he has won or lost a stipulated amount; or when the deck is exhausted.

Before the deal, each player, except the Dealer, places his counters or chips before him for a bet. This amount must not exceed the limit; in some localities it is limited to 1 or 2 counters. In one variation, the player is allowed to look at the first card dealt to him before betting. Another allows a player, when he receives a pair on the deal, to separate the two, and place separate bets on each. The Dealer makes no bet; as the banker, he bets against each player the amount the player stakes.

The dealer gives each player 2 cards, face down, in rotation to the left, one at a time.

Object of the Game.—To hold cards whose collective pip value is 21, or the nearest number below 21, without exceeding it.

Drawing and Settling Bets.—Each player examines his cards. If the Dealer's cards consist of an Ace and a court card or 10 (which together count to 21), they constitute a Natural; thereupon each player, unless he also has a Natural, loses twice the amount he has bet. If a player has a Natural and the Dealer none, the Dealer must pay double his stake to the player. In some localities, the player holding a Natural is allowed to take all stakes on the table, but this method is not general. Naturals are settled for forthwith.

After the Naturals are settled for, or if no player has received a Natural except the Dealer, each player in turn may ask for a card, so as to bring the pip value of his hand to 21 or as close to this as possible. The drawing begins with the player left of the Dealer. He draws one card at a time until he is satisfied (that is, content not to draw another card lest his total exceed 21); or until his hand counts higher than 21 (a burst or bust), in which case he abandons his hand and pays his bet to the Dealer. The next player to the left then draws similarly; and so on until each player is satisfied or overdrawn. The Dealer then faces up his two cards, and draws more if he so wishes. If the Dealer overdraws, he pays each player who has not overdrawn the amount of his bet. If the Dealer has 21 or less, players counting to the same number are tied, and neither win nor lose. Those holding less lose their bet; those holding more than the Dealer, but not more than 21, win the amount of their bets.

A player having 2 Aces may separate them, making a bet on each. For Naturals based on these, the banker must pay double for each Natural, if he does not draw a Natural; if he does, they are tied, neither winning nor losing.

When a player splits a pair, he finishes drawing to the first before he draws to the second.

The next deal is made from the Stock, that is, the remainder of the pack left over from the previous deal. When the entire pack is dealt out, all discards are gathered and shuffled, and the deal continues. [The deal passes when another player is dealt a

Natural, the Dealer having none, or after an agreed number of rounds. 21 or under on 5 or more cards pays double, in some localities.]

MACAO

Macao is a variation of Black Jack, in which only one card is dealt to each player. Aces count 1; court cards and 10's do not count. The number to be reached is 9, not 21. A player receiving a 9 in the deal is paid 3 times the amount of his wager; an 8, twice the amount; a 7, the amount of his bet. These are the three Naturals.

Drawing is the same as in Black Jack. If no Natural is shown, the players draw until they stand (that is, are satisfied), or overdraw, and so bust.

FARMER

EQUIPMENT: A 45-card deck, the 52-card deck with the 4 8's and the Diamond, Club and Spade 6 discarded.

OBJECT: To reach 16, or as near below it as possible.

Each player places 1 chip in the center, to form a pool called the Farm. The players bid in rotation left to right for the Farm and the privilege of being Dealer and banker. The highest bidder must deposit in the Farm the amount of his bid.

One card is dealt to each player. Each player must draw one card, and may draw more, as in Black Jack—the object being to reach 16 or nearest under, and not above. Court cards count 10, and numeral cards their pip value, from 10 for the 10 down to 1 for the Ace. If a player overdraws and busts, he does not announce it until the hands are exposed at the end. Any player having exactly 16 wins the Farm and all the counters it contains. If two or more have 16, the one holding the Heart 6 wins. If no player has this card, the one with the fewest cards wins. If this is a tie, the hand nearest to the Dealer on his left side wins.

If no player has exactly 16, the Farmer still remains in possession of the Farm, and he holds it, deal after deal, until some one wins it by holding exactly 16.

Whether the Farm changes hands or not, after the hands are exposed, all who have overdrawn pay the Dealer 1 counter for each pip they hold over 16. These chips are the Farmer's own property, and do not go into the Farm pool. Those holding less than 16 pay nothing to the Dealer; but the one nearest to 16 receives 1 chip from each of the other players. Ties are decided by the possession of the 6 of Hearts; the fewest cards; or the first hand on the Dealer's left, as above. When the Farm is won, it is emptied by the winner, and a new pool is formed and sold, as above.

SEVEN AND ONE-HALF

Equipment: A 40-card deck, the 8's, 9's and 10's being omitted.

Players: Any number.

Rank of Cards: Cards have only a counting ranking. Spot cards rank from the 10, 10 points, down to the Ace, 1 point; King Queen and Jack count one-half point each.

Preliminaries.—Either one player is selected to act as banker, and deal first; or the cards are dealt around face up, one at a time, left to right, the first player receiving an Ace dealing. The Dealer deals one card faced down to each player, in rotation left to right, beginning at his left. Before further cards are dealt, each player examines his card, and bets any amount within the agreed betting limit. The Dealer, after examining his card, may then require all players to double their bets. There is no redouble.

Object of the Game.—To hold cards whose collective pip value is 7½ or nearest to it, without exceeding it.

The Draw.—The player to the Dealer's left, after the bets have all been made, may stand on the card dealt to him or draw one or more cards, as he chooses. Cards may be drawn until he is satisfied, or the collective pip value of his hand exceeds 7½. This fact must be announced at once, the player abandoning his hand, and paying the amount of his bet to the Dealer. All cards drawn are dealt face up. One by one, in rotation to the left, each player stands or draws similarly. The Dealer then turns his card face up, and either stands or draws. If he decides to stand, he takes all bets from players having an equal or less number of points in their hands; and pays to those having a greater number, not exceeding 7½. If he overdraws or busts, he must pay all players who have not previously overdrawn.

If any player draws to total exactly 7½, he must announce this at once and expose his entire hand. If the Dealer fails to draw exactly 7½ after this has been done, and after the remaining players have been served in their turns, he must pay to each player making 7½ double his bet. If the Dealer draws exactly 7½, he collects double the bet of each player who has not already overdrawn, whether or not one or more of these players also has a 7½ hand.

If the first card drawn by a player is of the same value as the original card dealt him, and their combined pip value does not exceed 7½, he may split the pair, betting on the second card an amount equal to his bet on the first. Cards are served to both cards of the pair, but one hand must stand or bust before cards are served to the second. The first card served to each card of the split pair is served face down. If either of these first cards served to the split pair is of the same value as the original card, this pair can be split as above, and drawn to.

Change of Deal.—The first player to the Dealer's left to expose 7½, when the Dealer fails to draw a similar hand, takes the deal. If more than one 7½ hand is dealt, in rotation the players to the left have the option of dealing or declining the deal. If all decline, the Dealer deals again, but must pay double on all these hands. In some localities, a player who does not wish to deal when he has won the right may dispose of the deal to another player, or may pool his chips with another player. In this case, only 1 card is served to both players whose chips are pooled, they being regarded as one player. When the deal is lost, the chips in the pool are equally divided.

There is no misdeal; but a player is not required to accept a card exposed during the deal. The rules of Black Jack cover all other points.

BACCARAT

In this variety of Black Jack, one player is the Banker; the others, from 3 to 11, are the Punters. Three decks of cards are shuffled together, and used as one. Counting value of the cards: 9, 9 points, down to Ace, 1 point; court cards and 10's, nothing.

OBJECT OF THE GAME.—To secure cards whose total pip value most nearly approaches 8 or 9. An 8 made with 2 cards is better than a 9 made with 3 cards.

The players take their seats, half on the right of the dealer, half on the left, drawing for choice of position. Players make their bets on the right or the left of the table, any amounts they please, before the deal begins. These bets are that the player sitting on the banker's right, or on his left, will beat him. A player wishing to bet on both sides at once, right and left, meaning that both will beat the dealer, places his money on the line, or *à cheval.*

The banker deals the first card, face down, to the player on his right; the second card to the player on his left; the third to himself. This is repeated, so that each player has two cards, faced down. The three players then examine their two cards, to see how near they are to 8 or 9.

If any of the three has 8 or 9, he shows it at once. If the banker has 8 or 9 and neither punter has as much, the banker wins everything on the table. If either player has an 8 or 9, and the banker has less, he must pay. If no one has 8 or 9, the banker decides whether or not to offer a card, with a view to taking one himself. If he offers one to the players, he offers first to the player on his right, who may either take it or refuse it; it is then similarly offered to the left. If both refuse it, the banker must take it himself; but if either player accepts it, the banker is not required to take a card himself. If the player on the right takes the card, the player on the left may ask for one also. If offered cards are taken, they are left face up on the table; only one card is offered to each.

All the cards are now faced up. Ties are a stand off; but the Banker pays all bets on the side of the punter who has nearer

9 than himself, and wins all on the side that is not as near as himself; so that he may win from both, or lose to both. All bets on the side of the table on which the right and left player sits must be paid or lost according to the success or failure of the player holding cards who sits on that side.

Any player holding nothing but court cards, or such cards as 7 and 3, which equal 10 precisely, is Baccarat, or "nothing." If, however, a player has more than 10, such as 14, the 10 counts for nothing, so his point is 4.

When there is not enough money left in the bank to pay all the bets made, those to whom the hands are dealt must be paid first. Then come the players immediately behind them in their order; and the spectators last, as far as the counters will go.

Any player at any time may propose Banco, which means that he will individually bet as much as there is in the bank on one coup. This takes precedence of all other bets. If the bank loses, the bank is busted, and must be put up again. Usually the privilege of being Banker is auctioned off to the player who will put up the largest amount. If the Banker wins in a Banco, the same player may go Banco again; but he is not allowed to go Banco more than twice running.

When a player on the right or left loses a coup, the Banker deals the following hand to the next player in order beyond the one who lost. If the player wins from the bank, the cards are dealt to him again. Deals after the first are taken from the top of the stock, without further shuffling or cutting. The process of progressing from the player who loses a coup to the one beyond him is continued to the last player on the side, when it comes back to the one next to the banker.

CHEMIN DE FER

This is a variation of Baccarat in which six decks are used, and each player in turn to the left becomes the Banker, the deal passing as soon as the Banker loses a coup. Cards are given only to the player on the right, and to the Banker himself. As long as the banker wins, he deals again. If the point is a tie, all bets are off and the Dealer may pass the bank to the next player in turn, provided he has not given a card on the last deal.

QUINZE

This is a variation of Black Jack for two players, in which 15 is the objective, instead of 21. Court cards count 10, and the Ace 1 only. The play is for an agreed and equal amount each deal. The Dealer deals one card to his opponent and one to himself, and the non-Dealer may stand upon his card, or draw to it. The Dealer stands or draws in his turn, and the one nearer 15 wins. If it is a tie, or if both pass 15, the stakes are doubled, and the deal passes. Each deals in turn, and there are no Naturals.

ROUGE-ET-NOIR

EQUIPMENT: 6 decks of 52 cards each, shuffled together and used as one.

PLAYERS: Any number, as Punters against the Dealer, who is the Banker.

The Punters make their bets on one or the other of two large diamonds, one Red and one Black.

The Dealer shows down first for Black, turning up the top card of the deck and announcing its pip value. Court cards and 10's count 10 points each, and the others rank from 9 down to Ace (1 point). The Dealer continues to turn up cards, one by one, announcing the sum of those already turned up, each time, until he reaches or passes 31. The number never exceeds 40.

He then shows down for Red the same way. Whichever comes nearer to 31 wins. If there is a tie, all bets are a standoff. If exactly 31 is dealt for each, the bank takes half the money on the table.

PLAYING THE RACES

EQUIPMENT: A full deck of 52 cards, ranking Ace (high), King, Queen, Jack, 10, etc., down to 3, 2 (low). The suits rank: Hearts (high), Diamonds, Clubs, Spades (low).

PLAYERS: Any number playing against a Banker, usually selected by his offer to put up the highest amount against which to play.

The Layout is as follows:

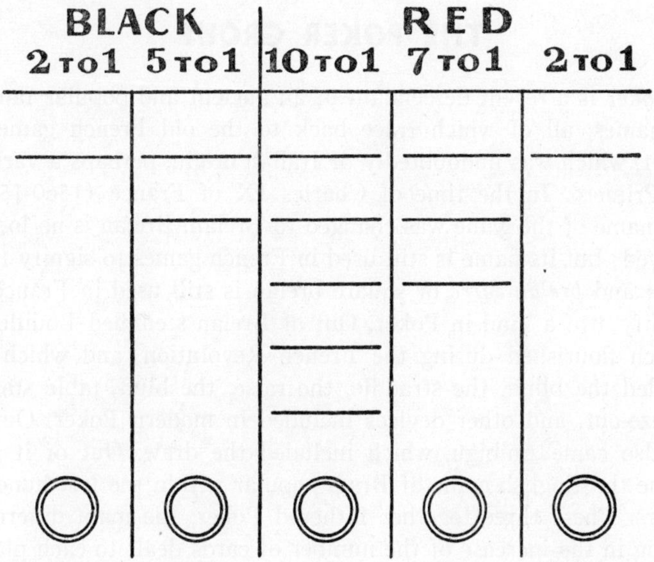

Bets are made with counters, 5 whites equalling 1 red; 5 reds, 1 blue; 5 blues, I yellow. There is usually a betting limit. There are two types of bets: all bets placed on Black or Red pay even money, and are on the color of the card bringing in the winning horse; the figures at the top of each column show the odds to be paid on each horse if he wins. The five checkers at the bottom represent the horses.

After shuffle and cut, the Dealer burns the bottom card by turning its face to the pack, then faces up 5 cards, 1 at a time, below the 5 horses, one for each. High moves its horse to the bottom line above him. Ties are decided by the rank of the suits. Five more cards are dealt the same way, and this continues until one of the horses has crossed the line. It takes only 2 moves for one of the 2 to 1 chances to win; and so on up to 6 moves, for the

10 to 1 shot. The Dealer pays at the odds given to the winner; pays Black or Red, depending on which colored card sent the winner over the line; and collects all other bets.

THE POKER GROUP

Poker is a recent descendant of an ancient and popular family of games, all of which trace back to the old French game of Gilet, which was undoubtedly of Italian origin, perhaps a variety of Primero. In the time of Charles IX of France (1560-1574) the name of the game was changed to Brelan. Brelan is no longer played; but its name is still used in French games to signify triplets; and *brelan-carré* or square brelan is still used in France to signify 4 of a kind in Poker. Out of Brelan stemmed Bouillotte, which flourished during the French Revolution, and which included the blind, the straddle, the raise, the bluff, table stakes, freeze-out, and other devices included in modern Poker. Out of it also came Ambigu, which included the draw. Out of it also came the English game of Brag, popular within the last hundred years. These three together fathered Poker, the main difference being in the increase of the number of cards dealt to each player from 3 to 5. *Brelan-carré*, or 4 of a kind, could only be made in the old games by combining the 3 cards in a player's hand with the card which was sometimes turned up on the stock or talon. The element of bluffing, so important in the armory of the adept at Poker, is found in Brag and the rest of the old games.

A number of card games retain the features of pairs, triplets, sequences, and flushes, but omit brag or bluff, and hence are at best only collateral members of the Poker group. Whiskey Poker, for instance, has little in common with the true spirit of Poker, and is simply the ancient game of Commerce played with 5 cards instead of 3. Early descriptions of this game indicated its French origin: in the use of the piquet pack; the French habit of cutting to the left and dealing to the right; and the use of such words as *brelan* and *tricon*. By 1835, the 52-card deck had come in, and the combinations were renamed Pairs-royal, Sequences, and

Flushes. The date and reason for the change from 3-card to 5-card hands are both uncertain.

AMBIGU

EQUIPMENT: A 40-card deck, the Kings, Queens and Jacks being omitted.

PLAYERS: Any number, up to eight.

After the cut for deal, low winning, and Ace being low, and after shuffle and cut, 2 cards are dealt in rotation left to right to each player, beginning at the Dealer's left. After examining them, each player is entitled to discard one or both cards, and draw to replace them.

The stock is then shuffled, and each player is given 2 more cards, on which he may play or pass. Those who play must bet; and any bet may be seen or raised by those who stay in, as in Poker. The players then discard and draw again, and are ready for the final betting on the hands of 4 cards each.

The 7 counting combinations, beginning with the lowest, are:

	Wins
Point, total pip value of 2 or more cards in any suit	1
Prime, 4 cards of different suits	2
Sequence, 3 cards in suit sequence	3
Tricon, 3 cards of the same denomination	4
Flush, 4 cards of the same suit	5
Doublets, any hand containing a double combination; as 4 cards in Sequence and suit; Tricon and Prime; or Sequence and Flush. Winner is paid for both.	
Fredon, 4 of the same denomination, if below 9's .	10
if Grand Prime, 4 9's, or 4 10's	11

The best hand wins the pool, and is then paid for the combinations he holds, the Dealer winning all other bets.

BOUILLOTTE, or BRELAN

EQUIPMENT: A 20-card deck, the Ace, King, Queen, 9, 8 in each suit. If five play, the Jacks are added; if only three, the Queens are omitted also.

PLAYERS: Four (or five, or three, as above).

RANK OF CARDS: Ace, King, Queen, 9, 8 (low).

PRELIMINARIES.—Each player purchases an equal number of counters, usually 100, called his Cave (French for cellar, store or reserve). When this is exhausted, he may purchase another 100; before then, as long as a single counter remains, he must call for a sight, just as in Freeze Out or Table Stakes in Poker (which see).

Before the deal, the Dealer puts up a Blind, usually of 5 counters. The player to his right has the privilege of straddling (see Draw Poker); and if he straddles, he may be straddled again. This goes around, until the Dealer has the last chance, and the straddling must then stop.

To select the Dealer, one Sequence (Ace, King, Queen, 9, 8) is dealt out, and whichever receives the King deals; if no one, the highest. The cards are then shuffled and cut by the player to the Dealer's left; and 3 cards are dealt to each player, face down, one at a time, from right to left, as in French games. The 13th card, called the Retourne, is then faced up on the stock.

THE BETTING AND SHOWDOWN.—The betting is as in Poker. In rotation, right to left, beginning with the player to the right of the Dealer or to the right of the last Straddler, a player may equal the amount of the ante; raise it; or pass. Any bet made must be equalled or raised. A player may call for a sight for the amount left in his Cave, as in poker, the balance of the pool being played for by the other players. If a player bets and no one equals his bet, he takes the pool.

RANK OF THE HANDS: from the highest down,

Brelan Carré—4 of a kind: 3 in the hand, the fourth the Retourne. If any player holds a Brelan (3 of a kind) ranking higher than the Brelan Carré, he may turn up the card under the Retourne; and, if it makes a Brelan Carré, he wins.

Simple Brelan—3 of a kind in hand, ranking Ace down to 8. A Brelan Favori is 2 cards in hand with the Retourne.

The Point—the highest card of the winning suit when there is no Brelan.

The holder of a wining Brelan Carré wins the pool, and also 4 white counters from each player. The holder of a winning Brelan wins the pool, and also 1 white counter from each player. The holder of a Brelan Favori, whether he wins or not, receives 1 counter from every other player. If two players hold Brelans, neither pays the other. If the Brelan Favori wins the pool, its holder also receives 2 counters from each player. If two Simple Brelans are held, the higher wins the pool; and both must be paid by the players who did not hold Brelans.

If no Brelan is held, all four hands are exposed; which, with the Retourne, makes 13 cards. The pips for each suit are then counted: Ace, 11; court cards 10 each; 9's and 8's by pip value. The suit with the highest value shown is called the Suit That Wins; holder of high card in it wins the Point, and takes the pool. If the holder of the high card has dropped out of the betting, his high counts for the player who has the highest card of the suit among those who bet. If no player still active has a card of the Suit That Wins, the Point is scored by the next highest suit, counting all the pips exposed, the high of this suit winning.

BRAG

Equipment: A full deck of 52 cards.

Players: Three to twelve.

Each player is dealt 3 cards, one at a time, after the cut for deal (low winning), the shuffle and the cut. The Dealer antes up (see Poker), and each player must equal the amount or throw up his hand. An ante may be raised, in which case later bettors must equal the raise or raise it, as in Poker.

The only scoring hands are Triplets and Pairs. There are 3 cards called Braggers: the Ace of Diamonds, the highest Bragger; then, the Jack of Clubs; and last, the Nine of Diamonds. A Bragger may be called by its holder any card he pleases, as if it were a Joker. A 3 or pair made without a Bragger ranks one made with a Bragger. If a player makes a bet which is not met, he wins the pool.

THREE-STAKE BRAG

Three pools are made, by equal contributions from the players.

The first 2 cards are dealt face down; the third is faced up. The highest card showing wins the first pool, Ace being high. A Bragger ranks all other cards of the same denomination.

The second pool is won as in regular Brag.

For the third pool, the pip value of the hand is counted; and the one nearest 31 takes the pool. In case of ties, the hand nearest to the Dealer on the left wins.

AMERICAN BRAG

In this variation, there are 8 Braggers: all the Jacks and 9's, none outranking the others. Threes or Pairs made with a Bragger outrank those made without one.

POKER

In General

Equipment: A full deck of 52 cards. The Joker may be added by agreement.

Players: Any number, from two to eight, or more.

Rank of Cards: Ace, King, Queen, etc., down to 4, 3, 2. The Ace may be ranked below the 2 in forming sequences. The suits are of equal rank.

Rank of Hands: Beginning with the highest:

1. Five of a Kind (denomination)—possible only when the Joker is used.

2. Royal Flush—the Ace, King, Queen, Jack, 10 of any suit.
3. Straight Flush—5 cards of a suit in sequence, ranked by its highest card. Thus 10, 9, 8, 7, 6 of any suit is called "Straight flush, 10 high."
4. Four of a Kind. It is ranked by its denomination; the fifth card in a hand can be disregarded.
5. Full House—3 cards of one denomination, 2 of another. It is ranked by the triplet, regardless of the ranking of the pair..
6. Flush—any 5 cards of a suit, not in sequence. It is ranked by the highest card, as King high, 10 high, etc.
7. Straight—a Sequence of 5 cards in various suits, ranked by the highest card. An Ace may begin or end a Sequence.
8. Threes—any 3 cards of the same denomination. The 2 odd cards may be any two unmatched cards.
9. Two Pairs. Any two pairs of any denominations, ranked by the highest pair. Thus, with 2 Jacks and 2 5's, this could be "Two Pairs, Jacks up." The fifth card of the hand may be disregarded.
10. One Pair. A pair of any denomination, with 3 unmatched cards. It is ranked by the denomination of the pair.
11. High Card. A hand containing none of the foregoing combinations, ranked by the highest card in it.

THE STRIPPED DECK.—With a small number of players, the 2's and 3's, and even the 4's, may be removed. This does not interfere with a straight in which Ace is low. Thus, with 2's, 3's, and 4's removed, an 8-high straight would be 8, 7, 6, 5, Ace.

OTHER HANDS.—In some localities, certain other hands rank. A Blaze is any 5 court cards, and ranks Two Pairs. A Tiger is 7 high and 2 low, without a Pair, Sequence, or Flush, and ranks above a Straight. A Dutch Straight or Skip is a Sequence of all even or odd cards, such as Jack, 9, 7, 5, 3, and ranks Two Pairs and a Blaze. A Round-the-Corner Straight uses the Ace to unite such cards as the 2, 3, etc., with court cards: such as King, Ace, 2, 3, 4; Jack, Queen, King, Ace, 2, etc. It ranks Three of a Kind, but not a regular Straight.

Ties.—Ties in Royal Flushes or any Straights divide the pot. If the highest cards in Flushes tie, the cards next below in order decide. If these are all equal, the players divide the pot. In case Two Pairs are a tie, the fifth card decides it. In case One Pair hands tie, the 3 outside cards in order decide it, the highest first. In case the High Cards are a tie, the rank of the remaining cards in order decides it. In all absolute ties, the pot is divided. In ties between two hands where one contains the Joker, the hand without the Joker ranks above the one with it.

Preliminaries.—Three preliminaries are usually agreed upon before beginning to play: the amount of the ante (the preliminary bet) (from the French *entrer,* to enter); the betting limit by which any bet may be raised; and the time set for ending the game.

The Seating.—As a rule, the players sit as they please. At the end of each hour's play, any player may demand that the cards be dealt around, face up, for choice of seats. The one receiving low sits to the left of the Dealer; the next lowest to his left; and so on. Ties sit side by side, or cut again for choice. If a newcomer enters at any time, room may be made for him; or the cards may be dealt between each two players already in the game, and he sits where the low falls; if there are 2 lowest cards, where the first of these fell.

Counters.—One player is usually named Banker; he takes charge of the chips or counters. These latter are usually of three colors, the white being the lowest amount that can be put into the pool at any one time, and the red and blue having agreed values.

The Deal.—Choice of deal is decided by dealing the cards around face up, the first Jack dealing. As a rule, two decks are used, one being shuffled by the previous Dealer while the other is being dealt. The shuffle and cut are as in all card games. The cards are dealt one at a time, left to right in rotation, beginning with the player to the Dealer's left. The last card cannot be dealt.

In the case of misdeals, the same Dealer deals again with the same pack. If a card is exposed in cutting or reuniting the packs, the deck must be shuffled again. It is a misdeal if the deck was not cut, or was improperly reunited; if a card is found faced in the deck; or if the deck is proved to be imperfect. If a sixth card is inadvertently dealt to the player on the Dealer's left, it must be restored to the stock at once. If one card not faced up in the pack is exposed during the deal, the player to whom it is dealt must take it; if 2 cards, even to different players, there must be a new deal.

Irregular Hands.—Any hand of more or less than five cards, any part of which has been looked at, is a foul hand, and must be abandoned, the player forfeiting all he has put into the pot, if it is won on that deal. If a player, without looking at any card announces that he has too few, the Dealer must remedy this from the top of the stock; if too many, the Dealer on request must draw the cards from the hand necessary to leave it at 5, placing such card or cards on the bottom of the stock. But if more than one hand is irregular in number, there must be a new deal; however, if one player has 6 cards and another one has 4, and neither has looked at his hand, the Dealer must be called upon to draw from the 6 hand one card, to complete the 4 hand. If one has looked and the other has not, the one who looked has a Foul Hand.

A deal out of turn, or with the wrong pack, must be stopped before it is completed, or it stands. No player who has looked at any of his cards may demand a new deal, except for an imperfect deck.

STRAIGHT POKER, or BLUFF

This standard game of Poker, from which the other varieties are derived, was originally played with only 20 cards in the deck, the Ace, King, Queen, Jack, 10 of each suit, all of which were dealt out to four players. It is still popular, especially for two-handed Poker.

The Buck.—The buck was originally some object used to mark the position of the player whose turn it was to put up the agreed amount, the ante, for the whole table. Each player in turn to the left, on being passed the buck, puts up the ante on each succeeding deal. This ante never varies in amount.

The Betting.—After the deal, each player examines his cards. Beginning with the player to the Dealer's left, each player may bet any amount within the agreed limit, by pushing the requisite counters to the center of the table; or he may pass. As soon as a bet is made, the player to the left must meet it with a stake of equal amount, raise it to a greater amount, or throw down his hand. Any player who passed before a bet was made can come in again on the next round of betting.

If no one will see (that is, meet or equal) the bet made, the bettor wins without having to show his hand. If it is met without being raised, those who are in the betting expose their hands face up, and the best poker hand wins the pool. The buck is then passed, the ante put up by all the players, and the winner of the pool deals the next hand.

DRAW POKER

The Blind and Straddle.—The player to the left of the Dealer puts up the required amount, usually a white chip, as The Blind. The player to his left can Straddle, if he wishes to, by putting up 2 counters; and, in turn, the player to his left can Straddle again, by putting up 4; and so on. No player can Straddle unless he sits next to the Blind or a Straddler. The player to the left of the Dealer has the privilege of raising his bet after the others have come in.

Coming In.—When each player has been dealt his hand of 5 cards, the player beyond the player who put up the Blind, or the one to the left of the last Straddler, if any, must put up the amount of the Blind or the last Straddle as an ante, if he wishes to draw cards to improve his hand. If not, he discards his cards into the center of the table, as a Trash Pile. If he comes in, he can raise the ante any amount within the betting limit; and any player in rotation after him may raise him again the same way, or simply "see" the amount, that is, put in the same amount. If the player to the left of the Dealer wishes to come in, he must put up as much as will make his Blind equal to any other player's bet. Any player who is raised must meet the raise; and he may raise again, if he so wishes.

The Draw.—Those who wish to draw cards having put up equal amounts in the pool, the Dealer asks the player nearest to him on the left how many cards he wishes. A player may discard any or all of his original 5 cards, and ask for an equal number; or he may stand pat, that is, he may retain his original hand unaltered. All who are in the pool are then offered cards in the same way.

Irregularities in the Draw.—The stock must not be disturbed between the original deal and the end of the draw. A faced card must be exposed to all the players and then placed among the discards. If a card is faced during the deal to the players drawing, it must be exposed to all players and not replaced until all the players have been served. A card once discarded may not be restored to the hand under any circumstances. If a player asks for too few or too many, this may be corrected if discovered before the player looks at any drawn cards and before the next player draws; otherwise, if an overhand, he must discard so as to keep them; if an underhand, it is foul, and must be abandoned. If the fault is the Dealer's, the error must be corrected the moment the Dealer's attention is called to it, provided the player has not looked at his cards drawn. If the excess cards are in the Dealer's hand, he must take them.

If a player lets a player to his left draw out of his proper turn, he must play the hand without drawing, or abandon it. If he has discarded, his hand is dead. If a player sees the face of a card or of cards about to be dealt to him, he must take them, unless another player has seen it or them and can name it or them. The last card must not be dealt; instead, the discards must be regathered and shuffled, and the draw continued from them. Neither the Dealer nor any player is allowed to give information as to how many cards a player drew; but if a player asks the Dealer how many cards the Dealer drew, and the player asking is in the pool and has not yet bet, the Dealer must inform him.

Betting after the Draw.—The influence of the Straddle dies out after the draw. The second player to the left of the Dealer makes the first bet, or passes, even if the player to the left of the Dealer is out of the play. If this player will not bet, or is out of it, the opportunity passes to the left. If no one bets, the player to the left of the Dealer takes the pool. If any player bets, each in turn to the left must see the bet, raise it, or drop out. Any player who is raised may raise again in his turn, or see the bet, or drop out.

Irregularities in Betting.—A player who bets or raises out of turn must let his chips stay in, even if the player whose turn it was to bet raises the bet to the limit. A bet is made only by putting the chips out; merely saying "I call you" does not constitute a call. Chips can never be withdrawn from the pot, or cards from the discard.

The Showdown.—As soon as the amounts put in by all the players still in the betting are equal, all the hands must be shown down on the table. A player in the call is not allowed to concede that he is beaten and conceal his hand. If the last bet made is not called, the player takes the pool without showing his hand. If two or more hands are shown in a call, the best hand wins, regardless of how the player calls it. Two players who are betting only against each other may agree to split the pool, but their hands must be shown on the table to the other players. If one player erroneously admits that another hand is better than his, and that hand takes the pot, it is too late to correct the error, as there is no pot left about which to dispute. Only cards and chips talk, in poker.

Whangdoodle.—It is sometimes agreed in advance that after a hand of certain rank, such as Four of a Kind or a Full House, is shown, a Whangdoodle or Jackpot must be played—a hand in which nothing lower than a pair of Jacks can open; or a Whangdoodle may be agreed upon to be the last hand of the play. Again, Jackpots are sometimes played when no player makes an ante. At times, a premium is agreed upon for all hands of high value, such as Fours, Straight Flushes, etc.

TABLE STAKES

Table Stakes is an agreement to raise the betting limit to the amount any player has on the table before him at the time. No player may raise the amount of his Table Stakes after looking at any of his cards. If any player has not enough counters left on the table to call, he may call a sight of the last bettor's cards for what he has, and separate that part of the pot from the rest; so that other players may go on and call a sight for their pile, or call the entire bet, or raise it. If the one who calls for a sight has the winning hand at the showdown, he takes only his part of the pot; the others decide the rest of the pot on the merits of their hands.

FREEZE OUT

In Freeze Out, each player starts with an equal number of chips. As soon as any player loses all his chips, he retires from the game, which continues until one player has won all of the chips.

JACK POTS

In Jack Pots, each player must ante on every deal. If the pool is not opened, it is usual to "sweeten" it by anteing up each time until it is opened. Each player to the left of the Dealer in turn, has the privilege of opening the betting, provided that he holds a pair of Jacks, or better, but, having Jacks or better, he is not compelled to open.

In turn, the other players, after the pot is opened, may meet the bet or raise it, whether their hands hold openers or not. Players who pass do not discard their hands, as they have an interest in the pot until it is proved that it was properly opened. Their hands are retained as a remedy against a foul hand.

When the bets are equalized, those still in the pool discard and draw more cards, if desired, to improve their hands. If the opener remains in the pool, he must place his discards under the chips in the pool. He is then at liberty to draw as he pleases, and may split his openers, if he wishes to, without being compelled to announce that he is splitting them. If the opener will not meet a raise, or no one comes in before the draw, he must expose his 5 cards, to establish that he had proper openers of a pair of Jacks, or better. If he has, he takes the pool; if not, he is a false opener, and forfeits his right to the pot. Those who came in under the impression that the pot was properly opened stay in, regardless of the value of their hands. The player to the left of the false opener now begins the betting. If the opener is not called after he has drawn cards and made a bet, he need show only his openers. No one may see what he has drawn, unless he pays to see it. Even if the opener has a foul hand, 4 or 6 cards, he takes the pot, unless some player has held a fair hand with which to dispute it with him. In that case the pot remains, and the player who has drawn to false openers must ante for all the others at the table for the next Jackpot.

THE DOUBLE-UP GAME

This is a betting variation which is usually confined to Jackpots. Each player to the left of the Dealer, in turn, is allowed to bet as much as there is in the pool at the time. The limit is usually fixed at a point that would stop at about six successive doubles.

POKER WITH THE JOKER, or MISTIGRIS

The Joker may be used in any game of Poker. Any player holding the Joker may call it anything except a duplicate of a card held in a Flush hand. Thus it is possible to hold Five of a Kind, which ranks all other hands. Hands otherwise equal, one containing the Joker, are ranked so that the hand without the Joker is the higher.

DEUCES WILD

In Deuces Wild, which may be played with or without the Joker, each 2 ranks as a Joker, and may be called anything except a duplicate of a card held in a Flush hand. Hands of the same denomination are won by the hand containing the least wild cards; if these tie, the highest natural card wins.

THE WILD WIDOW

In this variation of Deuces Wild, after 4 cards have been dealt to each player, a card is faced up, and then the fifth card is dealt to each. The other 3 cards of the same denomination as the faced card are now wild, as in Deuces Wild. The play is otherwise as in Deuces Wild. The Joker may be used, if desired.

SPIT IN THE OCEAN

In this variation of Deuces Wild, only 4 cards are dealt to each player, and then a card is faced up. The 3 other cards of the same denomination are now wild. The draw is based on 4 cards only, the faced up card being regarded as wild, and as belonging to each hand in turn when the showdown comes.

STUD POKER

Each player antes, or one player antes up for all. One card is dealt in rotation left to right to each player, face down. The cards may be examined by their owners, and then faced down again. Then one card face up is dealt around. The player with the first best card (that is, highest Ace being high) showing must bet, or throw down his cards. If he abandons his cards, the next best card bets or passes, and so on. Any bet made may be called or raised by any other player who still holds cards. When the bets have been made equal, another card is dealt face up to each player still in the pool, and the betting is resumed as before. When there are 2 or more faced up, the highest showing poker combination has the first betting opportunity each time: thus, a Pair outranks a high card, a Three outranks a pair, and so on. If a card is exposed from the stock before the betting is ended, the Dealer buries one card for each player, including the exposed card. As long as two or more players are in the pool, the cards are dealt out as above, until each has 4 exposed cards and one "in the hole." Final bets are then made, followed by a showdown, in which the best Poker hand wins.

STUD POKER WITH A DRAW

In some localities, after the Stud hands have been completed as above, each player has a right to draw once, as in Draw Poker. Betting takes place both before and after the draw.

PEEK POKER

Peek Poker is a variation of Stud, with two variations of its own. It may be played as 7-Card Peek or 8-Card Peek. Each player is dealt 2, or in 8-Card Peek, 3 cards, face down, and he inspects them to inform him what he has "in the hole." Then 5 cards, face up, are dealt, one at a time, betting on these taking place as each round is dealt, as in Stud. High card or high combination in each case has the first bet, each player in turn calling, raising, or abandoning his cards. When the final call is made, the players collect their hands and strip them down to 5 cards each. The highest hand of 5 cards wins.

HIGH-LOW POKER

This is a variation of Draw Poker, in which the pot is divided each time between the holder of the high hand and of the low hand. An odd chip always goes to the high hand.

A Runt is permitted—hands of different suits, of less value than a pair. The lowest possible Runt is 2, 3, 4, 5, 7. The highest card determines the ranking of a Runt. Runts are decided by the rules governing Flushes.

WHISKEY POKER

The Dealer deals as in regular Poker, except that he deals an extra hand, the widow, just before his own hand. Each player, beginning at the Dealer's left, has the privilege of exchanging his hand for the widow; keeping his hand and drawing to it; or playing it as it is, that is, "standing pat." If a player exchanges his hand for the widow, he places his own hand face down on the table, and takes up the widow, his own hand thereupon becoming the widow. If a player prefers to draw to his own hand, he says "I pass," and the privilege of taking up the widow passes to the left; and so on around. To play the hand as it is, a player knocks on the table, which also passes the privilege of taking up the widow.

If any player takes the widow, the next player on his left may do any one of three things: discard from his hand, replacing the discard with the same number of cards from the widow, and facing down his discard as a part of the widow; exchange his entire hand for the widow; or play the hand as dealt to him, and knock. The next player in turn has the same option, and so on, until some player knocks.

If all pass on the first round, the Dealer faces up the widow; and in rotation, left to right, each player in turn has the privilege of drawing from it, or exchanging his entire hand for it. After a player knocks, the others may have one more draw from the widow in turn, or may play their hands without drawing. No player can draw after he has knocked.

After the knock and the final round of draws, the hands are all shown, the highest winning the pot, if there is one; or the lowest pays a forfeit agreed upon in advance.

STRIP POKER

A popular variation of Poker, especially in the summer, is Strip Poker. In this, either the low hand each time, or all hands except the high, must remove one garment, or some article worn on the body, each time a hand is lost. Men discard such things as watches, cuff-links, handkerchiefs, a shoe-lace, and so on; articles carried in the pocket, such as pencils, letters, and so on, are not considered removable. Women discard hairpins (if any) and articles of jewelry. In some localities, the men play in one room and the women in another.

PATIENCE POKER

Patience Poker is a combination of Poker, Patience or Solitaire, and the party game known as Word Squares. It may be played by one player; or, better, by several players in competition, each with a complete deck of 52 cards. When two or more compete, one is the Caller, this privilege passing to the left.

The Caller, after shuffle and cut, faces his top card, and announces its suit and denomination. The other players, having their decks arranged in suit and sequence, pick out the identical card. Each places it before him on the table. The Caller repeats with a second card, placing it so that it touches the first card, on one of its four sides. The other players repeat: but they need not place it in the same position, so long as it touches the first card on some one side. This is continued, until each player has before him a Layout of 5 rows of 5 cards each, or 25 cards. A card once placed on the Layout cannot thereafter be removed.

The object is to form ten Poker hands, of as high rank as possible: five in the horizontal rows, left to right, five in the vertical, top to bottom. The hands are scored by the following table, high score at the end of an agreed number of deals winning. Note that Flush and Three of a Kind are rated below Straight.

	English	*American*		
Straight Flush	30	30	or	75
Four of a Kind	16	20		50
Full House	10	12		25
Straight	12	9		15
Three of a Kind	6	7		10
Flush	5	5		20
Two Pairs	3	2		5
One Pair	1	1		2

MATRIMONY

This is an ancient showdown game, which contributed the elements of Matrimony or Marriage, and also of Intrigue (in Bézique and Pinochle) to the Bézique family of games, and also to Pope Joan.

EQUIPMENT: A full deck of 52 cards; or the deck stripped by removing some of the lower cards.

THE LAYOUT: A layout of paper, cardboard or some other suitable material, divided into 5 compartments:

Matrimony.	Intrigue.	Confederacy.	Pair.	Best.

PRELIMINARIES.—Any number can play. The Dealer announces a number of counters he will stake, and places them as he pleases on the various compartments of the Layout. Each other player in turn left to right places as he pleases one less counter than the Dealer.

THE DEAL AND THE SHOWDOWN.—The Dealer deals one faced down card to each player, left to right in rotation, beginning at his left, and then a second card to each, faced up.

If the Ace of Diamonds, the Best, is faced up, its holder takes all the counters on the Layout. If it has not been faced up, the counters on Best remain until it is faced up in some subsequent deal.

The players then turn up their cards faced down. Any player holding any King and any Queen as his 2 cards, takes the counters on Matrimony. Any player holding any Queen and any Jack takes the counters on Intrigue; a King and a Jack, the counters on Confederacy. The highest Pair shown takes the counters on Pair. The Ace of Diamonds can only function, if a down card, as one of a Pair. If any of these combinations fail to turn up, the counters remain on the appropriate compartment in the Layout until, on some later deal, they are won. Where there is a tie, the tieing player nearer to the left of the Dealer wins.

The deal passes to the left. Each Dealer may announce as many counters as he chooses for his contribution to the Layout, the players each time individually contributing one less. A time limit is usually fixed in advance for the session.

AUTHORS

EQUIPMENT: A full deck of 52 cards. The game was originally played with special cards bearing the pictures of authors and other notables, and four different quotations from each.

Players: Any number; five to eight makes a good table.

Rank of Cards: The cards have no rank, any four of a kind being the equal of any other four of a kind.

Preliminaries.—Any player deals the cards around, face up. The first player receiving an Ace deals the first hand. The deal passes to the left. The cards are dealt around, one at a time, beginning with the left of the Dealer, from left to right, until the entire deck is dealt out.

Object of the Game.—To secure the largest number of tricks, each trick consisting of 4 cards of the same denomination. In the case of a tie, the higher denomination of the top trick wins—Ace being high, King next, etc.

The Play.—The player to the left of the Dealer begins by asking for a certain card, naming its suit and denomination, and asking any particular player he pleases. When he asks, he must have at least one card of the same denomination in his hand. If the player asked has the card, he must hand it over, and the successful asker then asks the same or another player for a specified card of a denomination and named suit, always having at least one of the same denomination in his hand.

If the player asked has not the card which was requested, the privilege of asking passes to this player. The moment a player has dealt to him or collects 4 cards of the same denomination, he lays them faced down before him, as one trick counting for him. The game ends when all the cards have been faced down in tricks of four of a kind.

LIFT SMOKE

Equipment: A full deck of 52 cards.

Players: Not more than six.

Rank of Cards: Ace (high), King, Queen, etc., down to 2 (low).

In the cut for the deal, low wins, Ace being low in the cut. After the shuffle and cut, for the four- or six-handed game 6 cards are dealt one at a time to each player in rotation left to right, beginning at the Dealer's left; if five play, five cards are dealt to each. The remaining cards constitute the Stock. The last card dealt to the Dealer is faced up for the trump, and the Stock is placed in the center of the table.

The hand to the left of the Dealer leads to the first trick. The others must follow suit if they can; if not, they must trump if possible; if impossible, they must discard. The highest card of the suit led wins the trick, unless it is trumped; in which case the highest trump wins. The winner of each trick draws one card from the Stock; the losers draw nothing. The winner of each trick leads to the next trick.

The player who ends up with one or more cards, while his opponents hold none, wins the game. If two players remain with one card each, the winner of this trick draws a card from the Stock, and so wins.

FARO

Faro is one of the oldest of banking card games, and probably originated in Italy. It belongs to the same general group which contains Lansquenet, Florentini and Monte Bank. Under the name of Pharaon, said to have been derived from the picture of an Egyptian pharaoh on one of the cards, it was a favorite in France during the reign of Louis XIV (1643-1715), and came to American by way of New Orleans. As originally played, the Dealer held the cards in his left hand, and any bets put down could not again be taken up until they were decided. The Dealer collected for splits, as in Stuss today; and also took hockelty, the payments for the Hock or In Hoc, the last card left in the box. The Layout today is far more elaborate.

Equipment: A full deck of 52 cards, having no rank, the denominations alone counting.

Players: Any number, playing against the Banker, who is usually selected by his offer to put up a certain amount for which to play.

Counters: All bets are made and paid in counters: 5 whites to 1 red; 5 reds to 1 blue: 5 blues to 1 yellow. There is always a betting limit, and this is doubled only when 1 card of a denomination remains in the dealing box; this card is called a Case Card.

THE LAYOUT: The Layout is a complete suit of Spades, consisting either of cards from another deck placed on a table (attached or otherwise), or of enamelled designs on green cloth. Sufficient space is left between the cards or designs for the players to place their bets. The arrangement is:

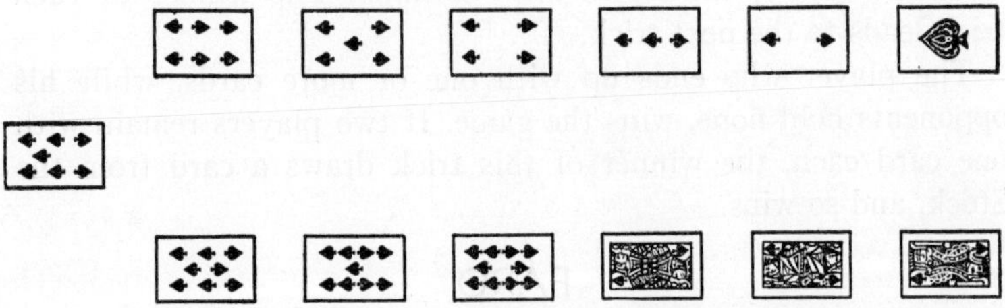

PLACING BETS: There are many ways of placing bets at Faro. A player may make bets of 21 different combinations of cards, all playing the 10 to win, as follows:

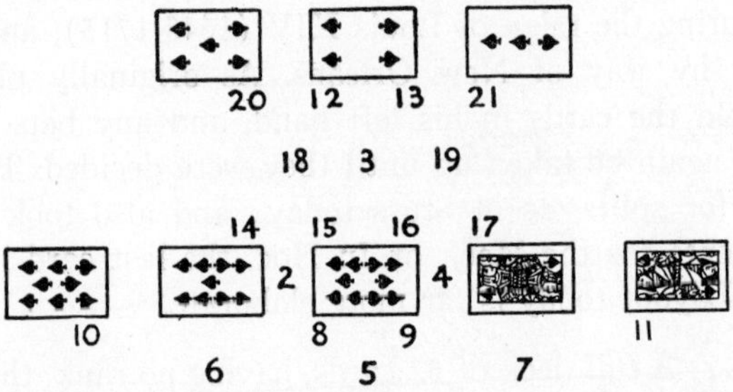

(In the diagram, bets 10, 8, 9, and 11 are at the touching *bottom* of the Sp 8; of both sides of the Sp 10; and of the Sp Q.)

Of these bets, 1 is flat on the 10 itself; 2, 3 and 4 take in the card next to the 10; 5, the cards on each side of it; 6 and 7, the three cards behind which the bets are placed, each including the 10; 8 and 9, the 10 and the card one remove from it in each direction; 10 and 11, the same, but placed on the other card; 12 through 17, the right angled triangles of which the bet is made inside the right angle; 18 and 19, the four cards surrounding them; 20 and 21 Heeled Bets, in which the bottom counter is on one card, the balance of the counters tilted diagonally toward the second card played to win, the 10. Two Heeled Bets might also be placed on the 10 toward the 5 and 3. There could be other Heeled Bets playing the 10 to win and the other cards to lose. Bets may also be strung behind odd or even cards on the side next the dealer: showing that the player bets that the next Case Card will win if it is even, and lose if it is odd—that is, if the string is placed behind an even card.

The Deal.—After shuffling and the cut, the cards are placed faced up in a dealing box, from which they can be withdrawn only one at a time. A spring usually presses the stock up to the opening in the box; and, one card at a time, the cards are slipped one at a time through a slit in the side.

The top card is called the Soda. The Dealer pulls out 2 cards, laying the Soda about six inches away from the box, the card beneath it right beside the box. This leaves one card faced up in the box. The card left in the box on the first Turn is the winner; the card next to the box, the loser. Players place their bets upon whether the next card of any denomination will win or lose: that is, be in the winning or losing position.

The Bets.—A bet placed flat upon a card bets that it will win, when next its denomination shows. A bet with a marker, called a Copper, placed on it, says that the card will lose, when next its denomination shows. Bets may be placed in many combinations, as shown above. If any card in the combination wins, the bet is won, or lost, if the bet is coppered. A player having the bet on 2 cards, one to lose and one to win, and losing both bets, is said to be whipsawed. The same denomination both winning and losing on a turn is a Split. If it is desired to place a bet on 2 remote cards, the Dealer furnishes an ivory marker to mark the second of these cards, the bet being placed on the first; or two markers may be used.

After the Dealer has waved his hand preparatory to pushing the top card from the box, no bet can be altered or made. After each Turn, which consists of 2 cards, a winner and a loser, all bets are settled, and new bets made. Between each Turn, a player may alter his bets in any way.

Keeping Cases.—As the cards are withdrawn from the box, they are marked on a Case-keeper, which is a suit of 13 cards, with 4 buttons running on a steel rod opposite each of them. As the cards come from the box, these buttons are pushed along, so that the players may know at a glance how many of each denomination are still to come, and what cards are left for the last Turn. A bet placed or left upon a card of which none are left in the box is called a Sleeper, and is public property; the first player that can get his hands on it keeps it. Waiting for Case Cards and then betting high on them is not regarded as the best form. Covering big bets by opposition small bets, or betting small chip bets all over the board, is called a piking game, and the player a piker.

Each player should also have a score sheet, to keep tab on the denominations as they come out. This has the denominations to the left; and after this the player marks a 1 for a win, and a 0 for a loss. The Soda is marked with a ., splits with an x, and the Hock with a -.

The Last Turn.—If 3 different cards are left for the last Turn, the players may call the Turn, naming the order in which they think the cards will appear. There are 6 possible ways. The odds against any one of these are 5 to 1; the Dealer pays 4 to 1 for them. In calling the Turn, the bet is strung from the selected loser to the selected winner. If a third card intervenes, the bet is strung away from it, to show that it goes around the Layout to the other end.

If there are 2 cards of the same denomination in the last Turn, it is called a Cathop; as it can come only 3 ways, the Dealer pays 2 to 1 for it. If 3 cards of the same denomination are left, the call is by the color, and is paid 2 to 1. These bets are placed on the Dealer's right for red first; on his left for black and red, and in front of him for 2 blacks, where there are two black and 1 red; and the reverse, where there are 2 red and 1 black.

STUSS

In Stuss, the cards are dealt from the hand, instead of a box. The Dealer wins on Splits. Otherwise, the game is the same as Faro. The name is colloquial German for "nonsense," derived from the Yiddish.

LANSQUENET

Lansquenet gets its name from the German *Landsknecht*, a foot soldier; and is said to be a game introduced into France by these soldiers, during the Franco-Prussian War.

EQUIPMENT: A full deck of 52 cards; or two such decks shuffled together and used as one.

PLAYERS: Any number.

PRELIMINARIES.—The deal and privilege of being the Banker is cut for, low winning, and Ace being low in the cut. The deal passes to the left, unless the Dealer gains a second deal. After the shuffle and cut, the Dealer faces up the 2 top cards and places them aside, as the Hand Cards, which determine whether the deal passes or not. No bets may be made on the Hand Cards.

The Banker then faces up one card for himself; and one card for the group of players. If his or their card matches one of the Hand Cards in denomination, it must be placed beside the card it matches, and another dealt, as all bets must be made on unmatched cards. All bets made upon the players' cards must be covered by the Banker at once.

THE SHOWDOWN.—The Banker proceeds to face up the cards from the top of the Stock, one at a time. As long as his own card remains unmatched in denomination, he wins. If he draws one of the same denomination as the players' card, he takes all bets made upon it. If he matches his own card, the players win all they have staked. If the card he draws matches neither, it is placed beside the players' first card, and they can then bet upon it also, the Banker covering each bet at once.

As soon as one of the players' cards is matched, the Banker withdraws the pair and places them beside his own card, so as to separate them from exposed single cards; but he cannot withdraw his own card. If a card is faced which matches either of the Hand Cards, it is placed upon the card it matches. If both the Hand Cards are matched before either the players' first card or the Banker's card is matched, the Banker wins all bets, gathers in all the cards, and deals again.

MONTE BANK, or SPANISH MONTE

This is a favorite Spanish and Spanish-American gambling game, using the Spanish deck of 40 cards.

EQUIPMENT: A 40-card deck, omitting the 8's, 9's and 10's.

PLAYERS: Any number.

PRELIMINARIES.—One player is selected to be the Banker, by cut or otherwise. After shuffle and cut, the Banker, holding the deck face down, draws out the 2 bottom cards, and faces them on the table for the Bottom Layout. He then draws the 2 top cards from the deck and faces them on the table for the Top Layout. The players then bet on either Layout all they wish, up to the limit that the Banker is willing to risk.

THE SHOWDOWN.—After all bets are made, the deck is turned face up. The card in sight is called the Gate or Port. If it is of the same suit as either card in the Top Layout, the Banker pays all bets on that Layout. If it is the same suit as either card in the Bottom Layout, the Banker pays all bets on that Layout. If both, he pays both. If there is no card of the same suit in either or both Layouts, the Banker collects all bets placed on the one or both of them.

After all bets are settled, the deck is faced down again, the 4 Layout cards and the Gate being discarded. Two fresh Layouts are made, bets are laid, and a new Gate is shown; this continues until the deck is exhausted.

THREE-CARD MONTE

EQUIPMENT: 3 cards, 2 red and 1 black; usually the red Aces and the Ace of Spades.

The cards are usually slightly bent lengthwise, so as to be picked up easily by the ends. They are faced down on the table separately. The black Ace is shown by the Banker to the other players. Then the Banker shifts the cards about, face down, by a few skillful passes, so as to confuse the players as to which is the black Ace when the cards are finally allowed to come to rest.

Bets are then placed as to which card is the black Ace. If the Banker pays even money, he wins on the average; if he pays 2 to 1, the chances are even.

COMMERCE

EQUIPMENT: A full deck of 52 cards.

PLAYERS: Three to twelve.

Each player chips in for a pool. The Dealer is selected by a cut, low winning, Ace being low. After the shuffle and cut, the Dealer deals three cards to each player, one at a time, left to right in rotation, beginning with his left.

The player left of the Dealer then bids to "buy" or "trade." If he buys, he hands one of his cards and a counter to the Dealer, and draws a card from the top of the pile in its place. If he trades, he passes a card to the player on his left, who must give him one in exchange, before looking at the card passed to him. If a player will not buy, and does not wish to exchange, he stands, and that ends his alteration of his hand. If he buys or trades, he may buy or trade again, always trading to the left. As soon as any player stands, all exchange ceases, and the hands are shown.

There are three classes of hands:

Three of a Kind, the highest: Aces high, Deuces low.

Sequence Flushes. The higher card decides ties. The Ace can be used above the King or below the 2.

The Point—the greatest number of pips on two or more cards of the same suit: the Ace, 11; King, Queen, Jack, 10, 10 each; the others their pip value. If the point is a tie, one of 3 cards will beat one of 2. Otherwise, the player nearest the dealer on the left wins.

MY BIRD SINGS; or, MY SHIP SAILS

In this variation, there is no buying from the Dealer, but only exchanging with the player on the left. The only winning hand is three cards of one suit, regardless of rank. If there are two such, the pips decide. After two rounds, if none is shown, the highest point among two-card flushes wins.

SPECULATION

EQUIPMENT: A full deck of 52 cards.

PLAYERS: Two to ten.

RANK OF CARDS: Ace (high), King, Queen, etc., down to 2 (low).

Each player contributes equally to a pool. In the cut for deal, low winning, Ace is low; after the shuffle and cut, 3 cards are dealt faced down one at a time to each player, in rotation left to right, beginning at the Dealer's left. The next card is faced up for trump.

If the card faced up is an Ace, the Dealer takes the pool at once. If it is a King, Queen or Jack, he offers it for sale to the highest bidder; but he need not accept any offer unless he so desires. If he sells, he passes it to the buyer; if he does not sell, he retains it. Then all the cards are faced up, and the holder of the highest trump takes the pool.

If the faced up trump is a numeral card, the Dealer offers it for sale, as above, before any player looks at his hands. Whether it is sold or not, it must be left faced up on the table. The player to the Dealer's left then faces up his top card; and this continues in rotation to the left, around and around, until a higher trump than the faced one is turned. The purchaser of the original trump does not face any cards until this trump is beaten. If a better trump shows, it is offered for sale, as above; and the rest of the unfaced cards in the hands are turned face up one by one, until a better trump shows, or all have been exposed. The holder of the best trump at the end takes the pool.

BLIND HOOKEY, or DUTCH BANK

EQUIPMENT: A 52-card deck; or this with additional 11's, 12's and 13's added.

PLAYERS: Any number; usually only four or five are active, the others making outside bets, as at Baccarat.

RANK OF THE CARDS: Ace (high), King, Queen, Jack, 10, down to 3, 2 (low).

PRELIMINARIES.—After the shuffle and cut, the Dealer (who has been chosen by a cut, low winning—Ace low on the cut), divides the cards into as many packets as there are players. There must be at least 4 cards in each packet, these being left faced down. The player second to the left pushes any packet to the Dealer, who must accept it as his. Bets are then made on the other packets, any player betting on any he pleases. The object is to bet that the bottom card of the packet bet on is higher than the bottom card of the Dealer's packet.

When the bets are made, one by one the packets are turned face up. If the Dealer's faced card on the bottom of his packet is higher than the faced card on the bottom of any other packet, he takes all bet on it; if lower, he pays. In case of a tie, the Dealer wins.

RED DOG, or HIGH-CARD POOL

EQUIPMENT: A full deck of 52 cards.

PLAYERS: Any number from three to eight.

RANK OF CARDS: Ace (high), King, Queen, etc., down to 3, 2 (low).

PRELIMINARIES.—In the cut for deal and choice of seats, low deals and has choice of seats, the others sitting the next lowest to his left, and so on. Ace is high in the cut. After the shuffle and cut, each player contributes one counter to the pool. If any player wins the entire pool, all contribute at once to form a new pool, 1 counter each.

The Dealer deals in rotation left to right, beginning at his left, until he has dealt 5 cards to each player, including himself. Cards are dealt 1 at a time. The remainder of the pack, the Stock, is faced down.

THE BETTING AND SHOWDOWN.—The player on the Dealer's left bids first. He may pass, abandoning his hand into a Trash Pile (called the Deadwood) and paying 1 counter to the pool; or he may bet any amount not exceeding the full value of the pool, that he holds in his hand a card of the same suit as the concealed top card on the Stock, and of higher denomination. As soon as he puts up his bet, the Dealer faces the first card on top of the Stock.

If the player can show a higher card in the same suit than the one faced, he wins from the pool the amount of his bet; if he cannot, his bet goes into the pool. He is allowed to show only one card. The card faced from the Stock, and also the player's hand, goes into the Deadwood. The next player to the left now has a chance to bet or pass, as above. When all have bet or passed, including the Dealer, the deal passes to the left. Any chips remaining in the pool are added to by each player making an ante, as before.

To make a safe bet, 2 high cards in 2 different suits are required; 4 Aces constitute a certainty.

HAVANA

This is a swift and fascinating gambling game, whether played with counters or for stakes. It has elements in it resembling Keno or Lotto, in the bets on vertical and horizontal lines of the Layout.

EQUIPMENT: A 33-card deck (Ace through 7 of each suit) and Joker.

PLAYERS: Any number, four or more making it more interesting.

PRELIMINARIES.—In the cut for the privilege of banking, low wins; the Joker and Aces are high in the cut. After the shuffle and cut, the Banker faces down 4 rows of 8 cards each for the Layout. The Layout locations rank as follows:

1st Row, Spades: Ace, King, Queen, Jack, 10, 9, 8, 7
2nd Row, Clubs: Ace, King, Queen, Jack, 10, 9, 8, 7
3rd Row, Hearts: Ace, King, Queen, Jack, 10, 9, 8, 7
4th Row, Diamonds: Ace, King, Queen, Jack, 10, 9, 8, 7

The Betting.—The Banker now calls for the bets. These may be made with chips of different colors for each player, or by other means indicating who makes each bet. A better way is to have printed or multigraphed copies of the Layout (one for each player every deal) on which the bets are marked down, as shown in the diagram below.

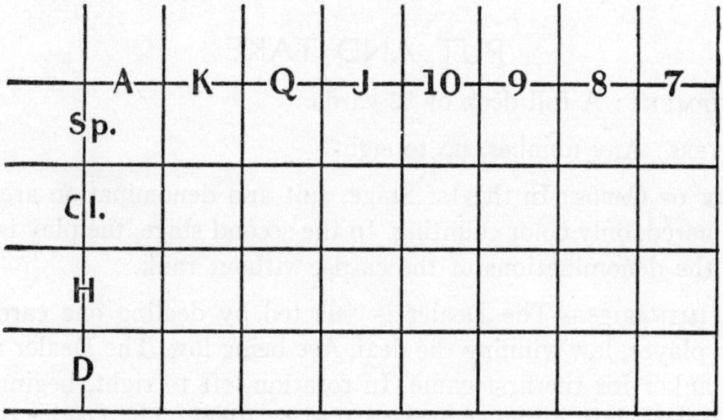

Bets are made on three things: on individual cards; on vertical rows of 4 cards; on horizontal rows of 8 cards.

The Showdown.—After all bets have been placed, the Banker faces the one card remaining in his hand, the Playing Card. It must be placed at once in its appropriate place in the Layout, and all bets made on that card paid. The faced down card removed to make room for it becomes the next Playing card. The showdown continues in this fashion until the Joker is turned, which ends the showdown. If the Joker is turned as the 33rd card for the Playing Card, the Banker collects all the bets, without further showdown.

Settling Up.—The Banker, in settling up, pays even money on any cards faced up; 4 to 1 on vertical rows of 4 cards faced up; 8 to 1 on horizontal rows of 8 cards faced up. The Banker also collects all bets on individual cards not faced up, and on vertical and horizontal rows not entirely faced up.

The banking passes to each player in turn on the left.

When used for betting, a copy of this Layout may be used for each game, printed, multigraphed or drawn. Bets on individual cards are placed in the appropriate one of the 32 rectangles, these paying even money. Bets on vertical rows (paying 4 to 1) are marked or placed above the vertical row bet on; bets on horizontal rows (paying 8 to 1) are placed to the left of the horizontal row bet on. The Layout locations of each card can easily be determined from this Layout.

PUT AND TAKE

Equipment: A full deck of 52 cards.

Players: Any number, up to eight.

Rank of Cards: In the 1st Stage, suit and denomination are ignored, only color counting. In the second stage, the play is by the denominations of the cards, without rank.

Preliminaries.—The Dealer is selected by dealing one card to each player, low winning the deal, Ace being low. The Dealer acts as Banker for the first game. In rotation left to right, beginning at Dealer's left, a player bets on Red or Black. The Dealer deals him 5 cards face up. If there are 3 or more red cards, Red wins; if 3 or more black, Black wins. The Dealer collects or pays the first bet, and then follows the same procedure with the other players until all have been served. Each player retains his 5 cards, faced up.

The Second Stage.—The Dealer faces up the next card, and calls on all players holding 1 or more cards of the same denomination to pay 1 chip to the pool for each card of this denomination. He repeats this, with 9 more cards: 2 chips for 2nd card turned, 3 for the 3rd, and so on up. On the 11th card, the players take out of the pool 1 chip each for every card of the denomination turned; 12th, 2 chips; 13th, 3; and so on. Anything left in the pool goes to the Dealer; or, if the pool becomes exhausted, the Dealer pays. The deal passes to the left.

BOOK TWO

OTHER SPECIAL EQUIPMENT INDOOR GAMES

DICE and MILITARY GAMES

It is impossible to know what informal games primitive man started with, in the various lands he came to occupy, although the games of existing savages throw some light on the problem. At first, a stone, a stick, a coconut, anything, must have been played with, the way that monkeys, cats and other animals play today. Any utensil or weapon, in moments of relaxation, could be used as the basis of a game. Slowly a number of games were formalized in two directions: as physical contests, and as contests of shrewdness. We are still playing games of both types that woke the shouts of victors beside the Yangtze, the Ganges and the Nile before Greece flowered or Rome thundered across the continents.

Many of these games are buried in mists of ancient forgetfulness. We know that the American Indians, in addition to polished stones like quoits or discuses, and stone balls for throwing, had flat pebbles cryptically marked for some sort of game; but the game itself is forgotten. Out of the ancient mists two types of games emerge especially: a group of games using the religious symbols used in casting lots before the gods; and games, physical or mental, symbolizing military strategy.

The drawing of lots, still used in many games, including the draw in cards, and such devices as spinning or tossing a coin (to determine which side it falls on), is based on primitive religious practice: that is, an invocation to the gods, especially the goddess of fortune, to select between the contestants. A kindred device, perhaps as ancient, persists in our use of dice. Dice are said to be derived from knucklebones, which very anciently became a distinct game. If so, they originated from knucklebones tossed to decide the will of the gods. The Urim and Thummin of the Hebrews, before the time of David, were objects used to ascertain the will of the gods. Later they were worn by the high priest in his breastplate, as ceremonial stones. The first sacred dice may have contained merely symbols indicating Yes or No. The cubical type with which we are familiar is found in the tombs of ancient Egypt; in classic Greece; and in the Far East. The Greek word for dice and games played with them came from *astragalos,* or ankle-bone. The game of Odds or Evens was probably played with pebbles almost as soon as man began to develop. Although Herodotus says that the Lydians invented dice during a famine in the time of King Atys, dice are mentioned as a game in the Rig Veda; and probably they originated either in Asia, fertile womb of the races, or independently in many ancient cultures.

In one direction, dice developed recently by being flattened into Dominoes, the face of a domino representing the two numerals faced up on a throw of two dice; similarly, the royalty and other persons in Chess were flattened anciently into cards. Dominoes are first recorded in 18th Century Italy. At some indeterminate period Mah Jong developed in China in like manner, each tile bearing a single symbol, like a card, and the tiles being handled like Dominoes. In another direction, possibly influenced by the great group of military strategy games represented by Chess and Checkers, the god-directed throw of the dice was used to determine the space that symbols representing soldiers could be moved, always in retreat into a fortress of safety: and this gave us Backgammon.

As in Chess, Checkers, and cards, Backgammon represents a warfare between the black and the red armies—for all that other differing colors were substituted later for these first two colors that primitive man differentiated. The origin of Backgammon is vaguely attributed to ancient Persia, to Ur of the Chaldees, to Egypt long before Tutankhamen, who had his board buried beside his body. In India, it was the parent of the simple four-player Parchesi; Japan knew it two thousand years ago; and the Greeks taught it to the Romans, who spread it over Europe. The Aztecs of Mexico played a recognizable variation of the game long before the conquest of Cortez, which points to an ancient Mongolian or Asiatic origin, or an independent invention of it in these widely separated lands. Chaucer and his associates played it, calling it Tables. Three centuries ago, it was rechristened Backgammon in England, the word simply meaning back-game; however, some authorities insist that it comes from the Welsh or Saxon word for "little battle." In the meantime, it had also been called Ticktack and Tricktrack; and Tric-Trac in France. It is a game determined by the fall of the dice primarily, the shrewdness coming in only in utilizing the numbers vouchsafed by the dice. Essentially it is the game of masterly retreat, no one having yet invented a dice game involving military conquest.

Chess is the parent of the present games of mental military strategy: even of cards, which stem remotely out of an ancient Indian variation of chess called the Four Kings. It was invented before recorded history began in India, as a conventionalized battle between two equal armies of soldiers, to train young princes and nobles in the rudiments of warfare. The goddess of fortune was sternly eliminated, for all that she still presides over Backgammon and cards. In India, its primitive form was called Chaturagna; it is mentioned in the Hindu Puranas as early as 3000 B.C. It spread eastward first through Burma to Tibet, Siam, China, Malacca, Java, and Borneo, and ultimately to Japan, where the board has 81 squares. Westward it reached Constantinople, passing through Persia in the 6th century A.D. The Arabs took it during the next century, to Mecca and Medina, Syria and then Byzantium. Byzantine bodyguards carried it to Scandinavia and the North, from which places it gradually spread over Europe. The object of the game is to capture the enemy's general, and the game ends when this is accomplished.

Checkers or Draughts is an ancient offspring of Chess, played in Egypt and Nubia 2000 B.C., where the circular men had a knob on them almost like chess pawns. Both names are illogical: Draughts, akin to "draw," being more applicable to dominoes or certain card games; while Checkers comes from the check and checkmate used in Chess, but unknown in Checkers. It is the game of utter annihilation of the enemy, the ranking into pieces of various powers being eliminated, at least until a piece has reached the king line and been crowned as a king. Everything points to its being a subsequent simplification of Chess. Go-Bang, a Japanese form of Checkers, requires a special board of 324 squares.

The other special equipment games, many of them exciting and popular, are of various antiquities.

BACKGAMMON

Equipment: A special backgammon board, as in Diagram I. The board is divided by a line from player to player called the bar. In front of each player are 12 triangles, called points, 6 on each side of the bar. The points are numbered from the outer edge of a player's inner table; points 1 through 6 being on the inner table, points 7 through 12 on the outer table.

Each player has a dice cup and two dice; and also 15 men, of differing colors, today usually red and white or black and white. The board is set up according to Diagram I. Each player has 2 men on his opponent's 1 point; 5 on his opponent's 12 point; 3 on his own 8 point; and 5 on his own 6 point. The opponent's men are set up opposite these. The direction of play is from opponent's inner table, through opponent's and then player's outer table, into player's inner table, until they can be borne off. The opponent moves similarly in the reverse direction.

Preliminaries.—Each player casts one die. The higher throw wins choice of men and location of inner table. The inner table was once the table nearer the light. With modern lighting, the inner table may be to the opponent's right or left, as he chooses. The table directly opposite this becomes the opponent's inner table. In case of a tie, the dice are thrown again, one die at a time by each player, until the tie is broken.

Throwing the Dice.—Each player must throw his dice into the open section of the board at his right. If a die rests upon another die, it is cocked; if it is not upon another die but is not resting fair and flat upon the board, it is fouled. Cocked or fouled dice must be thrown again.

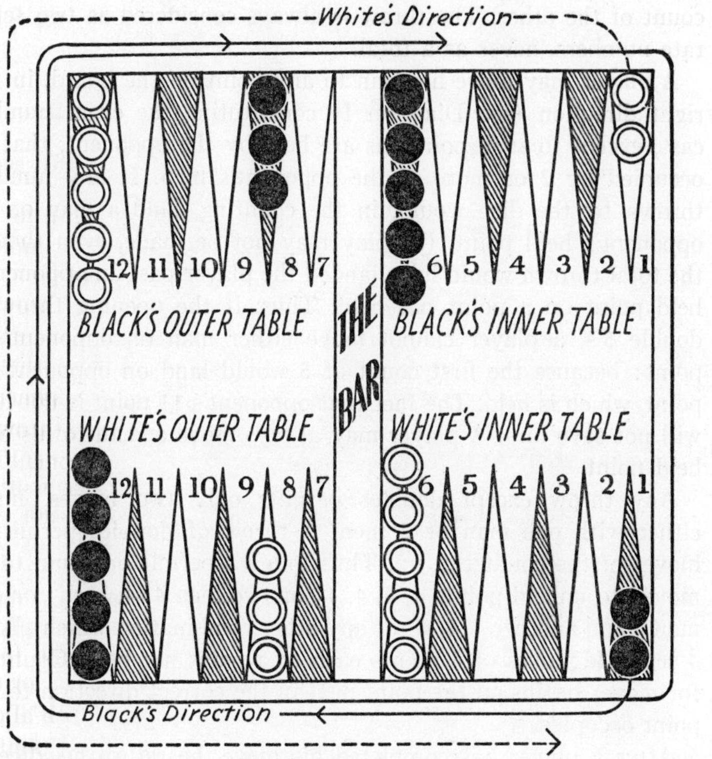

Backgammon: I

THE START.—When the board is set up and the choice of position and men determined, each player throws a single die. If the result is a tie, each throws a single die again, and so on until the tie is broken. The player receiving the highest number plays first. He may either let his first play consist of the two dice thrown by himself and his opponent; or he may throw both his own dice over again for the first play. The first method is the only one allowed in most clubs. Each game is started in this fashion.

THE PLAY.—Each player moves his men according to the individual numbers on the two dice thrown. He may move one man first the count of one die, and then the count of the other; or may move one man the count of one die, and another man the count of the other. The throw is always considered as two separate numbers, never as a total.

A player may move his man to any point on the board, in the right direction (see Diagram I) constituting the exact number cast, except to such points as are held by the opponent, that is, occupied by 2 or more of the opponent's men. If any number thrown by the dice would, in the counting, land a man on an opponent's held point, the play may not be made, even though the total thrown would have landed the player past an opponent's held point on a point not held. Thus, if the opening throw is double 5's, a player cannot move either man on opponent's 1 point; because the first count of 5 would land on opponent's 6 point, which is held. The fact that opponent's 11 point is not held will not save him. A player may always move a man to his own held point.

Any throw except doubles permits only two moves, made either with one man or 2 men. A throw of doubles permits 4 moves of the count thrown. Thus four 4's permit one man to be moved to unheld points 4, 4, 4, 4; or two men 4, 4, each; or one man 4 and another 4, 4, 4; or any other combination which allows 4 separate moves of 4 points each to a point not held. Counting for moves begins on the point next in the correct direction to the point occupied.

After a player has completed his move, he return his dice to his dice-cup, and the opponent casts and moves. The plays continue alternately in this manner until one player has brought all of his men to his inner table, and has borne them all from that table. The player's aim is to do this, and at the same time to block and handicap his opponent as much as possible.

A single man resting on a point is called a blot. It may be hit, that is, picked up, and placed on the bar. Such a man must be reentered in the opponent's inner table, by a throw of a die corresponding to some point not held: either blank or containing an opponent's blot, or one or more of his own men; from that reentry point it must start afresh on the journey home. A man may be hit on a blot only when the exact count of one of the dice thrown lands an opposing man on the blot. If a man on a blot is 4 points away, a throw of dice containing a 4 or some combination counting up to 4, which does not stop on a held point, will hit it; but any other throw will not. It is not compulsory to pick up a man on a blot, unless the player has no other move open to him. A player must play both or all counts of his throw, if these may be played in any way. If he can play only one of the two counts thrown, he must play the higher.

If a man is on the bar, a player owning it cannot make any other move until it has been reentered on a point not held by the opponent. If all six points are held, he may not even throw, until some point in the opponent's inner table is blank, or contains a blot. A player may enter on an opponent's blot, thereby placing the opponent's man on the bar. He may enter on a point in the opponent's inner table occupied by one or more of his own men.

When a player has brought all of his men into his own inner table, he starts bearing off, that is, removing his men from the board. This is done according to the casts of the dice. If a 6-4 is thrown, the player may remove a man from his 6 point, and another from his 4 point. He must play each count; but he is not required to bear off, if he can play the count down toward the outer edge of his inner table; as, for a cast of 4, from his 6 point to his 2 point. If there is no man on the point whose count is cast, he must move a man down from a higher point to the proper count cast. When all the men have been removed from the 6 point, a throw of 6 requires a man on the next lower point occupied to be thrown off; and so on, if point 5 is vacant and a 6 or 5 is thrown, etc. When doubles are thrown, the player throws off or moves down the count four times; or combines these moves in any way he chooses.

The player bearing off all of his men first from his inner table wins the game. As long as a man is on the bar or outside of the inner tables, no other man of that player may be borne off.

Scoring Games.—A single game is one in which both players have borne off at least one man before either wins, and counts 1. A gammon or double game is one in which one player wins before his opponent has borne off a single man, and counts 2. A backgammon or triple game is one in which a player wins while one or more of the opponent's men are on the bar or in the winning player's inner table, and counts 3. When the players gamble, the loser pays double for a gammon, and triple for a backgammon.

DOUBLING.—If, by agreement, doubling is permitted, either player, after the game has started, but before any throw of the dice at any stage of the game, may double the stake for which the game is played, by announcing that he doubles. The opponent must accept the double, or resign the game at once and pay the original stake. After the first double, only the player who accepted it may double next. In turn, if he has doubled and his double has been accepted, his opponent may double again; and so alternately, without limit. Where a double is not accepted, the player resigns and pays whatever the stake amounts to at that stage of the game.

Some players use also an automatic double. This occurs during the throw for the first play, the stake being doubled automatically each time the throws of the single die by each player are a tie Since this forces play for higher stakes, many consider it objectionable.

RECOMMENDED OPENING MOVES.—The following are recommended as the safest and best plays on the opening throws. (A player's bar point is his 7 point, just beyond the bar and outside his inner table.)

Double 6's: 2 men from opponent's 1 point to his bar point; 2 men from his 12 point to player's bar point. A powerful opening throw.

Double 5's: 2 men from opponent's 12 point to player's 3 point. A weak opening move. Any held point beyond a player's 3 point practically puts the pieces too far to maneuver.

Double 4's: 2 men from opponent's 1 point to his 5 point; 2 men from his 12 point to player's 9 point. The second best opening, when doubles are thrown.

Double 3's: 2 men from opponent's 1 point to his 4 point; 2 men from player's 8 point to his 5 point. A good opener.

Double 2's: 2 men from opponent's 1 point to his 5 point. A good move.

Double 1's: 2 men from player's 8 point to his bar point; 2 men from his 6 point to his 5 point. The best of all openings.

6-5: 1 man from opponent's 1 point to his 12 point. Called "Lover's Leap." A good opener.

6-4: 2 men from opponent's 1 point to his 5 point and bar point. A poor throw.

6-3: 2 men from opponent's 1 point to his 4 point and bar point. A poor throw.

6-2: 2 men from opponent's 1 point to his 3 point and bar point. A poor throw.

6-1: 1 man from opponent's 12 point to player's bar point; 1 from player's 8 point to his bar point. The second best throw with uneven dice.

5-4: 1 man from opponent's 1 point to his 5 point; 1 man from opponent's 12 point to player's 8 point. A poor throw.

5-3: 1 man each from player's 8 and 6 points to his 3 point. A mediocre throw, like double 5's; too far to maneuver.

5-2: 2 men from opponent's 12 point to player's 11 and 8 points. A poor throw.

5-1: 1 man from opponent's 1 point to his bar point. A poor throw.

4-3: 2 men from opponent's 1 point to his 5 and 4 points. A poor throw.

4-2: 2 men from player's 8 and 6 points to his 4 point. A good throw.

4-1: 2 men from opponent's 1 point to his 5 and 2 points. Poor.

3-2: 2 men from opponent's 1 point to his 4 and 5 points. Poor.

3-1: 1 man each from player's 8 and 6 points to his 5 points. The best throw with uneven dice.

2-1: 1 man from opponent's 1 point to his 4 point. The worst throw.

From these recommended throws, several facts are obvious. The best point to hold is your own 5 point; second best, opponent's 5 point; third best, your bar point; fourth best, opponent's bar point. At each move of the opponent, the advantage of these throws alters. The recommended throw for double 1's, for instance, becomes highly unwise if the opponent has moved a man to your 2 point, since it exposes a blot on your 8 point, within a 6 throwing range of your opponent. The same is true of all blots when placed within easy range. Held points, the more the better, are always wise.

CHANCES.—Here is the table of odds against being hit by any given throw of the dice, provided the space between the blot and the opponent's man is clear. If the player has one or more held points between his blot and the opponent's man, the odds against the blot being hit are greatly increased.

2 to 1	against being hit by a	1
2 to 1	"	2
3 to 2	"	3
7 to 5	"	4
7 to 5	"	5
Even	"	6
5 to 1	"	7
5 to 1	"	8
6 to 1	"	9
11 to 1	"	10
17 to 1	"	11
11 to 1	"	12
35 to 1	"	16, 20 or 24

Knowing these odds will aid the player in deciding his course if forced to leave a blot. The chances of reentering an opponent's table after any man has been placed on the bar are:

35 to 1,	if the opponent has	5	free points
8 to 1	"	4	"
3 to 1	"	3	"
5 to 4	"	2	"
4 to 9	"	1	"

These chances apply to any given throw, and knowing them aids a player in deciding whether to take a chance and risk being hit.

HOW TO SCORE BACKGAMMON PLAYS

The method of scoring Backgammon, for matches, tournaments, instruction, and permanent record, was originated in 1937 by Gloria Goddard and Clement Wood. This makes it possible, for the first time, to record games played by the masters for subsequent study; and to teach the game play by play, with play by play discussion of the reasons for or against various possible moves.

The 12 points in Black's inner and outer tables (see diagram, Backgammon: I) are numbered, right to left, B1, B2, B3, B4, up to B12; those in white's tables, W1 up to W12. The throw of the dice is recorded to the left: 3-1, 6-6, etc. For throws except doubles, if two men are moved, this is scored (in a 4-3 throw, for instance), B1-B4; B1-B5. If one man is moved the full distance, this is scored (as in a 3-2 throw) W6-W3-W1 or W6-W4-W1. When doubles are thrown, each move made by the one, two, three or four men moved is similarly scored. If several pieces are moved together, their number is expressed to the left of the space they move from; as (in a 5-5 throw) 3 B8-B3. Other symbols are: PU—pickup; BO—bear off; Out—man on bar, unable to enter; Out —same, because of a solid side prime in the inner table; W6 etc.—man on bar enters on the point encircled. If doubling is used, each double is indicated by a D. The summary at the end of the game includes who won; whether a single, double, or triple game, etc.; and the number of opponent's men left on at the end of the game, and their position: whether in the player's inner table, one of the outer tables, opponent's inner table, or on the bar.

A typical game, fully scored, with notes on the more important plays, is as follows:

Game No. ....

White—Player		Black—Player	
Throw	*Plays*	*Throw*	*Plays*
		2-1	W12-B10[1]
4-3	B1-B4; B1-B5		
		5-4	W12-B8; B10-B6
6-5	B4-B10; B5-B10[2]		
		6-1	W12-B7; B8-B7[3]
6-4	B10-W9; B12-W9		
		4-2	B8-B4; B6-B4
5-3	B10-W10; B12-W10		
		4-2	W1-W3; W1-W5
5-2	B12-W8-W6		
		5-3	B8-B3; B6-B3
3-2	W6-W4-W1		
		6-2	W3-W5; B8-B2
6-3	W8-W2; W6-W3		
		6-4	W5-W11-B10
6-1	W10-W4-W3[4]		
		5-5	W5-W10 PU; B7-B2; 2 B6-B1
6-5	B5 ; W8-W2		

Game No. . . . .

White—Player		Black—Player	
Throw	*Plays*	*Throw*	*Plays*
		5-1	B10-B5 PU-B4[5]
5-2	B5 ; B5-B7 PU		
		6-1	W1 PU; W12-B7 PU
5-2	B5 ; 1 out		
		3-3	W12-B10-B7; W1-W4-W7
5-2	B5 ; W8-W6		
		6-5	W7-W12-B7
3-1	B12-W10 PU-W9		
		5-4	W5 ; B7-B3
4-3	B5-B9-B12		
		6-3	W5-W11-B11
3-1	B12-W12; B9-B6		
		4-3	B11-B7-B4
5-3	B5-B10-W12		
		6-3	B7-B1; B7-B4
6-1	W12-W7-W6		
		6-3	BO 6, 3[6]
6-1	W12-W11; W9-W3[7]		

Game No. . . . .

White—Player		Black—Player	
Throw	*Plays*	*Throw*	*Plays*
		5-2	BO 2; B6-B1
5-3	W11-W6; W9-W6		
		6-6	4 BO 4
6-2	W12-W6; BO 2		
		6-4	BO 4, 3
3-2	BO 3, 2		
		6-3	BO 3, 2
6-5	BO 6; W6-W1		
		6-2	2 BO 1
4-3	BO 3; W6-W2		
		6-3	2 BO 1

	Won by	*Extra Games*	*Opponent's Men on*
Game No.	Black		10

1—The preferred opening is W1-W4. This is more aggressive, showing an aim at a blocking game.

2—Forming a strong held point. White is playing the position game.

3—Although White is apparently escaping, Black builds toward a side prime, not abandoning his blocking game.

4—This dangerous exposure in a 5 range loses the game. Either W10-W4; W10-W9 or W9-W3; W9-W8 would have been wiser.

5—A bounce-to-safety pickup, very valuable.

6—If White had played his second last throw, 5-3, differently, Black could only have borne off one piece here.

7—Probably W9-W8 is preferable to W12-W11.

When a match is completed, a summary score is prepared of the results of all the games in the match, similar to the one-line summary at the end of the scoring of this game.

PLAYBACKGAMMON, DUPLICATE BACKGAMMON

Playbackgammon or Duplicate Blackgammon was invented in 1937 by Gloria Goddard and Clement Wood. It increases the interest in each game; eliminates the unfair advantage of continuously lucky dice-throwing, while putting a premium on skilful play; it is the inevitable method to be used in Backgammon matches and tournaments; and furnishes the best instruction in play possible. The method of neutralizing the luck of the dice is by having each player in turn play the same dice, thus permitting actual matching of skill.

The First Round.—A regular game of Backgammon is played, and is scored throw by throw on an improvised or printed scorecard thus: The dice-throws are recorded in the first columns of White's and Black's side of the scorecard. In the column headed "First Round," pickups (PU), bearing off (BO), and the other incidents of the game are scored, as explained in the section How to Score Backgammon Plays. A line across the scorecard marks the ending of the First Round. At the end, the winner of the game is marked down; whether or not extra games are won; and the number and position of opponent's men left on. If doubling is used, this is scored (D) in the same columns.

THE PLAYBACK.—After an interval, either on the same or a subsequent evening, the Playback occurs. In this, White plays the dice already thrown by Black during the First Round, and Black plays the dice that White threw. The numbers are read off to the players; or a concealing card or sheet of paper is moved down the score of the first round, revealing only one throw at a time. Pick-ups and other incidents of the game are now recorded in the columns headed Playback. At the end, the details of winning are scored as above. Finally, a recapitulation gives the First Rounds and Playbacks of all the games in the match. If extra throws of the dice are needed to complete a game, as often happens, the original player of White throws these for White, and the original Black for Black. A typical scorecard is:

PLAYBACKGAMMON—*Scorecard*

Game No. . . . .

White—Player			Black—Player		
Throw	*First Round*	*Playback*	*Throw*	*First Round*	*Playback*

&c.

Game No.	*Won by*	*Extra Games*	*Opponent's Men on*
First Round			
Playback			

Recapitulation

Game	*First Round*	*Extra Games*	*Opponent's Men on*	*Playback*	*Extra Games*	*Opponent's Men on*
1.						
2.						
3.						
4.						
5.						

Total Games Won: White........ Black........

Total Points Won: White........ Black........

SCORING.—Each single game counts 1 point; double games, 2; triple, 3; double games, the number of games (1, 2, 3) won, multiplied by the doubling figure: 2, 4, 8, 16, 32, 64, etc. This applies to both First Round and Playback. If each player wins the same number of points on a game in both First Round and Playback, the player whose opponent has the largest number of men on in a single game wins 1 point; the player whose opponent has the largest number of men outside of his inner table, in a double game, wins 1 point; the player whose opponent has the largest number of men in opponent's inner table, or, if any are on the bar, the largest number on the bar, in a triple game, wins 1 point. If there is a tie in any of these cases, the actual count of total numbers needed to bear off (6 for a man on the 6 point, 24 for a man on opponent's 1 point, 25 for the bar, etc.) is taken, and the player whose opponent needs the largest total to bear off wins 1 point. Absolute ties must be played off.

ROUND ROBINS.—Playbackgammon gains in interest, when played as a round robin of three or more players. One game played in a round robin of three players means 6 games: A vs. B and their playback, A vs. C and their playback, B vs. C and their playback.

With four players, a round robin of one game calls similarly for 12 games to be played; with five players, one of 20 games, etc. With four or more players, the first game can be scored with carbon paper, and two tables can be run thereafter, playing the same dice both ways between each pair of players. Thus the best 3 out of 5 games, for 3 players, calls for 30 games; for 4 players, 60 games; for 5 players, 100 games, etc.

Playbackgammon Parties.—Playbackgammon parties may use round robins of three or more players at each table; or may progress by individual winners in elimination contests, as in many duplicate card games. Or each player may play 1, 3 or 5 games against each other player, with playbacks. A Playbackgammon tournament may be conducted by either of the two last mentioned methods; or by round robins of three or more players at each table, the highest one or two moving up, until by elimination the champion is selected.

Subsequent Playbacks.—Subsequent playbacks furnish the most fascinating and instructive aspect of the game. When the throws have been entirely forgotten, as a week later, the games once scored may be played over and played back. Here comes the major surprise of the game: the enormous difference a differing play on any throw of the dice may make in the result of the game. The dice thrown in certain games may mean victory if played as a position game, and defeat if played as a running, blocking, or back game. This cannot be known in advance. One game may result in anything from a single to a triple game for either side, depending on crucial plays. This is most thrilling when complete scoring is done of each First Round and Playback, and the causes of victory or defeat analyzed. Since the same dice are played each time by each player, the accident of lucky dice is eliminated in the result.

Here is a typical game and its playback, without full scoring. On the simpler First Round, White won a single game. On the playback, Black's pickups at the right time won for him a double game.

Game No. . . . .

White—Player			Black—Player		
Throw	*1st R.*	*PB*	*Throw*	*1st R.*	*PB*
			4-4		
6-3					
			6-2	PU	
4-1					
			6-3		
2-2					
			4-1	PU	
5-5					
			3-3		PU
6-3		out			
			6-1		
5-2		out			
			5-1		
6-3		out			
			5-3		
4-4		out			
			4-1		
4-1		PU			
			2-1		PU
6-2		out			
			5-4		
3-1					
			6-6		
2-1	PU	PU			
			6-1	out	PU
4-2		out			
			6-3	out	
4-1					
			2-2	out	
6-3		out			
			6-1	out	
6-1					
			6-4	out	
3-1	BO				

Game No. ....

White—Player			Black—Player		
Throw	*1st R.*	*PB*	*Throw*	*1st R.*	*PB*
			6-1	out	BO
4-2					
			2-1	out	
3-2					
			5-3		
3-2		PU			
			6-1		
4-3					
			2-1		
6-5					
			6-3		
4-2					
			5-2		
4-3					
			6-5		
5-3					
			6-5		PU
3-2					
			6-6		
5-2					
			2-1		
6-2					
			4-2		
6-3					
			6-1		
3-2					
			5-4		
6-6					

	Won by	*Extra Games*	*Opponent's Men on*
1st R.	White		10
PB	Black	Double	15 & 2

And here is the fully scored Playback of the game already given under the section, How to Score Backgammon. That was won by Black, with 10 of White's men on; this is won by Black, with only 5 men on White's inner table at the end. This means that the former Black won by 5 men, giving him 1 point. This victory can be settled for by point score, or by so much per man remaining.

Game No. ....—Playback.

White—Player		Black—Player	
Throw	*Plays*	*Throw*	*Plays*
		2-1	W1-W3-W4
4-3	B1-B4; B1-B5		
		5-4	W1-W5; W12-B8
6-5	B4-B10; B5-B10[1]		
		6-1	W5-W11-W12[2]
6-4	B12-B7-W3[3]		
		4-2	W12-B9-B7[4]
5-3	B12-W8; W6-W3		
		4-2	W12-B9-B7
5-2	B12-W8-W6		
		5-3	W4-W6-W12
3-2	W8-W6; W8-W5		
		6-2	W12-B7-B5
6-3	W8-W2; W6-W3[5]		
		6-4	W12-B7; B8-B4
6-1	W8-W2; W6-W5		
		5-5	3 B8-B3; B7-B2
6-5	B10-W10; B10-B9		
		5-1	B7-B2; B7-B6
5-2	W10-W5; W9-W7		
		6-1	W12-B7; B5-B4
5-2	B12-W8; B12-W11		
		3-3	W12-B10-B7-B4; B7-B4
5-2	W11-W6; W8-W6		
		6-5	BO 6; B6-B1

Game No. ....—Playback.

White—Player		Black—Player	
Throw	*Plays*	*Throw*	*Plays*
3-1	W7-W6; BO 3		
		5-4	BO 4; B6-B1
4-3	W5-W1; BO 3		
		6-3	BO 6, 3
3-1	BO 3, 1		
		4-3	BO 4, 3
5-3	W6-W3; BO 5		
		6-3	BO 6, 3
6-1	BO 6; W2-W1		
		6-3	BO 6; B4-B1
6-1	BO 6-1		
		5-2	BO 4, 2
5-3	BO 5, 3		
		6-6	BO 2, 3 BO 1

	Won by	*Extra Games*	*Opponent's Men on*
Playback	Black		5

1—An excellent held point.

2—A running game. It wins in this case. W12-B7; B8-B7 is probably better.

3—White adopts a running game in answer. B10-W9; B12-W9 is probably better.

4—Black continues the running game. B8-B4; B6-B4 would be better.

5—Instead of the inexplicable W6-W3, W8-W6 would be better.

RUSSIAN BACKGAMMON

In this variation, the men belonging to both players start off the board, and are entered by throws of the dice on the same board, by the reverse system to that by which they are borne off in Backgammon. The home table for both players is the one directly opposite the entering table. All the men move in the same direction. Bearing off is the same as in regular Backgammon.

After a choice of entering table and men, as in Backgammon, the winner throws both his dice to open play. If his first throw is a double, he enters 4 men on the point thrown. After the first throw, the players are entitled to play both faces of the doublets. After playing the first four, he turns the dice over and plays the four on the reverse. If all of the first four cannot be played, he cannot play the reverse four. After the doublets, the player is entitled to cast again; if doublets are thrown a second time, both sides of these are played, and the player continues to cast and play until he does not secure doublets, in which case he plays the numbers thrown, and the throw passes. If, at any time, all four numbers on the reverse side cannot be played, the player loses his second cast.

Blots are hit, as in the regular game, and when a man is on the bar, he must be reentered as above; before he is reentered, the player may not move another man. A player may not enter the entering board on any point held by his opponent. Once a player has entered 2 or more men, he may play these before entering any others; or he may alternate playing these and entering others at will, except in the case of a man on the bar. Men must be borne off by the exact number cast; that is, with no man on the 6 point, a throw of 6 will not permit bearing a man on a lower number. A player may move down in the home board, as in regular Backgammon; otherwise, the rules of regular Backgammon apply.

TABARD BACKGAMMON

In this variation, the men are set up at the start of the game on the same points as in regular Backgammon, but all of White's men are set up in Black's inner and outer tables, none of his men being in his own tables; the same number of pieces are on the same points as in the regular game; similarly, all of Black's men are set up opposite these, in White's inner and outer tables. Otherwise, the game is played as regular Backgammon.

PARCHEESI

Parcheesi (also spelled Parchesi, Parchisi, Pachisi) is a variation of Backgammon originating in India, for four players. In the original form, it was played on a cross-shaped board or cloth, with six cowrie shells for dice. Each player had a cone of some distinguishing color. The object of the game was to move the cone along the spaces into which the arms of the cross are divided, and into the center.

In the European variation of the game, small colored disks, of pasteboard or some similar material, are used instead of cones, and dice instead of cowrie shells. Each player has four of these disks, which start in the four corner circles of the board, colored the same as the disks. By throws of the dice, these men are brought out of their circles and moved around the spaces down and around each arm of the cross-shaped board, until they have made a complete circuit, gone up the central spaces, and entered the center. The first player to finish wins. The detailed rules accompany each set.

CHESS

Equipment: The board is the same as that used in Checkers—a square board containing 64 smaller squares, the alternate squares being black and red, or any two contrasting colors. Each player has 16 men: 1 king, 1 queen, 2 bishops, 2 knights, 2 castles or rooks, and 8 pawns. One player's men are of one color, the other's of a contrasting color. For convenience, they will be referred to hereafter as black and white. Here is the standard appearance of the various pieces, and the symbols used in print to designate the black and the white pieces:

Black

king queen bishop knight rook pawn

king queen bishop knight rook pawn

White

Chess: I

The Start.—Choice of men for the first move is drawn for, one player presenting to the other player a black pawn concealed in one hand and a white pawn in the other. The other player chooses one, this determining his color. The white moves first. The right of first move thereafter alternates with each game. The men are moved alternately until one king is checkmated, or the game is declared a draw.

The Set-Up.—The corner and square on each player's right must be of the light color. The pieces are placed as in the diagram, Chess: II. Queen is placed on her color: thus the black queen is on the right center of the player with the black pieces, and the white queen is on the same file, but to the left center of the player with the white pieces. The kings are placed on the other central file beside their queens; and to each side a bishop, a knight and a rook are placed in that order. The 8 pawns occupy the second row in front of the major pieces.

The vertical lines of squares extending between the players are called files, and are named by each player from his piece standing on the end row when the game opens. Thus, left to right, White's eight files are named queen's rook's file (QR), queen's knight's (QK), queen's bishop's (QB), queen's (Q), king's (K), king's bishop's (KB), king's knight's (KKt), and king's rook's (KR). From left to right on Black's sides, his files are named the reverse of this, starting with KR and ending with

QR. Pawns are indicated by P. K4 means king's fourth square QR3, queen's rook's 3rd square, etc.

Black

QR QQt QB Q K KB KKt KB

QR QKt QB Q K KB KKt KR

White

Chess: II

THE MOVES.—*Pawns* move only in one direction, straight forward, one square at a time. There are two exceptions to this. A pawn's first move may consist of 2 squares straight forward, instead of one. A pawn captures only on the next diagonal square on either side. On reaching the eighth row, a pawn may become any piece, except the king. It is usually made a queen; and this is called queening the pawn. When a pawn has crossed the middle of the board into the opponent's territory, it is called a *passed pawn.* If an adverse pawn attempts to pass this pawn by moving

2 squares on its first move, it may be captured *en passant,* that is, in passing.

The knight alone can jump over other pieces to reach the square to which it moves. Its move is 2 squares away in any file or row, then one square at right angles to the line of the first 2 squares. Its move always ends on a different file and row from those on which it started. It is the only major piece that can move before the pawn row is broken, at the beginning of the game. Its threat is greatest when it is near the center of the board; for then it threatens 8 other squares. It can threaten any piece, except an opposing knight, while remaining safe from attack itself. It and all the pieces except pawns can move forward or backward with equal facility.

The bishop moves along the diagonal squares of the color it first occupies, any distance that is clear. The maximum move of bishops, rooks and queens is 8 squares. Each player thus has one bishop permitted to move on the black diagonals, and one on the white; and these may never move to the other color.

The rook or *castle* may move any number of squares that are clear, along the vertical file or horizontal row that it occupies.

The queen combines the moves of bishop and rook. She can move any clear distance along any file, row or diagonal she occupies.

The king has the same move as the queen's, limited to one square only in any direction. The king may capture any piece on any of these 8 adjoining squares, but may not himself be captured. Thus he cannot capture a piece protected by another piece. This is called moving into a check. For the same reason, kings cannot approach within one square of each other.

Castling the king may occur only when the intervening pieces between king and either rook have been removed, provided that neither the king nor the rook has previously been moved; that the king does not pass over an intervening square menaced by any piece; and that the king is not in check at the moment of castling. Castling consists in moving the king 2 squares toward the rook, and then placing the rook on the other side of the king.

Capturing.—There is no jumping, as in Checkers. A man capturing another piece occupies in its place the square previously occupied by the captured piece, which is removed from the board.

Check.—When a king is menaced by an opposing piece, so that if he were not a king he could be captured on the next move, the opponent says "Check." The king must now either move out of check; interpose a piece to break the check; or take the menacing piece. If he cannot do any of these things, he is checkmated, and the game is lost.

It is never compulsory to capture a piece; except in the case of a king, who has no other way of getting out of check.

A smothered mate occurs when movement of the king is completely blocked by his own men, and one opponent's man, as for instance a knight, checkmates him.

Perpetual check, when the king cannot get away from being checked on any square to which he moves, but cannot be checkmated, is a draw.

A stalemate occurs when the king is not at the moment in check, but cannot move into any square without moving into check; and when the player has no other piece on the board free to move except the king. Stalemate is a draw.

Miscellaneous.—Moves are denoted in writing by the symbol for the piece or pawn to be moved, followed by a hyphen and the symbol for the space to which it is moved: P-K4, Kt-KB3. White's move is always given first, and Black's second. The symbol X between the symbols for pieces signifies that the former takes the latter.

A move is completed when the hand is withdrawn from the man moved. When an adversary's man is touched, unless it obviously needs rearranging and the player says the equivalent of "I arrange," it must immediately be captured, if it can be done. When it cannot be captured, the offending player must move his king, if that can be done. For playing a man to a square to which it cannot legally be moved, the opponent may require a proper move of the man, or that the king be moved. For touching more than one man of an opponent, the latter may choose which one is to be captured. If only one can be captured, the opponent may choose whether this be captured, or the king moved. If neither can be captured, the opponent may require the king to be moved. For attempting to castle illegally, the opponent may require the offending player to move either the king or the rook.

A player moving into check may be required to move his king elsewhere, or to make some other move of his own selection. For uncovering a king and discovering check on his own king, the player must either move the man touched illegally, or move the king, at his opponent's option. If neither can be done, there is no penalty. While in check, for touching or moving a man which does not cover the check, the player may be required to cover with another piece, or move the king, as the opponent chooses.

While the hand remains upon a man, it may be moved to any square that it commands, except such squares as may have been touched by it during the deliberation on the move. If all these have been touched, the opponent may select to which it is to be moved.

Where a player persists in repeating a particular check or series of checks, or any particular line of play which does not advance the game, or if a game-ending is doubtful as to whether it is a win or a draw, either player may demand judgment of an umpire as to its being a proper game to be determined as drawn at the end of 50 additional moves on either side, with no checkmate. At the end of these 50 moves, the other player may demand an additional 50 moves. At the end of this, unless checkmate has been effected, the game is a draw.

A time limit for each move shall be agreed upon. The beginning of each player's time shall be registered each time; and, if the agreed time limit is exceeded, the offending player forfeits the game.

Famous Openings.—A gambit means the sacrifice of a pawn or piece, or several successively, for an advantage in position. Among famous chess openings and responses are:

Alekhine's Defense: P-K4, Kt-KB3; P-K5, Kt-Q4; P-QB4, Kt-Kt3; P-Q4, P-Q3.

Caro-Kann Defense: P-K4, P-QB3; (usually) P-Q4, P-Q4

Evans Gambit: P-K4, P-K4; Kt-KB3, Kt-QB3; B-B4, B-B4; P-QKt4, B x KtP. ("x" means "takes.")

Falkbeer Counter Gambit: P-K4, P-K4; P-KB4, P-Q4; KP x P, P-K5.

French Defense: P-K4, P-K3; P-Q4, P-Q4.

Giuco Piano: P-K4, P-K4; Kt-KB3, Kt-QB3; B-B4, B-B4.

Queen's Gambit: P-Q4, P-Q4; P-QB4, P x P.

Queen's Pawn's Game: P-Q4, P-Q4.

Réti's Opening: Kt-KB3, P-Q4 or Kt-KB3.

Ruy Lopez: P-K4, P-K4; Kt-KB3, Kt-QB3; B-Kt5.

Sicilian Defense: P-K4, P-QB4.

CORRESPONDENCE and CONSULTATION CHESS

Chess may be played by correspondence, with or without consultation; or with consultation. In either case, the especial rules regulating the game must be drawn up in advance, and adhered to by both players.

THE KNIGHT'S TOUR

This is a chess problem, the object being to place the knight on any square on the board, and then move it so that it touches every square on the board only once, and as its last move returns to the starting-point. There are a number of ways of doing this, one of the simplest being:

14	29	34	55	12	27	24	49
35	56	13	28	33	50	11	26
30	15	54	51	58	25	48	23
41	36	57	32	61	52	63	10
16	31	40	53	64	59	22	47
37	42	1	60	19	62	9	6
2	17	44	39	4	7	46	21
43	38	3	18	45	20	5	8

CHECKERS, DRAUGHTS

EQUIPMENT: The board is the same as that used in Chess—a square board containing 64 smaller squares, the alternate squares being black and red, or any two contrasting colors. The corner end square on each player's right must be of the light color. Each player has 12 men, one set being dark and one light, turned, and round, not less than 1 inch nor more than 1¼ inches in diameter. For purposes of convenience. the two sets of colors shall hereafter be referred to as black and white.

THE START.—Choice of men is drawn for, one player presenting to the other player a black man concealed in one hand and a white man in the other. The other player chooses one, thus determining his color for the first game. Black always makes the first move. In games thereafter, the players alternate colors at the beginning of each game.

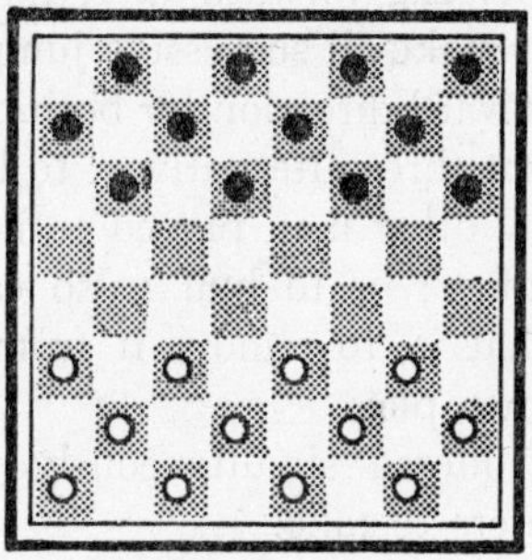

Checkers: I

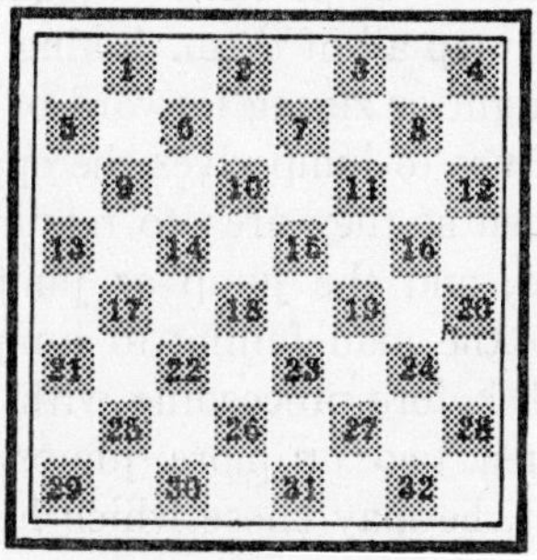

Checkers: II

THE SET-UP.—The black men must be placed on the 12 black squares nearest the black player, and the white men must be placed on the 12 black squares nearest the white player, as in Diagram I. For convenience, the squares are numbered from 1 to 32, as in Diagram II.

THE PLAY.—The opening move is made by Black's moving any of his foremost men one square, along one of the black diagonal lines of squares. Black's foremost men are on 9, 10, 11 and 12; one of them must be moved to an adjoining square, among 13, 14, 15 or 16. To denote a move, two numbers separated by a hyphen are given. Thus 11-15 indicates that a man (which must be black, at the opening set-up) has been moved from 11 to 15.

Thereafter, the players move one man alternately, always along the black diagonal lines, toward the opponent's back line. Moves are made to unoccupied black squares. When a man reaches the opponent's back line, it becomes a king, and the opponent places a captured man on top of it, to indicate this. It is indicated on a checkers diagram by drawing a circle around the man. A king can move forward or backward along the black diagonal lines; and, in jumping, both ways in succession on the same jump.

If a man is next to an opponent's man ahead of his progress, with a blank black space adjoining ahead in the same direction, he must jump this man, landing in the unoccupied space, and removing the opponent's man from the board. If there are several successive jumps in a straight or zigzag forward direction, he must jump all of them. A king must make all successive jumps in a straight or zigzag forward or backward direction, or both.

Failure to jump gives the opponent three alternatives: to leave the men as they are; to require any other man played to be replaced, and the jump or jumps taken; or to huff (also called blow) the man failing to jump—that is, to remove it from the board, before proceeding with his own play.

When two or more jumps are offered simultaneously to a player, he may chose which he prefers to take.

Time of Play.—When a player delays five minutes without playing, "Time" must be called; and if the move is not made in one additional minute, the game is forfeited for delay. When there is only one way of jumping one or more men, time shall be called at the end of one minute; and if the move is not made in one additional minute, the game is forfeited for delay.

Miscellaneous.—Either player may arrange any man in the center of its proper square, by giving notice that he is doing so; otherwise, he is warned at the first touch, and at the second forfeits the game. In all other circumstances, any piece touched must be played, or the opponent may dictate the offending player's next move. If any part of a playable man is moved over an angle of the square on which it is stationed, the move must be completed in that direction. A jumping play is completed when the hand is withdrawn from the man played, whether all possible jumps have been completed or not. All possible jumps must be completed, or this becomes a failure to jump. The man becoming a king completes his move on reaching the back or king row, and cannot continue jumps backward on this move, or be huffed for failing to do so.

Win and Draw.—A player wins when he has removed all his opponent's men from the board, or else so pinned them up that they cannot move. When neither player can do this, it is a draw. Where only a few men remain, either party may insist that the other win in 40 moves (unless 20 is the number agreed on), or declare the game a draw.

Conduct of Players.—In this, as in most other games, neither player is permitted to do anything that might annoy or distract the attention of the other: such as making signs or sounds, pointing or hovering over the board, or leaving the room during play without permission being granted. After warning, the player so offending forfeits the game. Any spectator giving warning in any way shall be ordered from the room.

The Standard Openings.—The most famous standard openings are:

Alma: 11-15, 23-19; 8-11, 22-17; 3-8.
Ayrshire Lassie: 11-15, 24-20.
Bristol: 11-16, 24-20; 16-19.
Center: 11-15, 23-19; 8-11, 22-17; 15-18.
Cross: 11-15, 23-18.
Defiance: 11-15, 23-19; 9-14, 27-23.
Double Corner: 9-14.
Dyke: 11-15, 22-17; 15-19.
Fife: 11-15, 23-19; 9-14, 22-17; 5-9.
Glasgow: 11-15, 23-19; 8-11, 22-17; 11-16.

Laird and Lady: 11-15, 23-19; 8-11, 22-17; 9-13.
Maid of the Mill: 11-15, 22-17; 8-11, 17-13; 15-18.
Old Fourteenth: 11-15, 23-19; 8-11, 22-17; 4-8.
Paisley: 11-16, 24-19.
Second Double Corner: 11-15, 24-19.
Single Corner: 11-15, 22-18.
Souter: 11-15, 23-19; 9-14, 22-17; 6-9.
Switcher: 11-15, 21-17.
Whilter: 11-15, 23-19; 9-14, 22-17; 7-11.
Will-o'-the-Wisp: 11-15, 23-19; 9-13.

SPANISH CHECKERS

This is the same as American checkers, except that (1) the board is placed with the corner end square to the player's left of the light color—the reverse of the position of the American board, as if it were seen in a mirror; (2) a king can move over any number of unoccupied squares on the same diagonal; and (3) where two or more groups of jumps offer, it is compulsory to take the jump which yields the largest number of jumped pieces.

ITALIAN CHECKERS

The Italian game was probably derived from the Spanish game. The king has the same move as the king in the American game. The maximum capture by jumping is compulsory. But the king is immune from capture by a man. The board is placed as in Spanish Checkers. The game is similar to the American game, until a player has a king.

POLISH DRAUGHTS

Polish Draughts was developed in Paris about 1721; it received its name from the fact that a Pole was one of its chief exponents at the beginning. It is played on a board of 100 squares, only the 50 dark squares being played on. The corner end square on each player's right must be of the light color. There are 20 men to each player. The men move forward, as in the American game; but they take forward or backward. A crowned man becomes a Queen or Dame, not a king. The Queen has the same move as the Spanish king, extended to the larger board. The maximum take is compulsory. In a capturing play, an uncrowned man may jump into and out of the back or king row, without being crowned, if further pieces remain to be taken. The huff or blow has been abolished. In capturing, the Queen takes any unguarded man or queen on any diagonal she commands, leaping over the captured piece and remaining on any unoccupied square of the same diagonal beyond. If, however, there is another unguarded man or queen, she is bound to choose the diagonal on which it can be taken. A capturing Queen or man must take all of the adverse pieces that can possibly be taken. In view of the intricacy of certain moves, it is usual to remove each piece as it is taken. As sometimes played, the huff or blow is used as in the American game.

GERMAN DRAUGHTS, DAMENSPIEL, MINOR POLISH DRAUGHTS

This is the same as Polish Draughts, played on a board of 64 squares.

RUSSIAN DRAUGHTS, SHASHKI

This variation of Polish Draughts is identical with German Draughts, except that the choice of capture is free, as in the American game. Also, a man reaching the back or Queen (king) row becomes at once a king, and continues to function as one.

MONTREAL DRAUGHTS, QUEBEC DRAUGHTS

This is a major form of the Polish game, with 144 squares on the board, of which 72 are played on; and 30 men to a side. It is played also by British soldiers in India.

TURKISH DRAUGHTS

This is played on a 64 square board. The men move to the side or forward, but not backward, in a straight direction, instead of diagonally. All 64 squares are played on. There are 16 men to each side; none on the last row to start with, and 8 each on the 2nd and 3rd rows. Captures are done to the side or forward. The maximum take is compulsory; pieces are removed one by one when captured. The king has a sweep of any number of squares.

LOSING CHECKERS

In this variation (which can be applied to any game of checkers), the object of each player is to give away all his men first, or to get them so pinned up that he cannot move one of them. The player who does this first wins. Huffing and all other rules of regular Checkers apply to the losing game. It is similar to Nullos and the Hearts group, among card games.

GO BANG

Go Bang is a Japanese game, played on a square board containing 361 squares, 19 on each side. Two, three or four players are provided with counters of distinguishing colors. The object of the game is to get 5 of one player's counters in a row, vertically, horizontally or diagonally. The game bears some resemblance to Tit-Tat-Toe, and to the English game of Nine Men's Morris, Morelles or The Mill, played before Shakespeare's time.

MORELLES, THE MILL, NINE MEN'S MORRIS

The layout appears from the diagram. Each player is provided with 9 men, of distinguishing colors. Each places one man in turn upon the layout; the object being to get 3 men in a line by occupying any of the intersections, corners, or meetings of the lines on a sheet of paper.

The first to succeed getting 3 men in a line can remove from the board any one of his adversary's men that he chooses; except that he cannot remove one of three already in a line, unless there are no others on the layout. As soon as all 9 men are entered, the player can move to any adjoining space, provided it is vacant. The moment a new line of 3 is formed in this way, an opponent's

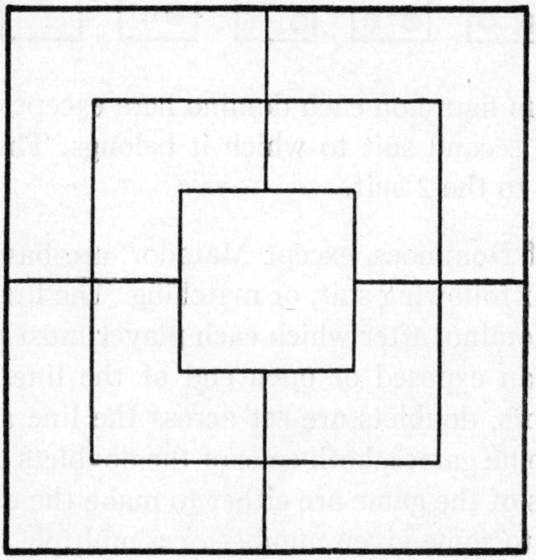

Morelles: I

man can be lifted. Sometimes one player can form and reform two lines alternately several times.

This continues until one player has only 3 men left. Any of these 3 men can then hop over to any vacant square on the board. As soon as an opponent is reduced to 3 men, he also can hop. The moment any player is reduced to only 2 men, he loses the game.

DOMINOES

EQUIPMENT: A set of dominoes is described by the number of pips on the highest dominoe or "bone" in the set. The standard set is the double-six set, containing 28 bones. Some players use the double-nine set, which of course includes all the bones in the double-six set as well. In the double-six set, there are seven suits, each named after some number from six to blank. Except for the doublet, each bone in a suit belongs to another suit as well. Here is the six suit:

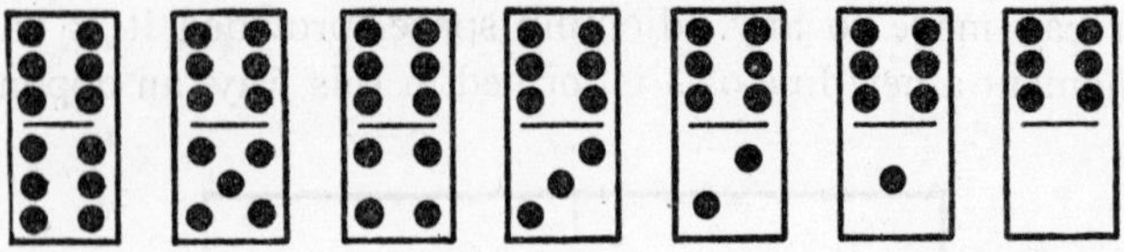

The bottom figure on each domino here except the double-six shows the second suit to which it belongs. Thus the 6-2 belongs also to the 2 suit.

All games of Dominoes, except Matador, are based entirely on the principle of following suit, or matching. The first player plays out a certain domino, after which each player must play a domino that matches an exposed or open end of the line. In all games except Matadors, doublets are set across the line at right angles to it; and in some games, both ends of the doublets may be played to. The objects of the game are either to make the ends of the line or lines equal to some given number or a multiple of it; to block the game so that the adversary cannot play; or to make both ends of the line the same. The player first getting rid of all his bones is "Domino."

At the beginning of any game, the dominoes are faced down and thoroughly stirred around to shuffle them. Each player then draws from the group the number of dominoes he requires for each game, with which to start. These dominoes may be stood on edge facing the player, or held in the hand, or both. It is usual to sort them into suits, as far as is possible. The player who has drawn the highest doublet usually plays or "sets" first.

ALL FIVES, or MUGGINS

Each player alternately draws a domino until he has 7 in all. The remaining bones are held on the side of the table, face down. This is called the boneyard, or bone pile. The player having the highest doublet plays it out, that is, "sets" it.

If the first doublet set is double-5, that counts 10 at once for the player playing it. The object is to play dominoes so that the sum of the numbers exposed on the ends of the line totals 5 or some multiple of 5; this at once scores that sum for the player playing the domino which completed the sum. After both sides of the first doublet set have been played to, the ends of this doublet may also be played to. After a doublet has been played to on one or both ends, all three or four ends of the line must be counted, in arriving at a sum that will score. Here is a position where the ends score 25:

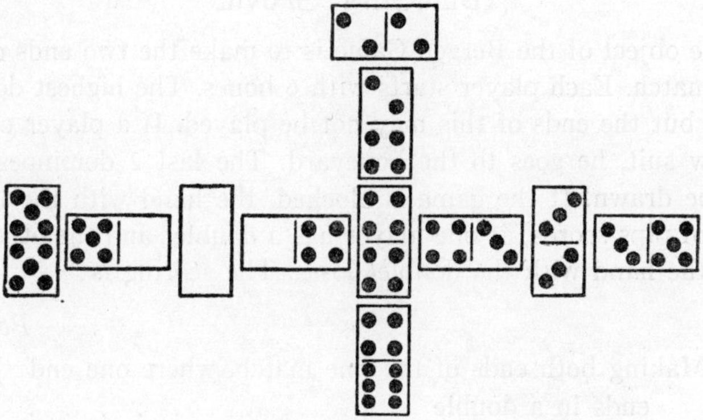

Only the first doublet set may be played from on all four sides. If a play entitles a player to claim some multiple of 5, and he fails to claim it, an opponent may say "Muggins," and score the sum for himself.

When a player is unable to follow suit, he must draw from the boneyard until he is able to play. The last 2 dominoes may not be drawn. If he so desires, a player may also draw in order to improve his hand, even when he could have followed suit. When a player plays his final bone, he says "Domino." The opponent or opponents then face up the dominoes they have left; and their pip value is added up, and the total scored to the player who went domino in this fashion: by scoring the nearest multiple of 5. Thus a 46 would be scored as 45; but a 49 would be scored as 50. The game is 100.

If the game is blocked, so that neither player can play, the pip value of the dominoes in the hand of each player is totalled, the lower score is deducted from the higher, and the difference is scored for the player with the lower sum.

ALL THREES

This is similar to All Fives; but the object of play is to make the sum of the end values on the lines 3, or a multiple of 3. The game is 60.

BERGEN GAME

The object of the Bergen Game is to make the two ends of the line match. Each player starts with 6 bones. The highest doublet sets; but the ends of this may not be played. If a player cannot follow suit, he goes to the boneyard. The last 2 dominoes may not be drawn. If the game is blocked, the hand with the lowest sum of pips scores; if one player has a doublet and the other has not, the hand with the doublet loses. The scoring is:

	Points
Making both ends of the line match, where one end ends in a double	3
Making both ends match, where neither ends in a double	2
When hands are blocked, lowest pip total; or hand without a doublet, if only one hand has doublet	1

The game is 15 points.

BLOCK GAME

This is played by two players, with hands of 7 bones each. Any domino may be set; right to set first should be drawn for by the players. The object is to block the adversary so that he cannot play further. There is no drawing from the boneyard. When a player cannot follow suit, he says "Go" and opponent continues to play. If he cannot follow suit, the player must continue to say "Go" each time his opponent plays a domino. If either player goes domino, he scores the sum of the pips remaining in the other player's hand. If the game is blocked and both have dominoes, the remaining dominoes in each hand are counted up and their difference scored to the lower hand.

DRAW GAME

This is a variation of the Block Game, in which a player, when it is his turn to play, may draw from the boneyard as many dominoes as he wishes, so long as the last 2 are not drawn. If a player cannot follow suit, he is required to draw until he can, so long as the last 2 bones are not drawn. This is true, even when there is no possibility that he can draw a playable domino. There is no playing from the ends of any doublet, in either this or the Block Game. The game is scored as in the Block Game.

SEBASTOPOL, or THE FORTRESS

This is a variation of the Block Game and the Draw Game. Double-6 sets; and nothing but 6's can be played until both sides and both ends of the Double-6 are played to, as in Diagram I. When the double-9 set is used, nothing but 9's can be played until there are eight ends open for play, as in Diagram II:

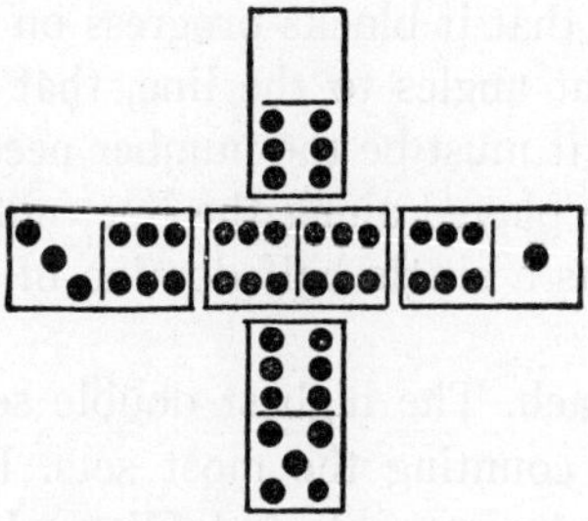

Sebastopol I

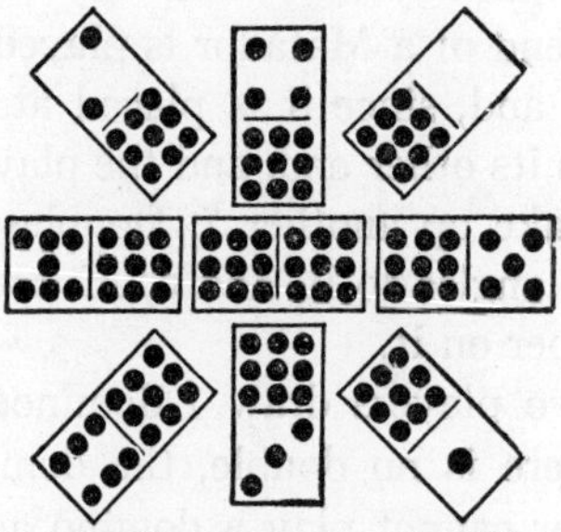

Sebastopol II

Four players compete, each drawing 7 dominoes. After the central fortress is completed, as in the diagrams, the game proceeds as in the ordinary Block Game or Draw Game.

POOL DOMINOES

Any number of players from three to six form a pool, to which each contributes an equal number of counters. They draw one domino apiece to decide who will have the first set, low winning. The dominoes are shuffled, and the players draw, one at a time, in rotation left to right, until there are 8 left in the boneyard. The player who has won the draw sets any domino he pleases. The ends of doublets may not be played to. When a player cannot follow suit, he says "Go." The first player to go domino wins the pool. If the game is blocked and no one can go domino, the hands are faced up, and the lowest count takes the pool. If two or more players tie, the pool is divided between them.

MATADOR GAME

This differs from all other domino games, in that adjoining dominoes do not match in suit; but the two adjoining numbers must in every case add up to 7. To a 6, a 1 must be played, and vice versa; to a 5, a 2; to a 4, a 3. Since no number from 1 through 6 can be played to a 0 to make 7, there are 4 especial dominoes, the trumps or Matadors, which can be played anywhere, at any time; and they alone can be played next to a blank. One end of a Matador is played so that it blocks progress on the line; and, since it is placed at right angles to the line, that exposes its other end, and the play to it must be the number needed to make up another 7. Doubles are played along the line, not at right angles to it, and count only as a single half domino of the number on it.

Two players draw 7 dominoes each. The highest double sets; if there is no double, the domino counting the most sets. If a player cannot play a domino adjoining an end of the line whose touching half makes up a 7, he must play a Matador, or draw until he gets a domino that will play: one completing a 7, or a Matador. The last 2 bones may not be drawn.

In the following instance, double-6 led. Double-1 was played next, 6 and 1 making 7—and doubles counting in play as single numbers. The play of a 1-4 made another 7 with the double-6. A 6-5 made another 7 with the double-1. A 3-2 completed a 7 with the exposed 4. The second player had neither a 5 nor a 2; but he had a 4-3, a Matador. He might play either end of this on either the 5 or the 2, blocking the line at that point. He played it to seal up the 5. This left the 4 exposed at one end of the line, and the 2 at the other. The leader completed a 7 by playing double-3 to the 4:

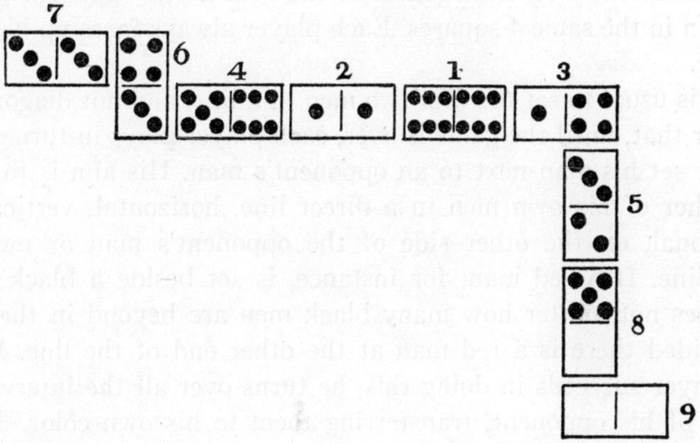

The next player drew a 5-0, and completed a 7 by playing it to the line ending with 2. The leader had been holding his double-0, the most powerful Matador, for just this emergency, and he now played it. Only a Matador can be played against it, and therefore this end of the line was blanked permanently, until a Matador is played.

When the game is blocked, or when a player makes domino, the hands are faced up, the one scoring less receiving either the difference between the hands, or, if he has gone domino, the total pip value of the opponent's hand. Game is usually 100. If a player can play and does not do so, he forfeits all right to any count from that hand. All blanks are valuable, since they seal an end of the line until a Matador is played there, and the double-0 is the most valuable bone of all.

The game is also often played by three or four players.

REVERSI

This is played on a board of 64 squares, 8 to each side: a checker-board will do. Each man has 32 men or counters, each counter being red on one side and black on the other.

The one who gets the first play (which may be determined by a player's calling which color is turned up unseen on one counter placed on the table by his opponent) places one of his counters on one of the 4 central squares of the board. His opponent places a man in the same 4 squares. Each player always faces up his own color.

It is usual to set the first two men in a line, and not diagonally. After that, until the game is over, each player plays in turn. Each must set his man next to an opponent's man. His aim is to have another of his own men in a direct line, horizontal, vertical, or diagonal, on the other side of the opponent's man or men on the line. If a red man, for instance, is set beside a black man, it does not matter how many black men are beyond in the line, provided there is a red man at the other end of the line. When a player succeeds in doing this, he turns over all the intervening men of his opponent, transferring them to his own color. Sometimes the placing of a man at an angle may turn two or three lines of the enemy at once.

As soon as each player has played out all 32 men, a count is made of each color then on the board. The player with the highest number of his color showing wins.

DICE GAMES

True dice are exact cubes, of uniform weight and material throughout. To test the numbering, when the 1 is on top and the odd numbers face you, the 3 should be on the left and the 5 on the right; when the 2 is on top and the even numbers face you, the 4 is on the left and the 6 on the right. A dice cup, usually of leather, is advantageous, but not necessary. The dice must be thrown level on the surface on which the play takes place. A dice landing on another is said to be cocked; one not landing level on the surface, and not on another die, is said to be fouled. Both cocked and fouled dice must be thrown again, without penalty.

CRAPS, or HAZARD

In this game, 2 dice are used, the players alternating with them as soon as each run of throws is completed. A betting limit should be set. The player casting the dice covers whatever bet, within the limit, the opponent makes. First throw may be determined by each player throwing 1 die, the highest winning first throw. Ties are thrown again until they are broken.

The player shakes the dice in his hand or the cup, and casts them fair on a flat surface. The total on the top surface of the 2 dice cast constitutes the throw. If the first throw is a 7 or an 11, this is called a natural or a nick, and immediately wins the bet, or 1 point. If a 2, a 3 or 12 is thrown, it is termed a crap; the thrower loses the bet, but retains the dice, and throws again.

If neither of these is cast first, or after either of them has been cast and scored, the next number thrown is called the point—that is, the number which the caster must make, to score, before a 7 is cast. A 2, 3, 11, 12 or any number not the point may be thrown, without penalty; the caster continuing to throw until his point is thrown, or a 7. If he throws his point before a 7 is thrown, he wins, and collects, and goes through the whole process again as if starting the game. If a 7 is thrown after a point has been arrived at to be thrown, the caster craps out, loses the money wagered, and the dice pass to the other player. This alternates as long as the game continues.

ACES IN THE POT

Each player starts with 2 counters. In rotation, each player makes a single throw with 2 dice. If he throws a 1, he puts 1 counter in the pot; if 2 1's, both counters. If he throws a 6, he passes 1 counter to the player on his left, as well as the dice. Double 6's pass both counters. Each player to the left throws in turn, until there is only 1 counter left out of the pot. As long as a player has no counter in front of him, he does not throw.

The player left with a single counter makes 3 consecutive throws. If he gets a 6, he passes the counter to the next man, who makes his 3 consecutive throws. This is continued until a player makes 3 throws without getting a 6; thereupon he wins the pot.

BASE BALL WITH DICE

I. Each player throws 3 dice. As long as he throws a 1, he scores a run. Every 1 is a run. If he fails to throw a 1, he is out Nine times out loses the game.

II. A layout is marked with the four bases of the diamond, marked 1, 2, 3 and 4 for the home plate. Each player in rotation throws a single die. If a 1, 2 or 3 is thrown, a marker is put on

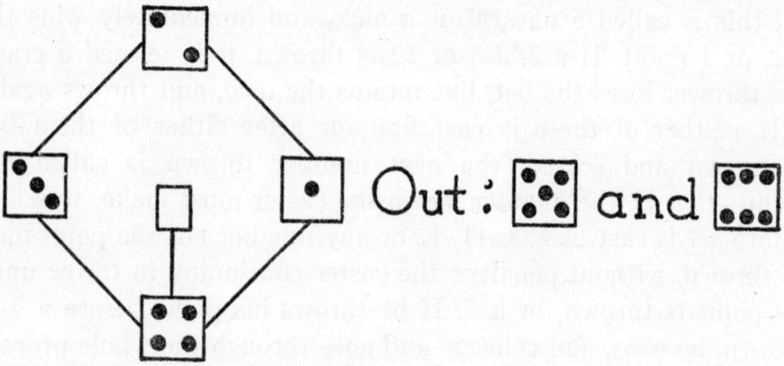

the appropriate base. A throw of 4 is a home run, bringing in all men on bases. Subsequent throws of 1, 2 or 3 advance appropriately all runners on bases. A throw of 5 or 6 is an out. Three outs retire the side. If a 6 is thrown with men on bases, the batter is out, but the men on bases are safe. If a 5 is thrown with men on bases, it is a fly ball, and the leading man on base, if any, is also out. In some localities, this is played thus: 1 man on bases, out; man on 1st, out; man on 3rd, always safe; men on 2nd and 3rd, both safe; men on 1st and 2nd, the man on 2nd is forced out, the man on 1st being safe; men on 1st and 3rd, the man on 1st is out.

At the end of an agreed number of innings, the high score wins, as in baseball.

CENTENNIAL

A layout, of 12 compartments numbered 1 through 12, is marked on paper or some similar material. Each player throws 3 dice. A 1 must be thrown first, to put a player's marker on compartment 1; otherwise the dice pass. When a 1 is thrown, a

1	2	3	4	5	6	7	8	9	10	11	12

2 or the combination equalling 2 (two 1's) must be thrown on this or the next throw, or the dice pass. This continues until each player's marker has traveled from 1 to 12, and back again to 1. The one finishing first wins. If a player throws a number that he needs and overlooks it, his opponent may use it, if it is the number he needs. The excitement comes from using a 1-2-3 throw, for instance, as 1; 2; 3; 4 (3 + 1); 5 (3 + 2); 6 (3, 2 and 1).

GOING TO BOSTON, NEWMARKET, or YANKEE GRAB

A pool is contributed to equally by the players, each of whom has 3 throws with dice. On the first throw, the highest die must be retained, and the 2 others discarded. On the second throw, the higher die is kept and the lower rejected. When 2 dice are tied for high, one must be discarded. The sum of his 3 dice after the third throw constitutes each player's total.

MULTIPLICATION

This is Going to Boston, with the last die thrown used as a multiplier of the sum of the 2 former ones, to arrive at the score. Thus, if a 6 and 4 are the first 2 throws retained, and the last die is a 5, the score is 5 times the sum of 6 and 4, or 50.

ROUND THE SPOT

This is a variation of Going to Boston, in which dice with no center spots (2, 4 and 6) count as blanks; and the dice with a center spot count only the spots around them (1 being blank, 3 counting 2, and 5 counting 4).

HELP YOUR NEIGHBOR

Six players, each selecting a different number from 1 through 6; or 3 players with 2 numbers each; or 2 players with 3 numbers each. Each player starts with 5 counters. The one who gets rid of his counters first wins.

In turn, each player throws 3 dice; and the players whose numbers appear put counters in the pool, 1 for each time their number comes up. If the player who has chosen the number 1 throws a 3, 4 and 5, he does not help himself at all; but players 3, 4 and 5 each contribute a counter to the pool. Two of a kind call for 2 counters from a player; and triplets, 3. The player who first gets rid of his counters wins the pool.

PASSE-DIX

Each player, in rotation, becomes the banker, holding his position as long as he wins. The moment he loses, the dice pass to the left. The players bet as much as they please, below the betting limit, that the banker cannot throw 10 *or more* with one cast of 3 dice. The advantage slightly favors the banker, since the average throw is 10½, and he wins also with a 10.

POKER DICE

Poker Dice is played with 5 dice, either of the usual type, or especial dice marked with the Ace, King, Queen, Jack, 10, and 9 as in cards. The object is to secure the best possible poker hand, in as many throws of the dice, not exceeding 3, as the first caster uses.

The poker hands rank:

Five of a kind, 6 being high and 1 low.

Straight, 5 dice in numerical sequence, one headed by a 6 ranking one headed by a 5.

Four of a kind, the higher ranking determining ties; and in case of ties with the same numeral, the 5th die determining.

Full House, 3 of one denomination, 2 of another; in ties, ranked by denomination of the triplets; if these tie, of the doublets.

Three of a kind, highest denomination ranking. In case of a tie, the higher of the other 2 dice ranks; if these tie, the lower.

Two Pairs, ranked by the denomination of the higher. In case of a tie, by the second pair; if both pairs tie, by the 5th die.

One Pair, ranked by its denomination; in case of a tie, the highest of the non-tieing other dice is the determining factor.

Highest Denomination, where the hand lacks even a pair; or, the highest of non-tieing other dice.

After the first throw, and again after the second, the first player may recast all the dice, or any lesser number, keeping any he chooses with which to build; the dice thus retained are set to one side. Any die set aside on one cast may be picked up and recast on the 3rd throw. In case of an absolute tie in any of these hands, each player recasts the dice once again, and the best throw wins. The players after the first may cast as many times as he casts, 1, 2 or 3, and no more.

In some localities, Straights and Full Houses have no value. In the East, 1's are high, 6's next; in the West, 6's are high.

POKER DICE WITH ACES WILD

The 1's or Aces in Poker dice may be played wild, like Deuces Wild in Poker. Hands with natural denominations rank higher than tieing hands with Aces Wild in them; and the one with the fewest aces wild, where both tieing hands have these, wins.

TEN-PINS WITH DICE

Each player takes turns for 2 throws with 2 dice. The count thrown equals the same number of pins down. If 10 is made on the first of the 2 throws it is reckoned a strike; on the second throw, a spare: the score is counted as in Ten-Pins. A throw above 10 takes down all the pins, but does not count as a strike or spare. A count below 10 on the first throw permits a second throw. The second throw is the last permitted a player. A game consists of 10 frames.

UNDER AND OVER SEVEN

This requires a layout:

U	7	O

The bets are placed in one or more of these compartments. Two dice are thrown. Bets on U or O pay even money; bets on 7 pay 3 to 1 if thrown by the banker.

SPOT 'EM

The Layout consists of the numbers 2 through 12:

2	3	4	5	6	7	8	9	10	11	12

The Banker throws 2 dice, and places a coin (the spot) over the number on the Layout which is the sum of the pips thrown. The player then throws, and must throw higher than this number in one throw, or lose. If the Banker throws doubles, he loses automatically. The Banker pays for doubles, and loses or wins one stake each time a player throws.

TWENTY-SIX, HOOLIGAN

In this popular game, 10 dice are shaken from a cup. Before the first shake, the player picks his pip, any number from 1 to 6, and this is recorded by the Banker, the other player. The player then has 13 tries, in which to win he must throw his pip 26 or more times. The total number of times this pip has so far been thrown is scored in one of 13 successive squares, representing his 13 tries; thus:

Pip Chosen	*Player*	*1*	*2*	*3*	*4*	*5*	*6*	*7*	*8*	*9*	*10*	*11*	*12*	*13*	
6	A.	1	2	6	7	8	10	12	15	17	17	19	20	21	Lost
1	B.	0	2	6	6	7	10	13	17	18	22	26	27	30	Won

The first player lost, and had to pay for his round. The second player won. A player who wins receives four times the agreed amount of the stake. The odds are 6 to 5 in favor of the Banker, in each round.

VINGT-ET-UN

The players make up a pool, but there is no banker. Each in turn throws a single die, and continues to throw until he stands under 21, or reaches it, or passes it—a burst or "bust." The player reaching 21 or nearest below it wins the pool. In case of a tie, the pool is divided. Most players throw again at 17, or less, but not at 18 or more.

CARGO

A special scoreboard is used, with twelve blank rows headed by the numbers 1 through 12, and the names of the players listed beneath at the left. Each player in rotation casts twelve rounds, using 2 dice. He may either stand on any throw as his score for

	1	2	3	4	5	6	7	8	9	10	11	12
Player A												
Player B												
Player C												

Cargo: I

any round, or may cast over one or both dice, to improve that score. For 1's through 6's, he scores the pip value of the one or two of the number thrown. For throwing 7, 9 or 11, or 8 or 10 without doubles, he scores the pip value. 8, 10, and 12, when thrown with double dice, are Cargo, and score twice the pip value thrown. On each round, the player must select which compartment to score in, after his casting is completed; and a score once entered may not thereafter be altered. When two or more rows can be scored, the player may choose which to score in. Thus a throw of 3-4 can be scored as 3, as 4, or as 7, if these numbers are unscored. When only one number may be scored on a round, it must be scored. When no number may be scored on a round, the player must choose which number to take a blank in. The highest score after the 12 rounds wins.

EVEREST

Everest is a dice game, in which each player or team must fill in, in any order he prefers out of the thrown dice, the numbers from 1 to 12, and from 12 back to 1 again. Three dice are used, and player or team must stand on the numbers thrown on the first throw each time. The scoreboard is marked thus:

Player	1	2	3	4	5	6	7	8	9	10	11	12
Player A	→											→
Player B												
Player C												
Player D												

Player	1	2	3	4	5	6	7	8	9	10	11	12
Player A	←											←
Player B												
Player C												
Player D												

Suppose the first throw were a 6, 6, 1. This could be scored as a 1 and 2 6's; as a 6 and a 7; or as a 1 and a 12. By all odds the wise thing to do is the 1 and the 12; since 12 is the hardest number to throw, 11 the next, and so on. A choice once made cannot thereafter be altered. As soon as any player or team has filled in the going and returning blanks, 1 through 12 and 12 back through 1, he wins. If a player throws dice where he can use only one combination or one number, the other numbers thrown must be ignored; if he can use none, the throw passes without his scoring anything. In general, it is wise to fill out the going numbers before reduplicating with returning numbers; since it is easier to throw, at the end, a 9 and a 10, than two 10's. This game grows tensely exciting at the end, when each player or team has only one or two numbers to throw, and may fail to throw them for several rounds. In some localities, the team that first fills in its going numbers receives an extra throw; but this gives an unfair advantage. First throw is determined by each player's casting one die for highest.

SARATOGA

Saratoga is a horse-racing game, using the Everest scoreboard as a racetrack. Thus each player has a lane in which to race to 12 and back, in numerical sequence, the one first completing the course winning. Three dice are thrown; and the numbers thrown can be used in any combinations, to secure the needed numbers. A 1 must be thrown before the player's horse can move at all; then a 2, a 3, etc., to 12, the returning 12, and back to the returning 1, which is the finishing line. If a 1 or the number needed is not thrown, the player receives one upright toward a hurdle. A second failure gives a 2nd upright; a third, the complete hurdle. When thereafter the proper number is thrown, the horse moves *two* spaces forward, plus any further moves he is entitled to. When there are two hurdles, the horse moves *three* spaces forward, etc. When the desired number is thrown, the horse is moved forward the proper number of spaces; and the player then throws over, and continues this until he throws a group of numbers on which he cannot move forward. First throw is determined, as in Everest, by each player throwing one die, highest winning choice of position and first throw, etc. The ideal starting throw is a 1, 2, 4. For this gives these combinations: 1; 2; 3 (1 and 2); 4; 5 (1 and 4); 6 (2 and 4); 7 (1, 2 and 4). Thus on an opening throw of 1, 2, 4 the player's horse moves from 1 through 7; and he still has another throw. Hurdles are most valuable as the turning 12 is neared. It is possible for a player to win before the other players have had a single throw; though there is no record that this has ever been done. And a horse apparently left at the post can suddenly start running and win, no matter how far ahead the others are. Betting is done as in any horse-racing game.

CRAG

Crag shares with Yacht the supremacy among sequence dice-casting games. At each throw, 3 dice are cast, and in order to improve his score a player is allowed to score his 3 dice as cast, or to throw over 1, 2 or all 3 of them a second time. A special scoreboard is used as above. Each player in rotation is allowed thirteen rounds. 1's through 6's score the pip value of those numbers thrown in any round; Odd Straight (1-3-5), Even Straight (2-4-6), Low Straight (1-2-3) and High Straight (4-5-6) score 20 each; any Three of a Kind scores 25; any throw of thirteen without doubles scores 26; and Crag, or a throw of thirteen including double 4's, 5's, or 6's, scores 50. On each round, the player must select which compartment in the scoreboard to score in, after his casting is completed; and a score once entered may not thereafter be altered. When 2 or more compartments may be scored in, the player may choose which he will use. When only one compartment on the scoreboard may be scored on a round, it must be scored. When no compartment may be scored, the player must choose the compartment in which to take a blank. The highest score after the thirteen rounds wins.

The highest score that can be thrown is 244. The last 7 compartments are the most difficult to secure, and should be aimed for first. Great skill is required, in choosing which die or dice to set aside to give the largest possible chance to score a high combination. Thus, a throw of 1-4-6, by setting aside the 1, could be thrown for an Even Straight or a High Straight; and by setting aside the 4, for a Crag (1-6-6). Since the odds are the same, the

	Scores	Player A	Player B	Player C	Player D
1's	Pip value	1	2	2	2
2's	"	4	2	4	2
3's	"	6	3	3	6
4's	"	..	8	8	4
5's	"	10	15	10	5
6's	"	12	12	6	12
Odd Straight	20	20	20	20	20
Even "	20	20	..	..	20
Low "	20	..	20	..	20
High "	20	20	20	..	..
Three of a Kind	25	..	25	25	25
Thirteen	26	26	26	26	..
Crag (Thirteen with a Double)	50	50	..	..	..
Total		169	153	104	116

Crag: I

higher-scoring Crag should be aimed for in this case, unless the caster has a dice sense that indicates that a 2 or a 5 is likely to come up; in which case he will probably ignore the odds, and throw for a Straight.

YACHT

A special scorecard is also used for Yacht, similar to that used in Crag. The top left line lists Events, and, heading separate columns, the names of the players, any number from 2 upwards. On 12 successive lines, 12 Events are listed: ones, twos, threes, fours, fives, sixes, Full House, Four of a Kind, Little Straight, Big Straight, Choice, Yacht; the line below is marked Total.

The first throw is decided by each player throwing one die; the highest wins, 6 being high. If ties occur, the tieing players throw again, until the ties are broken. The leader, and then in rotation each player to the left, has 3 throws to arrive at the best score under the event decided upon. These events are scored:

1's through 6's the added value of all the numbers from 1 through 6 player is throwing for, received in 3 throws. Other numbers disregarded.

Full House (3 of a denomination, 2 of another), Four of a Kind and Choice (any 5 dice): the added value of all 5 dice.

Little Straight (1, 2, 3, 4, 5), Big Straight (2, 3, 4, 5, 6), 30 each.

Yacht (any 5 of a kind): 50.

In throwing, each player at any first throw may stand on the throw, and score it as above; or he may retain as many dice as he chooses, from 1 to 4, and throw to remainder again. After this second throw, he may stand or set aside the same or other dice, and throw again. A player is allowed only 3 throws in each round. An event once scored may not thereafter be thrown again. In any throw, if no event is unscored which the throw shows, a blank must be marked on any event that the player selects.

Yacht, the two Straights, Four of a Kind and Full House are the hardest to throw, and should be aimed for first; failing one of them, the lowest number is usually the wisest to score. The highest score possible is 302. Each player has 12 rounds of 3 or less throws, but no more. The highest score wins.

COOTIE

This game is played by tables of 4 players, the partners being divided as in Bridge, Euchre, or any progressive form of these games. Each table needs a special die marked B (Body), H

(Head), L (Leg), A (Antenna), E (Eye) and T (Tail); or 1 may be B; 2, H; 3, L; 4, A; 5, E, and 6, T, when a regular die is used.

The Leader at each table throws the die first. Unless B (1) is thrown, the die passes to his left. The Body of the Cootie must be thrown before the Head, Leg or Tail may be added to it. The Head must be thrown before the Eye or Antenna is added to it. Partners play together to complete their Cootie, which must have 1 Body, 1 Head, 2 Eyes, 2 Antennae, 6 Legs, and 1 Tail. Where partners compete, one partner alternately marks the throw, while the other is scoring the throw on the drawing. A player continues throwing until he throws a number or letter he cannot use; the die then passes. Each item scored marks 1, 13 being the complete score. Here are two drawn Cooties, the first a completed one, scoring 13; the second incomplete, scoring 8:

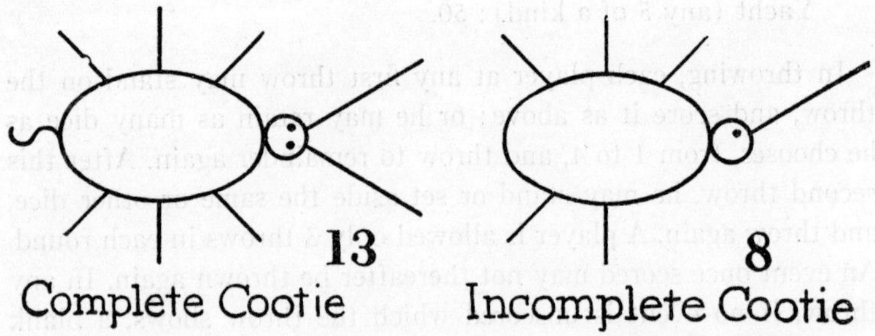

As soon as a player or partnership completes a Cootie, the game ends, the score at a table being the difference between totals made by the pairs of partners. In Progressive Cootie, as soon as the Head Table completes a Cootie, the others stop playing, and tabulate their scores as of that time; except that the players at any other table where a complete Cootie has meanwhile been made have previously stopped play and tabulated their scores. The winners progress as in Progressive Bridge or Euchre. Usually 10 to 12 rounds are played in an evening.

In one variation, 2 dice are thrown at each throw; otherwise, the above rules apply.

FIFTY

The players may be two, three, or four (playing as partners, two against two); or the game may be Progressive, with tables of four, as in Progressive Bridge, Euchre or Cootie. Each table requires 2 dice, and may have a dice-cup. Beginning with the Leader, each player has 1 throw, the dice passing to the left. The scoring is:

		Points
Double 1, 2, 4 or 5		5
Double 6		25
Double 3	Cancels whole score	
Any Other Throw		0

The game is 50 points. In Progressive Fifty, as soon as the Head Table goes game, the other tables stop play and tabulate their scores, as in Progressive Cootie; except that if a table reaches 50 before the Head Table, play stops there and the scores are tabulated. In progressing, the methods used in Progressive Bridge or Euchre are employed, winning couples changing partners with losing couples for each game. Ten games are usually completed in one evening.

ONE HUNDRED

In this variation of Fifty, all throws except doubles score the combined value of the pips; double 1, 2, 4 or 5 score twice the combined value of the pips; double 6's score 25; double 3 cancels the whole score. The game is 100.

HEARTS DICE

Hearts is a dice game, using 6 dice, each marked with the letters H, E, A, R, T, and S. However, 6 regular dice may be used, 1 being H; 2, E; 3, A; 4, R; 5, T; and 6, S. Beginning with the Leader, each player in rotation to the left throws the dice once only, scoring by the following method, if these combinations are found among the dice thrown:

	Points
1, 2	5
1, 2, 3	10
1, 2, 3, 4	15
1, 2, 3, 4, 5	20
1, 2, 3, 4, 5, 6	25

If three 1's are thrown, the entire score of a player or a partnership is cancelled. The game is 100. The game may be played by two, three, five or more players individually; four, as partners of two each; or by progressing tables, as in Progressive Bridge, Euchre, Cootie or Fifty.

WOODEN HORSE RACE, STEEPLECHASE

Equipment: 2 dice and dice-cup; or 2 lawn dice (say 4 by 4 inches) for the larger courses. Special equipment is necessary: a race-track with 6 lanes for the 6 competing horses to race on; and about 40 crosswise lines, dividing the track into 42 equal distances; three of the lines, numbers 11, 22 and 33, should be marked Hurdle. The length of the track may be the length of the floor (using marked canvas tracks) or the length of a table; in either case, it is furnished with horses of appropriate size, numbered from 1 through 6; the horses may have tiny jockeys mounted on them. All this equipment may be purchased, or may be home-made. The game may also be played on a course lined out on paper, with 2 dice.

Preliminaries.—The horses are lined up at the starting line. Each player, or group of players, buys a horse, or selects or wins one by lot. One horse may be regarded as the property of the house. In addition to ownership, bets may be laid, using the pari-mutuel or any other betting system. When all bets are placed, the dice are thrown.

The Race.—The horses are moved forward, depending upon the throw of the dice. Thus a throw of 3-4 means that horses numbered 3 and 4 each move forward one cross square. When doubles are thrown, the horse whose number is thrown moves forward

2 squares. The horse crossing the finishing line first wins. In case of a tie in crossing the finishing line, the tieing horses start over again and race from 1 to 10, or until the tie is first broken thereafter.

HURDLE RACE

A Hurdle Race is run off similarly; except that a hurdle (cross lanes 11, 22, 33) may only be jumped by having doubles of a horse's number thrown. Many horses arrive just before one of the hurdles and never cross it. To speed up the race, only two hurdles (cross lanes 15 and 30) may be used. Other rules are the same as above.

CHUCK LUCK, or SWEAT

This is a dice game, with a layout as in the diagram, requiring 3 dice. Bets are placed on the various compartments on the diagram; and the odds that are paid are shown on the lower line of each portion of the layout. Bets on single numbers refer to the face of any of the 3 dice when cast. If the number bet upon

High — Low

Even Money					
Single Numbers					
1	*2*	*3*	*4*	*5*	*6*

18	*17*	*16*	*15*	*14*	*13*	*12*	*11*	*10*	*9*	*8*	*7*	*6*	*5*	*4*	*3*
180	60	29	18	12	8	6	6	6	6	8	12	18	29	60	180

Raffles

Odd — Even

1	2	3	4	5	6
180 to 1					

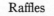

comes up once on a throw, the banker pays even money; if it comes up twice, he pays double; if three times, it is a raffle, and the banker pays 180 to 1, collecting all other bets. All throws from 11 through 18 are high; from 3 through 10, low. High and low, as well as odd and even, pay even money.

GRAND STEEPLECHASE

In this variation, 5 dice are used. Horses move forward 1, 2 or 3 cross spaces when 1, 2 or 3 of their numbers are thrown. A hurdle must be crossed only by a throw of 3 of the number. A throw of 4 of a kind sends the player of that number back 4 spaces, and is regarded as a spill. A throw of 5 of a kind moves the horse whose number is thrown 10 cross spaces forward, including any intervening hurdles, and usually wins a race.

KENO, LOTTO

In Keno and Lotto, a number of special cards in 9 vertical rows, and 3, 4 or 5 horizontal rows are spread around the table The vertical rows represent, respectively, numbers from 1 through 10, 11 through 20, etc., to 81 through 90. On each horizontal row 5 figures and 4 blanks appear. No number is duplicated on a card; and each number appears in its appropriate vertical row. A typical card, using 3 horizontal rows, might be:

3			31		52		73	81
	11	23		45		64		86
7		27		49		69	78	

Number 169

The number of the card is sometimes stamped across its center. Each player pays an agreed amount for as many cards as he cares to play.

There are also 90 numbered disks or balls; in Keno, balls are always used. In Lotto, after being thoroughly shaken, these disks or balls are usually drawn at random from a container, and are announced aloud one by one as they are drawn. In Keno, they must be rolled one by one out of the spout of the container, called the Keno Goose. When a player has on any card a number announced, he places on his number a marker—a grain of corn, a bean, or a pasteboard marker. The player first covering all the numbers in any horizontal row calls out "Keno" or "Lotto," and wins the prize. This is either the total sum paid for all the cards, or this less a share for the house. If two players go Keno or Lotto at the same time, the prize is divided.

The announcer has before him a chart containing all the numbers from 1 through 90; and when Keno or Lotto is claimed by a player he must call back his numbers, so that the announcer can make sure that Keno or Lotto has in fact been made. For an incorrect call, there is no penalty; and the announcing proceeds.

BINGO

This is a popular modern variation, where each card contains no blanks, but has 5 horizontal rows, all but the central one containing 5 figures; and the central row has 4 figures with "Free" marked in the center. There are no blanks on the cards. The central horizontal row goes Bingo when its 4 numbers are announced and covered. The balls roll one at a time out of a whirling wire ball, like a squirrel cage. "Bingo" is called, as in Lotto or Keno.

CHINESE FAN TAN

This is a banking game, in which the layout consists of a card or marked area on the table, numbered in its corners 1, 2, 3 and 4.

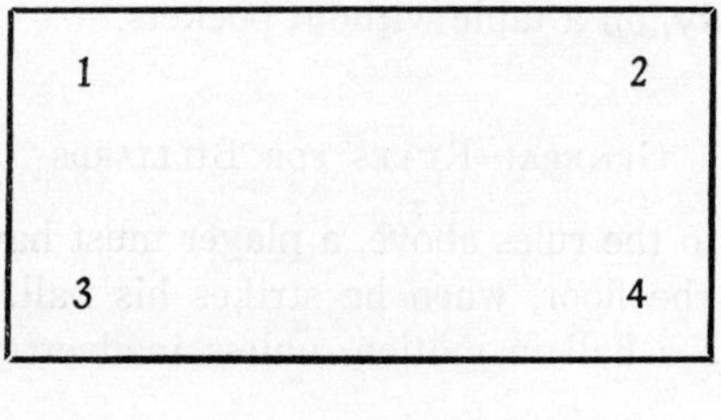

The players bet any number of counters, within the betting limit. A bet placed upon a corner is a bet upon a single number; a bet placed on a side, between two numbers, is a bet upon both of them, as against the two on the opposite side of the card.

The banker, after the bets are completed, takes a handful of beans or small counters of any kind from a bowl, and places them on the table. He counts them off, 4 at a time, with a little stick. All complete 4's are disregarded; the number of counters left at the end determines the bets. If the counters run out in even 4's, bets on 4 win; otherwise, the remainder, 3, 2 or 1 wins. As a rule the counters are withdrawn before the bets are made, and covered until the bets are placed, and then counted.

Bets on a single number pay 3 to 1; on the side, on double numbers, even money is paid.

BILLIARDS and POOL

The origin of billiards is lost in the mists of antiquity. The game is mentioned in the will of a 2nd centry Irish king; it was referred to by Spenser and Shakespeare; and was the fashionable game in France during the reign of Louis XIV. As originally played in America, 4 corner pockets were used, and 4 balls. The 2 red balls. one light and one dark, were placed each on its own spot; and each player had a white ball, one of which bore a spot to distinguish it. The counts were 3 and 2 for each shot, off the red and off the white respectively, as in the English game; game was 100 points. The pockets were abolished and the string was reduced to 34 buttons, which it still is in many localities. Since 1870, Americans have adopted the French carom game, played with 3 balls only, on a table without pockets.

General Rules for Billiards

In addition to the rules above, a player must have at least one foot touching the floor, when he strikes his ball. He is not allowed to strike a ball in motion, unless inadvertently, in which case the balls must be replaced and the shot taken over. Playing with the wrong ball, if claimed before the player makes another shot, is also a foul stroke; and so is touching the cue ball more than once, or touching another ball except by striking it with his cue ball, as above.

FRENCH CAROMS

The standard table is 10 feet by 5; at times a table 9 by 4½ feet is used. At the outset, each player plays a ball with his cue from the head of the table—the end with the maker's name upon it—to the cushion at the other end, so that it will return to the head. The player whose ball is closest to the head cushion must then decide whether to play first or not.

The red ball is spotted at the bottom of the table, that is to say, it is placed on the spot marked there. The non-striker places his ball on the spot at the head of the table, on a mark midway of the crosswise line called the balk line. The striker must then place his own ball anywhere within the balk line, but not more than six inches from the spotted ball of the opponent. The object of the game is for the player to drive his own ball with the point of the cue, so that it strikes both the other balls, either together, one after the other, or with the intervention of a cushion. In the opening shot, the red ball must be struck first; after that, either may be struck first, and a ball may be struck any number of times; provided always that the cue ball strikes or is struck by both the others. Every such stroke counts 1 point. If both balls are missed, the non-striker scores 1 point.

A number of shots in succession is called a break or run. Push shots—shots where the cue does not strike the ball clearly—are barred. When the balls touch each other, they are said to be frozen; and they must then be respotted. Each player has his own cue, which in length should reach from the player's chin to the floor, and in weight should be between 14 and 22 ounces, 18 ounces being the average.

If the red ball is forced off the table, it must be replaced on its own spot, if this is unoccupied; otherwise on the middle spot. If the striker's ball is forced off the table, it is spotted at the head of the table. If the carom was made before the ball jumped off the table, this scores, and the player plays from the spot; otherwise the non-striker plays. If the non-striker's ball is forced off the table, it is spotted at the head of the table. An agreed number of points constitutes the game.

BALK LINE BILLIARDS

To prevent large breaks being made with the aid of the cushion, chalk lines are drawn at an agreed distance parallel to the ends and sides of the table; and a player is forbidden to make more than one or two caroms within the space between the balk lines and the cushions, without driving one of the balls out of that space. This type of game takes its name from the distance between cushion and balk line: thus there is a 10-inch, 12-inch, 14-inch, and 18-inch balk line. If only one shot is allowed within the balk space with an 18-inch balk line, the game is called 18-1; if 2, 18-2, etc.

CUSHION CAROMS

A variation which makes the game more difficult is to require that the ball must touch a certain number of cushions before completing the shot. The cushions may be touched before the first ball is hit, or between hitting the 2 balls, or partly one and partly the other. The most popular game of this type is Three-Cushion Caroms.

BANK-SHOT BILLIARDS

It may be agreed that the cue ball must strike a cushion before touching the object ball; this is called Bank-Shot Billiards. Any number of cushions may be struck afterwards. If the cue ball strikes an object ball before touching a cushion, the stroke is foul.

MAN-OF-WAR GAME

Three players play this game, each with his own white ball. The red ball is spotted, as in French Caroms. At the start, one white ball is placed on the balk-line spot, and the other is in the middle of the rail, tight against the cushion, at the bottom of the table. The first striker may play from any position behind the balk-line.

ENGLISH BILLIARDS

The table is 16 feet by 6, with 6 pockets in it. The balls are only 2⅟₁₆ of an inch in diameter, and the cues lighter than in America. The red ball is spotted 12¾ inches from the bottom of the table; and the white ball for the opening shot must be spotted within the "D" at the head of the table, this D having a 11½ inch radius, and being a semicircle within the balk area, with the middle point of the balk line as a center.

The opening shot is made with only these 2 balls on the table. The winner of the stringing for choice usually lets his opponent play first, so as to get all 3 balls on the table for his own shot. The first player usually lays his ball safe against the cushion, halfway between a side-pocket and the balk line; but it must be driven out of balk, even if it returns within the balk line again.

The two shots that score are called cannons and hazards. A cannon is a carom which hits both object balls with the cue ball. A hazard is driving a ball into any pocket. If the object ball goes in, it is a winning hazard; if the cue ball, a losing hazard. If the red ball is pocketed, it must be placed on its own spot; or, if that is occupied, upon a spot near the bottom corresponding to the balk-line spot, called the pyramid spot; and, if this also is occupied, upon the center spot. If the cue ball falls into a pocket, it must be played for the next shot from within the D. If the non-striker's ball goes into a pocket, it is said to be in hand, and stays off the table until the non-striker's turn to play, when it is played from the D.

If a ball is forced off the table, the stroke is foul. The other player may then play the balls as they lie; or spot the red and play; or ask his opponent to play, as at the beginning of the game. To score, cannons and white hazards count 2 points each; red hazards, winning or losing, 3 points each. A red losing hazard is one in which the cue ball first strikes the red ball and then goes into a pocket, whether it makes a cannon in between or not. If the cue ball strikes the white ball first, and then the red, and then goes into a pocket, this is a white hazard, and the shot counts 4 only: 2 for the cannon, 2 for the white hazard. The highest score possible on one shot is 10: a carom, followed by driving all three balls into pockets.

A push shot means keeping the point of the cue in contact with the cue ball when it strikes an object ball. If a player makes two winning hazards in succession off the red ball while it is on its spot, it is spotted on the center spot for the next stroke. If the balls are frozen, the red ball must be spotted, the non-striker's ball spotted on the center spot, and the player must play from the D. If the non-striker's ball is in hand when the other two balls are frozen, only the red ball is spotted, the striker playing from the D.

If a player pockets his own ball or forces it off the table without touching another ball, it is a coup, and costs him 3 points, which the adversary adds to his score. If any ball but the cue ball is forced off the table by a stroke, the non-striker scores 2. If the striker makes a miss, it counts 1 point for the non-striker. The general rules are the same as French Caroms; except that striking the red ball with the cue forfeits the game; and that if a player playing from the D strikes a ball in balk with his cue ball before it strikes another ball or a cushion, he cannot score, and the opponent has a choice of remedies similar to those in French Caroms.

AMERICAN PYRAMID POOL

The game is played with 15 balls, numbered from 1 through 15, and a white cue-ball. The player opening the game plays from any point inside the strike, that is, the balk line; after the opening shot he plays the cue-ball from wherever it lies. Each ball counts 1 point; in match or two-handed games, the player first scoring 8 points wins.

The balls are arranged in a pyramid, its apex toward the head of the table, and the apex ball resting on the pyramid spot. The opening stroke, whether direct or banked, must strike the pyramid hard enough to cause 2 object-balls to touch a cushion, or at least one object-ball to go into a pocket. Failure to do either forfeits the stroke and one ball to the table. If the player has no ball to his credit, the first ball he scores shall be placed on the deep-red spot, or as near to it as possible. All balls pocketed on the opening stroke count, without being called.

After the opening stroke, each player must call the number of the ball he intends to pocket; but need not call the pocket. If the ball called is not pocketed, no ball pocketed on the stroke is counted, but must be placed on or as near to the deep-red spot as possible; the player's hand is out, but he incurs no penalty. Should more than one ball be called, and one or more of these not be pocketed, none can be counted. There is no penalty for failing to hit a called ball, provided any other ball is hit.

If, after the opening stroke, a player fails to pocket a ball, or fails to make at least one object-ball, or the cue-ball, after striking an object-ball, strike a cushion, one ball is forfeited. If the player also pockets the cue-ball, after one of these failures, he forfeits only one ball on the stroke. When the ball called is pocketed, all other balls pocketed on the same stroke score for him.

When more than two players compete, the game ends when the balls remaining on the table are not sufficient to tie the second highest score; and the game is settled in accordance with the standing of each player when pool is called. A player forfeits one ball for making a miss, pocketing the cue-ball, forcing it off the table, or failing as described above. A stroke is a foul if made when any ball is in motion, and a ball is forfeited. The next striker may play the balls as he finds them, or have them replaced. When the cue-ball is struck twice, the next striker has the same choice, the striker forfeiting one ball.

BOTTLE POOL

Bottle Pool is played on a pool table with one white ball, the balls numbered 1 and 2, and a leather pool-bottle. The 1 and 2 balls must be spotted at the foot of the table, at the right and left diamond nearest each pocket. The pool-bottle is placed standing upside down on the center spot. When it falls, it must be set up, if possible, where it rests.

Carom on the two object-balls counts 1 point; pocketing the 1 ball counts 1; pocketing the 2 ball, 2; carom from ball and upsetting the bottle counts 5 points. A game consists of 31 points. The player with the lowest score at the end of a game is the loser. Any number of players can play; and the rotation of the players is decided at the beginning of the game. A striker must strike either the 1 or 2 ball, before he can score a carom on the pool-bottle. If a legal carom on the bottle turns it upside down and sets it on its base, he wins the game at once. If the 1 or 2 ball touch the bottle, and in the same play the cue-ball caroms legally against it, or sets it on its base, the stroke does not count. If a player forces the bottle off the table or pockets it, the bottle must be spotted as at the beginning of the game, and the player forfeits 1 point and loses his stroke. A player who makes more than 31 strokes is burst, and must start his string anew, scoring all that he has made above 31 on his new strike, and the next player playing instead of the player who went burst. In some localities, this last rule is omitted.

CHICAGO POOL

The equipment is the same as in American Pyramid Pool. The balls must be played upon and pocketed in their numerical order. In laying out the pyramid, the 1 ball is placed against the end cushion at the first right-hand diamond sight at the foot of the table; the 2-ball at the center diamond sight on the same cushion; and the remaining 13 balls are placed in the orders of their numbers at the succeeding diamond sights. The three sights on the end rail at the head of the table are not occupied by balls.

The order of play is determined by throwing out small numbered balls. The first striker strikes the cue-ball from any point within the string, or balk-line. The opening stroke must strike the 1 ball. If that ball is holed, the player scores it; and he continues his hand until he fails to score. In continuing, each stroke must play upon the lowest numbered ball left upon the table. If a player plays upon the proper ball, any other balls pocketed on the same stroke count to the player's credit. If a ball is so surrounded by other balls that it may not be hit in a direct line, a bank play (against a cushion) or massé (jump-over shot) etc. may be resorted to; but the proper ball must be hit first, or the player forfeits 3, receiving a scratch.

If a ball is holed by a foul stroke, it is replaced upon the spot it occupied at the beginning of the game. If the 8, 9, 19 or 11 ball is holed so, they being within the string, and the cue-ball in hand, the balls listed are placed upon the pyramid or red-ball spot; and, if that is occupied, as near to it as possible. The player with the lowest total score is regarded as the loser.

COLOR-BALL POOL, ENGLISH or FOLLOWING POOL

The white ball is spotted. The red ball plays upon the white; the yellow upon the red; the green upon the yellow; the brown upon the green; the blue upon the brown; the pink upon the blue; the spot-white upon the pink; the spot-red upon the spot-white; the spot-yellow upon the spot-red; the spot-green upon the spot-yellow; the spot-brown upon the spot-green; the spot-blue upon the spot-brown; and the white upon the spot-blue. The English D or balk semicircle is used in this game.

The players play progressively, as the colors appear above, the top color being No. 1. Each player has three lives at starting. No. 1 places his ball on the "winning and losing" spot; No. 2 plays at No. 1; No. 3 at No. 2, and so on. Each player plays at the last ball, unless the striker's ball is in hand, in which case he plays at the nearest ball.

When a striker loses a life (that is, one of his granted shots), the next in rotation plays at the ball nearest his own. If this player's ball is in hand, he plays at the ball nearest to the center of the balk line, whether it is in or out of balk. The distance should be measured, in case of uncertainty. The balk is no protection. A player loses a life when he pockets his own ball off another; runs a coup; misses the ball played on; plays with the wrong ball; forces his own ball off the table; plays out of turn; strikes the wrong ball; or has his ball pocketed by the next striker. If a player pockets the ball he plays at, but in the same stroke pockets his own ball or forces it off the table, he loses a life, and the player whose ball was pocketed does not. If a player strikes the wrong ball, he pays the same forfeit to the person whose ball he should have played, as he would have done if he had pocketed himself. If a player misses the ball he is required to play at, and by the same stroke pockets another ball, the striker loses a life, and not the player whose ball was pocketed; and in this case the striker's ball is taken up, and both balls remain in hand until their turns to play.

A player at any time may ask and receive information as to which is his ball, and whether it is his turn to play. If misinformed, the striker does not lose a life. In this case, his ball is replaced, and the stroke is played again. If any balls intervene between the striker's ball and the one at which he must play, these balls are taken up until the stroke is concluded, and then replaced; and the same is true if the ball or balls are in the way of the striker's cue, so that he cannot play at his ball.

When a striker takes a life, he continues to play as long as he can pocket a ball, or until the balls are all off the table; in this case he replaces his ball on the table, as at the beginning. The first player who loses three lives may buy, with the amount of his original stake, as many lives as the lowest number on the board. This is called starring. If the player first out refuses to star, the second player out may do so; and this continues until only two players are in the pool. Only one star, however, is allowed in any one pool.

Moving any ball while striking is a foul. No player can lose a life on such a stroke, except the offender. If a striker's ball touch the one he has to play at, he is at liberty to play at it or any other ball on the table; but the striker loses a life if he pockets his own ball, or forces it off the table. If a ball is removed and the ball struck should stop at the place it occupies, the owner of the ball removed, at his turn to play, must give a miss from balk, without penalty. When three players, each with one life remaining, remain, and one misses, the others divide the pool without a stroke.

CONTINUOUS POOL

This game differs from other games of pool in scoring and otherwise, and is usually used in championship matches. For the layout, use a triangular frame to spot the 15 balls. The 15 ball is placed at the apex of the pyramid, and the 1 and 5 balls are at the bottom corners. Each ball counts 1 point. The game is scored on a string of buttons as in billiards, and penalties are deducted from this, and not by surrendering balls. The game consists of any number of points agreed upon. When the game lasts more than one night, the balls shall be played off until none remains, even after a player has reached the quota for the night; but, on the final night, play ceases when the winner reaches the fixed quota.

COWBOY POOL

In this game, a cue-ball is used, and 3 colored balls numbered 1, 3 and 5. To begin the game, these 3 colored balls are spotted respectively on the balk, center and pyramid points. When an object ball is pocketed or forced off the table, it is replaced as at the beginning. The opening player plays from any spot inside the strike, but must strike the 3 ball first, or forfeit his turn. The object is to score 101 by the cowboy method. That is, the first 90 points may be scored by caroms or pocketing any numbered ball, which counts its number: A single carom counts 1; a double one, 2. When 90 is reached, the next 10 points must be by caroms only; and the 101st point must be by pocketing the cue ball (after touching the 1 ball) into a designated pocket, without touching another ball, or pocketing any object ball. At a scratch, miss, or foul, the player loses all points previously made on that hand, and the hand passes to the next player.

If a player pockets the cue ball twice without striking an object ball, he forfeits the game. During caroming, if a player pockets a ball, the hand is out, and any points made on that run are lost. Whenever, except on the final stroke, the cue ball is pocketed or forced off the table, the hand is out, points scored on the run are lost, and the cue ball is in hand for the next player, who must play it outside the string line, or else on some point of the cushion outside the line. If the spot on which a pocketed ball belongs is occupied, it must be left off the table until the spot is unoccupied; except on the last shot, when a player may demand, if the 1 ball is pocketed and its spot occupied, that the lay-out be as at the beginning of the game, and he shall play with his ball in hand. Fouls are the same as in other games of Pool. Pushing is allowed during the caroms for the first 90 points, but not during the following 10 strokes; and the 101st shot must be a clean stroke without pushing.

During the first 90 points, if the cue ball is frozen, the cue ball may be pushed, and the carom allowed.

ENGLISH PYRAMIDS, or SHELL OUT

This is played with one white ball, and 15 red balls, pyramided as in other games of Pool. The player pocketing the greatest number of balls receives from each other player the difference between their lives and his. Only winning hazards count. One point or life is reckoned for each winning hazard. The striker loses a point if he pockets the white ball or forces it off the table, or gives a miss, or runs a coup—running the cue-ball into a pocket or off the table without hitting a ball. For every losing hazard (pocketing the cue-ball, a miss, or a coup), a point is taken from a player's score, by replacing a ball on the pyramid spot, or, if it is occupied, immediately behind it. If a striker forces a pyramid ball off the table, he scores nothing on the stroke, and the ball must be replaced. The last hazard counts 2. When all the colored balls but one are pocketed, the player who made the last hazard plays with the white ball, and his opponent with the red, each player alternately, as at single pool. If one of these pockets his own ball, or makes a miss, the game is ended, the opponent adding 1 to his score. A player whose ball is in hand may play from the D or semicircle at any ball on the table.

FIFTEEN-BALL POOL

This is played with 15 balls numbered 1 through 15, and a white cue ball. The lay-out consists in the balls arranged in a pyramid, the 15 ball at the apex toward the head end, the higher balls nearest it, and the lowest at the base. The score is derived from the number on each ball, which is credited to the striker pocketing it. The sum total of the numbers is 120; and, when only two play, whoever scores 61 by legally pocketing balls wins. The rules are the same as in other games of Pool, especially American Pyramid Pool. If the first stroke fails, 3 points are forfeited and the hand passes. Thereafter, 3 points are forfeited for any stroke which does not pocket a ball or make an object-ball strike a cushion, or when the cue-ball strikes a cushion after contact with an object-ball. Three forfeitures in succession lose the game. For pocketing the cue-ball, the forfeit is 3 points. When more than two play, the game ends when the aggregate of the numbers of the balls remaining do not amount to enough to beat or tie the score beneath the winner's. All misplays forfeit 3 points.

FORTY-ONE POOL

This is played with the regular Fifteen-Ball Pool equipment. The object is to pocket a sufficient number of the pool balls which, added to the private small ball, exactly score 41. The small balls are thrown first, one to each player; and the number received by a player is not revealed. The play is as in regular Pool, the game ending when exactly 41 is made by a player, including the count on his small ball; the player most distant from 41 being the loser. Play also ends when all the balls are pocketed, the nearest to 41 being the winner, the most distant the loser. A miss or pocketing the cue-ball is a scratch, and costs the player a ball to the table, the player choosing which ball, of those he has, is to be spotted; if he has none, he thereafter spots the first ball he pockets. More than 41 is a burst, and all balls scored must be spotted, the last ball being nearest to and behind the spot, etc. The player in this case is entitled to a new small ball, if he wishes.

HIGH-LOW-JACK-GAME

The equipment is the same as in Fifteen-Ball Pool. Any number may play, the order being determined by small numbered balls. The 15 ball is High, the 1 ball is Low; the 9 ball is Jack; and the highest aggregate, Game. Generally, 7 points constitute a game. The ball first pocketed, in case of a tie, goes game. In the lay-out, the 3 counting balls are placed in the center, High at their head. When each needs one to go game, only one ball is placed in the line of spots, a ball's diameter from the bottom cushion, and it must be pocketed by banking, to win.

THE LITTLE CORPORAL

This is the regular Three-Ball Carom Game, with a small pin added, as in Pin Pool, placed on the center spot. The caroms and forfeits are as in the regular Three-Ball Carom Game; but knocking down the pin scores 5 for the striker, who plays until he fails to effect a carom or knock down the pin. A ball must be hit by the cue-ball before the pin can be scored. It must be set up where it falls; but if it goes off the table or lodges on top of a cushion, it must be spotted as at the beginning of the game. A pin leaning against the cushion is scored as down. Where the pin lodged in the corner of the table so that it cannot be hit with the ball it is spotted as at the beginning. A game is 100 points, or a number agreed upon.

PIN POOL

The equipment is 2 white balls and one red one, and 5 wooden pins set in a diamond shape, their value being according to the numbers:

4

3 5 2

1

The 5 pin is black; the others natural wood. Numbers for the outer pins should be chalked on the cloth. The red ball is spotted as in the Three-Ball Game, and the second white ball occupies the pin pool spot, at the foot of the table, 3 inches from the center diamond of the end rail. The pin spots are far enough apart for a ball to pass between them without touching a pin. Each player receives a small numbered ball, and conceals its number. Pool consists in knocking down pins of a value which, added to the number on the concealed ball, total 31.

Caroms from ball to ball do not score. A clean miss or ball off the table only loses the stroke; the ball is placed on the pin pool spot, or the nearest unoccupied spot if this is occupied. The player leading off plays from any point within the string, and may play upon either the red or the white ball; or, in lieu of any other stroke, he may place the cue-ball upon the string spot. Players thereafter may play with and upon either ball. A counting stroke is made by the cue-ball caroming from an object ball on the pins, or by driving an object-ball into the pins.

Pins knocked down otherwise do not count, and are replaced, the player's ball being placed on the pin-pool spot at the bottom of the table, or, if this is occupied, on the nearest unoccupied spot. When balls are frozen, a player may play either ball direct at the pins, and score. When a legal stroke knocks down the 4 outside pins and leaves the center one (5) standing, this is a Natural or Ranche, and the player wins the pool at once. When a player makes more than 31, adding the count on his small ball, he bursts, and his score is reduced to his small ball; he may then draw another small ball and choose between the two, returning one. If a player fails to claim pool (31) before the next player shoots, he cannot claim it until it is his turn to shoot again. A pin counts if knocked down, or if entirely removed from the place it occupied, while still remaining perpendicular. In any other case, it must be replaced.

SNOOKER POOL

This game requires the 6-pocket table, 15 red balls being set up in the regulation pyramid; 6 other colored balls are then placed as follows:

Brown, on the balk-line spot; counts 4.

Yellow, 10 inches to the right of the brown; 2.

Green, 10 inches to the left; 2.

Blue, on the center spot; 5.
Pink, at the apex of the pyramid; 6.
Black, halfway between the base of the pyramid and the bottom cushion; 7.

All shots are made with the white ball. The first stroke must be from balk, and must touch a red ball. After the first stroke, the balk is not protection. Each player must pocket a red ball, or lose his turn; each red ball pocketed scores 1. After pocketing a red ball, he must play upon any other colored ball he chooses. If he pockets this, he must next play upon a red ball; and so alternately until he misses. The value of balls other than red, except the white ball, are scored to the striker's credit, and then must be respotted. Red balls, once pocketed, remain off the table. If the proper spot for a colored ball, not red, is occupied, it must go to the nearest unoccupied spot.

As soon as the last red ball is pocketed, there is no further spotting of the colored balls; they must be played upon and pocketed in upward numerical sequence. When a striker cannot play upon a ball he is bound to hit first, he is snookered. He is penalized for failing to hit, or hitting another ball first. The penalties are: for hitting a colored ball, not red, when he should have played upon a red, the value of the colored ball is forfeited; pocketing the white ball, without striking anything, 3 (unless it was his turn to shoot at a colored ball scoring higher than 3, in which case he forfeits the value of the ball); if, after pocketing a red ball, he aims at a colored ball and pockets the white, or makes a clear miss, the forfeit is the value of the ball at which he aimed; a clear miss when playing a red ball loses 1.

If a player strikes a red ball when playing upon a ball of another color, he forfeits the value of the ball at which he aimed. If he hits the wrong colored ball when playing upon them in rotation, he loses the value of the higher ball; and this penalty also applies to pocketing a wrong ball, even if the right ball is hit first. Pocketing a colored ball when a red ball is played upon or pocketed is a foul stroke, forfeiting the value of the ball not red. The same applies when the player pockets a red ball when playing upon or pocketing a colored ball. If 2 or more red balls are pocketed when it is a player's turn to pocket one, all score; afterwards, however, he must alternate as above. If a player plays upon a ball not red and pockets 2 or more, he forfeits the value of the higher ball, unless the ball he should have played on is higher than either, in which case he forfeits that higher value. When the last ball is off the table, the player with the highest score wins; or, the one with the lowest score loses, according to the object of the game.

THE SPANISH GAME

This is played with 2 white and one red ball, and 5 pins as in Pin Pool. The red ball is placed on the red-ball spot, and the first player shoots at it from within the balk D or semicircle. The game is scored by winning and losing hazards, caroms, and by knocking over the pins. It is usually played for 30 points or more.

A player knocking down a pin after striking a ball scores 2; two pins, 4; and so on, 2 for each pin knocked down. The middle pin alone knocked down scores 5. Pocketing the red ball scores 3; and 2 is scored for each pin knocked down during the same stroke. Pocketing the white ball scores 2; and 2 is scored for each pin knocked over at the same stroke. Carom scores 2 points.

A player who knocks down a pin or pins with his own ball before striking another ball loses 2 for each pin so knocked down. Pocketing a player's own ball without hitting another ball forfeits 3 points. Missing altogether forfeits 1. Forcing one's own ball off the table without hitting another ball forfeits 3; if this is done after making a carom or pocket, the player loses as many points as he would otherwise have gained. Otherwise, the rules of the Three-Ball Game apply.

RONDEAU

This is a banking game, played on a pocket billiard table, with 9 small balls. These are rolled, by means of a stick placed behind each, from one corner diagonally to the pocket at the other corner. The players bet on odd or even, as to whether the number of balls left on the table will be odd or even; the banker takes ten per cent of all bets as his share. At least one ball must go into the pocket, and at least one must stay on the table, or the bets are held over until the next round.

ROULETTE

Roulette is the aristocrat among gambling games. It was driven out of France in 1836; and, after a stay at Baden and Homburg, its world center today is Monte Carlo, in the tiny principality of Monaco.

The roulette wheel is spun slowly upon its axis, like a large flat top. It spins in a hollow dish; and in the contrary direction a small ivory ball is thrown, which finally comes to rest in one of the small pockets on the edge of the wheel, these being alternately red and black; except for one green pocket, marked 0. Each pocket has a number above it, the numbers at Monte Carlo running in this order—the heavier-faced numerals representing the black, the others the red:

0	32	**15**	19	**4**	21	**2**	25	**17**	
34	**6**	27	**13**	36	**11**	30	**8**	23	
10	5	**24**	16	**33**	1	**20**	14	**31**	
9	**22**	18	**29**	7	**28**	12	**35**	3	**26**

The Monte Carlo wheel thus has 36 numbers and one 0. Some wheels have only 27, 30, or 33 numbers; and, in addition, they have a 00, or a third 0, called Eagle Bird, these zeros being all green. Some European wheels have a red 0 and a black 0, the single red 0 being counted as odd and below 19; the double black 00 being even, and above 18. Bets on these are not paid, but remain until the next spin and roll, when the player receives double or nothing. The 0 at Monte Carlo takes everything except bets on itself.

The layout for the betting is as follows:

		0		
	1	2	3	
Passe	4	5	6	Manque
(19-36)	7	8	9	(1-18)
	10	11	12	
	13	14	15	
	16	17	18	Impair
Pair (Even)	19	20	21	(Odd)
	22	23	24	
	25	26	27	
Noir	28	29	30	Rouge
(Black)	31	32	33	(Red)
	34	35	36	
P M D				P M D
12 12 12				12 12 12

There are many ways of placing bets. At Monte Carlo, the bets, and the odds paid on them, are as follow:

Any single number, or upon the green 0, 35 for 1.
On a line between 2 numbers, 17 for 1.
On an intersection, taking in 4 numbers, 8 for 1.
Right or left of a line of 3 numbers, 11 for 1.
On the line between 2 rows of 3 numbers, 5 for 1.
At the bottom of a vertical column, 12 numbers, 2 for 1.
On the line between two vertical columns, ½ for 1.

P, Premier, on the numbers 1 through 12, 2 for 1.
M, Milieu, on the numbers 13 through 24, 2 for 1.
D, Dernier, on the numbers 25 through 36, 2 for 1.
On the line between any two of these chances, ½ for 1.
Impair, or odd: even money.
Pair, or even: even money.
Manque, on the numbers 1 through 18, even money.
Passe, on the numbers 19 through 36, even money.
Rouge, that the color of the number will be red: even money.
Noir, that the color of the number will be black: even money.

A wheel with a smaller number of chances pays less in proportion. Thus a 27-number wheel would pay 26 for 1 on single numbers.

When 0 comes up, the bank pays bets on the 0; and takes up all bets but those on an even chance. These are shifted into a "prison," and the next roll decides them, the bettor winning the stake back or losing it. This is equivalent to the bank's taking half of the amount on the 0 roll, and requiring the player to bet the other half on the same even chance the next time.

E. O.

This extreme simplification of Roulette was popular in the early 19th century. The outer part of a circular table about 4 feet in diameter is marked with compartments alternately marked E, even, and O, odd, the bets being placed in these compartments. Inside this is a stationary sloping gallery around which the ball is rolled. Centering the table is a circular section divided into 42 compartments, marked alternately E and O, except for 2, which are bar-holes. The circular inner section is turned about with handles, while the ball rolls around the gallery. The ball rolls into one of the compartments or niches, and this determines the bets. One bar-hole is marked E, and one O. If the ball rolls into a bar-hole, the banker wins all bets upon the opposite letter, while those betting on the same letter merely regain their stakes.

BAGATELLE GAMES

BAGATELLE

Bagatelle was originally played on a special table 6 to 10 feet long, and 1½ to 3 feet wide. At the upper end are 9 holes or cups, 8 in a circle and 1 in the center, and numbered as below.

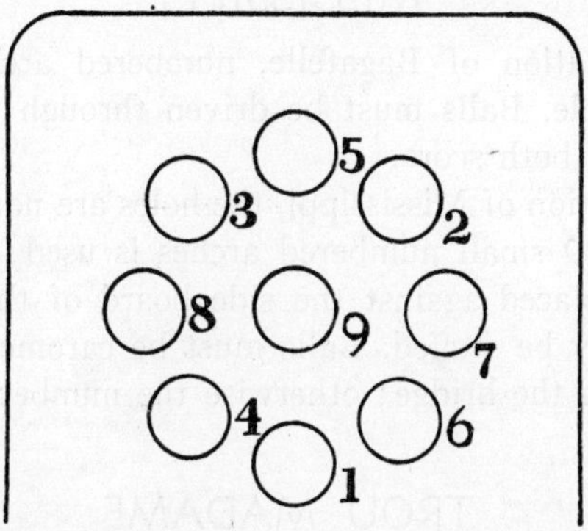

There are 4 red balls, 4 white balls, and 1 black ball. As usually played, the black ball is placed 9 inches in front of cup 1; and on his first shot the player hits with the point of his cue a red ball, which must strike the black ball; and thereafter he shoots to sink as many balls as possible into the cups, shooting one by one all the rest of the balls. The black ball counts double the value of the hole in which it falls. The usual game score is 120. The game is merely simplified pool.

A mace may be used instead of a cue, with which to strike the ball. To determine the lead, each player drives one ball up the board; and whoever scores the highest has the lead. Any number of rounds may be played for game, agreed upon in advance. The score is determined by the number beside each hole.

SANS EGAL

This is a game for two players. One player takes the 4 red balls, and one the 4 white balls. The black ball is placed as in

Bagatelle, and counts the same as in that game. The leader shoots one of his balls, and then his opponent shoots one, and so alternately. A player counts toward his own game all of his own balls holed by himself or his opponent; and also the black ball, if he holes it. The player who makes the most points in a round leads to the next. The game is 21, or 31, as agreed in advance.

MISSISSIPPI

In this variation of Bagatelle, numbered arches are placed before each hole. Balls must be driven through the arches into the holes; and both score.

In one variation of Mississippi, the holes are not used; instead, a bridge with 9 small numbered arches is used; and two small cushions are placed against the side board of the table, or the whole side may be stuffed. Balls must be caromed off a cushion before entering the bridge; otherwise the number counts for the opponent.

TROU MADAME

In this variation of Mississippi, using both arches and holes, the former are scored to the player making them, and the latter are scored against him.

In one variation of Trou Madame, the cups are not used; instead, the bridge is used as in the variation of Mississippi. There are no cushions, and balls are played straight from the end of the board through the bridge.

RUSSIAN BAGATELLE, or COCKAMAROO TABLE

Russian Bagatelle, in which the board slopes upward, begins the development into modern Bagatelle games. It can be best understood from the diagram.

The cups count the numbers marked on them. The 50 cup has a bell suspended from the arch above it. A ball which passes through and rings the bell counts double wherever it lands thereafter; but not if it fails to pass through, and merely lands in the 50. The pegs are brass pins standing 1½ inches high. The balls

are shot from the two slightly lowered alleys on each side of the board. At the base are cavities into which the balls may run, counting as they are marked.

Each player shoots one ball for lead; the highest score winning. The leader chooses his alley; and shoots; thereafter the players shoot alternately, except as below. Each player shoots one ball only, scoring each shot. If a ball gets stuck on the table not in a scoring position, alternately thereafter both players use the remaining ball. Whoever looses the ball so lodged, scores for both. If both balls are lodged, the ball last lodged must be taken up, and the game continued.

A player leads as long as he continues to lodge a ball in a cup. When he fails, the ball passes. The game consists of 100 points or more, as agreed on in advance. Playing into the top 100 hole ends the game at once. If the ball goes around and down the opponent's alley, the player loses 5 points and the ball. If the ball returns down the player's alley, he loses 1 point and the shot. The winner of one game leads in the next.

HOMEMADE BAGATELLE

As played today, each player has a definite number of balls or marbles, and one once rolled scores and remains where it scores until the player's turn is completed. A homemade board can easily be made, sloping slightly upward, with any variation of obstacles and scoring. Balls may be struck with homemade cues, or marbles rolled, shot, or tapped up the alley, with tiny nails as obstacles.

BOARD BAGATELLE

The small Bagatelle boards easily obtainable, and so popular in hotel lobbies and elsewhere, usually have the marbles shot by a plunger equipped with a spring, the plunger being drawn back and released. Scores are usually from 10 to 500 for each cup, or zero if the ball lands back in the trough beside the player. Variations of the game include boards resembling baseball fields, race tracks, football gridirons, and so on.

BAGATELLE FOOTBALL

This is a combination of Bagatelle and Bowling or Tenpins, scored as in Football. On the floor, draw chalk lines to represent the 10 yard lines on a football field 100 yards long. Off to one side, set up 10 Indian clubs, ten-pins, or the like, as in Bowling or Tenpins. Mark a different score on the bottom of each, such as:

1. Line plunge, gain 5 yards.
2. Penalty for offside, 10 yards.
3. End run, 15 yards.
4. Penalty for holding, 10 yards.
5. Forward pass, 30 yards.
6. Penalty for slugging, 15 yards.
7. Penalty for intercepted forward pass, 10 yards.
8. Safety, score 2.
9. Field goal, score 3.
10. Touchdown, score 6.

Divide the players into two teams, preferably of 11 men each. A referee rearranges the order in which the ten-pins are set up whenever he thinks necessary, so that the players cannot remember which they are throwing at; or this element may be eliminated. A score-keeper, while a team is rolling, moves a marker representing that team's ball up and down the chalked football field, and marks down all scores made. He is usually kept busier than any player. Each player has one roll with a basketball or indoor baseball at the clubs. When one team has made all the scores it can in one roll to each player, the quarter is over, and the other team gets the ball. As many quarters or rounds as are desired may be played.

BAGATELLE BASEBALL

This is played as Bagatelle Football, except that a baseball diamond is drawn, and baseball scorings are substituted. For instance, 1 base hit, out on caught fly, 2 bagger, out stealing bases, 3 bagger, out on caught foul, home run, out on three strikes, base-runner steals home (scored only if man is on base), out at first. Nine players should make up a team, and different markers must be used by the scorer for moving a team's men around the base. Any one player can retire his side in one roll by getting three out; but all scores made are counted before the outs are counted. Three outs retires a side. Nine or more innings may be played.

INDOOR ARCHERY

The target is similar to that used for outdoor archery. The arrows may be the regulation type, or be pointed to stick in the target, or have suction cups to stick where they hit. Played otherwise as outdoor archery.

INDOOR DARTS

Indoor dars may be played similarly.

MAH JONGG

Mah Jongg originated in China, perhaps very anciently. There is a Chinese legend that for centuries Chinese royalty played the game, keeping knowledge of it from commoners. Other legends ascribe its origin to a Chinese general, who invented it to entertain his soldiers during a prolonged siege; or to Chinese sailors, who played the game to ward off seasickness. The game is similar in play to certain forms of the card game Rummy. The pieces, called tiles, resemble dominoes, except that each stands for one value only, and none are double, as in dominoes.

The Players.—Mah Jong is usually played by four persons. Two, three, five or six may play, but the standard game is for four players.

Equipment.—A complete outfit consists of 144 tiles, as the pieces are called; 108 suit tiles, 28 honor tiles, and 8 Flowers, also called Seasons. The Seasons may be omitted in play.

There are 3 suits: Bamboos, Characters and Dots (sometimes called Circles). Each suit has 36 titles: 4 each of 9 denominations, numbered from 1 through 9. No suit outranks another. The 1's and 9's, called Terminals, in certain cases outrank the other denominations, which are often called Simples. The Honors do not constitute a suit. They are the Winds and the Dragons: 4 each of the 4 Winds, East, South, West and North, making 16; and 4 each of the 3 Dragons, Green, Red and White. East Wind designates both a tile and the player so designated. There are special values scored when a player holds tiles of his own wind. During the first round, East is the prevailing wind; during the 2nd, South; 3rd, West; 4th, North. Players sit at the table in the order of winds given above. There are 4 red Seasons and 4 green ones: the 4 of each color are numbered 1 through 4 or marked E, S, W, and N. The four 1's or E's are East's Seasons; the 4 2's or S's are South's and so on. (See design on opposite page.)

Preliminaries.—There are no partners; each player is for himself. One of each of the 4 Wind tiles are shuffled together, and each player draws one; and the players sit: East; to his right, South; and then, in rotation, West, and North. East retains his position until some other player has won a game. When positions are shifted, the order remains the same. Deal and play start with East; and, in settling, East pays or receives double. A round ends when each player has held and lost the East position. At the

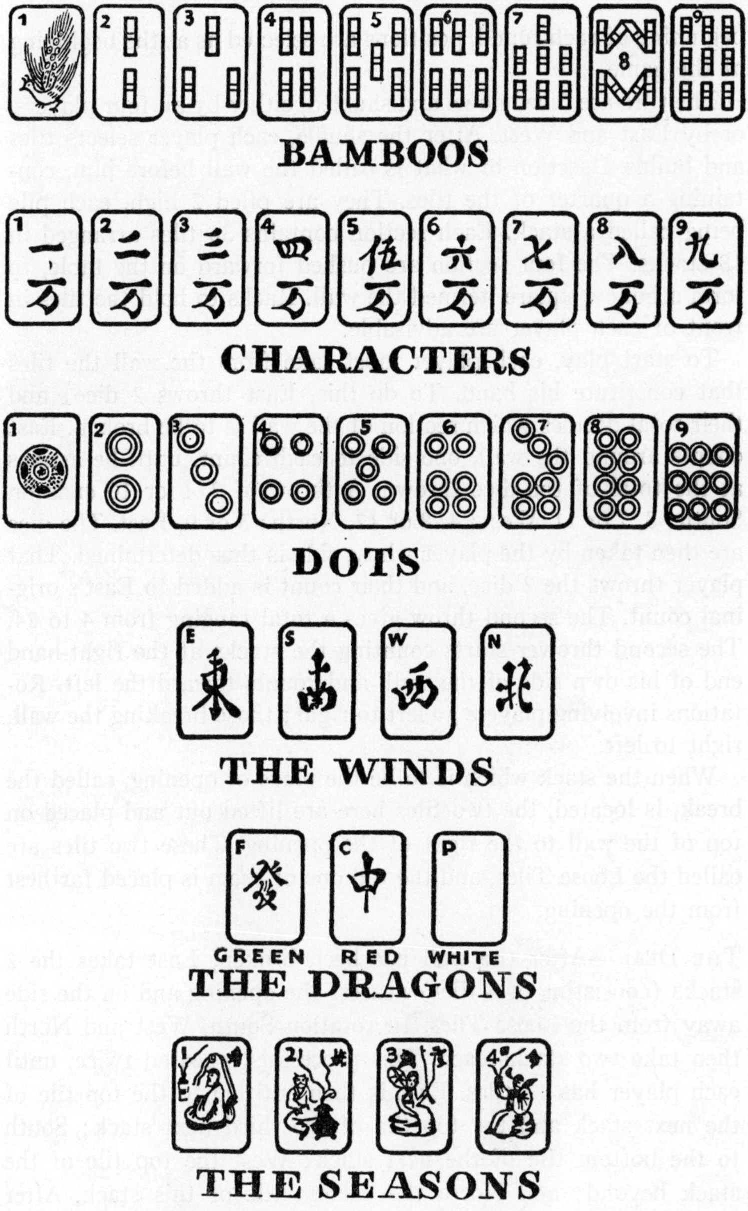

Design Showing Mah Jongg Characters

beginning of each round, positions are selected as at the beginning of the game.

The tiles are faced down and shuffled, either by all four players, or by East and West. After the shuffle, each player selects tiles and builds a section of what is called the wall before him, containing a quarter of the tiles. They are piled 2 high, each pile being called a stack. Each section contains 36 tiles arranged in 18 stacks. The four section are pushed forward on the table, to form a hollow square, termed the wall. Racks to hold the tiles in front of each player are advisable.

To start play, each player must take from the wall the tiles that constitute his hand. To do this, East throws 2 dice; and their total decides which section of the wall is to be broken. East counts around the wall, one side to each count, until he arrives at the total of the dice thrown. A throw of 2, 6 or 10 ends on South, 3, 7 or 11, West; 4, 8 or 12, North; 5 or 9, East. The dice are then taken by the player whose side is thus determined. That player throws the 2 dice, and their count is added to East's original count. The second throw gives a total ranging from 4 to 24. The second thrower starts counting the stacks at the right-hand end of his own side of the wall, and counts toward the left. Rotations involving players go left to right; those breaking the wall, right to left.

When the stack which is to be the place of opening, called the break, is located, the two tiles here are lifted out and placed on top of the wall to the right of the opening. These two tiles are called the Loose Tiles, and the top one of them is placed farthest from the opening.

The Deal.—After the wall has been broken, East takes the 2 stacks (consisting of 4 tiles) nearest the opening and on the side away from the Loose Tiles. In rotation South, West and North then take two stacks each. This process is repeated twice, until each player has 12 tiles. East is then entitled to the top tile of the next stack and the top tile of the third next stack; South to the bottom tile of the next stack; West the top tile of the stack beyond; and North the bottom tile of this stack. After play begins, the first tile drawn is the bottom tile of the stack left undrawn by East; and then in rotation the top, followed by the bottom, of each stack in the direction away from the Loose Tiles.

THE PLAY.—East now has 14 tiles, and the other players 13 each. Each player arranges his tiles so that he can see them, but the other players cannot. Any Seasons in any hand are at once faced up, and tiles are drawn to replace them. These Seasons belong to the players facing them up, and their value is counted later in reckoning the scores. It is East's play first. If he has a Hand from Heaven, which will be described later, he faces his whole 14 tiles, and wins the game at once. If he has one or more Four-of-a-kinds, he may face them, but is not required to do so. He draws a loose tile for each Four exposed, and discards one tile, no matter how many Fours were faced. If unable to do either, East must discard. A player discards by facing up the tile to be discarded near the center of the table.

CLAIMING DISCARDS.—The order of precedence in claiming a discard is intricate. If South can use East's discard to Woo (from the Chinese word meaning "peace"; meaning here to Mah Jongg, or win the game), he may claim the discard as against any other player for any other purpose. The same right then passes to West and North. A player who can Woo takes precedence over any player who cannot. If no player can use the discard to Woo, in rotation a player may claim it to Kong a Four, or Pung a Triplet. Kong means using a discard to complete a Four; Pung, to complete a Triplet; and Chow, to complete a Sequence. If no player claims the discard for Woo, Kong, or Pung, South may use it to Chow. Only the player next right to the discarder has this right. Lastly, if South does not wish to claim East's discard, he must draw a tile from the wall. A player is never obliged to Woo, Kong, Pung or Chow.

This procedure governs each subsequent discard. Any player may always claim a discard to Chow, when this permits him to Woo. A pair may be completed by claiming a discard, only if this permits the player to Woo. A time limit is given for deciding on whether to claim a discard or not. This time limit is usually the time before the player next in rotation has completed the first stage of his play, whether drawing and discarding, quitting a Season, or completing a Four; or before a Chower has quitted the 3 cards of his sequence; or to Woo, before a player beyond him, who has claimed it to Woo, has completed his Wooing. When a player's hand is withdrawn from a tile, it is quitted.

THE PLAY.—A tile must be drawn whenever a Four is faced. The fourth tile of a faced Four is not a numerical part of the hand. A "concealed" Four must be faced up; and a Four may thus be both "concealed" and "exposed," as will be explained later.

A Sequence is a combination of 3 suit-tiles in order as to denomination; one of these must be from a discard, and each must be of 3 tiles only. A Chow is completed when its 3 tiles are faced up and the discard is quitted. A Triplet is 3 tiles of the same suit and denomination, or 3 Dragons of the same color, or 3 Winds of the same direction. Seasons cannot form Triplets. Punging is forming a Triplet by using a discard, and is completed when the Punger's tile is quitted in discarding. Konging is similar, forming a Four by using a discard; and is completed when the Konger's tile is quitted in discarding. A Four may also be completed by drawing a fourth tile to a concealed Triplet; when placed with the 2 end tiles faced down, this is a concealed Four. A Four may also be completed by drawing a fourth tile to a Triplet faced up; but not by adding a fourth tile discarded to a Triplet faced up.

THE MAH JONGG OR WINNING HAND.—When a player builds up a hand of 14 tiles, consisting of 4 Triplets and a pair, he is in position to Mah Jongg. He must do this immediately after Punging, Chowing, drawing, or drawing a loose tile, and before discarding. A player may not Mah Jongg immediately after declaring a Four or drawing a Season, since this gives him only a 13-tile hand, and he needs 14 to Mah Jongg. Another player may Mah Jongg by a process called Robbing the Kong or Stealing the Fourth to Win. When a player adds a tile to a Triplet faced up, that is, grounded, another player who can use the tile to complete a Sequence which gives him four sets (of 3 tiles each, Triplets or Sequences) and a pair, may Woo; but this must be done before the Konger draws a tile from the wall and quits it. A Four formed by adding a fourth tile, discard or draw, to a concealed Triplet, may not be robbed.

The pair completing a Woo is called The Eyes.

Scoring.—There is a bonus of 20 for Wooing. The winner collects the full value of his hand from each non-winner, and pays no one. When East wins, he collects double from each non-winner; when East loses, he pays double to the winner. For "filling the only place to win," drawing 1 tile which alone enables a player to Woo, he gets 2 points extra. When a player Woos by drawing a tile, he counts 2 points extra. When a player Woos by drawing a tile to replace a Season, he counts 2 points extra. When a player Woos by drawing the last tile, he counts 10 points extra, or a double, depending on whether he plays the Cleared-Hand game, the Mixed-Hand game or the One-Double game. When a player Woos on Sequences and a pair, this scores as in drawing the last tile; the same is true for Wooing without a Sequence.

Winners and non-winners score 4 for each Season exposed; and 2 each for a pair of Dragons, Own Winds, and Prevailing Winds. They score also for the following: a Wind pair of one Own and one Prevailing counts 4. Triplets count:

	Grounded	*Concealed*
Simples	2 points	4 points
Honors or Terminals	4 "	8 "

Fours similarly count 8 and 16; and 16 and 32.

A Cleared Hand gives one double to all players in the One-Double and Cleared-Hand Games; in the Mixed-Hand game, one double to winners only. Other doubles are:

An All-Heads Hand (all Honors and Terminals) the same.

A 1-suit hand: the same, except 3 doubles, instead of 1.

An All-Honor Hand (Winds and Dragons only) when not a Wooing hand, 3 extra doubles in the first two games. If a Wooing hand, it is a Limit Hand in all games.

An All-Terminal Hand: a Limit Hand if Wooing; otherwise, 3 doubles in the first two games.

Own and Prevailing Wind: a Triplet or Four of Own Wind gives a double; the same with Prevailing Wind; of both winds, 2 doubles, to all players in all games.

Dragons: Each Triplet or Four of Dragons, 1 double to all players in all games.

Seasons: Own Season, 1 double; pair, 2 doubles; Bouquet without other Own Season, 4 doubles; Bouquet with other own Season, 5 doubles; all 8 Seasons, 8 doubles. These are computed after scoring 4 for each Season faced. All doubles double the total score of the player.

All-Sequence and No-Sequence Hands: 1 double, in the Mixed-Hand and One-Double Games.

In scoring, 10's only are counted (after doubles have been reckoned) all below 5 being eliminated, and all above being counted as 10.

The Mixed-Hand Game is usually played; this requires any four sets (Triplets, Fours or Sequences) and a pair. In the Cleared-Hand Game, the hand that Woos must contain all Honors; all Honors and suit-tiles of 1 suit only; all Terminals; or all Honors and Terminals. The One-Double Game requires the Wooing hand to contain at least one double, outside of Seasons.

The penalty for a false declaration of Mah Jongg is half the limit. The scoring by the official rules is:

All Hands

(First count for grounded; second for concealed)

Triplets: Simples, 2 and 4; Terminals, 4 and 8; Honors, 4 and 8. Fours, 4 times as much in each case. Pair of Dragons of any color, Player's Own Wind, Prevailing Wind, 2, 3. Own Wind when prevailing, 4, 4. Each Season, 4 only when grounded.

Doubles for All Hands

Triplets or Fours of any color of Dragons, or Player's Own Wind or Prevailing Wind, 1 double. Own Wind when Prevailing, 2 doubles. Own Season, 1 double; Bouquet of 4 Seasons, 4 doubles (including the double for own Season).

Winning Hand Only Scores These Bonuses

Mah Jongg, any game: 20. Drawing winning tile, 2 (all these until otherwise stated in any game). Filling only place, 2. Winning with last tile or subsequent discard, 1 double; except in Cleared-Hand Game, 10.

The same for winning with tile drawn after Kong; robbing a Kong; a hand of all Sequences and a non-scoring pair; and a hand of no Sequences. When all the tiles are of 1 suit, with honors, 1 double in any game; except in the Mixed game, non-winners also score this. The same for All Terminals with Honors. All 1 suit, no Honors, 3 doubles: in all but the Mixed Game, allowed to all players. All Terminals or all Honors, the hand is a Limit. In all but the Mixed Hand Game, these score 3 doubles for non-winners, in addition to any other doubles the hands contain. The Limit is arbitrarily fixed, usually at 1,000 for East, and 500 for any other hand.

Limit Hands.—These include:

I. Hidden Treasure: 4 Triplets or Fours and a pair, all drawn.

II. All Honors: The same, all of Winds and Dragons.

III. All Terminals: The same, all of Terminals.

IV. All Green: The same, made up from Green Dragons, and 2, 3, 4, 6 and 8 of Bamboos.

V. Three Great Scholars: Triplets or Four of each of the 3 Dragons, Red, White, and Green, with any set and pair.

VI. Four Large Blessings: Triplets or Fours of all 4 Winds, and any pair.

VII. All Kongs: 4 Fours, and any pair.

VIII. Nine Gales: A concealed hand all of one suit, with denominations 1, 1, 1, 2, 3, 4, 5, 6, 7, 8, 9, 9, 9: completed by draw or discard.

IX. Thirteen Orphans: 1 of each Wind, 1 of each Dragon, one 1 and one 9 of each suit; with a tile pairing with any of these.

X. Hand from Heaven: when East Woos before discarding.

XI. Hand from Earth: When a player, other than East, Woos with East's first discard.

XII. Moon from the Bottom of the Sea: When a hand is completed by drawing the last tile, which is a Dot.

XIII. Plum Blossom on the Roof: When a hand is completed by a tile drawn after a Kong, and this tile is the 5 of Dots.

XIV. Scratching a Carrying-Pole: When a hand is completed by Robbing a Kong; and the tile is the 2 of Bamboos.

XV. Kong on Kong: When a player draws after a Kong; and the tile completes another Kong; and he draws another tile, which completes the hand.

XVI. Heavenly Twins: a hand of 7 different pairs of Honors; or 7 different pairs all of one suit. The final tile may come from draw or discard.

A hand of 7 different pairs of one suit and Honors, or of Terminals and Honors, scores half the limit. The final tile may come from draw or discard.

TWO-HANDED MAH JONGG

The two players sit opposite each other, and alternate as East and West. Each player builds the side of the wall in front of him, and also on his right. In throwing to determine which breaks the wall, odd selects East, and even, West. A discard cannot be Chowed. East does not pay nor receive double. The non-winner pays the full amount of the winner's score.

THREE-HANDED MAH JONGG

The West Wind tile is omitted in the preliminary shuffle and draw for seats. The positions are the same, with West omitted. Each player builds his own side of the wall, and draws 12 tiles toward building the last side. Otherwise, in all these variations, the rules of Mah Jongg apply.

FIVE-HANDED MAH JONGG

A suit tile is shuffled with the 4 Winds for the draw for suits. The player who draws it sits out during the first game. After each game, East retires; and the player sitting out enters as North.

SIX-HANDED MAH JONGG

A 1 and a 9 tile are shuffled with the 4 Winds. These players sit out the first game. On the 2nd, the one who drew the 1 tile becomes North; East retiring each time. On the 3rd, the one who drew the 1 becomes North. The player who has sat out longest re-enters the game thereafter.

CROKINOLE

EQUIPMENT.—The board is the size of a bridge table, with a wooden rim surrounding it half an inch high. The playing area of it is a circle of polished wood, with a radius an inch less than the distance from the table's center to the nearest point on its edge. On this playing area three concentric circles are marked, the outer one half an inch inside the circle that constitutes the board, the distance between the two outer circles marked on the board being the radius of the inner circle. There are 8 posts or pegs around the inner circle at equal distances from each other, each one covered with rubber to deaden the impacts of the disks. In the center of the board is a depression slightly larger than a disk. A trough lies between the circle that is the playing board and the rims. There are also 24 Crokinole disks, 12 of one color, 12 of another.

THE PLAY.—The game is played by two, three or four players, four being divided into two partnerships of two each; and if three play, one playing against the other two as partners. Choice of color and seat is determined as in Chess or Checkers; or by having each player shoot with his released finger one piece toward the center, the closest to it winning. To determine first shot, the same process is repeated. The winner can elect to go in any position, last being the most advantageous, as in Croquet.

The object of the game is to win points by shooting the disks so that they remain on the highest scoring circles on the board at the end of the game, with opponent's disks shot off. The points score:

	Points
Between outer circles	5
Between 2nd and inner circle	10
Within inner circle	15
Within central depression	20

Touching a ring counts as inside it; but a disk must lie fairly inside the central depression to score 20. The game is 100 points. The first shot must be for the center; thereafter, each shot must be aimed at an opponent's disk, if one is on the board. A man landing fairly in the center scores 20 at once; 20 more if it is knocked out and immediately falls back in again; and 20 more if it is there at the end of the game. At the end, the scorers are totalled, and the first player or side reaching 100 wins.

INDOOR CROQUET

This game is played with a miniature Croquet set placed on the floor. The rules are the same as Croquet.

PIT, FLINCH, MONOPOLY, EASY MONEY, CAMELOT, Etc.

Such copyrighted card or board games as Pit, Flinch, and the later Monopoly, Easy Money, etc., as well as recent games like Camelot, all have instructions accompanying the cards or board.

TIDDLY-WINK

In its simplest form, this game requires disks of bone or ivory, which are snapped by pressure of a larger disk against their edges, into a cup or container. Each player has an equal number of small disks, and scores 1 for each disk snapped into the container. The winner is the first player to snap all his disks into the container.

More complicated layouts are often used, with concentric rings: the cup scores 5, the rings 4, 3, 2 and 1. An agreed score determines the winner.

JACKSTRAWS

Jackstraws require special equipment. The straws may be matches or toothpicks, with two of these used to move or flip the straws from the pile; or the fingers may be used. A Jackstraws set has colored sticks of wood a little longer than matches, and a little stick with a tiny wire hook at one end, to aid in removing the straws. The first player holds the straws over the center of the table, the bottom ends touching, and releases them so that they fall in a complicated pile. The player to the left plays first, and removes as many straws as he can, without causing any other straw to move. When another straw moves, the player must replace the straw he was removing, and the play passes to the player next on the left. This continues until all the straws have been removed. The player with the most straws wins.

FOUR-FIVE-SIX, PICK UP STICKS; WOOD PILE, Etc.

A set of larger jackstraws may be purchased, under one of the names above; each stick resembles a knitting-needle, 6 to 7 inches long and tapering at both ends. The sticks have different scoring values: as, black, 20; blue, 10; green, 6; red, 5; and yellow, 4. Fingers must be used, until the black stick is obtained; in which case it may be used, only by its owner, to help lift off the other sticks. A yellow, red and green stick in order doubles the value of the three. Otherwise the game is played as above. In one variation, each player in turn must remove all the sticks from the pile, if possible; when he misses, the whole pile is released at the center again, and the next player tries.

GAMING WITH COINS

TOSSING or FLIPPING COINS

From time immemorial, disputed matters have been settled by tossing or flipping coins. When familiar coins are tossed, the custom is to call "Heads" or "Tails." The coin must fall flat on the tossing surface or hand; otherwise it is a fouled toss, and must again be tossed. The one calling names whether he expects Heads or Tails to face uppermost; the tosser takes the one not called, and wins the toss if the caller was wrong in his guess.

LAGGING COINS

A lagging line is drawn on the ground, 10 to 25 feet away from the players, who stand on a throwing line. Coins—pennies, dimes, nickels, quarters, halves or dollars—are thrown by the players, the one whose coin is most nearly lying across the lagging line winning.

BOOK THREE

PARTY GAMES FOR ADULTS AND JUNIORS

THESE are the games that are enjoyed by everyone from high school age to ninety. Here are the games that call upon the brain to function swiftly and accurately. Here, also, is a large group of guessing games and amusing games, which give the guests ample opportunity for amusement and laughter. And finally, there is an interesting and varied collection of hilarious games and stunts. These will insure the success of any party. Even the most sedate person will find delight in testing his skill and nimbleness in these uproarious pastimes.

I. BRAIN TESTERS

THESE are quiet games that require intelligent concentration. Any one of them makes an ideal interlude in the midst of more strenuous entertainment. Most of them require some advance preparation, and pencils and papers for the guests.

There are two usual ways of scoring. When things are to be identified, the guest making the longest list of identifications may be called the winner; or the winner may be the first to make the correct identification.

Unless otherwise stated, each guest is provided with a paper and pencil for the following games.

AFFINITIES

Within a stated time, each guest must write down as many familiar affinities—words commonly joined by *and*—as possible Examples are, Adam and Eve, tried and true, etc. The player with the longest list wins.

Split Affinities: Each player is provided with a list of unfinished affinities, such as: Mutt and ———, mother and ———. In a limited time, these are to be filled out. The player with the longest correct list wins.

A list of typical affinities might include:

Adam and Eve
Alpha and Omega
Anthony and Cleopatra
Army and Navy
Assault and Battery
Bag and baggage
Ball and bat
Bed and board
Bigger and better
Black and blue
Black and white
Bow and arrow
Brave and bold
Bread and butter
Brother and sister
Butter and eggs
Cain and Abel
Cakes and Ale
Cap and gown
Cash and carry
Cash and credit
Cat and dog
Check and double-check
Checks and balances
Cheese and crackers
Coat and hat
Coat and vest
Collar and tie
Comb and brush
Come and go
Cream and sugar
Cup and saucer
Damon and Pythias
David and Goliath
David and Jonathan
Day and night
Death and taxes
Down and out
East and West
Ebb and flow
Fair and warmer
Far and near
Fine and dandy
Fire and water
First and last
Fruit and nuts

Gas and oil
Gold and silver
Good and bad
Half and half
Ham and eggs
Hammer and nail
Hammer and tongs
Heaven and Earth
Heaven and Hell
Hit and run
Home and fireside
Horse and wagon
House and lot
Ice cream and cake
In and out
Jack and Jill
Jonah and the whale
King and Queen
Knife and fork
Light and dark
Liver and bacon
Lock and key
Long and short
Macaroni and cheese
Man and beast
Meat and potatoes
Moonlight and honeysuckle
Moonlight and roses
Mother and father
Mutt and Jeff
Needle and thread
North and South
Nut and bolt
Oil and water
Open and shut
Paper and pencil
Pat and Mike
Pen and ink
Pick and choose
Pluck and luck
Poet and peasant
Pork and beans
Put and take
Right and wrong
Rod and reel
Romeo and Juliet
Saddle and bridle
Salt and pepper
Scotch and Soda
Shoes and stockings
Shot and shell
Snow and ice
Soap and water
Son and daughter
Spaghetti and cheese
Stars and Stripes
Stocks and bonds
Sword and shield
The just and the unjust
Thunder and lightning
Time and tide
Touch and go
Tried and true
Whiskey and Soda
Wholesale and retail
Widows and orphans

SIMILES

Within a stated time, each player must write down as many familiar similes as possible; such as, white as snow, red as a rose, etc. The player with the longest list wins.

Split Similes.—Each player is provided with a list of incomplete similes: as, Crazy as ________, green as ________, etc. The player wins who fills in the largest number of these correctly, within a stated time.

A list of typical similes might include:

Bitter as gall.
Black as coal.
Black as night.
Black as pitch.
Black as sin.
Blind as a bat.
Bold as brass.
Brave as a lion.
Bright as a dollar.
Bright as a new penny.
Bright as the sun.
Brown as a berry.
Brown as a nut.
Busy as a bee.
Busy as a one-armed paper-hanger.

Calm as a clock.
Clean as a whistle.
Clear as a bell.
Clear as crystal.
Clear as daylight.
Clever as a monkey.
Cold as ice.
Cozy as a bug in a rug.
Crazy as a loon.
Cross as a stick.

Dead as a doornail
Deep as a well.
Deep as the ocean.
Dry as a bone.
Dull as ditch water.

Fair as a rose.
Fat as a pig.
Finicky as an old maid.
Fit as a fiddle.
Fits like the paper on the wall.
Flat as a pancake.
Fleet as a deer.
Frolicsome as a lamb.
Full as a tick.
Funny as a circus.
Funny as a monkey.

Good as gold.
Green as grass.

Happy as a lark.
Hard as a rock.
Hard as flint.
Heavy as lead.
Honest as the day is long.
Hot as fire.
Hot as Hades.
Huge as an elephant.

Innocent as a babe in arms.
Irish as Patty's pig.

Jumpy as a flea.

Light as a feather.

Mad as a hatter.
Mad as a March hare.
Mean as a miser.
Mean as gar broth.

Merry as a church bell.
Miserable as a wet hen.
Modest as a violet.

Neat as a pin.
Nervous as a cat.

Old as Methusaleh.
Old as the universe.
Old as Time.
Ornery as a mule.

Plain as a pikestaff.
Plain as a pipe stem.
Plain as the nose on your face.
Playful as a kitten.
Plump as a partridge.
Poor as a church mouse.
Pretty as a picture.
Proud as a peacock.
Proud as Lucifer.
Pure as a lily.

Quick as lightning.
Quick as a wink.
Quiet as a mouse.

Red as a beet.
Rich as Croesus.
Rich as Midas.

Safe as a church.
Safe as the Bank of England.
Sharp as a razor.
Shy as a violet.
Skittish as a colt.
Slick as glass.
Slick as lightning.
Slippery as an eel.
Slow as a tortoise.
Slow as molasses in January.
Sly as a fox.
Smooth as butter.
Soft as velvet.
Sound as a bell.
Sour as a lemon.
Spry as a spring chicken.
Stiff as a board.
Stiff as a poker.
Still as a mouse.
Strong as an ox.
Stubborn as a mule.
Stupid as an ostrich.
Sweet as honey.
Sweet as sugar.
Swift as a hare.
Swift as an eagle.

Tall as a giraffe.
Tall as a tree.
Thick as molasses.
Thick as thieves.
Thin as a rail.
Tight as a drum.
Tough as shoe leather.
Transparent as glass.

Ugly as sin.

White as snow.

Yellow as gold.

EARTH, AIR, FIRE, WATER

The guests are seated in a circle. The leader throws a handkerchief in the lap of any one, saying "Earth," or "Air," or "Fire," or "Water," and starts counting 10. If he says "earth," the player with the handkerchief must name an animal that runs on the earth. If "air," a creature that flies; if "water," a creature that swims; if "fire," the player remains silent. Failure to name a proper creature, or speaking when "Fire" is said, gives the player a black mark. Three such marks call for a forfeit. No creature once named can be named again.

If "Earth" requires a mammal, "Air" a bird, "Water" a fish, the game is more difficult.

TANGLED TALES

Provide each player with a list of 15 to 25 incorrect statements, with space for corrections, such as:

Franklin Roosevelt is Secretary of State.
The Empire State Building is in Boston.
Rex Beach is a bathing resort.
Cleopatra was the wife of Henry VIII.
Moses was a Mahometan.
Paraguay is the capital of Brazil.
The Mississippi River flows into the Pacific Ocean.
Grapes grow on trees.
Paris is on the River Marne.
The Great Lakes belong to the United States.

The winner is the player with the most corrections during the time limit. An erroneous correction deducts 1 from a player's score.

Right or Wrong?—This game may be varied by having half of the statements correct, and half wrong. Give a credit of 1 for each accurate correction, and a penalty of 1 for altering a correct statement.

WHICH?

Provide statements with three alternatives to each. In each case, the player crosses out the two wrong ones. Thus:

Ambition is a noun, an accident, a country.
Dogs, sing, bark, talk.
Sweden is in Africa, Australia, Europe.

Score as in Tangled Tales.

QUESTIONS AND ANSWERS

Any *Questions and Answer Book* may be used. A questionnaire is chosen, and the questions read slowly, one at a time, allowing the players time to write their answers. The questions are then corrected. Score for correct, ½ for half or more than half correct, 0 for less than half correct.

It is more amusing to have the players read their questions aloud, in rotation, permitting the other players to say whether the answer is right or wrong. Then give the correct answer.

Home-Made Questions and Answers.—These may be prepared in advance, either a typed list for each player, or one list to be read as above. The advantage of this is that the lists may be made to suit the occasion or group, or can deal with something in which the guests are interested, such as: Do You Know Your Boston (or whatever your city is)? Do You Know Your State? Do You Know Your History? Do You Know Your Rivers? Do You Know Your Plants? etc.

Trick questions can be thrown in, and add to the amusement. Such as:

Where was Walter Scott when he wrote The Star Spangled Banner? (He didn't; Francis Scott Key wrote it).

Why was Lincoln called the Father of his Country? (He wasn't; George Washington was so called).

Where did Friday accompany Don Quixote? (He didn't; Sancho Panzo accompanied him).

What was John Bunyan's real name? (John Bunyan).

How long was Moses in the ark? (He wasn't; Noah was in it).

Caucus Race.—Start with a written Elimination Questionnaire of from 6 to 10 questions. Choose six to eight players who scored highest—half boys, half girls, for the finals. Line up the Finalists on a starting line. Read 20 to 30 questions aloud, one at a time. Answers are written and corrected at once. Winners move a full step forward; half winners, half a step; losers remain where they are. The Finalists progress in this manner, step by step, after each question. The one in the lead at the end wins. This is a gay dramatization of Questions and Answers.

Baseball Questions and Answers.—Divide the guests into teams of nine. Draw circles for the home plate and the three bases on the floor. Each player gets one question in turn; first player to bat. If he answers accurately, he goes to first base; if not, he is one out for his side. Players move on bases at each correct answer, and score when the fourth answer is correct, since the man on third base comes home. When one side has three outs, the other team comes to bat.

NUT QUESTIONNAIRE

Provide silly questions. Score is given for the cleverest answer in each case. Possible questions:

Who killed the Dead Sea?
Why is the Fourth of July? (Y is the fourth letter of July).
On what date is March 1st in Siam?
Who is the Admiral of the Swiss navy?
Which is the other side of the street?
What is the diameter of a square?

HIDDEN ANIMALS

Provide each guest with a list of sentences, each concealing the name of an animal. Thus:

The Real Estate *Co. w*ants more business. (Cow)
There is too much a*do g*oing on here. (Dog)
Mary and John bot*h are* here. (Hare)
If you take a di*p ig*nore the cold. (Pig)
He labore*d on key*note speeches. (Donkey)

Verti*go at*tacks the head. (Goat)
To such as *she, ep*aulets are marvelous. (Sheep)
Men ab*hor se*dentary games. (Horse)
He*r at*tachment was merely temporary. (Rat)
He mu*st ag*gravate all who know him. (Stag)

Within a given time, the animals must be discovered and written down. Deduct nothing for a blank, 1 for a wrong answer. The longest correct list wins.

Hidden Birds.—Played in the same manner, the sentences concealing names of birds.

Hidden Fish.—Played in the same manner, the sentences concealing names of fish.

QUOTATIONS

Prepare lists of familiar quotations, or one list from which they may be read; a list for each guest is better. Within a stated time, the players are to identify the quotations by writing the names of their authors. Thus:

The proper study of mankind is man. (Pope.)
If winter comes, can spring be far behind? (Shelley.)
As idle as a painted ship upon a painted ocean. (Coleridge.)
Her voice was ever soft, gentle and low, an excellent thing in woman. (Shakespeare.)
A man's a man for a' that. (Burns.)
The quality of mercy is not strained. (Shakespeare.)
A little learning is a dangerous thing. (Alexander Pope.)
A thing of beauty is a joy forever. (John Keats.)
Men may come and men may go, but I go on forever. (Alfred Tennyson.)
If the people can't eat bread, let them eat cake. (Marie Antoinette.)
Give me liberty or give me death. (Patrick Henry.)
Veni, vidi, vici. (Julius Caesar.)
War is hell. (General Sherman.)

A rose by any other name would smell as sweet. (Shakespeare.)
Only God can make a tree. (Joyce Kilmer.)
Beyond the Alps lies Italy. (Julius Caesar.)
I'll fight it out on this line if it takes all summer. (General Grant.)
We must all hang together; or assuredly we will all hang separately. (Benjamin Franklin.)
Government of the people, by the people, and for the people. (Abraham Lincoln.)
Forward the Light Brigade! (Alfred Tennyson.)

A book of famous quotations will aid in this game.

Broken Quotations.—Prepare lists of incomplete quotations, and give the players a stated time in which to complete them. Thus:

The proper study of ________
________ spring be far behind?
Her voice was ever soft, gentle and low, ________

LIST THE STATES

Require each player to list as many of the 48 states as possible in a limited time. The longest list wins.

State Capitals.—List state capitals instead of states. It is more difficult if the players list the cities, and the rivers they are on, if any.

The game can be varied by listing different things: military conquerors, lakes of the world, great events of any year, capitals of the various countries, fish, flowers, animals, vegetables, evil omens, etc.

ADVERTISING SLOGANS

Provide each guest with a list of 20 or more familiar advertising slogans to be identified. Such as: Ask the man who owns one. (Packard.) Eventually, why not now? (Gold Medal Flour.) It's dated. (Chase and Sanborn's Coffee.) Be nonchalant; light a ________. (Murad Cigarettes). When better cars are made, ________ will make them. (Buick.) Not a cough in a carload. (Old Gold Cigarettes.) The watch that made the dollar famous. (Ingersoll.) The Ham What Am. (Armour's Star Ham.) Just a real good car. (Dodge.) Going, going, gone. (Herpicide.) The skin you love to touch. (Woodbury's Soap.) Reach for a ________ instead of a sweet. (Lucky Strike Cigarettes.) When it rains, it pours. (Morton's Salt.) Keep that schoolgirl complexion. (Palmolive Soap.) It hasn't scratched yet. (Bon Ami.) I'd walk a mile for a ________ (Camel Cigarettes.) Four out of every five have it. (Forhan's Tooth Paste.) They're mild but they satisfy. (Chesterfield Cigarettes.) Your best friend won't tell you. (Listerine.) Nature's internal beauty bath. (Pluto Water.) It chases dirt. (Old Dutch Cleanser.)

FAMOUS NICKNAMES

Provide, for identification, lists of famous nicknames, such as: Honest Abe (Abraham Lincoln), Old Hickory (Andrew Jackson), The Big Stick (Theodore Roosevelt), Old Rough and Ready (Zachary Taylor), Blood and Iron (Bismarck), The Lone Eagle (Charles Augustus Lindbergh), Old Rowley (Charles II of England), Buffalo Bill (Colonel William F. Cody), Hell and Maria (General Charles Dawes), The Good Grey Poet (Walt Whitman), The It Girl (Clara Bow), etc.

Nicknames of States.—Played the same way, using the nicknames of the states, such as: The Empire State (N. Y.), The Old Dominion (Va.), the Lone Star State (Tex.), the Buckeye State (Ohio), the Keystone State (Penna.), the Nutmeg State (Conn.), the Hoosier State (Ind.), the Pine Tree State (Me.), the Sunflower State (Kan.), the Palmetto State (S. C.), the Granite State (N. H.).

City Nicknames.—This is more difficult, but is played the same way. Thus: the Windy City (Chicago), the Druid City (Tuscaloosa), City of Brotherly Love (Phila.), Beantown, or the Hub (Boston), Gotham, or Bagdad-on-the-Subway (New York), City of Elms (New Haven), the Magic City (Birmingham), etc.

WHAT DID SHE WEAR?

A girl enters the room, wearing as many things as possible, besides her regular attire: hat, rubbers, coat, gloves, handbag, umbrella, etc. The players have been told to watch her carefully. She walks around, and then goes out. It is permissible to mislead them by telling them to watch what she does. When she has left, the players are told to list the things she wore. The longest correct list wins; penalize 1 for each thing listed that she did not wear.

Fashion Plate.—A man fills the rôle in this similar game.

NAME THE TUNE

Provide from 10 to 20 numbered phonograph records. Play a short strain from each. The guests must write down the name of the music, identifying by number. They may be required to add the composer's name.

The music may be played on the piano, the pieces being selected in advance and numbered.

The choruses of old popular favorites may be played through once. The players must identify the song, the approximate date of its appearance, and the play, if any, from which it came.

Name the Picture.—Tack on the wall copies of 10 to 20 famous pictures, numbered, such as Maxfield Parrish's *Castles in the Air*, Burne-Jones' *Sir Galahad*, da Vinci's *Mona Lisa* and *The Last Supper*, Reynold's *Age of Innocence*, Raphael's *Sistine Madonna*, etc. Have the players identify these.

Advertising Pictures.—Display such pictures as the Gold Dust Twins, Aunt Jemima, etc., and have them identified. Pictures of automobiles may be used.

FAMOUS DATES

Provide lists of historical dates for identification, such as: 1066 (Battle of Hastings), 1492 (Columbus Discovered America), 1620 (Landing of the Pilgrims), 1776 (Declaration of Independence), 1861 (the Civil War), 1898 (the Spanish American War), 1914 (the World War), etc.

Suggestive Numbers.—Intersperse the dates with logically suggestive numbers which the players must reasonably identify. For instance, 10 (Nights in a Barroom), 12 (Apostles), 7 (come Eleven), 100 (in the shade), 60 (minutes in an hour), 640 (acres to the square mile), etc. Any appropriate ingenious answers are correct.

FAMOUS CHARACTERS

Tack up numbered pictures of historical persons, such as Abraham Lincoln, Queen Elizabeth, Queen Victoria, Theodore Roosevelt, Franklin Roosevelt, Henry VIII, Longfellow, George Washington, Beethoven, Walt Whitman, Julius Caesar, Napoleon, etc. The guests write their identifications. Identification games may all be scored as above.

Name the Stars.—Do the same thing with moving picture celebrities, stage celebrities, radio performers, etc.

Stamp Collecting.—Use stamps which bear the heads of familiar people instead of pictures: Franklin, Martha Washington, Sherman, Grant, Columbus, Washington, Edward VIII, Queen Victoria, Lenin, Hitler, etc.

POEM IDENTIFICATIONS

Tack up lines from familiar poems, using 2 to 4 lines of each, having each excerpt numbered. The guests write the name of each poem, and of its author.

MUSICAL ROMANCE

An amusing short story can be prepared, with blanks to be filled in by the names of songs, whose chorus openings are played on the piano. Ingenuity will suggest the details of such a contest. The winner is the one with the most correct identifications.

Similar short stories may be prepared, whose blanks are to be filled in with names of books, stories, novels, poems, flowers, etc.

IDENTIFICATIONS

Seeds.—Place in numbered saucers a few flower, vegetable and fruit seeds, each in its own saucer. Such seeds as sunflower, daisy, zinnia, etc.; pear, lemon, grape, etc.; onion, pea, Lima bean, corn, coffee beans, etc. The players write their identifications.

Twenty Objects; Sherlock Holmes.—Place 20 miscellaneous objects on a table: a book, a pencil, a blotter, a spool of thread, a peanut, a safety pin, a thimble, a calling card, a spoon, a handkerchief, a small box, a dime, etc. The players walk around the table once, then go into another room and write a list of all the objects they can recall. Penalize 1 for each object wrongly listed. Highest scorer is Sherlock Holmes.

Unseen Objects.—The players sit around a table, their hands beneath it. The leader passes, one at a time, from 15 to 25 objects without delay under the table. When the last has come back to the leader, the guests write their lists of what was passed. Score as above.

It Tastes Like.—Blindfolded, the guests taste 15 or 20 things, and later write their identifications. Score as above.

Fifteen Bottles.—Provide a row of fifteen identical dark bottles, uncorked, each containing a different liquid, such as vanilla, milk, cocoa, orange juice, grape juice, water, gasoline, vinegar, etc. The players pass before the bottles, smell each, and write down their identifications. Score as above.

Sniff.—Blindfolded, the players identify 15 or 20 things by odor: such as butter, coffee, yellow soap, nutmeg, cloves, ammonia, chocolate, banana, etc. After each sniff, the player whispers his identification to the leader or an assistant, who writes it down under the player's name.

HAWKSHAW

A murder is enacted before the players, after which the Murderer and the Victim leave the room. The guests then answer a list of 20 to 30 prepared questions, to test their powers of observation. Thus:

1. What was the weapon used?
2. How did the Victim fall?
3. What became of the weapon?
4. Did the Victim die immediately?
5. Was the Victim wearing earrings?
6. What color was the Murderer's necktie?
7. What did the Murderer do immediately after the crime?
8. Did the Victim have anything in her right hand?
9. What did the Victim say just before the crime?
10. Did the Murderer say anything after the crime?

The highest correct score wins.

PENNY WISE

Each guest is provided with a penny and a list similar to the following. In a stated time, the questions must be answered with the names of objects that appear on the penny. It is more difficult if the guests merely study the pennies for a few minutes, then answer the questions without having the pennies before them.

Slang for conversation	(chin)
A part of a needle	(eye)
What spans a river	(bridge (of nose))
In favor of, and to rasp	(pro-file)
A wreath	(garland)
Bright flowers	(tulips)
A narrow piece of land	(neck)
What "fresh" people have	(cheek)
Has knowledge	(knows)
What burglars pick	(locks)
A part of a hill	(brow)
A part of a river	(mouth)
What Patrick Henry wanted	(liberty)
Found in a post office	(letters)
Part of a nail	(head)

A numeral	(figure)
Used in tennis	(ball (of eye))
A messenger	(one sent)
A weapon	(bow)
Parts of a book	(leaves)
Conditions	(states)
A perfume	(scent)
The state of being married	(united)
One-third of the world's land surface	(America)
Part of a harness	(collar)
The fruit of maize	(ear)
Solitary	(one)
Big industrial combination	(trust)
Reverse of dog	(God)
A layer of paint	(coat)
An animal	(hare)
Part of ripe wheat	(beard)
Policeman	(copper)
A book of the Bible	(Numbers)
To take up weapons	(arm)
A connection	(tie)
A book by Lindbergh	(We)
A tavern	(inn)

II. ALPHABET GAMES

HERE are some of the oldest and most interesting of all the intellectual games. There is hardly a group of people anywhere who will not find delight in the majority of these brain teasers, if not in all of them. They have the added charm of definite cultural value. They are almost certain to add valuable facts to one's knowledge, while affording delightful entertainment. None of them is a game to be tried on mental sluggards.

For the first group, a pencil and paper must be provided for each guest.

ADDING LETTERS

Provide each guest with a list similar to the following. Set a time limit. The highest score wins.

Add one letter

1. To TEAR, and get weeds. (TARES)
2. To LOAN, and get solitary. (ALONE)
3. To ROAM, and get an ancient Italian. (ROMAN)
4. To BONE, and get carried. (BORNE)
5. To DINED, and get really. (INDEED)
6. To RENT, and get come in. (ENTER)
7. To MEETS, and get measuring units. (METERS)
8. To COME, and get the name of a wine. (MEDOC)
9. To NAGS, and get a girl's name. (AGNES)
10. To TIME, and get a Bishop's headdress. (MITRE)

Adding Two Letters.—This is a more complicated version of the same game. Adding three or more letters makes it even more difficult. For example, Add two letters to SEEM and get to plot: SCHEME.

Add a Letter.—Another way is to define the first word instead of giving it. Thus: Add a letter

1. To a Venetian official (DOGE) and get an automobile. (DODGE)
2. To a part of Moorish architecture (ARCH) and get suspicious. (CHARY)
3. To part of the face (NOSE) and get Norwegian. (NORSE)
4. To part of an automobile (TIRE) and get rows. (TIERS)
5. To a lane (PATH) and get to mend. (PATCH)
6. To an animal (BEAR) and get exposed. (BARED)
7. To decays (ROTS) and get runs slowly. (TROTS)
8. To an indefinite quantity (SOME) and get tiny specks. (MOTES)
9. To drags (LUGS) and get water birds. (GULLS)
10. To vice (SIN) and get insect eggs. (NITS)

For all of these games there should be at least 20 questions.

CHANGING LETTERS

The players are required to change one letter and get a different word. There should be about 20 problems. Score as above.

1. Corruptible (VENAL) and get a punishable offense. (PENAL)
2. A slight sin (VENIAL) and get a servant. (MENIAL)
3. A sweetmeat (CANDY) and get a foppish man. (DANDY)
4. Affection (LOVE) and get part of an ear. (LOBE)
5. A meat (VEAL) and get to guide. (LEAD)
6. A lane (PATH) and get a demonstrative pronoun. (THAT)
7. To change (ALTER) and get a hardship. (TRIAL)
8. Cozy (SNUG) and get a sudden puff of wind. (GUST)
9. A large quantity (MUCH) and get pals. (CHUMS)
10. Desire (WISH) and get learned. (WISE)

HASH, SCRAMBLED WORDS, ANAGRAMS

This game has several other names; Hashed Letters, Letter Hash, Scrambled Letters, Anagrams. Provide each player with a list of hashed words, all of which come under a single category, as Flowers, Animals, etc. Within a stated time, each must unscramble his list. Simple scoring gives one for each correct answer. Or one word called the Onion (a difficult word) scores 5; the Meat, 4; the Potato, 3; the Pan, 2. When this is done, the chosen words should all be slightly more difficult than the others, and their designations should be put after the scrambled word as; Defile Sam (The Onion). (Masefield) There should be 20 to 30 hashed words.

If the category chosen were Flowers, the scramble would be similar to this:

Sayid	Moss Co.	Haladi	Nepoy
(Daisy)	(Cosmos)	(Dahlia)	(Peony)

Hashed Poets.—1. N. B. Roy (BYRON) 2. Steak (KEATS) 3. Speak, Are She? (SHAKESPEARE) 4. Lem Rik (KILMER) 5. Til Mon (MILTON) 6. Thou Are (THOREAU) 7. Eppo (POPE) 8. Net No Syn (TENNYSON) 9. Tyb Ran (BRYANT) 10. Mush a Noe (HOUSEMAN) 11. Lov Nil (VILLON) 12. Sat So (TASSO) 13. Dew Il (WILDE) 14. Yew Li (WILEY) 15. Nee T. B. (BENET)

Hashed Fruits.—1. Anna A. B. (BANANA) 2. Per A. G. (GRAPE) 3. No Gear (ORANGE) 4. No Elm (LEMON) 5. Pep. Al! (APPLE) 6. Lo, Men! (MELON) 7. After U, Prig. (The Onion) (GRAPEFRUIT) 8. Rape (PEAR) 9. If G. (FIG) 10. Wyst Barrer (STRAWBERRY) 11. Serb, Parry! (RASPBERRY) 12. Eh, Cap? (PEACH) 13. Up, M. L.! (PLUM) 14. Great Man, Poe. (POMEGRANATE) 15. Pep Lean Pi, (PINEAPPLE).

This may be done with books of the Bible, names of popular entertainers, foods, etc.

Home-Made Hash.—Each player chooses a category, or all use the same one. Each then hashes five words, and the lists are passed once to the left. Within a given time, each must unscramble the five words he has received.

BACKWARD AND FORWARD

Provide each guest with a list of 20 or 25 sentences, each sentence having two blanks in it. In each case the words to be filled in are the same word spelled forward then backward. For instance:

1. ______ that rose, so I can ______ it on. (Nip, Pin.)
2. You'll paint a ______ picture, if you ______ the paint. (Bad, Dab.)
3. If the rain ______ her hat, she'll be in a ______. (Wets, Stew.)
4. From this ______ you can see the roof ______. (Spot, Tops.)
5. This ______ cheese is ______ from the freshest milk. (Edam, Made.)
6. He caught ______ in his ______. (Ten, Net.)
7. If it ______, there will be no outdoor ______. (Teems, Meets.)
8. There is a red ______ near that tall ______. (Deer, Reed.)
9. They put the stopper in the ______, ______ there was no water. (Tub, But.)
10. His master is a ______ to the ______. (God, Dog.)

Scrambled Word-Triplets.—This is a similar game using words having the same letters arranged differently. Prepare lists of about 20 sentences. In both games the players must fill in the blanks in a stated time. The longest correct list wins. Examples of Word-Triplets are: Seal, Leas, Ales; Leap, Pale, Peal; Veil, Live, Evil; Part, Trap, Rapt; Deal, Leda, Lead. A typical sentence is:

The ______ of the chapel bell, in the ______ dawn, made their hearts ______. (Peal, Pale, Leap.)

LETTER GOLF

This game is played in pairs. Each couple is provided with a pencil and six sheets of typewriter paper. The couples divide each sheet into three columns, numbering them one through eighteen. The leader dictates the following letters and par values, which the players write down at the top of each column, one for a column, G being the first.

G, 16; O, 16; L, 24; F, 23; F, 15; O, 15; R, 30; T, 22; H, 15; E, 20; B, 25; E, 18; G, 14; I, 18; N, 20; N, 16; E, 14; R, 20. The letters spell "Golf for the Beginner," and represent the 18 holes.

One minute is allowed to play each hole. At a signal, the couples start and write down all the words they can think of beginning with the letter at the top of the hole. At the second signal they switch to the second hole, and so on. After a hole has been left, no words can be added to it. A word already written in one hole cannot be repeated when the same letter is encountered at another hole. Plurals and other forms are permitted. Thus, if the player writes run, under an R, he should write runs running, ran, under succeeding R's.

The longest correct list wins.

Word Race.—This game eliminates the golf course. Within a limited time the guests write down as many words as possible beginning with a specified letter. Or a word is chosen, and they are given a minute each to write down as many words as possible beginning with each letter in the given word.

Alphabet Race.—The players are allowed one minute for each successive letter of the alphabet. In that time they write as many words as possible under each letter.

THE LETTER GAME

Provide each player with a list of about 20 problems involving the addition of letters to a given letter. Thus:

1. Add one letter to B, and get to exist. (Be)
2. Add 2 letters to B, and get evil. (Bad)

3. Add 3 letters to B, and get part of the face (Brow)
4. Add 4 letters to B, and get a tree. (Birch)
5. Add 5 letters to B, and get improved. (Better)

More letters can be added, but this makes the game more difficult. Set a time limit. The longest correct list wins.

CATEGORIES, or GUGGENHEIM

There are many variations of this game, which has a double object: to write a correct word under each classification, and, at the same time, one which no other player has written. Thus, if Animals were the classification, and L the letter, a player could write lion, lynx, leopard, llama, or lemur; but if any other player had chosen the same word, neither would score, or both would score less. The players must try to outguess each other.

One-Letter Categories.—In rotation, each player names a category or classification, such as Authors, Meats, Flowers, Trees, Countries, and so on. The players list these on paper, each having his own list. A letter is then chosen by cutting a deck of alphabet cards; or by a player, eyes closed, touching a letter in a book. Allow about 15 minutes for 20 categories. The players write one object under each category, each word beginning with the specified letter.

Thus, had B been chosen for the above, the following would be a correct list: Barrie; Bacon; Bridal Wreath; Beech; Bermuda. Only one name is permitted under each category. In rotation, each player reads his list. If a word is correct, and no other player has it, the score is 1 for each player in the game. If other players have it, the score is the number of players, less the number of those duplicating it. All the players having it get the same score for it. Scores are added, the highest winning.

Hearts of Lettuce.—The game is played as above, until the scoring. When there is doubt about the acceptability of a word, it is put to a vote; lobbying is permitted. Each player may give a brief speech in defense of his word; those favoring it may also give speeches, and those opposed speak against it. The word is then voted on. The name of the game comes from a player who, baffled by the letter H under Vegetables, wrote Hearts of Lettuce, and lobbied so successfully that it was allowed.

Square Categories.—Each player makes a rectangle, as per the diagram. It may be large or small, according to the wishes of the players. A 5-letter word is chosen (or 4- or 6-letter, according to the number of squares agreed upon). It is wise to avoid the letters J, Q, X, Z. Good 5-letter words are Atone, Adobe, Camel. This is a typical Square Category filled out:

	Trees	*Fruits*	*Animals*	*Countries*	*Vegetables*	
C	Cedar	Currant	Cow	Canada	Carrot	
A	Maple	Apple	Ass	Argentine	Asparagus	
M	Aspen	Melon	Monkey	Mexico	Mustard Greens	
E	Elm	Elderberry	Elk	Ecuador	Eggplant	
L	Larch	Lemon	Lynx	Lithuania	Leeks	

Score 1 for each correct word which no other player has written; 0 for all others. Alternatively, 1 for each word no other player has; and ½ for any that not more than 2 other players have; 0 for all others. The scoring for One-Letter Categories may also be used.

WORD SQUARES

Each player makes a block of squares 5 x 5. The block may be larger or smaller, if the players wish. If the party is large, divide it into groups of four, five, or six players; in this case, each group plays independently. In rotation, each player announces one letter, which is immediately written by all the others in any square. Once written, the letters may not be erased or moved. The object is to make, horizontally and vertically, as many 3-, 4-, or 5-letter words as possible. When 25 letters have been called, the players, in rotation, read their words and score 5 for a 5-letter word; 4 for a 4-letter word; 3 for a 3-letter word. The highest number of points wins. Here is a Word Square filled out:

A	T	O	N	E	5	
T	R	I	E	D	5	
T	I	L	E	I	4	(Tile)
I	N	E	P	T	5	
C	E	R	E	D	5	
5	5	5	4	4		(Neep, Edit)

The score for this is 24 across and 23 down: total 47.

HIDDEN WORDS

Select a word of ten or more letters, preferably one with plenty of vowels, as: Commemorate, Independence, Omnipotent, or the like. Within a stated time, the players must make as many words as possible from the long word. The words are usually limited to those of 3, 4, or 5 letters, though this is not necessary. Any letter in the long word may be used in a new one as many times as it appears in the original, but no oftener. No other letters may be used. Thus if Commemorate were the word chosen, M could be used in any new word 3 times, and T only once. Rat would be correct, but not Tat, since the latter word has two T's.

The player with the longest correct list wins.

Buried Words.—This game is played as above, except that a sentence is chosen instead of a word. Proverbs are good for this, such as "Look before you leap." Decide in advance whether the words to be made may be any length, or are to be limited to 3, 4, or 5-letter words. Score as above.

A TO Z

Provide each player with an alphabet dealing with a definite topic, such as Biblical Characters, Trees, Historical Characters,

Fruits, etc. Within a limited time, each player must write a proper answer to each problem. The longest correct list wins. If Fruits were the chosen category, the alphabet could start so:

A. A standard pie filling. (Apple)
B. Its skin is slippery. (Banana)
C. It provides light. (Currant)
D. Girls love them. (Dates)
E. This makes a fine wine. (Elderberry)
F. The fruit of Arabia. (Fig)
G. Popular for breakfast. (Grapefruit)
H. Another good pie filling. (Huckleberry)

I LOVE MY LOVE WITH AN A

Each player is provided with the following statements:

I love my love with a (an) ________ because he is ________.
I will send him to ________,
And feed him on ________.
I will give him a (an) ________ to ________,
And a bunch of ________ for a nosegay.

The first player fills his blanks with words beginning with A; the second, with words beginning with B; and so on down the alphabet. Thus the first player might fill in: ardor, amiable, Albany, artichokes, anteater, amble with, abalone.

A simpler game may be played without writing, and this simpler formula:

I love my love with an A. Her name is ________ (Agnes). She lives in ________ (Alsace), and I gave her an ________ (alligator).

For this the players sit in a circle and merely recite the formula, continuing around until the alphabet is exhausted.

RHYMED ALPHABET

Provide each player with a copy of a rhymed alphabet on any given subject, as below. Within a specified time, the answers must be written in. The longest correct list wins. Here is one on Animals: *

A lives on ants as a regular diet. (Anteater)
B is an ape who will rarely keep quiet. (Baboon)
C is the foe of the rat and the mouse. (Cat)
D is the guardian guarding the house. (Dog)
E is the hugest land animal known. (Elephant)
F is a wolf-cousin hunting alone. (Fox)
G is a thing we wish no one to get. (Goat)
H has a laugh you can hear ringing yet. (Hyena)
I is a wild goat that leaps in its glee. (Ibex)
J follows lions continually. (Jackal)
K keeps its young in the queerest of homes. (Kangaroo)
L has his hills in the sky where he roams. (Llama)
M lives in trees and can grin and can chatter. (Monkey)
N likes the kids, and to see them grow fatter. (Nanny-goat)
O walks around with its own incubator. (Opossum)
P, a big cat, is a real human-hater. (Panther)
Q wears his quills from his head to his tail. (Quill-pig, Porcupine)
R hops away, with his fluffy plume pale. (Rabbit)
S wears a fur that the ladies esteem. (Sable)
T frightens prey with his wild jungle scream. (Tiger)
U wore one horn—or, at least, so they say. (Unicorn)
V is a field mouse that nests under hay. (Vole)
W's a killer that's skinny and mean. (Weasel)
X a small even-toed beast no man's seen. (Xiphodon)
Y is an ox from the hills of Tibet. (Yak)
Z, a striped horse any zoo likes to get. (Zebra)

MAN TO NUT

Two words of equal length are announced, and written down by each player. In the fewest possible changes, changing one letter

---

* From *Let's Have A Good Time Tonight,* by Gloria Goddard and Clement Wood.

at a time, they are to change the first word to the second. Thus, Man to Nut:

Man	Man	Man	Man
Mat	Men	Ban	Ran
Mot	Met	Bun	Run
Not	Net	Nun	Nun
Nut	Nut	Nut	Nut

Four changes are necessary. Bad can be changed to Dun in three changes: BAD, DAD, DAN, DUN. It is amusing to use opposites, such as: Warm to Cold, Dry to Wet, Good to Evil, Black to White.

GAPS

Provide each guest with a list of 4-letter words giving only the first and last letter, thus: B--K (Book), L--E (Love), S--H (Such), etc. Where other correct answers are possible, these are permitted. Thus, Balk or Bank would do instead of Book.

A variation would be to use 5-letter words, giving the second and fourth letters: -I-I- (Livid), -N-E- (Anger), etc.; or the first, third and fifth letter may be given, thus: H-P-Y (Happy), etc.

The longest correct list wins.

ABBREVIATIONS

Provide each player with a jumbled list of letters which can be rearranged to form 25 familiar abbreviations. In a stated time they must unscramble the letters and arrange them in proper forms. Or the letters may be arranged alphabetically, using only those which will appear in abbreviations. Among common abbreviations are: T.N.T., T.V.A., K.P., N.G., A.D., A.W.O.L., D.A.R., Y.M.C.A., Y.W.C.A., B.V.D., K.K.K., A.O.H., R.F.D., K.C., R.S.V.P., S.O.S., I.O.U., B.P.O.E., A.A.A., B.C., U.S.A., I.O.O.F., O.K., P.S., M.D., etc.

The one with the longest correct list wins.

SHORTHAND

Give each player a list of definitions which can be answered by a letter of the alphabet. Within a stated time each must fill in his list, the longest correct one winning. There should be as least 25 definitions, such as:

One-Letter Shorthand.—Part of the head (I). An insect (B). A Scottish river (D). A beverage (T). A spring vegetable (P). A raucous bird (J). A printer's measure (M). A worm (S). An Oriental style of headdress (Q). Not so large as an ocean (C). Part of a house (L). A pronoun (U). A command to a horse (G). To be indebted (O), etc.

Two-Letter Shorthand.—An attractive girl (QT, Cutie). Cold (IC, Icy). A hot condiment (KN, Cayenne). A tent (TP, Tepee). A vine (IV, Ivy). Bedraggled looking (CD, Seedy). A make of automobile (SX, Essex). A girl's name (LC, Elsie). Not difficult (EZ, Easy).

The players write only the letters that express the word.

INITIAL STORIES

Provide each guest with a copy of a story, dealing with familiar subjects, using initials for familiar words they must identify. State what the story deals with, and set a time limit. The greatest number of correct identifications wins. A story dealing with Jack and the Beanstalk might run:

"J. went to market with a C., and returned with a bag of B.," etc.

TELEGRAMS

Each player writes down 10 letters as the leader calls them off. Each player must then write a 10-word telegram, each word beginning with one of the letters called, in the order called. A 10-letter word may be called out, instead of the 10 letters. The telegrams are then read aloud, the one voted best winning a small prize.

It is more amusing if the telegrams are for a specific event, such as a wedding anniversary; to a person going on a trip; an acceptance of an invitation to a week-end party, etc.

Cities.—Telegrams are written using the names of Cities. Each player must write a telegram of as many words as there are letters in the city, the words beginning with those letters in proper order. Thus, if the city were Atlanta, the telegram might read: "Alone, twice lately, a natty tailor absconded."

ALPHABET STORY

Allow ten to fifteen minutes for each player to write a story of 26 words, each word beginning with a successive letter of the alphabet, A through Z. The story voted cleverest wins.

MISSING RHYMES

Each player is given a set of couplet rhymes, in which the second rhyme is missing. They should be on obvious themes. Within a stated time, the players must locate the missing rhyme. The longest correct list wins. For example:

WEST INDIES CRUISE *

A couple took a trip one day,
Departing from the ________; (U.S.A.)

And for this all-important trip
They took the fastest streamlined ________; (Ship)

For nothing could be really finer
Than a well-furnished ocean- ________. (Liner)

Couples who travel much do not
Content themselves with a mere ________; (Yacht)

And they would really shriek and bawl
If forced to travel on a ________. (Yawl)

---

* From ***Let's Have A Good Time Tonight,*** by Gloria Goddard and Clement Wood.

They saw the natives down in Cuba
There on the dock all patting ________; (Juba)

They saw them do a languid tango
While munching on a ripened ________. (Mango)

There were no tariff dues to owe
When once they reached ________. (Curaço)

At New York hats they muttered "Bah!"
When they steamed into ________. (Panama)

There were no ice-skates to be had
When they'd arrived at ________. (Trinidad)

In bathing, they took many plunges
To capture floating wads of ________. (Sponges)

They felt their happy spirits droop
On smelling smells from ________. (Guadeloupe)

They felt a rapture all unique
At Mt. Pelée on ________. (Martinque)

There were no words that they could speak
When mounted on a wee ________. (Burrique)

And then, when they'd been gone a week,
The streamlined ship began to ________. (Leak)

They flew back without knife or fork,
Happy once more to see ____ ____. (New York)

VERSE AND WORSE

Each player is provided with lists of 2 rhyming words, or 4 rhyming words, and must write either couplets or four-line verses using the words as end rhymes. Set a time limit, and permit the guests to vote which verses are the best. The one having the largest number of best verses wins. There should be at least ten sets of rhymes given. For couplet rhymes the words could be: love, dove; ring, spring; deck, wreck; alter, falter; etc. For four line verses: run, sun, more, adore; abet, mind, forget, kind; etc.

LIMERICK CONTEST

Tack a typical limerick where all can see it, such as:

There was a young girl from Madrid,
Who cared not at all what she did;
She jumped on a chair,
And danced in the air,
Then eloped on the back of a kid.

Within a stated time, the guests must each write a limerick, the cleverest one winning. The limericks may be general, or upon a given subject. Or the first line may be given, as: "There was a bright lad named Lee," or, "There was an old man from Dundee." Or the last word of the first line may be given, as: king, Spain, Nome, etc.

Missing Line Contest.—In this game, the limerick is supplied, except for the last line. The players must each supply the missing line. The cleverest wins, usually decided by vote. Here is an incomplete limerick:

A man who was tall and quite thin
Went out one fine day for a spin.
He got in a jam
When he struck an old ram,
....

FAMILIAR POEMS

Give each player a copy of a familiar poem, or a group of stanzas taken from famous poems. There should be the equivalent of at least ten four line stanzas. Leave one blank in each line which, within a specified time, the players must fill in correctly. The one having the largest number of correct answers wins. The stanzas should look like this:

The day is done, and the ________ (Darkness)
Falls from the ________ of Night, (Wings)
As a ________ is ________ downward (Feather, Wafted)
From an ________ in his ________. (Eagle, Flight)

GHOSTS

The remaining games in this section as a rule do not require pencil and paper.

Ghosts is a spelling game. The players are seated in a circle. The first, thinking of a word, announces its first letter. The second, thinking of the same word, or another starting with the same letter, adds a second letter, and so on around the circle. When any player completes a word of 3 or more letters, any other player may call "That's a word!," and the player receives 1 black mark. Three black marks make the player a ghost.

When a player hesitates, the leader or the preceding player calls "Add or challenge." One minute is then allowed for the player to add a letter, or to challenge the preceding player. A player challenges when he believes the preceding player is misspelling, or has no word in mind. The challenged player must give the word he had in mind. If the challenger is correct, the preceding player gets 1 black mark; if not, the challenger gets the black mark. As a rule, foreign words, abbreviations, and proper names are prohibited. When a word is ended, or announced after a challenge, the next player starts a new word.

A player is out of the game when he becomes a ghost, except that he may try to make the surviving players speak to him. No surviving player may speak to a ghost, under any circumstances. If one does so, he immediately becomes a ghost. The winner is the one player who resists becoming a ghost, either through misspelling or speaking to an existing ghost. The winner starts the next round.

BACKWARD SPELLING

The players sit in a circle. The leader calls off words, and the players in rotation must spell them backward. There are three ways of scoring: One mistake eliminates a player; three mistakes eliminate a player; after three mistakes a player may become a ghost, as above.

HEADS AND TAILS GHOSTS

This is one of the most thrilling of all mental games. The rules are the same as for ordinary *Ghosts,* except that only words of four or more letters count. In this variation a letter may be added *before* as well as after the original letter. If added before, all the letters must be properly stated. Thus, if B is the original letter, and the next player merely says L, the letters stand BL. If the next player wishes to put O before them, he says OBL. Players are permitted to use paper and pencil to keep a record of the letters as called. Any hyphenated words found in a standard dictionary are permitted, the hyphen being omitted.

THE FAMOUS FEW

Select a letter of the alphabet. Write down all the famous people you can think of whose last names begin with that letter. Allow ten or fifteen minutes. Famous names include all those commonly known. For instance, Sears of Sears-Roebuck, Barnum of Barnum and Bailey. Names of kings, such as the Louis's of France, count as only one, unless some distinction can be made for each. Thus, the Louis's of France would count one, and Louis XI would count another one, if distinguished as St. Louis.

The player with the longest list wins. All fictional or mythological names are excluded. The post-mortem comparisons are amazing for their revelation of familiar names that each player forgot.

DUMB SPELLING MATCH

Start as above. In spelling the words, the players announce the consonants; the vowels are indicated, not spoken. A is indicated by raising the right hand; E, the left hand; I, by pointing to the eye; O, to the open mouth; U, to any other player. An error eliminates the player. The scoring may also be done as in Ghosts.

Five Fingers.—This is played the same as above, except that the vowels are indicated by the fingers: A, 1 finger; E, 2; I, 3; O, 4; U, 4 fingers and thumb.

LIVING LETTERS

The players are each given one letter or a group of letters, and are divided into teams. The teams hold duplicate letters. The leader calls a word, and the players holding the proper letters from each team run to opposite ends of the room and arrange themselves to form the word. The team doing this first scores one.

Double Living Letters, Living Anagrams.—The leader calls words which, rearranged, will form other words, that is, Anagrams. When the first word is formed, the leader instructs the players to form another word with the same letters. This calls for quick consultation on the part of each team. Examples: Dog, God; wed, dew; tam, mat; step, pets; veil, live; sent, tens; spar, rasp; steam, meats; teach, cheat; beard, bread; melon, lemon; march, charm; dramas, madras; tureen, neuter; loiter, toiler; erring, ringer; paired, diaper; souring, rousing; cheater, teacher; bolster, lobster; etc.

Switch the Letters, Anagram List.—This is a similar game played with pencil and paper. Give each guest a list of such words as above (using only one of each pair), and let them, within a time limit, rearrange each word to form another.

A WAS AN APPLE PIE

The players sit in a circle and, in rotation, add a verb beginning with the next succeeding letter of the alphabet. For instance, the leader says, "A was an apple pie. A ate it," in rotation the other players might add: "B bought it," "C cooked it," "D dunked it," and so on through "Z zoomed it." A player failing to follow properly gets 1 black mark. Three black marks eliminate the player.

ALPHABET TRAVELING

The players sit in a circle. The leader asks the first, "Where are you going?" The players must answer with the name of a place beginning with letters of the alphabet in rotation, and also state what they are doing there, using 3 words beginning with the same letter. Thus: (The numbers indicate the players.)

1. I am going to Albany, to acquire ancient archives.
2. I am going to Bermuda, to bewitch beautiful barracudas.
3. I am going to Chicago, to count Capone's cousins.
4. I am going to Dalmatia, to describe delightful dolmans.
5. I am going to England, to enjoy elongated eels.

And so on to the end of the alphabet. A player who fails to respond must pay a forfeit, or is eliminated.

INITIALS

Use alphabet cards for this (see page 430). The leader tells a story—a trip to France, an adventure, an airplane trip, etc. He stops suddenly and draws a card from a container, exposing it. The first player to name an appropriate word beginning with this letter wins it. The leader continues the story, and stops again, drawing a new card. At the end, the player holding the most cards wins.

The leader might start, "I took a walk in the woods. The first thing I saw was ______" He draws an L; one player might answer "Linden," and win the letter. The leader goes on, "And I met a ______." He draws an R; another player might answer "Rabbit," and win. The story may be long or short, as the group desires.

Oral Initials.—This is the same game, played without cards. The leader, when he pauses in his story, merely calls out a letter. The first player to respond correctly scores himself 1 point. Thus:

The leader starts, "Walking up the street, I saw a B____" ("Bus." or "Baby." might win.) The game goes on as above.

Initial Call-Out.—The leader announces a Category, such as Fruits, Trees, etc. He then calls a letter and points to a player. The player must respond immediately with a proper word under the Category and beginning with the letter. Or the players may respond in rotation. Score 1 for each correct answer, and 1 black mark for each failure. With 3 black marks, the player is eliminated.

GRAB ON BEHIND, ALPHA AND OMEGA

A Category is chosen, such as Countries, Rivers, Cities, etc. The first player names a word under the Category. Within one minute, the second player must name a word beginning with the last letter of the previous word. And so on around the circle. There are three ways to score: 3 failures eliminate the player; or make him a ghost, as in Ghosts; or three failures require a forfeit.

Thus, if Cities were the Category, the names might be: "Buffal*o*," "Omah*a*," "Alban*y*," "Yokohom*a*," "Akro*n*," "New Orlean*s*," "San Francisc*o*," "Oshkos*h*," "Hambur*g*," and so on. Names once used may not be repeated.

ALPHABETICAL ADVERBS

The players are seated in a circle. In rotation, they must repeat all that has been said before, and add an adverb beginning with the next letter. The leader might start: "Helen drives artfully." The second player would say, "Helen drives artfully, beautifully." Third, "Helen drives artfully, beautifully, consummately," and so on through the alphabet. An error eliminates the player.

Mary Jones Came to Town.—Each player must repeat "Mary Jones Came to Town," and add, in rotation, an adverb beginning with the next letter of the alphabet; then act the adverb. The first player might say, "Mary Jones came to town ardently"; and then act out *ardently.* The second, "Mary Jones came to town brashly," then act out *brashly.* And so on through the alphabet.

INITIAL ANSWERS

Each person must answer the question asked him with words beginning with his own initials in the correct order. Thus, if the first question were "What is your occupation?" and the player's initials were A.M.Y., he might answer "Aimlessly Mending Yawls." Each question should be different. Amusing questions are: "Where is your future husband?" "What is your favorite food?" "What were you doing at eleven last night?" Questions not answered, or answered incorrectly, call for a forfeit, or eliminate that player.

Excuse Me.—This is a variation. The Leader asks questions which call for an excuse. The answers must be prefaced by "Excuse Me," and must end with words using the player's initials in the right order. Thus, the question might be "Why did you come to the office late?" The above player might answer "Excuse me, I was Anxiously Matching Yarn." It is scored as above.

Sail My Yacht.—Each player, in rotation, says "I'm going to sail my yacht with a _______" adding words using his initials as above. Thus, if the initials were H. E. B., the player might say, "I'm going to sail my yacht with Hard Emery Boards"; if F. C. H., "I'm going to sail my yacht with Fancy Crochet Hooks," and so on. A player failing to sail correctly falls overboard, and must sit on the floor. The Leader has a Life Preserver, a cushion, which, from time to time, he tosses to a player on the floor. If the player then sails his yacht correctly, he returns to the circle.

INITIAL QUESTIONNAIRE

Each player is given a questionnaire, each question of which must be answered by words containing only the player's initials, used once only in their right order. Such a questionnaire, correctly filled out, might be:

1. Your name? Belle R. Harrison.
2. Who else would you rather be? Beauty's radiant heir.
3. Where do you live? By Rhine heights.
4. What do you think of the tariff? Better rather high.
5. What is your latest fad? Biting rose-haws.
6. Describe your character. Bitter Red-hater.
7. Your favorite flower. Beautiful ruddy heliotrope.
8. The height of your ambition. Billions, radiance, humility.
9. Your greatest accomplishment. Beautifying rickety houses.

NEVER SAY IT

The players agree to omit a certain letter. The Leader asks questions, and the answers must be given promptly in sentences of at least 6 words. If the forbidden letter were D, the Leader might ask a player "Are you going to Europe this year?" The player might answer, "I hope so, sometime before June or July," and be correct. But if he said, "We expected to leave next week, but we can't go till later," the player would get a black mark or be obliged to pay a forfeit, because of the D in *expected*. The players may be eliminated after 1 black mark, or after 3 such marks. The surviving player wins.

MRS. PETTIGREW'S TEA

The amusing part of this game is to guess the object of the game, which is not announced in advance. This object is to answer questions without using the letter T. The Leader says, "Mrs. Pettigrew doesn't like tea. What does she like?" The first three answers might be, "Apples," "Cocoa," "Peanuts." "Peanuts" contains a T, so the Leader says to this player, "You're out." The Leader continues to ask questions, varying them to include where Mrs. Pettigrew goes, what she wears, etc., until the object has been guessed. If it is not guessed, the Leader reveals it.

Our Cook Doesn't Like Peas.—This is the same game, with the letter P omitted.

The G Man Never Takes His Ease.—A similar game in which the Leader says, "The G man never takes his ease. What does he take?" It is played as above, E being the omitted letter.

RHYMING TOM

The Leader announces, "I have a word that rhymes with box." The players ask questions in rotation, each thinking of a word that rhymes with "box." The same words must not be asked about twice. The questions are indirect, and the Leader must promptly guess each word. The game goes as follows: Player, "Do they keep things safely?" Leader, "No, it isn't locks." Second player, "Is it derision?" Leader, "No, it isn't mocks." Third player, "Are they hard?" Leader, "No, it isn't rocks." Fourth player, "Is it a flower?" Leader, "Yes, Rhyming Tom, it's phlox." The person who identified the rhyme becomes the Leader and gives the next rhyme. If, at any time, the Leader cannot guess the rhyme demanded, the questioner becomes the Leader. If the Leader successfully outwits all the players, he remains Leader and gives another rhyme.

Dumb Crambo.—The players divide into two teams. The first team selects a word, say "Amuse," and announces that it wants a rhyme for "Lose." In another room, the second team consults, decides it must be "Abuse," returns and acts out the word. The rhyming team must guess the word from the acting and say, "No, it isn't abuse." And so on. If the rhyming team fails to guess the word acted, it gets a black mark. After 5 such marks, the acting team becomes the rhyming one. If, too, the latter team acts out the right word, it becomes the rhyming one. If the acting team cannot guess after ten attempts, a new word is chosen by the rhyming team, and the game starts again.

ZOO

In this game, the Leader tries to catch the players, and the players try to catch the Leader. The Leader says, "I am thinking of an animal beginning with C," (or any other letter). Suppose "Cow" is the animal. In rotation, the players try to guess the animal he refers to, each asking indirectly about an animal whose name begins with C. A player may say, "Has it whiskers?" The Leader must answer promptly, "No, it isn't a cat." If he fails to guess the animal to which the player refers, he loses, and another is chosen Leader. If he guesses, the next player may say, "Is it a beast of burden?" The Leader replies, "No, it isn't a camel." And so on until Cow is guessed, when the Leader must say, "Yes, it's a cow." If no one guesses, the Leader starts again. Otherwise, the one who guesses becomes the Leader.

If a player fails to name an animal beginning with a specific letter, or names one already given, or challenges incorrectly, he gets a black mark. With 3 such marks a forfeit is required, or the player is eliminated. The Leader or a player may challenge, saying, "There ain't no sich animal." If the challenger is correct, the one challenged gets a black mark; if he is wrong, the challenger gets the black mark.

Birdcage.—This game is played the same way, using birds. It can also be played using Flowers, Foods, Cities, etc.

SING AND SKIP

The players stand in line and each, in rotation, sings one stanza of a familiar song, singing two words, then omitting 2 more. If *America* were the song, it would go:

My Country ____ ____ thee,
Sweet ____ ____ liberty,
Of ____ ____ sing, etc.

The danger is in treating each syllable of a word of two or more syllables as a separate word.

III. GAMES FOR THE CLEVER

This group of games will test the wits of even the most hardened puzzle addict. They do not require any deep specialized knowledge, or a high-powered brain; but they do call for alert attention and a lively ingenuity. Most of them will call forth the amateur detective instincts latent in all of us. In many of them, the players must seek hidden objects. This is always a popular pastime. Everyone likes to hunt for something, particularly in competition. There is a real thrill in being the one who finds a thing that many have sought. Others test the wits in different ways. All of them will keep the average group of people amused for some hours.

HIDDEN TREASURES

Each player, or pair of players, is provided with a list of twenty objects hidden in the room, or in the house. The objects (such things as a penny, a needle, a match, a calling card, a pencil, etc.) are all visible, but are skillfully concealed. Thus, a needle could be placed on a flat tray with a number of straight pins. The players must locate the objects within a stated time, and write down the locations. When a player finds an object, he does not touch it, but moves on, and then writes down the location. The longest list wins; or, the game may continue until one person has located all the objects.

TREASURE HUNT

One or more prizes are concealed in the house or grounds. Each pair of players is given a list of identical directions, which are the first clue. The remaining clues are hidden in various places; there should be about ten of them. Each clue, hinting the location of the next, should be ambiguous, but decipherable. The last clue leads to the treasure.

The clues might run something like this: 1st, "Seek something that summons." The second could then be near a doorbell or a telephone. 2nd, "Look near a symbol of winter." The third clue then would be found near the ice box, close to the ice; and so on. When a clue is found, the couple does not remove it, but reads its instructions and puts it back. This should be done as secretly as possible, so that other couples will not observe. The game continues until all the treasures are found, these belonging to the finders. If the game drags, the Leader may give veiled hints.

BIG GAME HUNT

Animals crackers are hidden in the room or the house. The couple who finds the largest number wins; or the crackers may be numbered, and the numbers added to determine the winner. After the crackers are found, have the guests each select their favorite animals; each one is then asked to imitate the noise of the one he has chosen.

HUNTSMEN AND HOUNDS

The players are divided into two packs of hounds. Each pack selects a leader, the Huntsman, who is given a basket. Peanuts have been concealed throughout the house or the room. At a signal, the hounds start seeking the peanuts, hunting in pairs. When a peanut is found, the hounds do not touch it, but stand by, baying, until the Huntsman comes to collect it. The Huntsman must try to recognize the baying of his own hounds. When rival hounds find the same nut, each pair bays, and the Huntsman who gets there first wins the nut. The team collecting the most peanuts wins.

Hens and Chickens.—In this game small candy eggs or jellybeans are hidden, instead of eggs. The two Hens gather these, while the boys crow like roosters and the girls cluck like hens. Otherwise, it is played the same as above.

COBWEB TREASURE HUNT

Equal lengths of string, all starting at approximately the same place, are wound in and out among table legs, chairs, or any available place. The strings may be interwined with each other, but must not be knotted. On the other end of each string, which should be concealed, there is a small prize. Each pair of players, or each player, secures the free end of a string, and strives to untangle it without cutting or breaking it.

Cobweb.—The cobwebs may be tangled as above, without any prizes at the other ends. The couple, or player, whose string is first untangled, wins. The webs may be tangled separately, and each couple given a limited time in which to untangle theirs.

BLIND PIG

Provide each players with a sheet of paper and a pencil. One at a time, blindfolded, each must draw a pig without removing the pencil from the paper, except to draw in the eye. Starting at the tail, each one draws in the body, ears, legs. Then he must raise the pencil and draw in the eye. The best drawing wins.

CRAZY DRAWING

Provide each player with a sheet of paper and a pencil. Each draws a single line on his paper, straight, jagged or curved. The papers are then passed once to the left. Again each player adds a line, without erasing or altering the original one. The papers are passed to the left again, and another line added, and so on until each players has added a line to each drawing. The object is to create definite drawings. If a drawing has assumed form, the next player may not alter it, but must continue it.

AIRPLANE

Tack on the wall a large map of the world, or a homemade drawing of one. Give each player a small airplane cut from paper, with his name on it and a pin in it. Mark a large central spot on the map for the take-off. Line the players at the opposite end of the room, and put several obstacles in the center of the room, such as chairs and tables. Give each player a minute to study the location of the take-off on the map, and the obstacles. Blindfold him. He must then cross the floor without touching any of the obstacles, and pin his airplane on the map as far as possible from the take-off. If he touches an obstacle, it is a crash, and he is out of the race. If he pins his airplane in water on the map, it is considered lost. The pilot of the longest flight wins.

SCULPTURE

Provide the players with modeling clay, gum, soap or a similar substance. Each must model a specified object within a given time. The best wins a prize.

WHAT IS IT?

Write the names of animals on slips of paper, having as many slips as there are players. Mix these in a container, and have the players each draw a slip, without revealing to any other player what they have drawn. Have a blackboard or a large piece of Bristol board on the wall, and a supply of crayon. Provide the players with pencils and paper. The first player goes to the blackboard and draws the animal whose name is on his slip, and numbers the drawing. Each of the other players then writes the number of the drawing and his identification of the animal on his paper. The next player then draws his animal, and similarly it is identified by the others; and so on, until all have drawn. The player having the most correct identifications wins.

Another method is for the players simultaneously to draw their animals on small sheets of paper, number them, and then pass them around for identification.

CARD TOSS

Place a trashbasket, a bowl or a man's hat on the floor, and mark a line about 6 feet from it. Give each player 8 or 10 playing cards. Standing behind the line, each must toss as many cards as possible into the receptacle. The one who tosses in the most cards wins. In one variation, each player tosses a full deck of 52 cards, one at a time.

Toss Rummy.—Each player draws a specified number of cards from a shuffled deck or decks, and the game is then played as above. Cards landing in the receptacle count double their face value; cards landing face up outside count at face value; the highest score wins. Cards count: 14 for Ace, 13 for King, down to 2 for the deuce. Scoring may also be as in Rum; Ace 15, Court cards 10, others at face value.

Checker Toss.—The same game played with checkers, peanuts, buttons, poker chips, etc. The tossing line should be about 10 feet from the receptacle, which may be placed against the wall for bank shots. Players score one for each object landing in the receptacle.

Bounce Toss.—The same game played with small rubber balls. These must bounce once on the floor before landing in the receptacle. Allow each player 5 or 10 shots.

MAKE-UP CONTEST

Give each boy a length of ribbon or fancy cord, rouge, lipstick, powder, and eyebrow pencil. He must tie his partner's hands behind her and make her up for a Beauty Contest. The best make-up wins.

Girls of Tomorrow.—Have the boys make up the girls to represent what they think will be the fashion in 1960.

Isn't He Sweet!—Have the girls make up the boys, as above.

BIGGEST LIE

Each player in rotation tells a lie. The one judged the biggest liar wins.

Best Joke.—Instead of lies, tell jokes; judge as above.

Best Story.—Each tells a one minute story; the best one wins.

Declamation Contest.—Each player gives a brief recitation or declamation; the one judged best wins. Another method is to have each repeat the same recitation; the most dramatic rendition wins.

A CRIME THAT WAS COMMITTED

The Leader gives a summary of a tragedy: as, "Two girls went to the movies. When the show was over, one girl was dead, stabbed through the back with something like a hatpin. No weapon was found in the body." The players then collaborate to form a reasonable explanation of the crime. This might be: "No one near the girls was wearing a hatpin. Then man behind the dead girl was holding a package of knitting needles he had bought for his wife. They dropped, and he picked them up. Holding the last one he had retrieved, he leaned over the front seat to watch a thrilling part of the picture; the girl also leaned forward. Then she suddenly sank back in her seat, overcome by the picture, and fell against the knitting needle. The man, frightened, yanked the needle free."

The game ends when all are satisfied with a novel explanation of the crime.

NOTHING BUT THE TRUTH

For a stated period, each player must answer truthfully all questions asked. They must be answered publicly. A player failing to answer pays a forfeit. Ask questions in rotation, and make them as amusing and harmlessly personal as possible. An evasive answer requires a forfeit.

Truth Fishbowl.—This is played as above, except that the questions are written in advance and placed in a container. Each player draws, and must answer truthfully the question drawn, or pay a forfeit.

Truth Questionnaire.—Provide each player with a list of about 20 questions. The answers must be written truthfully, and are then read aloud.

TREE, FLOWER OR BIRD

The players are seated in a circle. The Leader, in the middle, says, "Tree, flower or bird—flower!," points to a player and starts to count. The player must name a flower before the Leader counts ten. If he fails, he pays a forfeit or falls out of the game. The Leader always varies the fifth word, saying *tree, flower* or *bird* as his final word each time. He should vary the order as much as possible.

RIGAMAROLE

The players sit in a circle, and the Leader repeats the first phrase, "One old owl." Each player in rotation repeats it. The Leader then says, "One old owl and two tame tigers tipping tables." Each player repeats the complete rigamarole, or falls out, or pays a forfeit. It must be repeated each time in the right order and without a mistake. Here are ten possible items:

1. One old owl.
2. Two tame tigers tipping tables.
3. Three threepenny thrushes thrashing thrashers.

4. Four funny fish flipping fins.
5. Five fast fouls finding figs.
6. Six simple sisters seeking soup.
7. Seven Severn sailors sailing sloops.
8. Eight aimless apes aiding aphids.
9. Nine noble nymphs nibbling nubbins.
10. Ten tiny toads trailing tadpoles.

These lists may be made simpler for some parties.

BACKWARD SENTENCES

The Leader gives sentences or phrases which the players must repeat backward. Start with simple sentences. Compound words, such as *bedridden, overall, woodchuck* add to the amusement, since some players are sure to divide them, which is wrong. If a player fails, he is eliminated or pays a forfeit, and the same sentence is repeated to the next player.

STREAM OF CONSCIOUSNESS

Provide each player with a sheet of paper and a pencil, and have him write the numbers 1 through 20 on the left side of the paper. The Leader opens a book or a magazine, and reads out the word his finger touches first. The others write rapidly, without thought, the first 20 words or phrases that come to mind. The lists are then read, and the associations explained, either by the writer alone, or with the assistance of the Leader.

REACTIONS

Provide each player with a list of 20 words, written on the left of the sheet. There should be key words such as Mother, Love, Home, Passion, Hate, etc., interspersed with unimportant words, such as Potato, Cake, Book, Wednesday, etc. As quickly as possible, without thought, the players write their first reactions to each word. These are then read as above.

BIOGRAPHY

The names of the players are written on separate slips of paper, and mixed in a container. Each player draws one name, and is given ten minutes in which to write a brief biography of the person whose name he has drawn, including a description and some illustrative anecdote, if possible. The player signs his name to the biography. The sheets are collected, shuffled and read, omitting the name of the subject and of the author. The players must guess who is the subject in each case; and who is the author. These are then announced.

APPLE PARING

Give each player an apple and a paring knife. The object is to see who can produce the longest, narrowest unbroken paring. The one who does so wins.

IV. GUESSING GAMES

Everybody likes to solve mysteries. An element of mystery piques the curiosity. Confront a group of people with a Where, Why, or What, and each immediately wants to know the answer. Each wants to be the first to guess the answer. Guessing games arouse a pleasant spirit of competition, and will keep a party happy for hours. In general, these games require nothing more than a good imagination and a lively curiosity. There are few people that lack these. Turn the guests loose on any of the following games, and the party will be a happy one.

CHARADES

The players are divided into groups of four or five each. The first group leaves the room, decides upon a word to act out, returns and acts out the first syllable, then the second, then the third, and finally the whole word. The other players must guess the word from the actions. If the word is not guessed, the same team enacts a second word. Otherwise, the group guessing the word select a word and act it out. The words chosen should be of three or more syllables, such as:

Penmanship	Pen; man; ship; then penmanship.
Cantaloupe	Can; tell; ope; then cantaloupe.
Masquerade	Mass; cur; aid; etc.
Longfellow	Long; fell; owe, or Oh.
Pilgrimage	Pill; grim; age.
Woodpecker	Wood; peck; err.
Microscope	My; crow; scope.
Antarctic	Ant; ark or arc; tick.
Anticlimax	Aunty or anti; climb or clime; ax.
Definite	Deaf; inn; it.
Decorate	Deck; oar; ate; or Deck; owe; rate.
Attenuate	At; ten; you; ate.
Almanacs	Awl or all; man; ax.
Innuendo	Inn; you; end; owe or Oh.
Benjamin	Ben; jam; inn.
Caricature	Carry; cat; your.
Ingratiate	Inn; gray; she; ate.
Independence	Inn; Dee; pen; dense.

Two-syllabled words may be used, but this makes the game harder. In any case, the words used should be accurately pronounced, to give the guessers every chance.

Some players permit acting two syllables at once, thereby having only two acts before the whole word is acted. As: Mayflower (May, flower); Penitent (Penny, tent); etc. This is more difficult.

Flower, Bird, Animal Charades.—This is played the same way, except that the subjects are restricted to the names of flowers; or of birds; or of animals.

State Charades.—In this variation, the names of states must be enacted. Cities, rivers, lakes, etc. may be used similarly.

ACTING GAMES

Mother Goose.—Mother Goose rhymes can be acted out in the same manner as Charades.

Proverbs.—This is played like Charades, with the teams acting out proverbs. This can be varied by cutting the proverb into several parts. Give each player a part, or let the players draw their parts. Then the players must locate the proverb. When players constituting a proverb have assembled, the group comprising it act it out for the others to guess. For a list of proverbs see page 522.

Titles.—The titles of books, plays, songs, or movies, etc., may be acted out in the same manner.

BURLESQUE

The names of stage or movie stars who can be easily mimicked are written on slips of paper and put in a container. Such persons as Eddie Cantor, Al Jolson, Mae West, etc., are ideal. Each guest draws a name, and then does the best possible burlesque of the person whose name he has drawn. The others must guess whom he represents.

The names of the guests may be similarly drawn, and each guest mimicks another. The others try to guess whom he is mimicking.

IN THE MANNER OF THE WORD

The players each write down an adverb, then fold and conceal their slips. In rotation, the players ask the first player to do ing at him the data learned: "It consists of six words. He's acting the fourth now." And soon, "Blank blank glitters blank blank gold." At any moment a player can call out the correct quotation: "All that glitters is not gold!" Whereupon the Timekeeper marks down the time for that team.

The actor indicates a negative ("Not the right word") by an outward gesture with his hands; encouragement ("Getting hot," or "hotter") by gestures toward himself; and "that's the word!" by crossing his hands, palms down, before his body, ending with each hand down with finality at its own side. If the word needs enlarging (as, a singular to a plural) he shows this by moving his hands from a position together to one further apart; if it is to be shortened, by the reverse process. Chopping up a word into syllables, or even letters, is shown by indicating which word it is, then a chopping movement with the right hand against the left forearm.

So played, the game is so fascinating that it has become the one parlor game of many groups.

"MY FIRST—"

This variation of *Charades* requires no acting. Single words are used. Each player in turn gives a word for the others to guess; indicating the word by giving definitions of, or synonyms for each syllable, and finally a definition of, or synonym for the whole word.

Thus, "My first is to caress, my second is a vowel, my third is an outer garment, my whole is part of a woman's attire." (Pet—e—coat; Petticoat) Or, it can be given, "My first and second is mean, my third is an outer garment, my whole is part of a woman's attire." (Petty—coat; Petticoat)

The charm of the game is that each player thinks up his own words, and invents his own definitions to puzzle the others. The more skillful the players become, the more involved and puzzling the definitions may be made.

ACTING GAMES

Mother Goose.—Mother Goose rhymes can be acted out in the same manner as Charades.

Proverbs.—This is played like Charades, with the teams acting out proverbs. This can be varied by cutting the proverb into several parts. Give each player a part, or let the players draw their parts. Then the players must locate the proverb. When players constituting a proverb have assembled, the group comprising it act it out for the others to guess. For a list of proverbs see page 522.

Titles.—The titles of books, plays, songs, or movies, etc., may be acted out in the same manner.

BURLESQUE

The names of stage or movie stars who can be easily mimicked are written on slips of paper and put in a container. Such persons as Eddie Cantor, Al Jolson, Mae West, etc., are ideal. Each guest draws a name, and then does the best possible burlesque of the person whose name he has drawn. The others must guess whom he represents.

The names of the guests may be similarly drawn, and each guest mimicks another. The others try to guess whom he is mimicking.

IN THE MANNER OF THE WORD

The players each write down an adverb, then fold and conceal their slips. In rotation, the players ask the first player to do something in the manner of the adverb: "Dance in the manner of the adverb"; "Speak in the manner of the adverb"; "Cross the floor in the manner of the adverb," etc. If the adverb written were "madly," the first player would do each of these things madly. The other players try to guess the adverb. The correct guesser scores 1. If no one guesses, after each has asked for one action, the actor scores 1. When the first player has finished, the second player acts his adverb, and so on.

The adverbs may be placed in a container and drawn for, then acted out as above.

HONEYMOON BREAKFAST, EMBARRASSING MOMENTS

The guests are paired. Each pair draws from a container a slip containing instructions to act out or represent some embarrassing moment. As:

The first honeymoon breakfast—and no eggs.
The old maid finds the burglar under her bed.
She is trying to make Him propose.
She goes to dinner with Him—and meets hubby.
William Tell's son (or daughter) eats the apple.

These may be amusing, or embarrassing. The acting must be pantomime, but wordless sounds, such as laughter, may be used. The other players try to guess the situation being acted. The correct guesser scores one. If no one guesses, the actors score 1 each High score for the evening wins.

Talking Honeymoon Breakfast.—This variation permits speech, but the spoken words must be ambiguous.

WHO AM I?

One player leaves the room. The others select a character he is to represent. The character may be real or imaginary, past, present, or future. He returns, and asks of each player: "Who am I?" He is permitted no other question, but he is allowed three guesses, such as: "Am I Mark Twain?" "Am I Shirley Temple?" "Am I George Washington?" He is permitted ten minutes in which to guess his identity. Then, another player is made the Victim. All the answers must be truthful, but should be as misleading as possible. For instance, if George Washington were the character chosen, the answers might be something like this: "You were a great cut-up"; "You surveyed the field admirably"; "You believed in being first"; etc.

WHERE AM I?

A player leaves the room; and the others decide where he is, and what he is supposed to be doing. Returning, he may ask any question that must be answered by "Yes" or "No." He must guess the answer within six to ten minutes by a process of elimination. The other players may only answer "Yes" or "No." If the thing hidden were, "You are hanging from the chandelier playing a saxophone," the questions and answers might go:

Q. Am I at this party? A. Yes.
Q. Am I in this room? A. Yes.
Q. Am I sitting down? A. No.
Q. Am I standing up? A. No.
Q. Am I flying? A. No.
Q. Am I hanging from something? A. Yes.

And so on, until the activity is discovered. When the time is up, whether or not the Victim has guessed what he is supposed to be doing, another Victim is chosen, and the game continues. It is not wise to make the hidden activity too difficult.

CONVERSATION

Two players leave the room, while the others decide on two intricate sentences, which are written down; as:

Balancing on a flagpole, a tall blonde was smoking cigarettes.
Many people jammed in the subway make breathing difficult and upset the indigestion.

The two players return, and each is given one of the slips containing a sentence. Each memorizes his quickly. They then start conversing with each other, bringing in the details of their sentences in a natural way. One might start, "Aren't these human flies wonderful? I even saw one balancing on a flagpole." The other would answer, "They certainly are, but I think it's more amazing to see the many people jammed in the subway at five o'clock." And so on, until one of the players has brought his whole sentence naturally into the conversation. The one doing this first wins.

HOT AND COLD

A player leaves the room, while the others select something for him to do, such as offering Fanny Adams a cigarette, or standing on a chair and opening the center window from the top. The Victim is not permitted to ask questions. When he is anywhere in the room except the right place, the others say, "You're cold." When he approaches Fanny or the center window, as the case may be, they say, "You're getting warm," "You're getting warmer," "You're getting hot." When he is close to the precise object, they say "You're hot." When he actually does it, they say, "You're sizzling—that's it!"

Hot Music.—This is a variation of the above. Instead of speaking, the players hum or sing a selected song—softly when the Victim is cold, louder and louder as he gets hot.

Tom Tom.—This is the most amusing version of the above game. The Victim is notified by the Leader's tapping on a metal bowl or a pot with a tin spoon. The taps are very soft when the Victim is cold, and become louder and louder and more insistent as he nears his goal.

TEAKETTLE

This game is based upon words which have the same pronunciation, but different meanings, as:

Break; brake (a type of fern); brake (part of a motor).
Sew; so; sow. Leak, leek.

Bear (the animal); bear (to support); bare.
Bored; board (a plank); board (to get on a boat); board (food).
Rent (to hire); rent (to tear).

With the Victim out of the room, the others choose a group of two or more such words and incorporate them in a sentence. When the Victim returns, the Leader repeats the sentence, using the word teakettle instead of the chosen words. Thus, instead of saying "If I went to board with Mrs. Smith, I would be dreadfully bored by her guests, and could never stand that ugly board floor in the dining room," the Leader would say, "If I went to teakettle with Mrs. Smith, I would be dreadfully teakettle by her guests, and could never stand that ugly teakettle floor in the dining room." The Victim is given about two minutes in which to guess the words, and score 1, or to fail. Then another Victim is chosen.

The players may be divided into two teams. One team then goes out, while the other selects. The one who guesses correctly wins for his team; then the other team goes out.

Or all the players may speak to the Victim, using the word teakettle instead of the chosen words.

Or the Victim may select the words and come in and pronounce the teakettle sentence. The player who guesses the words first is the next Victim.

COFFEEPOT

With the Victim out of the room, the other players select a verb (as walk, dance, sing, etc.) or a participle representing an activity (as walking, dancing, singing, etc.). The Victim returns and may ask questions of the players in rotation, using the word "coffeepot" to represent the verb or activity. If "walk" were selected, the questions and answers might go:

Q. Do *you* coffeepot? A. Frequently.
Q. Do you coffeepot alone? A. Sometimes, usually not.
Q. Do you like coffeepotting? A. Very much.
Q. Do you coffeepot at night? A. Sometimes.

And so on, until the Victim guesses the verb or activity. The next Victim is the one who has given the answer which enabled the first Victim to guess the correct word.

There are two variations. One requires that the questions be answered only by "Yes," "No," or "I don't know." The other permits objects to be used, instead of verbs or activities

PROPER NAMES

The players select a category or classification: Literature, Amusements, History, the Bible, etc. The Victim then goes out of the room, and the other players decide on some proper name that comes under the category. The Victim returns.

If Geography were the category, and "Liberia" the name chosen, the Victim might proceed this way: "Is it a city?" First player; "No, it isn't London." "Is it a river?" Second player; "No, it isn't the Loire." "Is it a state?" Third player; "No, it isn't Louisiana." Until finally, "Is it a country?" "Yes, it is Liberia."

The questions are asked in rotation, and each player must answer with a name beginning with L, or with whatever letter the chosen name begins. If he cannot, he pays a forfeit, or receives a black mark. Should he challenge the Victim, and the latter cannot name a word beginning with L under the category, he receives the black mark; if he can, the player receives it. Before the Victim replies to the challenge, he asks the question of the next player, and so on. If any player answers correctly, the game proceeds. If no one answers, and the Victim can name a correct word, all the others receive black marks. If the Victim cannot locate the word finally, he receives two black marks, or pays two forfeits.

TWENTY QUESTIONS

One player writes down the name of an object anywhere in the world. The slip is folded and placed in sight of all. The others in rotation ask twenty questions, and must guess the object by the time the twentieth question has been answered. Questions must be answered "Yes," "No," or "I don't know." The player naming the object selects the one to be questioned next.

A typical game, with the Empire State Building as the object, might proceed:

Q. Is it in existence now? A. Yes.
Q. Does it belong to the animal kingdom? A. No.
Q. Is it used by any members of the animal kingdom? A. Yes.
Q. Is it used by men? A. Yes.
Q. Is it something to eat? A. No.
Q. Is it something to wear? A. No.
Q. Is it a means of locomotion? A. No.
Q. Is it a public building? A. Yes.
Q. Is it in America? A. Yes.
Q. Is it in an Eastern city? A. Yes.
Q. Is it an office building? A. Yes.
Q. Is it a famous building? A. Yes.
Q. Is it in New York? A. Yes.
Q. Is it the Empire State Building? A. Yes.

Camps.—This is a variation of the above game. The players are divided into two camps, one at one end of the room, the other at the opposite end. One player from each camp goes out. This pair decide upon an object. They return and each joins the opposite camp. Each camp asks questions, as above, of the individual enemy in its midst. The camp first guessing the object wins, and keeps the first enemy and chooses another from the opposite camp, who must then join the winning camp. Two more players go out, and the game proceeds as above, until all the players are in one camp, or until one camp surrenders.

Vegetable, Animal or Mineral?—This is the old form of the above game. "Is it Vegetable, Animal or Mineral?" is the first question asked. The chosen object must belong to one of these kingdoms. Then twenty or thirty questions are asked. After the first answer, all answers must be "Yes," "No," or "I don't know." Proceed as above.

HIDDEN PROVERBS

With the Victim out of the room, the players select a proverb. (See page 522 for proverbs.) The Victim returns, and asks questions in rotation. The first answer must contain the first word of the proverb; the second, the second word; the third, the third word; etc. The Victim must discover the proverb within a stated time. If he fails he pays a forfeit. If the proverb were "Possession is nine points of the law," the questions might proceed:

Q. Is the proverb familiar to all of us? A. I am sure you are in *possession* of its every word.

Q. Ann, have you rouge on your cheeks? A. *Is* that a nice question?

Q. Have you ever been to France, Bob? A. No, but I've tried *nine* times to get there.

Q. Are you going away this summer, Ruth? A. Everything *points* to my having to stay at home.

Q. Were you home last night, Frank? A. What made you think *of* that?

Q. Do you like bananas, Amy? A. *The* very ripe ones, yes.

Q. Do you believe in kissing, Jim? A. There ought to be a *law* against it.

Q. Have you a handkerchief, Carrie? A. I have two in my *possession.*

And so on, until the Victim has discovered the proverb.

BLURBS AND SLAMS

While the Victim is out of the room, the others decide on an object in the room. He returns, and asks each player, "Why is the object like me?" The reply must be a compliment or a slam. Within a stated time the Victim must guess the object. If the object were a chair, the answers might be: "It's strong and sturdy." "It's frequently sat on." "It's a dependable support." "It's stiff and rigid." Whoever gives the revealing answer is the next Victim.

MURDER

One player is selected as the District Attorney. He may be sent out of the room, though this is not necessary. In advance, the Murderer and the Victim are selected and told what to do. The lights are flashed out, usually without warning. The Leader asks everyone to stand still. There is a sudden scream, and the thud of a falling body. The Leader counts ten, to give the Murderer a chance to escape. Then the lights are turned on, and the District Attorney attempts to solve the murder.

He is permitted to question everyone except the Victim. All must answer truthfully, except the Murderer. He may lie as plausibly as possible. The game continues until the District Attorney solves the crime.

Are You The Murderer?—Provide a deck of as many cards as there are players, including the Joker, the Ace of Spades, and the Queen of Hearts. Each player draws a card. Only the Leader may see what is drawn by each. The drawer of the Ace of Spades is the District Attorney; the Joker, the Murderer; the Queen of Hearts, the Victim. The Murderer is told who is the Victim, but the Victim does not know the Murderer. Proceed as above, the District Attorney counting ten, until the lights are flashed on again. Proceed as above, except that the Murderer may not lie if the direct question "Are you the Murderer?" is asked. The District Attorney may ask this question three times. If the murder is still unsolved, after he has asked the question three times, a new District Attorney is chosen, and the game continues until the murder is solved.

In one variation, the Victim and Murderer are notified in advance. The Murderer is given time to escape, then the District Attorney is appointed, and the game proceeds as above. The Murderer may not lie, but the question "Are you the Murderer?" may not be asked.

GUESS HOW MANY

Fill a bottle, bowl, jar, etc., with beans, grains of corn, or similar small objects. Within a given time the players must guess the number of objects in the container. The number of potatoes, apples, etc., in a large basket or a sack may also be guessed. The players may touch the container and study it from every angle.

LITERARY SALAD

Prepare in advance about one hundred green paper lettuce leaves. Write a familiar quotation or a line or two of verse on each, and arrange the leaves in a salad bowl. The Leader passes the bowl to one player at a time. The player takes a leaf, reads the quotation aloud, and must immediately identify it, telling from what work the lines come, and the author. If the player cannot identify it, he says "I don't know." Then anyone may identify it, the one doing so winning the leaf. The next leaf is then drawn, and so on, until the bowl is emptied. The one having the most leaves wins.

RUN AND DRAW

Divide the players into two teams, each with a captain. Each player writes something to be identified by drawing alone. These things should be difficult to draw: as the nebular hypothesis, a bachelor giving a baby a bottle, a seed growing, cornmeal mush. The slips are folded and put in a container, which is some distance from a table around which the two teams are grouped.

One captain withdraws a slip. He must rush to the table, and try to communicate what is on the slip by drawing alone. A stated time is allowed. He may make as many drawings as possible within the time. His teammates may make as many guesses as they choose, within the time limit. If he can transmit the idea by drawing and not speaking, his team scores 1. When the time expires, the second captain tries, then one by one, alternately, the members of the team withdraw slips from the containers and run and draw according to the instructions. The team scoring the most points wins.

LIKES AND DISLIKES

Provide each player with a sheet of paper and a pencil. Let each write his five favorite likes, and his five predominant dislikes. The papers are collected, shuffled, and read one at a time.

Each player tries to guess the writer, as each list is read. The correct guesser scores 1 each time. It is permissible to give one or two false likes or dislikes to throw off suspicion.

HANGMAN

Give each player a sheet of paper and a pencil, and instruct him to draw a scaffold with a rope hanging from it. A category or

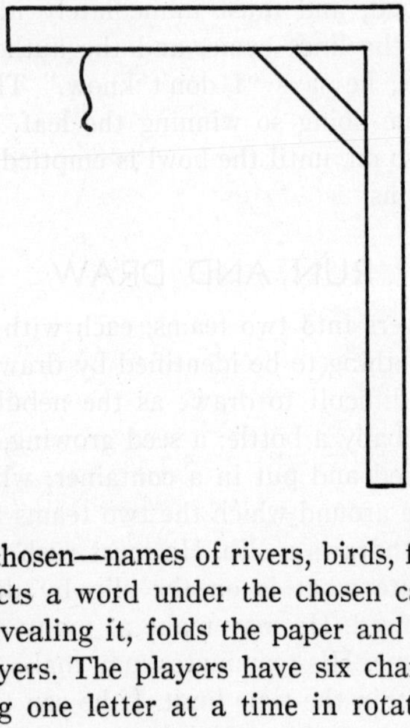

classification is chosen—names of rivers, birds, flowers, trees, etc. The Leader selects a word under the chosen category, writes it down without revealing it, folds the paper and places it in sight of the other players. The players have six chances to guess the word, by naming one letter at a time in rotation. Each player makes as many blanks on his paper as there are letters in the word.

If "trees" were the category, and the word walnut, the game might proceed in this fashion: First player, "Is there an A in the word?" (It is wiser to ask about the vowels first.) Leader, "Yes, it is the second letter." The players then write in the letter A in the proper place. Second player, "Is there an E in it?" Leader, "No. Draw your head on the rope." Each player then does so. If the third and fourth players ask about I and O, each player draws his body and one arm on the rope. Fifth player, "Is there a U in it?" Leader, "Yes, it is the fifth letter." And so on, until the word is guessed. For wrong guesses, each player adds to the

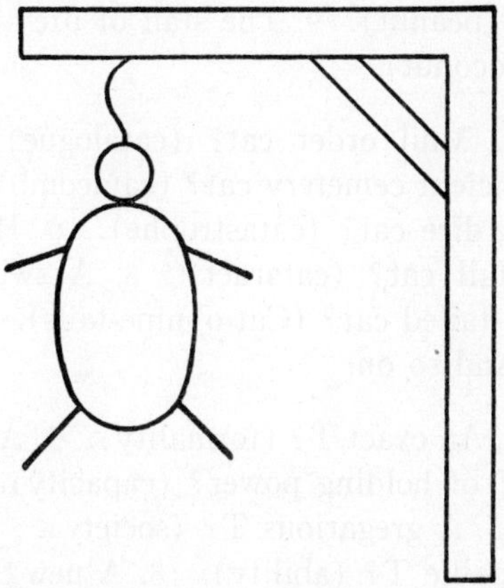

head, his body, the two arms, and the two legs. The object of the game is not to be hanged. The word walnut, partly filled in after the two correct guesses would look like this:

_ A _ _ U _

Before a letter is guessed, the player whose turn it is may ask one, and only one question, such as "Is it bamboo?"

The game may be played by one player at a time, sending him out as the Victim. The others decide on a word, and the game proceeds as above, with the Victim asking all the questions, and striving not to be hanged.

PUN QUESTIONNAIRES

These are questionnaires to which all the anwers are puns. Prepare a list of 20 or more for each guest. Within a set time they must fill in the answers. The one having the longest list wins.

Nut Questionnaire.—Each answer must contain the word "nut." This need not be told, provided the questionnaire is headed as above. 1. What nut is beside the sea? (beechnut). 2. A lighted nut (candlenut). 3. An uncooked bread nut? (doughnut). 4. A nut from the product of cows? (butternut). 5. A girl's name? (hazelnut). 6. A fruit? (grape nut). 7. A box nut? (chestnut). 8. A vegetable? (peanut). 9. The staff of life? (bread nut). 10. A hot drink? (coconut).

Which Cat?—1. Mail order cat? (catalogue). 2. Saucy cat? (catsup). 3. Ancient cemetery cat? (catacomb). 4. Flying cat? (catbird). 5. A dire cat? (catastrophe). 6. Horned cat? (cattle). 7. Waterfall cat? (cataract). 8. A swimming cat (catfish). 9. Many-tailed cat? (Cat-o'-nine-tails). 10. An aromatic cat? (catnip). And so on.

Done to a T.—1. An exact T? (formality). 2. An honest T? (sincerity). 3. A T of holding power? (capacity). 4.A changeable T? (variety). 5. A gregarious T? (society). 6. A religious T? (piety). 7. Capable T? (ability). 8. A new T? (novelty). 9. Political T? (Party). 10. A maidenly T? (modesty) And so on.

Many Nations.—1. An angry nation? (indignation). 2. A beguiling nation? (fascination). 3. A dreamy nation? (imagination). 4. A rebellious nation? (insubordination). 5. A finishing nation? (termination). 6. A gift nation? (donation). 7. A murderous nation? (assassination). 8. A quarrelsome nation? (recrimination). 9. A destructive nation? (ruination). 10. A ruthless nation? (extermination). And so on.

Pat Himself.—Prepare a pun questionnaire on words containing the syllable "pat," such as compatible, patent, patch, paternal, patrimony, pater noster, patter, pattern, etc.

Always Miss.—Use words containing the syllable "miss"—as misdeeds, mistakes, remiss, mission, amiss, missile, misconstrue, Mississippi, misdirect, misbegotten, etc.

The Dangerous Age.—Base the questionnaire on words containing the syllable "age," such as: cottage, dotage, carriage, marriage, luggage, average, mileage. acreage, courage, leverage, potage, etc.

Many-Sided.—This questionnaire is based on words containing the syllable "side," or a syllable pronounced similarly, as: coincide, countryside, broadside, patricide, sidereal, sidewalk, seidel, regicide, bedside, beside, etc.

Many other pun questionnaires can be devised, basing each upon a specific syllable.

RIDDLE QUESTIONNAIRE

Instead of being based upon puns, these questionnaires are riddles.

Your Body.—1. Part of the face? (eye—for I). 2. A tropical tree? (palm). 3. The fruit of maize? (ear). 4. A small animal? (hair—for hare). 5. Possesses knowledge? (knows—for nose). 6. To prepare for war? (arm). 7. What a carpenter uses? (nail). 8. A young animal? (calf). 9. Part of a shoe? (tongue). 10. What religions are concerned with? (sole—for soul). And so on.

Flower Riddles.—Make the questions either puns or riddles based upon the names of flowers, such as: buttercup, daisy, aster, marigold, lady's slipper, goldenrod, four o'clock, Sweet William, bleeding heart, forget-me-not, etc.

Questions can be devised using names of birds, animals, trees, and many other categories.

Riddles.—Provide a questionnaire of riddles, such as: 1. What has eyes and can't see? (A potato). 2. What runs and doesn't walk, has a tongue and can't talk? (A wagon). 3. What has legs and can't walk? (A table). 4. What is both a fruit and a time? (A date). 5. What has pains and doesn't ache? (A window). 6. What is full of holes and still holds water? (A sponge). 7. What grows larger the more you take from it? (A hole). 8. What is black and white and red (read) all over? (A newspaper). 9. What has a face and never washes it? (A clock). 10. What tells you how you look without speaking? (A mirror). And so on.

City Questionnaire.—Use the names of cities as the basis for the questionnaire, such as: Newark (new ark), Hartford (hart—or heart—ford), Hollywood, Little Rock, Palm Beach, St. Paul, Cleveland, etc. Names of states, countries, rivers, etc., can be used in the same way.

State Abbreviations.—For this devise riddle or pun questions on the abbreviations of state names. The names of Indian tribes can also be used in this way.

Hidden Author.—Base the questionnaire on the names of authors. Such as: 1. A happy man? (Gay). 2. A young grazing animal? (Lamb). 3. A denial of ability? (Kant). 4. The name of a country? (France). 5. A stream? (Brooke). 6. An old-fashioned head covering? (Hood). 7. A hard metal? (Steele). 8. What fire does? (Burns). 9. A maker of barrels? (Cooper). 10. An untamed thing? (Wilde). And so on.

V. STUNTS and GAGS

THESE brief stunt games and tricks are excellent to fill in lulls in the party, or to play between more formal games. They are sure to produce laughter and to spread gaiety over any group. The chief merit of most of them is that they start everyone laughing at everyone else.

There are certain groups which only the performer can do: such as magic and sleight-of-hand tricks. These, if well done, satisfy the performer's desire for attention, and keep the other guests interested. There are also mind-reading stunts, usually performed by two people in collusion to the mystification of the other guests.

Any party is improved by the addition of several of these stunts and gags.

BALANCING STUNTS

These stunts test toe poise and the stability of the nerves of the players; they also provide plenty of laughter.

Milk Bottle Balance.—Place a quart milk bottle in the center of the floor. The player must sit on top of the bottle; place his right leg straight in front of him; put his left leg over his right; then, a match in one hand and a cigarette or candle in the other, strike the match and light the cigarette or the candle, while keeping his balance. Or the player, when so balanced, may be required to write his name legibly on a card with a pencil.

Jug Balance.—Place a gallon jug, without handles, on the floor at right angles to the player's body axis. The player must sit on the jug, stretch his legs straight before him, take a match in one hand, a cigarette or candle in the other. He must then lift his legs from the floor and, before replacing them, light the cigarette or the candle. Once he has attempted to light the object, neither hands nor legs may touch the floor until the task is completed; should either touch, the stunt must be started again.

A variation is for the heel of one foot to be placed on the toe of the other before the legs are lifted.

This stunt is more difficult if the jug is parallel to the player's body.

Tin Can Balance.—Place an average size unopened tin can (about 5 inches tall) on the floor. Place a candle in a flat candleholder, and beside it a box of matches, and a match, the length of the player's forearm from the can. The player must balance on one foot on the can, with the other foot raised from the floor; in this position he must pick up the match and the match box and light the candle, without touching the floor with the raised foot.

Chair Balance.—Place a heavy straight-backed chair front down on the floor, and place a card on the central part of the outer edge of the back, so that it extends over the back. Place a cushion across the chair's back legs. The player must kneel on the cushion, grasp the sides of the seat, and lean forward and take up the card with his teeth, without falling or tipping the chair forward. Several cards may be placed as above, and the player required to remove all of them with his teeth.

Human Bridge.—Place three strong straight-backed chairs side by side. The player must lie with his head on the first chair and his feet on the third. Then he must fold his arms and stiffen his body. The Leader then removes the middle chair. If the player can maintain this posture for ten seconds, he passes. Or each player may be timed, and the one holding the posture longest wins.

Or the player may be required to remove the middle chair himself, fold his arms for ten seconds, then replace the chair.

Or he may be required to remove the middle chair, pick it up pass it over his body, and replace it on the other side.

Lighting the Candle.—Two players, each on a cushion, kneel on the floor facing each other. They must be far enough apart so that they must stretch their arms to reach each other. Give each a candle to hold in his right hand; one candle lighted, the other not. Now each player raises his left leg and grasps it in his left hand. So balanced, they strive to light the unlit candle with the lighted one. If either player touches his left knee to the ground, the stunt fails. The time required by each couple may be taken the shortest time winning.

Spearing Handkerchiefs.—Place two straight-backed chairs facing each other with a space between, and lay a broomstick from seat to seat. Hang a man's handkerchief over the two ends of each chair-back—four in all. Give the player a cane. He must balance himself seated cross-legged on the broomstick, lift the cane from the floor and, one at a time, remove the handkerchiefs. He may use the cane for balancing between spearings.

Pin in the Chair.—Use a strong straight-backed chair. Place a straight pin in the back of one of the rear legs, about two inches from the floor. The player sits in the chair; then, grasping it any way he chooses, balancing himself, with no part of his body touching the floor at any time, he twists around the rear of the chair, takes the pin in his teeth, and returns to his original position without falling or touching the floor. He may shift his grip as he pleases, so long as no part of his body touches the floor.

KISSING THE WALL BACKWARD

The player stands with his back to the wall, and about twenty inches from it. A tall player will have to stand farther away. He must then lean over backward until his lips touch the wall; then straighten up without losing his balance.

JUMPING OVER A STICK

The player, holding a stick in his two hands, tries to jump over it, without touching it. The trick is to push down with the arms as the legs rise, so that arms and legs are performing opposite motions at the same time.

After jumping forward, the player tries jumping backward. To contest, each player may jump forward and backward, without stopping, as many times as possible.

RINGING THE RING

Hang a ring, about two inches in diameter, suspended on a string, about shoulder high. One by one the players take a cane and, starting from the opposite side of the room, walk briskly toward the ring and try to spear it with the cane. Or the players may be required to run toward the ring.

RINGING THE WEDDING RING

Hang a plain gold ring on a piece of thread. The player holds this in his left hand, straight before him, elbow stiff. Holding a pencil in his right hand, starting with his arm straight out from his side, elbow stiff, he must without delay pierce the ring with the pencil.

FLIP

One player holds at arm's length a soda or ginger-ale bottle, with a cork or a lump of sugar balanced on top of it. Successively, the other players cross the room rapidly, and without pausing, flip the cork or sugar from the bottle by snapping the second or first finger from the thumb. The players may be required to run across the room. In either case, they may not pause at the bottle, but must do the flipping while walking or running.

STANDING HIGH JUMP

A player boasts of his skill as a jumper, builds up a discussion, and offers to prove it. Clever patter is essential. He studies the ceiling and wonders aloud if he'll hit his head. He places a floor-lamp or fire screen, at least four feet tall, in the center of the room, and drapes his handkerchief over it. He asks if the others believe he can jump flatfooted over it. When they deny the possibility, he quietly places the handkerchief on the floor, and jumps flatfooted over it.

PHOTOGRAPH

A Victim is chosen to have his photograph taken. The Leader is provided with a camera, and other properties, such as a flash-light, special light bulbs, or a special lamp. He prepares the room, giving an elaborate patter about the difficulty of taking indoor pictures. The Victim is told to sit in a chair. The Leader returns after blackening his fingers and proceeds to pose the Victim, turning his head, tilting his chin, and so on. "Turn your head a trifle to the left," the Leader might say, as he turns the Victim's head, leaving smudges where his fingers touch. When the Victim's face is thoroughly smudged, the Leader pretends to take a picture. Then he asks the Victim, "Would you like to see your photograph?," and hands him a mirror.

BARNYARD

A Victim is chosen, without knowing he is to be selected. The Leader tips off the others that, after the rehearsal, they are to be silent. He then assigns each the name of a barnyard animal, naming the Victim to be the donkey. They then rehearse, singly and in groups, the sounds made by the animals they represent. The Leader then instructs them all to perform their loudest when he raises his hand. When he does so, only the Victim makes a sound, braying loudly against the silence.

This can be varied by having all the players rehearse together, first as roosters, then as cows, sheep, dogs, and so on. The Leader then says that he will whisper to each what he is to impersonate when the signal is given. He whispers to all but the Victim, "Don't make a sound." To the Victim, "You are the donkey." Then the game proceeds as above.

WHO IS IT?

A Victim is sent from the room. The others decide on a player whom the Victim must locate by asking questions in rotation. The one chosen is the one to the left of the player who is being questioned. The Victim returns and questions the first player. He may not ask, "Is it this player or that one?" He must ask questions that can be answered by Yes or No. He might ask the first player, "Is it a girl?" The player (referring to the boy on the left), "Oh, no." The Victim to the second player, "Is it a boy?" The second player (referring to the girl on his left), "Oh, no." The Victim may ask such questions as: "Does it powder its nose?" "Does it play football?" "Does it wear a vest?" The answers should be baffling. Ultimately, a clever player guesses correctly, and may then ask some amusing personal questions before revealing his guess.

If the game is known to all, it may be varied by designating the chosen person in some other way, such as, the third on the left, or the first or second on the right, as each question is asked.

OPERA GLASS PROMENADE

This requires a large room. Stretch a string tightly down the length of the floor. Provide the player with a pair of opera glasses or field glasses. He must look through the opera glasses from the large end, and walk the string without stepping off it. If the room is large enough, and more than one pair of glasses is available, several players may try this at the same time.

TALKING TOURNEY

The Leader must be equipped with a watch. Two players stand back to back. At a signal, they face each other, and talk fast and furiously for thirty seconds, saying anything they please on any subject. At a second signal, they stop. The others vote as to which was the best talker.

Whistling Tourney.—The same, except that the players must each whistle a different tune for thirty seconds.

Song Tourney.—As above, the players singing a different tune.

Laugh Tourney.—As above, the players laughing for thirty seconds.

Whistling for Endurance.—Line up six good whistlers and see which can whistle the longest. The audience may laugh or clown in an effort to break down the performers.

THE DIME OF FORTUNE

The Victim stands facing the others with his eyes closed. The Leader dips a dime in water then presses it firmly into the Victim's forehead. The Leader says he is going to tell the Victim how long it will be before he is married (or, how many husbands or wives the Victim will have; or something equally amusing and pertinent). The Victim is told to bob his head forward, and try to dislodge the dime. Each bob counts one, until the coin falls.

The Leader then tells the Victim the next question that fate will decide. It may be, for instance, how many children she (or he) will have. It should be something ridiculous and personal, and something the Victim desires only in limited amount, or not at all. The Leader presses the coin in more firmly this time, but removes it. The Victim is then told to bob it off. Since it is not there, the Victim will bob and bob in vain.

FORTUNE-TELLING QUESTIONNAIRE

Give each player a sheet of paper and a pencil, and tell them to write the numbers 1 through 12 on the left side of the paper. The Leader instructs them to write "Yes" or "No," or any single word answer to the following questions:

1. Do you get much fun out of life?
2. Do you like money?
3. First name of girl or boy you like most.
4. Do you like anyone else?
5. Do you eat too much?
6. Do you like cheese?
7. Give a number from one to sixteen.
8. Are you healthy?
9. Give a number from one to fifteen.
10. Name your favorite color.
11. What is your favorite vegetable?
12. What other color do you like?

When the answers are written, the Leader reads the questions below, and the players, in turn, must give their written answers aloud.

1. Do you like kissing?
2. Do you get enough kissing?
3. From whom?
4. Does she (or, he) like it?
5. Does he (or, she) get enough?
6. Do you wriggle when kissed?
7. How many times do you get kissed?
8. Do you want more?

9. How many persons can you kiss at one time?
10. What color is your face after you've been kissing?
11. When you look in a mirror what do you see?
12. What color is your sweetheart's (husband's, wife's, father's) face when he catches you kissing?

SCRAMBLED QUESTIONS AND ANSWERS

The players sit in a circle. The Leader asks a question of each in rotation. He then says that hereafter each player must give that same answer to any question asked of him, without smiling or laughing. Then all the other players ask a question of the first player. Each time he must give his original answer. Then all the players question the second player, and so on around the circle. A player who smiles or laughs while answering pays a forfeit. The Leader's first question should be a trick one, to prepare for silly answers. He might ask, "What is your favorite dessert?" The answer might be, "Chocolate éclairs." To all subsequent questions, that player must reply "Chocolate éclairs," without smiling or laughing.

GRAB BAG ANSWERS

Let each player write a question, fold the slip of paper, and drop it in a container; then write an answer to the question, fold the slip, and drop it in another container. Mix these thoroughly. Then each player draws one question and one answer, which he reads aloud. The results might read: Q. Does John play the piano? A. Standing on his head balancing an umbrella with his toes. Q. Are you going to Paris? A. Boiled beef with horseradish sauce.

A variation permits the player to write one question, and an answer to any other question he may have in mind.

What Would You Do?—Each question must begin with "What would you do if ——"; and each answer must begin "I would ——"

Why and Because.—Each question must begin "Why?," and each answer must begin "Because."

FIRST AID

The players sit in a circle, and each writes a predicament, which he passes to the player on his left. Each then writes the remedy, or what he would do in the predicament; and passes it to the player on the right. In rotation, each player reads aloud the predicament he is holding, and the one on the left reads the remedy he is holding. The reading might be: Predicament: What would you do if you were lost in the woods? Remedy: Have my hair bobbed and get a permanent. Predicament: What would you do if you were drowning? Remedy: Take a mustard bath and go to bed.

PICKLED ADJECTIVES

Prepare a brief story, with blanks where the adjectives should be. The story should be personal—either about the party and the guests; or about something in which all of them are interested. Without knowing about the story, the guests are each told to write one pleasant, complimentary adjective, and one unpleasant, uncomplimentary one, and pass them to the Leader. The Leader then reads the story, filling in the blanks with the adjectives as they come. The result might read: "The hideous Helen Cobb gave a darling party this vicious evening for a number of her heavenly friends. Grisly Ruth Jones arrived with beautiful John Howard, who wore a gruesome tuxedo," and so on.

This may be varied by reading the story first with all the pleasant adjectives, then with all the unpleasant ones. Or have the players write only one adjective. Then the Leader reads a story from a well known author, from a magazine, or from any source, substituting the written adjectives in order.

CONSEQUENCES

Provide each player with a pencil and a sheet of paper. As each answer is written, the player folds the paper so that the next one cannot read the answer, then passes it once to the left. This is continued until all the answers are written. The papers are then passed once to the right, and the stories are read aloud in rotation. Here are the things to be written:

1. A girl's name.
2. A boy's name.
3. Where they met.
4. What she wore.
5. What he wore.
6. Where they went.
7. What she said.
8. What he said.
9. What she did.
10. What he did.
11. The consequences.
12. What the world said.

Art Consequences.—This is a similar game, using drawing. The method used is the same as above, the drawings being limited to approximately 1 inch. The players are told to draw: 1. The hat. 2. Upper part of the face. 3. Lower part of the face. 4. The neck. 5. The shoulders. 6. The waist. 7. The hips. 8. The legs. 9. The feet. The drawings are then exhibited.

Book Review.—Played as above, folding and passing the paper each time. 1. The name of a well known book. 2. The name of a famous author. 3 through 12. Single line reviews, written by each player in rotation. The first line should start "This is a story of ——," or "This book deals with ——," or some similar opening, and the other sentences then carry on the review. 13. Name of paper or magazine reviewing the book.

Last Will.—Played as above, folding and passing the paper each time. Write at the top of each slip "The Last Will and Testament of ——" 1. Name of girl making the will. 2. Name of boy jointly making will with her. 3 through 11. Items to be willed. 12. Name of the person who is to inherit.

THIS IS MY NOSE

The players sit in a circle, and the Leader stands before the first, pointing to one part of his body, and naming another. Thus he might say, "This is my nose," and point to his foot. The player must say, "This is my foot" and point to his nose before the Leader can count 10. If he succeeds, he becomes the Leader and turns to the next player. Articles of clothing as well as parts of the body may be designated.

GOING TO NEWPORT

The players sit in a circle, and the Leader announces that they are all going to Newport, and each must name one thing he intends to take along. When this is done, the Leader asks the first player, "What will you do with it in Newport?" He must answer in a complete sentence, naming the article he intends to take. In rotation the other players must repeat the same sentence, each naming his own object. Thus, the players might have airplane, Siamese cat, a pound of caviar, roller skates, etc. When the Leader asked, "What will you do with it in Newport?," the first player would answer, "I am going to fly my airplane." The second player would have to say, "I am going to fly my Siamese cat," and so on around. If a player laughs while answering, he is eliminated or pays a forfeit.

WHAT IS MY THOUGHT LIKE?

The players sit in a circle. The Leader says to the player on his right, "I am thinking about something—I will tell you what it is later. What is my thought like?" The first player answers, then the second, and so on around the circle, each naming some thing or person. The answers might run: Cornmeal mush, dominoes, Sam's necktie, chicken hash, the *Bremen,* etc. The Leader then says, to the first player, "I was thinking of Helen's fiancé. Why is Helen's fiancé like cornmeal mush?" The first player must answer immediately as cleverly as possible, as: "He's soft and always mushy." Each answers in rotation, drawing some clever parallel between his likeness and Helen's fiancé.

BOY OR GIRL

This is fun for a small group, particularly a dinner party; or several chosen Victims, half boys and half girls, may be selected from a large group. The Leader explains that everyone is part male and part female, since each inherits from a mother and father alike. This test is to establish what per cent of each the person contains. The Leader then has the Victims in rotation do the following:

1. Light a match.
2. Drink some water from a glass.
3. Look directly at me.
4. Look at your finger nails.

The Leader then tells whether the Victim is 25%, 50%, 75%, or 100% girl or boy.

These are the differences: A girl lights a match away from herself; a boy toward himself. A girl looks over the glass while drinking; a boy looks into it. A girl's eyes waver; a boy looks directly at you. A girl extends her hand palms down, fingers away from her; a boy extends it palm up, fingers folded in.

READING GAGS

Ask the players to read the complete phrase in this symbol:

0
Bed

The answer is, "A little darkey (dark *e*) in bed, with nothing over him."

Then ask them to read:

A B C D fish
L M N O fish
O S A R fish

a drawing of a fish may be substituted for the word "fish." The answer is, "Abie, see de fish." " 'Ell, 'em ain' no fish." "Oh, 'es, 'ey are fish."

MATCH TRICKS

1. A false equation:

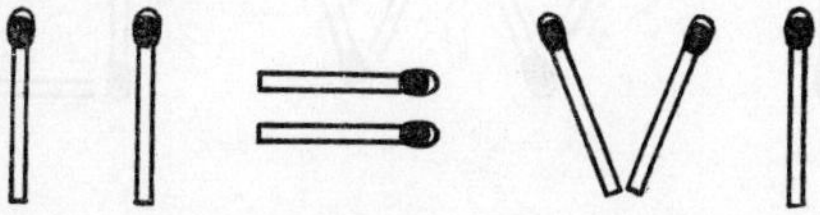

The matches forming the equality sign may not be touched. Only one match may be moved; and it must be moved from one side to the other side to form a mathematically true equation. There are two correct solutions:

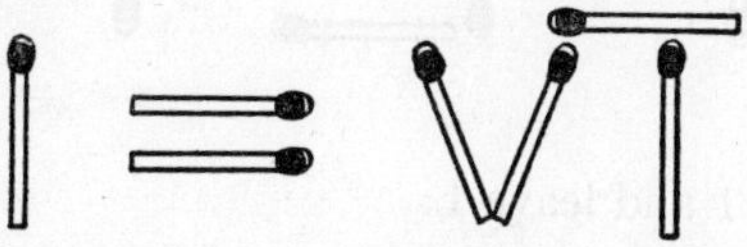

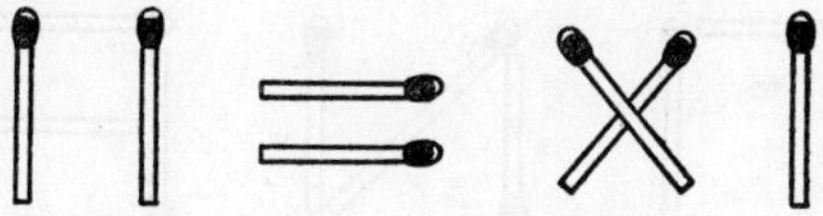

One equals the square root of one. 11 (Arabic numerals) equals 11 (Roman Numerals).

2. Make two squares and four triangles of 8 matches:

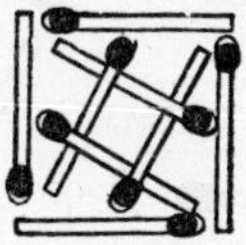

3. For the next three tricks, arrange 12 matches in three squares:

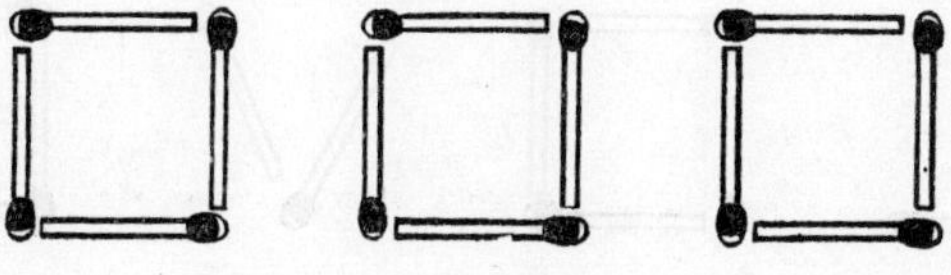

Take away 2 and leave 2:

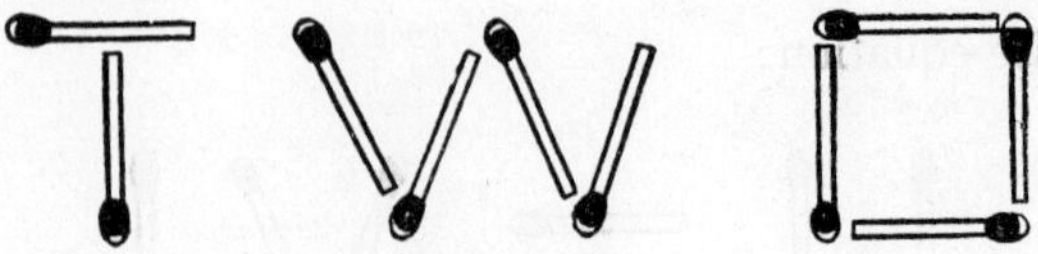

4. Take away 3 and leave 10:

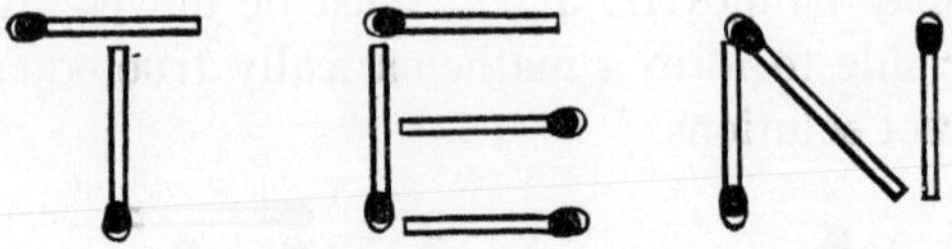

5. Take away 1 and leave 1:

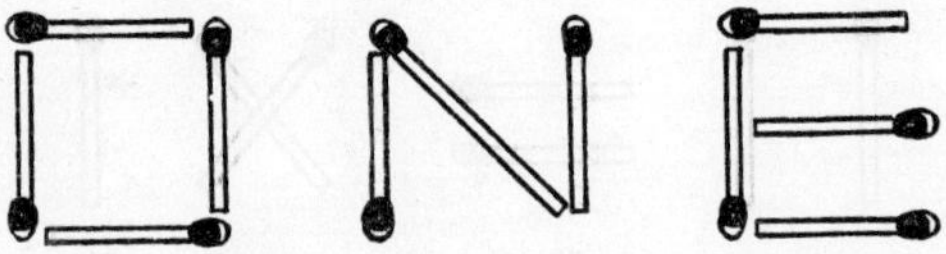

6. In the following arrangement of 12 matches move only 2 and get what matches are made of:

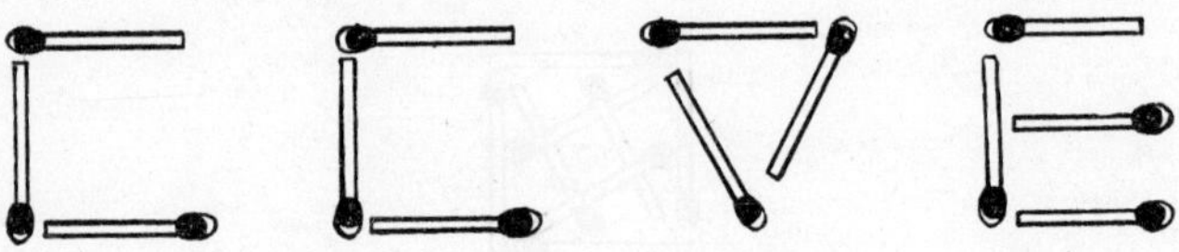

The answer is Love:

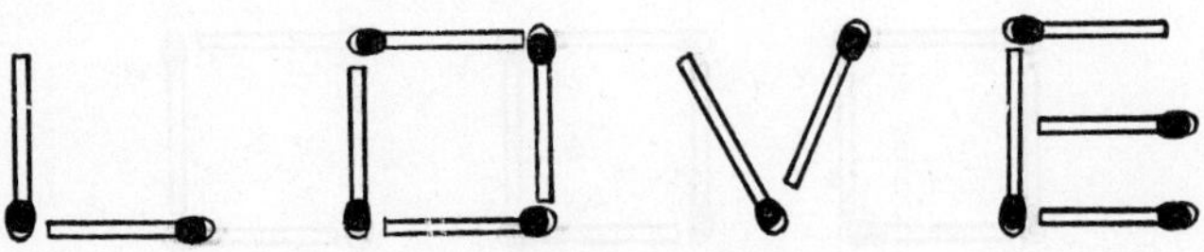

7. With 17 matches make two rows of three squares each, one above the other:

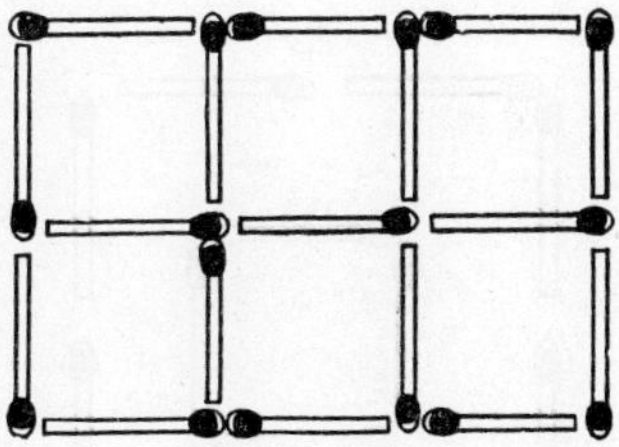

Remove 5 matches, touching no others, and leave three squares:

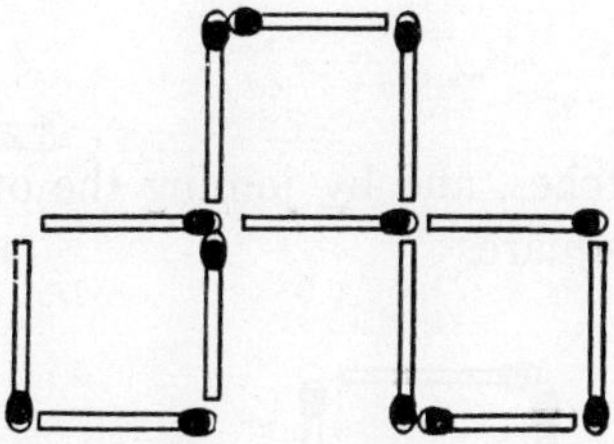

8. Form six squares with 17 matches:

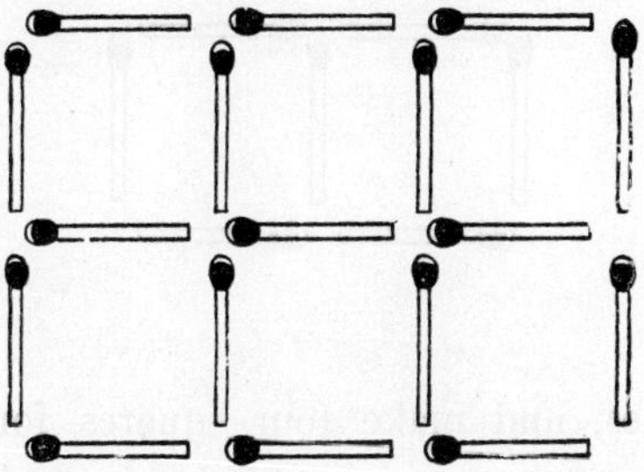

Take away 6 matches, and leave two squares:

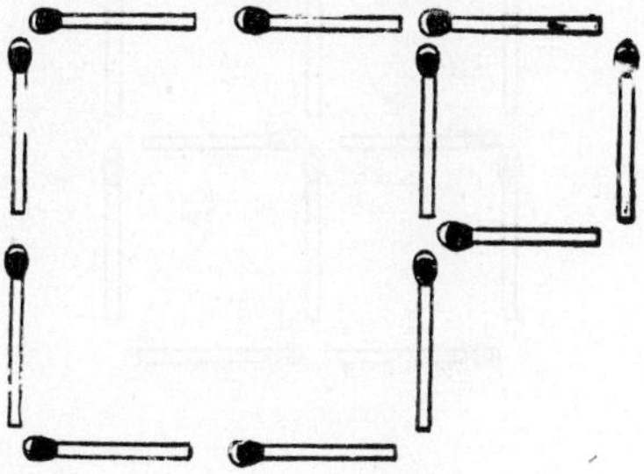

9. With 8 matches form a large square; then, with 4 matches form a small square within the first:

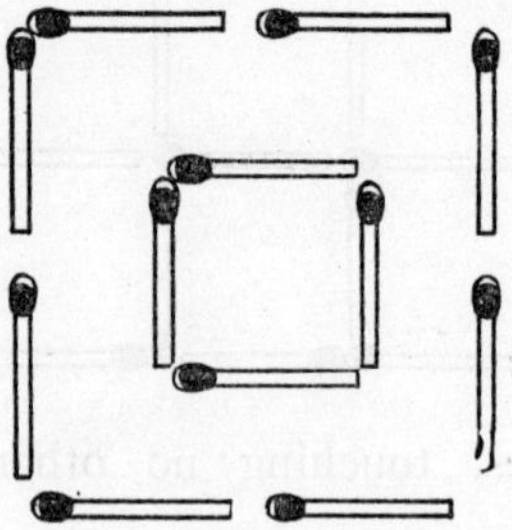

Take away 2 matches, and by joining the other 6 to the inner square, form three squares:

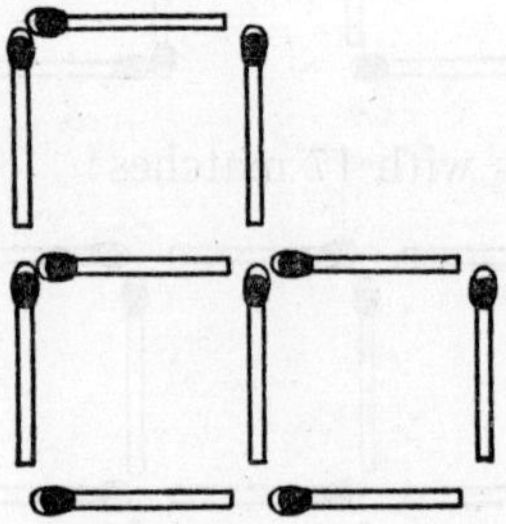

Add 2 matches, and make four squares forming one large square:

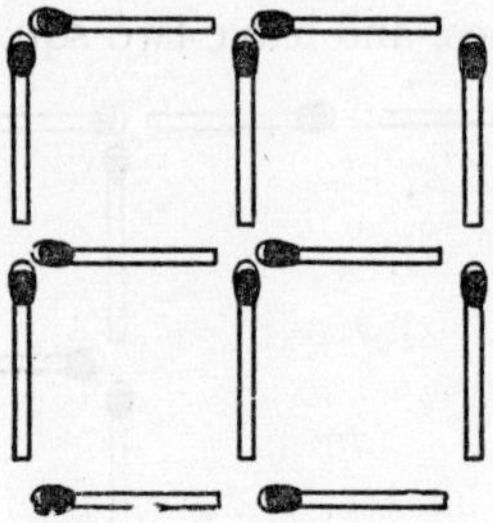

Remove 3 matches, and replace them, forming three squares:

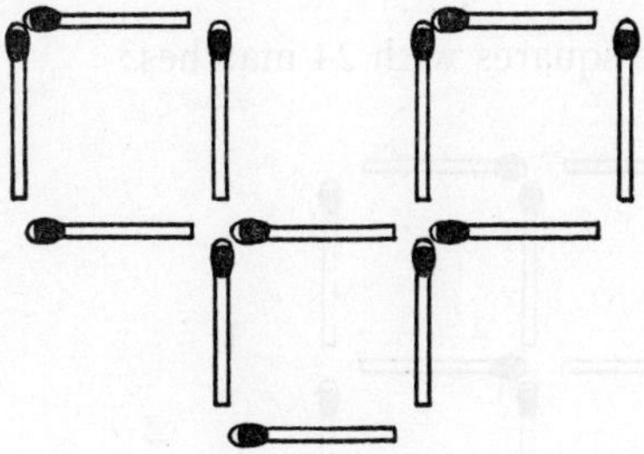

10. With 24 matches make three rows of three squares each, one above the other:

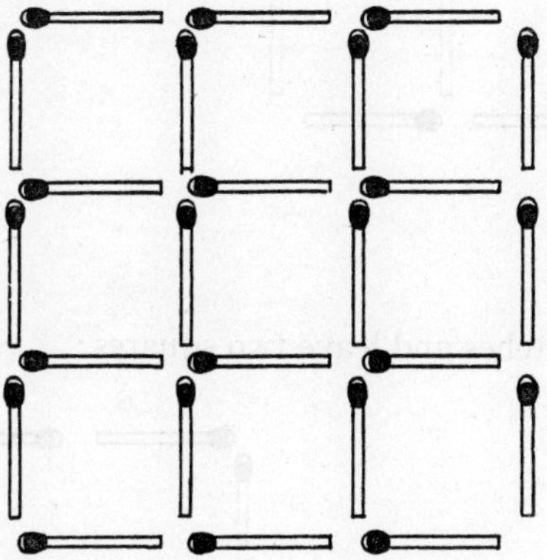

Remove 4 matches and leave five squares:

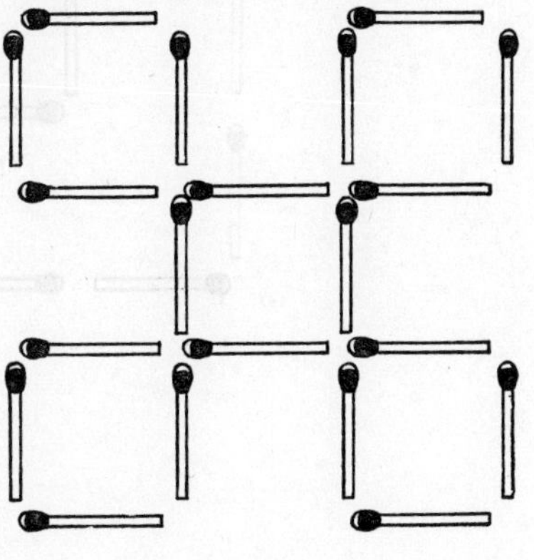

11. Form nine squares with 24 matches:

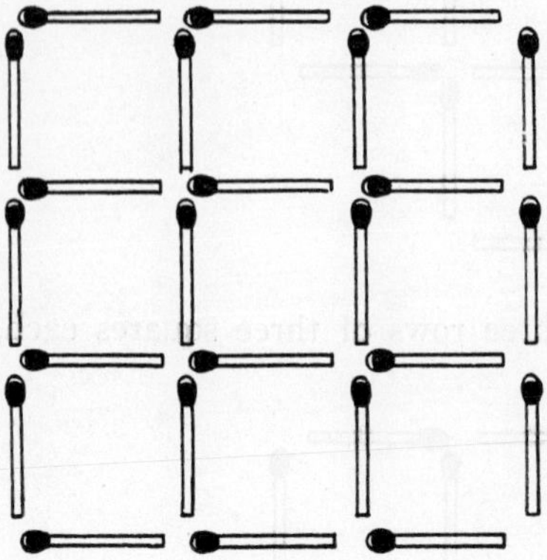

Remove 8 matches and leave two squares:

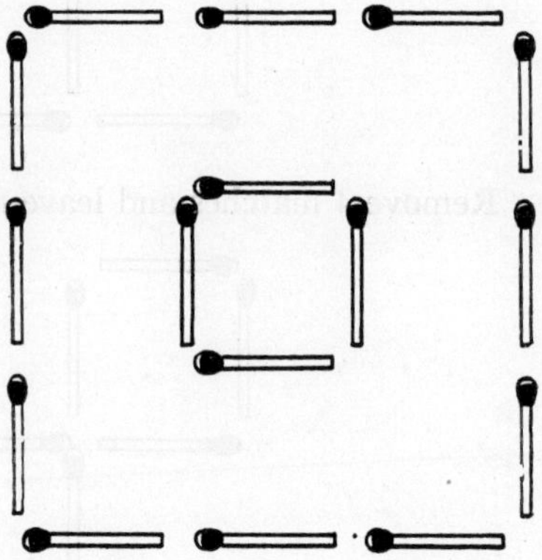

12. Form seven squares with 20 matches:

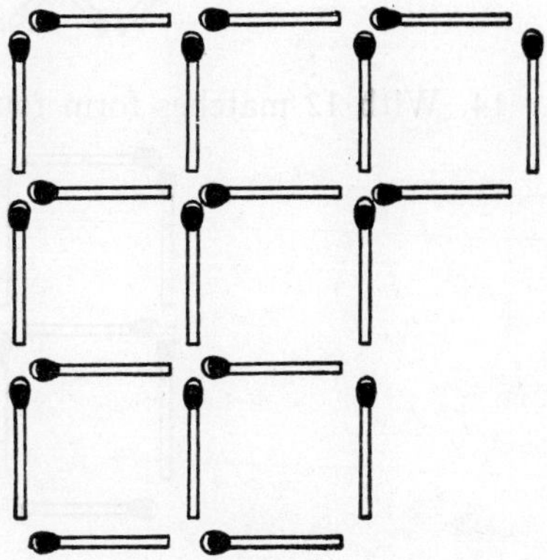

Remove 3 matches, and replace them so that there are only five squares:

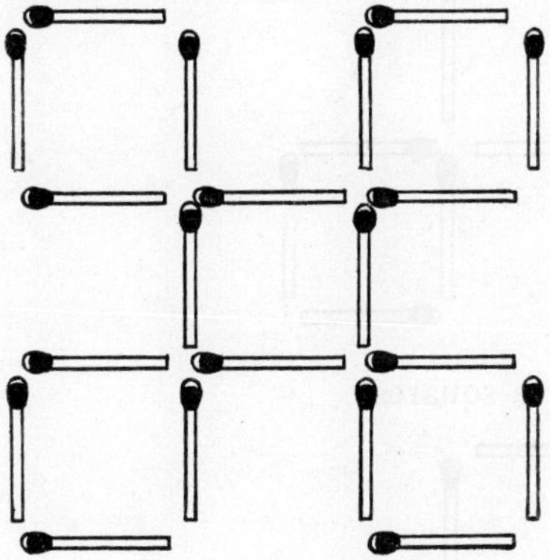

13. With 4 whole matches and 4 half matches form three squares. None of the matches may overlap:

14. With 12 matches form four squares:

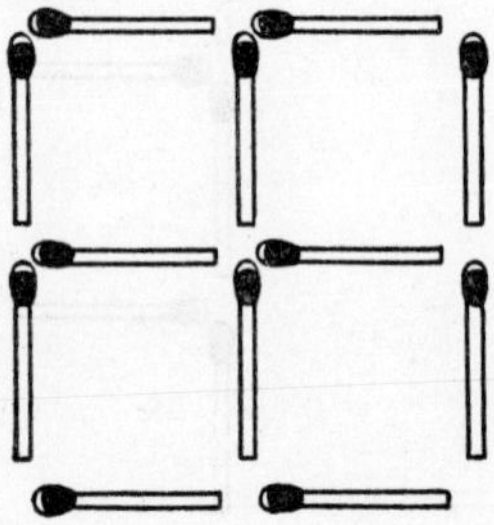

Remove 4 matches, and replace them leaving three squares:

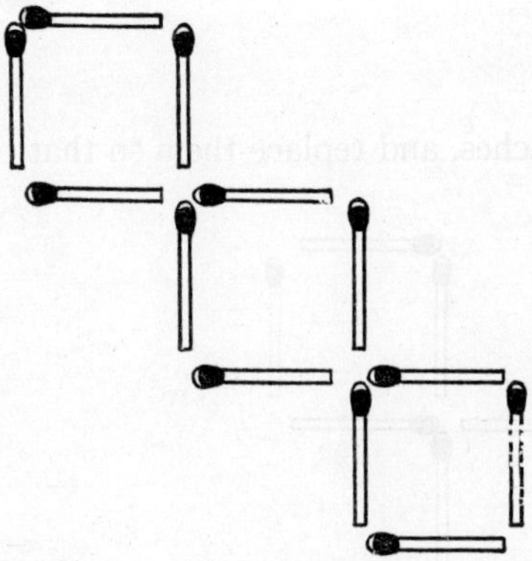

15. With 15 matches make five squares:

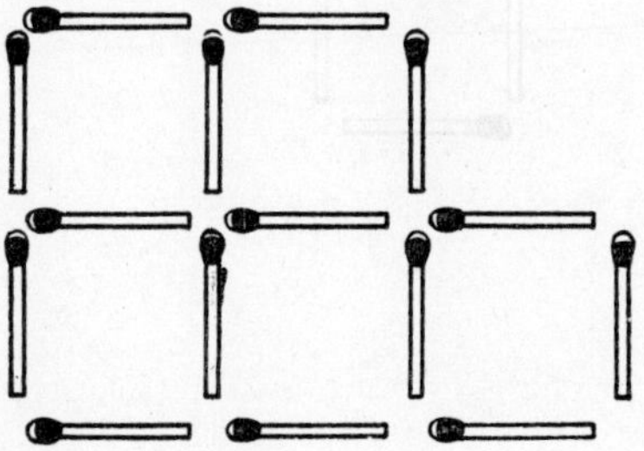

Remove 3 matches and leave three squares:

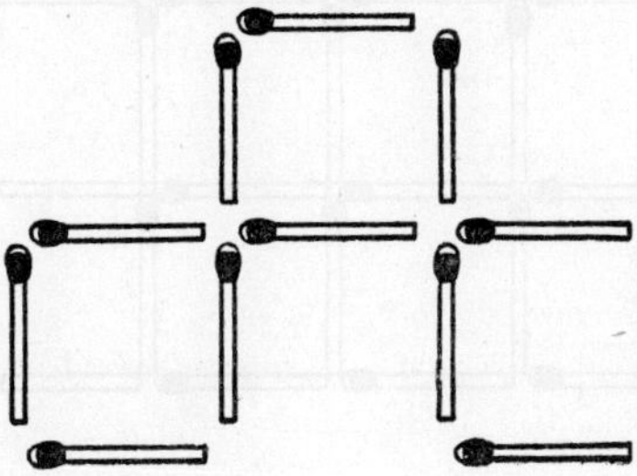

16. Form five squares with 16 matches:

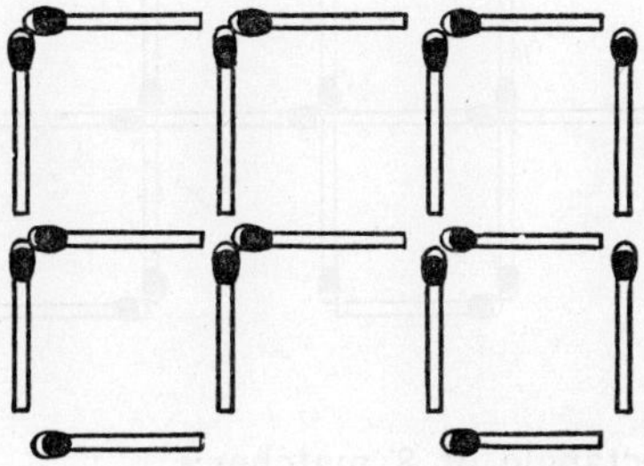

Remove 3 matches, and replace them to form four squares:

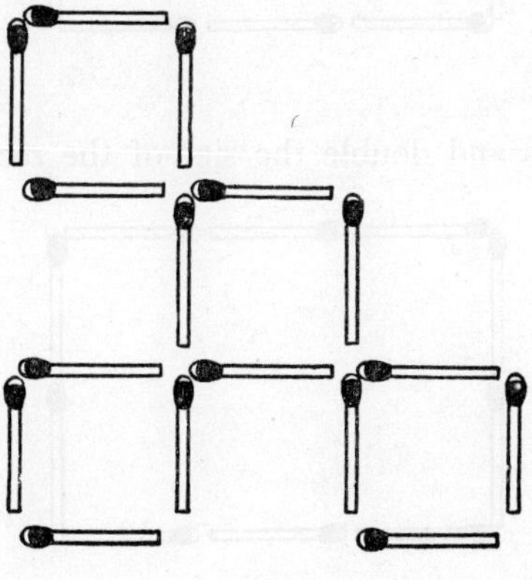

17. Form eight squares with 22 matches:

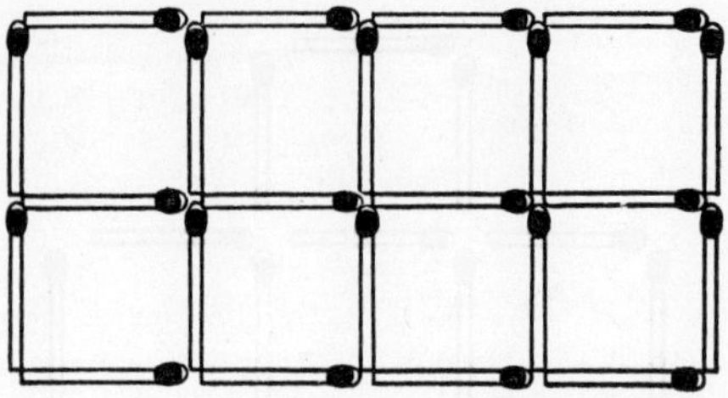

Remove 6 matches, and leave four squares:

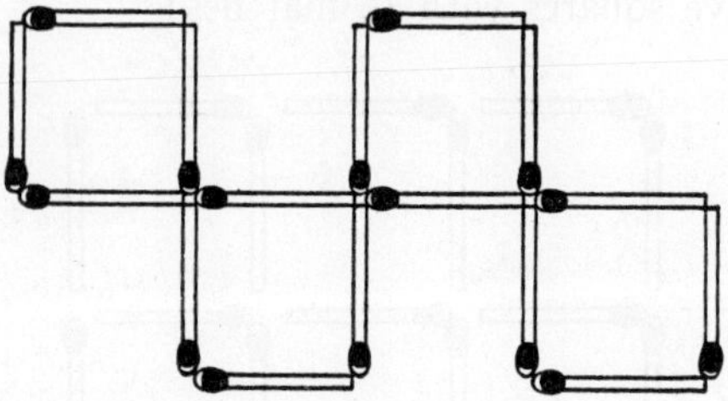

18. Form a rectangle of 8 matches:

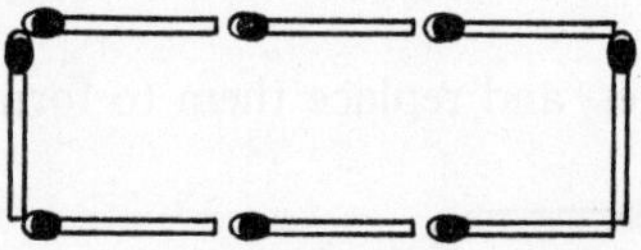

Add 2 matches and double the size of the rectangle:

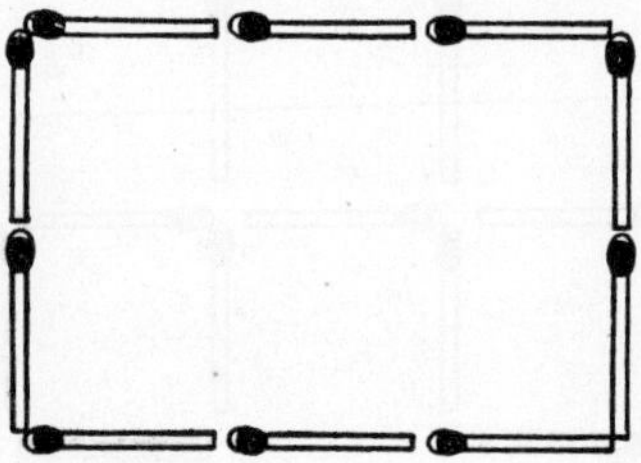

19. Form two equilateral triangles with 5 matches:

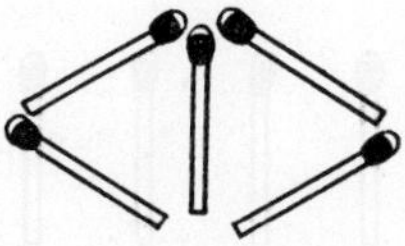

Add 1 match and form four equilateral triangles: (One triangle is the base; the others are held up from it.)

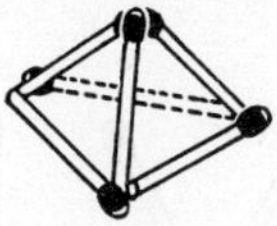

20. With 6 matches form "three and a half dozen":

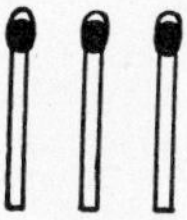

Three,

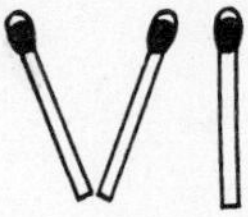

and a half dozen.

21. Give a player 9 matches, and request him to make 10, without breaking any:

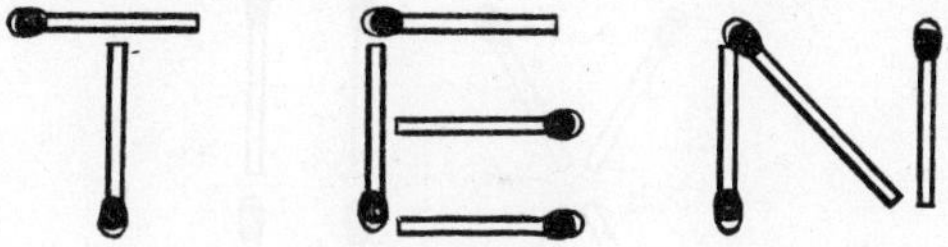

22. From a row of 7 matches take 1, and leave nothing:

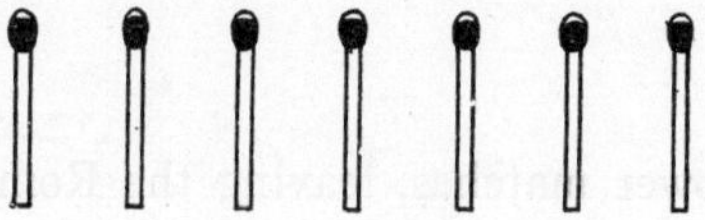

The answer is Nil (nothing):

23. With 6 matches make 11:

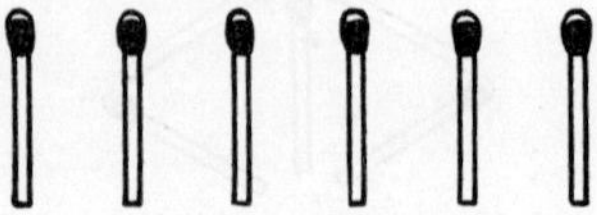

The answer is the Roman numeral XI:

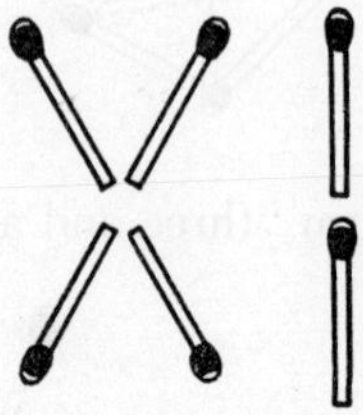

24. With 8 matches prove that half of twelve is seven. Form the Roman numeral XII:

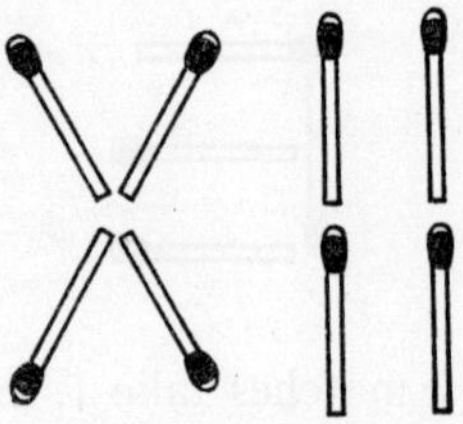

Remove the lower matches, leaving the Roman numeral VII:

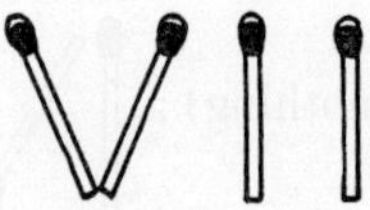

25. Form a row of 8 matches, and ask a player to remove 4 and leave 7:

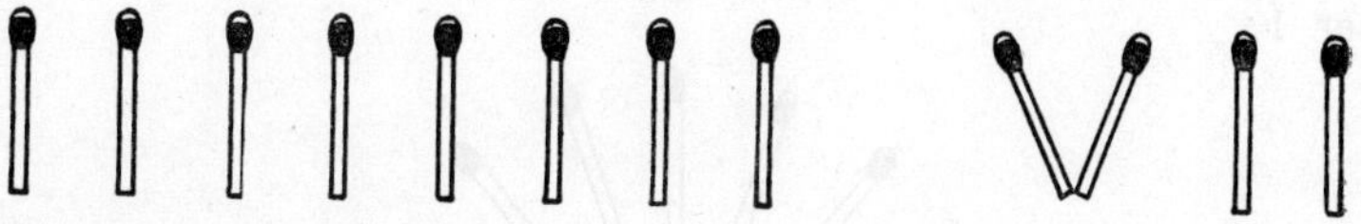

26. With 6 matches make 25:

27. Add 1 to 5 and make 4:

Or, add 2 to 1 and make 4:

28. Form a row of 6 matches:

Add 5 matches and make 9:

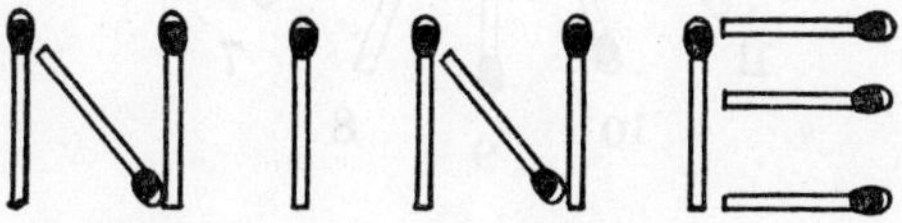

29. Arrange 18 matches in a circle, designating one as number 1:

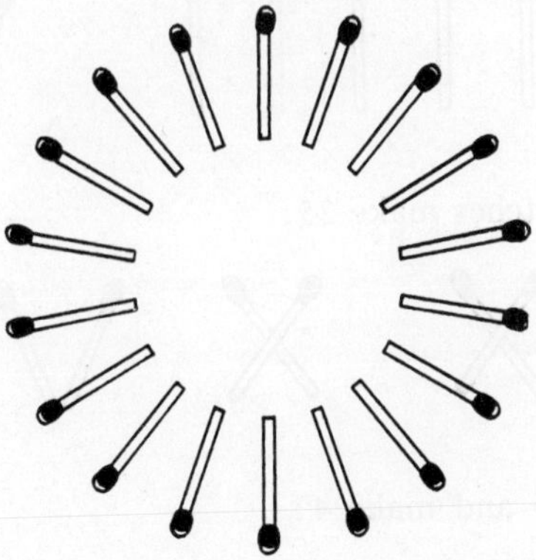

Problem: Rearrange the circle with some matches having their heads inside, and the others having theirs outside so that, starting with number 1, and counting nine each time, only the matches with their heads out will be eliminated. This is the correct circle:

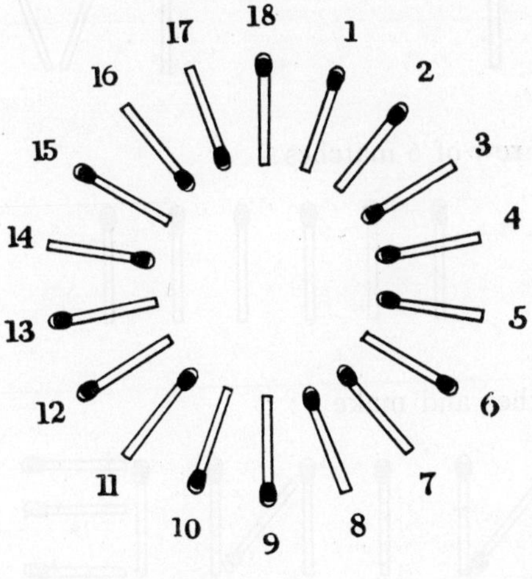

30. Arrange 10 matches in five lines of 4 matches each:

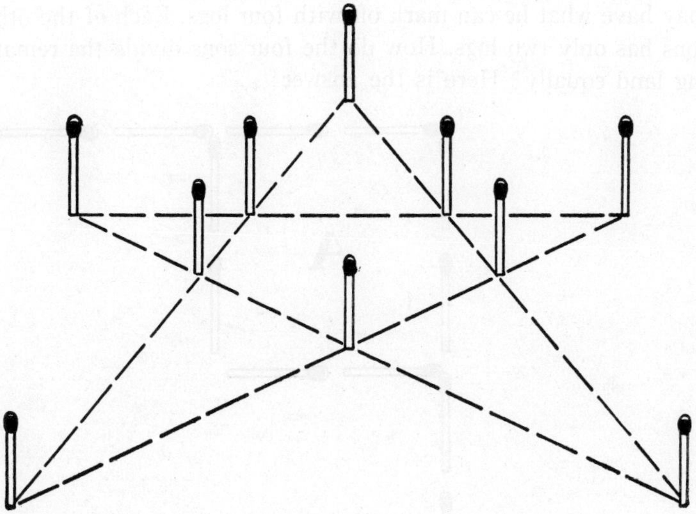

31. Form a large plot of land with 16 matches:

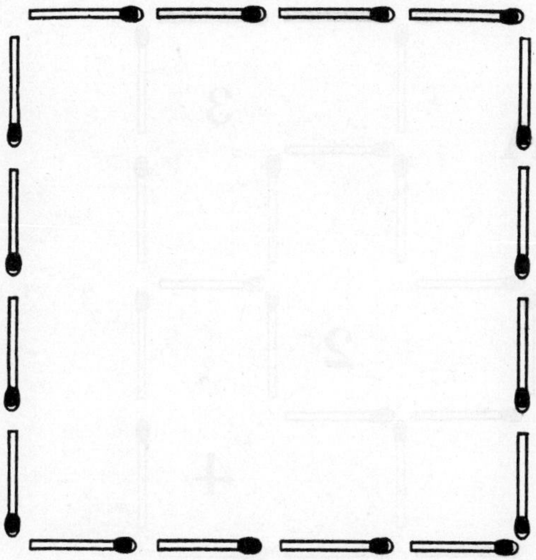

The land is to be divided among five sons; the eldest receiving the largest share; the others four equal shares. The eldest may have what he can mark off with four logs. Each of the other sons has only two logs. How do the four sons divide the remaining land equally? Here is the answer:

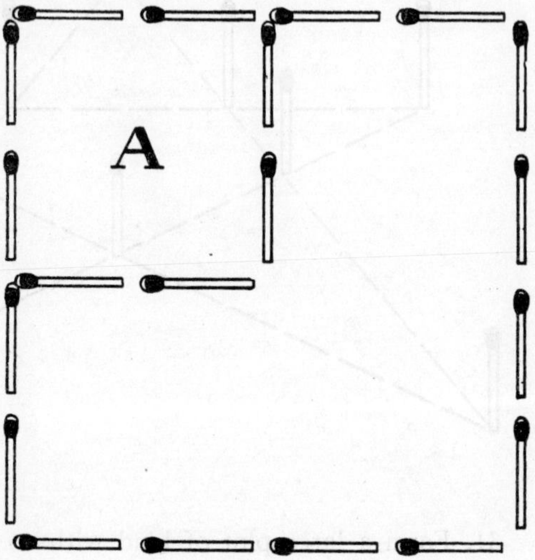

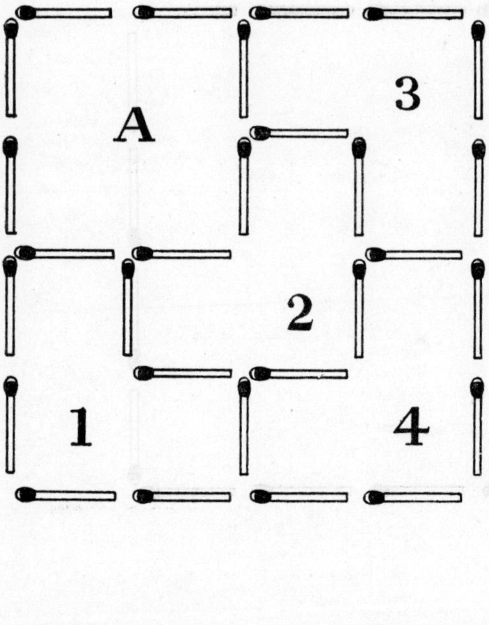

32. Make a small hole at one end of a safety match box, and place the box on a table on its broad side. Fasten a safety match in the hole, head up. Place a dime on the other end of the box. Angle another match against the first one, so that both heads are together, and the plain end of the second match rests on the dime. The object of the trick is to remove the dime without touching either match, or knocking either from position. To do this, light a third match, and ignite the center of the leaning match. Soon the two heads will ignite, and the leaning match will curl away from the dime so that it can be removed.

35. Place a safety match box cover on a table, with the striking surface up. Place the empty drawer across the cover, the narrow side down. Try to break the box by pressing down, or striking down on the top of the drawer. If the box is placed correctly, this is practically impossible.

34. Place 3 matches in a row. Request some one to remove the middle match from its central position without touching it.

Answer: Move the first match to the far side of the third, thus changing the position of the original middle match to first place.

35. Stand an empty safety match box, end up, on a table. Slightly raise the drawer, and insert a match on either side, with their heads up. Wedge a third match between the two heads. Ask the audience which of the upright matches will ignite first, if the horizontal match is ignited in its center. The answer: Neither will. The horizontal match, when lighted in the center, will jump free of the other two.

36. Place 15 matches in a row. The players may remove 1, 2, or 3 matches at a time, each working from the opposite end. The player who takes the last match loses. To win, leave 13, 9, or 5 for the opponent to take from.

37. Ask the guests if anyone can strike a wooden safety match on the sole of his shoe. To do this, thoroughly rub the striking surface of a match box on the sole of your shoe. The match will strike easily. Do the rubbing without being seen.

Pyramid of Matches.—Each contestant is given an empty bottle, and many matches. The object is to build up an inverted pyramid of matches on the bottle, so that they do not fall. One player from Cleveland, Ohio, succeeded in building 4,200 matches on top of his bottle, before the pile fell.

COIN TRICKS

1. Place six coins in a right angle. Move one, and have two rows of four coins each. Answer: Place lowest coin over corner one.

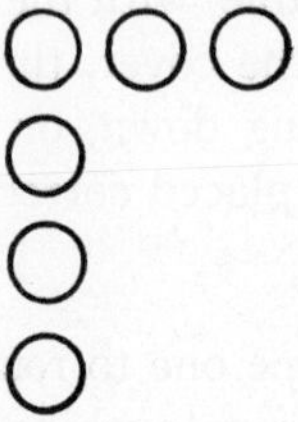

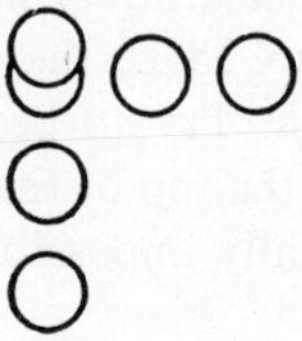

2. Form a cross of six coins. Move one, and have two rows of four coins each. Answer: Place lowest coin over center one.

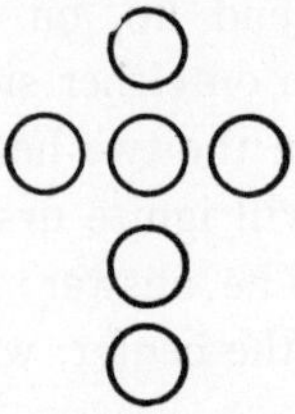

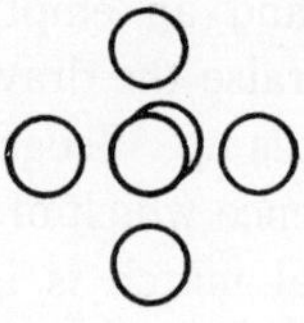

3. Which is higher, one dime on end, or 12, 14, 16 dimes in a pile? Ask the question, then let the players compare one dime on end with a pile of 12 or 14. The dime on end must not be held too close to the pile. Answer: A pile of 16 dimes is almost equal to a dime on end.

4. Place a dime in the bottom of a large wine glass, and a half dollar on top of the dime. Ask the players to remove the dime without touching the half dollar. Answer: Blow sharply down one side of the glass. The dime should jump out.

5. Ask the players to spin a coin on the bottom of a glass without touching the coin. Answer: Use a glass with a fairly large perfectly smooth bottom. Invert it. Place a quarter on it. Hold the glass in one hand at mouth level. Blow as hard as possible, so that the edge of the coin is lifted. When it rises it will spin. Keep blowing vigorously, and the coin will continue to spin.

BRAIN TEASERS

1. Seven men agreed to dine together every day, provided they could be seated in a different arrangement at table each day. How many dinners would be necessary? Answer: 5,040 times, requiring more than 13 years.

2. Ask the players to lift an ordinary medicine bottle with a soda straw. Method: Bend the straw and slip it into the bottle so that the angled end will slide into the shoulder of the bottle. It may then be lifted.

3. A owns a peacock. If the peacock laid an egg in B's yard, who would own the egg—A or B? Answer: Peacocks do not lay eggs.

4. A two-volume set of books is standing on a bookshelf in the right order. The pages of each are three inches thick; the covers, each one-quarter inch thick. A bookworm starts on the title page of Volume I and eats through to the last page of Volume II. How far did it travel? Answer: One-half an inch. He merely ate through two covers, since the first page of Volume I is next to the last page of Volume II.

5. A man owns a fox, a duck, and a bag of corn. He is on one side of a small river, with a boat only large enough for him to cross with one of these. If he leaves the fox and duck alone, the fox will eat the duck; if he leaves the duck and corn alone, the duck will eat the corn. How is he to cross safely with all three possessions? Answer: Duck over. Fox over, duck brought back. Corn over. Duck over.

6. A woman had fifty silk stockings, all of one size, 25 white and 25 black. She sent her blind maid to bring her one pair. What is the smallest number the blind maid must bring to be sure there is a pair? Answer: Three.

7. Smith gave Forty eight dollars for a horse, then sold it for sixty dollars. What was his profit? Answer: $52. The first seller's name was Forty.

8. Sisters and brothers I have none, but that man's father is my father's son. How is this possible? Answer: It is the speaker's son.

9. A farmer's wife was asked how many ducks she had. She replied, "As they ran down the path, I saw one duck in front of two ducks, a duck behind two ducks, and a duck between two ducks." How many duck were there? Answer: Three, one in front of another.

10. A beggar's brother died. But the man who died had no brother. How is this possible? Answer: The beggar was a woman.

11. At an engineers' club dinner, a Japanese engineer put this problem. Assume that the equator is 25,000 miles in circumference, and that a band of steel is fitted snugly around it. If 12 inches is added to the band, how far off the earth will the band be? Answer: A fraction under 2 inches all the way around.

This can be worked out mathematically. The size of the circumference makes no difference, it can be 25,000 miles, or 6 inches. A band 12 inches larger will always stand a fraction under 2 inches away from the original circumference.

12. There are two steel rails, each exactly one-half mile long, joined end to end, making the exact distance of one mile (5,280 ft.). The rails are firmly fastened at their farther ends. The sun's heat expanded them 12 inches. Since they are firmly fastened at the farther ends, the expansion causes them to buckle at the joining. How far off the earth did they buckle? Answer: More than 54 ft.

THE BAG OF PEANUTS

Five Italians arrived at an inn to spend the night, with a bag of peanuts and a monkey. They agreed to divide the peanuts in the morning. The first Italian, suspecting the others, slipped down to the room where the bag was stored, and divided the contents into 5 equal portions, taking his own with him. There was 1 peanut left over, which he fed to the monkey. The fourth Italian then slipped down and did the same, in each instance 1 peanut being left over, and fed to the monkey. Then the third, the second, and the first. When they gathered in the morning, there were exactly enough peanuts to divide into 5 portions, with 1 left over for the monkey. What was the smallest number of peanuts that the bag could have contained?

Answer: 3,121.

THAT'S

Make six sentences of this, punctuating it correctly: That that is is that that is not is not that that is is not that that is not that that is not is not that that is is not that so it is.

Answer: That that is is. That that is not is not. That that is is not that that is not. That that is not is not that that is. Is not that so? It is.

A less correct answer uses commas: That, that is, is. That, that is not, is not. That, that is, is not that, that is not. That, that is not, is not that, that is. Is not that so? It is.

TIT-TAT-TOE, NOUGHTS AND CROSSES

A design is drawn, as in Diagram I. One player draws circles; the other, crosses. The object is to get three circles or crosses in a

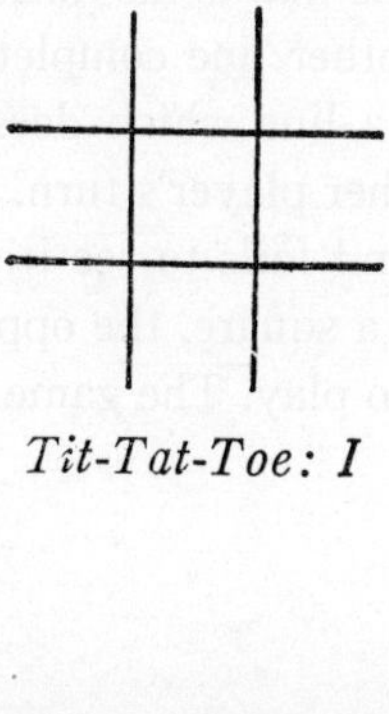

Tit-Tat-Toe: I

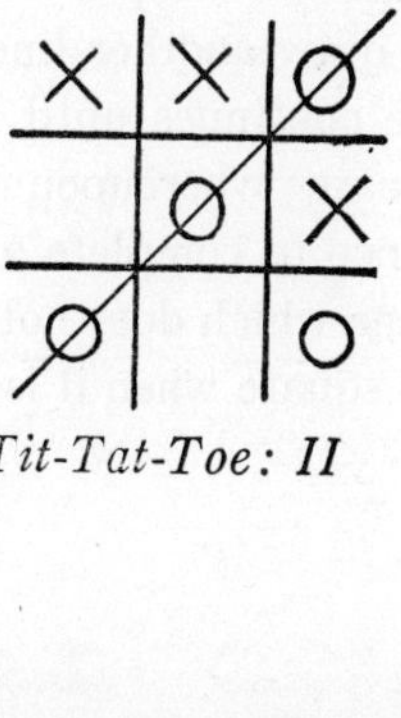

Tit-Tat-Toe: II

row, horizontally, vertically, or diagonally. One player draws first the first game; thereafter the players alternate in starting. To win requires great ingenuity. Diagram II shows a game won by the circles, which had the first play.

DOTS AND SQUARES

In this fascinating game, a number of dots are so placed on a sheet of paper, that lines connecting them will form a number of squares of the same size. Thus the layout might consist of 49 dots, which when joined would form 36 squares (see Figure 1); or it might be as many more as desired. The finished game need not consist of one large square containing smaller ones, as will result from the layout in Figure 1; it may be any other rectangle, or it may have dots permitting squares jutting out at irregular places.

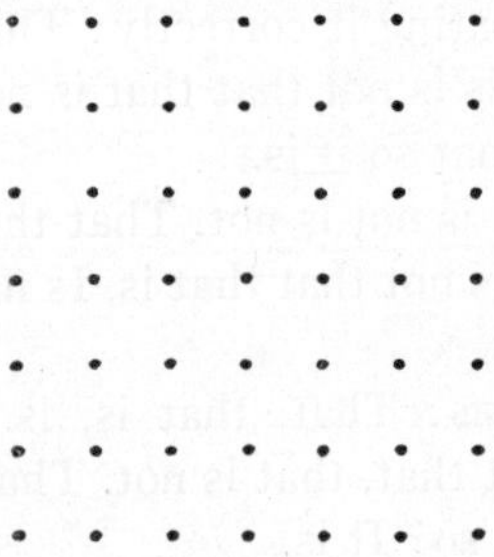

FIG. 1

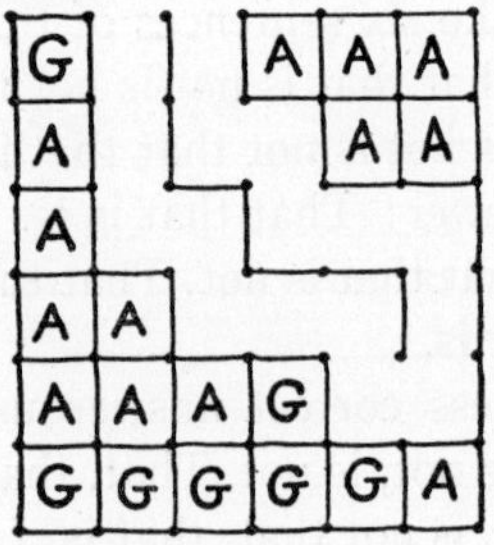

FIG. 2

One player now draws a line connecting any two dots. The other player does the same thing. This is continued alternately. As soon as a player's line completes a square, he marks his initial inside it, and must draw another line. If this other line completes another square, he continues until he draws a line which does not complete a square; whereupon it is the other player's turn. If a player has a chance to complete a square, and fails to see it, but draws another line which does not complete a square, the opponent may fill in this square when it is his turn to play. The game ends when all squares are filled in. Each player's squares are then counted, the largest number winning. In Figure 2, A has filled in 13 squares to G's 7. Notice that, whoever plays next, the turn after that must fill in all the remaining squares on the board. The game calls for great ingenuity.

THE SHORTEST CROSSWORD PUZZLE

1	2	3	4
5			
6			
7			

1 B	2 B	3 B	4 B
5 I	I	I	I
6 T	T	T	T
7 E	E	E	E

Give the first diagram to the players. Give them a stated time in which to solve it. The definitions: Across, 1. Insects; 5. Organs of the body; 6. To tantalize; 7. Comfort. Down, 1. What lions do; 2. What mice do; 3. What cats do; 4. What mosquitoes do. The down answers are all *bite.* The across answers are: *bees, eyes, tease, ease.*

HASTY SPEECH

(Say rapidly) A farmer had twenty sick sheep and one died. How many were left? Answer; Nineteen. (Not twenty-five.)

STRAWBERRIES WITHOUT CREAM

The Leader asks the players to repeat exactly what he says. He asks them to repeat "strawberries without cream." The answer is "Strawberries"—that is, strawberries *without* "cream."

Taxation Without Representation.—Similar.

BEAVER

An amusing English outdoor stunt game is Beaver. In this, each contestant scores 1 for each man with a beard at whom he first calls "Beaver." Only a beard is scored as a beaver; moustaches do not count.

CHOOSE YOUR BRIDE

In this outdoor stunt competition, the contestants take alternate blocks of a moderately crowded street, down which they are walking. The first contestant takes the first block, and must select from the girls who pass the one he would prefer to marry. The second contestant takes the second block. A third person is selected as referee, and decides which wins, from the general attractiveness of the girls selected.

AUTO POKER

This outdoor stunt contest consists in selecting oncoming automobiles, and making the best possible poker hands out of the first 5 numerals on the license tags: Five of a kind, four of a kind, full house, straight, three of a kind, two pairs, pair, and highest number ranking in that order.

MIND-READING

RAISE YOUR HAND

The Mindreader leaves the room, and says that, when he returns, he will tell which person raised his hand. From another room he calls, "Raise one hand." After a moment, "If the hand is now raised, cross your legs." After a moment, "If you have your legs crossed, lay the raised hand beside the other." He comes in quickly, and pretends to examine the feet of all present, then points to the correct hand. He knows this, because the hand held in the air for a time will be paler than the other, since the blood has run down.

READING THE WATCH

The Mindreader lays a watch face up on a table, and asks a player to choose an hour, and without speaking it, write it on a piece of paper and conceal it. He then tells the player to count, silently, beginning with the number one hour higher than the one chosen, while the Mindreader taps the watch with a pencil. When 20 is reached, the player is to say "Stop." The Mindreader's pencil will be pointing to the correct hour. This is the method: Tap 7 times at random. Beginning with the 8th, tap the hour of 12. Now tap counter-clockwise: 11, 10, 9, 8, etc. At "Stop," the pencil will be on the hour written down.

MAGIC ASHES

The Mindreader sits behind a table, with slips of paper before him. One at a time, the players approach him and name a famous person aloud. The Mindreader writes as each name is called, folds the slip, and places it in a metal bowl or pan. When all the names have been so placed, one player draws one slip, and holds it. The Mindreader burns the remaining slips. He studies the ashes, and announces the name that has been drawn. The method: He wrote the first name called on every slip.

WHAT TIME IS IT?

In the following mindreading games, the Mindreader has an Assistant. The Mindreader leaves the room, while the others decide upon an hour—say eight o'clock. The Mindreader returns and asks his Assistant, "What time is it?" The Assistant says, "I don't happen to have my watch with me." The Mindreader answers, "You don't need a watch. It's eight o'clock." Method: The first letter of the *third* word of the Assistant's answer told the answer, according to the following key:

Hour	*Key Letter*	*Hour*	*Key Letter*
1	A	7	G
2	B	8	H
3	C	9	I
4	D	10	J
5	E	11	K
6	F	12	L

The *third* word is "happen." "H" is the eighth letter of the alphabet, so the answer is eight o'clock.

This key may be varied by using the letters M through X to represent the hours 1 through 12.

THE MYSTIC CODE

The Mindreader leaves the room, while the group select a simple verb that the Mindreader must guess and act out. Such verbs as sing, leap, laugh, cough, etc. The Assistant is equipped with a cane. When the Mindreader returns, the Assistant starts an involved hocus-pocus with the cane. Suppose "leap" is the chosen word. The Assistant says, "Let's all concentrate." Then he taps twice with the cane. He pauses, and taps once, and says, "Please try to be quiet." After a silence, the Mindreader begins to leap about.

The method: The consonants are indicated by the first letter in each sentence spoken (L and P in the above); the vowels by tapping. 1 tap for A, 2 for E, 3 for I, 4 for O, and 5 for U.

Any word may be chosen, instead of a verb, and similarly guessed by the Mindreader.

Mystic Message.—This is done as above, except that the Assistant does not communicate the actual word chosen, but something closely allied to it. The Mindreader then guesses the connection, and names the word. Thus, if "Mussolini" were chosen, the Assistant could indicate "Italy," or "Duce," and the Mindreader might correctly interpret the word chosen. The names of cities or countries may be intoned in a jargon, instead of using sentences. In this method, the first letter, or the last one, of the city gives the consonant; and the vowels are tapped out.

Thus "George Washington" could be tapped out: The Assistant saying "Chicago, Honolulu," (2 taps), "Rome, Richmond, Yokohoma, Toronto, Rheims, (2 taps, pause 2 taps). This spells "Cherry Tree," and the Mindreader could easily announce "George Washington."

THIS AND THAT

The Mindreader announces that he will leave the room and, on returning, will name the object that his Assistant has touched. The Mindreader returns. The Assistant asks, "Did I touch this lamp?" "No." "Did I touch this door?" "No." "Did I touch this flower?" "No." "Did I touch that rug?" "Yes." Method: "This" is used before articles not touched; "that," before the article touched.

THE MAGIC SPOON

The Mindreader claims that he can photograph a face with a silver spoon. He mumbles some hocus-pocus over a bright tablespoon, and leaves the room. The guests sit in a circle on the floor. The Assistant pretends to photograph one player with the spoon, then places the spoon in the center of the floor, with the bowl away from the half of the group containing the person photographed. Returning, the Mindreader studies the spoon, and the faces of the guests, then announces whose face he sees on the spoon. The method: The position of the spoon tells him which half of the group contains the right person. The Assistant assumes the identical pose of the right person, changing his position whenever the person changes.

THE MYSTIC SIX

Line six objects on the floor—pencils, cards, small boxes, etc. The Mindreader leaves, and returns after the others have chosen one object. Without speaking, the Assistant points to various objects. The Mindreader says "No" until the right object is indicated. The method: The Assistant points to the correct object after pointing to one next to either end. If the selected object is next to either end, he points to the object next to the other end just before pointing to the right one.

THE MISSING PENNY

The Mindreader puts a penny under a plate, and leaves. The Assistant gives the penny to a player. When the Mindreader returns, he asks the players to place an index finger on the plate, one at a time. He then names the holder of the penny. The method: The Assistant places his finger on the plate directly after the holder of the penny.

THE MAGIC CIRCLE

The Mindreader announces that he will leave the room and, returning, name the person with whom the Assistant has shaken hands during his absence. The Mindreader intones, "The Magic Circle is now begun. Do you feel its influence?" He does not leave until several players have spoken. Returning, he names the player at once. The method: The Assistant shakes hands with the first person to speak after the Mindreader's chant.

BLACK MAGIC

While the Mindreader is out, the players select an object, either in the room, or anywhere else. Returning, the Mindreader answers the Assistant's questions, and names the article. The method: The Assistant names a black or blackish thing just before naming the correct one.

Red, White, and Blue.—An elaborate variation of the above. The first time played, the article is named after a red article; the second, after a white one; the third, after a blue one. This can be varied in several ways: as, first, after a flower; second, after a tree; third, after a vegetable.

READING THE COMPASS

Place four objects on the floor. The group selects one, while the Mindreader is out of the room. When he returns, the Assistant asks him these four questions, in any order, each time pointing to any one of the objects: "Is it this?" (intimating that the object closest on the right is the one selected). "Is it that?" (the object furthest on the left). "Is it this one?" (the object furthest on the right). "Is it that one?" (the object nearest on the left). The method: The first question reveals the object by phrasing, no matter which object is first indicated. The Assistant must ask the first question, the revealing one, and the others the rest.

READING THE NUMBER

A number is selected while the Mindreader is out. On his return, the Assistant calls off numbers, and the Mindreader identifies the right one. The method: The first digit of the first number called tells in what order the selected number will appear. Thus, if 45 were the number, the Assistant might call "39, 75, 45, 62." The Mindreader would reply "45 is the number." The first digit of 39, 3, told him that the right number would be the 3rd called. In one variation, the number designated must be multiplied or divided by 2, etc., to give the correct number.

READING SENTENCES

Each player writes a short sentence, folds it, and places it in a container. The Assistant pretends to do so, but does not. The slips are mixed, then the Mindreader draws one, places it against his head, and announces a short sentence. The Assistant admits that it is his. The Mindreader, nodding gravely, unfolds the paper and reads it. Doing this, he memorizes the sentence. He tosses the crumpled slip in a trash basket, and repeats the performance, this time repeating the sentence he has just memorized. When this is claimed by a player, he again repeats the whole performance. He does this about ten times, then claims to be tired. He must stop while there are several unread slips, otherwise the players would see that there is one slip less than the number of players.

READING THE GLOBE

This requires a globe or a map. While the Mindreader is out, the players select a city. He returns, and the Assistant names cities, one after another. When he says the correct one, the Mindreader announces it. The method: The Assistant names the correct city two cities after a two-word city, such as Baton Rouge, New York, etc. The trick can also be done with countries.

VI. HILARIOUS GAMES

When a party shows a tendency to go stale, it is time to introduce a few hilarious games. Even the most sedate party will loosen up and become gay after several of these fun-producing games. Anyone can play them, since they require no especial knowledge, nor any unusual wit. They are merely fun, and that is sufficient.

They call for practically no equipment. Most of them can be started as soon as they are suggested, without any fuss and bother. And they are certain to promote good-fellowship, which is the most important function of any game.

SARDINES

One player is selected to be It. The It hides anywhere in the house. After a few minutes—four or five—the players go to find the It, hunting separately. The first one who finds him, does not reveal the fact, but hides with him; whether he is hidden in a closet, under a bed, or behind a trunk in the attic. Successively, each player finding the Sardines, joins them, until all are hidden in one place. As a variation, this may be played in pairs.

BALLOON FOOTBALL

Divide the players into two teams. Use a table (or a chalked rectangle on the floor) for the field. A small balloon is the football. Players may move the ball only by blowing it. They may put their heads together and all blow at once, but they must not touch the ball. If the ball is blown offside, it is replaced in the center of the table across from the place where it went off. The object is to blow the ball against the goal line, or off the table, which scores a touchdown. Score 1 point for the goal line; 6 points for a touchdown. The team with the highest score wins.

Balloon Pushball.—The teams try to bat the balloon across the room, to touch the opponent's wall.

Balloon Volley Ball.—Stretch a string across the room, with a team on each side. The balloon is batted with the hands or with fans. Each team tries to keep the balloon off the floor on their side. When it touches the floor, it counts one for the other team. Game is 10 points.

Egg Football.—Mark a table to resemble a football field. Use a blown egg for the ball. It may be blown, or fanned with a fan, but not touched. Score as in balloon football. A pingpong ball may be used instead of an egg. Only two or three players on each team may blow at a time.

GETTING YOUR NUMBER

Arrange two rows of chairs facing each other. Number the chairs; the chair numbers do not change. The players take seats, each acquiring the number of the chair on which he is sitting. Number One calls any number but his own. That number must answer immediately by calling any number but his own. There must be no delay.

When there is delay; or when the wrong number answers a call; or when a player calls his own number, or makes any error; the erring player is demoted to chair Number One, the others moving up. Each player then acquires the number of the chair to which he has moved, and must respond to this new number. After several changes, it is difficult to remember your number.

WHO'S GOT THE WHISTLE?

One player is blindfolded, and the others form a circle around him. One player, with a whistle, slips up behind the It, and blows the whistle. The It must catch him, and identify him, by feel. If the It catches and identifies the whistler, the whistler becomes the It. If not, another player takes the whistle, and tries to elude the It.

Catch the Whistler.—The whistle is attached by a string and a safety pin to the blindfolded It's back. Successively, the players sneak up and blow the whistle, while the It tries to catch them. The first one caught becomes the It.

NAME ME

Each person has the name of a famous person pinned on his back by the Leader, and is given a paper and pencil to write down the names of those present, and whom they represent. He does this, while trying to conceal the name he is supposed to represent, as by backing against a wall, or lying on the floor. The one making the longest correct list in a given time wins.

ORCHESTRA

A player is chosen as the It. He assigns the name of a musical instrument to each player: drum, violin, piano, flute, etc. Standing in front of a player, he begins imitating one of the instruments—beating as if on a drum, fiddling as if on a violin, etc.

—making no sound. If he is not imitating the player's instrument, the player holds his finger to his nose. When the It imitates the player's instrument, the player at once starts imitating the It. The It moves from player to player. Anyone who plays at the wrong time, or continues after the It has switched, drops out. The survivor wins, and becomes the It for the next round.

WHO, SIR, I, SIR?

The players each having a number, sit in a circle. Number One says, "Someone has stolen my hat. Have *you* seen my hat?," and points to a player. The player jumps to his feet, and says, "Who, sir, I, sir?" Number One: "Yes, sir, you, sir." Player: "No, sir, not I, sir!" "If not you, sir, then who, sir?" "Number six, sir!" Before Number One can count 10, Number Six must rise and go through the same conversation. If a player does not respond in time, he becomes the It.

The Prince of Wales Has Lost His Hat.—The opening statement is, "The Prince of Wales (or, Prince of Paris) had lost his hat. Did you take his hat?" The game proceeds as above.

DUTCH BAND

The Leader assigns an instrument to each player, including himself, and names a popular tune that all know. At a signal, they all start playing, making the sounds with their mouths and the gestures with their hands. At any time, the Leader may switch to the instrument of one of the other players. This players must at once switch to the one the Leader has abandoned, or pay a forfeit. This game should be played rapidly.

KAZOO ORCHESTRA

A kazoo, or bazoo, is a small hollow instrument which is played by humming or singing through it, and may be bought in any five-and-ten store. Provide each player with one. A tune is decided upon, and the Leader leads the kazoo band. The amusement is greater if the players are required to imitate the sounds of different instruments through the kazoo.

THE CAT AND THE DOG

The players sit in a circle. The Leader holds two objects, as a pen and a book, an apple and a sponge, etc. He starts one object around to his right, and says:

One (the Leader): "I found the cat."
Two: "The what?"
One: "The cat.

Two hands the object to Three, and says:

Two: "I found the cat."
Three: "The what?"
Two (to One): "The what?"
One (to Two): "The cat."
Two (to Three): "The cat."

Three passes the object to Four, and the same questions and answers continue, the questions being referred back to One each time.

As soon as the first object has been started, One starts the second around to his left, saying, "I found the dog." Answers as above. When the two objects cross in the center, both sets of questions must be repeated accurately back to One each time.

DON'T LAUGH

The players sit in a circle. The Leader says, "I am going on a trip, and I am going to take my umbrella." Successively, the players repeat this, each saying a different article instead of "umbrella." The Leader then says, "I am going on a trip, and I am going to take my umbrella to keep the rain off." Successively, each player repeats this, substituting the article he has already named for "umbrella." If a player pauses at any time, he must pay a forfeit, or be eliminated, according to agreement in advance.

The Leader then makes his sentence longer: "I am going on a

trip and I am going to take my umbrella to keep the rain off, because wool shrinks in the rain, and my wool might shrink." The repetitions remain the same. There must be no laughter. The survivor wins.

JACK'S ALIVE

The players stand in a circle. One lights a match, saying "Jack's alive," and passes it rapidly to the next player. So on around the circle. Each player tries to prevent the match from dying in his possession. When it does, the holder says "Jack's dead," and pays a forfeit, or drops out, according to agreement in advance.

FIZZ

In rotation the players count—1, 2, 3, etc. When 5 or any multiple of 5 is reached, the player says "Fizz" instead of the number. The fifties are recited "Fizz-naught," "Fizz-one," etc. Players who miss are eliminated, until there is only one left. Or the scoring for Ghosts may be used.

Buzz.—The same, except that "Buzz" is said when 7, any multiple of 7, or a number containing 7, is reached.

Fizz-Buzz.—This is both games combined. "Fizz" is said as above, and "Buzz" is said as above. 57 is "Fizz-buzz," 75 "Buzz-fizz." Since it is a multiple of both, 35 may be said either way.

GOSSIP

The players sit in a circle, and the Leader whispers a brief personal item to the one next to him. Two whispers it to Three; and so around the circle. The item is whispered only once each time. The last player repeats aloud what he has just heard. The Leader then tells what he whispered. It is amusing to see how these differ. Each player may be asked to tell what he was told.

VENTRILOQUISM

The players are paired, a girl and a boy. The Leader asks the girls a question (or several) in rotation. The boys answer. The answers should be amusing. Thus: (to a girl): "Do you know how much you weigh?" Boy answering: "I weigh about five hundred pounds." The ventriloquist's position with his puppet may be assumed.

Then the Leader asks the questions of the boys, and the girls answer. Thus: (to a boy): "What are you going to do tomorrow?" Girl answering: "I am going to get a new permanent in the morning." The puppets to whom the questions are addressed may gesture, but may not answer.

POISON PENNY

The players sit or stand in a circle, while music is played. The Leader starts a penny around the circle. It must be passed as rapidly as possible. When the music stops, the holder of the penny drops out. If there is no music, a whistle may be blown. If the party is large, several pennies may be used.

HOT POTATO

A player is chosen as the It. He stands in the center, while the others sit in a circle. The players toss a handkerchief to one another, making many false moves and gestures. The It must touch the handkerchief while it is in the air. If he does so, the last to throw it becomes the It. The passing must not be delayed. This game affords wild excitement.

DUCKS FLY

When the Leader says, "Ducks fly," and flaps his arms, all the players must immediately flap their arms. The Leader goes on to say, "Cats meow," with appropriate sounds or gestures, which must be imitated as above. He may continue, "Hens cluck," "Horses trot," and so on, each time with appropriate gestures or sounds. When he chooses, he may substitute a false statement and motion: as, "Cows bark," "Elephants fly," and so on. If the player imitates the false motion, he is penalized. If any player makes a false motion or sound at any time, he is penalized, according to the method decided upon in advance. He may be eliminated after the first error; or he may be required to pay a forfeit. Or he may be given three chances, and after three errors be eliminated or required to pay a forfeit.

UNCLE JOSHUA

The players sit in a circle. The Leader says to the second player, "My Uncle Joshua died last night." The second replies, "That's too bad; how did he die?" The Leader says, "With one eye shut," and closes his eye. The second player repeats words and action to the third; and so on around the circle, until all the players have one eye shut.

The Leader repeats the ritual, adding "—and his mouth awry," and twists his mouth. This is repeated around the circle. The Leader adds, "One foot held high," and raises one foot. The fourth time he adds "—And waving goodbye," and waves one hand. Now each player has one eye shut, his mouth awry, one foot in the air, and is waving his hand. This must be played swiftly. The complete rhyme is:

"My Uncle Joshua died last night."
"That's too bad; how did he die?"
"With one eye shut, and his mouth awry,
One foot held high, and waving goodbye."

DO AND ADD

The players sit in a circle. The first makes a motion, as tapping his heels on the floor. The second does this, and adds a motion of his own, as waving one hand. The third does both of these, and adds a motion, as sticking out his tongue. And so on around the circle, each player repeating all previous motions and adding one of his own, until it comes back to the first, who must do all of the motions. Any player making an error drops out of the game or pays a forfeit. If he is eliminated, the next player takes up the motions where he left off.

FOX, GUN, MAN

The players sit in a circle, with the It in the center. The It makes this speech: "The fox is the sacred totem animal of the Fox Indians. The only thing superior to the fox is the gun, which can shoot the fox. The only thing superior to the gun is the man, who can shoot the gun. The only thing superior to the man is the fox, the sacred totem animal of the Fox Indians." This order of superiority must be remembered: fox, gun, man, fox, etc. The sign of the fox is thumbs to ears and fingers outstretched; of the gun, holding the arms as if shooting; of the man, standing up with one's hands on one's knees.

Standing before any player, the It gives the sign of one of the three. Before he can count 10, the player must give the sign of the immediately superior one, or become the It. If he gives the sign, the It must try again. Forfeits may be paid for failures, in which case the third or fifth to fail becomes the It.

I WENT TO THE CITY

The players sit in a circle. The Leader says, "I went to the city." The second player asks, "What did you buy?" The Leader: "A pair of shoes." He moves his feet slightly. The second player repeats the formula to the third, and so on around the circle, until all are moving their feet. Motions started must be continued throughout the game.

The Leader names something else, with an appropriate motion. This goes around the circle. Players failing in any motion, or failing to continue all motions, drop out or pay a forfeit. Some suggested objects and their appropriate motions are:

An umbrella—Make gesture of opening an umbrella.
A new tie—Gesture of tying a tie.
A new lipstick—Gesture of applying lipstick.
A fountain pen—Gesture of writing.
A box of candy—Chewing motion with mouth.

TOM THUMB

The players sit in a circle. The Leader says, "Tom Thumb got sick." The second player asks, "How did he get sick?" The Leader says, "Doing this," and slaps his right knee with his left hand. The second player repeats the formula to the third, and so on around the circle, until each player is slapping his knee.

The Leader continues to slap his right knee, repeats the formula, and adds a second motion. These are the motions in sequence:

1. Slap right knee with left hand.
2. Slap left knee with right hand.
3. Raise left heel up and down.
4. Raise right heel up and down.
5. Nod head vigorously.

Any player failing to continue all the motions drops out or pays a forfeit.

PROVERBS

The players divide into two teams, and sit on the floor, the teams facing each other. The Captain of one team announces a proverb. Before he can count 10, the other team must give a proverb beginning with the letter with which the first proverb ended. If they fail, the first team hauls a member of the other team to join it. The players are usually hauled by their feet. A proverb once given may not be repeated. The game ends when all the players are on one team, or when no one can think of another proverb. In which case, the team with the most members wins.

SHOUTED PROVERBS

Each team goes into a different room and one selects a proverb. Each word of the proverb is assigned separately to one or more players. The team returns, and at a signal each shouts his word. The other team must guess the proverb. When they have done so, they take their turn at shouting a proverb.

Singing Proverbs.—Start as above. The players sing their words to a familiar tune. It is better when each player selects a different tune.

Here are some of the most famous proverbs:

A bad penny always comes back.
A bad workman quarrels with his tools.
A barking dog never bites.
A bird in the hand is worth two in the bush.
A bold attack is half the battle.
Absence makes the heart grow fonder.
A cat may look at a king.
Accidents happen in the best regulated families.
A chain is no stronger than its weakest link.
A crowing hen never lays eggs.
Actions speak louder than words.
A dog knows his own master.
A drowning man will clutch at a straw.
A fair-weather friend changes with the wind.
A fat purse makes a soft pillow.
A fault confessed is half redressed.
A fool and his money are soon parted.
A friend in need is a friend indeed.
After a storm comes a calm.
After me, the deluge.
A good beginning makes a good ending.
A good book is the best companion.
A little knowledge is a dangerous thing.
A little pot is soon hot.
All good things come in small packages.
All good things must come to an end.
All is vanity.
All roads lead to Rome.
All's fair in love and war.
All's well that ends well.
All that glitters is not gold.
All the world loves a lover.
All work and no play makes Jack a dull boy.

A maid who laughs is half taken.
A man is his own worst enemy.
A man is judged by the company he keeps.
A man may dig a grave with his teeth.
A man of words and not of deeds is like a garden full of weeds.
A miss is as good as a mile.
An apple a day keeps the doctor away.
An army travels on its stomach.
An ass will deny more in an hour than a hundred philosophers will prove in a year.
An empty barrel makes the most noise.
A new broom sweeps clean.
An honest man's the noblest work of God.
A nimble sixpence is better than a slow shilling.
An open confession is good for the soul.
An ounce of discretion is worth a pound of wit.
An ounce of prevention is worth a pound of cure.
A penny saved is a penny earned.
A place for everything and everything in its place.
April showers bring May flowers.
A rolling stone gathers no moss.
A rose by any other name would smell as sweet.
A silver key can open an iron lock.
A soft answer turneth away wrath: but grievous words stir up anger.
As the twig is bent, the tree inclines.
A stitch in time saves nine.
A stumble may prevent a fall.
As you make your bed, you must lie in it.
A tree is known by its fruit.
A watched pot never boils.
A whistling girl and a crowing hen never came to any good end.
A word to the wise is sufficient.

Bad news travels fast.
Bear and forbear.
Beauty is only skin deep.
Be brave, my son, and let who will be clever.

Beggars and borrowers cannot be choosers.
Behind bad luck comes good luck.
Be sure you're right, then go ahead.
Better an open enemy than a false friend.
Better be safe than sorry.
Better late than never.
Better the leader in a village than second in Rome.
Better wear out shoes than sheets.
Beyond the Alps lies Italy.
Big churches, little saints.
Birds of a feather flock together.
Blood is thicker than water.
Boys will be boys.
Bred in the bone will out in the flesh.
Brevity is the soul of wit.

Care will kill a cat.
Carrying coals to Newcastle.
Cast your bread upon the water, it will return to you a hundredfold.
Charity begins at home.
Charity covers a multitude of sins.
Cheese is gold in the morning, silver at noon, and lead at night.
Children and fools speak the truth.
Children should be seen and not heard.
Circumstances alter cases.
Cleanliness is next to godliness.
Clothes make the man.
Consider the ant, thou sluggard, and be wise.
Contentment is better than riches.
Curiosity killed the cat.

Discretion is the better part of valor.
Doing everything is doing nothing.
Don't be a dog in the manger.
Don't borrow trouble.
Don't buy a pig in a poke.
Don't cast your pearls before swine.

Don't count your chickens before they're hatched.
Don't cross a bridge until you come to it.
Don't cry over spilt milk.
Don't cut off your nose to spite your face.
Don't fly in the face of trouble.
Don't give up the ship.
Don't kill the goose that lays the golden egg.
Don't lock the stable door after the horse is stolen.
Don't put all your eggs in one basket.
Don't put off till tomorrow what you can do today.
Don't rob Peter to pay Paul.
Don't start anything you can't finish.
Don't step into a dead man's shoes.
Don't teach your grandmother to suck eggs.
Don't wash your dirty linen in public.
Do unto others as you would have them do unto you.
Do well is better than say well.
Drunken days all have their tomorrows.
Drunk today and sober tomorrow.

Early ripe, early rotten.
Easier said than done.
Easy come, easy go.
Eat a peck of salt with a man before you trust him.
Eat to live, not live to eat.
Empty wagons make most noise.
Enough is as good as a feast.
Every ass loves to hear himself bray.
Everybody's business is nobody's business.
Every cloud has a silver lining.
Every dog must have his day.
Every Jack must have his Jill.
Every little bit, added to what you've got, makes just a little bit more.
Every man is the architect of his own fortune.
Everyone knows best where his own shoe pinches him.
Every rose must have its thorn.
Everything comes to him who waits.

Evil communications corrupt good manners.
Evil to him who evil thinks.
Experience is the best teacher.

Faint heart never won fair lady.
Fair exchange is no robbery.
Familiarity breeds contempt.
Fear nothing and shame the devil.
Feast today makes fast tomorrow.
Feed sparingly and starve the doctor.
Few words, many deeds.
Fine feathers do not make fine birds.
Fine words butter no parsnips.
Fingers were made before forks.
First a turnip, then a sheep, next a cow, and then the gallows.
Fond of lawsuits, little wealth; fond of doctors, little health.
Fools' names, like fools' faces, always seen in public places.
Fools rush in where angels fear to tread.
For conscience doth makes cowards of us all.
Forewarned is forearmed.
For the want of a nail the shoe was lost; for the want of a shoe the horse was lost; for the want of a horse the kingdom was lost.
Fortune knocks once at every door.
Four eyes are better than two.
From each according to his ability, to each according to his needs.

Give a calf enough rope and it'll hang itself.
Give a dog a bad name and he'll deserve it.
Give every man thine ear, but few thy voice.
Give the devil his due.
God helps those who help themselves.
God help the poor, the rich help themselves.
God is on the side of the largest army.
God made the country, and man made the town.
God takes care of babes and fools.
Goes up like a rocket, comes down like a stick.
Good clothes open all doors.

Good fences make good neighbors.
Great oaks from little acorns grow.
Green Christmas, white Easter.

Half a loaf is better than no loaf.
Handsome is as handsome does.
Happy is the bride whom the sun shines on.
Haste makes waste.
Health is better than wealth.
Heaping coals of fire upon his head.
Hear no evil, see no evil, speak no evil.
He jests at scars who never felt a wound.
He knows which side his bread is buttered on.
He laughs best who laughs last.
Hell hath no fury like a woman scorned.
Here today, gone tomorrow.
He that marries a widow will often have a dead man's head thrown in his dish.
He that would thrive must arise at five; he that has thriven may arise at seven.
He travels fastest who travels alone.
He who climbs highest falls farthest.
He who conquers himself conquers all.
He who dances pays the fiddler.
He who excuses himself accuses himself.
He who fights and runs away lives to fight another day.
He who smashes the window must pay the glazier.
His bark is worse than his bite.
History repeats itself.
Hitch your wagon to a star.
Home is what we make it.
Honesty is the best policy.
Hope for the best, get ready for the worst.
Hope is a good breakfast but a bad supper.
Hope springs eternal in the human breast.

Idleness is the mother of iniquity.
If an ass goes traveling he'll not come home a horse.

If at first you don't succeed, try, try again.
If every fool wore a crown, we should all be kings.
If the shoe fits, put it on.
If the mountain will not go to Mahomet, Mahomet must go to the mountain.
If you make your bed, you must lie in it.
If you talk to yourself, you talk to the devil.
If you want anything done, do it yourself.
If winter comes, can spring be far behind?
If wishes were horses, beggars would ride.
Imitation is the sincerest flattery.
In the kingdom of the blind, the one-eyed man is king.
In times of peace prepare for war.
In wine there is truth.
It is easier to give good counsel than to follow it.
It never rains but it pours.
It's a long lane that has no turning.
It's an ill wind that blows nobody good.
It's a wise father who knows his own child.
It's better to be right than president.
It's better to have loved and lost than never to have loved at all.
It's easy to steal from a cut loaf.
It's hard to swim upstream.
It's never too late to mend.
It's the shovel that laughs at the poker.
It takes a fool to call one.
It takes nine tailors to make one man.
It takes two to make a quarrel.
It will all come out in the wash.

Jack of all trades and master of none.
Judge not a book by its cover. (also, Don't—)
Judge not, that ye be not judged.

Keep your eyes open before marriage, half shut afterwards.
Kill two birds with one stone.
Kind hearts are more than coronets.

Laugh and the world laughs with you, weep and you weep alone.
Laugh before breakfast, cry before night.
Least said, soonest mended.
Let sleeping dogs lie.
Let the dead bury their dead.
Let well enough alone.
Lie down with the dogs, get up with the fleas.
Like calls to like.
Like father, like son.
Like master, like man.
Little pitchers have big ears.
Live and let live.
Live to learn and you will learn to live.
Look before you leap.
Look for dirt, and you'll find it.
Look not upon the wine when it is red.
Love is blind.
Love laughs at locksmiths.
Love me little, love me long.
Love me, love my dog.
Lucky in cards, unlucky in love.

Make haste slowly.
Make hay while the sun shines.
Make the best of a bad bargain.
Malt does more than Milton can to justify God's ways to man
Manners make the man.
Man proposes, God disposes.
Man's extremity, God's opportunity.
Man wants but little here below, nor wants that little long.
Man works from sun to sun, woman's work is never done.
Many a good tune is played on an old fiddle.
Many are called but few are chosen.
Many a true word is spoken in jest.
Many men, many minds.
Marriages are made in heaven.
Marry in haste, repent at leisure.
Might makes right.

Misery loves company.
Money begets money.
Money borrowed is money spent.
Money is a good servant but a bad master.
Money is the root of all evil.
Money makes the mare go.
More die by food than by famine.
Murder will out.
Music hath charms to soothe the savage breast.

Necessity is the mother of invention.
Necessity knows no law.
Nero fiddled while Rome burned.
Never bite off more than you can chew.
Never come between a man and his wife
Never howl until you're hit.
Never let the sun go down on a quarrel.
Never look a gift horse in the mouth.
Never make a mountain out of a molehill.
Never marry a widow unless her first husband was hanged.
Never put off till tomorrow what you can do today.
Never say die.
Never send a boy to do a man's work.
Never speak to deceive nor listen to betray.
Never spur a willing horse.
No cross—no crown.
No flies get in a shut mouth.
No garden without its weeds.
None but the brave deserve the fair.
No news is good news.
No pay, no piper.
Nothing is certain in this world but death and taxes.
Nothing ventured, nothing gained.

Oh what a tangled web we weave when first we practice to deceive.
Oil and water cannot mix.

Old birds are not caught with chaff.
Old books, old wine, old friends are best.
Old men for counsel, young men for war.
Once does not make a habit.
One cannot please all the world and his wife.
One good deed begets another.
One good turn deserves another.
One rotten apple spoils the whole barrel.
One swallow does not make a summer.
One touch of nature makes the whole world kin.
Only the slave can free himself.
Open locks, whoever knocks.
Out of sight, out of mind.
Out of the frying pan into the fire.
Overcome evil with good.

Paddle your own canoe.
Penny-wise and pound-foolish.
People who live in glass houses should not throw stones.
Please the eye and pick the purse.
Politics makes strange bedfellows.
Possession is nine points of the law.
Pour oil on troubled waters.
Practice makes perfect.
Practice what you preach.
Praise to the face is open disgrace.
Pretty words butter no parsnips.
Pride cometh before a fall.
Procrastination is the thief of time.
Promise little, do much.
Putting the cart before the horse.
Put your best foot foremost.

Rats desert a sinking ship.
Render unto Cæsar the things that are Cæsar's, and to God the things that are God's.
Rome was not built in a day.

Save for a rainy day.
Scratch a Russian and you find a Tartar.
Second thoughts are best.
See a pin, pick it up, all the day you'll have good luck.
Seeing is believing.
Self-defense is the first law of nature.
Set a thief to catch a thief.
Shoemaker, stick to your last.
Silence gives consent.
Silence is golden.
Sin in haste, repent at leisure.
Slow and sure.
Small beginnings make big endings.
Soft words break no bones.
Some are wise, and some are otherwise.
Sorrow treads upon the hells of mirth.
Sow the wind and reap the whirlwind.
Spare the rod and spoil the child.
Speak for yourself, John.
Speak no ill of the dead.
Steve Brodie took a chance.
Still waters run deep.
Straws show which way the wind blows.
Strike while the iron is hot.
Stuff a cold and starve a fever.
Sufficient unto the day is the evil thereof.
Sweets to the sweet.
Swim with the stream.

Talk is cheap.
Take care of the pennies, the dollars will take care of themselves.
Tell the truth and shame the devil.
The anvil lasts longer than the hammer.
The burnt child dreads the fire.
The cat loves fish but won't wet her feet.
The child is father to the man.
The clean bird doesn't foul its own nest.
The course of true love never did run smooth.

The cure is worse than the disease.
The danger past and God forgotten.
The darkest hour comes before the dawn.
The devil can cite Scripture for his purpose.
The devil finds work for idle hands to do.
The devil is beating his wife.
The devil take the hindmost.
The early bird catches the worm.
The end justifies the means.
The evil that men do lives after them, the good is oft interred with their bones.
The laborer is worthy of his hire.
The least said, the soonest mended.
The leopard cannot change his spots.
The nearer the bone, the sweeter the meat.
The new broom sweeps clean.
The only secret a woman can keep is her age.
The pen is mightier than the sword.
The pot calls the kettle black.
The proof of the pudding is in the eating.
The proper study of mankind is man.
The ripest fruit falls first.
The road to hell is paved with good intentions.
The shoemaker's children never have shoes.
The wages of sin is death.
The weakest goes to the wall.
The worm will turn.
There are more ways to kill a dog than hanging.
There are two sides to every question.
There is a destiny that shapes our ends, rough-hew them how we may.
There is honor among thieves.
There is no rest for the weary, the wicked need none.
There is nothing so bad but what it could be worse.
There's many a slip 'twixt the cup and the lip.
There's no use in crying over spilt milk.
There's no fool like an old fool.
There's no smoke without fire.

The watched pot never boils.
They can because they think they can.
Think before you speak.
Think first and speak afterwards.
This rule in gardening never forget: To sow dry and set wet.
Three moves are as bad as a fire.
Thrice armed is he who knows his cause is just.
Time and tide wait for no man.
Time was made for slaves.
To err is human, to forgive divine.
Tomorrow never comes.
Too many cook spoil the broth.
Too many irons in the fire.
To the pure all things are pure.
To the victor belong the spoils.
To thine own self be true, and it must follow as the night the day, thou canst not then be false to any man.
Trifles make up perfection, but perfection is no trifle.
Truth is stranger than fiction.
Two captains sink the ship.
Two heads are better than one.
Two's company, three's a crowd.
Two wrongs do not make one right.
Turn about is fair play.

Uneasy lies the head that wears a crown.
United we stand, divided we fall.

Vanity of vanity, all is vanity.
Variety is the spice of life.
Vice is a monster of so dread a mien, as to be hated needs but to be seen.
Virtue is its own reward.
Virtue which parleys is near a surrender.
Vows made in storms are forgotten in calms.

War is hell.
Waste not, want not.

We are never too old to learn.
Well begun is half done.
Well done is better than well said.
Whatever is worth doing at all is worth doing well.
What is one man's meat is another man's poison.
What's done cannot be undone.
What's sauce for the goose is sauce for the gander.
Whatsoever a man soweth, that also shall he reap.
When a man is wrapped up in himself, the package is small.
When Greek meets Greek, then comes the tug of war.
When in doubt, lead trumps.
When in Rome, do as the Romans do.
When one door shuts, another opens.
When poverty comes in the door, love flies out the window.
When the cat's away, the mice will play.
Where everyone goes grass never grows.
Where there's a will, there's a way.
Where there's smoke, there's fire.
Where water flows, man goes; where waters join, man builds a town; where water dries, man dies.
Where your treasure is, there will your heart be also.
While there's life there's hope.
Who counts without his host counts twice.
Whom the Lord loveth, He chasteneth.
Who serves everybody gets thanks from nobody.
Who steals my purse steals trash.
Willful waste makes woeful want.
Wisdom comes from the mouths of babes and sucklings.
Wise men change their minds; fools, never.
Wishes won't wash dishes.
Wonders will never cease.

You can catch more flies with honey than with vinegar.
You can lead a horse to water, but you can't make it drink.
You cannot have your cake and eat it.
You cannot serve God and Mammon.
You cannot serve two masters.
You can't make a silk purse out, of a sow's ear.

You can't teach an old dog new tricks.
You may choose your friends; your family is thrust upon you.
Young maids, "who"—old maids, "when."
Youth must be served.

VII. INDOOR ATHLETICS

This group of games will enliven any party. They require no particular equipment, and no practised skill. The novice frequently will triumph over the skilled athlete. Some of them are only advisable when a large room is available, such as a gymnasium, a barn, an attic, or a large basement. Others can be played in a constricted space.

Of course, all athletic games can be played outdoors. Practically all of the games in this chapter will be as successfully played outdoors as indoors. But not all outdoor games can be brought indoors. The games in this chapter are the ones that readily adapt themselves to indoor play.

The games in the first group are for individual contestants, wherein each player vies against all the others. The second group contains the games for teams. When the party is large, these team games are often preferable, since they permit a group of players as a unit to contest against a similar group.

It adds to the merriment of any gathering to play at least one of these games.

BLIND TOM OBSTACLE RACE

Select four or six players, who are lined up at one end of the room. Place obstacles on the floor: a pile of books, an overturned chair, bottles, a lamp, etc. Instruct the players to memorize the position of each object. The players then face the wall, and are blindfolded. While this is being done, the obstacles are quietly removed. The players are turned around and told to walk to the opposite wall without colliding with any of the obstacles. The audience gets considerable amusement out of this, particularly if the Leader offers clever suggestions to the blindfolded contestants.

WALKING THE PLANK

Place a plank on the floor, with a wide pan of water at one end. Tell the Victim he must walk the plank blindfolded, and jump over the pan of water. While he is being blindfolded, remove the pan of water. His efforts to jump over the missing pan are amusing. Several Victims may be chosen and sent to another room. They walk the plank one at a time.

One of the watchers may then be chosen to try to walk the plank. This time, leave the pan of water. Or permit a watcher to try the Blind Tom Obstacle Race, and leave an obstacle or two. This will not harm the performer, but his amazement will amuse the others.

BLINDFOLD BOXING MATCH

Draw a chalk circle on the floor. Provide two players with boxing gloves, and blindfold them. After turning each around several times, release them to box each other. The other players may act as teasers.

Blindfold Swat.—Instead of boxing gloves, provide each player with a rolled newspaper with which to swat the other. Otherwise, the game is played as above.

SCRAMBLED SHOES

The boys remove their shoes. These are then scrambled in the center of the room. At a signal, the boys rush to the pile, find their shoes, put them on and tie them perfectly. In the scramble, shoes may be tossed a reasonable distance.

The same thing may be done by the girls.

Off Again, On Again.—The girls sit at one end of the room. The boys, starting at the other end, race to their partners, take off their shoes, race to the end of the room and back carrying the shoes, then replace them on the girls' feet. The couple finishing first wins.

BUTTON YOUR COAT

Each boy must button his coat, unbutton it, take it off, put it on inside out and backward, take it off, right it, put it on correctly, and button it. The one finishing first wins.

The girls may contest, each wearing a boy's coat.

STANDING BROAD GRIN

The boys stand in a row, and each grins as broadly as possible. The broadest grin wins.

"DO THIS" RACE

The contestants are assigned ten stunts, which must be done in the exact order. The Leader, and two or three assistants, must watch the players to make sure that the orders are carried out correctly. The stunts should be varied and amusing. For instance: 1. Hop across the floor on one foot backward. 2. Write your name with your left hand. 3. Giggle for one minute. 4. Hop three times forward, twice to the left, once backward. 5. Stand on one foot and light a cigarette. 6. Walk an imaginary tight-rope. 7. Stand on your left foot, take off your right shoe, and put it on again. 8. Take a book from one table and put it on another. 9. Place a cigarette in an ashtray and walk sidewise to the opposite side of the room. 10. Recite the first stanza of "The Village Blacksmith."

MECHANICAL DOLL RACE

The girls stand perfectly rigid, as if they were mechanical dolls. Each boy lifts his partner's foot and places it forward, then the other foot. The couple to reach the turning point and return first wins.

LEGS CROSSED RACE

The contestant must cross his left leg before his right one, and keep it so while he races to the turning point. He then reverses, crossing the right leg before the left, and races back.

CRAB RACE

The contestants crawl backward, on all fours, to the turning point, and return to the starting point.

FREEZE

At a signal, each contestant runs three steps forward, then freezes. The players must now stand as long as possible without making any visible motion. Even swaying, winking, or swallowing is barred, and eliminates the contestant. The survivor wins.

RABBIT RACE

The contestants hop on all fours, rabbit-fashion, to turning point and back.

MUSH RACE, WHIPPET RACE

The contestants race on all fours to the turning point and back.

POTATO RACE

Place in front of each contestant five potatoes (or peanuts, or other objects), at even distances, such as 1, 2, 3, 4, and 5 yards.

The contestant must run from the starting line, pick up one potato, run back and put it in a basket, run and pick up a second, and so on. The potatoes may be picked up in any order. If a potato is dropped, it must be returned to its original position, and the contestant must start again to collect it. The one finishing first wins.

HOP HURDLE

Place a group of low hurdles or obstacles, such as small cushions, or piles of books, before each contestant. Each must hop to the turning point and back, hopping over the obstacles.

NEWSPRINT RACE

Provide each contestant with two sheets of newspaper. Each must race to the turning point and back, stepping only on his papers. He steps on one, lays the other in front of him, steps on it, moves the first forward, and steps to it, and so on.

MISSISSIPPI FLOOD RACE

Provide each contestant with a glass of water, full to the brim. Holding the glass, each must hop to the turning point and back. This is better if done one at a time. The one spilling the least water wins.

JUMPING CANDLES

Place twelve lighted candles on the floor. Each contestant must jump them, one at a time. The score is twelve, less the number blown out.

ATLAS RACE

Each player balances a book on his head, and walks rapidly to the turning point and back. If the book falls, it may be replaced, but otherwise hands may not touch it.

William Tell Race, Apple Race.—The same as above, using an apple to balance on the head.

TINCAN STILTS RACE

This should not be played on a polished floor. Provide each player with two tin cans, to which ropes have been tied; the ropes must reach above the knees. The contestant stands on the cans, holds the ropes to keep the stilts on, and races to turning point and back.

DIZZY PLANKWALK

Place about twelve sheets of typewriter paper in a line along the floor, narrow ends touching. One at a time the contestants are led to one end, spun around rapidly five times by the Leader, and then told to walk to the end of the paper plank, without delay, and without stepping off. In one variation, each contestant places his forehead on a cane placed against the floor, and spins himself around in this position before starting.

PEANUT RACE

Provide each contestant with a peanut. He must roll it along the floor with his nose from the starting line to the tape, about six feet. Only the nose may touch the peanut.

Peanut Toothpick Race.—Same as above, except that the peanut is rolled along the floor with a toothpick, instead of the nose. Potatoes, lemons, or any non-symmetrical object may be used.

DISHPAN RACE

Contestants race across the floor, each sitting in a dishpan.

HOP FOR THE CRACKER

Provide each contestant with four saucers, with one cracker in each. These are placed in a row on the floor. The contestant must hop from the starting line to the first cracker, get down on ali fours, eat the cracker, hop to the second, and so on to the end.

He must then hop back to the starting line. Crackers may not be touched with the hands. The one finishing first wins.

CRACKER RACE

Each contestant must eat four soda crackers, as fast as possible, without drinking water, and at the end give a college cheer, without spitting out any cracker dust. The one finishing first wins.

The contestant may be required to whistle a familiar tune instead of giving a college cheer.

POTATO ROLL

On the floor draw two circles, each four inches in diameter, about eight feet apart. Provide each player with a table knife and a potato. He must roll the potato across the floor into the first circle, then back again and into the other circle, using only the knife. Time this. The one doing it in the shortest time winning. Or have two circles for each player. The one finishing first wins.

Lemons or apples may be used.

THREADNEEDLE RACE

Each boy must run to a table, break off a piece of thread, thread a needle, lay it on the table, and run back to his place. The one finishing first wins.

One-Eyed Threadneedle.—Both girls and boys compete. The needle must be threaded with one eye closed. Otherwise, as above.

SNIP THE TAPE

Stretch lengths of tape about 9 feet long on the floor, one for each girl. Each girl, provided with a pair of scissors, must snip the tape lengthwise without ripping or tearing it. Boys may also compete. The one finishing first wins.

BUCKET RACE

Provide each contestant with a folded chair, an umbrella, and a lidded bucket containing a whistle. At a signal, each races with these things to the turning point, unfolds the chair and sits on it, opens the umbrella above himself, opens the bucket and takes out the whistle, blows it, replaces it, covers the bucket, closes the umbrella, folds the chair, and races back to the starting line with these objects. The first to complete these and touch the line wins.

BALLOON BURST

Each contestant is given a balloon of the same size. He must blow it up until it bursts. The first to burst his balloon wins.

KICKOFF

Provide each contestant with a balloon or a bag inflated with air. Mark a goal line twenty feet from the starting line. The contestant, on his hands and knees, must blow his balloon across the goal line. The one doing so first wins.

INDOOR SHOT PUT

Use balloons or bags inflated with air. The one who throws it farthest wins.

Balloon Shoot.—Provide each guest with a long balloon. He must blow it up, and release it, open end toward him, so that it shoots through the air. The one who shoots his furthest wins.

PASTEBOARD DISCUS THROW

Provide each contestant with a paper plate. The one throwing it furthest wins. This may also be done with playing cards. In this case, provide each with three cards.

RUBBER QUOITS

Rubber quoits or rope rings are used. The pin may be a regular quoits pin, a stick fixed upright, or any or all of the legs of an overturned piano stool or small table. Each player is allowed two or more tosses. Score: Quoit nearest pin, 1; both nearest, 2; one leaning against pin, 3; ringer, 5.

Rubber Horseshoes.—The game is played and scored as above, using rubber horseshoes. Outdoors, real horseshoes can be used.

BEN HUR CHARIOT RACE

Provide each contestant with two pieces of plank, about 12 inches square and one inch thick, with a piece of cord attached to the front end. Keeping a foot on each, the contestant must race to a turning point and back. The one finishing first wins.

NAIL DRIVE

Drive 16 or 20 penny nails about one-quarter of an inch into a piece of board. The nails must protrude evenly, and there must be one for each player. Object: Each must hammer a nail in straight, with as few blows as possible.

The board may be prepared with a quantity of small nails, 6 penny or less. Each player is permitted five blows, and must drive in completely as many nails as possible. Usually one blow is allowed for each nail.

Tack Drive.—Provide a large board, a hammer, and a pile of loose tacks. Each player must take tacks from the pile and drive them into the board. The one driving in the most in a given time wins.

INDOOR GOLF

Place nine containers around the house, at considerable distances apart. These are the nine holes. Place obstacles or bunkers between them. Use the whole house for an improvised links, arranging as many hazards as possible. Provide each player with a beanbag, an English walnut, a small ball, or some similar object. Each player must throw the ball into each hole, in rotation, in as few throws as possible. Keep accurate scores. Low score wins.

SEALED ORDERS OBSTACLE RACE

Four or six players compete. These may be the winners of previous contests. There should be ten obstacles, each marked with a number from 1 to 10. The contestants start from a given point and run to Obstacle 1. Here written instructions tell them how to reach Obstacle 2. And so on. The one first completing the tasks and returning to the starting point wins. Here are ten suggested directions:

1. Walk sidewise to Number 2, looking in the opposite direction.
2. Waltz to Number 3, while reading a newspaper item aloud.
3. Sing the chorus of a familiar song, while hopping to Number 4, holding right foot in left hand.
4. Crouch on your haunches and go so to Number 5.
5. Repeat three times "Meet my brother and sisters: Heza Nut, Sheza Nut, and Ima Nut." Hop three times, skip three times, then run to Number 6.
6. Race on all fours backward to Number 7.
7. Crow like a rooster, bray like a donkey, moo like a cow, while crawling on all fours to Number 8.
8. Balance a dime on your nose and walk to Number 9 without dislodging it.
9. Hop on the left foot and right hand, keeping right foot and left hand in the air, to Number 10.
10. Sit on a pillow (or a similar object) crosslegged, and propel yourself to the starting point with your hands only.

RELAYS

For all relays divide the players into teams, each headed by a Captain. Unless otherwise directed, only two teams are required for the following games, and the team finishing any event first wins.

Ball of String.—Each team, sitting or standing in a circle, is provided with a ball of cord. The Captain holds one end, while the ball is passed rapidly from hand to hand until it is unwound. It is then passed back and rewound. Variation: Each player wraps the string once around his body before passing the ball.

Tie the Handkerchief.—Provide each Captain with a large handkerchief. At a signal, he ties it between the left elbow and shoulder of Number Two. Number Two unties it with his right hand, and ties it in the same manner on Number Three. And so on, until the last player ties it on the Captain. Variation: The handkerchief is tied around the neck instead of the arm.

Clothespin.—Provide each Captain with five clothespins. At the signal, he places the pins on the fingers of Number Two's left hand, starting with the little finger. Number Two removes them and places them on the fingers of Number Three, and so on, the last player placing them on the Captain's fingers.

Card-Passing.—Each Captain has four cards. He must stick them, one at a time, between the fingers of Number Two's left hand. The game continues as above.

Fresh Eggs.—Provide each Captain with a hardboiled egg or a rubber egg, and each player with a spoon. Each team stands in a line, the players holding the spoons in their mouths. At a signal, the Captain places the egg in his spoon, then transfers it to Number Two's spoon without using his hands. And so on to the end of the line. If the egg falls, it must be picked up in the spoon held in the mouth. The hands may steady it.

Peanut-Passing.—Each team sits in a row, hands clasped to form a long line. Place 10 peanuts on a chair before each Captain, and place an empty chair before each last player. The Captain starts one peanut down his line. It must be passed by the clasped hands. If it falls, it must be picked up with clasped hands. As soon as he gets the first on its way, he starts the second, until all the peanuts have been passed and placed on the chair at the end of the line.

Neckties.—Provide each Captain with a necktie. He ties it around his neck, and shakes hands with Number Two. Number Two unties it, ties it on himself, and shakes hands with Number Three, and so on.

Lip Card.—Provide each Captain with a card. He holds the card between his upper lip and nose, and passes it to Number Two, who takes it in the same manner. And so on down the line and back again. If the cards falls, it may be held upright with the hands, but must be picked up with the upper lip and nose.

Barrel-Hoop.—Provide each Captain with a barrel-hoop. The teams sit, either on the floor or on chairs. The Captain passes the barrel-hoop over his head and down past his feet, then passes it to Number Two, and so on down the line. Standing is forbidden.

Chair-Sitting.—Provide each Captain with a chair. He sits in it, raises his feet from the floor, rises, and passes it to the next player. And so on down the line.

Bead-Stringing.—Provide each team with a basket of cheap wooden beads, and a length of string. At the signal, the Captain races from the starting line to his basket, strings a bead, returns, touches off Number Two, who runs to string the second bead. And so on to the end of the line.

My Rosary.—The same as above, except that a definite number of beads is allotted to each player, who must string these when he races to the basket.

Run and Sit.—Provide each team with a folding chair, placed ten to twenty feet from the starting line. At the signal, each Captain races to the chair, unfolds it, sets it upright, sits in it, lifts his feet, clicks his heels together, gets up, folds the chair, lays it on the floor, races back and touches off the next player. And so on.

Street-Cleaning.—Provide each team with a sheet of paper and a whisk broom. The Captain sweeps the paper across the room and back. Then Number Two does it, and so on.

Clothespin Jump.—Stretch a clothesline for each team. Stick on the line clothespins head downward, one for each player. Each player must jump for his pin, grasp it in his mouth, and drop it into a container. It is forbidden to use the hands.

Soap Bubble.—Provide a bowl of soap suds and a soap bubble pipe. Stretch a rope across the room, five feet from the floor. Each player must blow one bubble across the rope, only one blow being allowed to each. The team blowing the greatest number of bubbles over wins.

Locomotion.—Each member of the team must cross the floor, using a different method of locomotion: as running, hopping, skipping, crawling, etc. The corresponding members of the other team use the same method.

Y is for Yale.—The Leader calls a letter and what it stands for. Each team must arrange itself to form the letter. Variation: Players must lie on the floor to arrange the letter.

Taffy-Eating.—Provide each team with a bowl of wrapped pieces of taffy, one piece for each player. Each bowl is placed on a chair at the turning point, with a table between. At a signal, each Captain must run to his bowl, eat one piece of taffy, smooth the paper and lay it on the table, then run back and touch off next player.

Water-Drinking.—Played as above. Provide each team with a pitcher of water and a glass. Each player must fill the glass, drink the water, invert the glass, then run back and touch off the next player. Variation: Provide each player with a soda straw, through which the water must be drunk.

Candle-Lighting Time.—Provide each team with a candle and a box of matches. At the signal, each Captain lights his candle, runs to the turning point, returns, and hands the candle and box of matches to Number Two. And so on, until all have carried the candle. If it goes out, the player holding it must light it before proceeding.

Lights Out.—Provide each team with a box of matches. Place a candle for each team at the turning point. In rotation, each player runs to the candle, lights it, blows it out, and returns to give the matches to the next player, who must do the same thing.

Beans.—Provide each team with a spoon, a saucer containing two beans for each player, and an empty saucer. The first saucer is placed on a chair at the starting line, the second on a chair at the turning point. At the signal, each Captain carries two beans on the spoon to the empty saucer, places them there, returns, and passes the spoon to the next player, and so on. Only the spoon may touch the beans.

Toothpicks and Raisins.—Provide each player with a toothpick, and each team with a saucer containing three raisins for each player. In rotation, each player spears three raisins with his toothpick, one at a time, and feeds them to the next player. The last player feeds the Captain.

Bottoms Up.—Provide each with a handkerchief, and a chair at the turning point containing one or more milk bottles bottoms up. Each Captain races to his chair, places the bottles bottoms up on the floor, returns and passes the handkerchief to Number Two. Number Two must replace the bottles bottoms up on the chair. And so on, alternately. The last player returns the handkerchief to the Captain. If a bottle falls, the player must return and replace it.

Deuce to Ace.—Provide each team with a shuffled deck of cards, which are placed on a table. At the signal, each Captain runs to his deck, finds the deuce of spades and faces it, returns and touches off Number Two. Number Two finds the trey of spades and faces it. And so on, until the spade suit from deuce to ace is faced.

Sitting Card.—The teams are seated on the floor, each Captain holding a deck of cards. At the signal he finds the deuce of spades and faces it, then passes the deck. Number Two finds the trey, and so on, as above.

A to Z.—Alphabet cards are used, the alphabet being faced, as above.

Spelling Match.—Provide each team with a shuffled deck of alphabet cards, which are placed at the turning point. The Leader calls a word. Each Captain runs to the turning point, finds the first letter, faces it, runs back and touches off Number Two, who faces the second letter, and so until the word is spelled.

Living Words.—Provide each team with the same number of alphabet cards, chosen to fit the words the Leader will call. Each player holds one card. When the Leader calls a word, the proper players run to their places against the wall to spell the word.

Hopping to Spell.—Provide a blackboard or a large piece of cardboard or paper tacked on the wall. The Leader announces a word containing as many letters as there are players on each team. Each player on each team, in rotation, hops to the board, writes a letter, in proper sequence, hops back, and touches off the next player.

Button Your Vest.—The teams are composed of boys only. Each in turn is asked to unbutton his vest, then button it *up,* and tap the next player when he has finished. The next player then does it. The Leader must watch each one to see that he follows instructions. The team having the largest number of boys who obeyed instructions wins. They were instructed to button their vests *up,* not from top to bottom. Girls may play this, wearing boys' vests.

Mannequin.—Provide each team with a suitcase or box containing the same articles of clothing, such as hat, raincoat, scarf, gloves, vests, etc. Each Captain is the Mannequin, or model. At the signal, each Number Two opens his container, and puts one article of clothing on his Mannequin, who may not assist in any way. Number Three puts on the next article, and so on.

Reverse Mannequin.—When the Mannequins are dressed, play

as above, removing one article each time, and replacing it in the container.

Elopement.—Divide each team into pairs, one girl and one boy. Provide each team with a suitcase, containing similar men's and women's garments, and an umbrella. At the signal, the first couple runs to their suitcase; each dresses in garments of the opposite sex; the two race together under the opened umbrella to the starting line; undress; repack the suitcase; and touch off the next couple. This couple runs with the suitcase to the turning point, and repeats.

Burst the Bag.—Divide each team into couples, as above. Provide each team with a pile of paper bags. Each couple races to the bags. The boy blows one up, and the girl bursts it on his back. They race back to touch off the next couple.

Schnozzle Race.—Provide each team with a safety matchbox cover. Each Captain places it on his nose, and passes it to his Number Two, who must take it on his nose. And so on to the end of the line. If the match box falls, it may be replaced on the player's own nose with the hands; otherwise, the hands may not touch it.

Fish Race.—Provide each player with a soda straw, and each team with a fish cut out of paper. Each Captain fastens his fish on his soda straw by inhaling, and then passes it to his Number Two. Number Two inhales while the Captain exhales, thus passing the fish. And so on down the line, and back again. If the fish falls, it must be picked up by inhaling through the straw. Only the player from whose straw it fell may pick it up.

Cigarette-Paper Race.—Provide each team with a cigarette paper or a piece of tissue paper of the same size. Each Captain holds it to his nose by inhaling, and passes it to Number Two, by exhaling while Number Two inhales. Number Two, in turn, passes it similarly to Number Three. If the paper falls, the player may pick it up and replace it beneath his nose; otherwise the hands may not touch it. Or the player may be required to inhale the paper up from the floor.

Bean Race.—Provide each player with a soda straw and a glass, and each Captain with 5 to 10 beans, which he places in his glass. The Captain picks up a bean by inhaling through his straw, and passes it to the glass of Number Two. When all of the Captain's beans are passed, Number Two passes them to Number Three, and so on.

Speedway Race.—Provide each team with a ridiculous pullable toy—a fire-engine, an express wagon, a toy automobile. In rotation, the members of each team must pull it from the starting line to the turning point and back, then pass it to the next player. This may be placed as an individual race.

RACES FOR PAIRS

Pillow-Case.—Divide the party into pairs, one girl and one boy. Provide each pair with a cased pillow. The boy uncases it and holds the case; the girl slips the pillow in the case. Then the girl uncases the pillow, holds the case, and the boy slips it in. This may be done in teams, each couple in each team doing as instructed, then passing the pillow to the next couple.

Bicycle-Tire.—Divide the party into pairs, one girl and one boy. Provide each pair with a bicycle tire. Each couple slips the tire over their heads to their waists, run from the starting line to the turning point, and return. Luggage straps, barrel-hoops, circles of rope can be used. This may be played in teams, as above.

Sir Walter Raleigh.—Divide the party into pairs, as above. Provide each boy with two pieces of cardboard. He places them successively so that the girl steps on them. She crosses the room and returns in this manner. This may be played in teams, as above.

Apple Race.—Divide the party into teams of four. Provide each team with an apple and a paring knife. Each Number One peels the apple; Number Two quarters it; Number Three removes the core; Number Four eats it. No task may be started until the previous one is finished.

Candy Race.—Provide each team of four with an elaborately wrapped bar of candy. Number One unwraps it; Number Two halves it; Number Three quarters it; then each of these, and Number Four, eats one quarter.

Peanut-Eating Race.—A race for pairs. Provide each pair with 12 peanuts. The girl shells them one at a time, and, after each is shelled, feeds it to her partner, until he has eaten all of them.

Feeding the Baby.—A race for pairs. The girl feeds the boy a glass of milk, using a small spoon, giving him one spoonful at a time. Or she may feed him with a medicine dropper.

Chinese Stand-Up.—A game for pairs. A boy and a girl sit on the floor back to back, their arms interlocked. At the signal, they rise to their feet without unlocking arms. Variation: The players sit in chairs.

Siamese Twins Race.—A race for pairs. Each pair stands back to back, holding a cane between their legs. At the signal, they race from the starting line to the turning point, one running forward, the other backward. They return, the backward runner running forward this time.

Wheelbarrow Race.—A race for pairs. The boys down running on their hands, the girls holding their ankles. Or the girls may be the wheelbarrows.

Three-Legged Race.—A race for pairs. The near legs of each are tied together, and they race so.

Horseback Race.—The boy, on all fours, is the horse. The girl is the jockey. They race thus.

VIII. MIXERS

LARGE parties tend to start stiffly. People stand about gazing warily at each other, even if they are acquainted. Unconsciously they regard the party with suspicion, and each one is a trifle reluctant to drop his dignity and have a good time. This is true of all ages. Any two, four or six people may be close chums, and frolic together in their own small circle, but put those people in a large gathering and they will immediately be cloaked with formality. This is undesirable at any party where the aim is a good time. The chilled atmosphere must be warmed quickly, for the longer it persists, the harder it becomes to do so. To substitute warmth for this iciness, mixers have been devised. The host or hostess, or chosen leader, should start the party with a lively mixer as soon as possible, in order to get the party cheerfully on its way. Any of the following mixers will dispel formality in a few minutes.

PAPER BAG HANDSHAKE

As each guest arrives, tie a paper bag over his right hand, and instruct him not to remove it until he has shaken hands with all the guests.

MARCHING CIRCLE

The girls form a circle; the men form a second one outside of them. The leader gives the signal, "Ladies to the right, gentle men to the left. Forward march!" The music starts, and the two lines march until it stops. If music is not available, the two circles can be stopped by a whistle or the leader's call to halt. The members of the circles face each other, and each person shakes hands with the one opposite, tells his name, and talks until the music starts. There should be numerous and frequent stops.

At each pause, the leader announces some stunt to be performed, or a specific topic of conversation, such as:

1. What is the best movie you have seen, and why?
2. Imitate a soap box orator, a girl on her first date, a boy in his first long trousers, etc.
3. Tell your birthplace, parents, grandparents, hobby, dearest wish.
4. Girls skip around partners; boys hop around partners.
5. Tell your favorite form of amusement and why; your favorite radio hour, and why; your favorite movie actor or actress, and why.

The leader should think up many similar ingenious stunts. At the final whistle, the couples remain paired for the first game or dance.

I'VE GOT YOU

Start as above. When the circles halt, the leader announces that each person pairs with the one nearest him for the first game or dance.

LEFT-HANDED

Upon arrival, each guest is instructed to shake hands with all the others with his left hand, and to use only his left hand for any activity until all the guests are assembled.

AUTOGRAPHS

Provide each guest with paper and pencil and tell him to get the autographs of the other guests. The one getting the most wins a small prize. This is more amusing if the autographs must be written left handed.

FIND YOUR PARTNER

Cut pictures—illustrations, advertising pictures, postcards—in two pieces. The girls draw the top pieces; the boys, the bottom.

Those holding the matching pieces become partners. Or the girls may draw the whole pictures, the boys the proper titles for them. This may be done with other objects, such as paper hearts of differing colors, cut irregularly.

SPLIT PROVERBS

Proverbs are split, the girls drawing cards bearing one half; the boys, the second half. Thus:

Brevity is the / soul of wit.

There are matched as above. (A list of proverbs will be found on page 522). This may also be done with natural affinities:

Salt / and pepper,

or with similes: (See page 408 for list of affinities and similes).

Cold as / ice.

ODD OR EVEN

Provide the guests with varying numbers of peanuts, and instruct the girls to get as many as possible from the boys, and vice versa. A boy, concealing the peanuts in his hand, approaches a girl and says, "Odd or even?" If she guesses correctly whether he holds an odd or even number, she gets his peanuts, if not, he gets hers. The one getting the most in a specified time wins.

PULLING HEARTSTRINGS

Hang a large hoop or pasteboard heart from the ceiling, with equal lengths of string hanging down each side. Each girl takes a string on one side; the boys, those on the other side. At a given signal, all pull. Those pulling the same string become partners.

THE PYRAMID

In one room, the girls form a line, the shortest in front. In another room the boys form a line, the tallest in front. The lines are marched together so that the shortest pairs with the tallest, and so on.

FISHING

The girls' names are written on slips of paper and mixed in a bowl. The boys stand beyond an outstretched sheet, and are equipped with a fishing pole—a short pole, and a length of string with a bent pin attached. One at a time they toss the fishing line over the sheet and the leader picks a name at random and attaches it to the hook, thus pairing the guests.

The girls may similarly do the fishing for the boys' names.

ONE, TWO, BUCKLE MY SHOE

The girls, informally lined up, count aloud one number in ascending sequence apiece, until each has a number. The boys do the same. Matching numbers are partners.

FATE DECIDES

Favors are prepared in duplicates: two red carnations, two walnuts, two daffodils, two peanuts, etc. The girls draw from one pile, the boys from another, and so are matched as partners.

RUNNING THE GAUNTLET

The girls line up in one room, the boys in another, and then both lines march out together until they are side by side. The couples standing together become partners. Or the first girl may become the partner of the last boy, by marching the beginning of one line to the end of the other, and so on, until all are paired.

BLIND LOVE

The girls line up at one end of the room, with the boys at the other end. The boys are blindfolded, one at a time, and cross the room. Each becomes the partner of the first girl he touches.

The girls may be blindfolded instead of the boys.

GRAB BAG

Each boy brings a small favor, which bears his name hidden. These are put in a bag or a bowl for the girls to draw at random. They are then partnered with the boy whose favor they drew.

The girls may bring the favors, and the boys do the grabbing.

LOTTO OR KENO MIXER

Each guest is given a sheet of paper marked with as many squares as there are guests—thirty (6 x 5), twenty (4 x 5), etc. Each guest must get the autographs of the others, one in each square: or each may fill in his own squares with the names. When the squares are filled, the leader draws the names from a bowl, one at a time, and announces them. The one who first checks off a complete horizontal line calls "Lotto" or "Keno" and wins.

The guests in rotation may each call off a name for the checking.

PODUNK IS THE CAPITAL OF THE STATE OF MATRIMONY

Boys draw the names of states; girls, the names of their capitals, and match them for partners.

Paired objects may be used: bread and butter, cheese and crackers, strawberries and cream, etc. Affinities may be used: thunder and lightning, needle and thread, come and go, hook and eye, etc.

THE PRIZE GROUCH

Two leaders are required to keep the score. One tosses a handkerchief in the air a number of times, at a different level each time. All must laugh while it is in the air, but must scowl when it touches the ground. Those laughing at the wrong time, or failing to laugh at the right time, are eliminated, and may try to make the others laugh, and so join the eliminated. The leaders may try to provoke laughs at the wrong time. The survivor is The Prize Grouch.

CINDERELLA'S SLIPPER

Each of the girls removes one slipper, and the slippers are mixed into a pile. The men are lined up at one end of the room, and, at a signal, rush for the pile; each selects a slipper, thus securing his partner by restoring it to its proper foot.

The boys may pile up their shoes, and the girls do the selecting.

THE LUCKY TENTH

Distribute several quarters or dimes, unseen, one each to a few of the guests. At a signal, the guests start shaking hands, the holders of the coins passing them to the tenth person they shake hands with. The holders must keep accurate count.

ATHLETE'S FOOT, ZIEGFELD'S TEST

The boys sit behind a curtain or outstretched sheet, with one foot protruding. The girls select partners from the feet.

It is termed Ziegfeld's Test, when the girls are behind the curtain and the boys do the choosing.

KER-CHOO!

The guests are divided into three groups. The first group repeatedly practices saying "Hash"; then the second, "Hish"; the third, "Hosh." The three groups, in the same order then practice repeatedly, "Hashee," "Hishee," "Hoshee." At a signal, all repeat their final words in unison, giving the effect of a fat man sneezing violently.

MIXED CONFESSIONS

Four appointed messengers whisper to each guest as follows: The first, who the guest is supposed to be; the second, whom he is with; the third, where he is; the fourth, what he is supposed to be doing. The messengers move independently, and the guests are warned to remember what is told them. When the whispering is ended, the guests line up and announce what they have been told. For instance, a boy might say, "My name is Jim Browning. I'm with Alice Green, in Timbuctoo, making snowballs."

THE BIG SHOT SAYS—

On arrival, the girls are given even-numbered cards; the boys, odd-numbered ones. On each is written: "These are the Big Shot's orders; be sure to carry them out," followed by an amusing order, such as:

1. Find 6 and get her aid in selecting the handsomest man.
2. Find 11 and get his aid in listing all the jewelry worn.
3. List all the bald-headed men.
4. List the favorite pastimes of all the married women.
5. Find 8 and get her aid in listing the brands of cigarettes being smoked in the room.

PAT AND RUB

The leader instructs the guests, simultaneously, to rub the tops of their heads with their right hands, and at the same time to pat their stomachs with their left hands. He then calls, "Now reverse!" He continues, varying the time between commands. Those who fail are eliminated. The survivor is called Chief Osteopath.

YES AND NO

On arrival, each guest is given ten peanuts, beans, or similar counters. The guests are given a specified time in which to collect counters from the others, by getting one from each guest who answers "Yes" or "No" to any question. The one getting the largest number wins.

LISTEN CAREFULLY

The leader commands, "Listen carefully. Hold your left ear with your right hand. Now hold your nose with your left hand."

When all have done this, he commands, "Reverse." The ones who fail are eliminated. The survivor is called Teacher's Pet.

JOHN BROWN'S BABY

The leader sings, and all join in:

John Brown's baby had a cold upon its chest,
John Brown's baby had a cold upon its chest,
John Brown's baby had a cold upon its chest,
So they rubbed it down with camphorated oil!

to the tune of *John Brown's Body* (the *Battle Hymn of the Republic*).

He then gives the sign for baby: right hand on left elbow, and left arm swung as a cradle. The song is sung, using the sign, instead of the word "baby." The next time, "cold" is omitted, and a cough substituted. The next time, "chest" is omitted, and the guests tap their chests once with their right hands instead. The next time, "camphorated oil" is omitted, and the fingers are held close to the nose. Any one singing the wrong word, or giving the wrong sign, is eliminated.

NO LAUGHTER

The guests are seated in a circle and are told that this is a facial control test. Each is to repeat what is said by the guest to his left, adding one "Ha" each time, but never laughing. The leader begins by saying "Ha." The one to the left says "Ha ha," the third, "Ha ha ha," and so on. The laughers are eliminated. The survivor wins.

LAUGH, CLOWN, LAUGH

Two captains are chosen, who divide the guests into teams. By tossing a coin, one team becomes Heads, the other Tails. The leader tosses the coin, and calls its fall. This team must laugh, while the others remain serious. The laughing side tries in any way to make the other side laugh. Those on the opposing side who laugh join the laughing side. The coin is tossed continuously until all are on one team.

STRANGE SPELLING MATCH

Give each guest an alphabet card of one letter. These are easy to make, and should have many vowels, and no X's, Z's and Q's. Make every fifth player a leader. These each decide on a five-letter word, and choose four other players to help form it. When the guests are all divided, each group forms its word by holding up the cards. They are then told to reform another five-letter word with the same letters. The team rearranging itself first wins. (For words that can be rearranged see page 425).

SELECTING CAPTAINS

The leader may appoint captains; or they may be chosen by a ballot of the guests. If two or three are required, the two or three winning the most votes are chosen.

SELECTING TEAMS

The captains may choose in rotation. For first choice, flip a coin, or cut a deck of cards.

Have the guests count aloud in rotation. The even numbers form one team, the odd numbers the other. Or call the letters of the alphabet. A through M form one team, N through Z the other.

Form one team of those whose first names or last names begin with A through L, or whose first names or last names end with these letters; the rest form the other team.

Provide as many red cards and black cards as there are players, half of each color. The players draw the cards from a grab bag. Reds form one team; blacks the other.

SELECTING THE IT

The same procedure may be followed as in selecting captains, or a Counting-Out Rhyme may be used. (See Children's Games.)

IX. DANCES

DANCING is always a popular form of entertainment. The great problem at a dance is to keep the party general and the guests well mixed. Too frequently couples stick together through an entire evening, either through preference, or because one or the other does not know how gracefully to break away. There is also the problem of the shy person or the wallflower type who is not too popular. There are many ways of overcoming these difficulties and making sure that everybody has a good time.

RECEIVING LINE

This is usual only at a formal party, either a dance or a reception. On such occasions, the receiving line is formed of the host and hostess, the guest or guests of honor with their husbands or wives, and a few close friends of the host and hostess. Their function is to greet the guests when they arrive.

At a large party, where there are a number of guests who are not acquainted, an informal receiving line is helpful. This would be formed of several of the host's and hostess's close friends, and who, during the evening, would aid in getting the guests acquainted.

GRAND MARCH

This requires a good Leader, preferably one who knows the figures. It is the best way to start a dance and get the guests mixed. A simple Grand March is essential at a costume party, where the costumes are to be judged. Use any of the partner selecting mixers to get the guests paired. If they are already dancing, a whistle is blown, a leading couple selected, and the others told to fall in behind. The following are some of the simpler figures:

Two's, Four's, Eight's.—March line to far end of room, odd-numbered couples to left, even-numbered ones to right. The Leader and his partner may either fall out to direct, or one may lead one line, the other, the other line. Lines march down opposite sides of room, meet at the near end and march up the room in fours. Divide left and right again, and meet at the near end to march up again in eights.

Unwinding the Lines.—Reverse the process. Right half of eights to right, left half to left. March up opposite sides of room. Fours fall in behind each other and march down. Fours divide into twos and repeat.

Marching off the Lines.—The lines of eight are stopped by a whistle. The Leader and his partner march the couples off in twos, starting with the front line, and winding in and out of remaining lines.

Rose Arbor.—First couple reach near end of room, step apart, hands clasped in an arch. Each couple passes under, turns and makes a similar arch. When the last couple passes through, the first falls in behind, passes under the arch and marches off. The others follow in turn, until the line is restored.

The Labyrinth.—Lead the line into a watchspring, with enough room for the leaders to unwind it when completed.

Special Figures.—Any significant initial, letter or design may be formed; it is either unwound, or a whistle may be blown for dancing.

Grand Right and Left.—The line is led into a circle, and the couples face each other. After shaking hands, the boys then move to the right, the girls to the left, shaking hands in passing. When the whistle blows, each dances with the one with whom he is shaking hands.

Weaving.—The line is led into a circle, boys on the outside, girls inside. The girls join hands and are led in and out of the line of boys. At the whistle, each girl dances with the nearest boy. The boys may do the weaving instead.

Virginia Reel Figure.—The boys and girls form separate lines about twenty feet apart, facing each other. The boy at the foot of the line and the girl at the head march diagonally toward the center of the room, meet and dance away outside the lines. The boy at the head then marches to meet the girl at the foot. Alternate in this way until all are dancing.

Paul Jones.—Starting usually with Grand Right and Left, figures are thrown in during this dance as follows:

(1). *Dance with the Lady.*—The Leader blows a whistle to stop the dancing and calls "circle all." The couples come into a single circle. As the Leader calls, they slide to the right, then to the left, then skip to the center, then skip back. The Leader calls "Dance with the lady on your left."

(2) *Double Circle.*—The boys form a circle, and the girls another one inside, those in each circle joining hands. The boys move to the left, the girls to the right. At the stop signal, the Leader calls, "Dance with the lady in front of you."

(3) *The Basket.*—Start as above. At the stop signal, the girls step back, hands still joined, and step under the raised arms of the boys. Then all slide right, then left. At the next signal, the boys dance with the girls on their right.

(4) *Across the Circle.*—Form a single circle. Slide right, then left, then skip toward center. Boys choose each a girl from opposite side.

(5) *Ladies' Choice.*—Boys collect in a group in the center, and the girls dance in a circle around them. At a signal, the girls rush in and choose a partner; this may be reversed.

(6) *Kneel Before Your Lady.*—The dancers form a single circle. At the command, "Kneel before your lady," each boy drops to one knee before a girl. Girls then weave in and out among them. At a signal, each girl dances with the boy kneeling before her.

(7) *Reverse Circles.*—The couples form a circle and march around. At a signal, the girls turn and march in the

opposite direction; at a second signal, each dances with the boy opposite her.

SELECTING PARTNERS

The partner-selecting devices described in the previous chapter, *Mixers,* can be used for this purpose.

CALL-OUTS

The Leader blows his whistle, and calls a specified group to the center of the room: boys or girls from a certain school, or of a certain club; the single boys or girls; the married ones, etc. With such a group separated, the Leader blows the whistle, telling them to favor. Each chooses a partner from the other guests. This may be repeated, until, with the final whistle, the Leader announces, "All dance off."

WHISTLE CHANGE

Whenever he chooses, the Leader may blow his whistle, and call "Change partners. Dance with the nearest person," or some similar call.

CUTTING IN

This is an excellent way to keep the dancers well mixed:

Simple Cut In.—A boy approaches a dancing couple, touches the boy's arm, and dances off with the girl. Her former partner may then cut in on another couple. For variation, the girls may cut in. When there are a number of strangers present, the one cutting in should be instructed to introduce himself as he does so.

Lemon Dance.—Provide one or more of the boys with a lemon (or any piece of fruit). The holder of the lemon hands it to the boy of a dancing couple, and dances off with the girl.

Broom Cut In.—The boy is provided with a broom instead of a lemon. He dances with it until he wishes to cut in, when he passes it to the boy of the dancing pair. The broom may be dressed as a witch, a scarecrow, etc.

Doll Cut In.—Any doll, Teddy Bear, mannikin, etc., may be used instead of a broom.

Nigger Baby.—Use several soft rubber balls. Large gaily colored ones are best. The boy holding one rolls it toward a couple. If it touches them, he dances with the girl, leaving the boy to retrieve the ball and use it similarly. (Or girls may roll the balls instead.)

Hats On.—Provide several boys with dunce caps, sombreros, any humorous hats, or plain caps. When one of these boys cuts in, he places the hat on the dancing boy, and dances off with the girl.

Forfeit Cut In.—If the dance lags, the Leader may announce that, when the music stops, those holding the objects for cutting in must pay a forfeit. This will speed up the cutting in.

LEAP YEAR DANCE

For variation, the girls are instructed to do the things the boys normally do, seek partners, cut in, etc.

ELIMINATION DANCES

This is a system whereby a certain number of couples are eliminated at each blow of the whistle, the final couple being the winners:

Elimination Marathon.—Draw large chalk circles on the floor. When the whistle blows, any couple touching these is eliminated.

Blindfold Elimination.—A guest is blindfolded and provided with a large rubber ball. When the music stops he rolls the ball, eliminating all couples touched by it. Or he may move among the dancers, eliminating all whom he touches.

Who's Who.—The couples are provided with cards naming them famous individuals or famous lovers. The Leader draws from duplicate cards in a container, and calls out the couple drawn.

Or the couples may be scrambled, such as Nero and Shirley Temple.

Keno Dropout.—The couples are numbered. When the whistle blows, the Leader draws numbers from a container, and the ones drawn drop out.

Moonlight Elimination.—The dance floor is dark or dimly lighted. The Leader eliminates couples by turning a flashlight on them.

Joker Dropout.—The dancers draw cards, the girls red ones, the boys black ones. The Leader eliminates by drawing similar cards and calling out those who hold them.

Lotto Dropout.—The girls are given even numbers; the boys, odd ones. Duplicate even numbers are placed in one container, duplicate odd ones in another. The Leader draws several numbers each time, eliminating their holders. The remaining unattached dancers pair, and dance.

Balloon Rodeo.—A small balloon is tied to the left ankle of each girl. During dancing, each couple protects its own balloon, while striving to step on those of the other couples. As soon as a balloon bursts, the couple is eliminated, but must not step on other balloons while leaving the floor.

X. CHILDREN'S GAMES: INDOORS

Many of the games in other sections of this book can be played by children, and the games in this chapter can be played by people of any age. However, these games are especially suitable for young children. Most of them can be played outdoors or indoors. In the first group are the games more easily adaptable to indoors.

COUNTING-OUT RHYMES

These are used to determine who is to be the It, the Leader, the Blind Man, or whatever the game requires. The players stand in a circle. One player repeats the rhyme, slowly, pointing to each player in rotation, as he says each word. The player upon whom the last word falls is It.

One Two Three Four.—

One, two, three, four,
Mary at the cottage door,
Five, six, seven, eight,
Eating cherries off a plate.
O, U, T spells out!

One Two Three Four Five.—

One, two, three, four, five,
I caught a hare alive.
Six, seven, eight, nine, ten,
I let him go again.
O, U, T spells out!

Eeny Meeny Miny Mo.—

Eeny, meeny, miny, mo!
Catch a nigger by his toe!
If he hollers, let him go.
Eeny, meeny, miny, mo!

Eena Deena Dina Duss.—

Eena, deena, dina, duss,
Wattle, weela, wila, wuss.
Spit, spot, must be done,
Twiddlum, twaddlum, twenty-one.
O, U, T spells out!

Intry Mintry Cutry Corn.—

Intry, mintry, cutry, corn,
Apple seed and apple thorn;
Wire, briar, limber lock,
Three geese in a flock:
One flew east, one flew west,
And one flew over the cuckoo's nest!

Hickory Dickery Six and Seven

Hickory, dickery, six and seven,
Alabone, crackabone, ten and eleven,
Spin, spun, muskidun,
Twiddle 'em, twaddle 'em, twenty-one!

One-ery, Two-ery.—

One-ery, two-ery, ziccary, zan;
Hollow bone, crack a bone, nine-ery, ten;
Spittery spot, it must be done,
Twiddledum, twaddledum, twenty-one.

One for the Money.—

This rhyme is used for starting races.

One for the money,
Two for the show,
Three to make ready,
And four for the go!

RING GAMES

In this group of games the players stand or sit in a circle during the play. The first ones described are those wherein the players stand.

Drop the Handkerchief.—The player who is counted out as the It is given a handkerchief. While he moves around outside the ring, the others sing:

> A tisket, a tasket, a green and yellow basket,
> I sent a letter to my love, and on the way I dropped it.

At the word "dropped," the It drops the handkerchief behind one player, and starts to run around the circle. If he can make the complete circle before the player realizes the handkerchief has been dropped behind him, that player must go into the center of the ring—the Dunce Pen. If the player sees the handkerchief, he chases the It at once. If the It reaches the break in the circle before the other player catches him, the other player becomes the It. If not, the first It tries again. A player put in the Dunce Pen can only get out by later snatching the handkerchief from behind some other player, before that player can get it. The game may be played without singing.

Three Deep.—Two circles are formed, one inside of the other, with two players outside called the Chaser and the Runner. The Runner may weave in and out of the circles, with the Chaser pursuing him. When he chooses to, the Runner stops in front of a player in the inner circle, making it three deep. The player in the outer circle directly behind the Runner at once becomes the Runner, while the former Runner and the player behind him step into place in the circles. If a Chaser tags a Runner, the Chaser becomes the Runner, and the Runner the Chaser. Only a Runner may stop in front of the circles.

Cat and Mouse.—One player is the Cat, and another, the Mouse. The Mouse runs around the circle, with the Cat after him. The other players keep their hands clasped, and at any time will raise them to let the Mouse dodge in or out, but they try to prevent the Cat from getting through. When the Mouse is caught, he chooses another player to be the next Cat. The former Cat becomes the Mouse.

In and Out the Window.—The player who is It moves around outside the circle, while the others sing:

> Go round and round the valley, (repeated twice)
> As we are all so gay.

The players then drop their hands, and the It weaves in and out among them, singing:

> Go in and out the windows, (repeated twice)
> As we are all so gay.

It faces one of the players, who all sing:

> Go back and face your lover, (repeated twice)
> As we are all so gay.

It takes the hand of one player, and sings:

> Such love have I to show you, (repeated twice)
> As we are all so gay.

The player thus selected becomes It.

Miss Jennia Jones.—One player is the mother, another is Miss Jones. The mother sits on a chair in the center of the circle. Miss Jones stands behind the chair. One player dances in from the circle, then back, singing:

> I've come to see Miss Jennia Jones,
> Miss Jennia Jones, Miss Jennia Jones,
> I've come to see Miss Jennia Jones,
> And how is she today?

Mother sings:

> She's upstairs washing,
> Washing, washing,
> She's upstairs washing,
> You cannot see her today.

One at a time, the players dance in from the circle, singing the first verse. The mother repeats the second verse each time, substituting for "washing," baking, ironing, then scrubbing. Miss Jones now reclines as if ill, and the mother reveals that she is first ill, then worse, then dead.

All the players, except the mother and Miss Jones, sing:

What shall we dress her in,
Dress her in, dress her in;
What shall we dress her in—
Shall it be blue?

Mother sings:

Blue is for sailors,
Sailors, sailors,
Blue is for sailors,
So that will never do.

The verses are repeated, using Red. "Red is for firemen." Then Pink. "Pink is for babies." Then Green. "Green is forsaken." Then Black. "Black is for mourners." Then White.

White is for dead people.
Dead people, dead people,
White is for dead people,
So that will just do.

Then they sing:

Where shall we bury her,
Bury her, bury her,
Where shall we bury her?
Under the apple tree.

Miss Jones lies on the floor, and a sheet is thrown over her. The ring reforms, and the players sing:

I dreamed I saw a ghost last night,
Ghost last night, ghost last night,
I dreamed I saw a ghost last night,
Under the apple tree!

The ghost rises. The ring breaks up, and the players try to avoid being caught by the ghost. The one caught becomes Miss Jones.

Green Gravel.—The Messenger stands in the center of the circle, which dances around singing:

Green gravel, green gravel,
The grass grows so green,
The fairest of ladies,
Is fit to be seen.

As the Messenger approaches one of the players, the others sing:

Dear ———, Dear ———,
Your true love is dead;
The king sends you a letter
To turn back your head.

The player named turns his back upon the circle. One by one, the Messenger approaches the players, until all have their backs turned. Then, to each in turn, the following verse is sung, until all are again facing the circle:

Dear ———, Dear ———,
Your true love's not slain,
The king sends you a letter
To turn around again.

Blind Man's Buff.—One player is blindfolded to be the Blind Man, and stands within the moving circle of players. When he claps his hands three times, the circle must stop. He then points at one member of the circle. The player pointed at must come into the middle of the circle, and be chased until caught. When caught, the Blind Man feels the player's face, and tries to guess who it is. If he fails, he must try again. If he succeeds, the player caught becomes Blind Man.

Blind Man's Staff.—The same, except that the Blind Man is equipped with a staff, which must be long enough to reach from the center of the circle to its circumference. The Blind Man points his staff at one member of the circle, and the latter must take hold of it. The Blind Man asks, "Are you there?" The player must answer "Yes," but he may disguise his voice. The Blind Man then tries to guess who holds the staff. If he guesses correctly, that player becomes the Blind Man. If not, the Blind Man tries again.

In either of these games, music may be played. When the music stops, the circle stops. Or the Blind Man taps three times on the floor with his staff to halt the circle.

Handkerchief Catch.—The It stands in the center of the circle, holding a large handkerchief. He throws it in the air, and calls the name of a player. That player must catch it before it falls to the ground, or become the It.

Or the players may be numbered. Then the It calls a number instead of a name. Otherwise, as above.

Handkerchief Laugh.—Started as above. When the It throws the handkerchief in the air, and calls a player's name or number, that player must laugh while the handkerchief is in the air, and stop when it touches the floor. The It may specify the type of laugh—a gay laugh, a silly laugh, a giggle, etc. If a player fails, he becomes the It.

Or the entire circle may be required to laugh while the handkerchief is in the air, and to stop when it hits the floor. All failing pay a forfeit, the first one to fail becoming the It.

Porco, Italian Blind Man's Buff.—Play the same as Blind Man's Buff. When the Blind Man touches a player with his staff, the circle stops, and the Blind Man grunts like a pig, or imitates any animal he chooses. The player touched must repeat the sound. If the Blind Man identifies the player, the player becomes the Blind Man. If not, the Blind Man must try again.

Seated Blind Man's Buff.—The players sit on chairs in a circle. They may change their seats at any time, as quietly as possible. The Blind Man must sit on the lap of a player, and thus identify him. He may not grope, nor touch the player with his hands. The players must remain as quiet as possible, so that no giggle or whisper will aid the Blind Man in his identification. The players may try to baffle the Blind Man by putting pillows on their laps; or a boy may stretch the skirt of the girl next to him over his knees. When the Blind Man identifies correctly, the identified person becomes the Blind Man.

Here I Bake, Here I Brew.—One player is the Prisoner, and stands within the circle repeating this rhyme:

> Here I bake, here I brew,
> Here I mean to get through!

When he says, "Here I bake," he touches one pair of clasped hands; when he says, "Here I brew," he touches another pair; when he says, "Here I mean to get through," he makes a sudden rush to break through at some unexpected place. He continues until he succeeds, while the players in the circle try to prevent his escape. When he escapes, one of the players where he broke through becomes the Prisoner. If he is a boy, the girl at the break becomes Prisoner, and vice versa.

Blind Cat.—One player, the Cat, is blindfolded, and stands in the center of the circle. The Cat points to any part of the circle. If he is a boy, the nearest girl says, "Miaow." If the Cat is a girl, the nearest boy says, "Miaow." The Cat must identify the player who called. If he succeeds, he kisses the identified player, who then becomes the Cat. If not, he tries again.

He Can Do Little.—One player is the It, and stands within the circle, holding a stick in his *left* hand. He faces any player saying, "He can do little who can't do this." He thumps the floor with the stick, then hands it to the player. The player must repeat the motion, using his *left* hand, or It calls "Forfeit." If he does it correctly, the It says, "Good." In either case, the It passes to the next player. The It may make any motion with the stick, always using his left hand. The game continues until one player guesses the trick, or all have had a chance.

CLAP IN, CLAP OUT

The boys leave the room, while the girls form a circle, each with a chair in front of her. One girl names a boy, who is called in. He must decide which girl called him and sit down before her. If he is correct, the girls remain silent, if not, they clap, and he goes out. Another boy is then called, until all are seated. The girls then go out.

Clap In, Hiss Out.—The same as above, except that the girls hiss when a boy makes a wrong choice.

THIMBLE

The player who is the It stands in the center of the circle, holding a thimble. The other players clasp hands. The It moves around the circle, pretending to put the thimble in each pair of clasped hands, until he finally does put it in one pair. He then asks, "Who has the thimble?" The players guess in rotation, the one holding it being permitted to guess incorrectly without paying a forfeit. The others pay a forfeit if they are wrong, the first in error becoming the next It.

Button, Button, Who's Got the Button?—Similar to Thimble. The players sit in a circle. When the button has been passed, the It says, "Button, button, who's got the button? Whom do *you* say?" and points to any player. The game continues as above.

HUL GUL

Give each player a different number of beans, buttons, or similar small objects. No player should have more than 10, one or two may have none, and no player should know how many another has. The first player holds out his closed hand, and says to the player on his left:

Hul Gul.
Hands full.
Parcel how many?

The second player must then guess the number of beans held by the first. If he succeeds, he wins the beans. If he guesses too many, the first player demands enough to fill his number to the guessed amount. For instance, if the first player held 3 beans, and the second guessed 6, the first would say, "Give me 3 to make it 6." If the guess is too few, the second player must forfeit half of the beans he holds, provided he holds no more than 10. One player is allowed to win only 5 beans at a time. The play continues around the circle, until one player holds all the beans.

HUNT THE SLIPPER

One player is the Customer. The others, seated on the floor, are the Cobblers. The Customer gives one cobbler a slipper, and says:

Cobbler, cobbler mend my shoe;
Get it done by half-past two.

He then turns his back, while the cobblers pass the slipper around the circle, until one of them conceals it. The Customer returns, demands his shoe, and is told it is not ready. He pretends anger, and demands it as it is, and then tries to find it. The cobbler who has it must try to pass it without being observed by the Customer. When the Customer finds it, the cobbler who holds it must become the Customer.

STAGECOACH

In this, and the remaining ring games, the players sit in a circle. The Leader stands in the center, and gives each player the name of something connected with a stagecoach. The names might be: Horses, Harness, Bridle, Bit, Tongue, Whiffletree, Whip, Driver, Driver's Seat, Wheel, Spoke, Axle, Nut, Lantern, Door, Passengers, etc.

The Leader tells a dramatic, graphic story of a stagecoach journey. As he names each part of the stagecoach, the player representing that part must rise and turn around swiftly before resuming his seat. The Leader mentions all the parts as many times as he chooses. Suddenly he says, "The whole stagecoach turned over." All the players must rise at once and exchange seats. The Leader seizes the first free chair. The player left out becomes the Leader.

Blowout.—Played as above. Give the players names of things connected with an automobile: Windshield, Hood, Radiator, Carburetor, Wheel, Cylinder, Differential, Axle, Bumper, Gaskets, etc. The story deals with a motor trip. The cue for changing seats is, "And then there was a blowout!"

Airplane Crash.—Played the same way. Give the players names of airplane parts: Propeller, Wing, Strut, Radio, Fuselage, Motor, Wheels, Pilot, etc. The story deals with an air journey. The cue line is "The airplane crashed."

Western Stagecoach.—Played the same way. Use the same names as for Stagecoach, adding others such as: Guard, Lunch, Shotgun, Mailbag, Holdup Man, Big Chief, Indian, etc. The story deals with a Western trip, an Indian raid and a holdup. The cue is the same as in Stagecoach.

Train Wreck.—Played the same way. Give the players the names of things connected with a train. The cue is "The train was wrecked."

Football, Baseball, Basketball, Fumble, etc.—Played the same way. Give the players names connected with the chosen game. The Leader is the Radio Broadcaster. The cue is "The team fumbled."

Fruit Basket.—Played the same way. The players are given names of fruits, such as Lemons, Oranges, Figs, Pears, etc. Several players may represent the same thing. When the Leader calls "Lemons and Oranges," all players bearing those names change seats. The Leader tries to get a seat, as in Stagecoach. The Leader continues naming fruits in pairs until he gets a seat. If he doesn't get one, he calls "Fruit basket," and all change seats. The one left out becomes the Leader.

Bouquet.—Played as above. The players are named after four groups of flowers, as Peonies, Poppies, Asters, Forget-me-nots; or Roses, Lilacs, Violets, Lilies. The cue line is "Poison Ivy."

NUMBERS CHANGE

Played the same way. The players are numbered, 1, 2, 3, 4, etc. The Leader calls two numbers. These players must change seats quickly, while the Leader tries to secure a seat. He continues until he succeeds. The one left out becomes the Leader.

Blindfold Numbers Change.—The same as above, except that the Leader is blindfolded. If he touches one of the players who are changing seats, he gets that player's seat. The player becomes the Leader.

LOVE YOUR NEIGHBORS

The player who is the It stands in the center of the circle. He asks a player, "How do you love your neighbors?" The player answers, "Not at all." It asks, "Whom do you love?" The player names a boy and a girl. These must immediately change seats, while the It tries to secure a seat. If the players answers, "Very much," to the first question, all change seats. The one left out becomes the It.

Postman.—Played the same way. The Leader is the Postman. The players are given the names of cities. The Postman says, "I sent a letter from Boston to Detroit." These cities change places, while the Postman tries to secure a seat. When he says "Special Delivery," all change places.

SPIN THE PLATTER

Each player has a number. The Leader spins a plate or a platter in the center of the circle, and calls a number. That player must catch the platter before it ceases spinning, or become the Leader. This is usually played with the players seated on the floor.

Arithmetic Spin the Platter.—Played as above. It does not call a number directly, but a sum in addition, subtraction, multiplication or division whose answer gives the number. Thus player

16 could be called several ways: as 10 plus 6, etc.; 18 minus 2, etc.; 8 times 2, etc.; 32 divided by 2, etc.

Old-Fashioned Spin the Platter.—When a boy is the It, he spins the platter before a girl; when a girl is the It, before a boy. When the platter is not caught in time, the boy kisses the girl, and the one failing becomes the It.

Catch the Cane.—The It balances a cane upright on the floor, then releases it, calling a number. That player must catch the cane before it hits the floor, or become the It.

GOING TO JERUSALEM

Form a circle of chairs with their seats facing outward. There must be one less than the number of players. While music is being played, the players march around the chairs. When the music stops, they scramble for seats. The one left standing drops out, taking a chair with him. The game continues until only one player is seated. He has arrived at Jerusalem.

The game may be played without music, the Leader clapping when the players are to be seated.

Crossing the Lake.—A large broken circle is drawn on the floor. The broken space is the lake, and must be too wide for a player to jump. Played as above, either with or without music. When the music stops, players caught in the lake drop out.

SIMON SAYS THUMBS UP

The players sit around a table, with the Leader at the head. The Leader must start every order with "Simon says—." When he does so, the players obey the command; when he does not, the players remain motionless. Thus, the Leader says, "Simon says thumbs up." All thumbs go up. If he says, "Thumbs down," no one must move. Only when he says, "Simon says thumbs down," do the thumbs go down. He varies his orders as he chooses, says, "Simon says thumbs on heads," "Simon says wiggle-waggle," etc. If he omits the "Simon says—" the order must be ignored. All who obey at the wrong time, or who fail to obey at the right time, must pay a forfeit, or drop out.

TAG GAMES

These are games in which one player, who is the It, tries by some means to tag another, thus making the other player the It.

Last Couple Out.—The players form two columns, the boys in one, the girls in the other. The It stands about ten feet in front of the head of the columns, with his back turned. When he calls, "Last couple out," the last of each column run, one to the right, the other to the left. The It turns and tries to catch the girl before the couple rejoin at the head of the column. If he succeeds, the other boy becomes the It, and the first It joins the column with the girl. He continues until he does succeed. A girl may be the It and try to catch a boy.

Snatch the Handkerchief.—One player is the It. The others divide into two teams and stand on the opposite sides of the room. The players on each team are numbered 1, 2, 3, etc. The It places a large handkerchief in the center of the floor, its center pointed upward like a small tent. The It calls a number. The two players bearing that number, one from each team, run out to snatch the handkerchief. When one gets it, he must run back to his line without being tagged by the player from the opposing team. If the player is tagged before he reaches his line, the other team scores 1; if not, his team scores 1. The team having the highest score wins.

Wink and Tag.—The boys sit in chairs, the girls stand behind. There is an empty chair in front of one girl. When she winks at a boy, he tries to get to her chair before the girl behind his tags him. If he succeeds, the girl who lost him does the winking. If he fails, the first girl must continue to wink until she gets a boy in her chair. The game should be played rapidly.

The girls may sit in the chairs, and the boys stand behind them.

Puss in the Corner.—This game is meant for five players, but more can play it, if other objects are used for corners. For instance, the end of a mantle, a specified chair, a table, may be designated as corners. One player is Puss. The others choose corners, and try to change from corner to corner, without letting Puss steal a vacated corner. Puss can only get a corner when it has been left by its holder. When he succeeds in getting a corner, the player who lost it becomes Puss.

POST OFFICE

One player, the Postman, leaves the room. He knocks on the door, saying he has a letter for one of the girls. The girl asks, "How many stamps are to be paid?" The Postman may say any number under 10. The girl goes out of the room, pays for the stamps with kisses, and remains as Postmistress. The Postman becomes one of the players. The Postmistress repeats the procedure, saying she has a letter for one of the boys.

MIMIC

Two players go into another room, and call in another player. They tell him he must guess the game they are playing. They then imitate everything he says and does. When he guesses, he joins the first two, and another player is called in. Finally, everybody is mimicking the last player.

GOOD MORNING

The player who is the It is given two hats. He puts on one, and gives the other to any other player. The other player must now do the opposite of whatever the It does. If the It takes off his hat, the other must put his on; if the It walks across the floor, the other must stand still. When the other player makes a mistake, he becomes the It.

MY MASTER BIDS ME——

The Leader says to the second player, "My master bids you do as I do." Number Two says, "What did your master bid you do?" The Leader says, "To work with one," and starts pounding with his right hand on his knee. A motion once started must be continued to the end of the game. Number Two carries on the same conversation with Number Three, and goes through the same motions. and so on around the circle. The Leader starts the same conversation, ending with, "To work with two." He then pounds with his left hand on his other knee. This goes around the circle. The Leader then repeats the conversation adding, "To work with three," and moves his right leg back and forward. This goes around the circle. He then adds, "To work with four," and moves his left leg. Finally, he adds, "To work with five, there are no more," and bobs his head backward and forward. Any mistake calls for a forfeit. The complete rhyme is:

"My master bids you do as I do."
"What did your master bid you do?"
"To work with one, to work with two,
To work with three, to work with four,
To work with five, there are no more."

JUDGE AND JURY

One player is the Judge. The others are seated in two rows, exactly opposite each other. The Judge walks up and down between the rows, and asks a question of any player. He may say, "Did you go to school yesterday?" or "Have you ever flown a kite?" or anything he chooses. The player to whom he speaks must not answer. If he does, he must pay a forfeit. The player exactly opposite must answer before the Judge can count ten, or pay a forfeit. Answers must be three or more words, and must not contain these words: "Yes," "No," "black," "white," or "gray." Any answer less than three words long, or containing a forbidden word, calls for a forfeit. A player paying three forfeits becomes the Judge.

HOLD FAST!

One player is the Leader. The others are divided into groups of four. Each group stand in a square, holding a handkerchief between them, one player holding each corner. When the Leader says, "Let go!," the players must all hold fast. When he says, "Hold fast!," all must let go. He repeats these orders first slowly, then fast, to bewilder the players. When any player does the wrong thing he drops out, until only one player still holds a handkerchief. This last one then becomes Leader.

POOR PUSSY!

One boy is Pussy. He must kneel before a girl, and miaow three times. Each time the girl must shake her head and say, "Poor Pussy!" The Pussy tries to make the girl laugh, by mewing in different ways. If the girl laughs, she becomes the Pussy, and mews before a boy. If she does not laugh, the Pussy goes to another girl.

JERUSALEM AND JERICHO

The players stand in a long line. One is the Leader, and he stands before the others. When he calls "Jerusalem," all must bow deeply; when he calls "Jericho," no one must move. He tries to trick the players, by prolonging the first syllable, then ending quickly as, "Jee-e-e-e-er-rr-rusalem!" or "Jee-e-e-e-r-richo!" A player moving at the wrong time, or not moving at the right time, becomes Leader, and must pay a forfeit.

UP JENKINS

The players are divided into teams, one on each side of a table. Each team has a captain, who gives the commands. One team has a quarter, which is passed backward and forward under the table. When that captain says "Up Jenkins!" all hands must be raised. When he says "Down Jenkins," the hands must be struck palms down on the table. The one holding the coin tries to disguise its sound as it hits the table, or get it down without any sound. The other captain consults his team aloud, and signals up the hands, leaving until last the one he believes holds the coin. If he is right, his team gets the coin; if not, the other team tries again.

In a small group, one player may be the It, and make all the calls. When he locates the coin, as above, the player holding it becomes the It.

PINCHY-WINCHY!

A player is chosen the Victim, without knowing it. Another is the Leader, and sits on the Victim's left. The players sit in a circle. The Leader is provided with soot, lampblack, or some similar soft black substance, which the Victim cannot see. The Leader explains that this is a Follow the Leader game, and each must do exactly as he does. He also explains that there must be no laughing or giggling. He then pinches the right cheek of the Victim, saying, "Pinchy-winchy!" Victim does this to Number Three, and so on around the circle. The Leader then pinches the left cheek; the third time, the chin; the fourth time, the forehead; and finally the nose, each time saying "Pinchy-winchy!" His fingers, being blackened with the soot, have left marks all over the Victim's face. The Leader then looks in a mirror, and says "Pinchy-winchy!" Then the Victim looks in the mirror, and discovers the purpose of the game.

Skeegee-Weegee.—The same game, using the words "Skeegee-Weegee," instead of "Pinchy-winchy!"

THE DONKEY'S TAIL

A large donkey, with no tail, is drawn on a sheet, a blackboard, or a piece of cardboard, which is attached to a wall. Give each player a numbered donkey's tail with a pin in one end. In rotation, the players are blindfolded, turned around once or twice, and then required to cross the room and pin the tail on the donkey. The one pinning the tail nearest the proper place wins.

Whiskers on the Cat.—Draw a whiskerless cat, instead of a tailless donkey. Give each player numbered cardboard whiskers. Play as above.

Cupid's Arrows.—Draw a picture of a girl, with the heart outlined in the proper place. Give the boys numbered arrows. Play as above. The boy whose arrow is pinned nearest the heart wins.

YOUR FISH, MY FISH

One player is the Fisherman. He has a fish pole about three feet long, from which is suspended a heavy string of about the same length. There is a slip knot at the loose end of the string. The players sit around a table. The Fisherman spreads the loop of the slip knot in the center of the table, making a circle about three inches in diameter. When the Fisherman says "Fish, Fish!" all the players put their index fingers in the loop. If the Fisherman says "Your fish!" no one moves. If he says "My Fish!" he jerks the pole in an effort to catch the finger of a player. He repeats these phrases in any order, slowly, then rapidly, in an attempt to confuse the players. When he catches a fish, that player becomes the Fisherman. If a player withdraws his finger when "Your Fish!" is said, he drops out, or pays a forfeit.

SOAP BUBBLES

Clay pipes are usually used, but soda straws may be used with equal success. When using straws, make four slits, half an inch long, in one end of the straw, and bend back the cut sections.

To make the best soap bubbles, use the following solution: Fill a quart jar two-thirds full of hot water, add a heaping tablespoonful of finely shaved castile soap, or soap flakes; liquid castile soap may be used. Add four tablespoonfuls of glycerine, and a teaspoonful of sugar; olive oil or vegetable oil may be used. Shake vigorously, strain through a cloth, and let stand until cool. Water coloring may be added.

Over the Line.—Stretch a rope across the room, about five feet from the floor. Divide the players into two teams, one team on each side of the rope. Each player tries to blow one bubble over the rope. If he does so, it scores one for his team. Each player is permitted three tries. The team having the largest score wins.

Wicket Bubble.—Make a wicket by inserting the two ends of a piece of wire into the tops of two bottles. The wicket should be about 15 inches wide, and at least a foot high. Stand it in the center of a table. The players divide into two teams, one on each side of the table. Each player is given three tries to send a bubble through the wicket. Score as above.

Largest Bubble.—The player blowing the largest bubble, and releasing it, wins.

Strongest Bubble.—The players, standing in a row, simultaneously blow their bubbles and release them; each blows one bubble. The one floating for the longest time wins. A player may not touch another player's bubble, but he may blow at it with his lips and try to force it against a wall or the ceiling.

GRAB BAG

Place small gifts or favors in a large basket, bag, or similar container, and cover, leaving only enough space for an arm to enter. Each player reaches in and draws out a favor.

Partner's may be selected by this method, by putting the girls' names in a container, and letting the boys draw them.

Grab Bag for Instructions.—A grab bag may be used, to allow the players to secure sealed instructions, which they must read and carry out. These may require any ridiculous stunt, as in the chapter on Forfeits.

STUNT GAMES

Just Like Me.—The Victim is told to repeat "Just like me" to everything the Leader says. In turn, the Leader announces, "I went up one pair of stairs"; ("Just like me!" etc.) "I went up two pairs of stairs"; "I went into a room"; "I looked out of a window"; and finally, "And there I saw a monkey." "Just like me!"

I Am a Gold Lock.—The Victim is told to repeat exactly what the Leader says, except that he must say "key" where the Leader says "lock." The first statement and its repetition are,

"I am a gold lock."

"I am a gold key."

Then, after a lock and key preceded by "silver," "brass," and "lead," the final statement and its repetition are,

"I am a monk lock."

"I am a monk key."

Old Dead Horses.—The Leader announces that the Victim must repeat, after the Leader's first statement, what the Leader says next, using a number one higher each time. The Leader commences, "I saw an old dead horse. I one it." The Victim then says, "I two it." After three, four, five, and six are similarly stated, the final statements are:

Leader: I seven it.

Victim: I eight (ate) it.

Cross-Out Fortune Telling.—This is said to reveal the feeling of a girl for her boyfriend, and vice versa. The girl's full name is written down, and the boy's beneath it. Each identical pair of letters, one in her name, one in his, are then crossed out. Only one letter in each name is cancelled out by cancelling out one in the other; thus if there are three A's in one name, and only one in the other, only one is crossed out in each. When all possible pairs have been crossed out, the remaining letters in each name are counted off by this count, allowing one word to each letter: Friendship, Love, Indifference, Hate. The word, among these four, that falls on the final letter not crossed off, indicates that person's feeling toward the other person. For example, to take two famous lovers:

C L E O P ~~A~~ ~~T~~ ~~R~~ ~~A~~
M ~~A~~ ~~R~~ K ~~A~~ N ~~T~~ O N Y

This leaves 5 letters in Cleopatra's name not cancelled: which would bring her to Friendship, as her feeling toward the eloquent Roman; and 6 letters in Mark Antony's name not crossed out; which would bring him to Love, as his feeling toward the sorceress of the Nile. A tip to the lovesick: if it doesn't work with full names, try usual names; if it fails with these, and with nicknames, change your name, as in Numerology.

XI. HOLIDAY GAMES

HALLOWE'EN GAMES

THESE are the games that are usually played on Hallowe'en. They are especially designed for that night of ghostly events. They may be played at any time, but the quality of forecasting that surrounds most of them is particularly suitable for Hallowe'en. Since Hallowe'en is, according to ancient belief, the one night when all the spirits are liberated and free to roam the world, it is the ideal time for fortune-telling. The majority of Hallowe'en games deals with fortune-telling in one way or another. The fortune-telling games that follow are among the oldest and most popular of the forecasting pastimes.

THE WITCH'S CAULDRON

The Witch sits in a dim room before a cauldron, under which there is a real or an artificial fire. She has a lighted candle. There should be as many fortunes as there are guests. The fortunes are written on slips of paper, which are folded with the writing inside. These are placed in the cauldron. One at a time the guests approach, put their hands in the cauldron and draw out a fortune. When a guest opens the paper, there is nothing there. The Witch says she can read the apparently blank paper. She holds it above the candle, with the invisible writing nearer the flame. Slowly the words, which have been written in milk, become readable as the flame scorches the milk. The paper must not be held too close to the flame, or it will burn.

THE WHEEL OF FORTUNE

Make a large cardboard circle, and divide it into thirty to fifty pie-shaped segments. Write a fortune in each segment, such as: You will elope with a red-head; A blonde and a brunette are going to fight for your affections; You will be the parent of sextuplets. The fortunes should be humorous. Make an arrow of cardboard, fasten it on a heavy pin, and stick the pin firmly into the center of the Wheel of Fortune. The arrow must be about one-quarter of an inch above the wheel, and loose enough to spin. Each guest spins the arrow once. When the arrow comes to rest, he reads his fortune.

The Lucky Top.—Mark a large square of cardboard in small squares like a checker-board. Write a fortune in each square. Each guest spins a top on the board. The square in which it comes to rest reveals his fortune.

THE LOVE-APPLE

Give each guest an apple and a paring knife. Each tries to pare his apple without breaking the peeling, and when this is accomplished, he throws the peeling over his left shoulder. The initial formed is that of the beloved. If the paring breaks, the person will have no beloved.

THE LUCKY CAKE

Place in a loaf cake batter the following articles: a wedding ring, a small chain, a dime, a ring with a stone in it, a safety pin, a heart, a button, and a thimble, each wrapped in waxed paper. When the cake is served, each person seeks his fortune in his slice. The symbols signify:

Wedding ring—the first wedding in the group.
Small chain—chained for life.
Dime—wealth.
Ring with stone—first engagement in the group.

Safety pin—a baby.
Heart—a love affair.
Button—bachelor, or old maid.
Thimble—old maid, or bachelor.

THE PROPHETIC PUMPKIN

Mark a large smooth pumpkin into squares. Make a symbol in each square, such as: anchor, sailor; wings, aviator; %, banker; $, money; pen, writer; etc. Each of these signifies a boy's future. If a girl is playing, it signifies her husband's future. The pumpkin is suspended by a string in an open space, and twirled rapidly. While it is moving, the player jabs it with a hatpin. The square in which the pin sticks reveals the player's fortune.

THE MAGIC MIRROR

The boys stand on the stair landing holding candles. There must be no other light. A cellar stairway is best, but any other may be used, providing the floor below is darkened. A girl, holding a mirror before her, shoulder high, goes slowly down the stairs backward. At the bottom, she will see the face of her lover in the mirror. If she sees nothing, she will be an old maid.

THE LUCKY NEEDLE

Place a milk bottle on its side on the floor. The player sits on the bottle, holds his feet off the floor, and threads a needle. If the player succeeds, he will be married; if not, he will be a bachelor, or (in the case of a girl) an old maid.

HIDDEN FATES

Hide a wedding ring, a heart, a thimble, a button, a safety pin, a dime, a penny, a needle, and a tack in the room, each wrapped in paper so that they cannot be identified until the parcel is opened. The players must seek their fates in the room, and bring what they find to the Witch, who will interpret the meaning of the articles. The meanings are:

Penny—poverty.
Needle—shrewish disposition.
Tack—a tacky person, inclined to be sloppy.

The other articles have the same meaning as in The Lucky Cake.

FORTUNE-TELLING BY NUMBERS

Provide cards numbered from 1 through 100. Prepare a list bearing these numbers, with a humorous fortune written after each. The guests draw the numbers. The Witch draws duplicate numbers from her cauldron, and asks, "Who has 12?" She reads the fortune from the list. And so on, until all have drawn.

Many Mouths.—This is a variation in which the players tell each other's fortune. Prepare cards as above. The Witch has the duplicate set, and the players each draw one from the original set. The Witch draws a number from her cauldron, and says, "Who is the most popular person here?" Then she reads the number. The person having it says, "I am." That person then asks a question beginning with, "Who is—." The Witch draws another number and calls it. The person having it answers, "I am," and asks the next question. And so on. The questions may be as amusing as desired.

THE MAGIC SQUARE

Prepare a large cardboard square to resemble a checker-board, and in each square write a number. List the numbers on a piece of paper (with a fortune after each) from which the Witch will read. The player is blindfolded, and then places his finger on a square. The Witch reads him the fortune written after that number.

OTHER FORTUNE-TELLING METHODS

Apple Seeds.—Fasten two apple seeds to a person's forehead, after the person has given the name of an acquaintance to each. The seed that falls indicates that that individual will be faithless.

Apple Heart.—Halve an apple and count its seeds. 1, Old maid or bachelor. 2, early marriage. 3, a legacy. 4, wealth. 5, a long voyage. 6, fame. 7, heart's desire.

Wedding Ring.—Tie a wedding ring or a key to a silk thread and suspend it inside a glass so that it is held as motionless as possible. Repeat the alphabet slowly. Each time the ring strikes the glass, it reveals one letter of the beloved's name. Start the alphabet again after each strike.

The old-fashioned method used a strand of the fortune-seeker's hair, instead of the silk thread.

True Love.—Throw two hazel nuts into a fire, naming each aloud. If one bursts, that lover will be unfaithful.

Love is Blind.—Write the alphabet in large letters on a cardboard, and pin it to the wall. The player is blindfolded, turned around once, and made to walk to the board and touch a letter; this is the initial of his or her future beloved.

The Magic Feather.—The players stand in a circle, and in rotation, each releases a feather in the center of the circle. It will float toward the beloved.

Feather-Light.—Have three feathers—one white, one black, and one gray. The player blows each. The one floating farthest reveals the complexion of the beloved.

Four Saucers.—Place four saucers on a table, each containing one of the following: a little dirt; a ring; a little water; a rag. The player, blindfolded, walks around the table to touch one saucer. The one he touches reveals his fortune. Dirt—divorce; ring—marriage; water—a voyage; rag—poverty.

Combing the Hair.—By candlelight, each girl combs her hair before a mirror. The face of her beloved will appear in the mirror.

Four Bowls.—Similar to Four Saucers. The bowls contain, respectively, water, milk, vinegar, nothing. These signify, water—a happy life; milk—wealth; vinegar—poverty; nothing—old maid or bachelor.

What the Cards Reveal.—Write the name of each player on a blank card, such as a visiting card. The cards are shuffled by the player. He then lays eleven cards face down before him. He repeats the following rhyme, facing one card at each line, to learn his fortune:

One I love,
Two I love,
  Three I love I say;
Four I love with all my heart,
  And five I cast away.
Six he loves,
Seven she loves,
  Eight he loves and tarries;
Nine he courts,
Ten he sports,
  Eleven woos and marries.

APPLES ON A SPOON

Place a large basketful of apples at one end of the room, and a similar empty basket at the other end. Give each player a tablespoon. Each, without using his hands, must pick up an apple and carry it to the empty basket. The player carrying the most apples wins. If an apple falls, the player may pick it up with his hands, but must return it to the original basket, and start that round again.

APPLES ON A STRING

Stretch a clothesline across the room. Suspend apples on strings from the line, having one apple for each player. With his hands clasped behind him, the player tries to eat his apple. If the apple falls, the player is eliminated. The one who most nearly finishes his apple within a stated time wins.

DUCKING FOR APPLES

Place a large round washtub, filled with water, on a table. Float several apples on the water. In rotation each player tries to secure an apple in his mouth. He may not touch the apple with his hands, but it may be pushed against the side of the tub.

Variation: Put the name of a boy on each apple for which the girls duck, and the name of a girl on each one for which the boys duck. The one secured will bear the name of the beloved.

SOULS

Provide one sheet of tissue paper, about eight by ten inches, for each guest. Place on a table a platter or a tin pie pan. The Leader announces that this test is to determine whether or not the player's soul is going to heaven. The Leader makes a bag of a piece of the paper, by folding it in half the long way, then making a narrow fold along the long edge, and a similar fold across one narrow edge. Thus it is closed on three sides. The player breathes into the open end. The bag is then balanced on the platter on its open end. The player sets fire to the top corners at approximately the same time. While the bag burns, the players croon softly:

Heaven or hell, heaven or hell,
All is well, heaven or hell.
All is ill, heaven or hell,
Ill or well, heaven or hell.

When the bag is almost an ash, if it rises and floats through the air, the soul will go to heaven; if the bag fails to rise, the soul will not go to heaven.

EASTER GAMES

EASTER EGG ROLL

This is the only game that belongs entirely to Easter, and that is usually played only at that time. A smooth lawn, preferably with a downward slope, is the best place for an egg roll. But the game can be played indoors in a large room. Hardboiled eggs, or candy eggs of approximately the same size, are used.

Each player is provided with a basket and from two to six eggs. There are two ways of playing egg roll. The first is to roll the eggs down the lawn in an effort to strike another player's egg. The player whose egg strikes another one wins the second egg. The object is to strike and win as many eggs as possible. In the second method of play, the eggs are rolled for distance. In this case, the players stand behind a starting line, and endeavor to roll their eggs as far as possible. The one who rolls his farthest wins.

EASTER EGG HUNT

Quite as popular as Easter Egg Roll is an Easter Egg Hunt. The eggs are well hidden in advance by the hostess in the house or on the grounds. A prize is given for the largest number of eggs found; and there may be other prizes. The eggs belong to the players finding them.

XII. FORFEITS

The payment of forfeits affords amusement to young and old alike. If properly directed, this part of the party can be made the most exciting part of the evening. A number of games demand the payment of forfeits, and this feature can be added to other games.

FORFEITS

In general, the forfeits are all redeemed at one time, after the other events are ended.

A forfeit is any small object owned by the player: a handkerchief, a pin, a ring, an earring, a penknife, and so on. The Leader collects these at the time they are forfeited, and keeps them all together until the time for redeeming them.

When the time for redeeming arrives, a Judge is chosen from among the players who have forfeited nothing. He is given two prepared lists of forfeit stunts, one for girls and one for boys. He sits in a chair at one end of the room, with the forfeits and the Leader behind him where he cannot see either. The Leader selects a forfeit, and holds it over the Judge's head. He says, "Heavy, heavy hangs over your head."

The Judge asks, "Fine or superfine?"

The Leader replies, "Superfine," if the article belongs to a girl; "Fine," if it belongs to a boy. He continues, "What shall the owner do to redeem it?"

The Judge says, "Let the culprit—," and then announces the penalty required to redeem the object.

The person then pays the penalty, and redeems his forfeit.

Forfeits should be stunts which turn the laugh on the person doing them. Frequently, a clever person is able to turn the laugh on the Judge. Here is a list of popular forfeits:

1. Put one hand where the other can't touch it. (Hold one elbow with the other hand.)

2. Say six nice things about yourself.

3. Say "What am I doing?" thirteen times without taking a breath. At the end, the Judge says, "Making a fool of yourself."

4. Scramble like an egg. (The player goes to the center of the floor and tries to scramble like an egg.)

5. Kiss a book inside and outside without opening it. (Kiss it inside the room, then outside the room.)

6. Place three chairs in a row, remove your shoes, and do a standing high jump over them. (The "them" refers to the shoes, not to the chairs.)

7. "This pillow is your baby; rock it to sleep." The Victim croons a lullaby and rocks the pillow in his arms.

8. Tell the truth for two minutes, answering truthfully all questions put to you by Judge or players.

9. Smile, frown, laugh, weep, in that order, all in half a minute.

10. Say "mixed biscuits" rapidly ten times.

11. Lie on the floor, with a dime placed horizontally on your nose. Wriggle it off by moving only your nose.

12. Walk around the room, holding one ankle in your hand.

13. (Paying eight forfeits at once) Take the kings and queens from a deck of cards. Line up four boys and four girls, giving each boy a king, and each girl a queen. They must match suits and kiss.

14. Wrestle with Temptation. Similar to Scrambling like an egg.

15. Give a solo wrestling match.

16. Yawn until you make someone else yawn.

17. Give a sanitary kiss to three girls. (The Leader escorts the Victim. The Leader kisses the girls, and each time wipes the Victim's lips with a handkerchief.)

18. Tell why you like cheese and marriage.

19. Telephone to your sweetheart, using a chair for the telephone.

20. (For a girl.) Kiss Harry where Harry isn't. (Kiss the boy's shadow on the wall.)

21. Leave the room with two legs and come back with six. (Bring back a chair or a small table.)

22. Imitate a donkey. Bray; or imitate the Judge. The latter will turn the laugh on the player when he says, "Very natural."

23. Say the alphabet backward. (Turn your back on the Judge and start with "A.")

24. Confess your worst fault. If the Judge is not satisfied, it must be repeated.

25. Smile five ways; or, Laugh five ways; or, Snore five ways.

26. Transfer a book from hand to hand, with both arms extended at the two sides, without bending the arms at elbow or shoulder. (Slide the book off on a table, and slide the other hand under it.)

27. Put yourself through a keyhole; or, through a ring. (Write "yourself" on a slip of paper and pass it through the keyhole or ring.)

28. Give an imitation of one of these:

A person posing for a photograph.
Paderewski playing the piano.
A country boy proposing.
Rip Van Winkle waking up.
A Communist soapbox orator.
A drugstore cowboy as a girl passes.
A Salvation Army street-corner Captain.
A traffic cop at a busy corner.
A hick farmer on Broadway.
A small boy stung by a bee.
An efficient stenographer.
A girl seeing a mouse.

29. (For a boy.) Give Helen a camel ride. (Boy, on hands and knees, moves around the room, with the girl on his back.) Variation: Each boy kisses her as she passes.

30. Sit on the fire, or, Sit on a lighted candle. (Write "the fire" or "a lighted candle" on a slip of paper and sit on it.)

31. Ask a question which must be answered by "Yes." (The simplest question: "What does Y- E- S spell?")

32. Bite an inch off a poker; or, Bite an inch off a table knife. (Hold the poker or knife an inch from the mouth, and make a bite—an inch "off" or away from the object.)

33. Recite, or sing to the tune of *America,* the national anthem of Siam. First say, very slowly, syllable by syllable, "Oh, whah, tah, nah, si, am." Then repeat faster and faster, until it is "Oh, what an ass I am!" The Judge says, "We won't hold it against you."

34. (For two Victims.) Feed each other a saucer of icecream with two teaspoons, tied together with a six inch string.

35. Pick up a dime with your lips, without using your hands, when it is hidden in a saucer of flour. This is called the White Volcano.

36. Hobson's Choice. The Leader burns one end of a match; and blindfolds the Victim. Holding the match parallel to the Victim's shoulders, the Leader asks, "Which end will you have, left or right?" He asks the question three times, altering the

position of the match if he chooses. Each time he rubs the selected end first on the Victim's forehead; then on his nose; then on his chin.

37. Kiss your own shadow. (Kiss your shadow on the wall. A clever boy will kiss his shadow when it falls on a girl's face.)

38. Go upstairs with a girl and bring her down on a feather. (There is down on every feather.)

39. Go to market with a girl or boy, depending upon the sex of the Victim. The two stand eight feet apart. The Victim asks the other player if he likes chocolate, or a similar thing. If the answer is "Yes," the player takes a step toward the Victim; if "No," a step away. Then the player asks a similar question. The Victim steps forward at "Yes," backward at "No." They usually end by meeting and kissing.

40. Blow out a candle, while blindfolded. The Victim is shown the location of the candle; is then blindfolded, and turned around several times. He may not feel his way. He usually blows at everything but the candle.

41. Poke your head through a ring. (Hold the ring near your head, stick a finger through, and poke your head with your finger.)

42. Make love to yourself, propose to yourself, accept yourself.

43. Spin the Victim around vigorously, while he holds a dime over his own head. When the spinning stops, he must drop the dime and pick it up at once.

44. Act contrary. The Victim must do the reverse of five things the players tell him to do.

45. Make a speech telling how wonderful you are. The Judge may demand that this be done over, if he is not pleased.

46. Kiss the lady you love best, without letting even her know. (Kiss every girl in the room.)

47. Say "I am a donkey" four times, emphasizing a different word each time. The Judge will comment, "We agree."

48. Standing on a chair, make a one-minute speech on any subject selected by the Judge or the Leader.

49. Sing *America,* omitting every second word.

50. Laugh up an octave, then down it, without an error, in one breath

51. Kiss a candlestick. (Ask a girl to hold a candle, then kiss her. She has become the candlestick.)

52. Kneel to the prettiest, bow to the wittiest, and kiss the one you love best. (The Victim may do the opposite, if he chooses; that is, kneel to the homeliest, etc.)

53. Shake a dime off your forehead. The Leader dampens the dime and presses it firmly against the Victim's forehead, then removes it. The Victim shakes vigorously before he realizes the dime is not there.

54. Pat your stomach with one hand, while you rub your head with the other. Reverse, when told to do so.

55. (For two players.) Stand on a newspaper so that you can't touch each other. The newspaper may not be separated. (Place it over a door lintel, and close the door between the two players.)

56. Eat a moving lunch. Suspend an apple or a doughnut so that it just reaches the Victim's lips. He must eat it without using anything but his mouth.

57. Take a journey to Rome. The Victim announces that he is going to Rome to do penance, and wants a gift for the Pope. Each player gives him some unwieldy object. He must cross the room, without dropping anything, and deposit his burden in a corner.

58. Recite "Mary had a little lamb" or any familiar poem, counting from one up after each word. Thus: Mary 1 had 2 a 3 little 4 lamb 5, Its 6 fleece 7 was 8 white 9 as 10, and so on.

59. Place a pencil on the floor so that no one can jump over it. (Lean it against a wall.)

60. (For two players.) Shake hands blindfolded. The two Victims are blindfolded, and placed at opposite ends of the room. They must walk toward each other, meet, and shake hands.

61. Make a salestalk to a pretty girl (or, to a handsome man) about a cornplaster.

62. Sing a medley of one line each from five different songs, without pausing.

BOOK FOUR

OUTDOOR GAMES

I. THE BASEBALL GROUP

THE American game of Baseball, the English game of Cricket and many lesser games in the same group, originate from ancient playing devices, now found chiefly in games primarily for children: bases or goals; hitting a player with a ball; and tagging. The ancient game of Pussy Wants a Corner had the bases, and an Out-player who sought to steal one when the others interchanged bases. This developed into Four Corners, in which the Out-player tossed a small soft ball at one of the other players. He struck at it with his open hand; and, whether he hit it or not, each player immediately had to run to the next base. The Out-player picked up the ball as swiftly as possible, and sought to hit a runner with it before he reached his base: if hit, this put that player Out, and the former Out-player was allowed to occupy his base. Hitting a player with a thrown ball is a form of missile tag found in many simple games.

A century ago, English boys played a variation of this called Feeder, with several bases in a circular course; and, at times, the batsman used a small club. At about the time of the American Revolution, American boys played a game similar to One Old Cat, tagging the runner by touching him with a soft ball, or throwing and hitting him with it. This developed into Rotation, with three, four or five bases. In 1839, Abner Doubleday of Cooperstown, N. Y., devised the game we call Baseball. In 1845, President Curry of the Knickerbocker Club of New York assisted in drafting the first published rules of the game, and its Baseball club was the first recorded organization of Baseball players in the world. In the '70s, the ball was made so hard that hitting a player to tag him was dropped. Hitherto the pitcher had only been permitted to toss the ball to the batter; after 1875, throwing was allowed. This brought in the necessity for gloves, masks, and breast and other protectors, and the pitcher's box was moved further back. In 1887, George W. Hancock of the Farragut Boat Club of Chicago invented Indoor Baseball. In 1927, Playground Baseball or Softball was standardized. There are countless minor variations.

Cricket apparently originated from an ancient 12th century game called Stool Ball, in which one In-player stood by a three-legged stool, which he tried to protect while the other players threw a ball at it. The In-player scored 1, every time he hit the ball with his hand; an Out-player went In in place of the In-player, whenever he hit the stool or caught a hit ball. By 1593, the game was called Krikett, named from the Old French word for the game stake in the game of Bowls. Later, the In-player used a bat; and still later, the stool was replaced by a crude wicket. As early as the 17th century, the game was played by formally constituted teams.

The ball must meet the specifications as required in the Official Playing Rules. The bat must be round, not over 2¾ inches in diameter at the thickest part, nor more than 42 inches in length, and entirely of hardwood. Except for catcher's and 1st baseman's glove or mitt, all other gloves are regulated in weight and size.

BASEBALL

TEAMS: Two teams of nine men each. When fielding, these men are called Pitcher, Catcher, First Baseman, Second Baseman, Shortstop, Third Baseman, Right Fielder, Center Fielder, Left Fielder. When at bat, each member of the team in planned rotation becomes the Batsman or Batter.

THE FIELD: The field should be level, and 325 feet square; often it is smaller. A 90-foot square is marked out near one end of the field; this is called the diamond. At first base and third base the lines forming the diamond are continued to the outfield to indicate fair and foul territory. At the corner of the diamond nearest the end of the field the home plate is placed: a slab of wood or rubber set flush with the top of the ground, of the dimensions

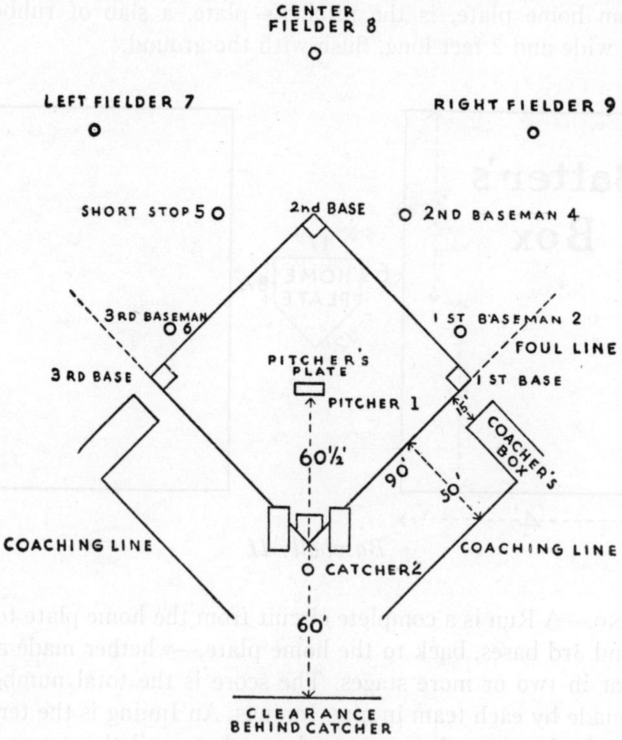

Baseball: I

shown in the second diagram. There should be no obstruction within 60 ft. of the corner of the diamond in which home plate is located. On each side of home plate is a batting box, for right-handed and left-handed batters.

On playgrounds and open fields it is often necessary to place a backstop behind the catcher in order that spectators and passersby be protected. This is usually a wide frame covered with wire netting. If the backstop is less than 60 ft. from home plate a ground rule will be necessary.

The other corners of the diamond, proceeding counter-clockwise from the home plate, are 1st, 2nd, and 3rd bases. In each of these corners is a canvas bag 15 inches square and at least 3 inches thick, filled with soft material, and fastened by an iron stake entirely underground. In the middle of the diamond, 60½ ft. from home plate, is the pitcher's plate, a slab of rubber 6 inches wide and 2 feet long, flush with the ground.

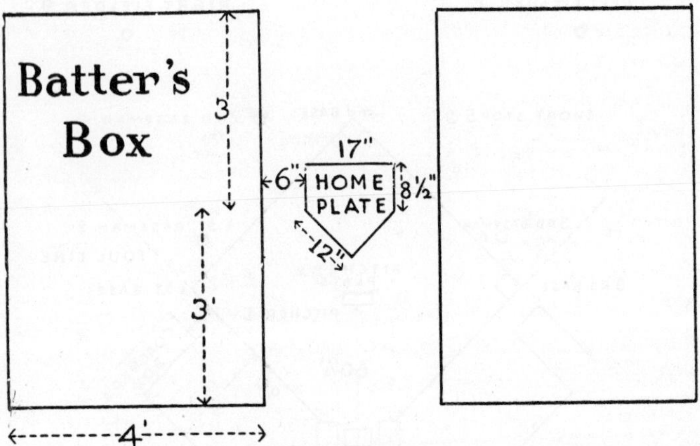

Baseball: II

Scoring.—A Run is a complete circuit from the home plate to 1st, 2nd and 3rd bases, back to the home plate,—whether made all at once or in two or more stages. The score is the total number of runs made by each team in nine Innings. An Inning is the term at bat for both teams. A team remains at bat until three men have been put out in its half of the inning. If the score at the end of nine innings is a tie, the game continues until one team makes a larger score in an extra inning, in which both teams have had their turn at bat. When weather or any cause stops the game before nine innings are played, the score at the end of the last completed inning is the final score, provided that at least five full innings have been played; but if the team last at bat has scored more runs in an unequal number of innings, then the total number of runs made by both teams shall determine the score.

The Batsman.—The batsman stands within his box, and bats at balls thrown to him by the pitcher. If he hits a ball to fair ground, he must run to 1st base before the ball is fielded there to avoid being put out. The Umpire declares a pitch a Strike, if the batsman strikes at it and misses it, or if the ball passes over home plate at a height between the batsman's shoulder and his knee. When three strikes are called, the batsman is out, provided the catcher holds the ball on the third strike and does not permit it to fall to the ground. If the catcher misses the third strike, the batsman may run to 1st base; and he is safe if he reaches there before he is touched with the ball in an opponent's hand, or before the ball is held by an opponent touching the base. However, if a runner is on first base and there are less than 2 out, the batsman is out whether the catcher holds or misses the third strike. If a pitched ball does not pass within the area of a strike, the Umpire declares it a Ball. Four balls entitle the batsman to go to 1st base. If the batsman is hit by a pitched ball, he is entitled to 1st base. If the pitcher makes a movement as if to throw the ball to the batter and then does not do so, this is called a Balk, and all runners on bases are advanced on base; but the batter is not affected.

Fair Hits and Fouls.—If the batter hits a pitched ball so that it settles on fair ground within the diamond, or that is over fair ground when it bounds from the diamond to the outfield, or that flies to the outfield and falls on fair ground, the Umpire declares it a Fair Hit, and the batter at once becomes a base runner. If a batted ball is caught by an opponent before it touches the ground, the batter is out. If it strikes the ground and is fielded to 1st base before the batter arrives there, he is out. He may also be tagged out before reaching 1st base. An infield fly also puts the batter out. An infield fly is a fair fly ball that can be handled by an infielder, provided 1st and 2nd bases, or all 3 bases, are occupied; and that 2 men are not already out. The umpire shall declare the hit ball an infield fly. Runners may advance as on any fly ball, at the risk of being thrown out. An attempt to bunt in the same circumstances is not to be called an infield fly, if the ball rises in the air instead of falling direct to the ground.

Any ball hit outside the limits of fair territory is a Foul Ball. Fouls that hit the ground before being fielded count as strikes until there are two strikes on the batter; thereafter no such foul counts as a strike. The batter is always out if a foul fly is caught by a fielder. If a ball strikes in and rolls out before reaching 1st or 3rd base, it is a foul; if it strikes out and rolls in, it is fair.

An entire circuit of the bases on one hit is called a Home Run. A hit which is made by the batter holding his bat so that the ball strikes it and falls directly to the ground, is called a Bunt.

Base Runners.—At any time the ball is in play a runner on any base may attempt to steal the next base but he is out if tagged before reaching that base or getting back to the base he had left. If a batter hits fair, a runner on 1st base must go to 2nd to make room for the batter at 1st. This is called a Force Play. In such cases any runner forced to advance is out if the ball is fielded to the base before he reaches it.

When a batted ball is caught before it touches the ground, a runner who is advancing must return to the base he occupied. If the ball is fielded to the base before the runner can get back, he is out. In all other cases, a base runner must be tagged with the ball to be put out. A runner is permitted to advance to the next base when the umpire calls a balk; when a fielder interferes with the runner; or where the batter is given 1st base, as on four balls or for being hit by a pitched ball. If a ball is hit foul and not caught, all runners must return to the bases they occupied, without liability of being put out.

The Pitcher.—The ball must meet the specifications as required in *Official Playing Rules*. The catcher, when the pitcher delivers the ball to the batsman, must stand in his assigned position within a triangle formed by continuations of the foul lines and extending 10 feet back of the corner of home plate. Except for catcher's and 1st baseman's glove or mitt, all other gloves are regulated in weight and size. When pitching to the batsman, the pitcher must keep both feet on the ground; at least one foot must be kept in contact with the pitcher's plate; neither foot may be back of pitcher's plate; and he may not take more than one step during delivery. With a runner on 1st or 2nd base, the pitcher must face the batsman with both hands holding the ball in front of him. He is never allowed to apply a foreign substance to the ball; spit on it or on his glove; rub the ball on his glove, body or clothing; deface it in any way; but he may dry his hands on an official sealed bag containing powdered rosin. Any ball unfairly delivered to the batsman is called a ball by the umpire. The pitcher may not delay the game by throwing to basemen, except in attempts to retire runners. If this is repeated after warning from the umpire, the pitcher must be removed from the game. For any delay longer than 20 seconds in delivering the ball to the batsman, the umpire calls one ball on the pitcher. There are 12 varieties of balks, and each advances the base runner or runners one base.

Scoring Record.—Each individual batter's record is kept, on this sort of scoring record:

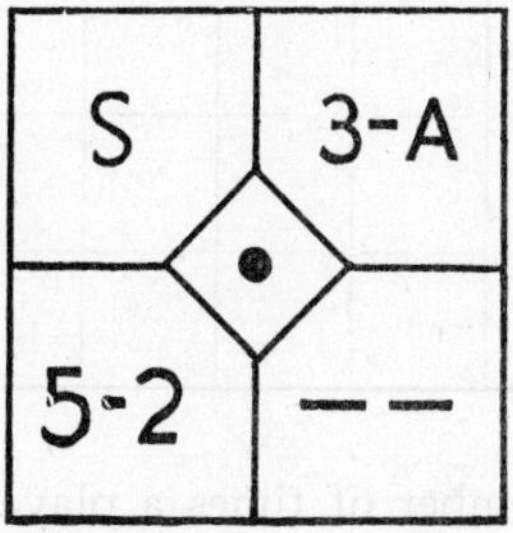

Baseball: III

The symbols used are:

——	Single—1 base hit	H	Hit by Pitcher
†—	Double—2-bagger	W	Wild Pitch
††—	Triple—3-bagger	P	Passed Ball
†††—	Home Run	.	Run
K	Strikeout	FC	Fielder's Choice
S	Stolen Base	E	Error
B	Base on Balls	BK	Balk
A	Assist		

The diagram above tells whether the batter reached 1st base, and how, in the lower right hand space; 2nd base, in the space above this; 3rd base, in the upper left hand space; home, in the lower left hand space; the center space being reserved for a period (.), when the runner scores a run. In the diagram filled in above, the batter reaches 1st base on a single; reached 2nd when the 1st baseman (3) assisted (A) in putting out a batter; stole 3rd base; and reached home on an out of the shortstop (5) to the catcher (2). The dot in the center of the diamond indicates one run. When a runner is put out, a number, 1, 2 or 3, is placed inside the diamond, indicating whether he was the first, second or third player put out in that inning.

The Box Score is the summary, often printed in the newspapers as the final tabulation of the game. After each player's name, listed in the batting order, determined by the manager or captain, the record as follows:

Player	AB	R	H	SH	SB	PO	A	E

AB—At Bat. The number of times a player came to bat; omitting the times he was given a base on balls, hit by a pitched ball, or made a sacrifice hit.

R—Runs. The runner is required to touch all the bases legally, home plate last, before three men of his side are out.

H—Hits. A safe hit is a fair hit ball not caught by an opponent before it touches the ground, or one which does not cause the runner to be put out at 1st base, or cause a base runner to be forced out; provided that the fielder does not make an error that permits a runner to reach base safely. When a batted ball hits the umpire or a base runner on fair ground before being touched by fielder, it is scored as a hit.

SH—Sacrifice Hits. A sacrifice hit is made when the batter bunts and usually is put out in an effort to advance a runner or runners.

SB—Stolen Bases. A stolen base is credited when a runner advances a base without the aid of a batter or the error of an opponent.

PO—Put Out. A put out is credited to the opponent who completes the play putting out a batter or runner.

A—Assist. An assist is credited to each fielder who handles the ball as part of the process of putting out an opponent.

E—Error. An error is charged against a fielder who makes a misplay that enables a runner to advance, or that prolongs the time at bat of a batsman.

The percentage for games played is ascertained by dividing the number of games won by the total number of games played. This also applies when computing pitchers' percentage of games won and lost. Batting averages are determined by dividing the total number of hits by the total number of times at bat. Fielding averages are arrived at by dividing the total number of put outs and assists by the combined number of fielding chances: put outs, assists, and errors.

In regulation games, there are two umpires and a scorer. At times, only one umpire is used. When two are used, one stands behind the catcher and calls the balls and strikes; decides whether a hit is fair or foul; whether a batter is out or not; whether a runner has reached home safely or not. The other umpire, located on the diamond, decides whether runners are safe or out, on all bases except the home plate.

SOFTBALL, PLAYGROUNDBALL, RECREATION BALL

Softball is coming into increasing popularity as a game for amateurs, and is suitable for both sexes. It differs from regular Baseball in the following particulars:

Size of Diamond: From base to base, 60 feet. Pitching distance, 37 feet 8½ inches, or 40 feet. At times, the baseline distance is only 45 feet, the pitching distance as above. Where the baseline is only 35 feet, the pitching distance should be 30 feet; where it is 27 feet, the pitching distance should be 24 feet.

EQUIPMENT: For the 60-foot diamond, a 12-inch softball; for the 45-foot diamond, a 12- or 13-inch softball; and for the 27-foot diamond, where men play, a 14-inch softball. The tendency is toward requiring an inseam ball, rather than an outseam one. Official softball bats are shorter and not as thick as regulation baseball bats. Spiked shoes are prohibited.

THE GAME.—The game consists of seven innings. Where a game is called, five innings must have been completed, or the game does not count.

PITCHING.—The pitcher must come to rest, with both feet on the pitcher's plate, facing the batter. An underhand pitch is required, the arm passing parallel to the body with the ball not more than 6 inches from the body. The ball must be thrown with a full arm swing, following through with the arm parallel to the body, and the hand below the hip as it passes the body. A snap or jerky release of the ball at the hip is forbidden; a final wrist motion is allowed. While pitching, the pitcher may take one step. One foot must be kept on the plate until the ball is released. After this, the pitcher may advance. A quick return pitch is forbidden. An illegal pitch is called a ball, unless it is struck at; in which case it is regarded as legal. No balks are called, unless there are runners on the bases and a pitcher while pitching drops the ball intentionally or otherwise; such a throw is called a ball, and runners may not advance.

THE BATTER.—Bunting is forbidden; and a batter attempting a bunt is out. A bunt is a ball not swung at, but met with the bat, or tapped slowly within the infield. A pitched ball which hits a batter while in his box is a dead ball; unless the batter strikes at it, or intentionally allows it to hit him. It is called a ball; and the batter does not take his base on it, unless it is a fourth ball, nor may a runner advance. After three strikes, the batter is out, and may not run to 1st base. A batter is out on a foul only if it is a foul fly, rising higher than his head, and caught by an opponent.

The infield fly rule is the same as Baseball: a batter is out and no runner may advance, nor can a play be made on a base runner, if the batter hits a fly to the infield before two are out, with 1st and 2nd base, or 1st, 2nd and 3rd bases occupied.

STEALING BASES.—Stealing bases is forbidden while the pitcher is in proper position to pitch, and before the pitched ball has reached or passed the batter. A runner taking his foot from the base before this has occurred is out.

OVERTHROWS.—In case of an overthrow at 1st or 3rd base or the home plate, if the ball strikes an obstruction or a spectator, the runner is given one base. If it does not strike such an obstruction, the runner is entitled to advance to the base to which he is running and one additional base, if he can make it. The advance of the runner is determined by the base which he occupied when the pitch started.

TEAMS.—There are ten men on a team, not nine, the tenth being a roamer, called a short fielder, usually playing behind second base. Except for the pitcher, the players may be stationed anywhere on the diamond that is deemed most advantageous.

Indoor Baseball.—Indoor Baseball is Softball played indoors. The size of the diamond is regulated by the floor space; and the pitching distance is regulated according to the baseline length, as described in Softball. Otherwise, the game is the same.

MINOR BASEBALL TYPE GAMES

ONE OLD CAT

This game is played with only one base beside the home plate, this being placed where 1st base appears in Baseball. There is only one batter. The other players are, in seniority, catcher, pitcher, 1st fielder, 2nd fielder, and so on. The batter is out when he strikes three times; or when a pitched ball is struck at and caught by the catcher on the fly or first bounce; or when a foul or fly is caught. When a hit is made, the runner must run to 1st base and back to home before the ball is returned to the catcher, who must touch home to put the runner out.

When a batter is put out, the other players move up in rotation in the order of seniority, the catcher becoming the batter, and the former batter the last fielder. A player catching a fly exchanges places with the batter.

TWO OLD CAT

With enough players, two batters are used. In this case, a batter making a hit and reaching 1st base safely may remain there until the other batter hits, when he must return to home.

THREE OLD CAT

In this variation, with enough players three batters are used, and all the bases, as in Baseball.

ROTATION, SCRUB, WORK UP, ROUNDERS

Either Baseball or Softball equipment may be used. There are one, two or three batters. The rules of Baseball apply. When a batter is put out, the players move up in rotation, from lowest to highest being Right Fielder, Center Fielder, Left Fielder, Shortstop, 3rd Baseman, 2nd Baseman, 1st Baseman, Pitcher, Catcher. When a fly ball is caught, the catcher of it exchanges places with the batter. When all the batters are on base and there is none at bat, the runner nearest home must reach home before the ball is thrown there; otherwise he is out. The object of the game is to stay in bat as long as possible. In England, it is played with a tennis ball and a cricket stump, other stumps marking the bases.

THREE GROUNDERS OR A FLY

Either Baseball or Softball equipment is used. One player is selected as the batter; the others are fielders, stationed wherever they please. The batter tosses the ball up and bats it out; the fielders try to field it. The fielder who catches one fly or three grounders—balls that strike the ground and bounce or roll—becomes the batter, and the batter becomes in turn a fielder. Once a ball has been touched by a fielder, no other fielder can score it. When each new batter comes to bat, the fielders lose all part scores already made.

HOT RICE

This game is the same as Three Grounders or a Fly, except that, when a ball is caught off the ground, the fielder, without moving a step, throws it at the batter. The batter must keep one foot on home base, and may avoid the ball by dodging or hitting it away with the bat. If he is hit by the ball, the player who hit him becomes the batter, and the batter a fielder.

CROSS-OUT BASEBALL

This is a variation of Softball, with one additional method of retiring a runner: throwing the ball across his path ahead of him. Otherwise, the same as Softball.

DONKEY BASEBALL

This hilarious variation of Softball originated in the Southwest States, where burros and donkeys are plentiful; but it has spread to all amusement centers of the United States. The game might be described as Baseball on donkeyback. Since donkeys are stubborn and move rapidly only when the notion strikes them, a potential home run may be hit and the player never reach first base; or an unfielded infield hit may be stretched into a home run.

The game is played on a Softball diamond, with 1st, 2nd and 3rd bases designated by circles about 6 feet in diameter. Softball equipment is used. The pitcher and catcher have no donkeys, but they are not allowed to leave their boxes to field a ball. The batter bats on foot, an attendant across the home plate holding his steed ready for him. There are no balls and strikes; the batter stays at bat until he gets a fair hit. He then mounts, and starts to ride to 1st base.

When a ball is hit, a mounted player must field it, and throw it to the pitcher, who throws it for the out. A fielder or baseman must ride to the ball, and may then dismount to pick it up, but must remount before throwing it. If a baseman dismounts and makes a fair catch, it does not count, and the runner may keep going. When there are two or more runners on bases, a fielder may use fielder's choice in throwing directly for an out. In all other cases, he must throw first to the pitcher, who throws for the out.

Human Donkey Baseball.—This variation of Donkey Baseball has each fielder mounted on a player who acts as his steed. Even the batter, pitcher and catcher may be so mounted. The players who are the donkeys are not permitted to field the balls. Otherwise, the game is played in the same way as regular Donkey Baseball.

PEGGING FIRST

This simplification of Baseball or Softball is played with the equipment of one or the other. One team is at bat, and the other in the field. The batter attempts to hit the pitched ball, and run to the one base, placed where 1st base is in Baseball. If he succeeds, he scores 1 for his side. If he is put out before reaching 1st base, the fielding side scores 1 point. The players of the batting side bat in order, until all have had one turn at bat. Then the teams reverse their positions, and the fielding team goes to bat. The team wins which scores the most points, at the conclusion of a number of innings agreed upon in advance.

BEATBALL

This game is played on a Softball diamond, a volley ball or sport ball being used. The batter does not bat the ball, but throws it into the field. He then runs the bases in regular order, keeping going until he reaches home, or is put out. Whichever fielder gets the ball, throws it to 1st base; the 1st baseman throws it to 2nd, the 2nd baseman to 3rd, and the 3rd baseman home. If the runner reaches home before the ball does, he scores 1 point for his team; otherwise he is out.

Interesting variations of this game require the batter to stand sideways and throw the ball behind his back; or to face backward and throw it between his legs; or to raise one leg and throw the ball under it; and so on.

Hand Beatball.—In this variation of Beatball, the pitcher pitches the ball, and the batter bats it with his open hand. Otherwise, the game is the same as regular Beatball.

Bowl Beatball.—In this variation of Beatball, the pitcher rolls the ball to the batter, who kicks it instead of throwing or batting it. Otherwise, the game is the same as regular Beatball.

BASEBALL TWENTY-ONE

This game is played on a regular Softball diamond. It differs from Softball chiefly in the way in which it is scored. The batter hits the ball as in Softball, and runs the bases as in Softball until he is put out. If he is put out at 1st base, he scores nothing; if he is put out at 2nd base, he scores 1 for reaching 1st; if at 3rd, he scores 2; if at home, he scores 3; if he makes a home run, he scores 4. After three outs, the team at bat changes positions with the fielding team. The first team reaching 21 points wins.

TOMBALL

Tomball is played like Softball, with the following two exceptions. There are no foul balls, and a batter becomes a base runner the moment his bat touches the ball, no matter where it goes; so the fielders must be stationed so as to cover all balls touched. In addition to the Softball methods of retiring a runner, he is retired if a ball is caught on first bounce; if it is held on any base ahead of him; or if it is thrown on his path between bases, as in Cross-out Baseball.

TOWNBALL

Townball is a variation of Baseball or Softball, using the equipment of either, in which all fielders except pitcher and catcher occupy any position they please; a batter is out on three strikes or a strike caught by the catcher; a runner is out on a caught fly or on a ball thrown across his path from base to base; and a team remains at bat until all its members have been put out. When only one batter is left and he scores three runs, he may call in to bat any member of his team that he chooses.

LINEBALL

The playing field consists of two parallel lines 45 feet apart. Each team lines up behind its line, equipped with a bat. The end player of one team bats the ball across the field, bouncing it no higher than the heads of the other team. If he bats it across the opponent's line, his team scores 1 point. Then the end player of the opponent's team bats the ball back similarly. The play continues until each player has batted once; the team with the highest point score wins.

SPEEDBALL BASEBALL

Speedball Baseball, introduced by the Department of Physical Education of Maryland, combines Baseball and Softball. The object is to complete five innings in a short time. Only four batters may face the pitcher in any inning. The inning ends when three players are out, or when the fourth batter makes a run, a forced out, or is put out by the ball reaching a base ahead of him. Unless he is put out at 1st base, runs driven in by the fourth batter score.

Bases may be stolen, as soon as the pitcher begins to move his arm to pitch. Base runners may steal home, even on a throw from catcher to pitcher. Balks are called, as in Baseball. Bunting is permitted. If the bases are empty, a runner may run first to either 1st or 3rd base. When a player is given a base on balls by the umpire, this does not count as a player at bat. In all other respects, the Softball rules apply.

HITBALL

This variation follows the rules of Speedball Baseball, except that an inflated ball 19½ inches in circumference, or a soccer ball, is used. This is batted with the hand. The game is usually played on a 45-foot Softball diamond.

HAND BASEBALL

This is played on a Baseball diamond whose baseline distance is 35 feet or less. The distance from the pitcher's plate to the home plate is 15 feet. Instead of a baseball or softball, a basketball, soccer or sport ball is usually used. The players are divided into teams, as in Baseball. The pitcher must pitch with an underhand motion; the batter strikes with his fist or open hand. The runner may be put out with a thrown ball which hits him; stealing bases and bunting are not allowed. Otherwise, the rules of Baseball apply.

Bounce Hand Baseball.—A small soft rubber ball is used. The pitcher stands 25 feet away from the home plate, and throws the ball overhand, so that it bounces once and passes the batter at striking height, between the shoulders and knees. The batter bats with his hand. There is no catcher, the batter catching and returning any ball he does not try to hit. One strike or two fouls put the batter out.

In one variation, the pitcher stands about 6 feet one side of the batter and tosses the ball so that the batter can hit it, making no effort to strike him out.

BASEBALL PUNCH BALL

This variation of Softball is popular, especially among girls. The diamond is 35 feet from base to base. There is no pitcher's box, and home plate is 3 feet wide. The catcher of the fielding team, standing 6 feet to one side of the batter, tosses the ball to him. The batter hits the ball into the field with his fist, and runs bases as in Baseball. A runner is out if the catcher, holding the ball, touches home base before the runner reaches 1st base; or if he steps off base and the catcher, holding the ball, touches home plate and calls out the runner's name; or if a fly ball, (fair or foul) hit by him is caught. Runners are thus put out only on a caught fly or by the catcher at home base, no matter which base the runner is on. In all other respects, the rules for Softball govern.

KICK BASEBALL

The diamond for Kick Baseball is 40 feet from base to base; the pitcher stands 30 feet from the home plate. A soccer ball, codeball or sport ball is used. The pitcher rolls the ball to the batter, who kicks it out instead of batting it. The kicker stands directly behind the home plate. A ball is good and may be called a strike if it passes directly over the home plate, not higher than the kicker's knee. A pitched ball which hits the kicker above the knee is a dead ball, counted as a ball unless the kicker makes no effort to avoid it, in which case it is a strike. A base runner may not advance on such a ball. When boys play, a runner may be put out by being hit with a thrown ball.

SOCCER BASEBALL

A 45-foot Softball diamond is used for Soccer Baseball. The 2nd base is placed 3 feet closer to home than its regular position on the diamond. Instead of 1st and 3rd bases, a marker is placed 25 feet from the home plate on the line leading to 1st base and to 3rd, and these markers are connected with a line, termed the foul line. A soccer ball is generally used, but a sport ball or codeball may also be used. Team division and length of game are the same as in Baseball.

The kicker, corresponding to the batter in Baseball, holds and kicks out the ball, which is not pitched. He may punt, drop-kick or place kick it, from the home base or either side of it, but he is not allowed to step in front of the home base until the ball is kicked. The ball must cross the foul line, to be a fair kick. After kicking, the runner runs to the one base, and then back to the home base. A fair ball must go beyond the foul lines and inside the boundary lines (1st and 3rd baselines) until it passes 1st or 3rd base. It is a foul when a fielder holds or trips a runner; enters the foul zone before or after a kick, except to retrieve a ball; plays in foul territory before a kick; or takes more than two steps while holding the ball. For each foul, one run is scored for the other team. In all fouls favoring the runner, he must complete his run.

If a slow kick, untouched by a fielder, comes to rest in the foul zone, it is a foul; if it rolls into fair territory, a fair kick. A runner commits a foul when he runs into a fielder, runs outside the 45-foot diamond, or intentionally kicks the ball after he has become a runner. For any of these fouls, the runner is out. When two fouls occur in succession, the first takes precedence. The kicker is out if he kicks two fouls. The runner is out if a ball kicked by him, fair or foul, is caught; if hit by a fairly thrown ball or touched by the ball before touching home base after ending his run, provided three clear catches have been made by the fielders before touching him; if a player of his own team is on the diamond or the fielding area; if he fails to touch center base or home; if after three completed passes a player holds the ball on center base and runner fails for ten seconds to touch center base; and if he commits a running foul. Notice that three distinct passes must be made from fielder to fielder, each one a clear catch, before the runner can be hit with the ball to put him out.

One point is scored each time a runner makes a safe run and touches center base and then home plate without being put out. A referee and score keeper are usually required.

Variation.—In a simpler variation of Soccer Baseball, a regular Softball diamond is used. The kicker place-kicks the ball from the home plate, and runs the bases as in Baseball. A runner is out if a fielder holding the ball touches the base toward which the runner is running, before the runner reaches it. Base stealing is allowed at all times, except when the kicker has the ball preparatory to kicking it.

Washburn Ball.—The diamond is the same as that used in Soccer Baseball. The kicker may throw, drop-kick, or place-kick the ball; but each kicker must use a different method from the kicker who immediately preceded him. The fielding and running are the same as in Softball.

TRIANGLE BALL

Triangle Ball is usually played when there are too few players for more elaborate games. The home plate consists of a triangle 3 feet each way, with one angle toward the pitcher's box. The only base, 1st base, is 20 feet from home base. The pitcher's box is 25 feet from the home plate. A softball is used.

The catcher functions as a backstop only. The fielders stand where they choose on the diamond. The batter hits the pitched ball, runs to 1st base, and returns home at once, as in One Old Cat. When a fielder fields the ball, it must be thrown to the pitcher, who tries to throw it into the home plate triangle before the runner arrives home. The ball may be rolled or thrown toward the triangle, but must touch the ground inside the triangle. If this is done, the runner is out; if the runner reaches home before the triangle is hit by the pitcher with the ball, he scores 1. After three putouts, the teams change sides. The game may be played without teams, by the rotation method used in One Old Cat and Rotation.

Variations.—At times a sport ball, codeball or soccer ball is used, which the batter strikes with his open hand; or it may be rolled by the pitcher to the batter, who must then kick it out instead of striking it with his hand.

KICKING HOME RUNS

The members of the teams are numbered. As Batter No. 1 takes his place at the home plate, Fielder No. 1 places himself anywhere on the diamond, which has baselines of 35 or 45 feet. The kicker placekicks, and then runs the bases. The fielder fields the ball, and runs for home base with it. The runner scores 1 for each base he touches in order before the fielder reaches home with the ball: thus he may score 1, 2, 3 or 4 points. If the ball is caught on the fly, he scores nothing. If he fails to score 4 points, he is considered as out. Then Batter No. 2 and Fielder No. 2 repeat the same thing, until three batters have been put out; the other team then comes to bat.

KICK-THE-BAR BASEBALL

This is played on a Softball diamond, with baselines of from 45 to 65 feet. Instead of a ball, a 1-foot section of an old bicycle tire, termed the bar, is used. Each team consists of 7 players: 6 fielders beyond the bunt line, drawn from 1st to 3rd base; and a bartender, at the home plate.

The batter stands at the home plate and kicks the bar toward the bunt line. He may kick at it any number of times, provided he fails to touch it. A kick into foul territory, or failing to kick the bar beyond the bunt line, puts the batter out. Once a fair kick is made, the runner runs the bases as in Baseball. Whoever fields the bar throws it to the bartender, who touches it to home base. If the bar touches home base before the runner reaches the base to which he is moving, he is out. The bartender must call out the base toward which the runner is running, as he touches home with the bar. Otherwise, the rules of Baseball apply. A game consists of seven innings.

LONG BALL

Long Ball requires a home plate, a pitcher's box 30 feet away, and a Long Base, 3 feet by 6, 30 feet beyond the pitcher's box, in a straight line. Two teams of three to ten players each play. Every hit is fair, and the runner must at once run to the long base, and remain there or return home. So long as there is one player at bat, the rest may remain on the long base. All these may return home on a hit, a run being scored by all who reach home safely. If a runner leaves the long base, he cannot return to it unless on a caught fly. A batter continues at bat until he hits the ball. A runner is out when a fly ball he hits is caught; when a baseman holds the ball with a foot on either base toward which the runner is running; when he is tagged off base by a fielder holding the ball; or when he is hit off base by a ball thrown by an opponent. After three outs, the teams change places.

SPRINTBALL

Sprintball is played on a court 40 feet wide and 60 to 80 feet long. One end is known as the baseline; the other, as the sprint line. Midway of the court is a lengthwise center line. At the baseline, 3 feet right of the center line, is home base—12 inches square, placed with one corner 6 inches behind the baseline. Two batter's boxes, 3 feet by 4, are marked out on each side of it. The pitcher's box is 25 or 30 feet from the home plate. A sport ball 19 inches in circumference is used.

The fielding side has a pitcher and a catcher, and the rest are fielders. The batter stands in his box and hits the pitched ball with his hand. The ball is pitched underhanded, as in Softball. After a hit, an uncaught third strike, or four balls, the batter runs to the sprint line, running on the right side of the center line. When he returns, he must return on the left side. He must run to the sprint line and back without being hit by the ball. Any number of players may remain behind the sprint line, provided that a player must have come home before it is his turn to bat again. After leaving the sprint line, a runner cannot return to it unless on a caught fly ball, and then only at the risk of being put out.

A batter is out when a fly ball is caught, a third strike is caught, or he hits the ball when standing outside of his box. A runner is out when the ball is held by an opponent on the sprint line before the runner arrives; when he is touched or hit by the ball in the fielding area; when the ball is held on the baseline by an opponent after runner has left the sprint line; or if he crosses the center line in either direction. Three outs cause the teams to change places. Four innings constitute a game. An umpire and a scorer are needed.

GERMAN BATBALL

The home plate is 2 feet square; and there is a post placed 40 feet away. A soccer or sport ball is used. The fielding team scatters over the fielding area. The batter stands by home base, tosses up the ball, strikes it with his fist or open hand, and at once runs to the post, around it, and back to the home base. The fielders secure the ball and attempt to hit the runner with it. No fielder may take more than one step while holding the ball, nor hold it longer than 5 seconds; nor may any two fielders pass the ball back and forth between them more than twice, before passing it to another player. Breaking a fielding rule scores a run for the runner. A batter is given three attempts to hit the ball; if he fails on the third try, he is out. A runner is out if a fly ball batted by him is caught, or if he is hit with the ball before he reaches home base. After three outs, the sides change. A run is scored for each player who reaches home safely.

Batball.—In this elaboration of German batball, a volleyball is used. The court is 40 by 72 feet, its two ends known as the serving line and the baselines. At 10 feet from the serving line a scratch line is drawn across the court; in the center of the baseline, a goal post is placed. Not more than two of the fielding team (each team of from six to ten players) may stand behind the baseline.

The serving team must serve in definite rotation. The server must stand behind the serving line, and bat the ball with open hand, fingers extended. A served ball must land inside the court beyond the scratch line; if it hits the floor inside the scratch line, the server gets another serve; if it falls out of the court, he is out. After serving a fair ball, the runner must run to the baseline, circle the goal post, and return to the scratch line, without being hit by a thrown ball. The runner may not hesitate behind the scratch line more than 5 seconds, or behind the baseline more than 20 seconds. If he sees no opportunity to circle the post, he may re-enter the playing area and go behind the baseline again, with another 20 seconds in which to try to circle the post.

The fielding is as in German Batball. A fielder cannot bounce the ball. If a ball goes out of bounds, a fielder may retrieve it and bring it to the boundary line, but must pass it thereafter. Two points are scored for each safe return of a runner to the scratch line; one point, for a foul committed by an opponent. A runner keeps on running after a foul, and scores both for his run and one point for each foul. In addition to the fouls in German Batball, fouls by fielders include: for having more players than two behind baseline, one point for each extra player; running across scratch line; and hitting a runner before he crosses the scratch line. A runner must keep running after entering the fielding area; it is a foul, one point, if he fails, and two such fouls put him out. The runner is put out as in German Batball; and is also out if he runs outside the boundary lines, exceeds his time limit behind scratch line or base line, stops running more than once after crossing the scratch line, serves outside the boundary lines, fails to serve fairly as above, or fails to serve across the scratch line in two tries.

Three outs cause the sides to change. Game, seven innings.

FLASHBALL

This differs from Batball in a few particulars. The ball is batted with the fist. The batter stands on a batting line midway of the serving line. The pitcher, a member of the batter's team, stands on the serving line 6 to 8 feet from the batting line. A strike is called if the batter misses a ball, fails to strike a ball within batting range, hits a foul, or hits the ball so far out of bounds that it cannot be put in play immediately. A foul is a ball falling short of the scratchline. The batter is out on three strikes; when a fly ball he hits is caught; or when he bats out of turn. After a safe hit, the game proceeds as Batball. There is no goal post, and the runner merely has to cross the baseline and return. He is not allowed to remain behind the baseline more than 3 seconds.

Bounce Dodgeball.—The same as Batball, except that the server drops the ball to the ground, and hits it on the rebound.

Schlagball.—A variation of German Batball, in which the batter is a kicker, punting the ball into the field. He is not allowed to kick it from the ground. Rules are the same, except that the runner is out if the ball is held by an opponent on the home base before he reaches home.

Kick Dodgeball, German Kickball.—The same as Batball, except that the ball is kicked, instead of being batted.

Pick-up Kickball.—A variation of Kick Dodgeball, in which a ball kicked along the ground may not be picked up. It must be kicked by a fielder upward into the air and caught by him or another fielder, and only when caught in the air may it be thrown at the runner.

HIT-PIN BASEBALL

A Softball diamond is used, with baselines 45 feet or less. A soccer ball is used. The home plate is a circle 6 feet in diameter; the other bases are 1 foot square. The pitcher's box is a rectangle 4 by 12 feet, the narrow side toward the home plate, and 20 feet from it. An Indian club is set up on each base, which may be made firmer by being screwed to wooden blocks 5 inches square and 1½ inches thick.

There are two teams of nine players each, placed as in Baseball. The batter stands in the home circle, and kicks the ball tossed to him by the pitcher. The runner must then run outside the bases, not entering the diamond. To put the runner out, fielders throw the ball from base to base in regular rotation, to permit the baseman to knock down the club with it before the runner reaches the base. When three outs are made, the sides change.

A missed kick at a pitched ball is a strike, and so are the first two kicks into foul territory; and a tossed ball that hits in the home circle and at which the player fails to kick is also a strike. Three strikes put a player out. A pitched ball that hits the batter is dead, and can not make him a runner. Any pitched ball not classified as a strike or dead ball is called a ball; and 4 balls entitle the batter to a free kick from placement inside the front half of the circle. Each club knocked down in rotation must be replaced before the ball is thrown to the next base. A kicker is out when he kicks a foul on a free kick awarded him; when he knocks down the club on home base; when a foul fly is caught; or when a ball pitched by the pitcher knocks down the club on home base. The runner is out on a caught fly; on being hit by his own kicked ball before it touches anything else; when his kicked ball knocks down a club before it touches anything else; when he knocks down a club in running; when he steps inside the diamond or interferes with a player there; or, as above, when a club is properly knocked down before he reaches a base. Interfering with a kicker by the catcher gives the kicker a free kick; interference of him by a fielder gives him a run.

BULL'S-EYE BASEBALL

On a wall, a series of rectangles are drawn, as follows:

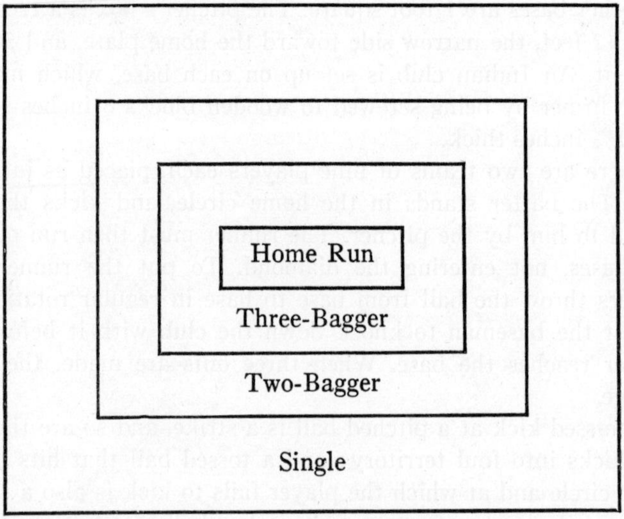

Home base is placed 25 to 35 feet from the wall, opposite the middle of the rectangles. A softball and bat are used. Teams should be preferably of three players only. The pitcher stands with his back to the wall, and pitches to the batter at the home plate. The batter attempts to bat so that his ball comes within a rectangle. He is credited with the number of bases his ball earns. If the ball misses the wall or is caught by an opponent, he is out. After three outs, the sides change.

TIP CAT

This game derives from American pioneer days. The cat, kitty or piggy is a 4-inch stick 1 by 1 inches, whittled down to a point at each end. The bat is a 4-foot stick, broomstick size. A kitty stick of the same thickness, 2 feet long, is also needed. A 3-foot circle is drawn for the goal; or a tree may be used. About 30 feet from it a pitcher's line is drawn.

One batter is selected, and the other players scatter as fielders. The batter sets the kitty stick on end perpendicular to the ground in the center of the goal circle, or in front of the tree. The pitcher throws the bat at the kitty stick. If he knocks it over, the batter is out. If not, the batter lays the cat on the ground within the circle, or a bat's length from the tree. He taps it on end so that it flies into the air, then tries to bat it as far as possible. If the cat is caught in air, the catcher of it exchanges places with the batter. If not, the fielders field it, the one getting it throwing it as near as possible to the circle goal or the tree, not more than a bat's length away from the tree. If he succeeds, the batter is out, and the fielder becomes batter. If the thrower fails, the batter scores one point for each bat's length distance away the cat lies from the circle or the tree. If the batter knocks the cat behind the goal, he is out, and chooses a new batter. The individual scoring the most points wins.

Variation.—As frequently played, especially in England, there is no kitty stick and no pitcher. The fielders stand where they prefer, entirely around the batter. He taps the cat so that it flies into the air, then knocks it as far as possible. A caught cat lets the catcher exchange places with the batter. If not caught, the cat is fielded and thrown to the player nearest the home circle, and he must touch the home circle with it before the runner returns, to put him out. As soon as the batter hits the cat, he runs to a base 30 feet or so away, and must return to the home circle before the cat is returned, to score one.

There are other variations of the game in some localities.

Nip.—The batter fields the cat, and seeks to return to the home circle and touch out the other players, who are required to run to the base and back before he has fielded the ball and returned home.

Rollies.—After the cat is hit out, in the variation called Rollies, the batter lays his bat at right angles to the place where the cat is fielded. The player fielding it rolls the cat from this point; and, if it strikes the bat, the batter is out.

CRICKET

Cricket is the national game of England and most of the British colonies, and is increasing in popularity in some sections of the United States.

The Field.—The playing field, commonly called a bowl, requires a space approximately 150 by 100 yards. Centering this two wickets are placed, 66 feet apart. Each wicket consists of three posts, called stumps, 27 inches high and 8 inches apart. The stumps are grooved at the top, and in the grooves two small sticks called bails are lodged to bridge the spaces between the stumps. A line 8 feet 8 inches long is drawn, with the wicket in the center; this is called the bowling crease. This marks the position of the pitcher, called the bowler. Four feet in front of this line and parallel to it, a line of the same length is drawn, called the popping crease; this defines the area for the batter, called the batsman.

Equipment.—The ball, of leather or composition, measures not less than 9 nor more than 9¼ inches in circumference. It must weigh 5¾ ounces. The bat is flat on its striking surface, and is approximately 3 feet long, with a handle 12 inches long; the blade is 5 inches wide, 3½ inches thick at the end, and tapering down to 2 inches thick where the handle begins. The handle is wrapped with twine, or corked.

The Players.—There are two teams, of eleven players each. The positions of the fielders vary with the kind of bowling and the known ability of the batsman, as in Baseball; the approximate positions are shown in Cricket Diagram I. This shows the positions when the batsman is right-handed; if he is left-handed, the fielders shift so that fielders 5 and 11 go to the opposite side of the bowl. The captain winning a toss determines whether to bat first or to put in his opponents to bat. Weather prospects and the condition of the ground (wet or dry—a "slow" or "fast" wicket) are factors governing his decision.

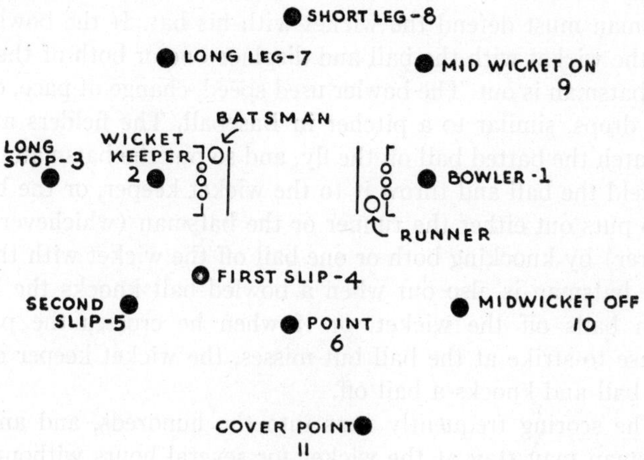

Cricket: I

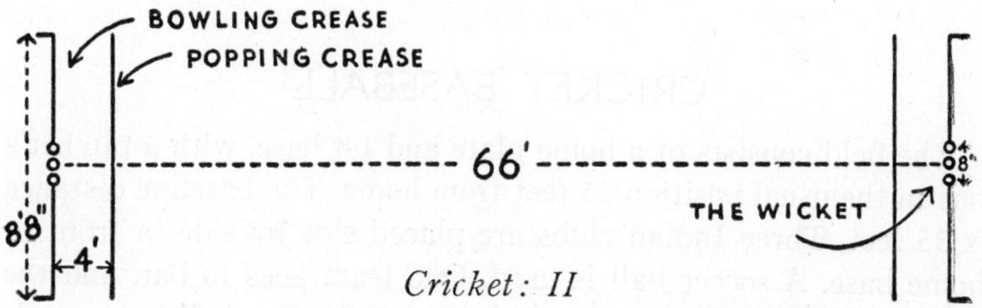

Cricket: II

THE PLAY.—The bowler stands at one wicket. The batsman stands at the other, behind the popping crease; and another member of his team stands at the opposite wicket, beside the bowler, it being required that his bat touch the popping crease. The batsman attempts to hit the ball. As soon as he does so, he runs to the opposite wicket, and his teammate, the runner, runs to the wicket at which the batsman stood. The bowler pitches the ball straight-armed, so that it will reach the batsman on the first bounce; and the bowler's front foot must not go beyond the bowling crease. One exchange of batsman and runner constitutes one run. If the hit was a long one, the two runners continue to race back and forth between the wickets, scoring a run each time. A maximum of six run are possible on one hit.

Any hit is fair, and the fielders must cover the entire field. The batsman must defend the wicket with his bat. If the bowler can hit the wicket with the ball and displace one or both of the bails, the batsman is out. The bowler used speed, change of pace, curves, and drops, similar to a pitcher in Baseball. The fielders attempt to catch the batted ball on the fly, and so put the batsman out; or to field the ball and throw it to the wicket keeper, or the bowler, who puts out either the runner or the batsman (whichever is the nearer) by knocking both or one bail off the wicket with the ball. The batsman is also out when a bowled ball knocks the bail or both bails off the wicket, or if when he crosses the popping crease to strike at the ball but misses, the wicket keeper catches the ball and knocks a bail off.

The scoring frequently runs into the hundreds, and an adept batsman may stay at the wicket for several hours without being put out. Two innings constitute a game, as a rule; and it may take three or four days to complete this.

CRICKET BASEBALL

The field consists of a home plate and 1st base, with a pitcher's box in the usual position 25 feet from home. The baseline distance is 35 feet. Three Indian clubs are placed side by side in front of home base. A soccer ball is used. One team goes to bat, and the other in the field. The batter, holding a light Baseball bat, stands just in front of the Indian clubs. The pitcher rolls the ball toward him; and he tries to bat it out and run to first base and back. The fielders try to field the ball and throw it to home base, knocking down one of the Indian clubs before the batter returns. The batter or runner is out if he has three strikes; if a pitched ball knocks down a club; if a fly ball is caught; if he is tagged by a ball held by a fielder; or if a fielder returns the ball home and knocks down a club before his return. After three outs, the sides change.

BUCKET CRICKET

In the center of a circle 40 feet in diameter a bucket is placed upside down. The fielding team stand outside the circle, and batter No. 1 stands on top of the bucket, bat in hand. A softball or a tennis ball may be used. Any member of the fielding team, standing outside of the circle, may throw the ball at the bucket. The batter tries to defend it, by hitting the ball. The batter is out when the bucket is hit; when a fly ball that he hits is caught; or when he falls off the bucket. The batter continues at bat until he is out, and a side continues at bat until each player has had a chance. Two runs are scored each time the batter hits a ball that is not caught; and one run each time the ball is thrown at the bucket and misses it, or is not batted.

CAN CRICKET

Two cans are placed on the ground 60 feet apart, or less. The pitcher stands by one; the batter beside the other; and the runner by the can beside the pitcher. The other players scatter as fielders. The pitcher pitches the ball to knock the can over, and the batter attempts to hit the ball. If the can is knocked over, the batter is out. When the ball is hit, the batter runs to the other can, and the runner runs to the batter's can. They continue to run back and forth as long as they think they can make the other can, without being put out. A runner is out when a batted fly is caught, or when a fielder knocks the can over with the ball before the runner reaches it. When a batter is out, the fielders move up in rotation, and the catcher or wicket-keeper becomes the batter.

II. THE TENNIS GROUP

Court Tennis, Racquets, Squash Tennis and Squash Racquets date back at least to a 14th century game, Jeu de Paume or Longue Paume, played by French and Italians. It apparently stemmed out of ball games played by the Greeks and Romans. Throwing, catching and batting the ball were used in these, and the orator Isocrates as a boy, as a statue of him indicates, held a horn or horn-shaped implement called the keras, probably used in playing an ancient game of ball. Cinnamus, the 12th century Byzantine historian, described a ball game in which the players used a sort of racket strung with cords. In medieval Italy, the game was called Guioca della palla. At first played indoors, the game was moved outdoors. In France it was played with a cork ball struck by the hand, with or without a glove, over an earth bank two feet high, the equivalent of the modern net. A racket, a crude wooden frame and handle with gut strings, soon replaced this, and it was in this fashion that the game reached England.

Major Walter C. Wingate of the British Army invented and, in 1874, patented Lawn Tennis, as we know it, calling it Sphairistike. By the next year, the Marylebone Cricket Club formulated the first rules for the game, renaming it Lawn Tennis. By 1877, the first Wimbledon tournament was held, and these have been continued since. The shape and size of the court, the height of the net, and other details were constantly altered.

Racquets began in England during the 18th century, popular first in debtors' prisons. In 1822, it was introduced into the English public schools. Squash Racquets originated in England during the early 19th century, at Harrow School. Fives, played at Eton and Rugby, vied in popularity with Squash; it is similar to Handball, and is played either with gloved hands or with a wooden bat. Squash Racquets of today evolved from Rugby Fives and Racquets. The original name of the game was Baby Racquets; the change to Squash Racquets occurred in 1886. The youngest member of the family is Squash Tennis, originating in Boston, but now centered around New York City.

The two oldest games in the group are Court Tennis and Racquets; and the later games derive mainly from these two, divided into the net games and the wall games.

COURT TENNIS

Court Tennis is played in a special court having stone walls, a roof, and galleries for spectators on two sides of the playing space. It is more complicated than the other games, and is not in general use. There are perhaps a score of these courts in existence today, chiefly in continental Europe.

LAWN TENNIS

THE COURT: Lawn Tennis, the most popular of all Tennis games, is played on a level court 78 feet by 36 feet, divided, according to the diagram, into four service courts, two alleys, and

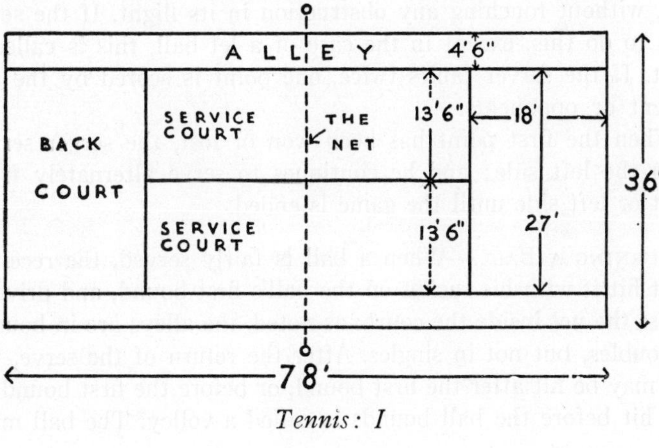

Tennis: I

two back courts. The alleys are used only in doubles,—that is, when two partners play against two other partners, or against a single opponent, in which case he uses the alleys, and they do not. EQUIPMENT: Regulation tennis balls and rackets, of the size and weights specified by the rules, are used. The net is attached to the posts at a height of 3½ feet, and must be 3 feet high in the center. The net must be kept at this height.

THE PLAYERS, AND PRELIMINARIES.—In singles, one player plays against one opponent, the alleys being unused. In doubles, two partners against another pair, the alleys being used. When one player plays two, the alleys are used by the two only. To decide the choice of side and service, a racket tossed rough or smooth (determined by the small threads of colored gut woven into the racket near its upper end); the racket is spun up with a whirling motion, and rough or smooth is called while it is still in the air. The choice of court may be for alternate sets, or for a change after every odd-numbered game, as is agreed on in advance.

SERVING.—The server first ascertains that the other side is ready. A ball served before they are ready must be served over. To begin the play, the server tosses a ball up, and hits it over the net with his racket. The first serve is from the right-hand side of the court. The server must stand with both feet behind the backline, and the ball must fall within the service court diagonally opposite him, without touching any obstruction in its flight. If the serve fails to do this, except in the case of a let ball, this is called a fault. If the server faults twice, one point is scored by the opponent or opponents.

When the first point has been won or lost, the server serves from the left side; and he continues to serve alternately from right or left side until the game is ended.

RETURNING A BALL.—When a ball is fairly served, the receiver must hit it with his racket on the ball's first bound, and drive it across the net inside the court: as noted, the alleys are in bounds in doubles, but not in singles. After the return of the serve, the ball may be hit after the first bound, or before the first bound; a ball hit before the ball bounds is called a volley. The ball must not be played until it has passed the net. A player touching the net with his racket or any part of his body loses a point. The play continues after each service until a player fails to return a ball properly: that is, he misses it, nets it, drives it out of bounds, or lets it hit his body. In this case, a point is scored by the other side, and the server serves again.

Scoring.—The first point made is called out as 15; the second, 30; the third, 40; and the fourth, game; except in a deuce game as described below. The server's score is always called first. The word "love" denotes a score of nothing. If the server wins the first point, the score is fifteen-love; if the other side wins, it is love-fifteen. When the scores are equal, they are announced as fifteen-all, thirty-all, etc. When both players reach forty, the score is called "deuce." Thereafter, a player must score two consecutive points to win the game. The first point won is called "advantage"; advantage in, if server wins it; advantage out, if the other side wins it. If a player who has advantage wins the next point, it is game; otherwise the score again returns to deuce.

A set is won by the side first winning six games; except where the score reaches five-all, in which case two games must be won in succession after a deuce score, to win the set: as, 7-5, 8-6, etc.

Let Balls.—A let ball (often incorrectly called a net ball) means a hindered ball; it counts nothing and the ball must be served again. A served ball that touches the net and then falls into the service court is a let ball. If it falls into the wrong court, it is not a let ball. When a player is prevented from making a play by interference from outside, this is a let ball: as when an outsider crosses the court, or a dog seizes the ball. A ball hitting the net and falling in bounds after the serve is not a let ball, but a legal return.

Out of Bounds.—A ball which strikes the ground or some permanent fixture outside the court is out of bounds, and loses the point for the player who drove it out. A ball on the line is good, and not out of bounds. A player stopping the ball with his hand or racket, clothing or body, and claiming that it was going out, loses the point; the ball is regarded as good until it falls out.

Order of Serving.—In singles, the players serve alternately. In doubles, each team selects which player shall serve first; but, once arrived at, the order must be maintained throughout. In a three-handed game, one against two, the singles player serves every other game.

Points.—A point is won when an opponent fails to return a fair ball; volleys a served ball; when server double faults; when a player allows a ball in play to hit him; touches the net during play; or strikes a ball before it has passed the net.

Matches.—Usually two out of three sets wins the match. In finals of a tournament, three out of five is usual. In team competitions, either four singles matches and two doubles matches, or six singles matches and two doubles matches, are usual. When several teams are competing, or in an individual or pairs tournament, an elimination tournament is usually arranged, in which the winners of each match play the winners of the next, in an arranged order. In team matches, a winner in any match scores one point for his team, thus allowing individual as well as team championships. This applies to both singles and doubles.

PING-PONG, TABLE TENNIS

Ping-Pong or Table Tennis is a miniature type of Tennis, played on a table with a small celluloid ball. It developed out of indoor tennis, played with web-covered balls on the floor, at about the beginning of the present century.

The Table: The table is 9 feet long and 5 feet wide, painted dark green, with a three-quarter inch white line around the outer edges, and lengthwise down the center. The table should be 30 inches above the floor. In home play, tables 8 feet by 4 may be used. The net is dark green with white tape at the top, and is stretched crosswise across the center of the table, with its top 6¾ inches above the table.

Equipment: Official celluloid Ping-Pong balls are used. The rackets have a solid blade 5¼ inches wide and 6¼ inches long, attached to a 5 inch handle; and may be surfaced with rubber, cork, leather or sandpaper, as the player prefers.

Service and Court.—Choice of serving or receiving, or of court, is determined by toss. The loser has the remaining choice of these. At the end of each game, the players change ends of the table. The player who serves first at the beginning of the first game receives at the beginning of the second.

The server stands behind his end of the table and strikes the ball with his racket so that it bounces from the table on his own side of the net, passes over the net, and bounces upon any portion of the table on the receiver's side. The server's racket and the ball must be behind the end line of his court and between the imaginary extensions of the side lines when he strikes the ball in serving. If he misses the ball entirely, he loses the point. When the score is anything except 20 all or higher, the server becomes the receiver and the receiver the server after each 5 points. When the score is 20 all, server and receiver alternate after each point.

The Play.—When the service is good, the receiver endeavors to make a good return, and so on alternately until a point is scored. A good return must consist of striking the ball upon its first bounce, so that it passes directly over or past the end of the net, and touches the playing surface of the opponent's side of the table. The ball may be struck only once by a player before it is his opponent's turn to strike it.

Scoring.—A player loses a point (a) if he fails to make a good service; (b) if he fails to return a good service or a good return; (c) if he or his racket touch the net while the ball is in play; (d) if he moves the table while the ball is in play; (e) if his free hand touches the playing surface while the ball is in play; (f) if he touches a good return before it has touched the playing surface; or (g) if the ball touches him before it has touched the playing surface on a good return.

It is a let ball, and another ball is served, (a) if a service otherwise good touches the net or its supports before touching the playing surface; (b) if receiver has not announced that he is ready —though an attempt to return establishes that the player was ready; or (c) if either player loses the point because of an accident not under his control.

The player first winning 21 points wins the game; except that when the score is 20 all, the player wins who first thereafter scores 2 points more than his opponent. A match is the best 2 out of 3 games. Tournament finals, if agreed upon, are 3 out of 5 games.

PING-PONG DOUBLES

In doubles, the pair who are to start determine which player is to serve for the first 5 points. The lengthwise center line divides each side into two minor courts. First 5 services are from the right side, diagonally across to the minor court at the server's left across the table. The second 5 services are made by the receiver of the first 5 to the server of the first 5, diagonally across the court. A server must be behind his own minor court when he serves. Then the third and fourth services of 5 serves each are made in rotation by the two partners; and thereafter this order is repeated until game is won, or the score is 20-all; in which case each server in order delivers one service each, until the game is won.

PING-PONG WITH TENNIS SERVICE

Tennis service has been officially recognized until recently, and is still preferred by some players. In this, the service is made by each server diagonally, as in Ping-Pong Doubles; and alternately from his right and then his left courts, until his 5 serves are completed. Only one ball is served, unless there is a let ball; in which case only, a second is allowed. In the service, the ball must be hit in the position in regular Ping-Pong, except that when struck it must be below the level of the waist, and must hit first within the receiver's court diagonally across from the minor court from which the player serves. The racket, except the handle, must be below the waist or at waist level when the ball is struck. An entire miss of the ball does not count; a touch, however slight, is a service. If a player serves out of turn, the mistake must be corrected when discovered; unless 5 consecutive serves have been completed, in which case the service passes to the opponent without penalty.

MINOR TENNIS TYPE GAMES

PADDLE TENNIS

Paddle Tennis was invented by F. P. Beal, and was standardized by him in 1920. The court is one-fourth the size of a Lawn Tennis court, with all dimensions of a Lawn Tennis court cut in half. Thus the court is 39 feet by 18; the alleys 2½ feet wide; the service courts 10½ feet by 6¾; the back courts 9 feet by 13½ feet, excluding the alleys. At the posts, the net is 2 feet 4 inches high, with a height of 2 feet 2 inches in the center. Official Paddle Tennis balls are used, made of light-weight solid sponge rubber. Paddle Tennis paddles are made of hard wood, usually three-ply glued. They are 14¾ inches long by 7½ inches wide. The rules are the same as Lawn Tennis.

SLAB TENNIS

This variation of Paddle Tennis uses, instead of a paddle, a circular disk of ½ inch wood, 9 inches in diameter, attached to the hand by a leather or heavy canvas strap tacked or screwed on. The court is the same as that for Paddle Tennis; the balls may be the same, or regulation Lawn Tennis balls may be used. The hand is slipped through the strap, and play proceeds as in Paddle Tennis.

SIDEWALK TENNIS

Four squares of sidewalk, each 3 feet square, in a straight row, constitute the court. There is no net, the central dividing line taking its place. The players stand midway of their outer squares or back courts. In serving, the server must not step over the line of his service square. He tosses the ball and bats it with the palm of his hand, so that it falls in his opponent's service square. Only one attempt at service is allowed each time. A served ball must bounce once before being returned. Thereafter it may either be played on the first bounce, or volleyed,—that is, met and hit before bouncing. The ball must always be hit with the palm of the open hand. Only the server may score, continuing to serve as long as he wins. He scores one for each failure of the opponent to return the ball fairly. The serve passes when the server (a) fails to serve into the opposing service square; (b) steps over the foul line while serving; or (c) fails to return a fair return into the opposing court. The game is 11 points; except that at 10 all, the server must win 2 points in succession to win. Service passes at the end of each game.

HAND TENNIS

A Paddle Tennis court and net are used. Service court lines are not used. Foul lines are drawn each side of the net and 3 feet from it. Any free-bounding soft rubber ball may be used. One or two players constitute a side. The ball is served from behind the rear line by dropping it to the ground and batting it on the first bounce over the net with an underhand swing. The ball must be below the waist when struck. Only one attempt is permitted. A let ball, hitting the top of the net and falling safe, must be served again. The server serves as long as he wins points; when he loses, the service passes. In doubles, the serving side starts with only one player serving. When the serve passes, both opponents serve before the serve passes again, the second partner serving when the first is out.

The ball is returned as in Lawn Tennis, except that it is batted with the hand. A player may not step across the foul line during play. Only the serving side scores, scoring one point each time the opponents fail to make a good return over the net within the opposing court, or when opponents step over the foul line during play. The server is out when his side fails to return a good return, or steps over the foul line during play. The game is 15 points.

Net Hand Ball.—This is played on a court 30 feet by 60, with 4 or more players on a side. The rules of Hand Tennis govern.

WHITTENNIS

Whittennis is played on a court 40 feet long and 15 feet wide, with a net 3 feet high. It resembles Lawn Tennis, but has a basket 2 feet in diameter, attached to the middle of the net. If a ball is served into the basket, this costs the server one point; during play after the serve, a ball into the basket scores one point for the player driving it in. In other respects, the scoring is as in Lawn Tennis

BADMINTON

Badminton was originated in India, and received its name from the seat of the Duke of Beaufort, in Gloucestershire. It is an older game than Lawn Tennis.

THE COURT: The court is 44 feet by 20, divided according to the diagram:

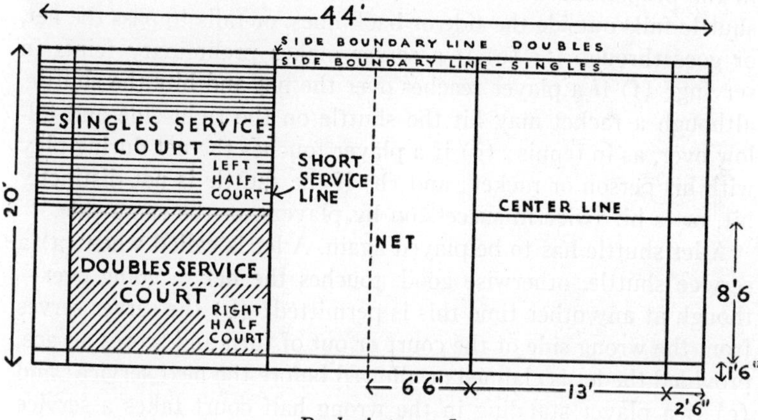

Badminton: I

The top of the net is 5 feet from the ground. Instead of a ball, an official shuttlecock is used, consisting of a piece of cork with feathers attached. The rackets are smaller and lighter than tennis rackets.

SERVING.—The server must serve with an underhand swing of the racket. The shuttle, at the moment it is struck, must not be higher than the server's waist. The server starts serving in his right half court, and serves diagonally to the opponent's right half court. If the server wins the point, he serves next from his left half court, always diagonally. The server continues to serve until an ace is scored against him.

In doubles, the server serves as in singles, and his partner stands in the other court on his side of the net. The side starting the serving has only one serve in its first inning. When the first server is out, the opponents serve, until each has been put out. Thereafter in all innings both partners serve.

FAULTS.—A fault made by the serving side puts the server out. One made by the receiving side scores a point, called an ace, for the serving side. A fault is made (a) if the service is overhand; (b) if the served shuttle falls into the wrong court, or short of the service line, or beyond the long service line, or outside the side lines; (c) if either server or receiver is not standing with his feet in the proper court for the service which is in order; (d) if the shuttle falls outside the side or back lines, or fails to pass the net, or goes through it; (e) if a server makes preliminary feints in serving; (f) if a player reaches over the net and hits the shuttle, although a racket may hit the shuttle on the right side and follow over, as in tennis; (g) if a player touches the net during play with his person or racket; and (h) if the shuttle is not distinctly hit, or is hit twice in succession by players on the same side.

A let shuttle has to be played again. A let is called when (a) a service shuttle, otherwise good, touches the net in going over—though at any other time this is permitted; (b) the server serves from the wrong side of the court or out of turn and scores an ace, provided the let is claimed or allowed before the next service; and (c) if a player standing in the wrong half court takes a service and wins the point, provided the let is claimed or allowed before the next service.

SCORING.—Points are scored only by the serving side. An ace is scored by the serving side whenever the receiving side commits a fault. When the serving side faults, the server is out. The game consists of 15 or 21 aces, when men play; when women, of 11. In a game of 15 aces, when the score is 13 all, the side first reaching 13 has the privilege of setting the game to 5, the side first winning this winning the game. When the score is 14 all, the side which first reaches 14 has the privilege of setting the game to 3, and the side first reaching 3 wins. In the game of 21 aces, 19 and 20 are substituted for 13 and 14; in the game of 11 aces, 9 and 10 for 13 and 14.

SPONGE BADMINTON

This is Badminton played with a sponge, instead of the shuttle. Either Badminton rackets or the paddles used in Paddle Badminton may be used. To make the sponge ball, secure a large natural sponge, and cut it down with scissors to a round ball 3½ inches in diameter.

PADDLE BADMINTON

Regulation Paddle Tennis paddles may be used instead of rackets. It is better to have smaller paddles, resembling Badminton rackets in size and shape. These are made of ¼ inch material, 16 inches long; the striking surface an oval 6 inches by 6, and the handle 10 inches long, 1½ inches wide at the end, and 1 inch wide at the blade. Either shuttlecocks or a sponge ball may be used.

Team Badminton.—Paddle Badminton may be played for six-man teams, by widening the court to 40 feet; by eight-man teams, by widening it to 50 feet. The rules of Volleyball apply.

AERIAL DARTS

Aerial Darts is played on a court 50 feet by 20, with teams of two or more players. Regular shuttlecocks are used, and the players use paddles, Tennis rackets or Badminton rackets. The rules follow those of Volleyball.

FEATHER BALL

No net is used in Feather Ball. A shuttlecock or feather ball is used. The court is 30 feet by 20, with a line drawn across the center, dividing it into two courts 20 feet by 15. The teams are composed of from two to six players each. The server bats the shuttle with his open hand to the opposite court, and it is returned in the same manner. The object is to keep the shuttle from touching the floor. Volleyball rules apply to serving, line ball, volleying, relaying the ball, and scoring. The game is 15 points.

VOLLEYBALL

Volleyball was invented in 1895 by William G. Morgan, director of a gymnasium at Holyoke, Massachusetts. The object was to secure an improved and less violent Basketball, permitting more players in the same space. The object of the game is to keep the ball in the air, by striking it forward and upward by one or both hands; and to score points.

COURT AND EQUIPMENT: The regulation court is 60 feet by 30, divided by a net into two areas 30 feet square. For girls and young players, the court may be reduced to 50 by 25 feet. The net is 32 feet long; it should be 8 feet above the ground to the top of the net for men; and, for less experienced players, 7½ feet. It may even be dropped lower, if deemed advisable. The ball is a regulation volleyball, 1 inch less in diameter than a basketball, and weighing from ⅓ to ½ as much; a sport ball may be used.

TEAMS: A team consists of six players, arranged as in the right half of the diagram. As many as twelve on a team may participate, arranged as shown in the left half of the figure. The players rotate each time their team does the serving. When a player reaches the highest number on his side, he shifts next to 1, and serves.

SERVING.—The player occupying position 1, standing with both feet behind his own backline, tosses the ball up, and bats it, with hand open or closed, forward over the net. It must not touch the net or any player on the server's side, must cross the net and be in bounds in the opponents' court. If the serve fails, the ball goes to the opponents. For men, only one serve is allowed; for other players, two attempts are allowed. A player serves as long as his side wins; when it fails to win, it is out, and the opponents serve. The players rotate in service, as above.

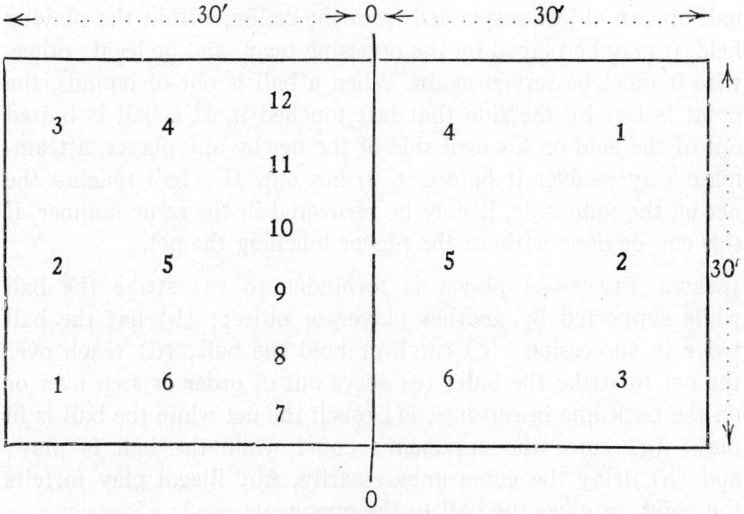

Volleyball: I

The Return.—When a ball is fairly served, the opposing players try to keep it in the air, and then bat it back across the net. Play continues in this manner until the ball strikes the floor, strikes a player below the hips, goes out of bounds, or is declared dead. Men use any part of the body above the hips in playing the ball; other players may use only the hands and arms. A served ball touching the top of the net is a let ball; otherwise, any ball touching the top of the net is still in play.

Relaying the Ball.—When two or more players on a side hit the ball in turn before it goes over the net, this is called relaying the ball. The ball may be relayed, provided that a serve is not relayed; that a player may not play the ball twice in succession without its being touched by another player; and, in the game for men, that a ball may be relayed only twice before it goes over the net. Violation of any of these rules forfeits the point to the opponents.

Out of Bounds.—A ball is out of bounds when it strikes the floor, wall, or any person or object outside the playing field. If the ball hits an object suspended from the ceiling within the playing field, it may be played by the opposing team, and be legal; otherwise it must be served again. When a ball is out of bounds, the point is lost by the side that last touched it. If a ball is batted out of the field on his own side of the net by any player, a teammate may recover it before it strikes out. If a ball touches the net on the same side, it may be recovered in the same manner, if this can be done without the player touching the net.

Illegal Plays.—A player is forbidden to (a) strike the ball while supported by another player or object; (b) bat the ball twice in succession; (c) catch or hold the ball; (d) reach over the net to strike the ball; (e) serve out of order or step over or on the back line in serving; (f) touch the net while the ball is in play; (g) enter the opponent's court while the ball is play; and (h) delay the game unnecessarily. Any illegal play forfeits the point, or gives the ball to the opponents.

Scoring.—Only the serving side scores. If the serving side loses, the service goes to the opponents. The serving side scores 1 point whenever a legally served ball is not returned, or an opponent makes an illegal play. The serving side is out whenever the server fails to make a legal serve; when the serving side fails to return a ball; or when any player of the serving side makes an illegal play. The game is 15 points; unless the score is 14 all, in which case a 2 point lead is needed to win the game. Among less experienced players, the game is won by the side scoring the most points in a 30 minutes playing period, usually consisting of two 15 minute halves.

At the end of each game, the teams change courts. If sun and wind affect the game, the captain of the team with a lesser score is entitled to demand a change of courts when the leading team has scored 8 points. Only one such change is permitted during a game. A referee, a scorer, and two linesmen, who stand behind the left end of each base line, are the usual officials.

GIANT VOLLEYBALL

Giant Volleyball is played on a regulation Volleyball court, with a cage ball 30 inches in diameter. Teams may number as many as 15 players each. A served ball may be relayed by two players. Otherwise, the rules of regular Volleyball apply. In this game, the ball is frequently played with the head.

BALLOON VOLLEYBALL

An ordinary toy balloon is used for the ball. A rope stretched across the room 6½ feet from the ground takes the place of a net. Side lines are drawn, and also a serving line each side of the rope and 6 feet from it. No back line is needed. In playing, two attempts are allowed; a served ball may be relayed once; and in play, a balloon may be relayed 5 times on one side of the rope, provided no player touches it twice in succession. Except for these, the rules of Volleyball apply.

Clubroom Volleyball.—This is a variation, played with a volleyball bladder covered with thin cloth. A rope 7 feet above the floor takes the place of a net. Volleyball rules govern play.

TOSS BALL

This is a simplification of Volleyball for children. Two or three players constitute a team. A light volleyball is used, and it is tossed and caught, or volleyed over the net. The rules of Volleyball may be modified, to make the game more entertaining.

DOUBLES VOLLEYBALL

Volleyball may be played with only two players on a side, by using a court approximately 40 by 20 feet, or one the size of a Badminton court. The regular Volleyball rules govern. In one variation, the ball may be bounced once in passing it between two players.

Singles Volleyball.—Played as Doubles Volleyball, with only one player on each side.

VOLLEY BOUNCEBALL

The net in Volley Bounceball is 4 feet high; the court, ball, and serve are the same as regular Volleyball. The return may be played on the fly or on first bounce. The ball may be played with the hands or with any part of the body above the hips. If it hits a player below the hips, it is a dead ball, and the point is lost by the side whose player was hit. With the low net, there is opportunity to drive the ball toward the legs of players, and so win a point. The ball may not be bounced over the net, but must cross it directly from the body of a player. Scoring is as in Volleyball.

BOUNCE VOLLEYBALL

A return must be made by hitting it over the net on the first bounce, the first time that it touches the floor. Prior to this, it may be relayed as often as the players desire, provided no player touches it twice in succession, and that the game is not unnecessarily delayed. Any violation of the rules scores one point for the serving team; or, if made by the serving team, the serve passes to the other team. Catching the ball and touching the net with any part of the body while the ball is in play are both illegal. In all other respects, Volleyball rules govern play. Scoring is as in Volleyball.

Fist Ball.—In this variation of Bounce Volleyball, the ball must be struck with the closed fist, both in service and in play. The server is allowed two tries; and his teammates may assist the ball over the net. If a first assisted serve does not land in the opponents' court, the server has no second try.

BOUNCE NETBALL

Bounce Netball is played on a Volleyball court, with the net 5 feet from the ground. The serve must strike inside server's court and bounce over the net, landing in the opposite court. Only one try is permitted. A let serve is served again. In the returns, each time the ball must be bounced over the net. Volleying is not permitted. Teammates may bounce the ball between them before one of them bounces it over the net; provided, however, no player hits the ball twice in succession, and the game is not intentionally delayed.

SPONGEBALL

Spongeball uses a ball made from an ordinary bath sponge, approximately 3½ inches in diameter. Tennis rackets or Paddle Tennis rackets are used. The game is played on a Volleyball court. A team consists of six players; the larger teams allowed in Volleyball are not permitted in Spongeball. The players stand and rotate as in Volleyball. The serve may be overhand or underhand. A second attempt is permitted. As in Tennis, the first return may not be volleyed; the ball must bounce once before it is returned. In serving, the service line must not be crossed. A player may not hit the ball twice in succession. More than three players may not hit the ball before it crosses the net. The ball may only be played with the paddle; and one paddle may not touch another player's paddle. Violation of any of these rules constitutes a foul, scoring one point for the serving side if the opponents fouled; or causing the serve to pass, if the serving side fouled. Only the serving side scores. The game is 15 points; except that at 14 all, the team wins which first thereafter secures a 2 point lead.

Tennis Volleyball.—In this variation, a Tennis or Paddle Tennis ball is used. Otherwise the rules are the same as for Spongeball.

LEEBALL

Leeball is a combination of Volleyball and Paddle Tennis. A Volleyball court may be used, or a court 6 feet shorter. The net is 5 feet high. Paddle Tennis paddles are used, and a sport ball 5 inches in diameter. Teams are of six players each; if more play, the court must be widened.

The players stand and rotate as in Volleyball. The server may serve with either an overhand or underhand stroke. Two tries are allowed. Touching the net with body or paddle constitutes a foul;

and so does crossing the service line in serving; batting the ball out of bounds; striking another player's paddle; hitting the ball twice in succession by the same player; or more than three players touching the ball before it is volleyed across the net.

Only the serving side scores, scoring one point for each foul committed by an opponent. When the serving side fouls, the service passes over to the opponents. The game is played in two halves of 15 minutes each. The teams change courts at half time. At the end of the second half, the team with the highest score wins. A referee and a combined timer and scorer are required.

BOUNCEBALL, VOLLEY TENNIS

The court is 50 feet by 36. A tennis net is used, 3 feet high at the center. The service line is drawn 18 feet back from the net, and parallel to it. A volleyball is used. Teams may be of from six to fifteen players; although with twelve or more the court should be widened.

The server stands midway of the service line, and serves by hitting the ball with the flat of the hand. The ball must cross the net before it touches the floor or a player on the server's side. The serve may be assisted not more than twice by one player only; but if an assisted serve fails to cross the net in bounds and hit fair if not returned on the fly, the server has no further attempt; otherwise he is given two attempts. A let service does not count, and is repeated.

The return must be made on the fly or on first bounce; but it must cross the net directly from a player's hand, not after bouncing. No ball may be hit after a second bounce. The ball may be relayed between members of a team, but must be hit each time with the hand, and may not bounce off a player's body. No player may hit the ball more than twice in succession until some other player has hit it. Hitting the ball downward, or dribbling, is not allowed. Reaching over the net is not allowed.

Only the serving side scores. It scores one point for each time the opponents fail to return the ball fairly. When the serving side fails, the service goes over to the opponents. The game is two halves of 14 minutes each, with an intermission of 2 minutes. Teams change courts during the intermission; but the side serving at the end of the first half starts serving in the second half.

RING TENNIS, DECK TENNIS

This game was originated by Cleve F. Schaffer, and first achieved wide popularity on shipboard. It is now quite as popular on land. It can be enjoyed the first time it is played. It differs from Tennis in that the ring is caught and thrown, and not batted.

THE COURT: The court is 40 feet by 18, and is marked out according to this diagram:

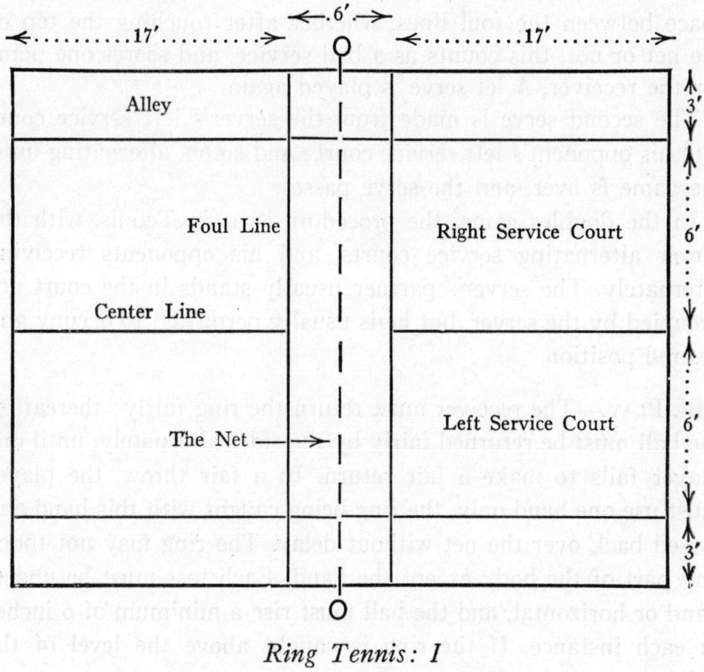

Ring Tennis: 1

EQUIPMENT: The ring is 6 inches in diameter, and may be of sponge rubber; inflated rubber; or of manila rope, ½ inch thick, with the ends spliced together.

SIDES.—One or two players constitute a side. In doubles, the entire court is used, the center line dividing the court into right and left service courts. In singles, the alleys are out of bounds, but the center line is retained in singles, and also the service courts.

SERVING.—In singles, the server stands behind the rear line of his right service court, and throws the ring for the first serve with an underhand toss across the net and into the opponents' right service court. Feinting is not permitted; once the hand holding the ring starts moving, the motion must continue until the ball is released, in service or return. The ring must be delivered with an upward flight of at least 6 inches. The server has only one attempt to make a good service. In some localities, he is given two attempts, as in Tennis. If the served ring falls into the space between the foul lines, whether after touching the top of the net or not, this counts as a bad service, and scores one point for the receiver. A let serve is played again.

The second serve is made from the server's left service court into his opponent's left service court; and so on, alternating until the game is over, and the serve passes.

In the doubles game, the procedure is as in Tennis, with the server alternating service courts, and his opponents receiving alternately. The server's partner usually stands in the court not occupied by the server, but he is usually permitted to occupy any desired position.

THE PLAY.—The receiver must return the ring fairly; thereafter, the ball must be returned fairly by the sides alternately, until one player fails to make a fair return. In a fair throw, the player must use one hand only, the ring being caught with this hand and tossed back over the net without delay. The ring may not touch any part of the body except the hand. Each toss must be underhand or horizontal, and the ball must rise a minimum of 6 inches in each instance. If the ring is caught above the level of the shoulder, it may be returned from where it was caught, provided it rises at least 6 inches. Holding the ring, even momentarily, taking one or more steps with it, feinting, or making false motions of throwing, are not allowed; however, the player's hand receiving the ring may move steadily with it in any direction, provided the sum of these movements does not exceed one complete circle. The ring must be firmly caught and returned in one attempt, and may not be juggled or batted.

SCORING.—The scoring is as in Lawn Tennis: 15, 30, 40, game. A score of zero is announced as "love." The server's score is always announced first: thus, "15-love," or "30-40." A score of 40-40 is termed deuce, and thereafter the winner of a point has advantage —advantage in for the server, advantage out for the opponent. When a player with the advantage loses the next point, the score returns to deuce. After deuce, a player must win two points in succession to go game.

A set is 6 games. If 5-all is reached, the winner must win 2 games in succession after this or any subsequent tie, to win the set.

A ring in the dead area, or out of bounds, or not touching the court or one of the boundary lines, counts one point for the other player. A ring touching a line is in play.

The players change side after each set; or, if there is decided advantage of side, due to sun, wind, etc., they may change sides after each odd-numbered game—1, 3, 5, etc.

Variation.—A variation of Ring Tennis scores the game as in Badminton or Volleyball. Only the serving side scores, and the serve passes when the server loses. In doubles, the serve alternates from side to side, in this order: 1st Server; 1st Receiver; Server's partner; Receiver's partner. The ring may be caught against the body, provided it is at once tossed back without the use of the other hand. The game is 15 points; unless the Long Game is agreed on, in which, at 14-all, a player must secure 2 points in succession after this or any subsequent tie to win. Matches are the best two out of three games.

QUOITENNIS, TENIKOIT

In this variation of Ring Tennis, the court is 19 feet by 16. There is a center line, and a service line 2½ feet beyond each rear line, used in service only. There is no dead area beside the net. The top of the net is 4 feet 8 inches from the ground.

A hollow air-vented rubber ring, called a tenikoit, is used. The serve is made diagonally, the server's foot touching the service line, which is used only during the serve. The serve is delivered alternately from the right and left service court lines. The receiver must stand toeing the back line, not the service line, and may not cross this line until the tenikoit has left the server's hand. In doubles, the two partners or server and receiver may stand where they please inside their own courts. The scoring is as in Lawn Tennis.

RING VOLLEYBALL

This variation is played on a Ring Tennis court, with Ring Tennis rings. Four to six play on each team. The game is played by Volleyball rules, except that the ring is caught and tossed as in Ring Tennis.

SWORD TENNIS

This variation of Ring Tennis derives from many ancient games, in which a ring is thrown and caught on a cane. A Ring Tennis court is used; but the dead line is placed 6 feet from the net. The net is 6 feet high. The ring, a hoop 6 inches in diameter, may be that used in Ring Tennis, or, better, an embroidery hoop. Each player holds a walking stick or a stick of the same dimensions.

The game is better for two players than for four. The server stands behind his end line, the hoop being thrust over the end of his stick. He tosses the hoop over the net, and his opponent catches it on his stick and tosses it back. A player loses a point if, in catching the hoop, he allows it to slide down the stick and touch his hand. It is a foul if a player steps over his deadline, costing a point; and a hoop falling into the dead area scores one point for the opposing side. Otherwise, the game is played like Ring Tennis.

THE WALL GAMES

In the wall games there is no net, and the court corresponds to one side of a Lawn Tennis court. The ball is batted against the front wall, and is played by the opposing side when it rebounds. Both sides use the same court, but alternately, the side not in play being obliged to keep out of the way.

HANDBALL: FOUR-WALL GAME

Handball originated in Ireland during the 10th and 11th centuries. The original court was larger than the one used today, and the ball could be struck by the hand or kicked. The game was brought to the United States soon after 1870, and is now firmly established; although the American One-Wall Game is extremely popular. The game is popular among the Latin races, especially in France.

The Court: The court consists of a room with four walls and a ceiling, the floor 46 feet by 22, the walls 22 feet high. A court 40 by 20 by 20 is permissible. The back wall is frequently only 10 feet high, leaving a space above for a spectators' gallery.

Midway of the court, and parallel to the front wall, a line is drawn on the floor, dividing the court into two halves of equal size. This is known as the short-line. A line 5 feet in front of and paralled to this is known as the service-line. At 18 inches from each side wall, and parallel to it, a line is drawn connecting the short-line and the service-line, thus forming two service boxes, one on each side of the court.

Equipment: The standard handball is of black rubber, 1⅞ inches thick. A tennis ball is often used in informal games. Gloves of soft material may be worn. Gloves with thumb and fingers webbed together are not allowed in official games. A team consists of one or two players.

The Serve.—In serving, the server must stand in the serving space between short-line and service-line. The ball must be bounced on the floor and struck on the first bounce. To be in

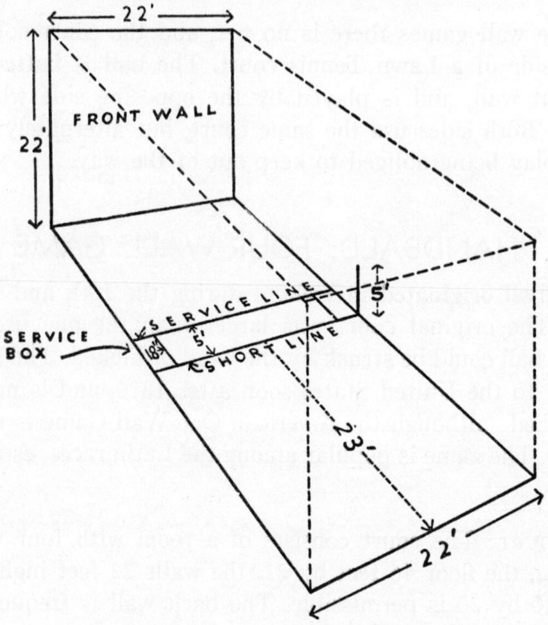

Handball: Four-Wall Game: I

play, it must first strike the front wall, and then rebound across the short line. The server is given two attempts to make a good service. If he serves a short ball or a long ball on the first attempt, he is allowed a second try. A short ball is (1) a served ball which fails to rebound past the short-line; (2) a service in which the server steps across either short-line or service-line; (3) a service in which the player's partner is hit by a served ball, while he is standing in the server's zone; and (4) a service in which server's partner fails to stand in the opposite box, back to the wall, until it crosses the short-line. A long ball is (1) a served ball which rebounds from the front wall and touches the back wall or the ceiling before touching the floor on or back of the short-line; and (2) a served ball which rebounds from the front wall, hits one side wall, and then hits the other side wall before touching the floor on or back of the short-line.

A short ball may be played, at the option of the receiver. A long ball may not be played. Two successive shorts, two successive longs, or a short and a long, put the server out.

The order of service is: Server; both opponents; then the other two, etc.

THE PLAY.—When a ball is fairly served, the opponents must return it to the front wall. It may be struck either on the fly or on first bounce; but after it leaves the player's hand it must not touch the floor before touching the front wall. A ball which hits the front wall and the floor at the same time is a miss. If a ball on its way to the front wall touches an opponent, it is played over. Either opponent may return a ball at any time. A ball may not be played by a player after it has touched his partner or himself. Hitting a partner with the ball counts as a miss for the side.

When a player is blocked or interfered with by an opponent, while attempting to play the ball, it is called a hinder. If the hindering is intentional, the offending side loses the point; if unintentional, the ball is served again without penalty. It is not a hinder when a player is interfered with by a partner.

SCORING.—The server wins one point if the receiving side fails to return the ball fairly. A game consists of 21 points. The serving side alone scores; when it loses, the serve passes to the other side. The serving side is put out when the server serves long or short balls in both attempts, unless the short ball is put into play; or when a player on the serving side fails to return the ball fairly during play; or when a player serves out of order.

HANDBALL: ONE-WALL GAME

One-Wall Handball originated in New York about 1900.

THE COURT: The wall should be 20 feet wide and 16 feet high. The court should be 20 feet wide and 34 feet long. The short-line is 16 feet from the wall, and parallel to it. Nine feet behind the short-line, markers are painted on the floor to designate the imaginary service-line. For outdoor courts, a 6-foot wire extension should be built above and to the sides of the wall, to backstop balls which miss the wall.

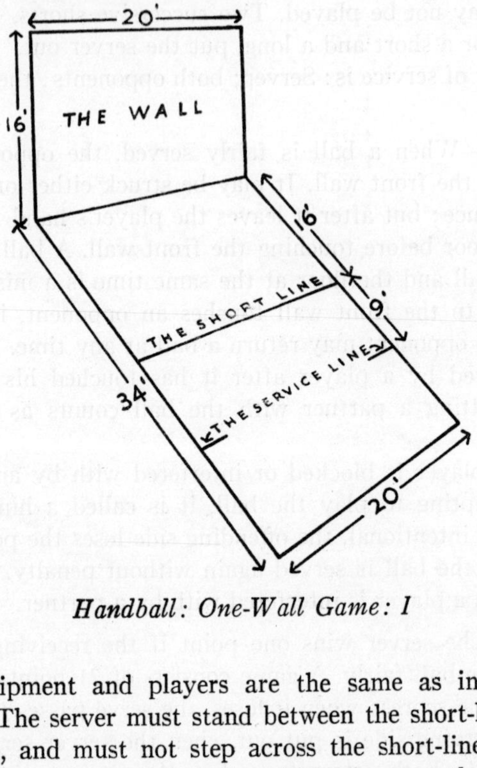

Handball: One-Wall Game: I

The equipment and players are the same as in Four-Wall Handball. The server must stand between the short-line and the service-line, and must not step across the short-line or outside the side lines while serving. Doing this twice puts the server out. The server's partner must stand outside the side lines while the ball is being served, and cannot enter the court until the ball has crossed the short-line. During service, the opponents must stand behind the short-line until the ball has rebounded across it.

The server is allowed three preliminary bounces before striking the ball; more than three puts him out. In serving, the ball must be bounced on the floor and struck on the first bounce, so that it strikes the wall and rebounds across the short-line into the court. The server is out, if the ball he serves strikes outside the side lines. A ball which fails to rebound across the short-line is a short ball; one which strikes the floor behind the back line is a long ball. If the first ball served is short or long, the server is given a second attempt. If he fails in both attempts, he is out.

The order of serving is the same as in Four-Wall Handball.

When a service is good, one of the opponents must return the ball to the wall. In a return, the ball may be played on the fly or on the first bounce; but it must strike the wall on a return before hitting the floor, and must rebound into the court. If it rebounds outside the court, the side that returned it loses the point. Hinders, scoring and all other points are regulated by the rules given for Four-Wall Handball.

COURT CODEBALL

Court Codeball was invented by Dr. W. E. Code, as a variation of Handball which preserved the element of kicking, and at the same time prohibited the use of the hands. A Four-Wall Handball court is used. The ball is the official codeball, an inflated rubber ball 6 inches in diameter and weighing 12 ounces—a fast bouncing ball. One or two players constitute a team.

THE SERVE.—The server must stand 3 to 5 feet back of the short-line, and may not step over it in serving. He drops the ball to the floor and kicks it on the first or second bounce. He is not permitted to drop kick, or to kick the ball on the fly. If the server misses the ball in serving, he is out. He may drop it three times before kicking, but failure on the third attempt puts him out.

The served ball must strike the front wall before it touches ceiling, sidewalls or floor. On the rebound, it must pass the short-line before touching the floor. Otherwise, it is a short ball, and may be played by the opponents; but, if they prefer, it must be served again. The server or his partner is not permitted to touch a short ball until the opponents decide whether to play it or not. Two short balls in succession put the server out.

If the served ball, after striking the front wall, strikes the back wall before striking the floor, the service is good. If it goes into the gallery, it is a dead ball, and is played over without penalty. When (1) the served ball strikes some other part of the court before striking the front wall, or when (2) the server or his partner touch or interfere with a short ball before opponents have refused to play it, or when (3) two short balls are served in succession, it is a "foot out," and the service passes to the other side.

The order of service is: Server; his two opponents, in succession; the other two players, in succession.

The Play.—After a ball is served fairly, one of the opponents must return it to the front wall, by kicking it on the fly, or on the first or second bounce. If it touches the floor before hitting the front wall, it is a "foot out." The ball can be played only by kicking it. If a player in attempting to foot the ball misses it entirely, he may still play it, provided it has not bounced more than twice. A ball may be relayed toward the front wall by the same player who footed it or by his partner, provided in the interval it has not touched any part of the court.

Hinders are as in Handball. If a server has one short serve against him and a hinder occurs during the second service, when he starts to serve again the short is not counted against him.

Scoring.—The server continues to serve as long as he scores points. He scores one point for each time the opponents fail to return a fairly played ball. The receiving side scores one point for putting out the server. In the doubles game, the receiving side scores only one point for putting out both servers.

A game is 15 points. At 13-all, the receiving side may set the game to 5 if he so desires; and at 14-all, to 3, provided this is done before another ball is served. Matches consist of the best two out of three games.

RACQUETS

The Racquets court is about 60 by 40 feet, surrounded by smooth walls of concrete about 25 feet high. Light is admitted through the roof. Doors are made to shut flush, leaving each wall perfectly smooth for playing. The front wall has a metal base 30 inches high called the telltale. The ball in play must strike above the telltale, or the point is lost. The ball is of solid rubber, and is struck by a light racquet with a small circular head.

Serving, play and scoring are as in Handball.

SQUASH RACQUETS

Squash Racquets, originating at Harrow School in the early 19th century, closely resembles Racquets, but is played on a smaller court built of wood.

THE COURT: The four-walled court is 32 feet long, 18½ feet wide, and 16 feet high. Across the front wall, a service line is painted 6½ feet from the floor, and a metal bar, the telltale, projecting 1½ inches from the wall, is 17 inches above the floor. A similar service line is painted on the back wall. A floor line or service-court line is painted parallel to the back wall, and 10 feet from it. A line drawn from this to the back wall divides that area of the floor into two equal rectangles. Two service boxes, one on each side of the court, are constructed by drawing an arc with a radius of 4½ feet connecting the floor line and the side wall toward the back wall. This is made clearer by the diagram.

The doubles court is 45 by 25 by 20 feet.

EQUIPMENT: The official Squash racquet is used, with a longer handle and a smaller head than the Tennis racket. The official Squash ball is smaller and less firm than a handball, and is not as lively.

THE SERVE.—The first service is determined by a spin of the racquet. As one player spins, the other calls "rough" or "smooth," this being determined by the rough or smooth side of the string in the throat of the racquet. Thereafter, the service changes whenever the server loses a point. The server may serve first from whichever service box he chooses; but thereafter he alter-

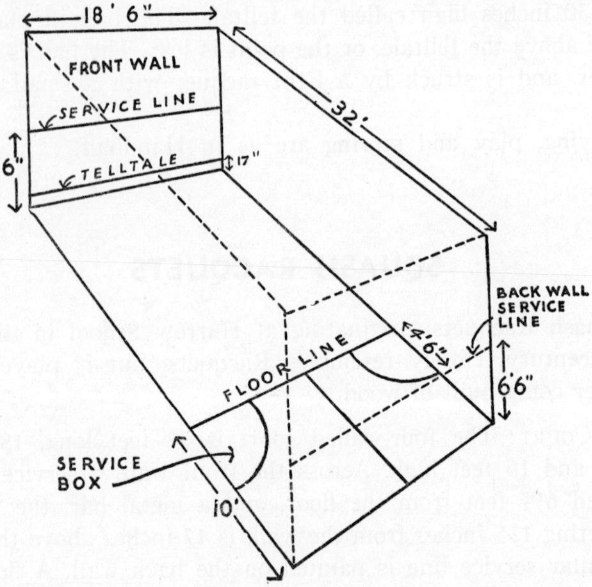

Squash Racquets: I

nates between the boxes until he loses the point. There is no penalty for serving from the wrong service box; but the receiver may refuse to receive the service, if he desires, and demand that it be served again from the right box.

The server must serve by standing with at least one foot in the service box. He serves by tossing up the ball and hitting it so that it strikes the front wall above the service line, before it has hit any other part of the court, and so that it rebounds to fall in the opposite service court before or after hitting any other wall; otherwise, it is a fault. If a served ball rebounds and hits the back wall before hitting any other part of the court on or above the back wall service line, or rebounds and hits the ceiling, it is a fault. Missing the ball in attempting to serve it also constitutes a fault. After one fault, the server serves again. When he makes two consecutive faults, the service passes.

The Play.—To constitute a good return, the ball must be hit on the volley or on the first bounce from the floor, and must reach the front wall on the fly above the telltale. It may touch any wall in the court before or after touching the front wall. The ball may be struck at any number of times, provided it has not been previously touched, and has not bounced more than once. If the ball hits above the back wall serving line on the first bounce from the floor, the point is played again.

Having hit the ball, a player must get out of his opponent's way, to give him a full view of the ball, and must not interfere with him in any way.

It is a let, and the play is repeated, if (1) a player is inadvertently prevented by an opponent from playing the ball; (2) a player cannot avoid being hit by a ball, because of the position of his opponent; (3) a player, because of his fear of hitting his opponent, refrains from striking at a ball; or (4) a player in the act of striking touches his opponent with his racquet. No let is allowed on any stroke made by a player (1) when he actually touches or is touched by his opponent; (2) when the striker could have made a good return; (3) or if the interference is merely with his vision.

If a fair ball touches either player before hitting the front wall, or before bouncing on the floor twice on a rebound from the front wall, the touched player loses the point. If a struck ball touches an opponent before reaching the front wall, the referee awards the point to the striker if, in his opinion, the ball would have reached the front wall before touching any other wall had the opponent not been in the way. If it would have hit another wall before reaching the front wall, it is a let. If the return would not have been good, the striker loses the point.

If the referee decides that the interference with the striker was deliberate, it is a balk, and a point is scored by the offended player. Unnecessary crowding constitutes a balk.

Scoring.—A game consists of 15 points; unless the score reaches 13-all or 14-all; in which case it may be set by the receiver. At 13-all, it may be set to 5 or 3 points. At 14-all, if it has not stood at 13-all, it may be set to 3 points. Each point by a player adds one to his score. A match consists of 3 out of 5 games.

Play is continuous until the match is over, except that between the 3rd and 4th games either player may request a rest of not more than five minutes.

Team Competition.—In Squash matches between two clubs, the teams consist of five players. The opposing players are paired, and each pair plays a match consisting of the best 3 out of 5 games. Each player winning his match scores one point for his team. When several teams compete, they are arranged in an elimination tournament. Two teams paired together as above play, as described above, and the surviving teams continue into the next succeeding round.

SQUASH TENNIS

Squash Tennis is essentially the same game as Squash Racquets, and is now played on a Squash Racquets court.

SQUASH HANDBALL

Squash Handball was invented by W. S. Slater in 1922. It is played on a Four-Wall Handball court, using the official Squash handball. The ball is hit by a Squash racquet. Otherwise, the rules of Handball apply. It may be played singles or doubles.

PADDLE BALL

The equipment is a Paddle Tennis ball and paddle. The game is played on a Four-Wall Handball court, with Handball rules applying, except in the scoring, which follows the system used in Squash Racquets. The server scores one point each time he wins a rally; the receiver or outplayer scores one point whenever he puts the server out. The game is 15 points.

WALL TENNIS

On a wall or building's end paint the outline of a tennis net, 27 feet long and 3 feet high. One-half of a tennis court is lined out in front of this, 39 feet long and 27 feet wide. The line dividing the back court from the service courts is 21 feet from the net; and from this line a line to the net divides the service court area into two equal courts. The size of the court may be lessened, if necessary.

The play is the same as in Lawn Tennis. The server serves first from behind the back line behind the right service court; and a fair serve must strike the wall above the net and hit in the left service court, from which his opponent must play it. Each ball must hit above the net; and any ball after the serve may be played on first bounce or on the fly. For the second serve, the players shift sides. The scoring is as in Lawn Tennis.

BATTLE-BOARD TENNIS

This game was invented by Mary K. Browne, and is popular as a winter indoor sport.

THE COURT: A board 18 feet wide and 12 feet high is covered with celotex to slow up the rebound and deaden the sound. A tennis net is hung 5 feet in front of it, the net being 3 feet high. A court 18 feet wide and 40 feet long is lined out on the floor. At 10 feet in front of the back line and parallel to it, a line is painted; and a second parallel line is painted 20 feet in front of the back line. A line connecting these two is drawn parallel to the side lines, creating two service courts 9 feet wide and 10 feet deep. A 3-foot service box is marked behind each service court, extending back into the back court adjacent to the side line.

THE PLAY.—Tennis balls and rackets are used. The server stands in the right service box and serves the ball against the board or wall, so that it rebounds into the left service court. When served from the other side, it must rebound into the right service court. Only one attempt is allowed for each service. After the serve, the ball may be played anywhere in the court. Any ball hit into the net is a lost point, whether hit directly or on the rebound. The players hit the ball alternately, as in Handball. If a player is hit by a ball, the play is lost by him. If a player is interfered with while endeavoring to play a ball, it is a hinder or let, and the play is played over without penalty. Merely obscuring a player's vision is not interference. The game is scored like Lawn Tennis.

FIVES

Fives is a game of the Handball type, popular in England. There are several variations of the game that are popular. The game is played by two or four players, in a court with three walls; four walls being sometimes used. As usually played, the court has a front and two side walls, but no back wall. The floor is paved. A line is painted across the front wall 4½ feet above the floor; and also a vertical line on it 3 feet 8 inches from the right hand corner.

The game is usually played by four players, and in general is similar to Four-Wall Handball. The server tosses the ball gently against the front wall above the line, so that it rebounds and hits the right wall, and drops onto the floor. The receiver may refuse any service he does not like. If he fails to return the ball above the line, no stroke is counted. After the service has been returned, the play proceeds as in Handball. The game is 15 points. At 13-all the game may be set at 5 or 3; at 14-all, at 3 points.

JAI ALAI, PELOTA

Jai Alai or Pelota is a popular wall tennis game played in Basque and Spanish countries, including Latin America. The regulation court is longer than a Handball court, with a front and back wall only; but the game can be played on a Handball court. The official bat is a basket-work structure strapped to the hand

and hollow on one side, so that the ball may be scooped up with it. This bat extends from the elbow to 8 or 10 inches beyond the finger-tips. The ball is slightly larger than a handball, and very fast.

The play is similar to Handball, but much faster. The ball may be hit with great speed, and is usually hit low on the wall so that it rebounds close to the floor. It is not permissible to play off the back wall; and the object is to hit the ball so that it will rebound past the opponents.

PALLONE

Pallone, the national game of Italy, was first played in Tuscany during the 14th century. The court is 100 yards long, and 17 yards wide. One of the long sides is backed by a high wall; the spectators sit on the other sides, protected by netting. A white line is drawn across the middle of the court. One end of the court is called the *battula,* the other the *ribattuta.* At the former end is a spring board, on which the player who is to receive the service stands.

The ball or *pallone* is an inflated ball covered with leather, 4⅜ inches in diameter. The players wear an oaken bat or gauntlet called the *brocciale,* tubular in shape and covered with long protuberances. It has a grip for the hand, and weighs 5 or 6 pounds. There are two teams, each of three players. A seventh player, the *mandario,* serves the ball and does duty for each team. The three players on each team are the batter or *battiore,* the back or *spalla,* and the third or *terzino.*

At the beginning, the batter stands on the spring board, and receives the ball thrown to him on the bound by the *mandario.* He is not required to play a ball until he receives one that he likes. He runs down the spring board and bats the ball over the center line toward the opponents. One of them must return it; and the play continues until a player fails to return the ball correctly, hits it out of bounds, or touches it with his person.

This scores one point for the opponents. A game consists of 4 points; the scoring being 15, 30, 40, and 50. The ancestor of tennis scoring is found here.

MISCELLANEOUS TENNIS GAMES

There are several games of the Tennis type which are neither net nor wall games.

TETHERBALL

Tetherball was invented in England in 1896. It requires an upright pole 10 feet out of the ground, and solidly packed at least 3 feet underground, to prevent vibration. The pole is usually 7½ inches in circumference at the base, and may taper toward the top. A 2-inch line is painted on it 6 feet from the ground. A circle with a 3-foot radius is drawn around the pole. A line 20 feet long divides the circle into two equal halves. At right angles to this line, and 6 feet on either side of the pole, two service spots are marked.

The ball is either a tennis ball enclosed in a net, or a ball with a soft padded center, resembling a baseball, and having a tape sewed on to attach it to the rope. It is attached to the top of the pole by a cord 7½ feet long. The ball is batted with tennis rackets, Paddle Tennis paddles, or wooden paddles. Metal tennis rackets are satisfactory, and so are Paddle Tennis paddles.

The object of the game is to wind the cord around the pole, by hitting it with the racket so that the ball will be above the mark on the pole, when the cord is completely wound. The opponent attempts to wind the cord in the opposite direction. There is one player on each side. The server, standing on his service spot, bats the ball gently toward his opponent. The advantage is with the non-server; the serve changes at each game, however. In some localities, the server is allowed to strike the ball with any force desired. If the server misses the ball or fails to knock it out of his territory, that is, across the 20-foot line dividing his territory from his opponent's, the service goes to the opponent, where any force is allowed on the serve. If the serve must be gentle, the server is required to serve correctly.

After the service, each player tries to bat the ball constantly, each in a different direction. The players must keep on their own side of the 20-foot line, and outside of the circle. A violation of this rule gives a free serve by him to his opponent, if the gentle serve rules; if not, a free serve to his opponent. The penalty for a cord wound around a racket is the same. If the cord winds around the pole below the 6-foot line marked on it, there must be a free hit by the opponent of the one last touching the ball, if the gentle serve is required; otherwise, the one in whose direction it is winding is given a free hit.

The game is won by the player who winds the cord around the pole so that the ball is above the mark on the pole.

Epic Tetherball.—To prevent the danger of players hitting each other with their paddles, Upton Sinclair in 1914 added the requirement of two parallel lines, marked by cords stretched 2 feet above the ground, to mark the bounds for the players. These lines should be at least 6 feet apart. No player is allowed to cross his boundary line, on penalty as above.

Doubles.—Tetherball is sometimes played with two players on a side. A circle 6-foot in radius is drawn around the pole. The partners alternate in service, as in Lawn Tennis. Before service, both partners of the serving side must stand outside of the large circle. The server immediately enters the 6-foot circle, and must stay in it during the play, and his partner outside.

Zel-Ball.—Zel-Ball is a variation of Tetherball, with a movable pole inserted in a metal pipe driven into the ground. It is played according to the same rules.

SPOTBALL

Spotball is played by two players. A circle 3 feet in diameter is drawn on the ground, and a line crosses it several feet on each side, providing a court for each player. A tennis ball or bounceable rubber ball is used.

Each player stands in his own court, and outside the circle.

The server serves by throwing the ball into the circle, so that it will bounce into the receiver's court. Each return thereafter must be made by striking the ball with the palm of the hand so that it strikes in the circle and bounces into the opponent's court. The play continues until a player misses. A player serves until he misses; thereupon the serve passes. The server alone scores, making one point each time his opponent misses. When the server misses, no point is scored.

Fouls include (1) stepping into the circle or over the line; (2) failure to bounce the ball from the circle into the opponent's court; and (3) catching the ball. Fouls by the receiver score one point for the server; fouls by the receiver cause the serve to pass. The game is 21 points. At 20-all, a player must score 2 points in succession above a tie to win. A set is the best 2 out of 3 games.

Ping-Pong Spotball.—The game can be played indoors, using a ping-pong ball. Otherwise it is the same as above.

CRAB VOLLEYBALL

The court is 50 feet by 25. Centering it, between the two teams, is a neutral zone marked by two parallel lines 6 feet apart. The teams can consist of any equal number of players.

The referee, standing in the neutral zone, tosses a soccer ball or cage ball in the air, so that it falls in the court of one of the teams. The players, while sitting on the floor, attempt to kick the ball over the neutral zone into the opponents' court. It may be relayed any number of times before being kicked across the neutral zone. When kicked into the opponents' court, the opponents attempt to kick it back. In moving about the floor, players can only move by the crab method—on hands and feet with their backs toward the floor. The ball may not be touched by the hands.

A team scores one point when the opponents (1) fail to kick the ball over the neutral zone into the opponents' court; (2) or commit a foul by moving other than by the crab method, or by touching the ball with their hands. A fter each point, the referee tosses the ball to the team that won the point. The game is 15 points.

HAND BATBALL

Two goal lines are drawn 150 feet apart. Draw a short service line for each team 50 feet from the goal line, midway of the imaginary lengthwise line centering the field. The players are divided into equal teams, any number of players on a team. They take any positions they please in opposite halves of the field, facing each other. One team takes the ball—a volleyball, soccer ball, or sport ball. One member of the team stands on the serving line, and with his fist or open hand bats the ball into the opponents' territory. The opponents attempt to catch the ball. The player securing it bats it back into the opponents' territory, from which it is in turn batted back. The ball is always batted from the deepest point it reaches. The team which first bats the ball over the opponents' goal wins.

TEN VOLLEYS

Two teams of an equal number of players compete, any number of players being permissible on a team. At the signal, the player who is given the ball first bats it to a team mate, who bats it to another, and so on. The object is to volley it ten times before the other side can touch it. It must not touch the floor. In rotation, as the players bat it, each calls out the number below ten that his stroke counts: "One," "Two," "Three," and so on. The opponents try to interrupt the ball and start their own sequence of ten volleys. Whenever the ball touches the floor, the count stops and must start from "One" again. A player who has volleyed the ball may not touch it again until it has touched another player or object, but not the floor. The team wins which first completes ten volleys.

III. THE FOOTBALL GROUP

An ancient game of football was played by Greeks of the classic period. The Romans acquired the game from the Greeks, and the soldiers of Julius Cæsar are credited with carrying it into England. Some authorities insist that a similar kicking game was played in Ireland a thousand years before the Roman invasion. Football, because of its turbulence, was forbidden in England by Edward II (1314), Edward III (1340, Tennis being outlawed at the same time, as interfering with Archery), Richard III (1388), and Henry IV (1409). Towns five miles apart would play each other, with their markets as the goals. At times a river had to be crossed; and once at least thirty players piled up in a scrimmage in the river, thirteen of them drowning.

The modern game developed into two distinct types of football: Association Football, usually called Soccer, and Rugby, which includes the familiar American College Football. In Soccer, a round ball is used, and is played chiefly with the feet, the use of the hands and arms being barred. In Rugby, the ball may be kicked, thrown, or carried in the arms, and a player carrying the ball may be stopped by tackling. The common belief is that the difference grew out of the fact that the playing ground at Rugby was soft, while at Eton and other schools it was hard and stony. The goals used in football and hockey games represent the gates of walled and fortified cities. The game was a symbolical battle of town against town; and driving or carrying the ball through a goal symbolized entering a breach in the fortifications. Each team defended its own gate; and thus a goal is considered as belonging to the team defending it.

Soccer is one of the most popular games in England, and entered the United States first. Princeton and Rutgers played it in

1869. Later (1874) the game was combined with Rugby, to form American Rugby, College Football, or American Football, the leading American intercollegiate sport today.

SOCCER, ASSOCIATION FOOTBALL

THE FIELD.—The field is a level rectangle, and may range from 130 by 100 yards to 100 by 50. Two posts are placed midway of the shortest lines, 24 feet apart, and a crossbar joins these at the top, 8 feet above the ground; these are the goals. A goal is said to belong to the team defending it.

An area 6 yards by 20 is marked out in front of each goal, called the goal area. An area 18 yards by 44 is marked out in front of each goal beyond the goal area and including it, called the penalty area. The half way line and kickoff circle are drawn as in the diagram.

For younger players, the field may be only 200 feet by 140, with a goal area 30 by 18 feet, and a penalty area 45 by 108 feet.

THE BALL: The official Soccer ball is round, and slightly smaller than a basketball.

THE PLAYERS: A regulation team is composed of eleven players, although any number may constitute a team. The players stand as in the diagram. The goalkeeper tries to prevent the ball from going between the goal posts. He may use any part of his body, so long as he remains inside the goal area. The two fullbacks act as extra guards for the goal, and remain near it during play. The three halfbacks keep behind the forwards, advancing or retreating with the ball during play. The five forwards advance the ball, and score goals whenever possible. The two outside forwards are called the right and left wings.

LENGTH OF GAMES: The professional game consists of two 45-minute halves, with a 5-minute intermission. For younger players, there may be four quarters of 10 or 8 minutes each, with rest periods of 1, 10 and 1 minutes.

The Kick-off.—The side winning the toss may either choose to kick off, or to select which goal it will defend first. The game

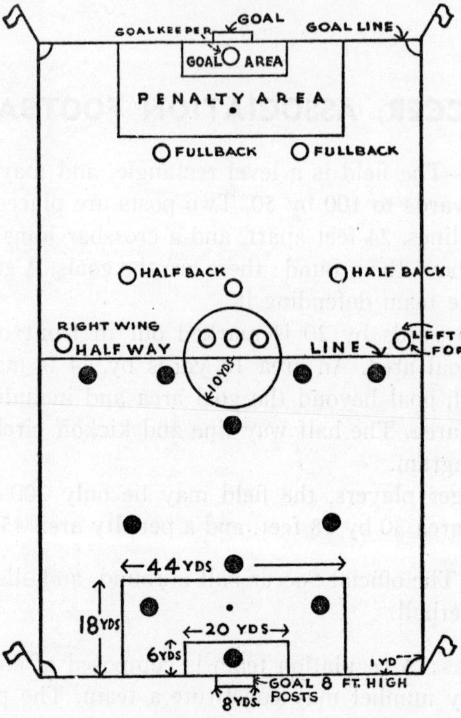

Soccer: I

begins by a place-kick from the center of the field, in the direction of the opponents' goal. To be a good kick, the ball must travel forward the length of its circumference. The opponents may not enter the circle until the kick-off. No player may pass beyond the center of the field until the kick-off. After the kick-off, the ball is kicked about the field until a goal is scored; or the ball goes outside the side or end lines; or until the referee blows his whistle for some other reason. After a goal is scored, the losing side kicks off from the center of the field. At the end of each playing period, the teams change goals. After a change of goals, the kick-off is by the opponents of the team kicking off at the beginning of the previous playing period. The Linesmen signal that a ball is going out of bounds, and mark the spot for the throw-in.

THE THROW-IN.—When the ball passes beyond a side line, either in the air or on the ground, it is a touch, and the ball is out of play. A wing or halfback of the side that did not put it out throws it in. This player must throw it in by standing with both feet on the side line, and holding the ball with both hands completely over his head. A goal may not be scored from a throw-in; and the thrower may not play the ball again until another player has played it. If this rule is broken, the opponents have a free kick from the place where the act occurred.

GOAL-KICK.—When the ball is driven beyond the goal line by a player of the opposite side, it is returned to play by the goal-keeper or a fullback, who kicks it into the field from the half of the goal area nearest which it passed over the line. No opponent may stand within 10 yards of the ball until it is kicked.

CORNER-KICK.—When a player of the defending side plays the ball, accidentally or otherwise, behind his own goal line, a corner-kick is given to the other side. This is taken from within one yard of the corner flag nearest which the ball was put out. A goal may be scored directly from a corner-kick. The kicker may not play the ball again until another player has played it. No opponent may stand within 10 yards of the ball, until the corner-kick has been made.

TIME OUT.—In case of time out, substitution of a player, or injury to a player, the ball is put in play again at the place where it was when time was called, by being thrown down by the referee. It comes into play when it touches the ground.

FOULS.—If any player, except the goalkeeper, touches the ball intentionally with any part of his hand or arm, this is a foul. The referee is the judge of this. It is a foul when a player violently or dangerously charges an opponent from behind, or pushes, holds, trips or jumps at an opponent. The referee is the judge of this, with wide discretion. Any technical evasion of the rules, such as playing the ball a second time before another player plays it, after a throw-in, free kick or penalty kick; being off-side; a goalkeeper's taking more than two steps while carrying the ball; playing the ball thrown down by the referee before it touches the ground; improper throw-in from a touch; not kicking the ball forward from a penalty kick; charging the goalkeeper when he is not holding the ball or obstructing an opponent, or when he is outside the goal area—though such charging must not be intentionally rough—all such technical evasions constitute fouls.

Free-Kick.—A free-kick is awarded for any foul committed outside the penalty area. No opponent may stand within 10 yards of the ball until it is kicked. The kicker may not play the ball a second time, until another player has played it. A goal may be scored directly from a free-kick, unless the foul is for one of the technical evasions of the rules such as listed above.

Penalty-Kick.—A foul committed by a defender within the penalty area, not a technical evasion of the rules as above, causes a penalty-kick to be awarded the opponents. The ball is kicked from a point 12 yards in front of the goal. The penalty area must be cleared of all players except the kicker and the goalkeeper. The goalkeeper must stay behind his goal line until the ball is kicked. The ball must be kicked forward, and a goal may be scored directly from it. The ball is put in play the moment it is kicked; but the kicker may not play it again until some other player has played it.

Scores.—Each goal counts one point. A goal is scored when the ball passes between the goal posts and beneath the bar; provided it is not thrown in, knocked in with the hands or arms, or carried in by an attacker. A goal may not be scored direct from a kick-off, or goal-kick, or from free-kicks resulting from fouls caused by such technical evasions of the rules as those listed above.

Substitutions.—The official rules do not permit substitutions of players. In informal play, this is altered to permit unlimited substitutions. On notifying the referee, a goalkeeper may change with another player.

Off-side.—A player is not off-side when in his own half of the field; when an opponent has last played the ball; while a goal-kick or corner-kick is being made; or when he is behind the ball. When a player is ahead of the ball and it has last been played by a member of his team, the player is off-side and may not touch the ball or interfere with an opponent, unless, at the time the ball was played, at least two of his opponents are between him and their own goal-line. As soon as he is again put on side, he is eligible to reenter the play. This strict off-side rule is often omitted in games with younger players.

Officials.—A referee and two linesmen are the officials.

SOCCER FOR WOMEN

As usually played by women, the field is made smaller, and the playing periods shorter. A player may block with any part of her body. If the blocking is at chest height, the custom is for the player to fold her arms across her chest, or meet the ball with the shoulder. A field goal counts 2 points; a penalty-kick one point.

LINE SOCCER

In this simple variation, no goals are used. The players line up on their goal lines. The referee drops the ball in the center so that it bounces. The two first players run out, and each tries to kick the ball over the opponents' line. Players on the line may use their hands to stop it, but may not throw it. As soon as one player scores a goal, the next two players compete; and so until all have had a chance. When a foul occurs, the other player is given a free kick for goal from the center of the field. Each time the player kicks the ball over the goal line, two points are scored. If another player, not one of the two competing, kicks it over, this does not count; and the ball is put in play as at the start of the game. For each free-kick that crosses the goal line, one point is scored.

A variation of this permits two backs to come out each time to aid the competing player for each team.

SOCCER TEN-KICKS

The object is to kick the ball to team mates 10 times in succession. Each player counts his number, "One," "Two," etc., as he kicks. The opponents seek to intercept the ball and start their own sequence. The hands may not be used at all. The team first making 10 consecutive kicks wins.

SQUARE SOCCER

The field is a square court, 35 feet on each side for younger players, larger for older ones. Each team lines up on two opposite sides of the square. The object is to kick the ball through the opposing line not higher than the head. It may be blocked with any part of the body except the hands. The players may only enter the court to secure the ball, and then return to the line to kick it. One point is scored each time the ball is kicked through the opposing line. The game is 10 points; or a time limit may be set.

CIRCLE SOCCER

Two concentric circles are drawn on the ground, the outer one 25 or more feet in diameter, the inner one 4 feet less. A diameter line is drawn. The players line up between the two circles, one team in each half of the intercircular space. The object is to kick the ball past the opponents, lower than the shoulder. Opponents score one point when a player touches the ball with the hands, steps over the inner circle when kicking, or kicks the ball through higher than the shoulders; and also when they kick it at proper height through the opposing line. The game is 21 points. The hands and forearms may not be used. If a ball goes through a player's legs or over his head, it is not a goal, and the player recovers it and puts it in play. After each play, the players on each side rotate one to the right.

GYMNASIUM SOCCER

This game is played on a Basketball court. Goals are jumping standards, 9 feet apart, the bar 6 feet from the floor. The section of the free-throw Basketball arc more remote from the goal is the penalty mark. An old basketball is used, inflated so that a good kick will send it the length of the court.

Six to nine players constitute a team. The scoring, fouls and throw-ins from out of bounds are as in Soccer. The side walls of the gymnasium may be considered as in bounds, to make the game faster. If the officials cannot determine who drove a ball out of bounds, the ball is centered as at the start of the game, at the point where it went out of bounds. It is usual to substitute for the kick-off a ball dropped by the referee between two players from the opposing teams, the ball being in play when it touches the floor.

SPEEDBALL

Speedball was invented in 1921 by E. D. Mitchell of the University of Michigan, as a combination of Soccer, Rugby Football and Basketball.

THE FIELD: The field is the same as that used in American College Football, 300 by 160 feet. The goals are placed on the end lines. The 50-yard line is called the middle line; and the two 40-yard lines the restraining lines. The 10-yard area between the goal line and the end line on which the goal stands is called the end zone and penalty area. Midway of the goal line, a penalty mark is placed. Official football goals are used. The size of the field can be proportionately reduced for younger players. A soccer field may also be used, if available.

PLAYERS AND EQUIPMENT: A team consists of eleven players, placed as in the diagram. On a smaller field, nine or seven players may constitute a team. The official speedball is a round ball slightly larger than a soccer ball, and slightly smaller than a basketball; a soccer ball may be used.

THE KICK-OFF.—The team winning the toss may choose to kick-off, or to receive at a goal it chooses. The game starts by a place-kick from the center of the field in the direction of the opponents' goal. Each player must stay on his side of the middle line until

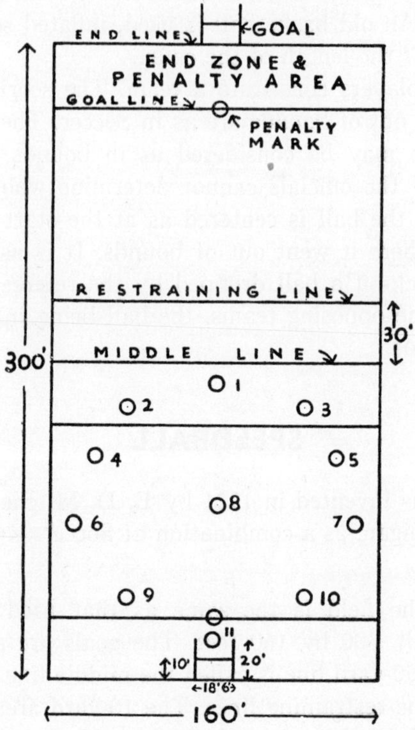

after the kick-off. The ball must move more than its own circumference. The kicker may not play it again until another player has played it.

THE PLAY.—Balls in play are either fly balls or ground balls. A fly ball is one that has been raised into the air directly from a kick. Such a ball may be played with the hands until it again hits the ground. A ground ball is one that is stationary, rolling or bouncing; or one that has touched the ground since being kicked or thrown. Ground balls may not be played by the hands or arms.

A ball may be given momentum by throwing, punting, drop-kicking, and dribbling with the hands or feet, under the proper conditions. A fly ball may be given momentum by any of these methods. A player may dribble a ball overhead, but may not score a touchdown by this method. A fly ball may be batted or tipped. A ground ball may be kicked into the air and caught as a fly ball by the kicker himself.

A player who is standing still when a ball is caught must get rid of the ball before the second step is reached. If running, he is allowed two steps; if at full speed, the referee decides whether he stops as soon as possible. Violation of these rules is called carrying the ball. A player cannot step over the goal line to score.

A player may guard an opponent who has the ball, but must play the ball and not hold the opponent. An opponent who does not have the ball may not be obstructed in any way. If two opponents hold the ball, or the referee is uncertain which side played the ball last before it went out of bounds, the ball is tossed up, as in Basketball.

Out-of-Bounds.—When a ball crosses the side lines, it is given to a player of the opposing team at the point where it went out. This player must throw it in, but no score may be made by this pass. A ball over the end line which results in no score is ruled as a touchback or a safety. If the offensive team put the ball over, it is a touchback, and is put in play by an opponent at the point where it crossed the line, by a punt, place-kick, or pass. If a defensive player last touched the ball before it crossed the end line, it is a safety; it is given to a member of the offensive team at the point, and is put in play by a punt, place-kick, or pass.

Scoring.—The points are scored as follows:

	Points
Field goal	3
Touchdown	2
End-kick	1
Penalty-kick	1
Drop-kick	1

A *field goal* is made when the ball is kicked or legally given impetus by the body over the goal line between the goal posts and beneath the crossbar. A *touchdown* is scored when a player standing in the end zone catches a forward pass. An *end-kick* is scored when a ground ball is kicked or legally given impetus over the goal line from within the end zone. A *penalty-kick* is awarded for a foul. The referee places the ball on the penalty mark, and the kicker attempts to kick it between the goal posts beneath the crossbar. Only one defender may attempt to guard the goal, standing on the end line between the goal posts. A *drop-kick* is scored when a ball legally caught is drop-kicked over the crossbar, provided the kick is made from the field outside the defensive zone area.

Fouls.—Personal fouls include (1) kicking, tripping, charging, pushing, holding, or blocking an opponent; and (2) unnecessary roughness. Technical fouls include (1) making an illegal substitution; (2) taking more than three time-outs in a game; (3) having more than eleven men on the field; and (4) delaying the game. Violations include (1) carrying the ball; (2) touching a ground ball with the hands; (3) making two successive overhead dribbles; (4) violating the kick-off rule; (5) violating the penalty-kick restrictions; (6) violating the rules in returning an out-of-bounds ball to play; (7) violating free-kick restrictions; (8) violating the tie-ball rule; (9) and the kicking or kneeing of a fly ball by a player, unless he has caught it.

Penalties.—The penalty for a personal foul committed outside the player's end zone is a penalty-kick by the offended player. If missed, a touchback is declared. If the personal foul occurs within the player's end zone, the offended player receives two penalty-kicks. The penalty for a technical foul committed outside the player's own penalty area is a penalty-kick by any member of the offended team. If missed, a touchback is declared. If the technical foul was committed inside the player's own penalty area, the penalty is the same. The ball is in play as soon as kicked. The penalty for a violation outside the player's own penalty area is the awarding of the ball out of bounds to any member of the offended team. The penalty for a violation inside the player's own penalty area is a penalty-kick by an opponent.

with the opportunity of a follow-up if missed. In penalty kicks, the referee places the ball in the penalty mark, and the kicker attempts to kick the ball between the goal posts under the crossbar. Where no follow-up is allowed, only the kicker and the goal guard are concerned, as above; where a follow-up is allowed, the other players may not encroach upon the end zone until the ball is actually kicked.

Length of Game.—Four periods of 10 minutes each, with intervals between them of 2, 10 and 2 minutes. The rest periods may be lengthened, if deemed advisable. In case of a tie, one or more over-time periods of 3 minutes each are played.

Miscellaneous.—A player may be taken out of the game and resubstituted once only during the game. A substitute must report first to the linesman, who waits until the ball is dead, and then blows his whistle to allow the substitution. The game is in charge of a referee and two linesmen. The referee has general charge of the game. The linesmen are stationed one on each side of the field, and assist the referee in calling fouls and out-of-bound plays.

SPEEDBALL FOR WOMEN

Where women play, it is usual to limit the field to 100 yards by 60. For younger players, the field may be still further restricted. The end zone is only 6 yards wide, and the penalty mark 12 yards from the goal. Other differences are: A drop-kick scores 2 points, not 1. When the ball is thrown in from out-of-bounds, a 2-handed throw, as in Soccer, is required. The guarding rules are as in Basketball for Women. The penalty for a violation is a free-kick, with the opponents at least 6 yards away. When the referee cannot determine which of two opposing players last touched a ball which has gone out of bounds, the ball is put in play by a throw down between the two players.

INDOOR SPEEDBALL

Indoor Speedball is played upon a Basketball court. The end lines of the court are the goal lines; the space beyond these is the end zone. The goals are two jumping standards 9 feet apart with a crossbar 6 feet from the floor. The basketball backboard is used for scoring drop-kicks. The penalty area is the space between the basketball free-throw line and the end line. The penalty mark is the basketball free-throw line. The ball should not be too lively; an old basketball inflated just enough to travel the length of the court on a good kick should be used.

Teams consist of seven players each. The game starts with a toss-up, as in Basketball. The same is used following each score and at the beginning of each quarter. End-kick is not scored. A drop-kick must be kicked from behind the penalty area. There is no free-kick; instead, the ball is awarded to the offended side out of bounds. The side walls may be regarded as in bounds, to speed up the game. In a safety, the ball must be returned to the nearest penalty mark, before there can be a score.

Basket Speedball.—In this variation, touchdowns are made by throwing the ball into the basket.

TAG SPEEDBALL

In this variation, running with the ball is permitted. No interference for the runner is permitted. When the runner is tagged, he forfeits the ball to the opponent who tags him; the latter puts the ball in play from out of bounds at the nearest boundary line. A touchdown may be scored by running over the goal line while carrying the ball, or by an overhead dribble.

FIELD-HANDBALL

This is a game of recent German origin, given international standing in 1927 by the International Amateur Athletic Federation, and scheduled as an event in the 1936 Olympics.

The game is played on a field approximately the same as a Soccer field, with minor variations concerning the goal and penalty areas. The ball is 24 inches in circumference. A team comprises eleven players. Any part of the body above the knees may be used by all players except the goalkeeper, who may use his entire body. He is only allowed to kick the ball when it is coming toward him. No other player may use any part of his body below the knees to strike the ball with. Scores are made when the ball is thrown through the goals.

A player is not allowed to hold the ball longer than 3 seconds, nor take more than 3 steps while holding it. He is not allowed to touch it twice in succession, until after it has touched another player or object. He is allowed to throw it on the ground and catch it again, while running or standing. The ball may be knocked out of a player's hand with the flat of an opponent's hand; but both hands may not be used, nor a fist. Blocking is allowed, but holding, stopping with the hands, hitting, pushing and charging from the rear are forbidden. Only the goalkeeper may occupy the goal area.

The penalty for fouls in general is a free-throw from the spot where the foul was committed. Corner-throw and penalty-throw rules resemble the corner-kick rule in Soccer.

The game consists of 2 halves of 30 minutes each, with an interval of 10 minutes between them. For younger players, the halves are 20 minutes each.

FIELDBALL

Fieldball, originated by L. R. Burnett, might be described as a combination of Soccer and Basketball, with the use of the feet in handling the ball eliminated.

THE FIELD: The field should be 180 feet by 100, or may be smaller if desired. The lining is shown on page 690.

Goals may be constructed with a rope stretched between jumping standards; or may be marked on the ground. A soccer ball is used. Teams consist of eleven players each: five forwards, three halfbacks, two fullbacks, and a goalkeeper, who may not leave the goal area.

THE START.—The captain winning the toss has the option of throwing off, or choice of goals. One member of the team which throws off tosses the ball into the opponents' territory. No mem-

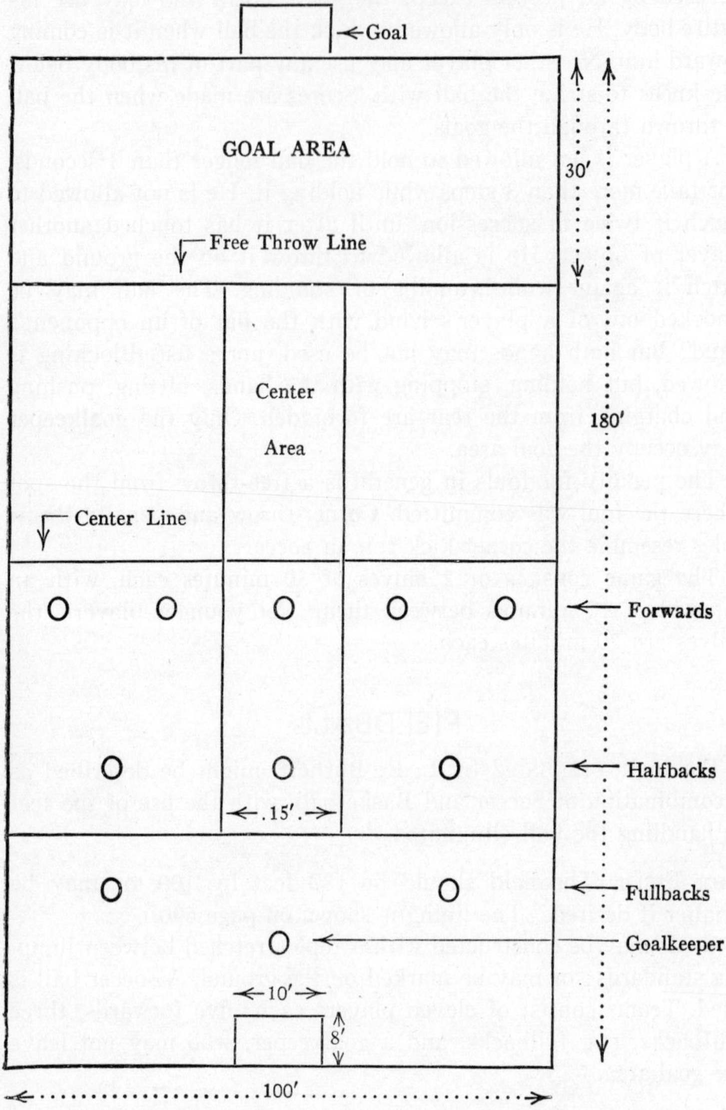
Goal
GOAL AREA
30′
Free Throw Line
Center
Area
180′
Center Line
Forwards
Halfbacks
15′
Fullbacks
Goalkeeper
10′
8′
100′

Fieldball: I

ber of his team may cross the center line until the ball has crossed it. Opponents may not block a throw-off within 15 feet of the center line; if they do, the throw-off must be repeated. At the beginning of the second half, the ball is put in play in the same way.

THE PLAY.—The ball may be thrown, batted, bounced or juggled in any direction. After a player has done one of these, he may not play the ball until another player has played it. The ball must be caught with both hands, but may be retained and thrown with one hand. It must not be held longer than 3 seconds. If the player falls to the ground, the time is counted from the time when all the weight is on the feet. The ball may not be handed or rolled from one player to another. The goalkeeper may run with the ball within the limits of the goal area. This area is open to both teams.

When a ball goes over a side line, it must be thrown back without unnecessary delay by a player of the opposite side from the points where it went out. It may be thrown or bounced back. When it goes over an end line, if the offending team drove it out, the goalkeeper throws the ball into the field from any point within the goal area; being allowed a running throw, if he does not step over the free-throw line. If the defending team drove it out, one of the opponents throws the ball in from a corner. The opposing players must stand at least 15 feet away until the ball is actually thrown.

FOULS.—Fouls include (1) taking more than one step while holding the ball (one foot must remain in place while throwing, unless both feet are off the ground during a jump); (2) throwing the ball while lying down; (3) kicking the ball, or touching it while held by another player; (4) center forward or center halfback stepping out of the center area, or any other player stepping within it; (5) the goalkeeper leaving the goal area while the ball is in play; (6) or any other violation of the rules. For any foul outside the goal area except intentional pushing, holding, interfering or using rough tactics, the ball is given to the nearest opponent on the spot where the foul occurred; he has an unguarded throw, with all opponents at least 5 yards away. For intentional roughness, as above, the fouled side is given a free-throw from the free-throw line. For a foul inside the goal area, if the defenders committed it, the offensive side is given a free-throw from any side of the goal area, except the end line; only the goalkeeper and fullbacks may then guard the goal, the other players being required to be outside. If the goal is not made, the ball is in play. Where the offensive side commits the foul in the goal area, the goalkeeper receives a free-throw from any part of the goal area, all other players being required to stand at least 5 yards away. When two opposing players commit fouls simultaneously in the goal area, each side is given a free-throw from the free-throw line, after which the ball is put in play as at the beginning of the game. If the fouls occur outside the goal area, the ball is tossed up between the two nearest opponents at the point where the ball is in play.

Off-Side.—If a player of the side throwing off crosses the center line before the ball does, there must be a new throw-off 5 yards further back. If the throw-off fails to go at least 15 feet into opponents' field, the same penalty applies. If these offenses are committed twice in succession, the ball goes over for the throw-off.

Scoring.—A team scores one point each time it causes the ball to go between the opponents' goalposts beneath the crossbar. It also scores if the defenders cause the ball to go through their own goal. If no crossbar is used, the score is made when the ball goes between the goal-post positions not more than 8 feet above the ground.

Length of Game.—The game consists of 4 quarters of 5 minutes each, with 2-, 10-, and 2-minute rest-periods. At the beginning of the 2nd and 4th quarters, the ball is put in play where it was when the last quarter ended. It is given to the player who last possessed it and he is allowed an unguarded throw; all players standing at least 5 yards away.

Officials.—In formal games, the officials are a referee, an umpire, a timer, a scorer, and four linesmen. Fewer may be used

PUNCH BALL

This is a variation of Soccer, played on a regulation Football field. The ball is advanced by slapping, punching, or butting it with the head. The goal lines constitute the goals. A sport ball 10 inches in diameter is used. Six to twenty players constitute a team. The game is started by hitting the ball with the fist from a point halfway between the punching team's goal and the center of the field. The ball may not be kicked; it may be tossed in the air before punching, but a runner may take only one step in doing this. No dribbling or running with the ball is permitted. A player may catch the ball, but may not take more than one step while holding it. Kicking, dribbling and running with the ball are fouls; the ball is given to the other side (on the side line nearest to the spot where the foul occurred) and is thrown in with the team on side. Out-of-bounds are thrown in by the team which did not send the ball out.

Scoring.—One point is scored each time the ball crosses the opponents' goal line. After a goal, the opposite team puts the ball in play. The game is four 10-minute quarters, with rests of 1, 10, and 1 minutes.

MASS SOCCER

In this variation, a regular Soccer field is used; but the goal lines constitute the goals, and goal posts, goal areas and penalty areas are not used. The game is started by the players lining up behind their goals. The ball is placed in the center of the field. The players rush for it, and attempt to kick it over the opposing goal. After each goal, the ball is put in play the same way.

When fouls occur, a free-kick is awarded the offended team at the point where the foul took place. Opponents stand at least 10 yards away. Unnecessary roughness eliminates a player from the game. When the ball goes out of bounds, it is thrown in by the referee. Each time the ball crosses a goal line, it counts one point for the offensive side. A game consists of two periods of 10 minutes each.

In one variation, goal posts are used, and one point is scored each time the ball is kicked through. There are four goalkeepers for each team; these alone may catch the ball and throw it, when it comes in the area of the goal.

PUSH BALL

Push Ball is played with a large inflated ball 5 to 6 feet in diameter. It may also be played with a 30-inch cage ball, an inflated canvas-covered bag. Two lines are drawn, 30 to 50 yards apart. Any number may play; the teams are usually large. One team lines up or masses behind each line. The ball is placed midway. At the signal, the players run for the ball, and attempt to push it across the opposite line. The team wins which pushes it across the opposite line first.

BALLOON PUSH BALL

In this, a toy balloon is tossed in the air in the center of the playing space. The two teams, massed at either end, rush for it at the starting signal, given when the balloon is tossed up, and attempt to bat it to the opposite wall. The team wins which first makes the balloon touch the opposite wall. When a balloon is broken, a substitute one should be tossed into the air where the incident occurred.

COLLEGE FOOTBALL, AMERICAN FOOTBALL, AMERICAN RUGBY

College Football, as commonly played in America, differs from English Rugby in many particulars. There is much mass play in the American game, while the English game is much more open. The use of mass play in the American game comes chiefly through the use of what is called interference,—a group of men sent ahead of the man carrying the ball, to protect him from opposing tacklers. In England, the players ahead of the ball are off-side, and passing to an off-side man is not allowed in English Rugby; this prohibits the forward pass. In America, a forward pass is allowed once in each play; although this innovation only came in in 1906.

THE FIELD: The field is 300 feet by 160, with an end zone at each end 30 feet by 160. This makes the whole space 360 by 160

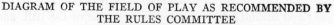

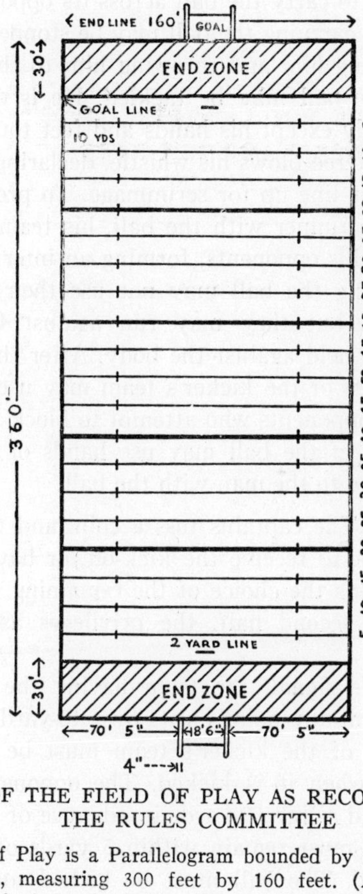

DIAGRAM OF THE FIELD OF PLAY AS RECOMMENDED BY THE RULES COMMITTEE

The Field of Play is a Parallelogram bounded by the side lines and the goal lines, measuring 300 feet by 160 feet. (All measurements should be made from the inside edges of lines marking boundaries.)

American Football: I

feet. Midway of the end lines are the goals, the posts $18\frac{1}{2}$ feet apart and joined by a crossbar 10 feet from the ground. Side lines, end lines, and lines every 5 yards are marked with lime, to aid the officials in measuring distances. The diagram makes these markings clearer.

The Ball: The official ball is a prolate spheroid, not a sphere.

In General.—The object of each team of eleven men is to defend its own goal, and to carry the ball across its opponents' territory, to score. A player carrying the ball may be stopped by tackling—that is, by grasping him and throwing him to the ground. Only the man with the ball may be tackled. He is down when any portion of his body except his hands and feet touch the ground; whereupon the referee blows his whistle, declaring the ball dead; and the two teams line up for scrimmage. To prevent opponents from tackling the runner with the ball, his teammates may run between him and his opponents, forming an interference. Players of the team having the ball may not use their hands to keep opponents away; but they may run against them with hip, shoulder, or arms held against the body. After the ball has been kicked, the players of the kicker's team may use their hands to ward or push off opponents who attempt to block them. The team not in possession of the ball may use hands or arms freely, to aid them in getting to the man with the ball.

The Kick-Off.—The captains toss a coin, and the winner may choose to kick-off, to receive the kick-off, or have the choice of goals. The loser has the choice of the remaining two options. At the start of the second half, the privileges as to choice are reversed.

At the referee's signal, the team having the kick-off place-kicks the ball from any point on its own 40-yard line, or behind it. The members of the kicker's team must be in bounds and behind the ball when it is kicked. The opponents must be in bounds and behind a line 10 yards in advance of the ball, and at least five players must remain within 5 yards of this line until the ball is kicked. The ball must be kicked to or beyond the opponents' restraining line (the line 10 yards in advance of the ball) to continue in play; the exception is when it is touched by an opponent. When the ball is kicked, the kicker's team is allowed to charge down the field toward the spot where the ball lands. A player of the opposing team attempts to catch or secure the ball, and run it back as far as he can before being tackled. The referee then blows his whistle, as a signal for play to stop.

During the 1 minute intermission before the 2nd and 4th quarters, the players change goals, but do not leave the field. The ball is placed in the same relative position, facing the opposite direction from which it was when the preceding period ended. Otherwise the play proceeds as though no change had been made, the number of downs and the distance to be gained remaining the same.

A Scrimmage.—Following the kick-off, after a player has been tackled in the field before the goal line has been reached, the players line up for a scrimmage. The positions are shown in the following diagram:

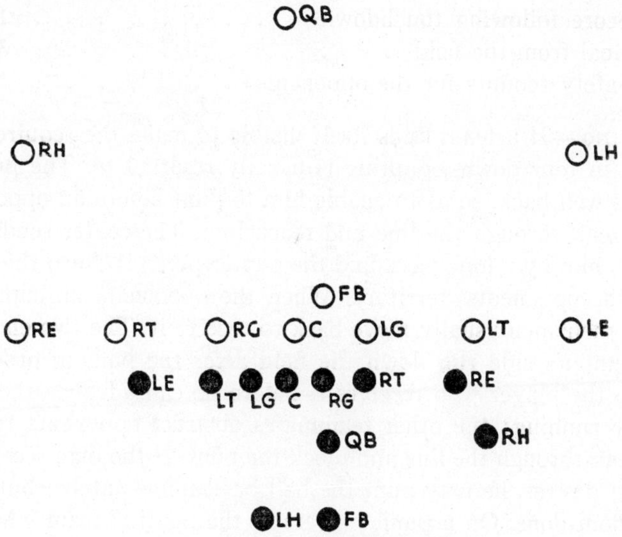

American Football: II

(The black team has the ball; the white team is defending. C, center; RG, right guard; RT, right tackle; RE, right end; LG, left guard; LT, left tackle; LE, left end; QB, quarterback; RH, right halfback; LH, left halfback; FB, fullback.)

The ball is held by the center. The captain or the quarterback calls a signal which the teammates understand as the call for a certain play, having rehearsed it in advance. Such a play usually begins by the center passing the ball to a back; and in many plays this back passes it to a third player, who runs with it, so as to advance it toward the opponents' goal.

A scrimmage ends when the player carrying the ball is tackled, falls so that one knee touches the ground, carries the ball over the goal line, or is forced out of bounds. Unless he has scored, a down is then declared. It is also a down if a forward pass strikes the ground before being caught. Four downs are allowed a side, in which to advance the ball the required 10 yards. In case this distance is made before the four downs are used up, a new first down is declared.

Scoring.—The scoring is as follows:

	Points
Touchdown	6
Score following touchdown	1
Goal from the field	3
Safety (counts for the opponents)	2

Punting.—If a team finds itself unable to make the required 10 yards in four downs, punting is usually resorted to. The punter stands well back, so as to enable him to punt before an opponent can break through the line and reach him. The center sends the ball to him by a long pass, and the punter punts it down the field into the opponents' territory. When the opponents anticipate a punt, their men usually move back to receive it. The two ends on the punter's side run down the field after the ball, in order to tackle the player who receives it before he can advance the ball far by running; the other teammates obstruct opponents trying to break through the line and block the punt. If the man receiving a punt desires, he may punt the ball back immediately; but this is seldom done. On a punt, players of the punting team who are ahead of the ball when it is kicked are off-side, and may not play the ball themselves until it has been first touched by an opponent.

Forward Pass.—The forward pass, or throwing the ball toward the opponents' goal, may be made by any player who is at least

5 yards behind his scrimmage line, and it may be caught by any player of the passing team who was at least a yard behind the line of scrimmage, or an end man on the line. An opponent is allowed to catch (intercept) a forward pass. After a forward pass has been touched by a member of the defense, and while it is still in the air, it becomes a free ball for either side. If the ball touches the ground, a down is declared, and the play starts once more from the spot of the preceding scrimmage, as an incompleted forward pass.

LATERAL AND BACKWARD PASSES.—A pass may also be made to a player on a line with the player passing (lateral), or behind him (backward); any number of lateral or backward passes may be thrown in succession, and any player may receive one. Following a completed forward pass, if a lateral pass is attempted and fumbled, the play is held to be an incompleted forward pass. In the same situation, if the attempted lateral pass goes forward, two forward passes have taken place; this is not allowed, and the ball is brought back to the point from which the play started.

A FUMBLE.—It is a fumble when a player holding the ball loses possession of it other than by passing or kicking it. A fumble can be caused by dropping the ball, permitting an opponent to snatch it, or failing to complete a backward pass. When a fumble occurs, the players of either team may recover the ball. If the team which fumbled recovers the ball, it may be advanced. If the opponents recover the ball after it strikes the ground, it is dead at the point of recovery; if recovered by the opponents before it strikes the ground, the ball may be advanced.

OUT OF BOUNDS.—The ball is out of bounds when the ball or any part of the player holding it touches the ground, an obstruction, or any person other than a player on or outside the side line or end line. When the ball goes out of bounds between the goal lines, except in the case of a kick-off or forward pass, or when it becomes dead within 10 yards of a side line, it is put back in play at a spot 10 yards from the side line, and on a line at right angles to the side line through the point where the ball became dead.

Penalties.—Most penalties for fouls provide that distance be given to the non-offending side. This includes fouls for holding, tripping, illegal use of the hands and arms in interference, rough play, off-side play in scrimmage, and technical fouls. The penalty for off-side in scrimmage is 5 yards; for holding or illegal interference by the offensive team, 15 yards. Some fouls include a loss of the ball to the offended side, without distance: as when a foul occurs when neither side is in possession of the ball, or where an off-side player on a punt touches the ball. When the defensive side is penalized, with a few exceptions, the distance is given to the offensive team, and a first down as well. When the offensive side is the offender, the distance penalty is given, setting the ball back; but the number of the down and the distance to be gained from the place where the first down started remain the same as before. An opposing team may refuse a penalty, if it so desires; this is usual where, on the play, the offensive team made more yards than the penalty would allow (as, for instance, in an off-side in scrimmage).

Touchdown.—When the ball becomes legally dead on, above or behind one of the goal lines, a touchdown is scored. The team scoring a touchdown then has the privilege of a try-for-point. To do this, the ball is placed in front of the center of the goal and 2 yards from it, and usually a kick from placement is attempted, which must pass over the crossbar of the goal to score. If the attempt succeeds, one point is added to the score. The opposing team lines up under the goal, and attempts to prevent the ball from crossing over the bar between the goal posts. The rules permit one down from scrimmage to make this score, by means of a field goal, carrying the ball across the goal line, or completing a forward pass in the end zone. After a touchdown and the try-for-point, play is resumed by a kick-off. The team scored upon may decide which team shall take the kick-off.

Field Goal.—When a team is in front of the opponents' goal and within kicking distance, a goal from the field is sometimes attempted. This must be a kick from placement or a drop-kick—one in which the ball strikes the ground before it is kicked; a punt is not permitted. In the case of a place-kick, the ball is passed back by the center, to the quarterback or some other back, who holds it for the kicker. If the kicked ball goes over the crossbar or a goalpost, a goal is scored, and play is resumed as in the case of a touchdown.

Safety and Touchback.—When a player with the ball is downed behind his own goal line, a safety is declared if the impetus which caused the ball to cross the goal line came from his own team. If the impetus came from the offensive team, the play is called a touchback, and no score is made. Following a safety, the team scored upon puts the ball in play by a free-kick from any point on or behind its own 20-yard line. Following a touchback, the team making it puts the ball in play by a scrimmage at any point on its own 20-yard line.

The Game.—The game consists of four periods of 15 minutes each. The rest intervals are 1, 15, and 1 minutes. The time may be shorter for each quarter, by agreement. Not more than 2 minutes each time is allowed for the purpose of completing a substitution of players. Each team is allowed three time-outs during a half. After the third time-out, a loss of 5 yards is inflicted for each additional time-out, unless it is caused by an injured player who is removed from the game.

Substitutions.—When a player is to be substituted for another, he must go out on the field only when the ball is dead, and must first report to the umpire before entering the play. He is not allowed to communicate with his teammates until after one down has occurred. A player taken from the game may not return in the same period or intermission in which he was withdrawn, but may return in the following period. A player disqualified or suspended from the game may not reenter it.

Officials.—The officials are a referee, an umpire, a linesman and a field judge. The referee has general charge of the ball, and is the judge of its position and progress. His whistle terminates and restarts play. He calls fouls. He stands behind the team having the ball. The umpire is judge of the conduct of the players, and calls fouls occurring near where he stands, behind the defending team. The linesman, under the referee's direction, marks the distance gained, and has jurisdiction over the positions of the players when the ball is put in play. He also watches for fouls involving personal conduct. He stands to the side of the play, and stands his stick even with the forward point of the ball. His assistants on the side lines have stakes marking the distance to be gained in each series of downs. The field judge occupies a position well back of the defending team, and toward the side of the field opposite from that occupied by the linesman. He relieves the referee of some of his duties in this part of the field; keeps time; and reports fouls not noticed by the other officials.

SIX-MAN FOOTBALL

This variation of College Football was originated in 1934 by Stephen Eppler, according to most accounts. Frank Wright, of the University of Florida, is also credited with its invention. It is increasingly popular throughout the United States, especially in the Middle West. In 1937, more than 500 teams played it. Its advantages over College Football are many. It has not yet been extensively commercialized; does not require expensive stadiums; and calls for far less equipment per player. It is ideal for small schools with less than 100 students, since a squad may consist of as few as ten players. There is less risk of injury, due to the requirement of passing the ball by the original receiver behind the line of scrimmage, and the added premium on field goals. Every man on the team is eligible for a forward pass, including the center, if he is placed at either end of the line; and this results in more rounded training for all the players.

The Field.—The playing field is 80 yards long by 40 yards wide, —one-fifth shorter than the College Football field, and more than one-fifth narrower. Side lines, end lines and lines parallel to the goals every five yards are marked with lime, as in College Football. End zones and goals are the same as in College Football.

In General.—The ball is the same as in College Football. Each team consists of six men, normally lined up as in the following diagram:

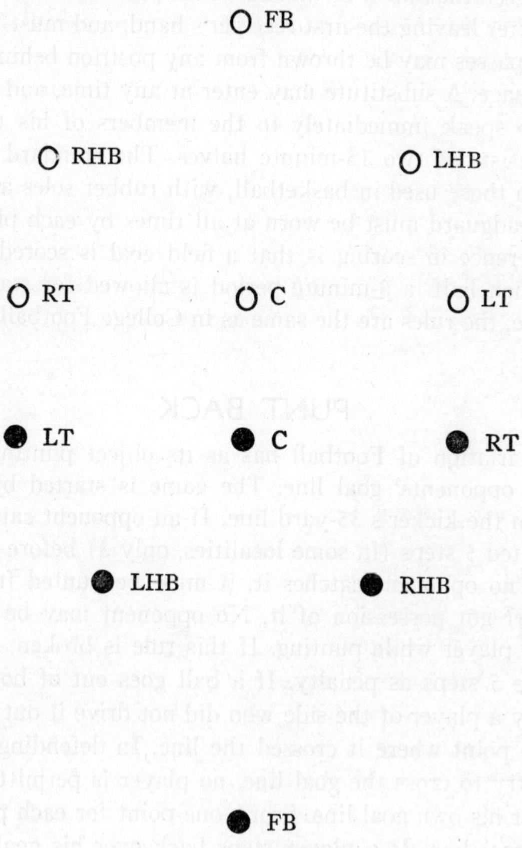

Six-Man Football: I

(The white team has the ball; the black team is defending. C, center; RT, right tackle; LT, left tackle; RHB, right halfback; LHB, left half-back; FB, fullback.)

The object is the same as in College Football. Kickoff and scrimmage are the same, except that the ball must be passed, and not merely handed, from the player who first receives it from the center, to a member of his team, before the player first receiving it has crossed the line of scrimmage. This passing must be through the air, after leaving the first receiver's hand, and must be visible. Forward passes may be thrown from any position behind the line of scrimmage. A substitute may enter at any time, and he is permitted to speak immediately to the members of his team. The game consists of two 15-minute halves. The standard shoes are similar to those used in basketball, with rubber soles and canvas top. A headguard must be worn at all times by each player. The only difference in scoring is that a field goal is scored 4, not 3. Before each half, a 3-minute period is allowed for warming up. Otherwise, the rules are the same as in College Football.

PUNT BACK

This variation of Football has as its object punting the ball over the opponents' goal line. The game is started by a place-kick from the kicker's 35-yard line. If an opponent catches it, he is permitted 5 steps (in some localities, only 3) before punting it back; if no opponent catches it, it must be punted from where the player got possession of it. No opponent may be within 10 feet of a player while punting. If this rule is broken, the kicker may take 5 steps as penalty. If a ball goes out of bounds, it is kicked by a player of the side who did not drive it out of bounds from the point where it crossed the line. In defending against a punt to try to cross the goal line, no player is permitted to step back over his own goal line. Score, one point for each punt crossing the goal line. If a player steps back over his goal line, this scores one point for the opponents.

In one variation of the game, only a drop-kick across the goal line scores; any other kick over the goal lines gives the defenders a free punt from the goal line.

In another variation, the ball must be drop-kicked so that it falls inside a goal area, 30 feet by 15, midway and behind the goal line.

Still another variation allows any type of kick from a caught ball; and only a drop-kick from a ball not caught. No steps are allowed.

Drop-Kick Drive.—This is played like Punt Back, except that all kicks must be drop-kicks. A drop-kick over the goal bar scores 3.

Forward Pass Drive.—In this variation, the ball is passed, and not kicked. Each time the ball is passed over the opponents' goal line, the side scores one point.

Kick-and-Pass Drive.—In this combination game, the ball may be advanced by punting, drop-kicking, or forward passing. The scoring is: drop-kicked goal, 3 points; forward-passed goal, 2; punted goal, 1.

TOUCH FOOTBALL

The field, ball, choice of goals, and kick-off are as in American Football. Nine players constitute a team. The four quarters are usually 15 minutes long each, with rest intervals of 3, 5, and 3 minutes. However, interference is not permitted to the team receiving the kick-off; and the ball must be advanced on the return by carrying it, kicking, or passing sideward or backward. Tackling consists only in an opposing player's touching with both hands the player carrying the ball; in some localities, one hand is sufficient.

In scrimmages, the offensive team must have at least five men on the line of scrimmage. The center passes the ball between his legs to one of the backfield men (a back), who endeavors to advance the ball by carrying it, kicking it, or passing it sideways, backward or forward. The backfield players may not move toward the line of scrimmage before the ball is snapped. If the offensive team has not advanced the ball 10 yards in 4 consecutive downs, the ball goes over; in some localities, 20 yards is the required distance.

If a player during a pass is interfered with by an opponent, the pass is ruled as completed. Any player is eligible to receive a pass; and any defensive player may interrupt one. Any play may be an attempted pass. An incompleted forward pass, even when preceded by a successful lateral pass, is returned to the point where the ball was at the beginning of the play. If a defender interferes during a forward pass, the penalty is 10 yards from the place the ball was at the beginning of play. If a player passes to himself, the play is dead from the place the pass started. An incomplete pass across the goal line is regarded merely as an incompleted pass. In some localities, two such incompleted passes cause the ball to go to the opponents on the 20-yard line.

An incompleted sideward, backward or pass from center which is fumbled is regarded as a dead ball, and scores one down against the offending side.

SCORING.—Touchdown, 6 points; safety, 2 points. There is no play-for-point after a touchdown. In addition to the usual fouls, others comprise tackling, use of hands or feet in attempting to block an opponent, intentional delay, and kicking or attempting to kick a free ball. Tackling is penalized 15 yards; and so is the use of hands or feet to block an opponent. The penalty for a substitute not reporting to the referee is 5 yards. For kicking or attempting to kick a free ball, the penalty is loss of the ball. For intentional delay, the penalty is 5 yards for the first two offenses; then, loss of ball.

BEEBALL

This variation is played on a regulation Football field, or one smaller. The ball is round, slightly smaller than a Soccer ball—22 or 23 inches in circumference. Goals are as in Soccer. A team consists of nine players: four forwards, four guards, and one goal guard. The game is usually two 20-minute halves. The kick-off from midfield must travel at least 10 yards. After the kick-off, the ball may be touched, batted, kicked or run with, if caught on the fly. A tackle consists of the player carrying the ball being touched with both hands by an opponent. Following a legal tackle or a foul, a free-kick is awarded the player tackled, the other players standing at least 5 yards away. When the ball goes out of bounds over the end lines, a corner-kick is awarded, provided a defender last touched it standing on the playing field. If no defender touched it, it is a touchback, and the defending side is awarded a free kick from the touchback mark, midway of the goal line. No ball may be touched by a player twice in succession, before a teammate or opponent touches it. Any violation of rules constitutes a foul, for which a free-kick is awarded the offended side.

Scoring.—One point for a field goal, a ball kicked between the goal posts beneath the crossbar; safety, 2 points; touchdown, (offensive player catching a fly-kick ball running across opponents' goal line; or catching a kicked ball behind the goal line) 3 points. The officials are an umpire and a referee.

FOOT VOLLEYBALL

The field is 100 by 200 feet, or smaller. A neutral zone centers the field, 20 feet wide. A soccer ball is used, or a regulation American football. Seven to fourteen players constitute a team. The players are scattered over their playing area. The ball is kicked-off by a punt from the middle of the offensive side, so that it falls in the receiving side's field. Only one try is given; if it fails, the ball goes over. Each team receiving the ball must catch it and punt back. Only the team that kicks off can score. It scores one point when the opponents allow the ball to touch the ground in their court; or kick the ball out of bounds, or into the neutral area, or within its own court. Each time a team receives a kick-off, the players rotate one position. This gives each player a chance to have a kick-off.

RUGBY FOOTBALL, ENGLISH RUGBY FOOTBALL

A Rugby schoolboy named William Webb Ellis is said to have been the first player to catch the ball and run with it, thus originating the distinctive Rugby game. This occurred in 1823. It was 40 years before the game was taken seriously by the football clubs of England. In 1872, Oxford and Cambridge competed in the game. At Rugby, the matches were called Bigside, with 40 to 100 players competing on each team. Later the number was reduced to 20 to a side. The game was rough and tumble, consisting chiefly of rough scrummaging, where the players might heave in a fierce mass for 10 minutes, struggling for a ball whose location was unknown. Kicking the opponents' shins was expected: this was called hacking-over. Intentional kicking elsewhere was called merely hacking. Mauling, or making a maul-in goal, meant a wrestling match for the ball between two opposing players behind the goal line, while the other players watched and cheered. Hacking was abandoned in 1866, and made illegal in 1871. In 1875 the teams were limited to 15 men. A new method, called wheeling or screwing the scrummage, became popular, though reviled at first. Then heeling came—kicking the ball back to the backs. Reviled at first, this became the clever process called hooking today. Passing came in among the forwards; then the halfbacks; then the three-quarters backs.

As played today, there are 15 players to a team; 8 forwards; 2 halfbacks; 4 three-quarters-backs; 1 fullback. New Zealand plays 7 forwards, 2 five-eighths backs, and 3 three-quarters-backs. The field is laid out as shown opposite.

The scrummage is no longer the dominating feature of the game; modern developments have been concerned primarily with the forwards. The three front forwards on each team, in the scrummage line-up, are shoulder to shoulder, with heads tucked down to watch the ball, as the scrummage halfback throws it toward them. Each central man is the hooker, who tries to sweep the ball back with his foot through the legs of his teammates behind him. Outside men are forbidden to hook. The three in the back row of the scrummage must break rapidly from formation and, if the opponents get the ball, rush the opposing backs, to anticipate any attack; or, if their team gets the ball, to follow up and support the backs as they pass.

As to the rules, at the beginning of the game and after each score the ball must be kicked across the 10 yard line or to it; and no opponent may advance over the line until the ball has been kicked. The 25 yard line comes in when the ball is dead behind the goal lines, without a score. The defenders may then take a drop kick from any point behind this line; and their opponents may not cross it until the ball is kicked. The broken line marked 5 yards each side each boundary (called a "touch line") came in

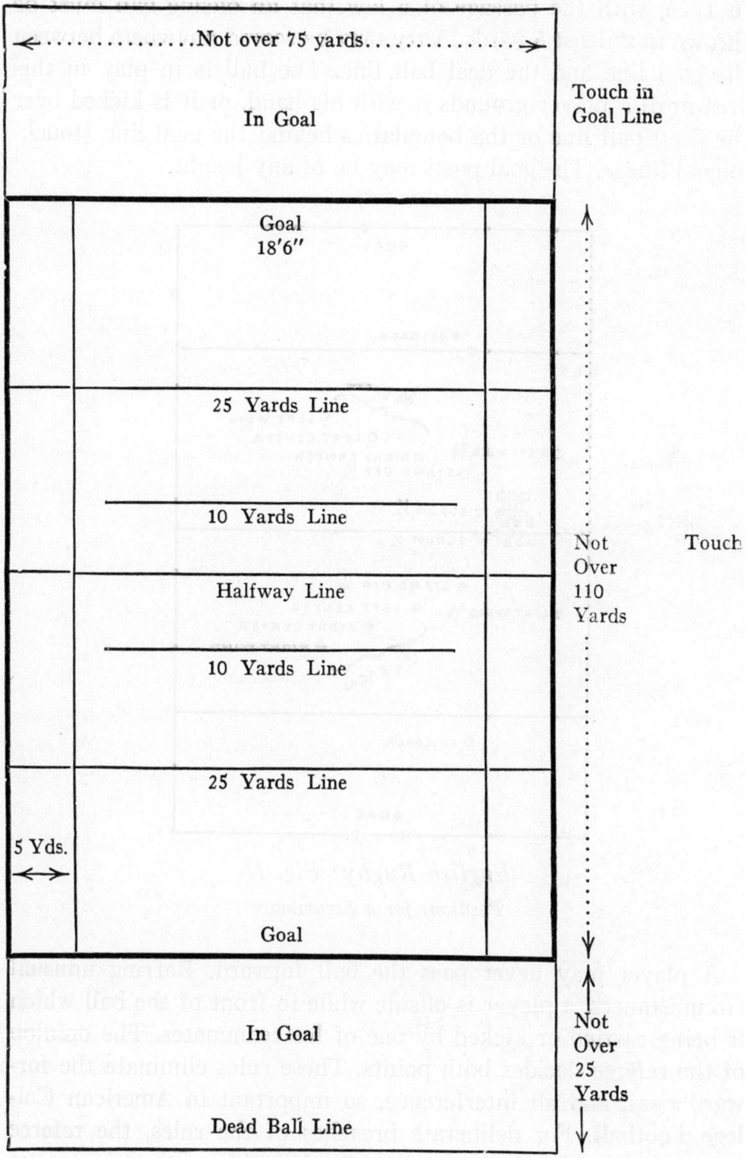

English Rugby: Fig. I

in 1926, with the passage of a law that an offside ball must be thrown in at least 5 yards. A try may be scored anywhere between the goal line and the deal ball line. The ball is in play in this area until a player grounds it with his hand, or it is kicked over the dead ball line or the boundaries behind the goal line (touch-in-goal lines). The goal posts may be of any height.

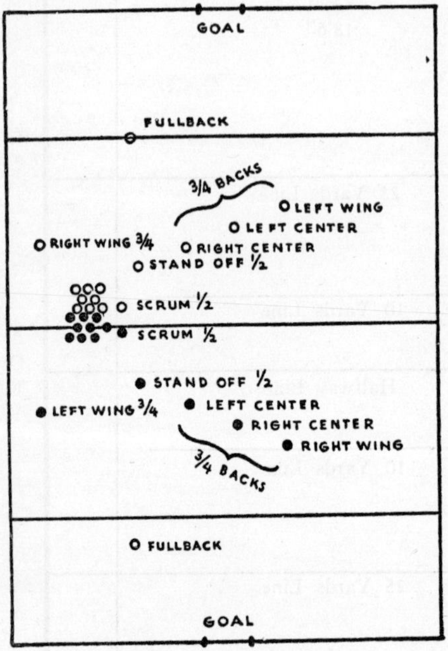

English Rugby: Fig. II

Positions for a Scrummage

A player may never pass the ball forward. Barring unusual circumstances, a player is offside while in front of the ball which is being carried or kicked by one of his teammates. The opinion of the referee decides both points. These rules eliminate the forward pass, and all interference, so important in American College Football. For deliberate breaches of the rules, the referee awards a penalty kick to the offended side; otherwise a set scrummage takes place, with the ball put in play by a half-back on the non-offending side. A player may only be tackled when he is in possession of the ball. He is tackled when he is so held that he cannot for the moment play or pass the ball. He must then play the ball. A place kick is generally used for goal after a try and after a penalty kick is awarded. A drop kick scores a goal at any time, and is often used for penalty and free kicks. A punt is chiefly used for kicking into bounds (into touch, to use the English phrase). A place kick is a kick at a ball placed and held on the ground; a drop kick, a kick of a ball that touches the ground before the toe touches it; a punt, a kick before the ball touches the ground.

The scoring system (adopted in 1905) is: Try, 3 points. Goal from a try, altogether 5 points. Dropped goal, not from free kick or penalty kick, 4 points. Goal from a penalty kick, 3 points. Goal from a "mark" (a free kick claimed by a player who makes a fair catch of an opponent's kick, or when the ball is knocked forward, or thrown forward, by an opponent), 3 points.

AUSTRALIAN RUGBY

In Australia, especially in Victoria, the game is played on an oval field whose greatest distances are 180 yards long and 120 yards wide. The goal posts are 7 yards apart, without a crossbar. There are two "behind posts" 7 yards away each side of the goal. A goal, scoring 6 points, is made when the ball is kicked at any height, without being touched, between the goal posts. A "behind," scoring 1 point, is made when the ball passes between the behind posts, or is touched before passing between the goal posts. Each team consists of 18 players; 17 of these scattered over the field, each paired against an opponent, somewhat as in lacrosse; the 18th a rover. The ball must be kicked or punched, and may not be passed with the hands; a player may not run with it more than 10 yards without bouncing it. There are no offsides, as in English Rugby.

THE ETON WALL GAME

This ancient form of English school football is played on a strip of ground running along a high wall. At each end is an area known as calx, equivalent to the area behind the goal line in Rugby. One is called "good calx," one "bad calx"; goals are marked at the back of each. A team consists of 11 players. A bully or scrummage of 5 players forms against the wall; the other players take up positions outside. The ball is put into the bully to start the game, and whenever it goes out of bounds. The object is to work it along the wall with the feet into the calx. When the ball has been forced into calx, the attackers attempt to get a "shy": lifting the ball with a player's foot against the wall and touching it there. This done, the ball may then be "shied" at goal. In scoring, one goal outweighs any number of shies.

THE ETON FIELD GAME

This equally ancient form of English school football requires two teams of 11 players each, though larger teams are sometimes used. The field is large, with goals at each end; the goals smaller than those used in Association football. The bully resembles an attenuated scrummage in Rugby; the forwards, the bulk of the team, do the dribbling; the behinds or backs are called on for long and accurate kicking. A goal may be scored by an ordinary shot, or by forcing a "rouge." A rouge, similar to a try in Rugby, is scored when an attacker touches the ball down behind the goal line. The ball is then brought out in front of the goal; a bully is formed; and the attackers try to force it through. A goal is scored as 3 points; a rouge with no goal following, 1 point.

THE HARROW GAME

This simple variation consists chiefly of dribbling by the forwards and long kicking by the backs. Two posts are set up at each end of the field, without a crossbar. A goal, called a base, is scored when the ball passes between them at any height. The ball may not be handled. It may be caught from a kick, whereupon its catcher must kick it, or drop it and begin dribbling it. Players must keep behind the ball; offside rules are similar to Rugby. As a rule, teams are 11 players to a side.

THE WINCHESTER GAME

The Winchester game is played on a small field about 80 yards by 25 yards. There are no goal posts; a goal is scored whenever the ball crosses the end lines. The ball may not be kicked more than 5 feet above the ground, unless it comes rolling or bounding toward a player direct from an opponent. There are 6 players to a team; sometimes more are used. The "hot" is similar to an old-time scrummage in Rugby; it takes place at the beginning of a game, or whenever the ball goes out of play. Dribbling forms no part of the game. A player is offside if he is in front of the ball. Passing is illegal.

IV. THE HOCKEY GROUP

A GAME that is the equivalent of Field Hockey was played by the Greeks of classic times, its origin lost in the mists of remote antiquity. Existing Greek murals show Athenians of the time of Pericles facing off for the game, two players with curved sticks hooking a ball, while the other players wait for the ball to be passed. The ancient Egyptians played a similar game. The Roman invasion carried their version of the game to the northern European countries. France already had a game similar to Hockey. The Roman importation became popular in England as Hockey; in Ireland, as Hurling; and in Scotland, as Shinny. At first a crude game with an indefinite number of players, it became formalized in England as Hockey about sixty years ago.

Polo is of Asiatic origin, and was played in Persia before the conquest of Alexander the Great. The word is the Tibetan Balti dialect word for the ball used in the game; cf. Tibetan *pulu,* ball. Tibet, India, and Japan played it for centuries, under rules similar to those used today. It was first played by Europeans in Calcutta in 1863. Lacrosse is one of the oldest native American Indian games, as a symbolic replica of war; whole tribes competed against each other, and the field often had the goal posts a mile or more apart. Ice Hockey is also extremely ancient, having been played by the Scandinavians from earliest times. Organized Ice Hockey dates from 1879, being invented in Montreal, Canada, by W. J. Robertson and R. J. Smith in imitation of Field Hockey.

FIELD HOCKEY

The Field: The field is a smooth level stretch of turf, clipped short and kept rolled. It is 100 yards long and from 50 to 60 yards wide. The boundaries and other lines are marked with lime, with a flag stationed at each corner. For younger players, the field should be 85 yards by 45. The goals, with posts 12 feet apart and crossbar 7 feet above the ground, are midway of the end lines. Three lines divide the field, as in the diagram. A 12-foot line is drawn 15 yards in front of each goal, and parallel to it; its ends are connected with circular lines with a 15-yard radius to the goal line, using the goal posts as centers. This constitutes the striking circle.

Equipment: The game is played with official Field Hockey balls and sticks. Sticks must not weigh more than 23 ounces, players on the forward line usually using lighter sticks. Metal spikes and cleats are prohibited.

Players: Each team consists of eleven players: five forwards (left wing, left inside forward, center forward, right inside forward, right wing); three halfbacks (left halfback, center halfback, right halfback); two fullbacks (left fullback, right fullback); and one goalkeeper. They line up as in the diagram.

THE BULLY-OFF.—Before the game starts, goals are chosen by lot. At the beginning of the second half the goals are changed. The game is started by two players, one from each team, usually the center forwards, together bullying the ball in the center of the field. Bullying consists in each player first striking the ground

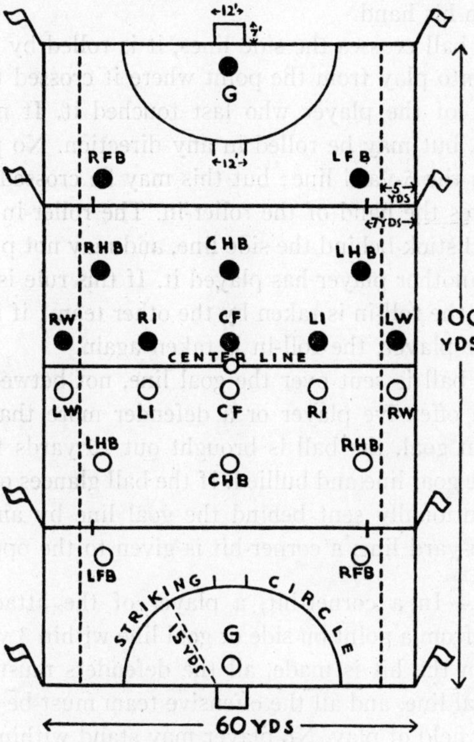

Field Hockey: I

on his own side of the ball and then the opponent's stick, alternately, three times. After this, one of these two players must strike the ball to bring it into play. The two players who are bullying stand squarely facing the sidelines, while every other player must be nearer his own goal line than the ball. If this rule is broken, the bully must be taken again.

THE PLAY.—The ball may be caught, provided it is released at once to fall to the ground, or stopped; but it may not be picked up, carried, kicked, thrown or knocked forward or backward, except with the stick. No person may use any part of his person to gain an advantage, except as it may result from stopping the ball. No player may interfere with the game in any way, unless his stick is in his hand.

When the ball crosses the side lines, it is rolled by hand along the ground into play from the point where it crossed the line, by an opponent of the player who last touched it. It may not be bounced out, but may be rolled in any direction. No player may stand within the 5-yard line; but this may be crossed as soon as the ball leaves the hand of the roller-in. The roller-in must have both feet and stick behind the side line, and may not play the ball again until another player has played it. If this rule is broken by the roller-in, the roll-in is taken by the other team; if it is broken by any other player, the roll-in is taken again.

When the ball is sent over the goal line, not between the goal posts, by an offensive player or a defender more than 25 yards from his own goal, the ball is brought out 25 yards from where it crossed the goal line and bullied. If the ball glances off the stick, or is unintentionally sent behind the goal line by any defender inside the 25-yard line, a corner-hit is given to the opponents.

CORNER-HIT.—In a corner-hit, a player of the attacking team hits the ball from a point on side or goal line within 3 yards of the corner. When the hit is made, all the defenders must be behind their own goal line, and all the offensive team must be outside the circle, in the field of play. No player may stand within 5 yards of the striker. A goal may not be scored from a corner-hit, unless the ball has been stopped (though not necessarily entirely) on the ground by one of the attacking team, or has touched the person or stick of a defender, before the last stroke of the attacking team. The striker may not play the ball again until another player has played it. If this rule is violated, a free-hit is given the defenders from anywhere within the circle. In case of a striker committing the foul called sticks (see below), the defenders are awarded a free-hit. A free-hit is also allowed for shooting at the goal before the ball has been stopped.

When a player hits or rolls the ball in any way, any other player of his side in the opponents' half of the field is offside; if he is nearer the opponents' goal line than the striker or roller-in; and if there are not three of his opponents nearer their own goal line than he. An offside player may not play the ball, nor in any way interfere with another player, until the ball has been touched by an opponent. No player may be penalized for merely standing in an offside position; the rule is broken only when an offside player gains an advantage, plays the ball, or interferes with another player.

Fouls.—In addition to fouls resulting from a violation of these rules, it is forbidden to play with the back or rounded side of the stick; to raise the stick above the shoulders in hitting a ball, called sticks; to undercut the ball or hit it in a dangerous way; or to strike an opponent's stick or interfere with it. Shoving, charging and obstructing an opponent also constitute fouls.

For fouls outside the striking circle, a free-hit is given an opponent on the spot where the breach occurred. During a free-hit, no player may stand within 5 yards of the spot from which the hit is made; and after the hit the player may not play the ball until another player plays it. Inside the striking circles, when the foul is committed by the attacking team, the defenders receive a free-hit from any point within the circle. When a defender fouls inside the circle, the penalty is a penalty-corner for the attacking team. In case of a wilful breach of the rule, or when a goal would probably have been scored but for the foul, a penalty-bully is given.

A penalty-corner is a hit by a player of the attacking team from any point on the goal line he chooses, not less than 10 yards from the nearest goal post. All defenders must stand behind their own goal line, and all of the attacking team must be outside the striking circle in the field of play. A goal may not be scored by the attacking team unless the ball has been stopped by one of this team, or the ball has touched the person or stick of a defender before the last stroke of the attacking team. A penalty-corner hit striker may not play the ball again until another player has played it.

A penalty-bully is played by the offender and any opponent on the spot where the breach occurred. All other players must remain beyond the nearer 25-yard line until the play is completed. If during the bullying the ball goes over the goal line, not between the goal posts, off the stick of the offender, the bully is taken again. If the ball goes between the goal posts off the stick or person of the offender, it is a penalty goal. In all other cases, as soon as the ball has passed wholly over the goal line but not between the goal posts, or outside the striking circle, the game is started with a bully on the nearer 25-yard line's center. A breach of any of these rules by the offender gives the attacking team a penalty goal. A breach of a rule by the attacker selected for the bully gives the defending team a free-hit.

SCORING.—To score, the ball must pass entirely over the goal line between the posts, as a result of a hit by an attacker, or of glancing off his stick. Each goal scores one point. The game consists of two 30-minute halves. These may be shortened, for younger players. Time out, not to exceed 5 minutes, may be taken for accidents. The officials are two umpires, two scorers, and two timekeepers. Each umpire has charge of half of the field.

ICE HOCKEY

THE RINK: The field, called a rink, is similar to that used in Field Hockey, but is smaller. It should be 200 feet by 85, but may be as small as 160 feet by 60; its floor is covered with ice. It should be surrounded by a board fence 3½ to 4 feet high, the banking board, to allow the puck to rebound, though it may also be played in an open space. A goal is placed at each end of the rink at least 10 feet and not more than 15 feet from the end. The goal is a stationary or movable cage made of wire or net, 6 feet wide and 4 feet high. A zone line is drawn 60 feet from each end line, and parallel to it. The center area is termed the center zone; and the end areas are the end zones. The squares in front of the goals indicate the spots on which face-offs take place.

EQUIPMENT: An official ice-hockey puck is used; this is a vulcanized black rubber disk, 1 inch thick and 3 inches in diameter. The players carry official Ice Hockey sticks, and wear ice-skates, shin guards to prevent injuries from the puck, and heavy gloves to protect their hands from blows from an opponent's stick, when

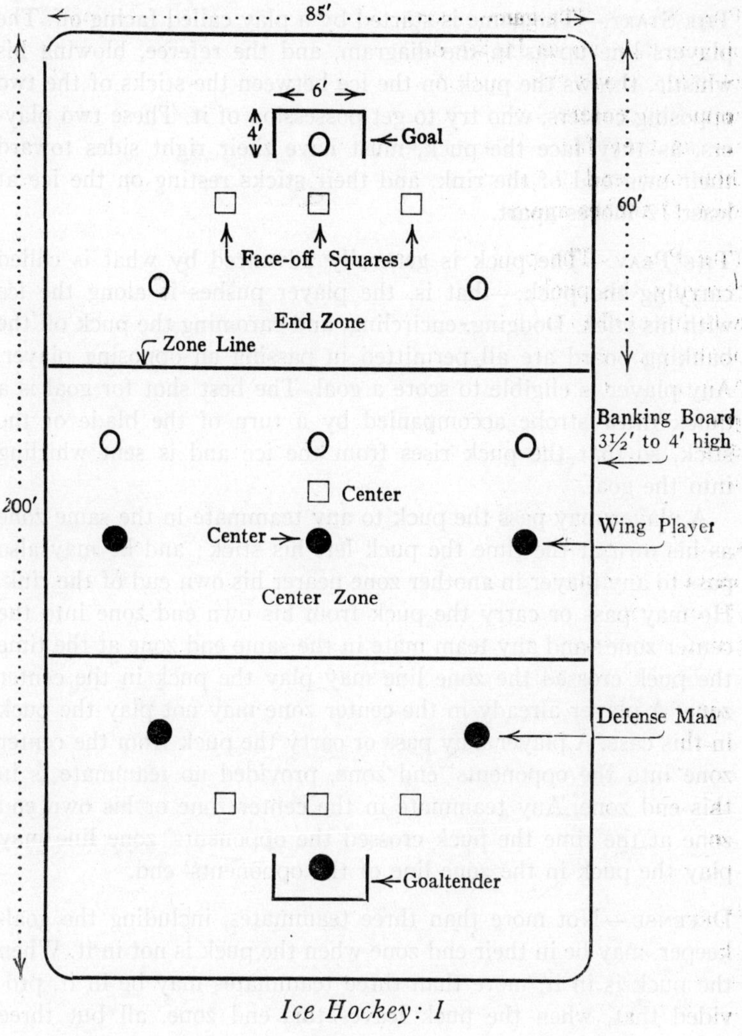

Ice Hockey: I

checked by an opponent. The goaltender is padded with a stomach protector and guards reaching from ankle to hip.

The Players: Each team consists of six players: three forwards (a center and two wing players), two defense men and a goaltender.

The Start.—The game is started by a play called facing-off. The players line up as in the diagram, and the referee, blowing his whistle, throws the puck on the ice between the sticks of the two opposing centers, who try to get possession of it. These two players, as they face the puck, must have their right sides toward their own end of the rink, and their sticks resting on the ice at least 12 inches apart.

The Play.—The puck is generally advanced by what is called carrying the puck,—that is, the player pushes it along the ice with his stick. Dodging, encircling, and caroming the puck off the banking board are all permitted in passing an opposing player Any player is eligible to score a goal. The best shot for goal is a quick draw stroke accompanied by a turn of the blade of the stick, so that the puck rises from the ice and is sent whirling into the goal.

A player may pass the puck to any teammate in the same zone as his own at the time the puck left his stick; and he may also pass to any player in another zone nearer his own end of the rink. He may pass or carry the puck from his own end zone into the center zone; and any team mate in the same end zone at the time the puck crossed the zone line may play the puck in the center zone. A player already in the center zone may not play the puck in this case. A player may pass or carry the puck from the center zone into the opponents' end zone, provided no teammate is in this end zone. Any teammate in the center zone or his own end zone at the time the puck crossed the opponents' zone line may play the puck in the zone line of the opponents' end.

Defense.—Not more than three teammates, including the goalkeeper, may be in their end zone when the puck is not in it. When the puck is in it, more than three teammates may be in it, provided that, when the puck leaves this end zone, all but three teammates must leave it at once. Additional teammates may enter the end zone ahead of the puck, if they are facing more toward their own end of the rank than their opponents' end, are covering opponents, and are not more than 5 feet away from such opponents. The defenders in possession of the puck in their own end zone must keep the puck moving. If there are no opponents in this zone, they must advance the puck toward the opponents' end of the rink; except that one defender in possession of the puck, before advancing the puck toward or across his own end zone line, may circle once only toward or behind his own goal line or cage.

Fouls.—For certain minor fouls, a player is suspended from the game for 2 minutes. These include striking an opponent with the stick; holding the stick in both hands against an opponent, called cross-checking; throwing the stick; swinging it above the shoulder; playing without a stick; charging, pushing, tripping, and similar bodily contacts; and handling or propelling the puck with any part of the body, instead of the stick. These rules apply to all players except the goalkeepers.

For certain major fouls, a player is suspended from the game for 5 minutes. These include roughing or interfering with the goalkeeper, pushing an opponent violently into the board, and throwing the stick to prevent a goal. Excessive roughness in the use of hands, feet or the stick is punished by suspension for the balance of the game.

The Face-Off after a Foul.—The puck is faced off, following a foul. At such a face-off, all players except the two who participate must be at least 10 feet from the puck, and nearer their own end of the rink than the puck. The place where the face-off takes place depends on the character of the foul, as the rules provide in each instance. This may be the spot where the foul occurred; in the center zone; or on the side face-off marks near the goals. When a foul occurs on a play that might have resulted in a goal. the puck is faced off on the penalty face-off mark directly in front of the goal.

Scoring.—Each time the puck fairly enters an opponents' goal, one point is scored by the offensive team. The largest score during the game wins. The game consists of 3 periods of 20 minutes each, with 10-minute intermissions. If the score is a tie at the end of the third period, after a 10-minute intermission there is an overtime period of 10 minutes. If the score continues tied, there is a 5-minute intermission and a second 10-minute overtime period. Only two overtime periods may be played.

Miscellaneous.—At any time when play has been officially stopped, substitutions may be made. Players who have been suspended may re-enter the game immediately upon the expiration of their penalty interval. In charge of the game is the referee, who is aided by an assistant referee. There are two goal umpires, who stand behind the goals and decide whether a scored goal is legal or not; a penalty timekeeper, who keeps time for suspended players with limited suspensions; and a timekeeper and his assistant, who keep the actual playing time of the game.

LACROSSE

The Field: The Lacrosse field is 120 yards long and from 70 to 85 yards wide. A center line is drawn across the middle, parallel to the end lines. A circle with a 10-foot radius centers the field. A barrier fence 10 feet from the boundary lines and at least 5 feet high should be constructed, to retain the ball. The goals are 80 yards apart, and midway between the side lines. The goal poles are 6 feet high and 6 feet apart, with a cross bar to which the net is attached. The net is of cord and has its central points staked to the ground 7 feet behind the center of the goal. An area termed the goal crease, 18 feet by 12, is marked out around the goal; and the goal is evenly distanced from the boundary lines of the goal crease.

Equipment: The official ball is of Indiarubber sponge, from 7¾ to 8 inches in circumference, and from 4½ to 5 ounces in weight. The Indians used a ball cut from white cedar or some other soft wood; and this may be used. The crosse resembles a longer loosely strung tennis racket, and is held in both hands.

It may be of any length to suit the player, but may not be more than one foot wide.

THE PLAYERS: A team consists of ten players: goalkeeper, point, cover point, first defense, second defense, center, second attack, first attack, outside home, and inside home. They stand as in the diagram.

THE START.—Before the game starts, the captains toss for goals. Play commences at the start of each quarter in the center of the field, by a play corresponding to the bully in hockey and to the toss-up in basketball; it is called facing. The two centers stand in the center circle, each having his left side toward the goal he is attacking, and his crosse touching the ground and parallel to the

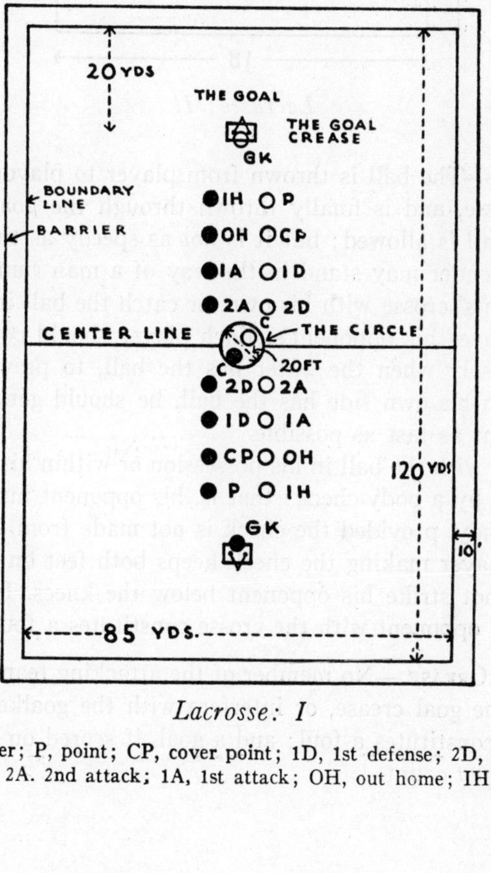

Lacrosse: I

GK, goalkeeper; P, point; CP, cover point; 1D, 1st defense; 2D, 2nd defense; C. center; 2A. 2nd attack; 1A, 1st attack; OH, out home; IH, in home

goal line. The ball is placed touching the reverse surfaces of the crosses, and resting on these reverse surfaces. At the signal, each player is free to try for the possession of the ball, by picking it up or driving it to a player on his own side.

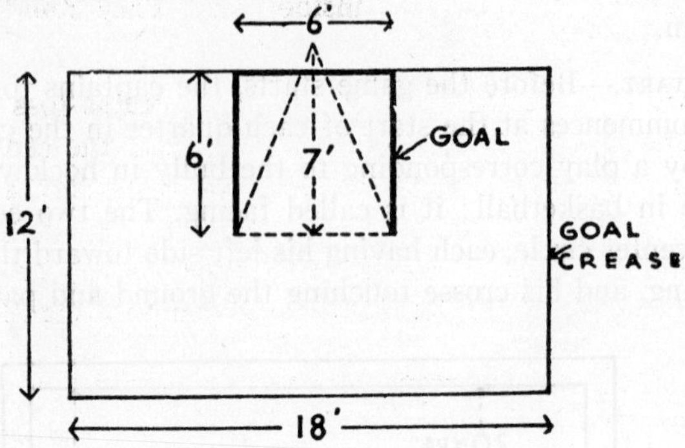

Lacrosse: II

The Play.—The ball is thrown from player to player by means of the crosse, and is finally thrown through the goal. Running with the ball is allowed; but it is not as speedy as throwing the ball. A defender may stand in the way of a man running, strike an opponents' crosse with his own, or catch the ball in his crosse when it leaves his opponent's. Each player should cover his opponent closely when the latter has the ball, to prevent a good pass. When his own side has the ball, he should get away from an opponent as fast as possible.

A player with the ball in his possession or within his reach may be stopped by a body-check; that is, his opponent may stop him with his body, provided the check is not made from behind, and that the player making the check keeps both feet on the ground and does not strike his opponent below the knees. In checking, hitting the opponent with the crosse constitutes a foul.

The Goal Crease.—No member of the attacking team is allowed to enter the goal crease, or interfere with the goalkeeper inside it. Either constitutes a foul; and a goal, if scored on such a foul play, does not count.

Offside and Out of Bounds.—At no time may a team have less than two men on the attack between the center line and the goal of the opponents; and at no time shall a team have less than two men, in addition to the goalkeeper, on defense between the center line and the boundary behind its own goal. Violations of this rule are called offside play.

When the ball goes out of bounds, the referee has the option of facing it 10 feet in from where it went out; or of allowing the nearest player to put it in play by a throw, or run from where it went out of bounds.

Fouls and Penalties.—Class A technical fouls include improper handling of the ball, such as touching it with the hands, lying on it, or causing it to go out of bounds; playing without a crosse, or throwing the crosse; and changing position during a time-out period. These are penalized by either a free-throw, or a suspension from the game of 1 minute. Other technical fouls call for suspension from 1 to 5 minutes. These include unnecessarily rough tactics, such as shouldering, clipping, tripping, body-checking or forcing an opponent into the fence; interfering with an opponent's play, such as holding his crosse, striking it, holding him with the crosse, and running or falling in front of him to keep him from the ball; and entering the goal crease or interfering with the goalkeeper.

A personal foul calls for suspension for the remainder of the game. Such fouls are called for deliberately striking an opponent, and for charging into an opponent with both hands on the crosse, so that the crosse strikes him—called cross-checking.

A free-throw is awarded to a team when it is fouled. The player fouling and the one fouled are placed at the same locations they occupied just before the foul took place, the player fouled having the ball in his crosse. At the signal, each is allowed to play in any legal manner. A free-throw may never be made within 20 yards of the opponents' goal.

Scoring.—One point is scored each time the ball is put through the goal from the front side.

Miscellaneous.—Substitutions may be made only when the play has been stopped for some other reason. A player taken from the game may return at any time except in the same quarter. When a player has been suspended for a personal foul, a substitute may be sent in to take his place, but not until the expiration of 10 minutes from the time of the suspension.

The game consists of 4 quarters of 15 minutes each, with 1, 10, and 1 minute intermissions between quarters. Shorter periods may be agreed upon. In the case of a tie, after a 5-minute rest an overtime period of 10 minutes is played. Only one overtime period is allowed. Time-out, not more than 2 minutes in duration, may be taken if a player is injured. The officials consist of a referee, a judge of play, two umpires, and two timekeepers.

LACROSSE FOR GIRLS

There are minor variations, when girls play. A team consists of twelve players, not ten. Players are allowed to propel the ball with the foot or leg. The use of arms or the crosse on an opponent's body is forbidden, and detaining an opponent must be by body-checking and no other method: that is, by placing the body in an opponent's way so she is merely impeded. There are certain restrictions on bodily contact that do not apply to the game when played by boys.

BOX LACROSSE

Box Lacrosse is played indoors or out on a field at least 160 by 60 feet, and not larger than 200 by 90 feet. The goals are 4½ feet high and the same distance apart, with a bar at the top. The net is cone-shaped, running to a stake 6 feet behind the center of the goal. The rear of the net rests on the end of the rink, midway between the side lines. The goal crease is a semicircle with a radius of 9 feet from the center of the line between the goal posts.

Sticks must not be more than 46 inches long or less than 42; except that the goalkeeper's stick may be any length. Each team consists of seven players: goalkeeper, right defense, left defense, rover, center, right forward, and left forward. The game has three 20-minute periods, with 10-minute intervals between playing periods.

The rules are as in Lacrosse, except (1) the ball may not be faced nearer than 15 feet from the goal crease or 10 feet from a boundary line; (2) no defender in possession of the ball may throw it back to the goalkeeper; (3) if the referee decides that a player deliberately threw the ball out of bounds, a free-throw is given to the opponents; (4) the penalties are suspensions of 2 and 5 minutes, or for the entire game (after 15 minutes the referee may permit a substitute in this last case, if he has announced it while pronouncing the suspension); and (5) players may be substituted at any time, provided the retiring player reaches the players' bench before the change is made.

POLO

THE FIELD: The field is 900 feet by 450. The side lines are boarded 11 inches high, to aid in keeping the ball in bounds. The goals are placed midway of the end lines, with goal posts 24 feet apart and 10 feet high, made of wicker light enough to break in case of a collision.

EQUIPMENT: Polo is played on horseback, and four ponies are usually required for each player, a pony being played one or two periods. The ball is of light wood, usually willow, covered only with white paint. Its diameter is 3¼ inches, and its weight 5½ ounces. The mallets have cane shafts and ash heads, set at an angle. In length, the mallets range from 48 to 52 inches.

THE PLAYERS: Four players constitute a team. Number 1 and Number 2 are primarily offensive players; Number 3 a rover, ready to aid in attack or defense; and Number 4 the back player, who usually stays near his own goal.

THE START.—At the start, the four players of each team line up in the middle of the field, facing the side boards. The referee rides toward them, throws the ball between them, and play is on. After each goal, play is resumed in the same fashion, the teams changing goals after each goal scored.

The Play.—In playing, the players strike the ball with the side of the mallet, endeavoring to drive it toward the opponents' goal and over the line between the goal posts.

Fouls.—The player who last hit the ball has a right to continue on its line of travel, and has the right of way over a player approaching at an angle. If the approaching player crosses in front of the former player, or close enough to cause him to swerve or check, it is a foul. The penalty may be a free-hit from where the foul occurred, or from the 30, 40 or 60 yard line, depending on the danger incurred and its effect upon a possible goal. In extreme cases, a goal may be awarded to the fouled side. Zigzagging in front of an approaching player, stopping on the ball, hooking with the mallet unless the ball is between two players, and dangerous riding, are also considered fouls.

Out of Bounds.—If an attacking player drives the ball over the end lines but not between the goal posts, a defender puts it in play by a free-hit from the point where it went out. In no case may the hit be made closer than 12 feet from the goal post. If a defender, attempting to prevent a goal, causes the ball to go over his own end line, a safety is called, and the other side is given a free-hit from the 60-yard line, at the point opposite the point where the ball went out.

Scoring.—A goal is made when the ball crosses the goal line between the goal posts, even if it is higher than the posts. The goalkeeper waves a flag overhead when a goal is made, and waves it parallel with the ground when the ball goes over the end line without scoring a goal.

Length of Game.—A game consists of eight periods or chukkers, of 7½ minutes each. The intermissions are 2½ minutes each; except that between the fourth and fifth chukker, which is 5 minutes. At the end of a period, the timekeeper signals the end of play; play continues, however, until the ball goes out of bounds, or a goal is made, or some point reached where play can be stopped without advantage to either side.

WHEELBARROW POLO

Each team consists of eight players, four to wheel the wheelbarrows, four to sit in them and play the ball. Each player has a house broom or toy broom for a mallet. An inflated ball, such as a soccer ball or sport ball, is used. The field should be about 80 by 60 feet.

The teams line their wheelbarrows up, as in the beginning of polo, about 10 feet apart, facing the side lines. The referee rolls the ball between the lines and sounds his whistle. The teams then play as in polo. A goal is scored when the ball is hit over the opponents' goal line. The pusher and his rider may exchange places at any time; but only the rider may play the ball, and may only touch it when in the wheelbarrow.

Kiddy-Kar Polo.—In this variation, each player rides a kiddy-kar. Six players constitute a team. Toy brooms are used. Otherwise the rules are the same as for Wheelbarrow Polo.

HOCKEY KEEP-BALL

The players are divided into two teams, the members of a team being marked so that they can be clearly distinguished. The area should be limited. The game starts by a bully in the center; and thereafter each team strives to keep the ball in its possession, and prevent the other side from obtaining or keeping it.

HOCKEY TEN-PASSES

This is a hockey adaptation of Ten Catches. Teams are divided and clearly marked. Each player has a hockey stick. The game starts with a center bully, and the object is as in Hockey Keep-Ball; except that the first player on a side who passes the ball to a team mate calls "One," the next "Two," and so on until 10 is reached, which wins the game; or until an opponent gets possession of the ball and starts a sequence toward reaching 10.

SHINNY

Shinny is similar to Field Hockey, but simpler. Any convenient field can be used, with side lines and end lines marked. The game may be played with a hard rubber ball, any ball not larger than a baseball, a block of wood, or a tin can. Regular hockey sticks may be used, or sticks improvised from sticks bent or crooked at the bottom.

The game is started by placing the ball in the center of the field as in Field Hockey, between two opposing players. After the ball is put in play, it is knocked down the field toward the opponents' goal. There are no offside rules. One is required to "shinny on his own side"; that is, one must face the goal toward which the ball is being knocked and hit the ball on the hitter's right side; otherwise another player may hit the offender on the shins with his stick. One point is scored each time the ball crosses the opponents' goal line.

Roller Skate Shinny.—A variation of Shinny, played in the same way except that the players wear roller skates.

Charley-Horse Polo.—This variation is played indoors on a basketball court. It is played in the same way as Shinny, except that a tennis ball or softball is used. The ends of the sticks may be wrapped with leather or string, to protect the floor.

SHINNY HOCKEY

Shinny Hockey may be played indoors or out. The court is 100 feet long and 75 to 50 feet wide; or a basketball court may be used. Goals 5 feet in width are marked midway of the end lines, the markers being two feet long at right angles to the end line. Shinny sticks, or light-weight Field Hockey sticks, are used, and an Ice Hockey puck or an informal wooden puck. Five to ten players constitute a team.

The bully-off is as in Field Hockey. Fouls include failure to "shinny on your own side"; hitting or tripping an opponent with the stick; shoving an opponent; raising or swinging the stick above hip level; handling the puck with the hands, or stopping it or playing it with the feet. A player of the fouled side takes the puck out of bounds, when a foul is committed, nearest to the spot where the foul occurred, and tosses it not over 5 feet to a team mate. No opponent may stand nearer than 5 feet while this is being done.

One point is scored each time the puck legally crosses the 5-foot goal line. Game may consist of the first 10 points scored; or may consist of four 5-minute quarters, with 2, 5 and 2 minute intervals between the quarters.

STICK POLO

The field is about 80 feet by 50, outdoors or in. Each player has a stick about 3 feet long. A soccer ball is used. The two teams, of any number of players, line up on their end lines. The ball is placed midway of the field. At a signal, both teams rush for the ball, and attempt to knock it over the opposing goal line. The ball may be moved with the stick only; kicking the ball or playing it with any part of the body is not allowed. The penalty for a violation of this is a free-hit for the opponents, with the other team's players at least 10 feet away. If the ball rolls out of bounds, it is rolled in by the referee at the point where it went out. One point is scored each time the ball goes over the opponents' goal line. A time limit must be set for the game, in advance.

FLOOR HOCKEY

This is an indoor game, using a gymnasium floor for a field. The goals are 72 inches long and 6 inches high, inside dimensions; and may be of one-inch galvanized pipe, or of wood. If of pipe, they should be attached to a 6-inch base of wood. An ice-hockey puck or its equivalent is used. A lighter stick than that for Ice Hockey is used. Each team has six players: goalkeeper, right and left guards, and center, right and left forwards.

The game is started by bullying-off, by placing the puck between the sticks of two opposing players, or by dropping it between them. The play follows the form in Ice Hockey. The puck may be stopped by any part of the body, but may not be carried, held, knocked on, or kicked; except that the goalkeeper may kick the puck away from the goal. No stick may be raised above hip level, or thrown. Charging, kicking, tripping or pushing an opponent is forbidden, on penalty of suspension from the game. No player is allowed to sit, lie or kneel on the floor in front of his goal, or place the full length of his stick on the floor before it. For violations of these rules, a player is to be suspended from the game for 1, 2 or more minutes, and no substitute may take his place. When the referee stops the game during a period, play is resumed by dropping the puck between the sticks of two opposing players at the point where it was last played. One point is scored by a team each time the puck passes through the opponents' goal.

BROOM HOCKEY

The field is approximately the size of a basketball court, and may be outdoors or in. The goal is two uprights 6 feet apart and connected by a bar 3 feet from the floor. Each player is equipped with a housebroom, approximately 31 inches long. A sport ball of inflated rubber, 5 inches in diameter, is used; a 6-inch codeball may be used instead.

Each team consists of five players: center, right and left forward, guard, and goal guard. The ball is placed midway of the playing field, the opposing centers standing beside it with their brooms touching the floor on either side of it. At a signal, they are free to strike the ball. The ball is returned into play each time the same way. The ball may be played only with the brooms; and no player but the goal guard may use any part of the body to advance or stop the ball. When a ball is knocked out of bounds, the referee brings it to the center of the field opposite the point where it went out, and it is put in play by two opposing players, as at the start of the game. The goal guard may not catch the ball, hold it, kick it, or hit it with his hands; but he may block it with any part of his body. He may propel it only with the broom. If a goal guard leaves his position in front of the goal, he loses the especial privileges of a goal guard. Holding, deliberately knocking the ball out of bounds, delaying the game, holding the ball with the hands or between the legs, unnecessary roughness, or any violations of the rules constitute a foul. The penalty is a free try for goal from a position midway between the side lines 10 feet from the goal, only the goal guard being allowed to stop it; he must have both feet on the ground at the time of stopping it, or it scores. However, in the case of unnecessary roughness, the penalty instead is 1 minute's suspension from the game for the offender, no substitute taking his place; and for deliberately striking an opponent, or for the third instance of unnecessary roughness on the part of a player, the suspension is for the balance of the game, and a substitute may be sent in.

One point is scored each time the ball is put legally through the goal. The game consists of four 5-minute periods, with intermissions of 1, 3 and 1 minutes. The officials are a referee and a timekeeper.

ROLLER-SKATE HOCKEY

The rink is approximately 90 by 60 feet. The goals are 5 feet wide and 4 feet high, and are placed 6 feet from the end of the rink, halfway between the side lines. All players wear roller skates. An Ice Hockey puck is used. The hockey sticks must not be more than 3½ inches thick at any part, and must be entirely of wood, with tape binding permissible. Six players constitute a team.

The game is started by facing-off, as in Ice Hockey. The rules are as in Ice Hockey, with the following exceptions: There is no offside; but loafing offside, that is, near the opponents' goal when the puck is at the other end of the rink, is prohibited. The goalkeeper may catch the puck, but must immediately drop it. The puck may be kicked at any time; but a goal may not be scored in this manner. For minor fouls, the penalty is suspension from the game for 2 minutes; for major fouls, 5 minutes. Grossly unsportsmanlike conduct is penalized by expulsion from the game, with a substitute allowed after 5 minutes.

A game consists of three periods of 20 minutes each; with a 5-minute overtime period in case of a tie, the first goal scored during overtime ending the game. A goal is scored only when the puck legally crosses between the goal posts; it may not be kicked or thrown across and score as a goal.

HAND HOCKEY

The court is a basketball court, or one of approximately the same size. The end lines constitute the goals; the basketball free-throw lines, extended across the court, form end zones. A volley-ball may be used; or a sport ball of similar size will serve. Each team consists of nine players: a center, five fielders, and three goalkeepers. The goalkeepers play in the end zones; the center starts in the center circle, but thereafter joins the fielders, playing on any part of the floor.

The game starts with the two opposing centers standing in the center circle, each with their left side toward the opponents' goal, and with one hand on the ball. At the signal, the centers try to roll or push the ball to their team mates. The ball must be played with the hand, not kicked; and only one hand may be used. The hand must be kept open. Goalkeepers alone may use both hands, and may pick up the ball and throw it back on the floor away from the goal. They may not take more than one step with the ball, or hold it longer than 3 seconds; nor may they step out of their end zone.

A violation of any of these rules is a foul, penalized by a free bat to the ball given to a player of the opposing team, from the spot where the foul occurred. Opponents must stand at least 10 feet away during this free bat. If a defender commits a foul within his own end zone, an opponent is given a free-hit at the ball from the end zone line, with his team mates behind this line and the defenders lined up behind their goal line until the ball is struck. If a ball rolls out of bounds, it is rolled back in by a member of the team that did not cause it to go out. The players may line up at right angles to the side line, but may not be closer than 3 feet to the spot where the ball is rolled in.

One point is scored for each time the ball legally crosses the opponents' goal line. The game consists of two 10-minute halves.

MASS FIELD HOCKEY

Any number of players participate, divided into two equal teams. The periods are 10 minutes each, one, two or more periods constituting a game. The play follows the rules of Field Hockey, except that: (1) Players are eliminated for fouls; (2) after a foul, the ball is returned to play by a bully-off at the spot where the foul took place; (3) there are no boundary lines, and hence no out-of-bounds plays; and (4) the offside rule is disregarded, and hence players can be in play at any part of the field at any time.

KONANO

Konano is a game remotely resembling Lacrosse, adapted by Theresa Anderson and L. E. Hutto from a game played by the Mesquaki Indians, among whom it was played by the women, while Lacrosse was played by the men.

THE FIELD: The field is 40 to 80 yards long, and 40 yards wide, For girls, it may be 50 yards by 30. The goals are 6 feet wide and 7 feet high, made of light strips of wood. There are no side or end lines; but a center line divides the field into two halves. At each goal there is a goal area marked, a semicircle with a 12-foot radius, measured from a point midway between the goal posts on the line joining them.

EQUIPMENT: Each player has a stick 42 inches long and about ¾ of an inch thick. The konano consists of 2 balls joined together by a thong or a strip of canvas. It can be made of canvas sacks stuffed with sawdust and sewn tight, forming balls 5 inches in diameter; joined by a canvas strip 1½ inches wide, and 10 to 12 inches long. The entire konano is about 20 inches long.

TEAMS: A team consists of ten players, or less. With ten on a team, there are five forwards, four backs, and one goal guard. The forwards and backs are not permitted to leave their half of the field during play, and the goal guard should remain close to the goal.

The Start.—The referee, called the watcher, tosses the konano high in the air between the two opposing forwards standing at the center line. These forwards try to secure the konano on their sticks, or knock it to a team mate. All players must be on their side of the center line at the toss, and may not come within the distance of an arm and an extended stick of the two forwards at center until the konano has been touched. As soon as it is put in play, the forwards of each team cross into their halves of the field.

The Play.—The object of the game is to catch the konano on a player's stick, and throw or carry it through the goal. The players are allowed to toss the konano back and forth, and to carry it on the stick until the player is in position for a throw for or a run through the goal. If the goal is missed and the konano goes behind the goal, the play continues as usual. No player but the goal guard is allowed in the goal zone, except in the case of an attacking forward who has possession of the konano, and who gained possession of it before entering the goal zone.

Fouls.—Fouls include (1) striking or slapping with the stick, or starting a stick movement above the shoulders (in carrying the konano or following through a swing, however, the stick may go above the shoulders); carrying or directly hitting the konano with the hand (if it slips down the stick and touches the hand, it is a foul only if it is not moved out at once); (3) forwards or backs crossing the center lines from their respective territories; and (4) entering the goal zone, except as permitted. Unless the foul occurred near the goal, the penalty is a free-throw from the spot where the foul occurred. If it occurred near the goal, the goal guard has the option of having the free-throw take place from the spot where the foul occurred, or from a spot 15 feet directly in front of the goal. No player may be between the player and the goal except the goal guard, who stands directly in front of the goal. If two opposing players foul at the same time, the konano is tossed up between them.

Scoring.—One point is scored each time the konano legally passes through the goal from the front side.

Length of Game.—The game consists of four periods of 5 or 6 minutes each, with 1 minute intermissions. The periods may be made as long as 8 minutes each.

V. THE BASKETBALL GROUP

Basketball is the youngest of major team contests. It was invented in 1891 by Dr. James Naismith, as a synthetic cross between Soccer and Lacrosse. It took hold at once, Yale organizing a team as early as 1893. The idea was to design an indoor variation of Football. Kicking was prohibited, and also running with the ball; the latter rule eliminating tackling and interference. The ball is advanced by passing or by dribbling—that is, a player's bouncing the ball against the floor, or tossing it in the air once and retaining possession of it.

It has given birth to more minor and practice variations than any other major sport.

BASKETBALL

The Court: The maximum size of the court is 94 feet by 50; it may be as small as 60 feet by 35. The goals, metal rings 18 inches in inside diameter, are rigidly attached to backboards 2 feet from the center of each endline, so that they reach out horizontally 10 feet above the floor. The diagram indicates the markings.

Equipment: An official basketball is used, round and slightly larger than a soccer ball.

The Players: A team consists of five players; two forwards, a center, and two guards. The forwards lead the attack, and specialize in goal-throwing. The center puts the ball in play, and assists forwards and guards. The guards safeguard the goal.

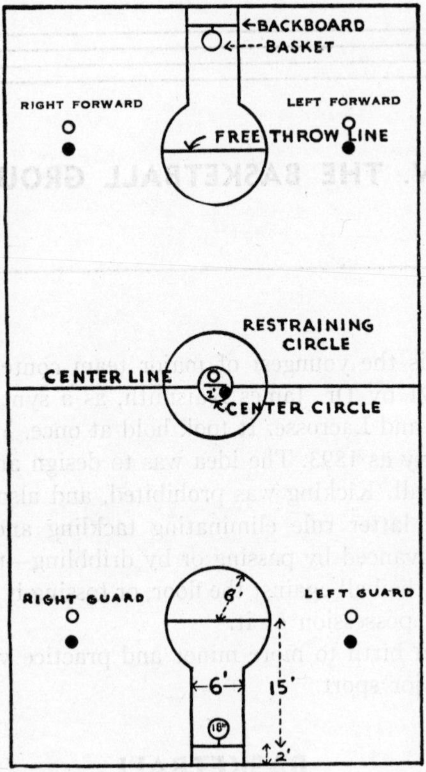

Basketball: I

The Toss-Up.—Each center stands inside his half of the center circle, at the beginning of the game. The referee tosses the ball up between the two centers to put it in play. A similar toss-up takes place when the ball is held in tie by two opposing players; the toss-up in this latter instance taking place at the point where the held ball was called, or at the nearer free-throw line if it occurs in the free-throw lane. After a field goal a player of the team scored upon shall put the ball in play from any point out of bounds at the end of the court where the goal was made.

The Play.—After the ball is put in play, it may be batted, rolled, bounced, or thrown in any direction, with one or both hands. A player is not allowed to kick the ball, strike it with closed fist, or run with it. Dribbling against the floor is permitted and the ball may be tossed in the air once during a dribble. When a player who is running receives the ball, he may take not more than one step with it before getting rid of it, on penalty of being charged with a violation of the rule forbidding running with the ball.

When a team gains possession of the ball on its own side of the center line, it must advance it legally into the front court within 10 seconds, unless the ball is touched by an opponent. Each time it is touched, a new 10-second period starts.

Out of Bounds.—When a ball goes out of bounds, it is thrown back into play by a player on the team who did not cause it to go out of bounds.

Violations and Fouls.—Minor infractions of the rules are called violations. When these occur, the ball is given to a player of the offended team at the nearest side line, to permit it to be thrown back into play. More serious violations are called fouls, whether technical or dealing with bodily contact. The penalty for a foul is a free-throw for goal from behind the free-throw line; unless the foul was committed against a player while he was throwing for a field goal, in which case the penalty is two free-throws if the field goal was missed.

Scoring.—For each goal thrown from the field, 2 points; for a free-throw resulting in a goal, 1 point.

Length of Game.—The game is usually two 20-minute halves, with a 15-minute intermission, which may be reduced to 10 minutes by mutual agreement. For younger players, it may consist of four 8- or 6-minute quarters, with intermissions of 1, 10 and

1 minutes, or 2, 10, and 2 minutes. A team is entitled to four time-outs during the game, which may be taken at the request of the captain whenever the ball is dead. Younger players may have five time-outs.

BASKETBALL FOR WOMEN

When basketball is played by women, the court is either a 3-division court ranging in size from 90 by 45 feet to 70 by 35 feet, the divisions being equal in width and separated by division lines 12 inches wide; or 2-division court 70 feet or less by 35 feet or less, equally divided into two halves. The trend is toward the 2-division court.

Teams consist of six players each; or they may consist of nine. In the 3-division game, there are two forwards, two centers, and two guards, who may not leave their divisions during the play. In the 2-division game, there are three forwards and three guards, one forward being designated to serve as center. Only forwards are permitted to throw goals.

The game is started by a toss-up, or by a center throw, whichever method is preferred being agreed on in advance. In the center throw, the referee hands the ball to the center who is to throw, and then blows his whistle to start the game. Each quarter starts with a play from center, unless a foul has been committed during an intermission.

The ball is advanced as in the boys' game, except that it may not be rolled, and may not be handed from player to player. It must be caught with two hands, but may be retained or thrown with one. A player may bounce the ball in air once, or dribble it against the floor once; but may not do both without an intervening play with the ball by another player. A ball must be thrown within 3 seconds after it is received. It is not permissible for a player to place a hand on the ball when an opponent holds it.

BUCKETBALL

In this variation, 2 buckets on the ground are the goals. Two points are scored each time the ball is put in the bucket and remains there. If the bucket upsets, no points are scored. In this and all subsequent variations, all Basketball rules apply, unless otherwise expressly stated.

Hobble Bucketball.—Played the same, except that each player has his ankles firmly tied together with a belt or piece of rope, and hence must jump or hobble.

KEEP-BALL, KEEP-AWAY, PIG

The object of this variation is to keep the ball from passing into the hands of the opponents. Any number of players may constitute a team. The ball may not be held longer than 5 seconds. A violation of a rule gives the ball to the opponents. There is no scoring.

The passes may be limited to bounce passes, or push passes, or one-arm passes, etc. It may also be played in a Nine-Court Basketball court, the players being forbidden to step out of their respective courts. It may also be played in a 3-division court, with similar restrictions.

TEN CATCHES

In this variation, the object is for a team to make 10 consecutive passes before the opponents can get the ball. Each player passing announces the number of his pass: "One," "Two," etc. When the ball is captured by the opponents, touched by them, or touches the floor, the numbering starts afresh.

The game may be played by scoring as winner the team that makes the most consecutive passes during play, announced as above.

GUARD BALL

Draw two parallel lines 10 feet apart on the floor, allowing 3 feet to each player behind the line. One team is placed between the lines; the other divided behind both lines. The object is for the team outside of the lines to pass the ball back and forth through the players in the center, below the height of the players' heads. One point is scored for each successful pass. The game consists of four 3-minute periods. The teams change positions after each period. Bounce passes may or may not be permitted.

SCORE-BALL

In Score-Ball, each side has a scorer; and the highest total of successful passes during play wins. This may be played on a Nine-Court Basketball court.

BOUNDARY BALL

Divide the court into two equal halves. Place half of each team in each half. A volleyball, soccer bail or basketball is used. The object is to pass the ball as in basketball, and then to roll or bounce it over the opponents' goal line. Throwing the ball over on the fly is prohibited. Players may not cross the center line. One point is scored for each legal goal.

CENTER MISS BALL

The players stand in a circle, with one in the center. Two balls are used. As the center throws one ball to a player in the circle, a player in the circle throws the other ball to the center. Thereafter the center must throw the ball to the players in rotation. When the center misses or fumbles, the player who caused this becomes center. Especial passes may be designated, as, push pass, one-arm pass, cross-chest pass, and so on.

TWO BALL GAMES

Most of these games may be played with two balls in play at the same time. A goal scored by each scores twice as much as one goal. This applies to Basketball, Soccer, Speedball, Beeball, Hockey, and their variations.

OTHER MINOR BASKETBALL GAMES

KING-BALL

The players line up on the four sides of a square about 30 feet wide, the player on the right of each line being called the king. The ball must be passed to a player in another line. A player fumbling the ball or making an uncatchable throw must recover the ball. While he is doing so the players below him on his line move one space each to the right, and the player recovering the ball takes the place on the extreme left of the line. The object is to remain as king.

PIN-GUARD

The players stand in a 20-foot circle. An Indian club is placed in its center, inside a 3-foot circle. One player is center and guards the pin, but may not step inside the circle while doing so. The players in the circle throw a basketball in at the pin. Any player knocking down the pin or causing the center to knock it down becomes center. If the center can get the ball, he may throw it beyond the circle, thus giving himself a rest. The player who remains center longest wins. Players may run for the ball, but must throw only from the circle.

Team Pin-Guard.—In this variation, the two teams are in two 30-foot circles; with a player of the opposite team inside each circle, as center and pin-guard. Each team throws with a soccer ball or basketball. The center may guard with hands, legs and body. The team that knocks down the pin first scores one, and play stops, while in rotation two more players become the centers, and so on. The team scoring the most points wins.

CIRCLE POLE BALL

Two circles are drawn as in Circle Soccer, one 20 to 25 feet in diameter, the other 4 feet less. A pole 12 to 15 feet high is placed in the center. Each team is divided into two parts, basemen and guards. One guard stands by the pole, to guard it. The guards stand in front of the basemen, inside the inner circle, the basemen between the circles—each team's basemen being restricted to their half of the inter-circular space, marked off by a diameter of the circles passing through the pole.

The toss-up is as in Basketball, between the two pole guards. The guards seek to gain the ball, and throw it to a baseman on their team, who tries to hit the pole with it. Guarding is as in Basketball. For any violation of a Basketball rule, the ball is given to a guard of the offended side. The same applies when the ball is out of bounds. One point is scored for each ball that hits the pole. The team with the largest score in a given time limit wins.

BOTTLE BALL

Draw a center line dividing a court 50 feet by 25 into two equal divisions. In the middle of each rear line place six Indian clubs or similar objects in a row. Each team occupies a court. One team is given a basketball, to start the game. Each team endeavors to defend its own pins, and knock down the opponents' pins with the ball. A pin knocked down is left down. The team wins which first knocks down all of the opponents' pins.

NEWCOMB

A net or rope 7 foot high divides a 50- by 25-foot court into equal parts. A volleyball or basketball is used. One team occupies each half of the court. The ball is thrown over the net, and must be caught and thrown back. This continues until a point is scored. The ball may not be relayed, but must be returned across the net each time by the person who caught it. The team which loses the point starts each fresh rally by throwing the ball over the net. If a player touches the ball, he is responsible for catching it, and cannot claim that it was going out.

Scoring.—One point is scored each time the ball drops to the ground in an opponent's court; and also for any of these fouls:

hitting the net with the ball; throwing the ball under the net; relaying the ball or having two players of the same team touch it in succession; or throwing the ball outside the opponents' court, provided it is not touched by a member of the opposing team.

The game consists of two 10-minute periods.

Volleyball Newcomb.—This is scored as in Volleyball. Only the serving side scores; it continues to score, until it loses. The service throw must be from behind the rear line. A game is 15 points.

Volley Newcomb.—Regular Newcomb, with Volleyball service.

Fence-Ball.—This is Newcomb, played across a fence, with no boundary lines. The general rules of Newcomb apply.

Forward-Pass Newcomb.—The court is 145 feet by 45. A neutral zone 30 feet wide is marked lengthwise of the court. Each team occupies its court. The object is to throw into the opponents' court a college football which will hit the ground without being caught. Score one for each such hit. A game is 15 points.

Goal Post Newcomb.—The two teams line up on opposite sides of a College Football goal, and endeavor to throw the ball over the bar and between the posts so that opponents cannot catch it. The ball may be relayed once to a team mate before a try for goal is made. Score as in Newcomb; or 15 points may constitute a game.

Ground-Ball.—A space 75 feet by 25 is divided by two cross lines into three equal courts. The central zone is the neutral area. A basketball or volleyball is used. The object is as in Goal Post Newcomb. A game is 15 points.

CURTAIN-BALL

A solid wall or fence at least 8 feet high separates the teams, with no boundary lines. A basketball or volleyball is used. The object is as in Forward Pass Newcomb. A game is 10 points.

CABINET BALL

This game was originated by Herbert Hoover while President, and was played with his Cabinet on the White House Lawn. A Volleyball court is used, with a net 8 feet high. The service line on each side of the net is 15 feet from it. The ball is a small medicine ball, 12 inches in diameter, weighing 6 pounds. Any number of players constitute a team, though in match games a team consists of nine players. The rules are the same as those in Volleyball, except that (1) in serving, the ball is thrown with one hand from the service line, and must be relayed once and then clear the net; (2) one or both hands are used in catching the ball, and the body may be used to aid; (3) the ball must be put in play immediately, either by relaying it to a team mate or throwing it over the net; and (4) the ball must be thrown in a rising direction. Fouls comprise: relaying more than once; holding the ball more than 5 seconds; walking with the ball; and stepping over the boundary lines.

CIRCLE STRIDE-BALL

The players stand in a circle, with legs wide apart, and their hands on their knees. In the center stands one player with a basketball or football. He endeavors to throw it between the legs of the players. Hands must be kept on the knees, until the ball leaves the center's hands. When a ball passes through a player's legs, he becomes center.

Partner Circle Stride-Ball.—The center has a partner outside the circle, who endeavors to throw the ball back into the circle through a player's legs, once it has come outside the circle. Both center and his partner change places with players in the circle as in Circle Stride-Ball.

Team Circle Stride-Ball.—This requires two circles, one of each team; with one opponent standing inside each circle as the center. When either center throws a ball through, play stops in both circles, and he scores one point for each such throw. New centers thereupon enter the circles, and so in rotation. The team first scoring 10 points wins.

ENDBALL

The court is 50 feet by 30, with a center line dividing it into two equal playing courts, and two base areas at the ends, made by drawing lines parallel to the end lines and 6 to 8 feet away. A basketball, volleyball, softball or sportball is used. The teams should have from twelve to fifteen players each. Two-thirds of each team occupy their respective playing courts outside of the base areas as guards; the other third are the basemen, occupying the bases of the opposite playing court.

The object of the game is for the guards to throw the ball over the heads of the opposing guards, so that their basemen may catch the ball. After each score, the players rotate, giving each player a chance to have his time as guard. A toss-up between two central guards opens the game. Baseman are not allowed to step over the baselines. There is one score for each ball caught by a baseman; but the ball, which must be returned immediately, does not score when the guards catch it. A guard may not run with the ball nor hold it more than 3 seconds. It may be relayed between guards before being thrown to the basemen. Play does not stop when a score is made. An out-of-bounds ball is returned by the nearest guardsman to a guard on his team; a ball over the end line is similarly returned by the nearest baseman. Fouls consist of stepping over a division line, taking more than one step while holding the ball, or holding it more than 3 seconds. One point is scored for each legal catch by a baseman, and for each foul by an opponent. The game is in two halves of 10 minutes each, the teams changing sides at the end of the first half.

CORNERBALL

The Cornerball court is similar to the Endball court, except that, in place of the base areas, there is in each corner a box 6 or 8 feet square. Rotation is similar. Scoring is one point for a legal catch by a corner man, and one point for a foul by an opponent. The rules of Endball apply.

CAPTAINBALL

Captainball was originated as Centerball in Cincinnati, Ohio, in 1896, by Dr. E. A. Poos. The field is 60 feet by 30, with a crosswise neutral zone 2 feet wide in the middle. Six circles are drawn in each playing court, each 4 feet in diameter. The rear

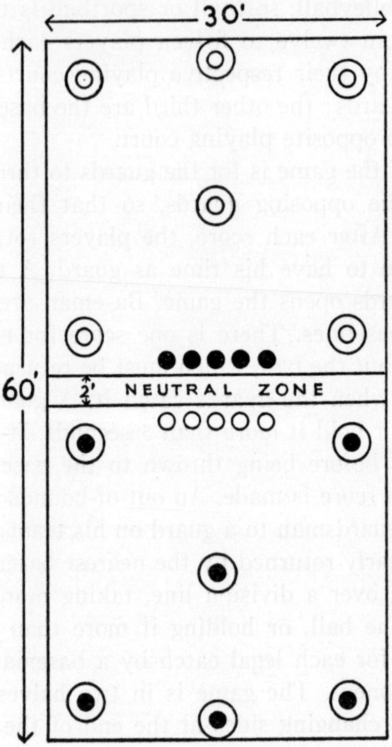

Captainball: Fig. I

middle circle touches the middle of each rear boundary line. There are four corner circles, 2 feet from the boundary lines of each playing court; and a center circle centering the four corner circles.

Each team has eleven players. They are arranged as in Fig. I: a center in the central circle, a player in each circle, and five guards, lined up: left front guard, left rear guard, center guard, right rear guard, right front guard. The object is to score one point for any player in a circle who legally throws the ball to center; or to score 3 points when the ball is passed by any player in a circle to the next circle, and so on around, until it has made a complete circuit of all the circles.

The game starts with a toss-up between two opposing guards. A ball out of bounds on either side is given to a guard on that side to put in play again. Fouls include direct interference; stepping into a circle to prevent a throw, in which case the ball is awarded to the offended player, even though this completes a scoring passing; indirect interference, stepping into a circle but not interfering with a play, the penalty being a free-throw, or, for three instances, 1 point; holding of arms over the space within the circle, or stepping out of the circles to interfere with a guard, a free-throw being awarded for either. If a guard knocks a ball from the hands of a circle player, the decision is to the circle player.

The game consists of two halves of 12½ minutes each, with a 10-minute intermission. The teams change fields between the halves. The scoring sometimes is 2 points for a throw from circle to center, and 1 point each time the ball is passed to a circle player in making the circuit of the outer circles.

Variation.—There is no center circle, all of the circles being placed along one huge circle reaching from the end line to two-thirds of the way to the center line. The Captain stands in the circle nearest the end line. The object of the game is to pass the ball to him, and to prevent the opponents from doing likewise. Only a throw from a circle player to Captain scores, or a free throw given to a fouled player, which he makes to the Captain. Fouls include those listed above, a guard's touching a ball held by a circle player, holding the ball longer than 3 seconds or taking more than one step with the ball, and bouncing the ball more than once before passing it. The circle men may relay the ball as long as they choose. A pass from a guard to the Captain does not score.

In one variation, a pass to a Captain scores 2; from 1 circle player to another, 1.

Captain Basketball.—In this variation, any circle player may, whenever he has the ball, try for a basketball goal, which counts 2 points if made.

LANE CORNERBALL

This variation of Cornerball has a court 50 to 90 feet long, and 30 to 60 feet wide. A lane 8 to 16 feet wide runs lengthwise down the court, and this lane may be occupied by guards of either team at any time, and throws to the corner men may be made from the lane or from the rear playing court. Basketball rules apply to handling the ball, running with it, and guarding.

TOUCHDOWN PASS BALL

Eight players constitute a team. The field is 78 by 45 feet. A basketball or sport ball is used. The object of the game is to pass the ball until it can be touched down behind the end line of the opponents. The rules are as in Basketball. A team fouled is awarded 1 point, and a pass touched down behind the end line counts 2 points. The game consists of two 5-minute halves, with a 2-minute intermission.

Drive Ball.—In this variation, a goal is scored by a fly ball that is thrown and falls to the floor behind the end lines. Whenever a ball is touched by an opponent, it becomes his ball at that spot, and from it a free-throw is allowed, with all opponents at least 5 feet away. A goal scores 1 point.

NINE-COURT BASKETBALL

To crosswise lines and two lengthwise lines divide the court into 9 equal courts. The court is otherwise a regulation Basketball court, which should be from 90 feet by 45 to 60 by 35. The courts are numbered from one corner court along the end line, up the side line, along the other end line, down the side line, with the central court as court 9. Nine players usually play on a team;

less or more may be used. If less than nine play, leave one or both courts flanking the central court empty. When more than nine play, place more than one player in certain courts. Each time a goal is made, the players rotate to the next highest numbered court, those in 9 returning to 1. The game is played in four 5-minute quarters, with 2-, 5,- and 2-minute intermissions. Points are scored as in Basketball for girls. Only the forwards may throw goals. Free throws are made only by the forwards in courts 2 and 6.

The rules are the same as in Basketball for girls, except that bouncing the ball is prohibited. If more than two players are in courts 2 or 6 when a free-throw takes place, only one is allowed in the court, the other players standing across the division line in a flanking court.

PIN BASKETBALL

A Nine-Court Basketball court is used. A circle 3 feet in diameter is drawn midway of each middle end court touching the end line. An Indian club is placed in each such circle. It should be attached to a block of wood 6 inches square, to give it greater stability. Nine-Court Basketball rules apply, except that a goal is scored by knocking down the Indian club with the ball, which must hit the floor before hitting the club. This scores 2 points. In free-throws, the ball is thrown at the club, and not rolled. Goals from free-throws score 1. Players must not step in the circles, on penalty of a free-throw for the opponents.

Post Ball.—In this variation of Pin Basketball, a player stands inside the circle; when he catches a ball thrown by one of his team mates, he scores 1 for his side. The player in the circle, called the post, may not step outside the circle, and other players may not step inside. If play is too vigorous, a restraining circle 6 feet in diameter may be drawn around the post circle.

BASKET ENDBALL

The court is a girls' Basketball court, but each of the three divisions is divided by another crosswise line into two divisions, making six divisions in all. Nine to twenty-one players constitute a team. One-third of each team are guards; one-third, centers; and one-third, forwards. The guards are in the two divisions nearest the end lines; the opposing forwards are in the divisions next to these; and the centers are in the two central divisions, the opponents in the one further from the basket they are attacking.

Toss-up as in Basketball. No player may leave the division he is placed in at the beginning, and may not step over a division line. When the ball goes out of bounds over an end line, it is given to a guard in the nearest division. Only forwards may throw for the goal. Fouls include: (1) carrying the ball; (2) dribbling or bouncing it; (3) playing it when an opponent has it; and (4) stepping over division lines. A free-throw is awarded to the opponents at a foul; any forward takes it, as in Basketball.

When the ball is passed into the hands of a forward, 1 point is scored. If a basket is made, 2 additional points are scored. A free-throw scores 1 point. The game consists of three periods of equal length. At the beginning of each period, the guards become centers; the centers, forwards; and the forwards, guards.

ONE-GOAL BASKETBALL

In this variation, only one basket is used, and both teams shoot at it. There are no out-of-bounds rules. The score goes to whichever team makes the goal. Basketball rules apply in all other instances.

In one variation, one player starts making free-throws for the basket, scoring 1 for each success. When a failure occurs, the ball is scrambled for; and a goal from field counts 2 points. The player making a field goal is the next free-thrower. The game is 21 points; and 2 games out of 3, constitute a match. The last point in the game must be from a field goal.

FOUR-GOAL BASKETBALL

When a gymnasium has four basketball goals, assign two adjacent ones to one team, and two to the other; when there are six goals, assign three to each. The entire gymnasium is used as a court. Any number of players constitute a team. The game is played otherwise like Basketball, any player being permitted to try for one of his team's goals.

CAGE BASKETBALL

A 30-inch cageball is used. The object is to cause the ball to hit the backboard of the Basketball goal, such a goal scoring 2 points. In case the players pile up on a ball, holding it to the floor, play is stopped and another toss-up occurs. This may also be played with four or more baskets, as in Four-Goal Basketball.

ONE O'GANG

In this game, only one basket is used. Five or six players take part. One boy is chosen as guard against the rest. The object of the game is to keep the ball away from the guard, using all permitted methods of Basketball advancement. A goal for a player counts 2 points. If a goal is missed, the player changes place with the guard. If a ball being passed is intercepted by the guard, the last person to touch it before the interception exchanges places with the guard. Each player keeps his individual score. The game usually consists of a score of 10, the winner being the first player to reach this.

In one variation, 2 points is deducted from the score of a player who misses a shot for goal.

VI. OTHER OUTDOOR GAMES

ARCHERY

THE FIELD: The field for men is 100 yards long, with other shooting lines drawn at 80, 60, 50 and 40 yards from the targets. The field for women is 60 yards long, with shooting lines drawn also at 50, 40 and 30 yards distance. Each shooting lane should be 16 feet wide. The field should run north and south, if possible, to prevent archers being forced to look into the sun.

EQUIPMENT: Targets 48 inches in diameter are used outdoors. On a circular piece of oilcloth covering the face of the target 5 concentric rings are painted. The central one, the bull's-eye, has a radius of $4\frac{4}{5}$ inches; each ring is of the same width. The target face is attached to a target made of sewn straw. The target is supported by a target stand of soft wood, so that the target leans back slightly. The center of the bull's-eye is 4 feet from the ground.

Arrows for men are usually 27 inches long; for women, 26; for children, 24. Standard bows are used.

STANDARD ROUNDS.—York Round for men: 72 arrows at 100 yards; 48 arrows at 80 yards; 24 arrows at 60 yards.

National Round for men and women: 48 arrows at 60 yards; 24 arrows at 50 yards. Junior National Round: the same number of arrows, at 50 and 40 yards.

American Round for men and women: 30 arrows at 60 yards; 30 at 50 yards; 30 at 40 yards. Junior American Round: 30 arrows at 50 yards; 30 at 40 yards; 30 at 30 yards.

Metropolitan Round for men: 30 arrows at 100 yards; at 80 yards; at 60 yards. For women: 30 arrows at 60 yards; at 50 yards; at 40 yards.

Columbia Round for women: 24 arrows at 50 yards; 24 at 40 yards; 24 at 30 yards. Junior Columbia Round: 24 arrows at 40 yards; at 30 yards; at 20 yards.

A double round consists in shooting any of the above rounds twice in succession.

SHOOTING.—Four archers are assigned to each target, and are numbered to designate the order of their shooting, 1, 2, 3, 4. Archer 1 shoots 3 arrows; Archer 2, 3 more; and so on. When all have shot 6 arrows, they go to the target for scoring. Archer 2 withdraws the arrows in the order in which the archers shot, and Archer 1 records the score. Each archer should have arrows marked differently from the others. As each arrow is withdrawn, the score is called and recorded.

SCORING.—The bull's-eye counts 9; the other concentric rings 7, 5, 3 and 1 in outward order. The score for each arrow is recorded on the scoreboard; then the number of hits, and the total score. Thus a score appearing:

9 9 5 3 1 1 6—28

would mean six hits, two bull's-eyes, one each in the third and second circles, and 2 in the outer circle. An arrow passing through the target, or rebounding from its scoring area, counts 5 in all cases. An arrow on a line counts as if within the higher scoring circle. An arrow which jumps off the string is counted as a shot, unless the archer can reach and touch it with his bow.

In tournaments, the archer with the highest score for all shots wins. Only the points made count; hits do not count. If there is a tie, the highest score at the longest range wins; if there is still a tie, the score at the next longest range decides.

In team matches, either all scores of team mates are added and divided by the number on the team, the average score for the team counting; or, by agreement, the four highest scores, or some other agreed number, are used in determining the team's score. Team rounds for men: 96 arrows at 60 yards; for women, 96 at 50 yards; for juniors, 96 at 40 yards.

Indoor Archery.—The usual distances are 15 to 20 yards. There should be a backstop behind the target, to prevent arrows from breaking. A 2-foot target would be used for 15 yards, and others in proportion.

ARCHERY GOLF

This combination of Archery and Golf may be played in any weather. A golf links, approach golf links, or field may be used. Targets may be bales of straw staked to the ground near the regular golf holes (at a distance of 100 to 300 yards between them). A cardboard disk 4½ inches in diameter is attached to each side of each bale. Three types of arrows are used: flight arrows for distance; approach arrows; and target arrows. For winter use, the arrows may have a spike or nail protruding from the end, to prevent skidding on snow or ice.

Standing at a target, each contestant shoots one arrow at the next. Each shot counts 1 point. Each succeeding shot is taken from the point where the first arrow stopped. When close enough, each archer shoots at the cardboard disk. If it is hit, he holes out; if he hits the bale but misses the disk, he holes out, adding 1 point to his score for missing the disk. Scoring is as in Golf.

CLOUT SHOOTING

A target 48 feet in diameter is marked on the ground. The radius of bull's-eye and width of each concentric circle is 4⅘ feet. A flag stands in the center of the bull's-eye. Men shoot from a line 180 yards away; women, 120 yards. Each round is 36 arrows per archer. Scoring: hitting the clout, 10; nearest to the clout, 5; next nearest, 3; third nearest, 1.

OTHER ARCHERY GAMES

Flight Shooting.—Shooting for distance, scored according to the distance shot.

Roving.—Either played with marked targets, called rovers, marked with paint or colored cloth; or unmarked targets, a bush, a tree, a spot on the hillside, etc. If the targets are not marked, the winner of each round at a target picks the next target. Where targets are marked, shooting takes place from the first place where it is sighted. Each archer is given 2 shots at a target, and scores 1 if his arrow is nearest to the target. The first archer to score 7 points wins.

William Tell Contest.—A wallboard boy is drawn and cut out, erected, and an apple placed on the head. The distance for shooting is from 15 to 30 yards. An archer hitting the boy is eliminated. The first archer to hit the apple wins.

Archery Balloon Contest.—Toy balloons inflated with gas are tied with string to the ground, so that they float in the air at heights varying from 6 to 24 feet from the ground. Each archer is allowed 3 shots at each balloon. The archers shoot in turn, one arrow each time. The archer breaking a balloon scores 1.

As a variation, the balloons may be inflated with air and hung from a horizontal rope, so that they hang 6 or 8 feet from the ground.

Rabbit Hunting.—Stuffed toy rabbits are hidden in the grass along a trail. Each archer sighting one scores 1; then rounds of 3 shots each are taken, an archer scoring 5 who hits a rabbit. If the rabbit is not hit, the nearest arrow scores 3.

Wand Archery.—The wands are 2 inches wide and 6 feet long, standing upright. Men shoot from 100 yards away; women, from 60. A round is 36 arrows. The archer who scores the most hits wins.

Still-Hunting the Buck.—A burlap deer is constructed, with two ovals marking its vitals, the heart being inside the larger oval. One player hides the deer, leaving a trail of kernels of corn dropped every yard. After 10 minutes, the hunters surge forth. The first to sight the deer calls "Deer!" He shoots 1 arrow from here; if he misses, in turn the others shoot 1 arrow each. If all miss, they take 5 steps and shoot again. This continues until they are 10 yards from the deer, or until it is hit; in which case further shooting is from the spot from which the hit was made. A shot in the heart scores 10, and ends the hunt. A shot in the large oval scores 5. A hit outside the large oval scores 2. If all shoot 10 yards from the deer without a hit, the hider scores 25, and the deer is hidden again. The hunter with the highest score wins.

Game Hunting.—A number of large game animals may be cut out from wallboard and placed on the archery range, or along a trail in the woods. Each has two ovals painted on it, as in Still-Hunting the Buck. An archer sighting game scores 1. Shooting is from that point. An arrow in the heart scores 5; in the large oval, 3; outside it, but hitting the game, 1.

SHOOTING CONTESTS

Shooting contests are usually done with .22 caliber rifles, using a rim-fire cartridge, and only metallic sights. Other contests may be held with shotguns, pistols, etc. There must be a backstop, either of a hillside without stones, or one constructed of dirt, 10 feet high, extending 6 feet on each side of the target, and at least 3 feet thick. A wooden target rack is placed in front of this, to which the targets are tacked. Indoors, steel plates ⅜ inch thick hung at an angle of 30 to 45 degrees are recommended as backstops.

Official ranges are 75 feet long, with 4-foot firing lanes. Official targets with concentric rings should be used. On the official targets, the rings from the bull's-eye outward score 10, 9, 8, 7, 6, 5. On a junior target with additional rings, these score 4, 3 and 2. Shots which touch a line score in the higher circle.

Junior Contest.—Each contestant shoots 40 shots from the prone position. The shots are fired in four strings of 10 shots each. The highest score wins.

Junior Gallery Contest.—Each contestant shoots 10 shots each in 4 positions: prone, sitting, kneeling, standing. Score all these contests as above.

Senior Gallery Contest.—This is in three stages, each to consist of two strings of 10 shots each. The first stage is prone, then sitting; the second, prone, then kneeling; the third, prone, then standing. There are two sections, at 50 feet and then at 75 feet.

Interscholastic Team Contest.—Teams of ten contestants each compete in three stages, each of two strings of 10 shots each. These stages are; two strings prone; one prone, one kneeling; and one prone, one standing. The highest aggregate score wins. For a record, the five high aggregate scores count.

String-Shooting.—A box of candy, or a box wrapped to resemble candy, is hung by a string in front of the target. Each contestant receives one shot in turn. Whoever drops the box wins. If it is dropped before all shoot, it is hung up again. In case there is a tie, it must be shot off. The winner gets the candy.

Crayon Shooting.—A strip of 2 by 2 lumber as wide as the backstop is erected horizontally before it. White crayons, one for each contestant, or more, are set up in holes bored in the plank. Each contestant is given 5 shots. The one breaking the most crayons wins.

Wand Rifle Shooting.—This is similar to Wand Shooting in Archery, the wand being a stick ⅜ of an inch thick stuck in the ground before the target. Each contestant is given 5 shots, and scores 1 each time the wand is hit.

Candle-Out Shooting.—Five candles are placed as the crayons in Crayon Shooting, and lit. Each contestant is given 5 shots to extinguish the candles. Shots which hit and knock over a candle score as misses. The highest score wins.

Match-Lighting Shooting.—In a board similar to that used in Crayon Shooting, insert ten non-safety matches. Each contestant is given 10 shots. Lighting the match wins; ties are shot off. If a match is not lit, high score goes to the player breaking the most matches.

Tack-Driving Shooting.—Five large-headed tacks are tacked lightly into a board before the target. Each contestant is given 5 shots. The one driving in the most tacks wins.

Pendulum Shooting.—A block of wood 4 inches square is hung before the target, and set swinging from a 3 foot cord. Each contestant is given 10 shots. Each hit scores 1.

Balloon-Shooting.—The balloons are arranged as in the Archery Balloon Contest. Each contestant is given 5 shots, each shooting 1 shot in turn. The one breaking the most balloons wins. The balloons may be floated from 20 to 100 feet high, to add interest.

Wooden Bird Shooting.—A 4-inch square block of wood is tossed into the air from behind the shooter, not more than 10 feet high. Each contestant is given 10 shots, and scores 1 each time the block is hit.

Tin Can Shooting.—Tin cans may be placed on a post before the target, or on a board horizontally erected there. First the sides should be shot at; then the circular head. The object is to hit the can so that it falls off. Ten shots to each contestant, each hit scoring 1, each knockoff scoring 2. Highest score wins.

Shooting Tournament.—Any five to ten of these events can be arranged for a novelty shooting tournament.

TRAP-SHOOTING

In Trap-Shooting, clay targets are thrown into the air by a mechanism called a trap, and are shot at with shotguns. The firing line should be 16 feet behind the trap. Standard clay pigeons are used. The standard for such contests is a 12-gauge gun.

Usually 25 to 50 pigeons are released. A contestant is not allowed to put his gun to his shoulder until the bird is in the air. A bird must be actually broken, to score. When the shooter calls "Ready," the clay pigeon is released.

This may be played without the shooter's calling that he is ready. Handicaps of distance may be given when the shooters differ in ability.

SKEET

In Skeet, two traps are used, 40 yards apart, so placed that birds shot from one will fly over the top of the other. Using a point midway between the traps as a center, a semicircle is marked on the ground connecting the two traps. On this are marked 7 shooting stations, equidistant from each other, with an 8th station midway between the traps. Each contestant shoots in rotation from each of the 8 stations, the angles of flight differing from each. Since 2 birds are released at once, the effort is to bring down both. Scoring is as in Trap-Shooting.

BOWLING

Bowling is one of a number of athletic showdown games in which the element of choice enters strongly.

Equipment: Standard bowling alleys, 41 to 42 inches wide, and 60 feet from the foul line to the No. 1 pin. Official pins are 15 inches in height. Balls must not exceed 27 inches in circumference, nor 16 pounds in weight. There are 10 wooden pins, and the object is to knock them down by rolling the balls down the alleys.

The Play.—Each bowler stands as far as he chooses behind the foul line, takes any number of steps he chooses, and rolls the ball. Should his foot or any part of his body touch the alleys beyond the foul line, it is a foul; this counts as a ball bowled, but the pins are replaced and do not score. Each player in turn is allowed to bowl two balls, unless he knocks down all the pins with one.

Scoring.—For each pin knocked down, 1. If all the pins are knocked down by the first ball, it is called a strike; and the score made with the first two balls in the next turn is added to the first score, as well as being counted in the second. If all the pins are knocked down with the first two balls, it is called a spare, and the score made with the first ball of the next is added to the preceding turn, as well as being counted in its own turn.

Each player begins each turn with his pins all up, and the alley clear of balls. Ten rounds make a frame. In scoring, the total is written down after each turn. X means a strike; /, a spare. A spare in the 10th round gives a player an additional throw; a strike, 2 additional throws.

Team Bowling.—Teams usually consist of five bowlers, but may consist of any number agreed upon. Competing teams bowl in adjoining alleys, one team to each. After each frame they alternate alleys. The team score is the aggregate score of its members. A team wins by winning 2 out of 3, or 3 out of 5 games; or the scores of the 3 or 5 highest games are added, and the highest aggregate wins.

DUCK PINS

In Duck Pins, the pins are 9 inches high, and the balls must not exceed 4½ inches in diameter. Each player rolls three balls in each frame, and two frames at a time. A ball delivered 10 feet beyond the foul line is declared foul. For a strike on the first ball, the bowler does not bowl his next two balls; but the score of the next two balls in the following frame is added to the score for this frame, as in Bowling. If all the pins are knocked down by the first two balls bowled, a spare is credited, the third ball is not bowled, and the score made by the first ball in the next frame is added to the score for the preceding frame, as well as scored in its own frame.

TENPINS

The pins are 9 inches high. They are set up as in Bowling, with the apex (pin No. 1) toward the bowler. The pins are 10 inches apart. The foul line is 20 to 40 feet away. The bowler uses a wooden ball or a softball. Each roller in turn has three rolls. Scoring is as in Duck Pins. Each turn constitutes a frame; and ten frames constitute a string. Three strings is a match.

Ball Bowling.—Ten Indian clubs or sticks of wood of similar size are set up as in Bowling. A basketball, volleyball, soccer ball, softball or croquet ball is used. Scoring is as in Bowling.

Soccer Bowling.—This variation of Ball Bowling has the ball kicked, instead of rolled; otherwise it is the same.

SKITTLES

Skittles is played like Tenpins, except that a wooden disk is used instead of a ball. The skittles may be thrown at the pins with a flat toss, as in Horseshoe Pitching, or they may be slid along the floor. The skittles are 4½ inches in diameter and about 1½ inches thick.

SKIDDLES

In this outdoors game, 5 pins or round sticks are needed, 4½ inches long and 1½ to 2 inches thick. In addition, 3 throwing sticks are needed, 14 inches long and 2 inches thick. A throwing line is marked on the ground. A 30-inch square is drawn 60 feet from this, placed cornerwise to the throwing line. A pin is placed on each corner of the square and in its center. The nearest pin to the throwing line scores 1; the one to the right, 2; to the left, 3; the farthest one, 4; the center one, 10. Players take turn in throwing the throwing sticks, each throwing all 3 sticks in turn. Each scores for the pins he knocks down. As usually scored, game is 100; and if a player exceeds 100, he must start again. A better game is to declare as winner the first to reach 100 or better.

TIRE BOWLING

This is Bowling, with automobile tires for balls, and Indian clubs or some equivalent as pins. Strikes and spares score as in Bowling. Highest score in ten frames or turns wins.

BOWLING ON THE GREEN, LAWN BOWLS

This game is similar to Curling. It is played on a smooth lawn called a bowling green, with a 6-inch trough surrounding it. Some lawns have a mound, or crown. Wooden balls called bowls are used, not round, but having one side with less curvature than the other. Round balls may be used with lead inserted in one side to give a bias. Each player has two of these bowls. A smaller ball, white in color, is called the jack.

The first player bowls the jack out on the lawn, as a mark for the bowling. In rotation the balls are bowled at the jack, and the scoring is as in Quoits, by the nearness of balls to the jack. It is permissible for the jack to be moved by another bowl in play. Bowls which roll into the trough do not score. The players bowl from a small rubber mat; and when a turn, called an end, is completed, the mat is carried to the opposite end of the green, and the bowling recommences from that end.

Bowl Spot-Ball.—This game is played with croquet balls or any similar balls. One ball, the spot-ball, is marked in some distinguishing way; and each player has one ball. A foul line is established near one end of the lawn. First roll is decided by lot. The winner stands behind the foul line, and rolls the spot-ball out on the lawn; he then rolls his own ball as near it as possible. Each of the other players then rolls in turn. The scoring is by the number of players. If five compete, the ball nearest the spot-ball counts 5; the next, 4; and so on. If a player's ball hits and moves the spot-ball, he scores nothing. If two balls tie, their score is added and averaged. On the second frame, the winner of the first rolls the spot-ball out, the others following in the order of their scores in the preceding frame. The game consists of 50 points.

BOCCIE *

Boccie is the Italian form of Lawn Bowls, with a method of scoring preferred by many players over the better known game. The cue ball is smaller than the balls used by each player in bowling. A game consists of 21 points, scored as follows. Each team, of 2 or more players, elects a captain. One captain, by toss-up or otherwise, secures the privilege of bowling first, or naming which of his team is to bowl first. He tosses out the cue ball, and then he or the chosen player bowls as near it as he can. The captain of the other team then designates a player, who may be himself or not, to bowl next for his team. If his ball does

* Italian for *bowls*. It is pronounced bôt′ chȧ (bawt′chuh).

not come to rest closer to the cue ball than the other team's ball, one by one his teammates, in an order he selects, must bowl, until one ball does come to rest closer than the other team's ball; or until all have bowled. When all have bowled and none has come closer, then the first captain designates the order in which his teammates bowl, until all have bowled.

The moment an opponent's ball comes closer to the cue ball than the first ball bowled, the opponent's team temporarily stops bowling, and the team that bowled first must bowl, in an order stipulated by their captain, until a ball is bowled closer than the closest opponent's ball. Whenever this happens, the bowling privilege passes to the other team; and so alternately.

At the end of the game, the team with the ball closest to the cue ball scores 1 for each ball closer than any opponent's ball. Thus, with 3 players to a team, the score may be 3 (all 3 balls closer than an opponent's ball), 2, or 1. The team winning each frame has first bowl for the next frame. The game ends when 21 points is scored. Only one team scores in each frame.

GOLF

Golf originated in prehistory, as a game played by shepherds, in which they used their crooks to drive a small stone to a goal in the fewest possible strokes. Scotland and Holland both claim the origin of the present game, Hollanders claiming that early in the 14th century the game was played there with a single club. It was established definitely in Scotland late in the 14th or early in the 15th century; and in 1457 Parliament legislated against both it and football, as interfering with archery. Additional laws were passed against it in 1471 and 1491; but James IV, who signed the latter law, became an enthusiast at the game. The St. Andrews Golf Club of Scotland was founded in 1552, and is regarded as the birthplace of modern golf. A full course of 18 holes requires about 100 acres; a 9-hole course, which needs only half as much, must be played twice for a full game.

THE COURSE: A golf course, also called a golf links, consists of 18 distinct links, or holes. Each hole comprises a tee, a fairway, and a putting green. The tee (where play toward the hole commences) is a section of well-clipped level turf, from 10 to 20 feet square; the fairway is a strip 150 to 200 feet wide of well-mowed meadow land, approximately 400 yards long, leading up to the putting green (where play at a hole concludes). There are hazards to the sides and across the fairway, consisting of such natural obstacles as trees, brooks, or ponds, or artificial bunkers of earth and sand traps. The putting green is a space 60 to 70 feet wide, level or slightly rolling, and near its center is a 4-inch cup or hole, its top set level with the ground; in the center of this cup is a slender pole a few feet high, topped by a flag indicating to the player the location of the hole. The links or holes vary in length from 75 to 600 yards, averaging 300 to 400; the total distance for the 18 holes is from 6,000 to 6,400 yards, or slightly more than 3½ miles.

EQUIPMENT: The most important clubs are a driver and a brassie, the wooden clubs, which are used for drives of from 160 to 250 yards; a mid-iron, mashie, and niblick, clubs with iron heads and more or less loft or pitch to them; and a putter, which is approximately straight-faced. The mid-iron is used for distances from 150 to 180 yards; the mashie for 75 to 150 yards; the niblick for lifting out of sandpits, bunkers, or high grass, or for pitches under 75 yards; and the putter for use on the putting green, to hole the ball. A player can use any club he pleases for any stroke. The ball is a hard white rubber ball, 1.68 inches in diameter and 1.62 ounces in weight.

THE PLAY.—The object is to drive the ball around the links and into each hole in the fewest strokes possible. If one or more other players compete, each drives his own ball, and interference is not permitted. The game is definitely of the showdown type. Order of drive-off from the tee is arranged by lot, team members alternating with their opponents. After the drive-off, the player furthest from the hole plays first. When all the balls have been holed, they are lifted from the cup and driven off once more from the next tee; the drive-off or honor goes to the lowest score on the hole just completed, the order of the others depending on the lowness of their scores. In case of a tie, the honor is retained by the player driving off from the previous tee.

Scoring.—In medal play, the lowest score for the course wins. In match play, the winner of a majority of holes wins. Each link or hole is played as a unit from the tee to the cup. If the scores, medal or match, are tied at the 18th hole, play continues on around again until a contestant wins a hole. In medal play, it is usual to play over at least 9 more holes.

Miscellaneous.—Par means the number of strokes at each hole required by a very good player; 72 strokes constitute par on most courses. A twosome is a game with one player on each side; a foursome is a match of four players, each playing his own ball. A two-ball foursome is a match in which there are two players on each side, each team of two using one ball and playing it alternately. In a regular foursome, the custom is to score both low ball and low total: the low ball for a partnership scores 1 for the side making it, and the low total scores another point for the side making it. If one side has low ball and the other side low total, neither scores. In professional foursomes, only the low ball is usually scored.

Team Matches.—A team match usually consists of four twosomes and two foursomes. The match is 18 points, divided: four twosomes, 3 points each, or 12; two foursomes, 3 points each, or 6. In the twosomes and foursomes, the winner of the first 9 holes scores 1; of the second 9 holes, 1; of the 18 holes, 1. In the Nassau System, when golf clubs meet, any number of players may compete, and the points are awarded as above. The aggregate score of the individual contestants on each team determines the winner.

CLOCK GOLF, ROUND-THE-CLOCK GOLF

Clock Golf is a putting game. A circle is drawn on the lawn, 20 to 24 feet in diameter; or it may be larger. Around the circle place 12 markers at regular intervals, these being the 12 numerals representing the hours on the face of a clock. The markers may consist of tin cans set flush in the ground, with the numerals painted on them. The putting hole is placed off center within the circle, so that the distance to the various numerals varies markedly. A tin can of approximately 4-inch diameter, open at one end, with holes punched in the bottom for drainage, and set with its open end flush with the ground, makes an excellent hole. Only putters are used. Each player needs a putter and a golf ball.

Two to four, or more, may play, each competing independently; or they may play in partnerships of two or more. A two ball foursome may be played, as in Golf. Each contestant in turn putts the ball from the one o'clock marker, to sink the ball in the hole in the fewest number of strokes. Play is as in golf, the ball farthest from the hole in each instance being played after the putt-offs. After all the players have holed from the one o'clock marker, they putt-off from the two o'clock marker; and so on around the clock. In scoring, the usual way is to add up all a player's scores, the lowest score winning. Or, as in match play, the number of holes won counts in deciding the final winner.

The twelve holes need not be around the sides of a circle, but may be at varying distances, depending upon the size and shape of the lawn. The green may be undulating, as in Golf.

MINIATURE GOLF, TOM THUMB GOLF

In this putting game, so popular a few years ago, 9 or 18 putting holes are placed on the lawn, with a putting distance varying for each hole, and with such obstacles in the form of hazards as ingenuity suggests. The putting lanes may be planked in or left open; in the latter case, certain obstacles, such as water pipes, may have to be shot through before the ball can be holed. The play and scoring is as in Golf. Only a putter and a ball are needed; in some instances a niblick is permitted, to chip in when a ball lies beyond the planked boundaries of the putting lanes.

APPROACH GOLF

This is regulation Golf, without the initial drive-off at each tee. The holes may be from 50 to 250 yards long, with such natural and artificial hazards as the ground permits. Either a separate green and hole may be made for each link or hole, or from one to less than 9 may be used, with different approaches which give the effect of different holes. The play and scoring are as in golf. The equipment is the same, except that the wooden driver is unnecessary.

BINGO GOLF

Bingo Golf is Golf with an altered scoring. On each hole, the longest drive scores 1 bingo or point; the first to reach the green, 1; the longest putt, 1; the first to make the hole, 1; the lowest score for the hole, 1. The player with the highest score wins.

GOOFY GOLF

This is Golf played with such improvised equipment as shinny sticks and an old tennis ball. The holes may be made of tin cans, punched as in Clock Golf.

CROQUET GOLF

This is Miniature Golf played with croquet mallets and balls, using for the holes tin cans 6 inches in diameter and 6 inches deep. The distances for the holes may vary from 30 to 90 feet. Hazards of great variety should be constructed. Except on the greens, the ball must be hit with the mallet between the legs. In some localities, any stroke with the mallet is permissible. In other respects, the rules of Golf apply. Par for holes under 35 feet, usually 2; 36 to 70 feet, usually 3; 71 feet and over, usually 4.

CROQUET AND GOLF

Many combination games are interesting. Thus, a croquet course may be played competitively between a player or team equipped with croquet ball and mallet, and a player or team equipped with a golf putter and a golf ball. In this case, the rules of croquet apply. Similarly, Clock or Miniature Golf may be played competitively with the same respective equipments, the golf rules applying. Other games can be combined similarly.

TIRE GOLF

This is an informal game of Golf, without golf equipment, Nine old automobile or bicycle tires, bushel baskets, or smaller containers, are placed at 9 different places on the lawn or in bounds, as far from each other as possible, and with natural hazards or bunkers between them. Each of these 9 holes should have a cardboard number prominently displayed above it.

Each player has a ball—a beanbag, a rubber ball, a tennis ball, a golf ball, or some similar object—and a scorecard and pencil. The object is to make the rounds of the course in as few throws as possible, throwing the ball entirely inside the hole each time, so that it stays there. A ball that bounces out after being thrown in must be thrown again. This game can be played individually or in teams of two or three, as in Golf; low score counts for each hole; or both low and high count; or players throw the ball alternately, each team using only one ball.

HORSESHOE PITCHING

In informal Horseshoe Pitching, two stakes are fixed 30 to 40 feet away from each other. New or discarded horseshoes are used. The first throw is determined by a toss. In turn, each contestant then pitches his two horseshoes. A foul line is drawn, and stepping over it disqualifies that throw. A ringer is a horseshoe that encircles the stake. The scoring is: ringer, 3; horseshoe leaning against stake, (leaner or hobber), 2; horseshoe nearest to stake, 1; both shoes nearest to stake, 2. The game consists of 21 points.

Tournament Play.—The stake is in the center of a pitcher's box, a wooden frame 6 feet square, of 2 by 4 inch planks, extending not more than 1 inch above the surface. For a distance of 18 inches around the stake, the box should be filled with potter's clay or a similar material to a depth of 6 inches, and kept moistened to a putty-like consistency. The stakes are of iron, 1 inch in diameter, 8 inches out of the ground, and inclined 1 inch from the perpendicular toward the opposite stake. They are 40 feet apart; except that in junior contests they may be 30. The horseshoes must not exceed 7½ inches in length, 7 inches in width, and 2½ pounds in weight, with toe or heel calks extending out not more than ¾ inch. The opening between the calks must not exceed 3½ inches, inside measurement.

A game is 50 points, and the first player scoring this total wins; a match is the best 2 out of 3 games. First choice between first pitch or follow is determined by a toss. At games thereafter, the loser of the preceding games leads. A contestant may not walk over and examine his opponent's shoes before pitching. A contestant who has pitched must stand back of the stake line and out of the pitcher's box, or forfeit the value of the shoes pitched. The front of the pitcher's box is the foul line, and any pitcher stepping over it in pitching loses the value of the pitch. A shoe striking the frame of the pitcher's box or any other object is called a foul shoe, and does not score. A ringer must encircle the stake enough to permit a straight-edge to touch both heel calks and clear the stake.

If a thrown shoe moves another, both are measured from their new positions. Closest shoe, 1 point; both closest, 2; ringer, 3; ringer and closest, 4; two ringers, 6. If each contestant has a ringer, these are not counted, except as pitches that nullify each other; and the next closest shoe scores. Two double ringers nullify each other. If one player has two ringers and his opponent 1, the former player scores 3 points only. If all four shoes tie, there is no score, and the player who pitched last again leads. A shoe leaning against the stake has no advantage over a shoe touching it while lying on the ground; such shoes tie. A leaner counts only as a closest shoe. Measurements are made by the use of calipers and a straight edge.

QUOITS

Quoits is similar to Horseshoe Pitching, except that a circular metal ring is used instead of a horseshoe. Otherwise it may be played as Horseshoe Pitching. In the official Quoits rules, the pin or stake is driven into the ground until the mott, the head of the pin, is level with the surface of the ground.

The official English and Caledonian distance from pin to pin is 54 feet; for juniors, 30 to 20 feet. The official quoit is a circular metal ring with a hole in the center 4 inches in diameter, a rim 2½ inches wide; it weighs not less than 3 pounds. For juniors, it may weigh less.

Variations from Horseshoe Pitching rules include: the pitcher may stand astride of the pin, provided his feet are back of the center of the pin, but may not step ahead of it in pitching. He may stand back and step forward before pitching, subject to the above rule. The quoits must be delivered with the convex surface, uppermost, but a quoit turned in pitching or by being struck by another quoit counts. A ringer is a pitched quoit encircling the pin; a hobber, a pitched quoit resting on the pin.

Scoring is as in Horseshoe Pitching, except that a ringer topped by an opponent counts 6 for the second player; and a triple ringer, 9 for the second player. A ringer topped by two hobbers counts 7 points for the person pitching the hobbers. A pitcher pitching a ringer and a hobber that is topped by an opponent scores 3 for his ringer. A ringer and a hobber count 5. A ringer topped by an opponent's hobber counts 3 for the person pitching the ringer. If a double ringer is topped by a hobber, the person pitching the last ringer scores 6. If a ringer is topped by an opponent's ringer and hobber, 8 points are scored by the opponent. A hobber counts 2. A hobber topped by another quoit counts 2 for the quoit nearest or resting on the pin. If two opposing quoits rest on the pin, they are removed, and the nearer remaining quoit counts 1. Two hobbers score 4, if both touch the pin. If neither a ringer nor hobber is made, the nearest pin counts 1; the two nearest by the same player, 2. If opposing quoits not ringers or hobbers tie, they are removed and the nearer remaining quoit counts 1. If 3 quoits are in contact with the pin, two are considered as tied, and the remaining quoit scores 1. Measuring is done with calipers from the center of the pin to the nearest part of the quoit. The game is 21 points. The player or pair first reaching 21 wins. Matches are the best 2 out of 3 games

TIRE QUOITS

Old automobile tires are used instead of quoits. The stakes are sturdy poles 30 feet apart, extending 18 inches out of the ground. Two or four players may play; if four play, they play as teams of two each, and one player of each team stands at each stake. A player rolls his two tires before the other player rolls his two. The scoring is as in Horseshoe Pitching. A winner throws first in the next round. A player may not step beyond the stake in rolling, but may run as far as he likes behind the peg before rolling. The game is 21 points.

SHUFFLEBOARD

The court is laid out on a hard surface—clay, plank, concrete, etc.—according to the diagram. Eight circular disks are required, 6 inches in diameter and 1 inch thick. Four are of one color, and four of another color. The cues have a 5 foot handle, with a head 3½ inches wide and curved to fit the disks. They must not exceed 6¼ feet in length.

Two or four players may play. If four play, they play as teams of two each, and one member of each team is stationed at each end of the court. The player who leads off shoots one disk from the 10 OFF space, his object being to land it in a scoring compartment. His opponent then shoots one, with the double object of striking the other player's disk and driving it into the 10 OFF space, or out of the scoring area; and of landing his own disk in a scoring compartment. The players alternate until each has shot his four disks.

A disk scores in the area in which it rests, after

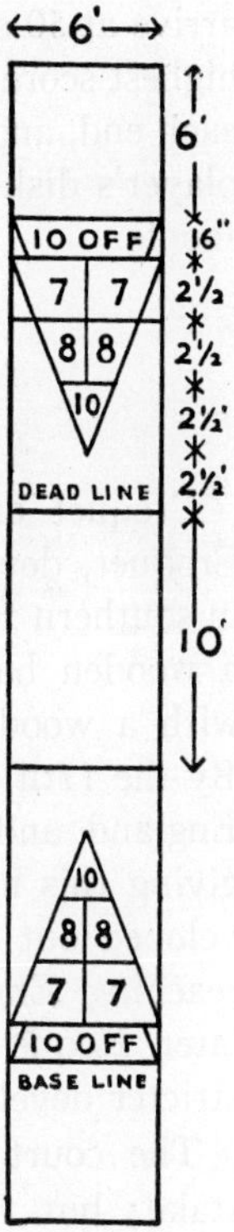

Shuffleboard: 1

all 8 disks have been shot. Disks resting on a division line do not score. Disks that do not cross the farther dead line are dead, and are removed at once. After the first round is scored, the same two players, or their partners in a foursome, repeat the shooting from the other end of the court. Penalty for not shooting from the 10

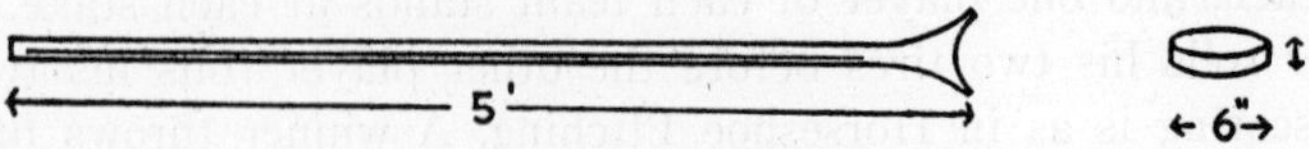

Shuffleboard: II

OFF space, 5 points off the score. If a player in shooting steps across the line bounding the 10 OFF space parallel to the base line, the penalty is 5 points. The game is 50 points. If both sides arrive at 50 or more points in the same round, the side having the highest score wins. In case of a tie, each side shoots one disk from each end, and the highest score wins. In this tie play-off, the first player's disk must be removed and scored before the second one shoots.

CROQUET AND ROQUE

Croquet and its two formalized forms, Roque and Modern Croquet, developed from the game of Paille-Maille, originating in southern France in the 13th or 14th century—a game in which a wooden ball 4 inches in diameter was driven down an alley with a wooden mallet. The name originally meant ball-mallet. By the 17th century, it was popular in France and Italy; and, in England and Scotland, under the name pall-mall; incidentally giving this name to a street in London. Croquet apparently developed out of this game in France in the early 19th century, reaching England about 1852, and the United States slightly later. Roque (pronounced Rōk) and Modern Croquet are recent stricter developments of the popular pastime.

The court is equipped with wickets and stakes, or a single stake; but the arrangement of these varies with almost every diagram encountered. Each croquet set carries its own directions, and these may be followed in laying out the court; or one of the standard arrangements given here may safely be followed. Published rules usually give balls of only four colors, in one of these orders: Red, White, Blue, Black, as in Roque; or Black, White, Blue, Red, as in Modern Croquet; or Blue, Red, Black, Yellow, as in English Croquet. The usual set comes equipped with eight balls of eight different colors, with mallets to match; and the order is always that painted in rings on the stakes, the top color usually shooting first, but the sequence always continuing the same as the colors on the stakes, from above down.

CROQUET

THE COURT: The court is a rectangle, its size depending upon the lawn space available. A size of 60 by 40 feet is usually satisfactory, but it may be smaller or larger. It should be level, with the grass mowed short. Two wooden stakes are placed at least six feet away from the end lines, and midway of the distance between the side lines. The wickets are usually placed as in Diagram I. On an imaginary line drawn from stake to stake, wicket 1 is placed two complete mallets' length from the home stake; wicket 2, one mallet length away on the same line; wickets 7 and 6 are similarly placed at the other end of the court; wicket 4 centers the court; wickets 9 and 3 are placed on a line at right angles to the imaginary line from stake to stake (this line being halfway between wickets 4 and 2, and approximately 15 feet left and right of the imaginary line from stake to stake); and wickets 8 and 5 are placed similarly left and right of the area between wickets 4 and 6.

The course of the ball through these wickets is shown in Diagram I. In one variation, the ball goes from right to left, going up and returning; through wicket 4; and back toward wicket 4 from wickets 5 and 9.

(Variation I. Two central wickets are used, crossing each other so that the square made by the points where they enter the ground has sides parallel with the end and side boundaries of the court. A ball going from the home stake is played either toward the turning stake, or from the area between wickets 8 and 9 toward the area between wickets 3 and 5; one returning from the turning stake is played either toward the home stake, or from the area between 5 and 3 toward the area between 8 and 9; diagram II illustrates this. In order to counter, a ball must pass

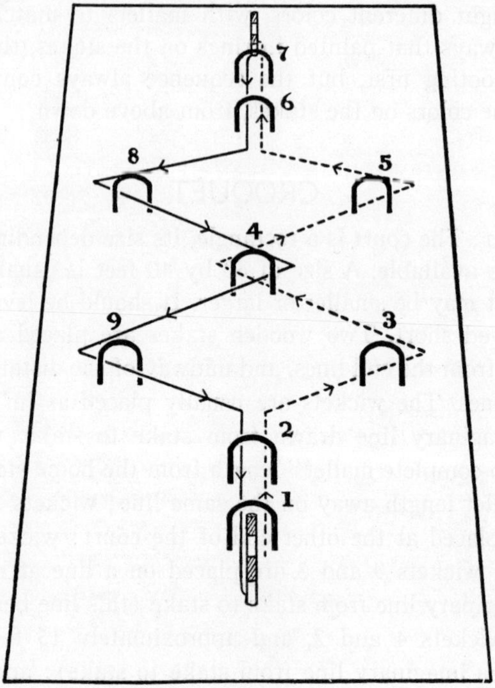

Croquet: I

under both wickets in one or more shots in one of these two ways, and in no other way; providing always that in the meantime the ball has not been knocked out of its position in one of these lines. Going through this double wicket gives the player 2 strokes, not 1.)

(Variation II. Two central wickets are used, placed as in Diagram III. The balls must be passed through as in the diagram, and legally passing through them gives the player 2 strokes. In this variation, wickets 5 and 9 are played differently; both must be approached and driven through from the far and not the near part of the court, that is, 5 from the side nearer the turning stake, and 9 from the side nearer the home stake.)

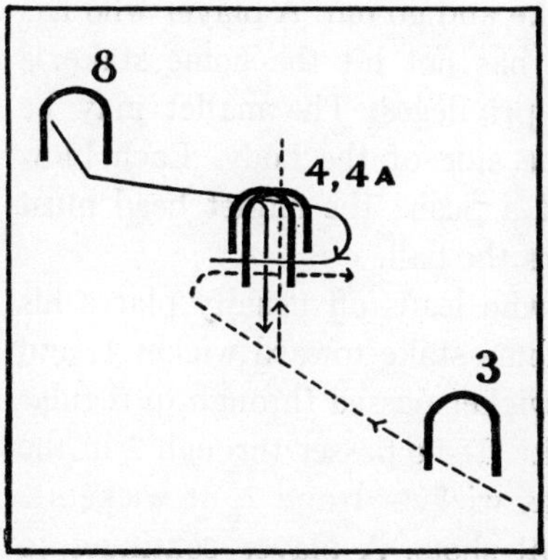

Croquet: II

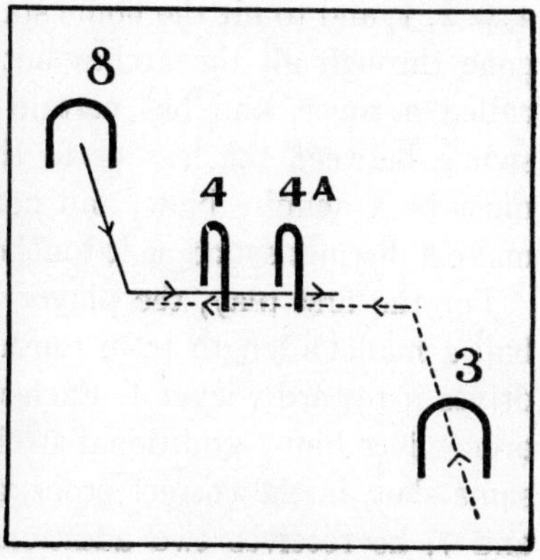

Croquet: III

Balls and Mallets: Wooden or hard rubber balls, approximately 3⅜ inches in diameter, are used. Mallets may be of any conventional size and style. The balls are distinguished by differing colors, as above; and the mallets by colors matching the balls. From two to eight players can play.

The Start.—To select choice of color, position, and partners, if partnership games are being played, the balls are rowed up on a line equidistant from the home stake and at least 15 feet from it. Each player hits one ball toward the home stake. It is not allowed, in this shot, to knock another player's ball away from the position near the stake it has reached; if, by inadvertence, a ball is knocked away, it must be replaced. The player nearest the stake has choice of color, which carries with it position in the shooting, the positions following the rings of color on the stake, the top color being first, and so on. The next nearest player chooses a color in sequence on the stake, and so until all have chosen. Alternating colors become partners automatically. Usually the winner of this shot chooses last rather than first position, in order to have more balls on which to play.

The Play.—The object of the game is to drive the ball, by hitting it with the face of the mallet, through the arches 1 through 7, then to hit the turning stake, then back through arches 7, 6, 8, 4, 9, 2, 1, and to hit the home stake and go out. A player who has gone through all the arches but has not hit the home stake is called a rover, and has certain privileges. The mallet may be swung between the legs or to the side of the body. Each blow must be a definite blow, and not a push; the mallet head must make a distinct sound as it touches the ball.

For the first play, the player who leads off usually places his ball a mallet's length from the home stake toward wicket 1, and drives it toward wicket 1. Each wicket passed through in regular order gives him 1 additional stroke. If he passes through 2 in the same shot, in the correct order, as wickets 1 and 2, or wickets 6 and 7, he receives two additional shots. A player continues to shoot until he can no longer pass through a wicket in a shot attempting to do so, or until he shoots for position, and fails to go through.

In rotation, the other players then play, starting as the first player did. Instead of shooting for a wicket, a player may hit the ball of an opponent or a partner. This gives him two strokes or one, depending upon his choice. He may place his ball against the ball he hit, and drive the two in any desired direction, and thereafter take one additional shot. He may place his ball against the ball he hit, with his foot upon his own ball, and so drive the other ball in any desired direction; and thereafter take one additional shot; but in this case, if his own ball moves at this shot, his play is ended. Or he may place his ball a mallet's head away from the place where the ball that he hit is lying, and take two shots from that point. Or he may, lastly, take one shot from the point to which his ball has rolled; (in some localities, he may take two strokes from this spot). Until he passes through another wicket or hits the turning stake properly, he is dead on the ball he has hit, and cannot gain any strokes by hitting it again.

A player is allowed to drive his partner's ball through the hole for which the partner is aiming. When a ball has become a rover, no ball is dead to it at the beginning of any play. Once during any play a rover may hit any ball, and gain two strokes by so doing. A rover that touches the home stake, whether driven there by an opponent, or partner, or its owner, is eliminated from further play; and thereafter, if only one ball is out, the rotation of shots continues according to the sequence of colors on the stake, so that the opponents receive two shots in succession to one for the surviving partner. The individual player, or the team, that first finishes the entire course, wins.

POISON CROQUET

A variation of Croquet, which speeds up the finish of the game, is called Poison or Blacksnake Croquet. In this, a rover has the power of putting out of the game immediately any ball that it hits, or any ball that it is driven into. A poison ball is put out of the game by being driven into the final post; or by driving through the wicket, or into the post. The last ball in the game wins for the side.

ENGLISH CROQUET

The ground is 105 by 84 feet. The rules are intricate. There are two arrangements of the court. In both, six wickets are used, and both have four corner wickets each 21 feet from both of its nearest boundaries. In the first setting, the two central wickets are on the lengthwise central line of the court, each 21 feet from the crosswise line joining the two corner wickets at its end; while the two stakes are midway of the lines joining these corner wickets. In the second setting, the turning stake is omitted, the home stake centers the court, and the two central wickets are each 21 feet from it, on the lengthwise central line of the court. The course of the play is as shown in the Diagrams.

Clips corresponding with the colors of the balls are placed on the top of the wickets or stake which the ball must go through next, until six wickets have been gone through; and thereafter on one of the uprights. It is not permissible for a player to place his foot on his ball in making a croquet, that is, a shot from another ball. Only a rover can drive another rover against the home stake.

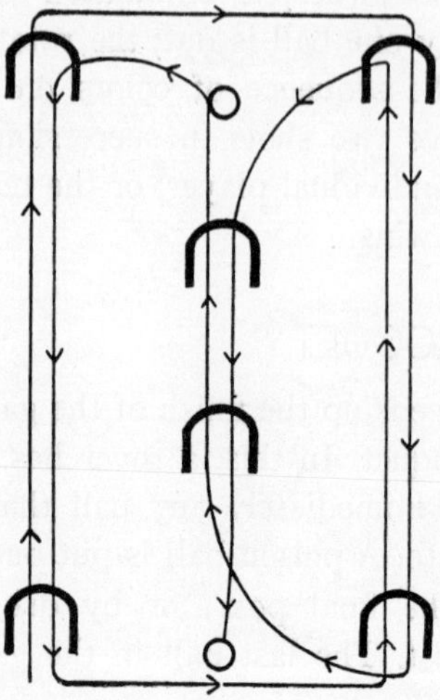

Croquet: IV

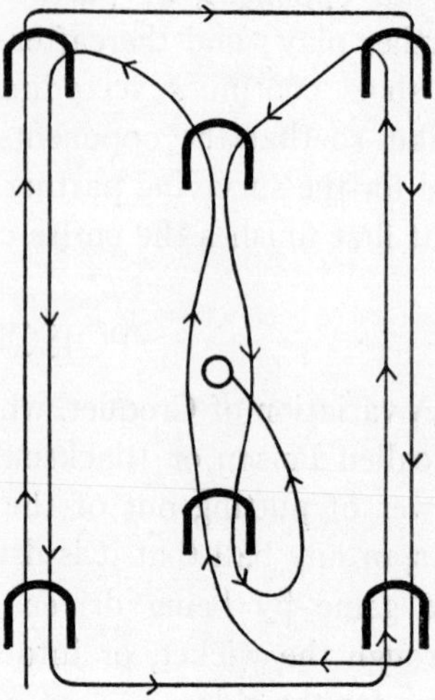

Croquet: V

ROQUE

The Roque court is 60 by 30 feet, with four corner triangles taken off, by drawing between two points on the end and side lines equidistant from each corner a line 6 feet long. A line 28 inches from the boundary lines is drawn inside them. The stakes, 1 inch in diameter and 1½ inches high, are just outside this inside line, midway of the crosswise portions of this inner line. The first wicket is 6 feet from the stake; the second, 6 feet from this, on the lengthwise center line of the court; the side wickets are 1 foot nearer the nearer end of the field than the wicket second from the stake, with its center 5 feet 9 inches from the boundary; the cage or double wicket in the center (see Diagram III) is 18 inches long, at right angles to the line drawn from stake to stake. The wickets in the cage are 3⅜ inches wide; the other eight wickets, 3½ inches. A 4-inch border board surrounds the court.

The following are the important differences between Croquet and Roque: There is no restriction as to mallets; and a player may change his mallet at any time during the game. After making a wicket, each player must change his clip on it to the next wicket; if he fails, he must make the same point again. To start the game, players shoot two balls toward the home end line. The nearest ball has choice of play and balls, provided the ball struck no object. The four balls which are in the game are then placed on the four corners of the field, the leader's partner diagonally across from the leader's ball; and all balls are in play.

If a player makes a point, (passing properly through a wicket or properly hitting the turning stake) and on the same stroke hits a ball, the point is made, and the ball must be used. If a ball hits another ball and thereafter makes a point on the same stroke, he must use the ball and reject the point. A ball making two or more points on one stroke counts the same as if only one were made. If a player hits a dead ball, the opponents may decide whether the balls are to be replaced, or whether to let them lie as they are. If a player strikes a dead ball, his play ceases. A ball shot over bounds must be returned at right angles from where it lies.

MODERN CROQUET

The wickets are of steel, not over 5 inches wide. Mallets weigh from 3 to 5 pounds. Split shots are forbidden. Only one ball may be hit by a player during a succession of points; when another ball is hit, the run is stopped, and no further points may be scored until the player's next play.

The two stakes, the lower stake and the final stake, are set 70 feet apart. There are 9 wickets, called arches, five on the lengthwise central line, the one nearest the stake 7 feet from it, the next nearest 7 feet from this wicket, and the central one midway between the stakes. The side arches, called wing arches, are 3 feet ahead of the arches second nearest to the wicket, and 14 feet left of the wickets on the central line. Arches are of $\frac{5}{16}$ inch steel rods, covered with rubber tubing; when in position they must be

11 inches high and 5 inches wide, or less, inside measurements. The stakes are wooden, or steel rods covered with hard rubber, 1 inch in diameter, and rising 11 inches above the ground. The court is arranged as in Diagram I, except that the corner or wing arches are only 3 feet ahead of the arches second from the wickets, rather than midway of the area between these arches and the central arch.

The balls are of hard rubber and 3⅜ inches in diameter. The colors, Black, White, Blue, Red, are always to be played in that order. Clips are used, to indicate through which arch a ball is next to be played. There is no restriction on the type of mallets used, except that the head must be cylindrical and brass-bound, and set midway of the handle. Choice of colors, partners and first play are decided by shooting from the center of the court to the final stake. The play starts with the four balls in play, as in Roque Strokes must be made with one hand only. When a ball is hit, a croquet may be taken from it; or the player may take one stroke from where his ball lies. Dead balls are treated as in Croquet. In croqueting a ball, the foot must be placed on the player's ball. If the player's ball slips, called a flinch, the play is at once ended. Only one other ball may be played on by a player in any one run of successive points. If the marker is not properly advanced, the point or points must be played again. A roquet occurs when a ball is touching another (the ball is said to be frozen) and the ball must be croqueted.

SPECIAL EQUIPMENT CONTESTS

BLOW-GUN CONTESTS

Blowguns should be 5 to 6 feet long, with an opening ¼ to ⅜ of an inch in diameter. They may be made of tape-wrapped glass. Arrows are bamboo splints 10 to 11 inches long, ⅛ of an inch in diameter, tipped with a piece of cork or wadded cotton the size of the tube opening. Targets should be 18 inches square, with concentric rings 3, 6, 9, 12 and 15 inches in diameter, scoring respectively 5, 4, 3, 2 and 1.

For accuracy, the shooting line should be 15 to 20 feet from the target. The cork end of the arrow is inserted toward the mouth, resting about an inch from it. Arrows score by the ring in which they are, or the outer line which they touch. Game is 50 points. In tournament play, each player gets 18 to 36 shots, highest score winning.

There may also be shooting for distance, each player receiving 3 trials.

CASTING CONTESTS

Accuracy Bait-Casting.—Use any casting rod, with free-running reel, and a ½ or ¼ ounce weight for bait. There are 5 circular targets 30 inches in diameter, 60, 70, 80, 90 and 100 feet from the casting line. Each player makes two casts at each target, starting with one cast at the 60, then one each up to the 100, then back in reverse order. A hit is a perfect score. Each miss is scored by subtracting not more than 10 demerits, 1 for each foot or fraction thereof. At the end, the demerits are added, divided by the number of casts, and this result is subtracted from 100, giving the percentage or score of the contestant.

Fisherman's Accuracy Bait-Casting.—The same, with a ⅝ ounce weight, and 5 targets ranging between 40 and 80 yards from the target.

Distance Bait-Casting.—Each player has five trials, their distances being added and averaged for the score. If a line breaks, the score counts 0. If a caster steps over the line, 1 foot is deducted from the distance for each foot or fraction thereof the caster steps over it.

Accuracy Fly-Casting.—The rod must not weigh more than 5 ounces, nor be more than 11 feet long. A leader between 6 and 12 feet long is used, to whose end a fly is attached, the point of the hook being broken off. Targets are 30 inch rings, stationed in water 45, 50 and 55 feet from the casting line. The player makes five casts at each ring. Scoring is as in Accuracy Bait-Casting. As a variation, hazards or obstructions may be placed between the casting line and the target rings.

TOP-SPINNING EVENTS

For Endurance.—At a signal, all players spin their tops. The one spinning longest wins. A top is considered as having stopped spinning when its side hits the ground.

For Accuracy.—A target, consisting of 5 concentric rings, 6, 16, 18, 24 and 30 inches in diameter, is drawn on the floor or ground. These score 5, 4, 3, 2 and 1 respectively. Each player has five trials from a line 3 feet away. He is credited with the ring in which his top lands, provided it continues spinning.

For Distance.—Similar to Golf Drive for Distance, each player having five trials, and the furthest distance winning, provided the top spins after striking.

Fifty-Foot Top Dash.—The players line up at a starting line, and at a signal throw their tops. Each runs to the point where his top is spinning, marks the spot, toes it, and spins again. Each continues until one player spins his top across a finishing line 50 feet away. If a top fails to spin, it must be thrown again from the spot from which it was thrown.

Foot-Spinning.—The top, duly wound, is placed on the ground, point up. Each player steps on the end of the cord with his left foot, and kicks the top with his right foot, thus making it spin. Each player has five trials; each success counts 1; and high score wins.

Stunt Spinning.—Each spinning top must first be picked up on the palm of the hand, and then the following motions added, as stunts 2 through 9; tossing the top up and catching it on the palm of the other hand; tossing it, and catching it on the back of the same hand; the same tossing hereafter, in each stunt, plus catching it on the back on the other hand; the same, plus causing it to spin on the index finger; the last event, followed by transferring it from the index finger to the palm of the hand; the same tossing, plus catching it on the thigh of the right leg; the same tossing, plus ducking under the top and causing it to land on the back; the same tossing, plus catching it on the top or back of the head.

KITE-FLYING CONTESTS

For Altitude.—Each contestant has 100 yards of string. The winner is the one whose kite is highest, when the strings of all contestants are fully out.

For Looping.—Each contestant has 50 yards of string. Contestants may run as far as they like, providing they stop on the flying line. When a reasonable time has been allowed for all players to arrive here, a 6-minute interval is given, and the winner is the player whose kite is made to loop oftenest in that period.

For Reeling-In.—When all kites are out on 50-yard strings, a signal is given, and players reel in, winding the string figure-8 fashion around a single stick. The one who completes this first, with all the string wound in, wins.

For Novelty.—Kites may be judged for novelty of construction, appearance, decorations, accessories, manner of flying, and behavior in the air.

For Artistry.—Kites may be judged for workmanship, neatness, shape and style, coloring, decoration, and beauty.

ROPE SPINNING

For a home rodeo, rope spinning is essential. The ropes should be 20 feet long, ⅜ inch in diameter, with a 3-inch loop or honda wired back. Among common rope-spinning tricks, which may be contested, are: The Flat Spin, to the side of the body; The Wedding Ring, in which the rope is spun from the ground with the spinner standing inside of it, and over his head; In and Out; Up and Over; Skip; Ocean Wave; and Jumping over the Rope. There are many more intricate tricks.

MODEL CONTESTS

Model airplanes, gliders, balloons, sailboats, and motorboats may be raced in competition for speed, endurance, distance, etc.

VII. TRACK AND FIELD EVENTS

ATHLETIC showdown games may be held in any of the fundamental physical movements, such as *locomotion:*

Running, Walking, Swimming, Skating, Riding, Jumping, Climbing.

and also in *handling objects,* including the mechanical:

Throwing, Catching, Striking, Kicking, Pushing, Pulling, Butting, Shooting, Archery, Boat-Handling.

Certain of these athletic showdown games have become highly standardized, and are called *track and field events.* Many unstandardized games of similar nature are as enjoyable and beneficial.

A. THE TRACK EVENTS

Track events are the sprints, the hurdle races, the middle distance runs, and long distance runs.

THE SPRINT

There are two standard sprints in interscholastic and intercollegiate meets: the 100-yard dash and the 220-yard dash. In the Olympic Games, the distances are from 100 meters up.

To prevent interference between contestants, sprint events should be run in lanes at least 3 feet wide, and clearly marked with lime. Positions in the lanes are determined by lot. Sprinters today use the crouch start, and increasingly favor the use of starting blocks, which afford firmer foot placement. The front foot is usually placed 8 inches behind the starting line; the knee of the back leg rests on the ground beside the instep of the front foot. The thumb and first finger of each hand are placed on the starting line, with elbows locked.

When the starter calls "Get on your marks," the contestants assume their starting positions. He then calls "Get set," at which each runner moves slightly forward and upward. When all are ready and motionless, and at least 2 seconds after "Get set," the starter discharges the starting pistol, or says "Go." If any part of a runner's body is moving just before the shot, this constitutes a false start. The offender is warned, and the start is taken again. If the runner breaks a second time, he is disqualified. In this and all such games, the runner crossing the finish line first, or touching the finishing tape first, wins.

When girls compete, the distances usually range from 40 to 75 yards; when younger boys compete, from 50 to 100 yards.

THE HURDLE RACES

The High Hurdles.—The distance is 120 yards, with 10 hurdles 3½ feet high. The hurdles divide the course into 11 parts, the two end parts being 15 yards each, and the hurdles 10 yards apart. The start is made as for a sprint. All hurdles must be attempted. Each hurdler has his hurdles in his own lane. Stepping out of the iane does not disqualify; but no interference is permitted. Two hurdles may be knocked over without forfeiting the race. A record cannot be made unless all the hurdles are left standing.

The Low Hurdles.—The distance is 220 yards, with 10 hurdles 2½ feet high. Each section of the lane is 20 yards. Otherwise the race is the same as the High Hurdles.

On indoor tracks, the distance may be shorter, down to 40 yards with 3 hurdles. Sometimes 440-yard hurdle races are run outdoors, using 10 hurdles, 3 feet high, 35 yards apart.

THE DISTANCE RUNS

The Middle Distance Runs are the 440-yard run, and the half-mile run. The Long Distance Runs are the one-mile run and the two-mile run. The 440-yard run is sometimes included with the sprints, and is run similarly. In the longer distances, lanes are not used. No runner may cross in front of another unless he is at least two full strides in advance.

CROSS-COUNTRY RACE

Cross-country Runs are from 1½ to 7 miles long; a good average distance is 2½ miles. The course should be marked with flags 1-foot square, on poles 2 to 4 feet from the ground. There are three flags used:

Red flag: turn to the left.
White flag: turn to the right.
Blue flag: straight ahead.

First place scores 1, 2nd, 2; 3rd, 3; and so on. The team with the lowest score wins. Five or some agreed number of runners must score on each team, or the team is disbarred. Each team must have at least one more runner than the number fixed to score per team.

MARATHON RACE

A Marathon Race is 26 miles, 385 yards long, commemorating the reputed run of the Greek messenger in 490 B.C., bringing from the battlefield of Marathon news of the Greek victory over the Persians. It requires superb physique and intensive training

WALKING RACES

Walking races were once standard events. It is difficult for the judges to decide whether a contestant is walking or running, and this has caused a decline in their popularity. They are still popular at picnics and informal meets. In walking, the heel of the advancing foot must be on the ground before the toe of the back foot leaves the ground. Distances are from 220 yards to 1 mile.

OTHER RUNNING RACES

NOVELTY RACES

Sore-Toe Race.—This needs a starting line, and a turning line 40 or 50 feet from it. At the signal, each runner raises one foot, grasps the toe with both hands, and hops on the other leg to the turning line. Here he raises the other foot, grasps its toe as above, and hops back to the starting line. In all these races, the one finishing first wins.

Hopping Race.—The contestants hop on one foot to the turning line, and hop back on the other foot.

One-Leg Race.—Holding one leg off the ground with both hands, each contestant hops to the turning line; and hops back, holding the other leg off the ground with both hands.

Skipping Race.—Each contestant skips to the turning line and back. Skipping means step on right foot, hop on right foot; then step on left foot, hop on left foot; and so alternately.

Crawling Race.—Each contestant crawls to a turning line 30 feet away, and returns similarly. Crawling must be on hands and knees; a contestant may not rise to the toe to propel himself.

Heel-and-Toe Race.—Each contestant advances by placing the heel of the advancing foot against the toe of the back foot on each step. The turning line should be 20 feet away.

Eskimo Race.—Each contestant advances, holding the feet together and the knees stiff, by quick toe springs. The turning line is 30 feet distant.

Heel Race.—Each runner runs on his heels. Contestants are not allowed to touch the toes to the floor.

Stiff-Knee Race.—Each runner runs to the turning point and back, keeping his knees stiff throughout.

Toe-Hold Race.—The contestant, leaning forward and grasping his left toe with his left hand and his right toe with his right hand, runs to the turning line and back.

Crisscross Toe-Hold Race.—The same as above, except that the contestant holds his right toe with his left hand and his left toe with his right hand.

Heel-Hold Race.—The runner holds his right heel with his right hand and his left heel with his left hand, and races in that fashion.

Rolling Race.—The contestant lies on the floor parallel with the starting line, and rolls to the turning line and back.

Dressing Race.—Draw four lines between the starting line and the turning line. The contestant runs to the first line and removes his shoes, to the second and removes his stockings, to the third and removes his belt, to the fourth and removes his shirt, leaving each article at the respective lines. He runs to the turning line, and returns, putting on each article in turn. Shirts must be properly buttoned, and shoes laced.

One Out.—Place stones, bean bags, sticks, or similar articles along the finish line, having one less article than there are players. The players race from the starting line to the finishing line, each trying to secure an article. The player who fails drops out, and an article is removed. The race continues until only one player remains.

Circle Race.—The runners, arm's length apart, form a circle, then face right. They race in the circle, each trying to pass the one in front. Passing must be done on the outside. When a runner is passed, he drops out in the center of the circle. The surviving runner wins.

Variation.—The Leader may order the runners to reverse, and run in the opposite direction.

Slow Motion Circle Race.—This race goes to the slowest, not the fastest runner. Start as above. Each runs as slowly as possible. If a racer touches the one in front, the former drops out. The runners are obliged to keep moving. The survivor wins.

Base-Running Race.—This is played on a baseball diamond, with one player racing at a time. The player crouches at home base. At the signal, he races around the diamond, touching each base in turn, and back to the home base. The players are timed. The one making the best time wins.

Bat and Run.—A pitcher and catcher take their places, with the contestant at bat. When the ball is pitched, the contestant must bat it and run to first. His time is taken from the crack of the bat to his touching first base. The contestant making the best time wins.

Human Top Race.—Each contestant lies on his back, raising his arms and legs vertically through a barrel hoop. The racers must maintain this position throughout the race, and may not use either hands or feet to move themselves forward. They rock themselves to the finish line.

Barrel Rolling Race.—In rotation, each player stands on the side of a barrel and tries to roll it. The winner is either the one staying on the barrel longest, or the one rolling it farthest.

Potato Race.—On the starting line draw a circle one foot in diameter for each player. Straight in front of the center of each circle place eight potatoes, stones, peanuts, or similar objects, each 2 feet apart, the first one 2 feet from the rim of the circle. Each player must run to a potato, pick it up, bring it to the circle, then run for another potato. When all are in the circle, he runs to the finish line. The potatoes may be picked up in any order, but once one is picked up it must be placed in the circle before an other is touched.

Variation.—At 5 yards from the starting line draw a 12-inch square; 5 yards farther draw a 6-inch circle; and 5 yards farther draw another 6-inch circle. Place a potato in each circle. The contestant runs from the starting line, picks up the first potato, and places it in the square. He then runs for the second potato, touches the square with it, and replaces it in the farther circle. He then takes the first potato from the square, puts it in the nearer circle, and returns to the starting line. The potatoes may not be thrown or dropped.

Indian-Club Race.—Played in the same manner as Potato Race, using Indian-Clubs instead of potatoes.

All-Up Indian-Club Race.—Draw two circles side by side, touching each other, each 3 feet in diameter. Place three Indian-clubs in one. The starting line is about 30 feet from the centers of the circles. Each player runs to the circles and, using only one hand, places the Indian-clubs upright in the other circle, and returns. This is done three times.

WHEELBARROW RACE

Divide the players into pairs, one girl and one boy. Provide each boy with a wheelbarrow. The boys race, with the girls riding in the wheelbarrows, from the starting line to the turning point, and return. If there are not enough wheelbarrows, the pairs may be divided into groups, the finalists in each group entering for the final race. The girls can race, pushing the boys.

In this race, as in all the others, unless otherwise stated, the team or pair first completing the event wins.

SACK RACE

Provide each contestant with a large burlap sack. He gets into it, holds it hip high, and runs or hops to the turning point and back.

BACKWARD RACE

The contestants race backward from the starting line to the turning point, and backward to the starting line.

KIDDIE KAR RACE

Provide each contestant with a kiddie car. These are raced from the starting line to the turning point, and back. If there are not enough kiddie cars, the players may be divided into groups, with the finalist competing to decide the winner.

AFROMOBILE RACE

This is popular at beach resorts. The boys push the girls in wheel-chairs from the starting line to the turning point, and back.

RELAY RACES

The standard track relay races are the ½-mile, mile, 2-mile, and 4-mile races; a quarter-mile and medley relay may also be used. Relay teams consist of four runners, no one of whom may run more than once in a relay race. Only contestants who compete in the trial heats may compete in the finals. Each runner carries in his hand a wand or baton, which he passes to his successor teammate within a 20-yard zone marked by lines drawn 10 yards on each side of the exchange line. The baton must be handed, not thrown, or the succeeding runner is disqualified. In the quarter- and half-mile relays, the teams draw for lanes and retain these throughout; in the others, the starting lanes from inside and outside are reversed at each exchange of the batons, the center lane only remaining the same.

For minor relays, captains may be selected and choose their teams; or the players may be lined up by height, and count off in groups for the number of teams desired: as, 1, 2, 3; 1, 2, 3; etc.

To prevent gaining advantage at the transfer, an object should be passed by each racer to his successor: a handkerchief, stick or stone. Another excellent method to prevent this is to have each runner run to a wall or line 15 feet behind the starting line, and then run and transfer the object to the next runner.

MINOR RELAY RACES

Any of the Novelty Races for individuals may be run as relays, for teams of four or more. Other amusing relays are:

Kangaroo Jumping.—Players hold a card or basketball between the ankles, holding it by the legs only, and jump to the turning point and back.

Gallop.—One foot is kept before the other during the racing.

Crab.—Each player is back toward the floor, supported on hands and feet, the feet toward the starting line.

Reverse Crab.—The same, with the hands toward the front.

Elephant.—Each racer is on hands and feet, with legs and arms absolutely stiff and rigid.

Bear-Walk.—Each racer moves right hand and left foot together, and then left hand and right foot, and so alternately.

Frog-Jumping.—Each racer holds his feet spread, with knees outside the hands, which are together. He advances by froglike jumps, landing on hands at each leap, then bringing the feet up.

Lame Dog.—Each racer runs on two hands and one foot, holding the other foot out behind.

Seal.—Each player moves forward on his hands, dragging his body and legs behind him. Legs should be kept straight and toes pointed.

Run-and-Sit.—Each racer runs to the turning line, sits, taps his heels together three times, and returns, tapping off the next.

Dizzy Izzy.—Each player puts his head on a cane leaning against the floor, runs around the cane five times, races to the turning line and back, and touches off the next racer. A baseball bat or umbrella may be used instead of a cane.

Leapfrog.—Line up each team, hands on knees. No. 1 leaps over each of the others leapfrog position, and takes the leapfrog position at the head of the line. Each player in succession does this, and the team first to have all of its players again in their original positions wins.

Miscellaneous.—Countless other relays may be devised: as, barrel rolling; tire-rolling; hoop-rolling; hoop-diving; somersaulting; rope-skipping; running in two pails; sitting in dishpans; walking on two chairs; oversized slippers relay; tin-can stilt relay; stilt relay; pogo-stick relay; broom-riding relay; wheelbarrow relay, with teams of two, one grasping the axle and the other grasping the first player's ankles; and so on. Similarly, striking, kicking and butting relays may be devised. Throwing relays and object-passing relays can also be devised, utilizing all of the throwing and object-passing games.

MASS CONTESTS

FILE RACE

Teams of six to twelve each race, one behind the other. No racer is permitted to pass his teammate ahead of him. The team finishing first wins.

CHINAMAN'S RACE

This is the same as File Race, with each player's right hand extended between his legs and grasping the left hand of the player immediately behind him.

TUG-OF-WAR

The usual method is to draw two lines on the ground 16 feet apart. A long rope is stretched out, with a handkerchief tied to its middle, midway of the 16-foot space. At a signal, the teams pull. The team wins which first pulls the handkerchief over its line.

Or the teams may pull for thirty seconds, and the one which has pulled the handkerchief on its side of the center at that time wins.

An amusing variation is to have each player mounted on another, and the rope pulled so. Any rider falling must let go of the rope until he is remounted.

MISCELLANEOUS

QUARTET RACE

Teams of four race, clasping hands. Any team failing to keep hands clasped drops out. The distance may be 50 to 100 yards. Instead of clasped hands, arms may be linked; or each team may have a stick, up to 8 feet long, which must be held in front of the chests with both hands on it throughout the race.

BACKWARD TRIO RACE

This is raced by teams of three, the central player facing forward; the other two, with arms linked, facing backward. The first team finishing intact wins.

RODEO RACE

Teams of three race, one player grasping another around the waist, the third player riding on the back of the front racer.

CENTIPEDE RACE

Teams of eight or more race, each with his arms clasped around the racer in front—a position that must not be altered during the race. The race should be around a turning line and back.

BUMP RACES

Any individual or group race may be run, putting one racer or group a certain distance behind the other. In this case, if the individual or group behind bumps or tags the front racer or group, it wins from them.

RIDING THE RAIL

Groups of four or more race, straddling a pole, which must be held with both hands by each player; the front racer having at least one hand on the rail in front of him, the rear racer at least one on the rail behind him. The race should be around a turning line and back.

Crew Race.—The same, except that all players face backward except the last one, who is coxswain, and steers.

CATERPILLAR RACE

The front racer of the team runs with his hands on the floor; each other racer grasps the ankles of the racer in front with both hands. The race should be around a turning line and back.

CHARIOT RACE

This is raced by teams of three, the horses racing on hands and feet, the driver guiding them with reins of cord. As sometimes raced, the horses merely clasp hands.

BLIND MEN'S RACE

This is raced by teams of three. Two are blindfolded, and clasp hands. The one not blindfolded holds their outside hands, and guides them down the course, around the turning post, and back to the starting-finishing line.

SNAP THE WHIP

Crack the Whip can be played on foot as well as on ice-skates. It is then called Snap the Whip. See description of the game, in the section on winter sports.

It is also admirable for roller-skates.

B. THE FIELD EVENTS

FIELD THROWING EVENTS

SHOT PUT

The shot is a round iron or brass ball, 16 pounds for adults and 8 or 12 pounds for younger contestants. A contestant stands within a circle 7 feet in diameter, which is indicated on the ground by an iron, wood or rope band; 4 feet of the circumference is marked by a toe board 4 inches high. Each contestant has 4 trials to qualify for his best put. One more than the places to be filled compete in the finals, each contestant having 4 more trials. Each scores his best distance in the 4 tries, measured from the nearest edge of the first mark made by the shot on falling to the nearest point in the circle. If any part of the body touches the stopboard or the ground outside of the circle during an attempt, this is a foul.

JAVELIN THROW

The javelin has a wooden shaft and a sharp metal point, and weighs not less than 1.765 pounds. It is thrown from behind a scratch-line 2¾ inches wide and 12 feet long. No throw counts in which the javelin point does not hit the ground first. The thrower must stand behind the line in throwing, and not cross it until the throw is marked. Rules for qualifying are as in Shot Put.

DISCUS THROW

The discus is a flat disk of metal and wood weighing 4½ pounds, thrown from a circle 8 feet 2½ inches in diameter. The Olympic rules call for 4 pounds, 6.4 ounces, and a circle 2.5 meters in diameter, which is the same size. Rules are as in Shot Put, except that throws to score must be thrown within a ninety-degree sector marked on the ground.

HAMMER THROW

The hammer is a metal sphere called the hammerhead, with a wire handle. The hammer must be not more than 4 feet long and must weigh not less than 16 pounds. It is thrown from a circle 7 feet in diameter. Shot Put rules apply, except that it must fall within a 90 degree sector, as in Discus Throw.

MINOR THROWING EVENTS

BEANBAG TOSSING

Beanbag Board.—Beanbag boards range in size from 18 by 24 inches to 24 by 30. They may have circular holes 4, 5 and 6 inches in diameter, cut in them, scoring 3, 2 and 1 respectively; or equilateral triangles 4, 5, 6, 7, and 8 inches to a side, scoring 5, 4, 3, 2, and 1; or squares of similar size, scoring similarly. The board is set up at a 45 degree angle. Players stand 10 feet away, and throw three standard beanbags at each turn. The game is 25 or 50 points.

Beanbag Bull's-Eye.—On the floor, three concentric circles are drawn, 1, 2, and 3 feet in diameter. These are marks, and score, 5, 3 and 1 respectively. From a distance of 15 feet, each player has 5 shots at the target. A bag touching a line scores as inside the higher scoring circle. Highest score in 5 tosses wins.

Beanbag Climb the Ladder.—At 6 feet from the throwing line a circle 1 foot in diameter is drawn; and, every 3 feet thereafter, another circle, until six are drawn. In rotation, the players have one shot each for the first circle. All who land in it have a shot for the second. The player scoring the most distant circle in this method wins.

Beanbag Tire Toss.—At 20 feet from the throwing line, an old automobile tire or barrel hoop is laid. Each player tosses three beanbags, scoring 1 point for each one inside; but nothing for a bag lying on the tire, unless a subsequent throw by any player knocks it in. Game is 11; or, in an equal number of throws, the highest number immediately beyond 11 points.

Rolling Tire Toss.—The players are divided into teams of four to six each. Two rollers, one from each team, stand 20 feet apart. One rolls the tire to the other; and each player attempts to throw his beanbag through it as he passes. Score 1 for each success. When each player has acted in rotation as roller, the team with the highest score wins.

BASEBALL THROWING

Distance.—Balls are thrown, with or without a running start, toward lines drawn 50, 60, 70, 80, 90 and 100 yards from a 3-foot throwing line. The target lines are 20 yards long. Any balls falling outside them is disqualified. The longest throw within bounds wins, a throw ending where the ball first hits the ground.

Softball Distance.—The same, using a 12-inch softball.

Accuracy.—On a board 6-feet square, concentric circles 1, 2, 3, 4 and 5 feet in diameter are painted, scoring 5, 4, 3, 2 and 1. The throwing line is 45 to 90 feet away. Each contestant has 10 throws. Touching a line scores in the higher ranking circle. The highest score for 10 throws wins.

Accuracy Pitch.—A target 15 inches wide, 24 inches high, and with its bottom 24 inches from the ground, is pitched from a distance of 45 to 60 feet. Each player gets 10 throws; all balls hitting within the target are strikes, and score 1 each.

Softball Accuracy Pitch.—The same, with throwing line 25 to 35 feet distant. The underhand pitch must be used.

Throw to Second Base.—On a regular baseball diamond, a barrel is placed firmly on 2nd base, its open end toward the home plate. Each player has 5 throws. Score, 3 for ball in on the fly; 2, 1st bounce; 1, second bounce. The open end of the barrel should be elevated 3 or 4 inches above the ground.

Fielder to Home.—From deep center, players throw three times to home. The nearest throw to home wins.

FOOTBALL THROWS

Accuracy.—Two ropes, 10 feet long, divide a football goal into 3 equal-sized zones. Players throw from the 20-yard line. Scoring: center zone, 2; outer zones, 1. Each player receives 5 or 10 throws. In one variation, an automobile tire is suspended 6 feet from the ground beneath the center of the crossbar. Each player is given 10 throws, scoring 1 for each ball through the tire.

Center-Pass.—From the snapper-back position, each player has 5 or 10 passes toward a tire 2 or 3 feet from the ground. Scoring 1 for each throw through the tire.

Distance.—From behind a throwing line, each player has one pass for distance, the longest throw winning.

SOCCER THROW

A soccer ball is thrown with both hands overhead. Each player is given 3 trials. In all these contests stepping over the throwing line is a foul. The longest throw wins.

SPEEDBALL THROW

This is the same as Soccer Throw for distance, using a speedball.

There may also be accuracy passes, as in Basketball Accuracy Passes; and Overhead Dribbles for Distance, each player having 5 to 10 trials, the longest throw and catch winning.

BASKETBALL THROWS

Distance.—Each contestant has 3 trials, the longest distance winning. The throws may be limited to one-handed throws; forward overhead throws with both hands; throws with the ball held by both hands in front of the chest; side throws with one arm; toss with both hands between the knees; or side underarm throws.

Accuracy Pass.—Each player has 10 throws at a circle on the wall 4 feet in diameter, 2 feet from the floor. Each hit scores 1.

Overhead Dribble.—Scored as in Speedball Overhead Dribble.

Foul Shots.—Each player has 25 foul shots from behind the free-throw line. Each basket scores 1.

Goal Shooting.—Each player has 10 or 15 throws from behind the free line, scoring 1 for each goal. Or throwing semicircles with radii of 10, 12 and 15 feet may be drawn, with a spot under the goal for a center, and 5 or 6 throws given each player at a time. Goals may be by clear throw or by bouncing in from the backboard.

Follow-Up Goal Shooting.—Each player is given 10 trials from the free-throw line. If the throw misses, the player runs up and shoots from the point at which he catches the ball, on the fly or on first bounce. Score for goal from free-line, or from ball caught on the fly on follow-up, 2; from ball caught on the first bounce on follow-up, 1.

In one variation, after each goal thrown the player recovers the ball and shoots for the goal from where he recovered it. Score, 1 for each goal. Each player has 3 to 5 trials. Highest score wins.

In another variation, each player gets 10 throws, the first from the free-throw line, each thereafter from where the player recovers the ball. Score, 1 for each goal. Balls out of bounds are returned to the free-throw line; or 1 minute may be allowed each player to shoot as in the last variation, goals scoring 1 each.

Basketball Twenty-One.—Played as in Follow-Up Goal Shooting, each player getting a free-throw line shot and a follow-up shot each time. Scoring, 2 and 1; maximum score on each round for each player, 3. The game is 21. In some localities, scoring over 21 causes the player to start again.

Variations.—Each goal from the long shot allows an extra long shot try; or this, with 1 for the first such goal, 2 for the second, 3 for the third, etc.; or each goal in succession from the free-throw line scores 2, a short throw 1, and this entitles the player to another throw from the free-throw line.

This may be played by teams of two, one player making the long shot, his partner the short shot, the first time; and thereafter the players alternate in this.

Elimination Twenty-One.—The first player throws from the free-throw line. The next player must catch the ball, whether a goal or not, before it hits the floor, or he is eliminated. If he succeeds, he throws from the point where he recovered the ball. If no player has reached 21 before all are eliminated, the last to be eliminated wins.

Five, Three, One.—In this variation, each player has 3 throws, one from the free-throw line, the others from the point where the ball is recovered. These 3 throws score respectively 5, 3, and 1.

BASKETBALL GOLF

Fifteen feet from the basketball goal, 9 circles are marked on the floor. Each player in turn throws from circle 1, until he has made a goal. His score is the number of throws he required. Then all throw from circle 2, etc. Low score for the 9 circles wins.

Six-Hole Golf Basketball.—This variation uses 6 holes, marked 1 through 6. Each player advances goal by goal until he fails. Holes 2 and 4 are marked "Safety." If a player is overtaken at any other hole, he must return and start again. After reaching Hole 6, he must return through Holes 5, 4, 3 and 2 to Hole 1 to win, scoring in the same manner. After 6 has been passed, the return is taken from Hole 6. not Hole 1. The first player returning to Hole 1 wins.

MISCELLANEOUS THROWING

Medicine-Ball Throw for Distances.—A 4- or 6-pound medicine ball is used. Each player has 3 throws. A tape-line measures the distance to the spot where the ball first touches the ground. Stepping over the throwing line counts as a foul, and is 1 trial.

As variations, the throws may be limited to two-handed overhead throws; the same, thrown backward; a toss with both hands from between the legs; the same, backward; a one-handed side overhead throw; or a one-handed put, as in shot-put.

Broomstick Throw.—Each player receives 3 trials. The broomstick is held at one end in throwing. The longest throw wins.

Dart Throwing.—Targets are 6 feet square, with 10 concentric rings, each with a radius 3 inches longer than the one next smaller; the center ring has a 3 inch radius. These score in points, center outward, 10, 9, 8, etc., to 1. The throwing line is 10 to 30 feet from the target. Darts on a line score the higher number. Each player throws once in turn, the darts being withdrawn after each round, and scored. Game is 100 points.

In tournament play, each player has 18 or 36 throws. Each player may throw his entire complement of throws first; or two players may be paired against each other, as in elimination tournaments, the winners competing against each other.

Roping Still Targets.—Use a lariat 35 feet long, of ⅜ inch manila rope. A wired 3-inch loop at one end, the honda, has the rest of the rope slipped through it. A chair or other target is placed 20 feet from the throwing line. Each player has 20 trials, scoring 1 for each circling of the chair with the noose. The lariat may be thrown with a wind-up, or a toss, the noose in this case lying flat on the ground before the throw.

Roping Running Targets.—The target is a player, running along a line 10 feet from the throwing line, and parallel to it. When circled, the noose should be relaxed, so as not to trip the runner. Scored as in Roping Still Targets.

Dart Baseball.—On a 4-foot target a 30-inch diamond is drawn, as in the diagram. The throwing line is 15 to 20 feet away. Teams are chosen, and one goes to bat, as in regular baseball. Each player leaves his dart in, until it is advanced by a base hit, or

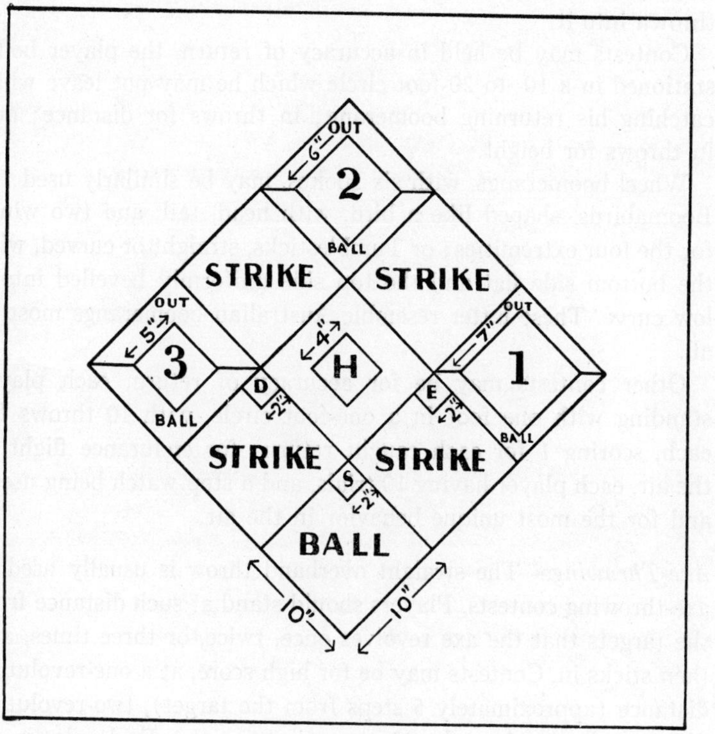

Dart Baseball: I

until a side has three outs. E (error) or D (dead ball) give a player his base. S is a sacrifice hit, the runner being out, the others on bases advancing. A dart that misses the diamond is an out; and so is one that fails to stick in. Nine innings or less are played. Scoring is as in Baseball.

Boomerang Throwing.—Boomerangs may be Cross-stick Boomerangs, each stick 12 inches long and 1 or 1⅛ inches wide, bevelled for the outer 4 inches toward each end, and bent up about ¼ inch at the tips; or larger, in proportion. These may be thrown whirling at head level, and made to return; or thrown along the ground, and made to circle into the air and return. A still day is best for throwing; if there is a breeze, the boomerang should be thrown into it.

Contests may be held in accuracy of return, the player being stationed in a 10- to 20-foot circle which he may not leave while catching his returning boomerang; in throws for distance; and in throws for height.

Wheel boomerangs, with six spokes, may be similarly used; or Boomabirds, shaped like a bird, with head, tail, and two wings for the four extremities; or Tumblesticks, straight or curved, with the bottom side flat and the top side uniformly bevelled into a low curve. These latter resemble Australian boomerangs most of all.

Other contests may be for accuracy of return, each player standing with one foot in a one-foot circle, with 10 throws for each, scoring 1 for each caught return; for endurance flight in the air, each player having 10 trials, and a stop-watch being used; and for the most unique behavior in the air.

Axe-Throwing.—The straight overhand throw is usually used in axe-throwing contests. Players should stand at such distance from the targets that the axe revolves once, twice, or three times, and then sticks in. Contests may be for high score, at a one-revolution distance (approximately 5 steps from the target), two-revolution distance (approximately 10 steps away), etc. Each player receives 25 throws, scoring 1 for each throw in which the axe sticks in the tree or board target. There may also be contests for the most consecutive good throws out of 25. Or there may be a contest for distance, in which all players who make a good throw out of 3 trials from the one revolution distance move back to the two revolution distance; then the winners in this event move on back to the three revolutions distance. The player who sticks in his axe at the greatest distance from the target wins.

APPLE THROWING

Use a tree or a post, or a small glassless window in an outbuilding, for the target. Each player gets 5 throws. Score 1 for each hit.

Or the target may be a row of tin cans or similar objects placed on a fence or some similar surface. Each player gets 5 throws. Score 1 for each hit, 2 for each knockoff.

Or the target may be an archery target, with four concentric rings. Rings score 5, 10, 15, and 20, from outermost to innermost. The bull's-eye scores 25.

Miscellaneous Throwing.—Stones, tomatoes, etc., may be used instead of apples. Or old baseballs.

ICE-PICK

The target is any wooden surface, such as a wooden wall, a tree, or the side of a barn. The player stands behind a line drawn on the ground about 20 feet from the target. The ice-pick is balanced in the palm of the hand and hurled toward the target. Score 2 for sticking in the target; 1 for sticking and falling out. Falling and sticking in the ground may be ½ point for the player; or may penalize him ½ point, according to previous decision. A chalked circle may be drawn on the target; in this case, score 3 for sticking within the circle, and 2 for sticking in the edge; otherwise scoring is as above.

KICKING EVENTS

Punt for Distance.—A football is punted, the longest punt winning. The measurement is to the spot at which the ball first hits the ground.

Place-Kick for Distance.—A similar event.

Place-Kick for Accuracy.—Each player has 10 trials to place-kick a football over the goal, scoring 1 for each success. The kicking line may be from 20 to 30 yards away.

Drop-Kick for Distance.—This is similar to Punt for Distance.

Soccer Kicking.—Similar contests may be held in Soccer place-kicks for distance, punts for distance, and place-kicks for accuracy.

Speedball Kicking.—These are similar events to the regular football events described above. There may also be a Kick and Catch contest, in which a player kicks into the air a ball rolled toward him, and has 10 trials to catch it in the air, scoring 1 for each such catch.

Codeball Kicking.—This is the same as Soccer Kicking, above, using a codeball.

Kick, Bounce and Catch.—A player is given 3 trials to kick a soccer ball or codeball, and catch it on the rebound at the farthest distance from the wall against which he kicks it. The player making the farthest catch wins.

HITTING EVENTS

Batting for Accuracy.—The players compete by tossing up baseballs from deep center field, and batting them as near the home plate as possible. A ball is counted from the place where it first strikes the ground. Flags marked with the players' names may be used to mark their closest hits. Each player has 3 trials, the one striking closest to home winning.

Tennis Serve for Accuracy.—A second tennis net is stretched 30 inches above the regulation net. Players serve one ball alternately into the left, then the right, service court, standing in the usual tennis serving position. Each is given 10 trials, scoring 1 for each good serve. Or a rectangle 30 inches wide by 13½ feet long may be marked on a wall, its bottom 36 inches from the floor. The service line is 38 feet away, and players must stand left or right of the 13½ feet along this line directly behind the rectangle. Score as above.

Tennis Stroke for Accuracy.—The center line in a tennis court is continued to the back line, dividing the court into right and left service courts, and right and left back courts. As the leader tosses a tennis ball to a contestant, he calls out one of these courts; and the contestant must hit the ball within the court designated. Score 1 for each success. Each contestant has 20 trials, each of the four courts being called 5 times, in random order. The highest score wins.

Volleyball Serve for Accuracy.—This event is similar to Tennis Serve for Accuracy, using Volleyball rules and equipment.

Golf Putting.—Each player has 10 putts toward the hole, from a line 6 feet away. Score 1 for each ball holed. Other contests may be from a longer distance; or from graduated differing distances.

Golf Approach.—Each player has 10 tries, from a point 100 feet from the hole. Scoring: in the hole, 10; within 10 feet of the hole, 5; between 10 and 20 feet, 3; between 20 and 30 feet, 1; beyond 30 feet, 0. The highest score wins.

Golf Drive.—Players have 3 trials, driving from a tee for distance, down a fairway 50 yards wide. The longest distance wins.

Hockey-Goal Golf.—This is played in the same way as Basketball Golf, using Hockey equipment.

Shinny Golf.—This is also the same, using shinny sticks and a paddle-tennis ball.

Hockey Drive.—Each player has 5 or 10 drives from a point 35 yards from the goal, each goal scoring 1.

Hit the Can.—Each player has 10 trials to hit a gallon tin can or water bucket on the ground between the hockey goal posts, the driving being from 15 yards away. Score as in Hockey Drive.

Hockey Drive for Distance.—This is the same as Golf Drive for Distance, using Hockey equipment. Each player has 5 to 10 trials.

JUMPING AND VAULTING GAMES

RUNNING HIGH JUMP

The high-jump pit is usually 14 feet wide and 10 feet deep. The uprights are 12 feet apart. The crossbar should be square, with bevelled edges, 1⅛ inches thick; or triangular, 1$\frac{3}{6}$ inches on each face. A light bamboo pole may be used in informal jumps. The crossbar should rest upon a standard 1½ inches wide and 2⅜ inches deep; standards with pins not over 3 inches long are often used.

Each contestant must clear the bar without displacing it from its supports. Each contestant has 3 trials at each height, and then the bar is raised. A contestant failing at any height in all 3 trials is disqualified. Each contestant is scored as of the greatest height at which he cleared the bar.

STANDING HIGH JUMP

This contest is similar, except that each contestant, standing with his feet in any position, must leave the ground one foot at a time in jumping. If a foot is lifted from the ground twice, or two springs are made without an attempt to clear the bar, this counts as one trial.

Standing Double High Jump.—Each contestant stands on both feet facing the bar, and jumps with both feet simultaneously. The body must face front squarely throughout, and the jumper must land on both feet simultaneously, with his back to the bar. Any violation counts as one trial.

POLE VAULT

The pit is 14 feet wide and 12 feet long. The uprights are 12 feet apart, and the crossbar must not be more than ½ inch thick, nor extend more than 3 inches beyond the uprights. The contestant's upper hand may not be raised after his feet leave the ground, nor may the lower hand be placed above the upper. One trial is counted whenever the competitor leaves the ground in an attempt, or passes under the bar. The bar must be cleared without displacing it.

RUNNING BROAD JUMP

The scratch-line is a take-off board 2 inches thick, 8 inches wide, and at least 4 feet long, firmly set level with the ground. The jumping pit should begin 5 feet in front of the take-off board, and be 6 feet wide and 25 feet long. It should be filled with 12 to 18 inches of sand, level with the take-off board. Each contestant may run as far as he pleases, but must jump from, or behind, the scratch-line. If ground is broken in front of the plank, this counts as a trial. The jump is measured with a tape from the board to the nearest point where any part of the jumper's body breaks ground. Each contestant has 4 trials. In the finals, one more than the places to be filled compete. Qualifying jumps count in the final tabulation of places.

Running Double Broad Jump.—This event is similar; the jumper must jump with both feet on the take-off board, and land on both feet.

STANDING BROAD JUMP

This is similar to the Running Broad Jump, except that the contestant stands with both feet touching the scratch-line. He may sway back and forth, but may not lift either foot before the jump. The jumper jumps with both feet and lands on both.

Standing Backward Broad Jump.—This is similar, except that the jumper jumps backward.

DOUBLE STANDING BROAD JUMP

This should be conducted on level ground, without a jumping pit. Each contestant toes the scratch-line with both feet, and makes 2 successive jumps, the second being immediately after and continuing the first. The distance is measured from the scratch-line to the nearest point touched by the contestant on his second jump.

Triple Standing Broad Jump.—This is the same, except for 3 jumps in succession.

Seven Standing Broad Jump.—This is the same, except that 7 continuous jumps are taken.

Standing Broad Hop.—This is the same, except that the contestant hops from the take-off board and lands on the same foot. He must retain his balance on land, and may not touch the ground with any other part of his body until the jump is completed.

Double, Triple, Seven Standing Broad Jump.—This is similar to these variations of the Double Standing Broad Jump.

RUNNING BROAD HOP

This is similar to Standing Broad Hop, except that the contestant runs to the scratch-line.

Hopping Broad Hop.—This is similar, except that the contestant hops to the scratch-line.

STANDING HOP, STEP and JUMP

Each contestant stands on one foot on the take-off board, takes one hop, landing on the same foot, steps once forward landing on the other foot, and jumps forward landing on both feet. This process must be continuous. It is measured like the Broad Jumps.

Running Hop, Step and Jump is the same, with a running start.

Standing One- and Two-Foot Jump.—This is a Double Standing Broad Jump, except that the first jump must land on one foot, and the second jump be taken continuously without touching the other foot to the ground.

Standing, Hop, Skip and Jump.—In this variation of the Standing Broad Jump, the first jump starts from and lands on one foot.

The contestant then swings the other foot behind the foot landed on and lands on it; then jumps forward, landing on both feet. This must be continuous.

Running Hop, Skip, and Jump.—This is the same as the last, except that the contestant takes a running start before his first hop.

Standing Broad Step.—From a standing take-off, the contestant hops from one foot and lands on the other.

Double, Triple, Seven Standing Broad Step.—This is the same, except that 2, 3 or 7 steps are taken.

Double Hop, Step and Jump.—From a standing take-off, each contestant hops twice, steps twice, and jumps twice.

POLE VAULT FOR DISTANCE

No cross-bar is used. Each contestant runs to the take-off line, places an end of the pole on the ground, and vaults as far as he can.

Bat Vault for Distance.—In this variation, a baseball bat is used instead of a vaulting pole.

STILT JUMPS

Running and Standing Broad Jumps on stilts, and Stilt Hop, Step and Jump, are conducted in similar fashion to the events without stilts, except that each contestant uses stilts.

ROPE SKIPPING AND JUMPING

METHODS

In all these, the contestant uses a standard short rope, turning it himself.

Skipping: Hop on right foot from standing position on right foot, passing rope under it; then on left foot; and so alternately.

Running: No hops are used, the rope passing first under the right foot, then the left, and so alternately.

Single Jump: Both feet together, no intervening hops.

Double Jump: Both feet together, with an intervening jump between each passage of the rope under the feet.

Backward Skipping or Jumping: Any of the preceding, backwards.

Skipping on One Leg: One leg is held off the floor; the rope is skipped on one leg.

Stiff-Leg Kick Forward: The same as Skipping, with a straight-legged kick forward after each skip.

Stiff-Leg Kick Backward: This is the same, with a straight-legged backward kick.

Spread Eagle: Jumping with feet spread widely, with or without a hop intervening.

Crossed-Foot Jump: The feet are crossed on each jump, alternately.

Buck and Wing: The heels are clicked together between jumps.

Click Handles: The rope handles are clicked together between jumps.

FIFTY SKIPS

This event is timed, the shortest time winning. Older contestants may be required to make 100 skips.

Rope Skipping, Thirty Seconds.—The number of jumps each contestant makes in half a minute determines the winner.

LONG ROPE JUMPING EVENTS

In these events, two players, the turners, swing the long rope, while the others jump it. Each player may compete in any one event until he misses, the one lasting longest winning. Or five or more events may be conducted simultaneously, the player completing all of these without a miss winning.

Against the Wall: The player runs in against the turn of the rope, and jumps as often as possible.

Rocking the Cradle: The rope is swinging about 4 inches above the ground; the jumper jumps from one side to the other, until he misses.

Double Rope: The jumper jumps as many times as possible over two ropes turned toward each other, one slightly after the other.

Over the River: This means running through the rope without being touched by it.

Building a House: This involves jumping, the rope being raised 2 inches after each jump.

Red, White, and Blue, Stars over You: At every fourth jump, the player stoops, and the rope is turned high over her head.

Hot Peas: The rope is turned as fast as possible, after the first four jumps (spelled H-O-T-S). Each jump is counted, 1, 2, 3, etc.

Keep the Kettle Boiling: Ropes radiate from the center of the playground, like circular hurdles. They start low, and then are gradually raised.

Swinging Rope: Like Keep the Kettle Boiling, except that the ropes are swung slowly.

Over the Waves, Serpents: Each rope is made a series of slow or fast waves, by a holder's arms moving up and down.

Over and Under: Each player jumps one rope and crawls under the next.

LONG ROPE SKIPPING EVENTS

In these, the rope is skipped, instead of jumped.

Double Dutch: The turners turn two ropes, which touch the ground alternately. The turners' arms are held as far apart as possible. The ropes may be turned toward the players or away from them.

Higher and Higher: Successively, the rope is turned higher and higher.

French Almond Rock: To the rhyme:

> Handy-nandy,
> Sugardy-candy,
> French almond rock.

the players jump over the rope, as it swings from side to side.

The rhyme is repeated, as they skip over it; then, as it swings over their heads; finally, as they skip it again.

Salt, Mustard, Vinegar, Pepper: At the word "pepper," the rope is gradually turned faster and faster.

All in Together: The players run in from the side or front, and try to continue skipping until all are in. When the last player enters, count is kept of the number of skips.

Running In: The players run in, skip an assigned number of skips, then run out again.

Over the Moon: This is either of the two last events, skipped backward.

CLIMBING GAMES

ROPE CLIMB

The rope should be 1¼ to 2 inches in diameter, hanging 18 feet above the floor. Tapes should mark 12, 16 and 18 feet. A stop-watch is used in timing the seconds required by a player to reach the height marker.

Arms Only.—This is the same as Rope Climb, except that only the arms may be used. Players start by sitting on the floor, not standing.

POLE CLIMB

The pole should be 20 feet high, and well greased with axle-grease. A strip of cloth is tied to the top. The winner is the one who unties it. In case of ties, repeat the climb.

VIII. PERSONAL COMBATS

BOXING and wrestling are almost as old as the human race. Schliemann's excavations at Mycenæ and Tiryns revealed that as early as 3,000 B.C. the Greeks had begun to formalize boxing. The Greeks wore a glove consisting of a thin thong 10 to 12 feet long, called the cæstus, wound around the hand, to increase the power of attack and prevent the knuckles from swelling. Among them, skill was the chief determinant. Among the Romans, brutal cruelty came in, with the cæstus replaced by a metal ball with several spikes on the end, one well-struck blow with which meant death. In the 18th century, boxing became popular in England; and by the middle of the next century the Queensbury rules replaced the more brutal earlier London rules. John L. Sullivan was in 1889, the last professional fighter to fight with bare fists.

Wrestling dates back quite as far. Early Egyptian tombs picture it. It was important in the Greek pentathlon, without restrictions, so that butting, gouging, kicking, strangling and hitting were used. The Greeks had two chief styles, the upright, in which the object was to throw the opponent to the ground; and the squirming, in which, after the contestants fell to the mat, they struggled until one acknowledged defeat. Rome never favored the sport. The Teutons had a mild form of wrestling, forbidding tripping and all holds below the hips. The Swiss had a form of wrestling called Schwingen, or swinging, in which the contestants wore strong belts, which were grasped and used to throw the opponent down, and thus win. In Japan, the first recorded match was in 23 B.C. In 858 A.D., the imperial throne was wrestled for by two brothers. Almost a thousand years later, Jiu Jitsu developed, a dangerous sport designed to cripple the adversary.

Japanese wrestlers put on all the weight possible, and victory goes to the one who forces his opponent to touch any part of his body, except the feet, to the floor. Excess weight is also at a premium in wrestling in India, but to win in that country, both shoulders must be touched to the ground. In England, Henry VIII is said to have been a powerful wrestler. There are many English styles. The Cumberland and Westmoreland style started with the opponents chest to chest, barred kicking, and was won when any part of the body except the feet touched the ground. The Cornwall and Devon required the contestants to wear loose jackets and grip above the waist; to constitute a win, two shoulders and a hip, or two hips and a shoulder, had to touch ground. The Lancashire style, or catch-as-catch-can, is now most prevalent in America. A win requires both shoulders to touch the ground at the same time. No kicking or hitting are allowed; strangling and crippling holds are barred; otherwise practically all holds are allowed. The so-called Græco-Roman style arose about 1860 in French wrestling schools; this style forbids tripping and holding below the waist.

Fencing is the game developed out of ancient warfare with the sword, as boxing and wrestling developed from weaponless hand-to-hand conflict. Commencing with short two-edged blades, of bronze first and then of iron, the sword became in the latter Middle Ages a two-handed weapon. The rapier, a piercing weapon only, with a finely tapering blade, was originated in the early 16th century, and by the next century it had become the preferred weapon for fencing and duelling. The foil and epee, both piercing weapons, originated in the rapier; the thrusting and cutting sabre developed out of the more cumbersome cavalry sabre and the cutlass. These three weapons are used in modern fencing.

BOXING

The Ring: The ring should be between 16 and 20 feet square. The floor should extend beyond the ropes for at least 2 feet on each side. The ring should be enclosed by at least three railings of rope, wrapped in cloth, with the posts properly padded. The floor should be padded for a thickness of at least an inch with matting, felt, corrugated paper, or some other soft material. The floor padding of an outdoor ring may be tight canvas over dampened sawdust. During a match, the ring must be cleared of all chairs, buckets and other objects.

EQUIPMENT: Standard boxing gloves must be used, weighing not less than 10 ounces; however, professional boxers frequently use 8- and 6-ounce gloves. Spikes and cleats on the shoes are forbidden. As a rule, sleeveless shirts and knee-length trunks are worn.

WEIGHT GROUPINGS: Weights are classified as follows:

	College	*Secondary School up to 95 pounds*
Flyweight	up to 118 pounds	" 105 "
Bantam	" 126 "	" 115 "
Feather	" 135 "	" 125 "
Light	" 145 "	" 135 "
Welter	" 155 "	" 145 "
Middle	" 165 "	" 155 "
Light-heavy	" 175 "	" 165 "
Heavy	over 175 pounds	" 185 "

SECONDS.—Each contestant is allowed two seconds. These are not allowed to signal, speak to or coach a contestant during the rounds, nor enter the ring between rounds. They may enter the ring only when the contest is over.

FOULS.—Fouls include: (1) hitting below the belt; (2) with the glove open; (3) with the inside or butt of the hand, wrist, or elbow; (4) hitting an opponent who is down, or who is rising after going down; (5) holding an opponent, or deliberately maintaining a clinch; (6) holding an opponent with one hand and hitting with the other; (7) pushing or butting with head or shoulder, or using the knee; (8) wrestling or roughing at the ropes, (9) going down without being hit; (10) striking deliberately at the part of the body over the kidneys; (11) using insulting or abusive language; (12) any action that may injure a contestant except by fair sportsmanlike boxing; (13) failure to obey the referee; (14) and coaching, advice or applause from spectators when, in the opinion of the referee and judges, the occasion warrants regarding these as fouls.

The referee has a right to disqualify immediately a contestant who deliberately fouls, in which case the decision is awarded to the opponent. The referee should not warn more than once for an unintentional foul which may incapacitate the opponent. In the case of minor fouls, the referee has the option of awarding the contest to the opponent, or not. For major and minor fouls, the judges penalize contestants in points.

A contestant is considered down when any part of his body other than his feet is on the floor; when he hangs helplessly on the ropes; or when he is rising from a down position. When a contestant is down, the opponent must retire out of striking distance, and may not resume boxing until the referee orders it.

Scoring.—A maximum of 20 points is awarded to a contestant in each round: 14 for attack (clean hits, aggressive action, and well-delivered partial hits) and defense (blocking, making the opponent miss, balance, and readiness for counter attack); 4 for generalship; and 2 for aggressiveness. Points are deducted for all fouls, and for stalling, covering up with the hands, and clinching.

Length of Contest.—A contest consists of three or more rounds. A round is 2 minutes long in college competition, and may be reduced for younger contestants. Intermissions between each two rounds are 1 minute each. If the judges disagree, an additional round may be ordered. A bout is ended if a contestant who is down fails to take his feet in ten seconds.

The officials are a referee, two judges, two timekeepers, and a medical officer. The referee is in general charge of the match. The judges are stationed at opposite sides of the ring, and their duty is to record the points and the rounds, and select the winner. If they disagree, the referee's vote decides. The timekeepers indicate the opening and ending of each round.

WRESTLING

EQUIPMENT: The regulation area of the mat is 20 feet square when ropes are used, and 24 feet square without ropes. The ropes should be 1 inch in diameter, well wrapped and stretched 4, 3, and 2 feet respectively above the mat. They are stretched from turnbuckles attached to the four corner posts, which are placed at least 18 inches from the corners. Three vertical ropes, ⅜ inch thick, are placed at equal distances on each side of the ring, to keep the ropes in position. Wrestlers usually wear full-length tights, sleeveless shirts, and gymnasium shoes without heels, laced through eyelets. The weight classification is as in boxing.

ILLEGAL HOLDS.—In college wrestling, these holds are illegal: (1) hammerlock above the right ankle; (2) twisting hammerlock; (3) over-scissors; (4) strangle holds; (5) full or double nelson; (6) toe hold; (7) body slams, unless the attacker's knee touches the mat before the opponent's upper body touches it; (8) holds over mouth, nose, or eyes; (9) interlocking of fingers, hands or arms around body or legs, while the contestants are on the mat; (10) bending or twisting of fingers to break holds, or for punishment; (11) any hold used for punishment only; and (12) striking, kicking, gouging, hair-pulling, butting, elbowing, strangling, or anything that endangers life or limbs. Except for these, all holds are legal. Among younger contestants, all slams from a standing position and the fall back (that is, falling backward when the opponent is on the contestant's back) are also forbidden.

FALLS.—To constitute a fall, any part of both shoulders must be held in contact with the mat for a 2-second count. If the head or one or both shoulders of the defending contestant are off the mat, it is not a fall.

MISCELLANEOUS.—If the contestants interlock off or on the edge of the mat, they should be brought to the center. If neither had an advantage when brought to the center, they resume in a standing position. If either held the advantage, the referee gives him a position with the same advantage in the center. If a fall was about to take place and the defensive wrestler intentionally left the mat, the contestants are given as nearly as possible the positions they were in when the referee stopped the bout. If a contestant continues intentionally to go off the mat, the match may be awarded to his opponent. Contestants are not allowed to stall; they must wrestle to gain a point of advantage, and then secure a fall. When a contestant in a position of advantage stalls, the referee should place both men on their feet in a neutral position. If a contestant in a neutral position on the mat is stalling, the referee should order both men to the floor in the referee's position, with the offender beneath.

In case of injury, the injured contestant is given a 3-minute rest, after which the bout continues as if he had gone off the mat. If the injury was accidental and the contestant cannot continue, the match is awarded to the opponent. If the injury resulted from a barred hold, the bout is forfeited to the injured player, and is scored as a fall.

Scoring.—If the time has expired without a fall, the decision is awarded to the contestant who showed the greater wrestling ability and aggressiveness, providing he has had a time advantage of at least one minute. A time advantage begins when a wrestler brings his opponent to the mat, and continues as long as he has a position of clear advantage, even though the opponent temporarily regains his feet.

When only one contestant secures a fall, he is awarded 5 points. If both secure falls, the fall in the shortest time scores 5, and the other fall 3. A decision counts 3. If a contestant scores more than one fall, he is scored for only one. In team contests, the team scoring the highest total of points wins.

Length of Bouts.—Wrestling bouts in college competition are 10 minutes long, unless a fall occurs. Where no fall occurs and the referee does not award the bout, two extra periods of 3 minutes each are allotted. At the end of the first 2 minutes of a 10-minute bout, if a contestant has his opponent on the mat and has secured a position of advantage, the bout becomes continuous to the end of the 10 minutes, or until terminated by a fall. If neither wrestler has a position of advantage within 2 minutes, the referee divides the remaining 8 minutes into two periods of 4 minutes each. By coin toss one wrestler is allowed to decide between the under and the over position when the wrestlers are placed in the referee's position on the mat. At the beginning of the final 4-minute period, the positions are reversed. A fall during the first 4 minutes terminates this period only, and the second period of 4 minutes must still be wrestled. If each wrestler scores a fall, the wrestler securing his fall in the shortest time is awarded the points for the fall. Between the 10-minute bout and extra periods, a 1-minute intermission is permitted. There is no intermission between the periods of the 10-minute bout. For younger wrestlers, bouts are 7 or 8 minutes in length. If neither wrestler secures an advantage in 2 minutes, the remaining time is divided into two periods, as above.

A referee starts the bouts, enforces the rules, decides when falls are legally made, and awards decisions. There are three timekeepers, one being assigned to each wrestler, to record the duration of his time advantage.

The Referee's Hold consists in each wrestler's placing one hand over the back of the opponent's neck, at the same time grasping with his other hand his opponent's arm near the elbow, with feet well spread and back out of reach; this is usually the first position assumed after the preliminary on guard position, where the wrestlers stand facing each other.

FENCING

Fencing takes place on a mat 40 feet long and 3½ feet wide. To start, the two contestants stand at the center facing each other. They cross swords, take one step back, and the referee announces "Fence!"

THE FOIL.—The foil is a thrusting weapon, and the fencer's object is to thrust at the opponent so that its point touches some part of the target. The target is a vest covering the fencer from the neck to the hip bones, and tapering down to the crotch.

There are eight standard thrusts (with parries for each) each thrust being designed to touch a different section of the target. Each thrust has many variations. Each contact of the target with the point of the foil scores 1 point. The head, protected by a mask, the arms, and the legs, are not parts of the target. The player wins who first scores 5 points; except at 4-all, 2 successive points being then required to win.

The Sabre.—The sabre is heavier than the foil, and is used for both cutting and thrusting. The rules are the same as fencing with foils, except that the entire body except the legs constitute the target, and that a fencer may score by touching with the front cutting edge and the upper third of the back edge of the sabre, as well as with the point.

The Epee.—The epee is heavier than the sabre, and is a duelling sword. The entire body is the target; the player making the first three hits wins; and, to start, only the points of the weapons are touched. Otherwise, the rules of foil fencing apply.

Team Competitions.—When a team consists of seven players, three use foils; two, sabres; and two, epees. Each in his group must meet all others in the same group. There are thus 9, 4 and 4 matches, or 17 in all. Each match scores 1 point, the team with the highest total winning. When the team consists of three fencers only, one fences with the foil, one with the sabre, and one with the epee. There are 3 matches, the best 2 out of 3 winning for the team.

The formalities of fencing are intricate, and a large number of terms restricted to this sport are used.

TILTING

Tilting is done by the contestants standing on stools with a 15-inch top and sturdy legs widely spread. It may also be done from the tops of medium-sized barrels or small wooden tubs. The spears are 6 to 7 feet long, with a hollow wooden disk 2 inches thick and 3½ inches in diameter pegged on to the lighter end, and then thickly padded with hair stuffing, covered with canvas and taped on. The spears should be about 2 inches thick at the heavy end.

The object is to dislodge the opponent from the stool, by pushing and punching him with the spear. A second stands behind each contestant, to catch him if he falls. The contestants may push, shove and punch each other with their spears above the knees and below the head. A spear can be pushed against the back of the neck; it may not be used as a club with which to strike the opponent, although it may be swung to cause the opponent to drop his spear. In defense, the spear, the hand, and movements of hips and body are allowed. Any violation of these rules is a foul; and so is rapping the opponent's hand to dislodge the spear, and grasping the spear with the hand, which may only be used to ward off the spear.

A contestant wins when an opponent touches the floor with any part of his body, or commits a foul, or drops his spear, or by the decision of the judge. If no fall occurs, the decision is based on blows struck, defense, and aggressiveness. The bouts are 1½ minutes long, with ½-minute rests between them. A bout consists of 3 rounds, or until terminated by a fall. Championship matches consist of 2 out of 3 bouts. Officials are a referee, two judges, and a timekeeper. The referee starts the bout, and passes on fouls; the judges select the winner, where there is no fall. If the judges disagree, the referee's vote decides.

MINOR PERSONAL COMBAT GAMES

PILLOW-FIGHTING

Pillow-fighting may take place on a bed. The contestants stand, each one equipped with a pillow. The winner is the player who first knocks the other player to his knees or flat, while remaining upright himself.

In summer camps, the contestants are seated on poles, high enough above the ground for a player to hang head downward and still miss the ground. Mattresses should be placed beneath. A player may not grasp his opponent's pillow or touch his body with his hand. Each bout is usually 3 rounds of 1½ minutes each with ½-minute intermissions, in which the players remain on their poles. If a player falls from the pole, he loses. If no fall occurs, the judges make the award on the number of blows struck, aggressiveness, and skill in defense. A fall scores only when a player falls from the pole; hanging upside down does not constitute a fall.

POLE-BOXING

This is the same as summer camp pillow-fighting, each player wearing one boxing glove. A player is defeated if he falls under the pole, even if he still clings to it.

SWING BALL

Each player stands on his own side of a center line, over which he may not step, and holds one end of a rope, at whose center a ball of the punching bag type is suspended. The ball is swung in a horizontal circular motion; and each player attempts to strike his opponent with it. For a slight hit, score 1; for a full hit, 2 points. A hit on the wrist does not score. Any violation of the rules is a foul, and play starts again. For repeated violations, the referee may award points to the fouled player. The game usually consists of an agreed number of rounds, or a stipulated number of points.

MINOR WRESTLING

Advantage Wrestling.—The players face each other. At a signal, they commence to wrestle, the winner being the one first to get behind his opponent's back, and hold him around the waist from behind. Only the arms may be used.

Square Hold.—Each player grasps his opponent's two arms, one near the shoulder and the other near the elbow. They wrestle facing each other, the winner being the one first to make his opponent lose his feet or his hold.

Elbow-and-Collar Wrestling.—The right hand of each player grasps his opponent's left elbow, and the left hand is placed behind the opponent's neck. Tripping is allowed. The winner is the player who first makes his opponent touch the ground with any part of his body except his feet.

Cumberland Wrestling.—The players stand, each with the right arm over the opponent's left shoulder, and grasping his own left hand. The winner is the player who first lifts the opponent entirely clear of the ground.

Tire Wrestling.—Each player wrestles standing in an antomobile tire. The winner is the one first to throw the other player out of his tire, while he himself remains on his feet inside his own tire.

Ring Wrestle.—The players wrestle in a 10-foot ring. The winner is the one first to push any part of his opponent's body out of the ring.

Shoulder Shove.—This is the same, the players standing each on one leg, with arms crossed, and using the shoulders for shoving. The winner is the one first to force the opponent out of the ring, or to cause him to drop his other foot.

Ring Free-for-All.—This is the same as Ring Wrestle, except that a 15-foot circle is used, with twelve to fifteen players competing. The one last remaining in the ring wins.

COCK FIGHT

Each player grasps his left foot raised to the rear with his left hand. The right arm must be kept close to the body with fist closed, and may not be used to pull, shove or strike. The winner is the one to upset the other, or to cause him to drop his left foot to the ground.

Free-for-All Cock Fight.—This is the same, up to ten players competing. The winner is the one to remain standing longest. For more than ten players elimination fights will reduce the number to ten for the finals.

Cock Fight on Stilts.—Two players compete on stilts in a 6-foot circle. The winner is the one first to force his opponent out of the circle or off of his stilts.

Hop Fight.—The players compete with arms folded, hopping on one leg, using the other leg as the sole means of upsetting the other player.

Cane Wrestle.—Two players grasp a stick 3 feet long. The winner is the one first to force his opponent to take both hands from the stick.

Wand Wrestling.—This is the same, the winner being the one first to force his opponent to release the wand, or to move either foot.

Double-Peg Fight.—Two pegs, broom-handle size, a foot long, are used, each player holding with one hand to each. The object is to take the sticks from the opponent. If one hand is released, it may not be used on either stick. A tie is played off by using one stick only.

Can Push or Pull.—Standing as in Double-Peg Fight, each player tries to force the other over one of two parallel lines drawn 6 feet apart.

Ball Struggle.—Two players face each other, each with both hands on a basketball or soccer ball held chest high between them. The winner is the one first to remove the ball from any contact with his opponent.

Hand Wrestle.—The opponents stand with their right feet braced against each other, and grasping their right hands. The winner is the one first to force his opponent to move either foot, or to touch the ground with any part of the body except the feet. For a variation, this may be wrestled holding left hands.

One-Legged Hand Wrestle.—This is the same, except that the left foot is held in the left hand; and touching the floor with any part of the body except the right foot, or letting go of the left leg, loses.

Individual Tug-of-War.—The two players stand each on his own side of a line. At a signal, they reach over and start trying to push the other player over the line. The winner is the one first to pull his opponent completely over the line.

Elbow Wrestle.—The two contestants sit on opposite sides of a table, each with his right elbow resting on the table, and with fingers interlocked with those of his opponent. The winner is the one first to force his opponent's hand back until it touches the table.

MINOR BOXING

Hat-Boxing.—Each player wears a farmer's straw hat. The boxing is with the open hand. The player wins who first knocks off his opponent's hat. It is not permitted to use a hand to fix one's hat on more firmly. This may also be played with paper bags for hats; or using a rolled newspaper to swat the hat off; or as a free-for-all, with up to ten players competing.

Balloon-Bursting.—Each player has a balloon tied to his ankle. Any tactics except unnecessary roughness are allowed. The winner is the one who, while protecting his own balloon, first bursts that of his opponent. The balloons may be tied to the wrists, or to the waists. Any of these may be played as a free-for-all or battle royal, the winner being the one retaining his balloon unburst to the end.

Cats on the Fence.—The two opponents stand on a piece of 2 by 4 lumber, 6 to 8 feet long, which rests on two chairs. The winner is the one first to knock off his opponent, his weapon being his right hand, which is used only to slap the rival's right arm from the hand to the shoulder.

Sparrow Fight.—Each contestant grasps both of his ankles with his two hands. The winner is the one first to upset the opponent, or to shoulder him out of a 6-foot circle.

Duck Fight.—This is the same, except that each contestant squats, with a 3-foot stick placed behind the knees, his hands reaching under the stick and clasped in front of his legs.

Heave Ho Boxing.—The two players are blindfolded, and connected with a 10-foot rope interval, the rope being tied around the waist of each. They are equipped with pillows or swatters, and are allowed to pull the opponent close enough to strike. The winner is adjudged for aggressiveness and defense.

Swatter Boxing.—Each player has a rolled newspaper, instead of boxing gloves. Three 1-minute rounds constitute a bout. It is judged as Heave Ho Boxing.

Are You There, Mike?—Each player is blindfolded, and equipped with a rolled newspaper as a swatter. Before each blow, he asks, "Are you there, Mike?" and the opponent must answer, "Yes." The questions and answers, and the blows, are given alternately. After an interval, the Leader may quietly unblindfold one player, and let the game continue.

Barrel Boxing.—The same as boxing, with each player standing in a barrel. As a variation, have them stand in burlap bags, tied around the waists.

Soot Boxing.—Blacken the boxing gloves with soot or lampblack. The winner is the one whose face is less black after 3 minutes.

Boxing Knights.—Each boxer is mounted on another player. The winner is the one first to unhorse his opponent, or to upset the opposing pair. The horses may only support the boxers.

KING OF THE MOUNTAIN

The top of a short steep grade, or a small square marked on a hillside, is marked off for the mountain; or a gymnasium mat may be used. A player is selected as King, and stands on the mountain. The other players mount the mountain, and try to throw the King off. If he is thrown off, the other players fight it out for possession of the mountain, unnecessary roughness being forbidden. The title of King of the Mountain goes to the one remaining last. When any part of a player's body goes off of the mountain, he is considered off.

IX. MISCELLANEOUS GAMES AND CONTESTS

HARES AND HOUNDS

Select one or two players to be the Hares. Furnish each with a bagful of pieces of paper about 2 inches square. The boundaries are indicated to all the players. The Hare is given a 5 or 10 minute start. Every 100 feet he must leave a trail—a piece of paper plainly displayed, on the ground, or not more than 5 feet above it, so secured that it will not blow away. The Hare's object is to leave a plain trail and yet elude the Hounds, and return to the spot designated as Home.

After the Hare has had his start, the Hounds go out, hunting singly or in groups. No Hound disturbs a trail he has found. He may follow it alone, or call others to join him. When the Hare is sighted, the Hounds usually try to surround him to prevent his getting Home. The Hare is caught when he is touched by any one of the Hounds. The game is over when the Hare is touched, or has reached Home safely. The first to touch him may be the Hare for the next game.

SCAVENGER HUNT

Each pair of players draws from a container a slip of paper on which is written something to be obtained. The articles may be obtained by any means except purchase or barter, and must be obtained within a stated time. The pair returning first with their article wins. It is up to each Leader to devise an ingenious list of articles to be obtained. Here is a suggested list:

1. An uncancelled Canadian stamp.
2. A live puppy, kitten, lamb, etc.
3. A year-old copy of a specified magazine.

4. A button from a policeman's coat.
5. A last year's local newspaper.
6. A hair from a collie's tail.
7. An Indian head penny.
8. A tail-feather from a goose.
9. The autograph of a local celebrity.
10. A piece of wedding cake from an actual wedding.

The list of required objects must be fitted to suit each community. They must be obtainable, but not easily so, in the locality in which the hunt takes place.

RAG BAG

This is a simpler version of the above game. Played as above, except that each guest must obtain five or more objects, easier to secure. They might include:

1. A wilted rose from a discarded bouquet.
2. A man's straw hat (In the winter).
3. A last week's *Saturday Evening Post.*
4. A flower from a florist shop.
5. A last month's commuter's ticket.

ANTI-NUDIST

This is played the same as above, except that each pair of guests receives an identical list of five men's garments and five women's garments, to be obtained in some house other than the one in which the party is being given. A guest may not obtain the garments from his own home; they may be borrowed. When the garments are secured, the player puts them on. The first couple to return, attired in the required garments, wins.

FOLLOW THE LEADER

A Leader is selected. He starts off, the other players following him and doing whatever he does: leaping into the air at a certain space on the lawn; touching a tree or post; missing or circling the next; running up and down stairs; hopping; and so on. The stunts are made gradually more difficult, a player falling out of line as he fails to do anything that the Leader does. When there is only one player left, this player becomes Leader, and the game commences afresh.

When played indoors, with grown-ups, the stunts are less strenuous and involve more clowning, such as hopping across the floor with a book balanced on the head, whistling one line of the *Star Spangled Banner* backward, and so on.

PULLING and PUSHING CONTESTS

Chinning.—Players start with the hands on the bar, palms forward and thumbs under the bar. With arms straightened at full length, and without kicks, snaps, jerks, or swings, the player must pull himself up until his chin touches the bar. After each chinning he must lower himself until his arms are straight. This is continued with a score of one for each time the chin touches the bar.

Push-Up.—Each player lies on the floor, face downward, hands open and close to the shoulders. The arms must be straightened and the weight supported on the hands and toes, with the back stiff; then the body must be lowered until only the chin touches the floor. Each similar push-up counts one. Any violation is a foul, and scores nothing.

Sit-Up.—Each contestant lies on his back, head against the floor, feet together, arms extended with palms of hands on thighs. Keeping his heels on the floor, and his knees and elbows straight, and sliding his hands down his legs, each contestant raises his trunk to a sitting position. He at once lies back to the first position again, and continues as long as possible, scoring one for each sit-up.

Chinese Pull-Up.—Two opponents face each other sitting on the floor, their soles touching. Each grasps a 3-foot broom handle with both hands, and tries, with a straight and steady pull, to pull the other off the floor, or make him break his hold.

Squat-Tug.—Two opponents squat, with knees fully bent, each holding one end of an 8-foot rope with both hands. The player wins who retains his balance and causes his opponent to fall.

Pull-Over.—Two opponents stand back to back, grasping each other's wrists with a wrist grasp. Each attempts to pull the other over a line 5 feet from the center of where they are standing.

GYMNASTIC EVENTS

Any standard gymnastic event may be used as a showdown athletic game. This may be without equipment: as in forward rolls; backward rolls; headstands; dives; cartwheels; snap-ups; headsprings; belly-rolls; round-offs (cartwheels ending with the body facing backward) and so on. It may also be any of the usual gymnastic events done on the horizontal bar, the side horse, the parallel bars, and other gymnasium apparatus. Such events may be scored as track and field athletic meets.

STILT CONTESTS

Stilts should be about 6 feet long, with the footrests 12 to 18 inches from the bottom.

Stilt Race.—The contestants race on stilts from the starting line to the finish line.

Backward Stilt Race.—The contestants race backward on stilts.

Obstacle Stilt Race.—Between the starting line and the turning line, stretch four light ropes at equal distances apart, one foot above the ground. The contestants step over the first rope, jump over the second, step over the third, jump over the fourth, and race to the turning line. They return in the same manner.

Zigzag Stilt Race.—Place eight or ten obstacles, such as milk bottles or sticks stuck upright in the ground, in front of each contestant, between the starting line and the turning line. The contestants zigzag down the course, going to the left of the first obstacle, to the right of the second, and so on. When they reach the turning line, they return in the same manner.

Circular Stilt Race.—Draw an 18-inch circle for each player. Holding his stilts within the circle, each mounts them and performs the following stunts: (1) turn completely around to the right; (2) turn completely around to the left; (3) jump ten times; (4) raise left stilt and stand on right for five seconds; (5) repeat, standing on left stilt; and (6) walk around the edge of the circle, keeping on the line. If a player falls, or steps out of the circle, one point is scored against him.

Block Stilt Race.—Draw a chalk rectangle about 6 feet wide and 20 feet long, with a central line dividing it lengthwise. Divide it crosswise with nine equally spaced lines, so that the rectangle contains twenty blocks, in two rows. Starting in the lower left-hand corner, number the first block one, then zigzag upward, using the odd numbers. Starting in the lower right-hand corner with two, number similarly with the even numbers. Thus:

19	18	15	14	11	10	7	6	3	2
20	17	16	13	12	9	8	5	4	1

The players walk through the rectangle in rotation, attempting the following stunts: (1) without touching a line, dismounting at the far end, remounting, and returning; (2) straddling the central lines; (3) stepping in every block, dismounting, remounting, and returning; (4) stepping only in the odd-numbered blocks, dismounting, remounting and returning.

Score one against a player if he touches a line; steps outside the rectangle; or falls or dismounts before completing a stunt.

ROLLER SKATING

For official contests, standard four-wheel steel roller skates are required. Rubber, wooden, or composition wheels may be permitted, at the discretion of the Leader. Since roller skating requires a smooth course, a skating rink, gymnasium, or paved street is essential.

Straight Roller Skating Race.—Run as any ordinary race over a distance of 50 to 400 yards.

Backward Roller Skating Race.—Run as any backward foot race for a distance of 100 to 200 yards.

Roller Skate Coast.—The contestants commence at a starting line, skate to a line about 50 feet beyond, and thereafter coast. The contestant's feet must be together on the ground when he hits the coasting line, and thereafter he may make no movement with any part of his body. The one coasting furthest wins

Single Skate Coast.—The contestants wear one skate each. They run about 50 yards, then coast on the single skates. No racer may touch his other foot to the ground after he begins to coast. The one coasting furthest wins.

Single Roller Skate Race.—The racers wear one skate each, and and race for 50 to 100 yards, by pushing with the free foot. The racer may not run. The one finishing first wins.

Zigzag Roller-Skating Race.—Arrange a course of 100 yards as for Zigzag Stilt Race. The race is run in the same manner.

Three-Legged Roller-Skate Race.—Run as a three-legged foot race. The racers wear skates on the outside feet only, and push with the inside ones.

Travelling on Roller-Skates.—Each racer carries an open umbrella in one hand and a suitcase in the other while he races. The distance should be about 100 yards.

Roller-Skating Obstacle Race.—Place the following articles each 25 yards apart, the first 25 yards from the starting line, the last 25 yards from the finish line:

> (1) a six-inch hurdle, which must be jumped; (2) a row of barrels, open at both ends, which must be crawled through; (3) a row of tables, which must be climbed over; and (4) a tennis net, which must be crawled under.

The contestant finishing first wins.

Tandem Roller-Skating Race.—The pairs of players stand side by side, holding right hands in right hands, left in left; and race so. A team is eliminated for releasing hands.

Variation: One player stands behind the other, holding the front one's waist.

Roller-Skate Potato Race.—The play and rules are the same as for the regular Potato Race, except that players wear skates.

Roller-Skating Lap Race.—This requires a skating rink or a gymnasium. Draw the starting line in the middle of one long side of the skating arena. In each corner place a marker out from each wall one-third the width of the floor. The racers must skate between the walls and the markers. The race may be from two to ten laps, and finishes at the starting line.

Roller-Skate Tug-of-War.—The play and rules are the same as for a regular Tug-of-War. The players are divided into teams of five, each player wearing one skate.

Paper-Throwing Contest.—Mark a line down the length of the course. Place five barrels on their sides, open ends facing the line, 25 feet to one side of the line, the barrels 25 feet apart along the course. The players contest in rotation, each provided with ten rolled newspapers, which may be carried in a bag.

BICYCLE EVENTS

Various racing events can take place while riding bicycles. A paved roadway is preferable, with the road closed to traffic.

Speed Races.—Distances, quarter-mile, half-mile, mile, 2 miles, 5 miles, and 10 miles. The procedure is the same as in running races.

Slow Race.—Course, 50 yards long. Each racer has his own lane, 3 feet wide. Leaving the lane, touching the ground with the foot, or touching another contestant, disqualifies a contestant. If no one finishes, the one going furthest wins.

Bicycle Plank Race.—The plank is 150 feet long, 5 inches wide, and 1 inch thick, smoothly joined. The start can be behind the beginning of the plank. When a bicycle leaves the plank, this place is marked. The contestant riding furthest wins. Ties are raced again. One contestant rides the plank at a time.

Bicycle Paper-Throwing Contest.—This is the same as the similar contest on roller-skates, except that bicycles are ridden. Score one for each paper thrown into a barrel; deduct one for each time a rider dismounts. In case of a tie, the shortest time wins. Papers may be carried in a bag.

Hill-Climbing Contests.—Short steep hills are best. A 25-foot start on level ground is allowed. The first to reach the top wins.

Bicycle Potato-Race.—Barrel hoops, one for each player, are placed on the starting-finishing line, and 10, 20, and 30 yards from it, a potato in each of the last three hoops. Players may dismount to pick up the potatoes. The race is otherwise the same as the potato race on foot. In one variation, riders have a pointed 3-foot stick, with which to spear the potatoes without dismounting. In another, instead of potatoes, 6-inch blocks of wood, with 2-foot broom handles sticking up, are placed in the three outer hoops, and players may not dismount.

Bicycle Tournament.—Each rider has a 10-foot bamboo pole, held within 3 feet of the rear end. At 25-foot intervals along a 250-foot course, 10 rings are so hung that they come off when speared. Score one point for each ring speared. The rings may be curtain rings, or others of that approximate size. Touching a foot to the ground disqualifies a contestant.

Bicycle Candle Race.—The course is 100 yards. Each rider carries a lighted candle, and the one first finishing with his candle still lit wins.

Bicycle Barrel Race.—Midway of a 150-yard course, an empty barrel lies in the course of each contestant. Each rider must ride to the barrel, dismount, dive through, and ride to the finish. The one finishing first wins.

Trick Riding.—Among stunts which may be competed for, and judged for the best riding, are: steering the bicycle with the feet; pedalling first on one side, then on the other; riding under the crossbar; holding the handlebar with the hands, and placing one foot on the crossbar; riding on one wheel only; and riding backwards, sitting on the handle-bars.

SCOOTER AND COASTER-WAGON CONTESTS

Among scooter contests, in which even adults may compete, are:

Standing Scooter Race.—50 to 220 yards; one foot propels.

Kneeling Scooter Race.—The same, except that the contestant kneels on one knee, and propels with the foot of the other leg.

Sitting Scooter Race.—The same, except that both feet are used for propulsion.

Backward Scooter Races.—The same as the Standing Scooter Races, except that the scooter is propelled backward.

Net Scooter Race.—A tennis net is placed midway of the course, and the scooter must be lifted over it both going and returning.

Pushing Scooter Race.—One of a team of two sits on the scooter and is pushed to the turning line; the other is pushed to the finishing line.

Zigzag Scooter Race.—A box is placed every 10 yards along a 100-yard course for each contestant. Alternately the boxes must be passed to the right and then to the left. The last box must be circled, and the zigzagging continued to the finish line.

Skipmobile Races.—Skipmobiles (roller-skate rollers attached to the ends of a board 3 feet long, 6 by 2 inches), with home-made handle-bars, may be run like Scooter Races.

Coaster-Wagon Races.—Coaster-wagons, or children's ordinary express wagons, may be used in racing as in Scooter Races.

Block-Wheel Wagon Races.—These wagons have solid blocks of wood for wheels, not more than 6 inches in diameter; they are raced the same as Scooters.

Chariot-Wagon Races.—These have two wheels only. Two players pull the chariot-wagon; one rides in it. The contests should be graded, depending upon the sort of wheels used. Distances up to 300 yards may constitute the course.

POGO-STICK CONTESTS

A pogo stick is an upright pole, with a spring on the bottom; and with foot rests at right angles to the pole, about a foot from the ground. The contestant holds the pole in his hands, mounts it with both feet, and leaps forward with it.

Pogo-Stick Race.—The course is 15 to 50 yards. If a contestant falls, he must remount before proceeding.

Backward Pogo-Stick Race.—This is similar to any backward race.

Pogo-Stick Broad Jump.—This is similar to the Running Broad Jump.

Pogo-Stick Lane Race.—The course is more than 20 feet long. The lane is 12 inches wide for the first 10 feet; 8 inches wide to 20 feet; and gradually tapers down to 2 inches. The player who stays in the lane longest wins.

Block Pogo-Stick Race.—This is conducted the same as the Block Stilt Race.

X. WATER SPORTS

SWIMMING RACES

SWIMMING races take place both in open water and in swimming pools. Lanes may be indicated by rope markers, buoyed up by wooden floats. The take-off should be flat, and not more than 18 inches above water level. Races commonly used are:

100-yard breast stroke.
50- or 40-yard free style.
220- or 200-yard free style.
100-yard back stroke.
100-yard free style.
200- or 160-yard relay.
180- or 150-yard medley relay.
Fancy diving.

The scoring is usually 5 points for first, 4 for second, 3 for third, and then 2 and 1 for fourth and fifth places. For relay races, the scoring is 8, 6, 4 and 2. In meets between two teams only, 5, 3, and 1 are scored for first, second and third places in individual events; and, in relay races, 8 and 4 for the free style relay, and 6 and 3 for the medley relay.

The start is by "Get on yours marks," requiring steady balance; and then "Go" or a pistol shot, to start the race. The winner is the swimmer any part of whose body first touches the finishing line. In relays, each contestant must touch the finishing line before the next team mate starts.

NOVELTY SWIMMING RACES

Finning.—The legs held still, hands by the sides, only the wrists moving.

Sculling.—The same as Finning, except that the hands must move in and out in a figure 8 motion.

Overhead Sculling.—The swimmer on his back, feet together, arms sculling overhead.

Flutter Finning.—The same as Finning, except that the legs are are allowed a flutter kick.

Bicycle Pedaling.—The swimmer on his back, hands on hips, movement is secured by pedaling with the legs.

Crabbing.—The swimmer on his stomach, using the reverse breast stroke, which moves the body forward with the feet first. The legs may frog kick, but may not exert pressure.

Spinning Swim.—A front and back crawl, in which the swimmer swims each stroke alternately on his face and on his back. The legs flutter kick throughout.

Log Roll.—With body, arms and legs in a straight line, the swimmer rolls in the water to secure movement.

Handicap Position.—This may be raced with one arm held out of the water, using a side stroke with the other; with both arms out of the water, swimming on the back; with one leg held vertically out of the water, swimming on the back.

Frog Race.—The swimmer is on his back, hands on hip, frog kicking to secure movement.

Steamboat Race.—The swimmer is on his stomach, arms and head in coasting position, swimming with legs only, the feet performing the crawl kick.

Ball-Between Knees.—The swimmers swim holding a water-polo or sport-ball between their knees; if they lose it, they must return and replace it before continuing.

Dog Race.—Swimmers line up, bark three times like a dog, and swim with the dog paddle stroke to the finish.

Umbrella Race.—Each swimmer races carrying an open umbrella. If it touches water, he is disqualified. Flags, fans with which the players fan themselves, or newspapers folded only once and read while swimmers swim on their backs, may be used instead.

Lighted Candle Race.—The swimmers swim to a turning dock or float, light a candle, and return with it lighted.

Japanese Lantern Race.—Each swimmer carries a Japanese lantern with a lighted candle in it. The winner is the swimmer who finishes first with his candle lighted.

Table-Waiter Race.—Each swimmer carries a tin or paper plate with a stone in it; the winner must have his stone still on the plate. Or a cork may be used; if it falls off, the swimmer may stop and replace it.

Spoon-and-Egg Race.—Each swimmer has a spoon held by the handle in his mouth and containing an egg or potato. A 50-foot course is long enough.

Banana-Eating Race.—Each contestant, in chest-deep water, stands holding a banana. At the signal, the banana is peeled, and must be eaten entirely under water. The contestants may come up for air as often as they please. No chewing or swallowing is permitted when they come up for air.

Straw-Hat Race.—The contestants wear farmers' straw hats. They jump in feet first, entirely submerging themselves; emerging, they regain their hats, and swim to the finishing line.

Distances up to 100 feet, or less, are best for most of those novelty races.

Water Balloon Race.—The contestants swim 25 yards, each holding an inflated balloon.

Water Ping-Pong Race.—Each contestant races 40 to 60 feet, blowing a ping-pong ball ahead of him. He may not touch his ball, splash water on it, or raise waves to carry it, on penalty of disqualification.

Water-Egg Race.—This is the same, except that each player blows ahead of him an egg blown out, its hole sealed with tape or wax.

Water Spearing-the-Ring.—Each swimmer has a 10-foot bamboo pole, with which he attempts to spear 10 curtain rings hung at intervals 3 feet above the water's surface. He may be required to carry the rings on his pole to the end; or may merely enter them with the tip of his pole, and then withdraw the pole, and proceed.

Log-Obstacle Race.—The logs are floated at definite distances. Players swim, diving over the first, under the second, and so on, around or over the turning log, and so to the end, returning over and under the obstacles, as above. If only one log is available, place it at the turn, where the swimmers dive under and crawl over.

Strip Race.—Each contestant wears pajamas over his bathing suit, shoes, a hat, and gloves, and carries an open umbrella. He swims to the turning float, climbs on to it, strips down to his bathing suit, and swims back. The race may be simplified by omitting everything but shoes and pajamas.

Threadneedle Under Water.—Each player is equipped with a piece of coarse thread and a large darning needle. At the signal, each ducks. The winner is the one who first threads the needle entirely under water.

Head-Carry Race.—This is raced in pairs. One of each team starts in the head-carry position, on his back, with arms folded and feet crossed, while the swimmer holds his hands over the first contestant's ears, and swims with his legs only. The race is 50 to 75 feet; the players change position at the turn, and swim back in this fashion.

Cork Harvest.—The players line up on the bank. About 100 corks having been scattered suddenly in the water, they dive in to retrieve them; the winner is the one who gathers in the most corks. As a variation, 24 to 36 corks or blocks of wood are scattered about 30 feet from the bank; the winner is selected as above.

Sunken Treasure.—This is the same, except that the objects are of types which do not float, such as teaspoons, golf balls, tops of tin cans, and the like. Or shining pennies may be scattered, and similarly gathered.

Team Swimming Relays.—Any of these races can be raced, with the first member of each team competing first; then the second; and so on, as in relays on land.

Inner-Tube Race.—Each racer sits in an inflated inner tube, and paddles with his hands to the turning point and back. For small contestants, tubs may be used instead.

NOVELTY WATER GAMES

Water Follow-the-Leader.—This is similar to the game on land.

O'Grady in the Water.—This is a water variation of Simon Says Thumbs Up. When the Leader prefaces a command by saying "O'Grady says," each player must follow instructions immediately; if he gives a command without saying "O'Grady says," no player must move. For each 3 points scored against him as penalties for failing in either manner, the player pays a forfeit. The commands may deal with any stunt in the water, such as, swim, float, duck the head, touch bottom, duck with feet out, and so on.

Push-of-War.—The players, divided into teams, line up on each side of a floating plank or a pole 5 inches in diameter. At a signal, they start kicking, to force the plank or pole and the other team backward. The team forcing the opponents back 10 feet wins.

Life-Buoy Throw.—Three blocks of wood,6 inches each way, are anchored so that they float 30 feet from the throwing line, and 2½ feet from one another, in a line. These represent the head and the two hands of a drowning man. A 17-inch life-buoy with rope attached must be thrown 3 times within 1 minute. A ringer on the first throw counts 5; on the 2nd, 3; on the third, 1.

DIVING CONTESTS

Accuracy Dive.—An inflated inner tube is floated below the diving-board. Each player receives 3 tries, scoring one for each dive through the tube.

High Jump Dive.—Conducted like High Jumps on land, both Standing and Running. The rope-holders raise the rope after each round of jumps. When a diver touches it, it should be released at once.

Broad Jump Dive.—This is similar, with the rope held ahead of the divers, to register distance, as in Broad Jumps on land.

Underwater Swim.—The players dive and swim under water, the one coming up furthest from the starting point winning.

FANCY DIVES

Diving contests may be held, with such fancy diving events as:

Indian Dive.—The diver stands upright, hands to side, and falls slowly forward, so that he enters the water like a spear. The legs must be kept straight throughout.

Hand-Stand Dive.—A dive from the hand-stand position, the arms thrown overhead after the grip on the plank is released.

Head-Stand Dive.—From a head-stand, the diver does a turnover, and enters the water feet first.

Cart-Wheel Dive.—The diver enters the water after a cartwheel, his feet touching water first.

Military Dive.—The diver marches to the end of the diving board, brings both feet to attention, jumps and strikes the board firmly, then enters the water feet first, with body rigid and hand at salute.

Back-Somersault Dive.—After a back somersault, the diver enters the water feet first.

Tandem Dives.—Two divers may dive together, facing each other with hands joined overhead for a side dive; or, one facing forward and the other backward, in relation to the end of the board, for a front-and-back dive; or, back to back, hands joined overhead, for a side or front-and-back dive.

Jacknife and other fancy dives may also be used. Various individual clowning and comedy stunts may also be introduced.

TANDEM SWIMS

Pairs of swimmers may engage in tandem swimming contests. They may do the Crawl with the legs of the front swimmer locked around the waist of the back swimmer; the Back Crawl (when on their backs); the Breast Stroke; or the Side Stroke. In the Crocodile Race, the rear swimmer places his hands on the hips of the front swimmer. In a Siamese Twin Swim, the swimmers race as a team, with inside arms interlocked. In the Three-Legged Swim, they race with their inside legs lashed together.

WATER POLO

Water Polo is played in an area between 57 feet square and 90 feet square. Goals, placed one foot behind the central part of the end lines, consist of two uprights 10 feet apart, and a crossbar 3 feet above the water. Each team consists of seven players. For the start, the players place themselves in line with their respective goals. At a given signal the ball is released at the center. Balls may be carried or thrown, and goals may be made in either manner. For each goal between the uprights and beneath the crossbar, one point is scored. The game is usually two halves of 7 minutes each.

The ball may not be touched with both hands at the same time; or held under water when a player is tackled; or struck with the clenched fist; or handled, after a referee's throw, until it has touched the water. Walking or standing on the bottom are permitted only for resting; nor may the bottom or sides be used to spring from to play the ball or tackle an opponent. Only the player with the ball may be impeded or interfered with in any way. An opponent may not be held or pushed off from, or kicked, nor may water be splashed intentionally on him. Within 6 feet of the goal, a ball may not be thrown or dribbled directly at the goalkeeper or a teammate. The goalkeeper may not go more than 12 feet from his goal. For any violation of any rule, a foul is called, and a free throw given to a player of the opposite side from the place where the foul occurred.

WATERBALL

Waterball is simplified Water Polo. The entire pool is required, and a water-polo ball used. There are seven men to each team, at the start lined up behind their respective goals. The ball may be advanced by throwing, batting, kicking, carrying, or otherwise. The players may touch the ball only when they are in the water. The only foul is unnecessary roughness, which disqualifies a player. A score is made when the ball is placed in the trough at either end of the pool, while the referee counts up to ten. The game is two 10-minute halves, with a 2-minute intermission. After each goal, teams change sides.

WATER-PUSHBALL

A 30-inch cage ball is placed midway between the two teams, lined up at goals 90 to 150 feet apart. Ducking and roughness are prohibited. The team wins which first forces its ball across the opponent's goal line.

CANOE TILTING

Each player has a pole 6 to 7 feet long, its end covered with a rubber suction cap, or padded as in land tilting, and covered with oilcloth. Each canoe has a paddler and a tilter. The tilter may stand on the front seat; on the gunwales at the front seat; or on a 2-foot platform placed on the gunwales over the bow seat. The object is to dislodge the opposing tilter, by pushing or punching him with the tilting spear. A paddler may not touch the other canoe or its occupants. In approaching a canoe, the paddler must keep the opposing canoe on his port side (or left).

Fouls include intentional blows above the neck or below the knees; against the opposing canoe; seizing the opponent's pole; touching the tilter's own canoe with his hands; any violation of the rules concerning the paddler, including driving his canoe against the other with intent to dislodge the tilter. When a tilter's foot slips to the floor, or he falls into the canoe or the water, or drops his spear, or he or his paddler commits any foul except touching the canoe with his hands, and this fouls is committed 3 times, the opponent wins. A match is the best 2 out of 3 falls.

RAFT BATTLE-ROYAL

A number of players stand on a raft or a squared end of the dock, and seek to throw each other off. The survivor wins. Players, in one variation, are allowed to climb back; all on the raft or dock at the end of 3 minutes win.

OTHER WATER EVENTS

Tag Games.—Any simple tag games may be played in the water. These may include Water Poison (the same as Poison Ring or Spot on land), Water Black and White, Water Crows and Cranes, Water Dodge-ball, Water Numbers Change, Water Spud, and so on.

Water Baseball.—Base-lines should be 27 feet long, with a soft-ball or cork water-ball batted with a bat. Or a 6-inch rubber ball may be used, which is batted by the hand. The rules of Baseball apply. Or a water-polo ball may be used, in which case a base swimmer may be put out by being hit by the ball while off base. The game is 5 innings. Sometimes 2 strikes put a batter out.

Water Volleyball.—The is similar to Volleyball on land; it is best played in water chest deep.

Water Basketball.—This is the same as Basketball on land, except that a player may swim with the ball. The goals, which may be made of bushel baskets, are 4 feet above the surface of the water.

BOAT RACES

Canoe Races.—Distances, 110, 220, 440, and 880 yards. Races may be one man in a canoe, single blade; two men, single blade; four men, single blade; one man, double blade; two men, double blade; four men, double blade.

Medley Canoe Race.—A 50-yard dash on land, a 50-yard swim, and then a 50-yard canoe paddling race.

Paddle and Tow.—Each contestant paddles out to a turning point 220 yards or less out, overturns his canoe, and swims back, dragging his canoe with him.

There are many other possible variations of stunt canoe racing. These include Bobbing or Pumping, which consists of moving the canoe forward by jerks while standing on the gunwales near the rear seat, without using a paddle; Canoe Tug-of-War, with the canoes tied 5 feet from each other and paddlers paddling in opposite directions; and Torpedo Race, with canoes turned over and swimmers racing under them, each holding a thwart and swimming with the feet.

Rowboat Races.—Any variety of the above races, and other races based upon the greater safety of rowboats, may be used. The boats may rise to the dignity of the shells used in college boat-races.

Sailboat Races.—Where sailboats are available, races between them may be arranged, ranging from races for such small classes of boats as dinghies, starboats, butterflies and small catboats, to races between yachts of the largest class.

Speedboat and Outboard Motor Races.—These are conducted similarly.

LOG-ROLLING CONTESTS

The log should be 15 to 24 inches in diameter, and 12 to 15 feet long. It should be anchored by a long rope in water about waist deep. Each contestant needs a balancing pole, which may be a slender sapling 12 to 15 feet long, and 3 inches in diameter at the larger end. It is held by the small end, with the other end a foot or so below the surface of the water. Great dexterity may be acquired in rolling the log, and in slowing up or stopping it.

Log-Rolling Contest.—The contestants throw for choice of ends of the log. On a signal, they begin rolling. The winner is the one who first rolls the other player off. Crossing the center mark on the log, or touching the opponent with pole or body, loses the match for the offender.

Distance Log-Rolling.—Each contestant mounts the log alone. The winner is the one who rolls it furthest before falling off.

Squatting on the Log.—Each contestant mounts the log alone, stands erect, squats, then continues these alternately. The winner is the one squatting oftenest before falling off.

Stump-Riding.—A section of log slightly longer than it is wide is required. It must be ridden end over end, not rolled on the side. The winner is the player who steps along it end after end the oftenest.

Barrel Riding.—This is similar, except that contestants may stand on the barrel in any position, the one staying on longest winning.

XI. HORSEBACK GAMES

HORSEBACK RACING

Horseback races are too familiar to need extended description; and, in general, are too expensive for average contestants. Among the most usual are trotting, pacing, and running or galloping races; and steeplechase races, in which various objects must be leaped, including hedges, fences and water obstacles. In addition to the vehicles drawn in trotting and pacing races, amusing races may be made by using farm horses instead of race-horses, drawing farm wagons and the like; coaching races, using modern coaches; and Roman chariot races, using two-wheeled chariots.

MISCELLANEOUS HORSEBACK GAMES

Mounted Potato Race.—This is similar to the Potato Race on foot. Each potato is 60 feet from the next, and each rider holds a 3½ foot stick, with a spike or nail at its lower end, with which to spear the potatoes; these may be speared in any order. In one variation, the first must be speared first; the second, second; and so on in rotation. In another variation, no spears are used, the riders dismounting to secure the potatoes, and dropping them in the finish box. If they roll out, the rider must dismount to replace them, before continuing. In another variation, 6-inch blocks of wood may be used, with projecting 3-foot sticks for grasping.

Tournament Spearing.—Each rider has a 10-foot bamboo pole, with which, as he rides around the course, he spears rings or doughnuts placed at regular distances. The rider spearing the most objects wins; he is not permitted to hesitate before a ring.

Horseback Zigzag Race.—Each rider zigzags around 5 or more poles placed 60 feet apart, and returns, also zigzagging them. The shortest time wins.

Other Horseback Games.—Among other games that may be played on horseback are: Obstacle races; anti-nudist race, in which at various stops identical garments must be put on by the dismounted riders, before proceeding; treasure hunts; paper-chase; polo drives for distance and accuracy; broom polo, using a soccer ball; mounted hat-boxing; mounted push-ball, the fore-feet of the horses doing the pushing; mounted Basketball, permitting carrying the ball; mounted tag; and many other tag games.

XII. WINTER ACTIVITIES

ICE SKATING

Straight Races.—Under the general regulations of track racing events, races of from 110 yards to 1 mile may be held. The track may be circular, with the turns marked by blocks of wood having flags affixed to them.

Backward Skating Races.—This is the same, except that the skaters race backward; distances should be from 110 to 440 yards.

One-Skate Race.—One foot only wears a skate. The players race 100 yards, using either foot as they desire.

Tandem Races.—Players compete in pairs. The inside legs may be tied together; or the pairs may stand side by side, with hands clasped across the body.

Candle-Lighting Skating.—The course is 100 yards. Each contestant has a candle and a box of matches. At a given signal, each lights his candle and skates to the finishing line. If the candle goes out, the skater must stop and relight it at once. This may be done in tandem, the girl carrying the candle, the boy lighting it.

Miscellaneous.—Potato Races and many other foot races may be done on skates. Obstacle races, including objects to be crawled under or over, hurdles, and so on, are always fascinating.

Ice-Hockey Contests.—Similar to Hockey contests on foot, Ice-Hockey contests for acucracy driving, distance driving, hitting the can, and so on, may be held.

SLEDDING CONTESTS

For Distance.—Each contestant takes a running start carrying his sled, lands on his stomach on it behind the starting line, and coasts as far as possible. The winner is the one who coasts the furthest.

Push and Coast.—With one boy seated on the sled, and one behind to push, they start as far as desired behind the starting line. At this line, the pushing boy must leap aboard and stand on the sled. If he falls off, the pair is disqualified. The winning sled is that which coasts the furthest.

Sled Swimming.—The course is 90 feet over level ice or ground. To start, each contestant lies on his stomach on the sled at the starting line. At a given signal, each must push with hands and feet. The player finishing first wins.

Sled-Pulling.—One player of each couple pulls to the turning point 150 feet away, while the other lies on the sled; on the return, they exchange places. The couple finishing first wins. As a variation, both players of each couple wear skates.

Sled Centipede Race.—Each team is of eight, one rider and seven pullers. Six of these hold on to the belts of the players in front of them. The sled rope is looped around the waist of the last man. The course is 100 yards, and back. The first team finishing with all players in position wins. As a variation, have the seven runners hold on to a 30-foot rope attached to the sled to pull it, and race 220 yards.

Miscellaneous.—A housebroom, with one player seated on it and one pulling it, or a chair, with one player seated and one pushing, may be used instead of a sled.

SNOWSHOE AND SKI RACES

Snowshoe Dash.—This is the same as sprints on foot, 60 and 100 yards being the distances.

Cross-Country Snowshoe Race.—The course should be 1 to 3 miles long, over rolling country. The course is marked, and the race scored, as in Cross-Country Races.

Ski Race for Speed.—This is the same as a race on foot, over a 50-yard straight course. As a variation, race 50 yards, turn, and return.

Uphill Ski Race.—An uphill course, of varying steepness, a quarter of a mile long, should be used. The method may either be step climbing, with skis at right angles to the slope; or the herringbone, with the skis angled out to prevent slipping.

Cross-Country Ski Race.—The course should be from one-half mile to three miles, laid out and raced as in the Cross-Country Snowshoe Race.

Skijorning Race.—One player is mounted on skis, and is drawn by two players on foot. Distance, 100 to 440 yards. This is also raced with the Skijorner being pulled by a horse.

SNOW CONTESTS

Snowball-Throw for Accuracy.—The throwing distance is 60 feet, against a 3-foot target. Each player has 10 throws, scoring one for each hit.

Snowball-Throwing for Distance.—Each player has 3 throws, the longest throw of each being his score. The longest throw wins.

Snow Tug-of-War.—A rope is run through a hole in a 4-foot snow wall. Each team endeavors to pull the other team through the wall, or to make them let go of the rope.

Snowball Tenpins.—Set up 10 sticks of wood 2 feet long, the way bowling pins are set up. The throwing distance is 30 feet. Each player throws 3 snowballs, scoring one for each pin knocked over. Ten frames or turns constitute a game. The highest score wins.

Hit the Pipe.—A snow man is erected, with a pipe in his mouth. Each team, equipped with a supply of snowballs, stands on a throwing line 20 feet each side of the snow man. At a signal, both teams throw. The team first knocking out the pipe wins.

Snowball Twenty-One.—Let the snowman's arms hold a barrel hoop parallel to the ground. From a tossing line 20 feet away, alternately players from each team try to toss through the hoop, scoring one point for each success. The first team to score 11 or 21 points wins.

Snowball-Rolling.—Each player starts with a snowball one foot in diameter. At a signal, all roll for 5 minutes. The snowballs are then measured, the largest winning.

Snow-Modelling.—Competitions may be held in modelling snowmen, snow animals, etc., and judged for construction and life-likeness.

CURLING

A section of ice 30 feet by 126 feet should be cleared for the rink. Two holes, the tees, 114 feet apart, are cut into but not through the ice. Two circles, 8 feet and 14 feet in diameter, are drawn around each; a sweeping score line is drawn across the middle of each tee; a hog score line is 21 feet in front of each; a middle line is drawn midway between the tees; and an 18-inch line, called the foot score, is marked 12 feet behind each tee.

Each player needs two "stones," spherical balls of granite weighing from 33 to 40 or more pounds. Each has a handle on top, and is finely polished beneath. Each player has a besom or broom, with which to sweep the ice. Each team comprises four players, including a captain or "Skip."

Standing behind a tee, the first player slides his stone toward the other tee. Alternately the players of the two teams throw, until each has thrown both his stones. The stones of the team that are found to be nearest to the tee score as shots. The game is 21 shots. The ice may be swept to aid the moving stones. Neither the captain nor the thrower may sweep. As soon as a stone passes the middle line, the Skip may order the ice swept ahead of it to clear its passage. Once a stone has passed the sweeping line, the sweepers may sweep ice in front of it, to stop its passage. The Skip alone may order sweeping, and without his orders no sweeping may be done.

MISCELLANEOUS WINTER GAMES

Ice Shuffleboard.—Five concentric circles are marked on the ice, with diameters 16, 24, 36, 48 and 60 inches. The central circle is marked 5; the others, outwardly, 4, 3, 2 and 1; or the "3" circle may be marked "3 Off." Each team of two players has regular shuffleboard cues and 6 disks. Scoring is as in regular Shuffleboard.

Ice-Shinny.—This is the same as Shinny, except that it is played on ice skates.

Ice-Hockey Variations.—Keep Ball and Ten passes may be played on skates, as in regular Hockey variations.

Crack the Whip.—The players on skates join hands, forming a line. At the head is the Snapper; at the tail, the Cracker. The line skates forward rapidly. Suddenly the Snapper skates back, endeavoring to snap the Cracker off. If he is snapped off, he becomes the Snapper, and the player next to the end the Cracker. If not, the whip is cracked again, until he is snapped off.

This is often played as an elimination contest, those snapped off being eliminated. The player, furthest from the Snapper, who stays on, becomes Snapper for the next game.

Roller-Skates Crack the Whip.—This game is popular on roller-skates.

Running Crack the Whip.—This is equally possible, running on the lawn.

Ice Baseball.—This is Playgroundball or Softball, played on skates.

Ice Basketball.—Two barrels are the goals. The players are on skates. Regular Basketball rules apply otherwise.

Tag on Skates.—Many Tag games are popular on skates, including Pom-Pom-Pull-Away and its variations, Black and White, Crows and Cranes, etc.

Tilting on Skis.—This is similar to Tilting, as already described.

Snowball Duck-on-the-Rock.—This is the same as Duck-on-the-Rock, except that snowballs are used instead of stones.

When there is sufficient snow, various games involving storming snow forts are always popular.

Ice Yachting.—Similar to yacht races on water.

XIII. CHILDREN'S GAMES: OUTDOORS

A. WITH SPECIAL EQUIPMENT

MUMBLETY-PEG

MUMBLETY-PEG consists of tossing a pocket-knife so that its blade sticks in the ground, so high that the referee can place 2 fingers between the ground and the knife handle. Players may sit or kneel, and throw with the right hand, unless otherwise provided. Here are the stunts of the game, in order:

1. Front.—The knife on the palm, with the blade toward the finger tips; toss the knife upward and inward.

2. Back.—The knife on the back of the hand; toss as above.

3. Punch.—Form the hand into a fist, the knife handle across the nails with the blade toward the thumb; twist the hand quickly toward the left.

4. Snaps.—Hold the blade between the thumb and forefinger of the left hand, with the handle pointing to the right; strike the handle sharply downward with the right hand.

5. Seven Pennies.—With the blade between the thumb and first finger of the right hand, and with the handle away from the contestant, snap the knife away from the player; this must be done 7 times in succession.

6. Around the Horn.—Holding the knife as in Seven Pennies, swing it, handle toward the ground, around the head from left to right; then snap away as in Seven Pennies.

7. Shave the Peg.—With the blade between the first and second fingers, and holding with the thumb, and with the handle away from the body and the point of the blade toward the tosser, snap the knife away from the tosser.

8. Cut Left.—Hold as in Seven Pennies; snap downward across the left arm, striking the left wrist with the right.

9. Cut Right.—The reverse of Cut Left.

10. Headings.—This is Seven Pennies, with the handle of the knife touched against the forehead before snapping.

11. Chinnings.—This is the same, except that the chin is touched.

12. Snaps.—This is Snaps (No. 4 above), done 3 times in succession.

13. Drop In and Pull Out.—Holding the handle between the thumb and forefinger, drop the knife through a hole made by joining the tips of the thumb and forefinger of the left hand. After the blade sticks in, pull the knife back through the hole by the blade, with the handle touching the ground, and the thumb and forefinger holding the blade. The snap is as in Seven Pennies.

14. Shave the Barber.—Hold the left hand with palm in and little finger nearest the ground. Place the knife flat against the palm of this hand, with the cutting edge toward the tosser, and the handle toward the ground. With the fingers of the right hand pull the blade toward the tosser, giving a downward snap.

15. Lady Dives.—Holding the right hand vertical, with its back toward the players, place the point against the heel of the hand, and the handle against the fingertips; push forward and upward, giving a looping effect to the knife.

16. Pinwheel.—With the handle at right angles to the right hand, the arm at right angles to the body, and holding the point loosely between the thumb and forefinger, flip the knife toward the left with a downward push of the thumb.

17. Kick 'em Out.—With the handle flat on the palm of the left hand, the blade protruding over the little finger side, strike the blade downward with the right hand.

18. Cop's Club.—Holding the knife as for Seven Pennies, flip it toward the tosser. At once strike upward with the same hand, spinning the knife in the opposite direction.

19. Tony Chestnut.—Starting at the toe, place the point of the blade on the end of the shoe, and snap away from the tosser; repeat this at the knee, then at the chest, then from the front of the head. When snapping from the chest, the toe may be elevated, and the point placed against the thumb.

20. Fingers.—This is the same as Seven Pennies, except that the blade is held between the thumb and each finger consecuitively; and two snaps are made with the forefinger and thumb, and one each with the thumb and the second, third and little fingers.

21. Johnny Jump the Fence.—Stick the knife into the ground at an angle; about a foot away, place the left hand with the palm toward the knife, and the little finger touching the ground; strike the knife up and forward with the right hand, causing it go over the fence, the left hand, before sticking into the ground.

22. O-U-T Period.—Place the point on the left wrist. With the right thumb and forefinger on top of the knife, snap it to the ground, saying "O." Repeat at the elbow, saying "U"; repeat at the shoulder, saying "T." Make a fist as in Punch, place the knife

along the nails, its blade toward the little finger; twist the wrist inward quickly, and say "Period." To complete the game, these must be performed consecutively.

This is called the Long Game. As often played, the game is far simpler. For girls, the Short Game is preferred, its order of stunts being: 1; 2; 3.

Rabbit's Ears.—With the index and little fingers extended, the two other fingers and thumb closed, and the knife resting on the extended fingers, its blade toward the side of the thumb, twist the wrist inwardly.

4; 5 (done 5 times, not 7).

Slice the Ham.—With the left palm toward the tosser, the point against the thick of the hand near the little finger side, and the handle toward the thumb side, the knife is pulled toward the tosser with the right forefinger and thumb end of the handle.

15; 7; 9; 8; and 22.

JACKSTONES, JACKS

Jackstones or Jacks is an ancient showdown game played with small stones. It was originally called in English *chackstones* or *checkstones,* from the English *chuck,* for pebble. There are those whose insist that *Checkers* received its name from the same stem, rather than from the *check* in Chess. Modern metal jacks, ¾ of an inch in diameter, have replaced the ancient stones. The equipment is 6 jacks and a semi-hard rubber ball about the size of a golfball. The game is played on any smooth level surface. The order of playing is determined by lagging, that is, by tossing a jack to a lag line 10 feet away. In sequence, the jacks nearest the lag line on either side have precedence in playing. The winner is the player who goes through these stunts with the fewest misses:

1. Baby Game, 1's through 6's. The jacks are first scattered. The ball is tossed up, and while it bounces once, the jack or jacks are picked up, and the ball caught before a second bounce. All this is done by the right hand. After the ball is caught, the jacks are transferred to the left hand. First all of the jacks are picked

up one at a time. Then by 2's; then similarly 3's; then 4 and 2, or 2 and 4; then 5 and 1, or 1 and 5; then all 6 at one pick-up.

2. Downs and Ups.—With all the jacks and the ball held in the right hand, the ball is tossed, all the jacks are laid down, and the ball is caught before its second bounce. On the second toss, all the jacks are picked up, and then the ball is caught as before.

3. Eggs in Basket.—This is the Baby Game, 1's through 6's, but with the jack or jacks transferred to the left hand before the ball has bounced once each time.

4. Crack the Eggs.—This is the same as the Baby Game, 1's through 6's, right hand only; except that the jack is cracked once against the playing surface after being picked up, and before the ball has been caught after its first bounce.

5. Upcast.—This is the same as the Baby Game, except that the ball is bounced between each pick-up to give time for the transfer to the left hand. The jacks, 1's through 6's, are only picked up by the right hand.

6. Downcast.—This is the same as Upcast, except that the ball is bounced downward, and not upward.

7. *Pigs in the Pen.*—The left hand, finger tips and wrists touching the playing surface, constitutes the pen. The thumb and forefinger may be raised while putting a pig or pigs on the pen; but any jack left outside the thumb constitutes a miss. Using the right hand only, play from 1's through 6's, putting the pig or pigs in the pen.

8. Pigs over the Fence.—The left hand, at right angles to the playing area, little finger on the ground, constitutes the fence. Using the right hand only, transfer 1's through 6's over the fence.

9. Sweeps.—During the bounce of the ball, each jack or group of jacks is swept toward the player's body and then picked up, before the ball is caught before its second bounce. Using the right hand only, play 1's through 6's.

10. Scrubs.—During the ball's bounce, using the right hand only, scrub the jack or jacks backward or forward across the playing surface, keeping the jack in the hand while catching the ball before its second bounce. Transfer to the left hand, and proceed, 1's through 6's.

11. Double Bounce.—This is the same as the Baby Game, but

the ball must bounce twice before it is caught. Play 1's through 6's.

12. Bounce, No Bounce.—This is the same as the Baby Game; except that, in transferring the jack or group of jacks to the left hand, the ball is thrown up, the transfer is made, and the ball is caught without bouncing. Play 1's through 6's.

Any violation of these directions constitutes a foul, and other fouls comprise: allowing jacks or ball to touch the clothing or body; touching another jack or jacks while picking up one or more; double grab; changing position after the jacks have been scattered; and failure to begin a turn with the proper stunt.

HOP-SCOTCH

Hop-Scotch, meaning to leap a line or scratch, is an ancient children's game, played widely with local variations. The court is laid out on a smooth surface, according to a design somewhat like the following two patterns. Convenient dimensions are 5 feet for the baseline, with from 10 to 15 feet between baseline and the beginning of the top semicircle. The puck should not exceed 3½ inches in length, width or other dimensions.

The play consists of tossing the puck into the numbered compartments first into 1, then into 2, and successively up to 10, and hopping or leaping until the compartment containing the puck is hopped into; then, while hopping, kicking the puck beyond the baseline, and returning to it by hopping or leaping, as below. In Diagram II, compartment 9 comes after 7; 10 comes next; and 8 comes last of all.

In progressing to a higher compartment, compartments 5 and 6 in Diagram I, and 1 and 2, 5 and 4, and 9 and 10 in Diagram II, must be leaped into, the left foot in the left compartment going up and returning, and the right foot in the right compartment. Thus going up, in Diagram I, to reach compartment 7, the left foot would go in compartment 5, the right foot in compartment 6; while returning, these would be reversed. Any number of hops may be taken inside the compartment containing the puck, before the kick is delivered by the hopping foot, and the return journey commenced.

The puck must be tossed each time while the player is on one foot, in the hopping position. The puck must land entirely inside its compartment, and may not touch a boundary line. The puck,

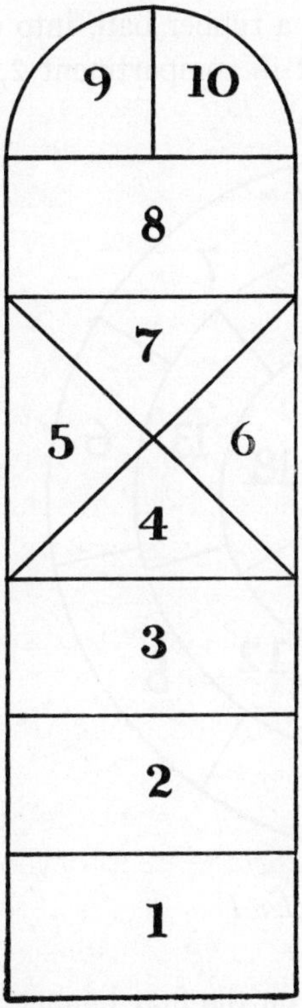

Hop-Scotch: I

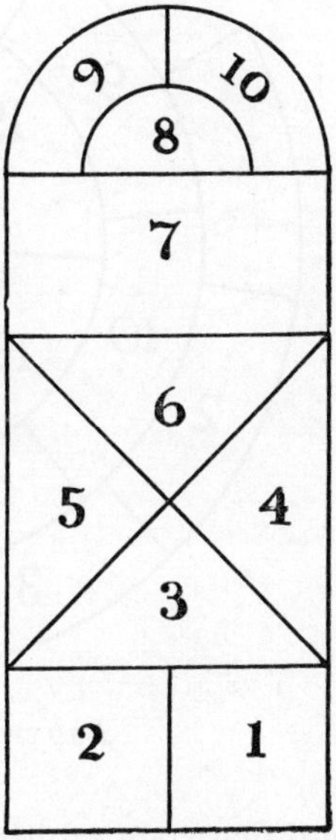

Hop-Scotch: II

on being kicked out, must entirely cross the baseline. The foot must never touch a boundary line in hopping or leaping. Any violation of the proper order of the game constitutes a foul, error or miss. This is a showdown game, in which all players may win.

Hop-Scotch Golf.—A Clock Golf Course may be used, or 9 tin cans may be sunk as holes in a circle 25 or more feet in diameter.

In rotation each player kicks a wooden puck from the center into Hole 1, then Hole 2, and so on, until all the holes have been made. All kicking must be done while players hop on one foot. Low score for the course wins.

Labyrinth Hop-Scotch.—Using a circular labyrinth design as in the diagram, each player hops, bouncing a rubber ball, into compartment 1; catches the ball, bounces it in compartment 2, and

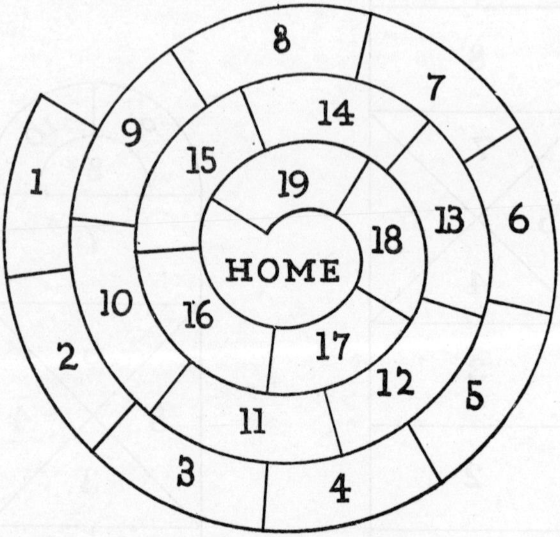

Labyrinth Hop-Scotch: I

hops into that compartment, catching it on the first bounce; and continues until the home is reached, after which the labyrinth is unwound, in the same manner. When a player misses, he must start again. The players completing the labyrinth in any one turn win.

O'LEARY

During the stunts in O'Leary, this rhyme is sung, to the tune of *One Little, Two Little, Three Little Indians:*

One, two, three, O'Leary;
Four, five, six, O'Leary;
Seven, eight, nine, O'Leary;
Ten, O'Leary, Postman.

Any small rubber ball is bounced once on each number, 1 through 9, while at the word "O'Leary" the required stunt is performed; at "Ten, O'Leary, Postman," the ball being given a high bounce, and caught on the last word. The stunt movements on the word "O'Leary" are as follows:

1. Swing the right leg outward over the ball.
2. Repeat with the left leg.
3. Swing the right leg inward over the ball.
4. Repeat with the left leg.
5. Grasp the edge of skirt or trousers, and make the ball pass upward between the opening thus made.
6. Repeat, letting the ball drop through the opening.
7. Grasp the right toe with the left hand, and make the pass pass upward through the opening thus made.
8. Repeat, letting the ball drop through the opening.
9. Grasp the right wrist with the left hand, forming an opening with the arms, and make the ball pass upward through it.
10. Repeat, letting the ball drop through the opening.
11. Touch thumbs and forefingers together, and make the ball pass upward through this opening.
12. Repeat, letting the ball drop downward through the opening.
13. After each word of the first three lines of the chorus, bounce the ball alternately to right and left of the right foot, moving it from side to side.
14. The same, except that the foot is not moved.
15. The same, passing the right leg outward over the ball at every bounce.
16. The same, using the left leg.
17. The same, passing the right leg inward.
18. The same, using the left leg.
19. To the chorus, whose first three lines are "Jack, Jack, pump

the water," and whose fourth line is "So early in the morning," bounce the ball as in No. 1, making a complete turn to the right on the last word.

20. The same, turning to the left.

21. The same as No. 1, except that the right leg is swung twice outward over the ball.

22. The same, using the left leg.

23. The same as No. 5, except that the ball is passed twice through the opening, upward.

24. The same as No. 1, except that the right leg is swung outward over the ball on each bounce.

25. The same, except that the right leg is swung inward.

26. The same as No. 5, except that the ball goes through the opening on every bounce.

27. On the word "O'Leary," make a scissors jump over the ball.

28. On the word "O'Leary," swing the right leg inward and the left leg outward over the ball.

29. The same, passing both legs over the ball at each bounce.

MARBLES

The variations in games of marbles are countless. The most familiar is:

Ringers.—Inside the central section of a ring 10 feet in diameter, 13 marbles are placed, one in the center, the others forming a cross, each marble 3 inches from the others. For first shot and order of precedence, the players shoot from a pitch line tangent to the ring on one side, to a lag line parallel to this tangent to the ring on the other side. The first player must knuckle down just outside the ring line, so that one knuckle touches the ground—a position that must be maintained until the player's shooter has left his hand. His object is to knock out one or more marbles from the ring. A marble whose center is on the line or outside is knocked out, and belongs to the player knocking it out. If the shooter remains inside the ring, after one or more marbles are knocked out, the player shoots from there; if his shooter goes outside the ring, he may take "roundsters," and shoot from any point around the ring. If he fails to knock a marble out on any shot, the player picks up his shooter and holds it until his next turn. The players shoot in the order determined by lagging. If a marble slips and the player calls "slips," the referee may order the shot shot over, if he is convinced it was a slip, and if the marble has not travelled more than 10 inches. The player first obtaining 7 marbles wins, provided his shooter goes out of the ring on knocking out the 7th marble. If it fails to go out, the marble or marbles knocked out on this shot are respotted, and the shot is counted as a miss. A match consists of 1, 3, or 5 games, scored as games and not by score. If there is a tie, the tieing players play off the tie. Any violation of the rules is a foul, and causes the player's turn to terminate.

MINOR MARBLES GAMES

Ringers Variations.—In a small circle, 1 to 2 feet in diameter, the marbles, contributed in equal numbers by each contestant, are bunched in the center. First shot is from a shooting line 6 feet or more away. Each player wins all the marbles he knocks out on one shot. The marbles are then rearranged, and shooting is resumed from the shooting line. Shooting is done with special larger marbles called reals, reels, shooters, agates, stoneys, etc.

Another variation has a circle 4 feet or more in diameter, and the marbles clustered in the center. Each player in rotation shoots until he can knock out no more marbles; or until his shooter goes outside of the circle, in which case the next player shoots.

In another variation, the marbles are not clustered, but are placed at regular intervals along a diameter of the large circle, at right angles to the shooting line. Shooting continues until a player knocks out no more marbles, or until his shooter rolls out of the circle. A player may hit another's shooter, thereby securing another shot at the marbles.

Knuckles Down.—Five holes are dug in the ground, about 6 inches in diameter, 6 feet apart, arranged:

1 2 3 4
5

In rotation the players shoot from 1 to 2, 2 to 3, so to 5, then 5 to 1, then returning the reverse direction to 1. The winners secure 3 free shots each at the knuckles of the loser, from a distance of 12 inches.

Stoney-Whop, Shooting for Reels.—This is a refinement o. Ringers, in which the Shooters are shot for, one or two only being placed in the ring by each player.

B. GOAL GAMES

There are many games, especially for younger players, in which the object is to get possession of a goal or base. It was games of this type, sometimes with the element of tagging added, which became the parents of most of the popular athletic games of today, such as baseball, cricket, football, basketball, hockey, polo, and so on.

Skip Away.—In this simple game, one player is selected to be the It. He runs around a circle composed of the other players, and tags one. Immediately he starts running around the circle in one direction, and the tagged player in the other. The one who fails to reach the gap first becomes the next It.

Hop Away.—This is the same, with the players hopping and not running.

Flying Dutchman, Partners Skip Away.—The players stand in couples around the circle, with clasped hands. One couple is the It. Otherwise, it is the same as Skip Away.

Circle Zigzag, Circle Weaving Race.—This is the same as Skip Away, except that the It and the tagged player weave in and out around each player in the circle.

Partners Zigzag.—This is the same, but with a couple as the It, and a couple tagged, before the weaving, which is done by couples around the other couples.

The Beater.—The It passes a knotted face towel or handkerchief in a player's hand, as he runs around the circle. He at once steps into the player's place in the circle, as the player starts swatting the player to his right, who runs around the circle, the Beater after him, swatting him as often as possible. When the beaten player returns to his place, the Beater becomes the next It.

Leaning Tower.—An It is selected, and given a cane or baseball bat. Standing in the center of the circle, he stands the stick upright. The players have previously been numbered. The It releases the cane, as he calls a number. If the player whose number is called does not catch the cane before it hits the floor, he becomes the It; otherwise, the It repeats, calling another number.

Rabbit-Hunting.—A player, selected to be the Hunter, asks, "Who would like to hunt rabbits with me?" He may name any animal he chooses. The other players, who have been seated, all answer "I!" and fall into line behind him. He marches the line around the room, until suddenly he says "Bang!" Each player then scrambles for a chair, the one left out being Hunter for the next round. This may be played indoors or out.

Pig in the Hole, Kettle Drive.—The pig is a small ball or other object. When the game begins, it is placed in a hole dug in the center of the group, twice the diameter of the pig. Each player has a stick the size of a cane. There is a 10-foot circle around the center, with one less small holes dug in it than there are players. To begin the game, all players place their canes under the pig, and at a signal give a heave. All then run and endeavor to get their canes into a small hole. The one failing becomes the Driver, and endeavors to drive the pig into the hole. The other players endeavor to prevent this, but at the risk of losing their holes; for at any time the Driver may put his cane in a vacated hole, in which case the player who has lost his hole becomes the Driver, and the game continues. A vacated hole may be taken by any player. If the Driver holes the pig, the game starts again.

Club Rush.—Place a number of Indian clubs at one end of the playing ground or gymnasium, one less than there are players. At a signal, all rush for the clubs, the one failing to get one being eliminated. One club is removed, and the game is continued until only one player is left, he becoming the winner.

Cap Rush.—This is the same, except that caps are used instead of Indian Clubs.

C. TAG GAMES

Simple Tag.—One player, selected to be the It, runs after the others. When he tags one, that player becomes the It.

I Have It.—This is the reverse of Simple Tag. The player who is the It runs away from the others, and attempts to remain the It as long as possible. When he is tagged, the tagger becomes the It.

Fox and Farmer.—One player is counted out to be the Fox; another, the Farmer. The Farmer runs to catch the Fox, who may dodge around the other players as he chooses. The Farmer must run around them exactly the same way that the Fox does, or a tag does not count. When the Fox is tagged, he becomes the Farmer for the next game, and a new Fox is counted out.

Cat and Rat.—Two players are counted out to be the Cat and the Rat. This dialogue takes place:

Cat: I am the cat.
Rat: I am the rat.
Cat: I will catch you.
Rat: Pray do.

The Cat then tries to tag the Rat. The other players assist the Rat by letting him pass under their arms, etc., and prevent the Cat from doing this. If one Cat cannot catch the Rat, count out a second Cat to aid him.

Pass and Change.—The player counted out to be the It stands in the center of a circle composed of the other players, equipped with a soft rubber ball or some soft ball. The It names two players in the circle, who must immediately exchange places. At the same time, the It throws his ball to a third player, who returns it to the It. As soon as the It catches it, he throws it at one of the players exchanging places. If he hits one before he rejoins the circle, that person becomes the It.

TOUCHING WOOD

The player selected as the It starts inside a circle of the other players on the lawn. A definite bounds is assigned, and a player who goes out of bounds immediately becomes the It. If the It tags a player inside bounds, he immediately becomes the It in turn, unless he is touching wood—the corner of the house, kitchen, or barn, a post, or even the wooden plank along a flower-bed. As a player tempts the It from one side of the circle, players from the other side leave the wood and run to new sections of the circle, even across the entire circle.

Touching Grass.—This is an excellent variation for the beach, or for a yard where the amount of grass is limited.

Touching Green.—This is similar to the above.

Touching Glass.—This is similar to the above.

Touching Water.—This variation is amusing, when there are bird-baths, fountains, lily ponds and other water containers handy.

FIREFLY

A circle is formed of couples, each boy holding his girl partner's hand. One couple, the Fireflies, runs around the outside of the circle, carrying a flashlight. Suddenly they flash it on one of the couples in the circle. They then try to run around the circle to the right, while the other couple runs to the left—both couples trying to arrive first to the only vacancy in the circle. The couple that fails gets the flashlight, and becomes the Fireflies. The game is best played on the lawn after dark, or in a large room with most of the lights turned off.

I SPY, HIDE AND SEEK

One player is counted out to be the It. He stands by the Home base, eyes closed, and counts by 1's to 20 or 30, or by 5's to 100. Then he calls out,

Hidden or not,
You shall be caught.

During this counting, the players hide. The It now goes out to look for them. If he goes beyond a player who is hidden, this player can run for Home; if he touches it first, he call out,

One, two, three,
I'm in free.

If the It sees a player before the player touches Home, he runs and tries to touch Home first. If he succeeds, he calls out, "One, two, three, Betsy," or whoever the player is; and the player then becomes the It. In one variation of the game, the search can continue until the last player has run Home free or gotten caught; the player first caught then becomes the It for the next game.

Kick the Wicket.—In this variation, a tin can or stick is leaned against the Home base, called the wicket. The players may hide nearer home. Even should a number of players be caught, if one player can run Home uncaught and give the can or stick a kick, all are free to run and hide again. The wicket should be kicked as far as possible, since the It must restore it to its position leaning against the Home base, before he goes seeking again. A tin can is preferable to a stick, for it can usually be kicked much further.

Run, Sheep, Run.—This variation of I Spy, and Hide and Seek, calls for a division of the players into two teams. Each team selects a Captain. One team stays at the goal; the other team is taken away by their Captain and hidden. He arranges with them a set of signals, such as "One," danger; "Two," come closer; "Three," caution; "Four," go on around the house; "Five," try to run to the goal. The names of colors, flowers, birds, or anything else, may be used for the signals.

After hiding his men, the Captain returns and joins the

searching team, whose Captain now starts his team after the hidden players. The Captain of the hidden team accompanies the seekers, and calls out his signals. When he thinks that there is a chance for a safe dash for home, he calls out "Run, Sheep, run!" No one can run for the goal until this is called out. The opposing Captain at once makes the same call. The player reaching goal first wins for his team. Then the hidden team become the team at the goal, while the others hide as before.

CHAIN TAG

Two lines are drawn about 50 feet apart. When the player counted out to be the It calls out "Run!," all the other players, standing on one line, must cross the danger territory to the safety line. All players caught by the It at once join hands with the It, and aid in the tagging. Only the outside pair of the chain can actually do the tagging. The game lasts until every player is caught; and then the first person tagged becomes the It for the next game. A definite out of bounds line must be established; and a player crossing this becomes at once tagged.

Squat Tag, Stoop Tag.—The other players, with hands joined, circle around the player counted out to be the It, chanting:

I am happy,
I am free,
I am down
And you can't catch me!

At "down," all release hands, and stoop or squat. As long as they are in this position, they are safe. They may at any time rise, run, hop or skip within bounds; stooping for safety when menaced. The first one caught becomes the It for the next game. In some localities, only 3 squats are allowed; thereafter, only running. Also, if the It retreats 5 steps from a squatter and comes at him again, he must run or may be tagged.

Variations.—Other variations in safety positions include, instead of squatting, lying on back with hands and feet in the air (Turtle

Tag); hands and knees, forehead to ground (Hindoo Tag); one hand holding nose, other holding a toe or under a knee (Skunk Tag); one hand on floor (Floor Tag); hanging by the arms, feet off the floor (Hang Tag); assuming a statue pose the It has previously designated (Statue Tag); holding another player's ankle, he however being subject to tag (Ankle Tag); or, played by pairs, sitting sole-to-sole with your partner on the floor (Sole-Mate Tag).

Cap Tag.—The It is counted out. One runner is given an old cap, and the It tries to tag him. When in danger of being tagged, the runner may pass the cap to any other player; in which case the It must try to tag that player instead. If the cap is dropped, the It may capture it, and the player who touched it last thereupon becomes the It. If a player holding the cap is tagged, he becomes the It.

Other objects may be used instead of a cap; in these cases the name of the game is changed to Handkerchief Tag, Ball Tag, etc.

Cross Tag.—After the It is counted out, a player is selected to be chased first. The moment a player crosses between the It and the player chased, this new player becomes the one to be chased. When a player is tagged, he becomes It, and the game starts again.

Stride Tag.—The player selected to be the It stands astride an empty tin can, a soccer ball or the like. The players come near the It, trying to kick the object out from between his legs. When it is kicked away, the It starts chasing the kicker. If at any time another player kicks the object, the It must chase him in turn. A player tagged becomes the It, and the game starts again.

Three Deep.—A player is counted out to be the It. The other players stand in two circles facing inward. A player is selected to be chased first. At any time, he may stand in front of a player in the inner circle, making the circles Three Deep here. Thereupon the rear player of the three becomes the one to be chased, and starts running; the other two step back, completing the circle as before. Either the It or the chased player may run across the circle.

In different variations, neither the It nor the chased player may cross the circle; or only the chased player may.

Two Deep.—This is the same, using only one circle.

Three Wide.—This is the same, except that the players stand in one circle with arms locked. The chased player may at any time lock arms with an outer arm of any pair, thereby making the further player of this pair the one to be chased.

Two Deep Leap-Frog.—This is the same as Two Deep, except that players in the circle stand with their hands on their ankles. The player who is chased may leapfrog over any player in the circle, whereupon the player leaped over becomes the one to be chased.

Crawling Three Deep.—In this variation of Three Deep, the players in the circles stand with their legs wide. To be safe, the player who is being chased must crawl under the legs of two players who are one behind the other in the circles, and stand inside; the back player then becomes the one chased.

Crawling Two Deep.—This is the same, with only one circle.

Partner Tag.—This is Three Wide without a circle, the pairs of players being scattered over the field. Otherwise it is the same.

Animal Cage, Basket Three Deep, Third Man.—In this variation, each couple of players faces each other, with their hands on each other's shoulders. To be safe, the player who is being chased gets inside such a cage. The player to whom he turns his back at once becomes the one to be chased.

Last Man It.—Any of the games of the Three Deep type may be played by having the released player at once become the It, the former It becoming the player to be chased.

Circle Ball.—A player is counted out to be the It. The others stand in a circle, passing a basketball or medicine ball at random from player to player. If the It can touch the ball, the last player touching it before him becomes the It, and the former It joins the circle.

In one variation, the ball must be bounced once from player to player, instead of being passed through the air.

Soccer Center-Ball.—This is the same, with a soccer ball kicked from player to player, the It attempting to touch it as it crosses the circle. If the ball is kicked over a player's head, the kicker becomes the It.

Steps.—A player is counted out to be the It, and turns his back on the other players, who are on a starting line 60 feet away. The It calls "Go!" and then counts up to 10 aloud very rapidly, and then turns. At the "Go!" the players start moving toward the It; but any one seen moving when he turns is sent back to the starting line. When a player gets close enough to touch the It, he wins.

Steps and Statues.—This is the same game, except that each player except the It must announce in advance what statue pose he will adopt, every time the It turns to see him. Any player seen moving or not in the right pose goes back to the starting line.

Shadow Tag.—Many simple games of Tag may be played by having the It step on the player's shadow, instead of touching him. This calls for sunlight or bright moonlight.

BARLEY BREAK

Divide the playing field into three equal zones in a line. The game is played in couples. One third of the couples is counted out to guard the central area, the Barley Field; the others are divided into two groups, each assigned to one of the flanking zones. The players in the Barley Field are required to keep their arms locked; the others need not do so.

Couples from the end zones enter the barley field, trampling down the grain and taunting the guardians of the field by saying, "Barley, break!" When one of these is caught, he remains an inactive prisoner in the Barley Field until his partner is captured. This couple then joins the Its, the custodians of the Barley Field, the couple who caught their last member going to the end zone from which they came. The It couples may not leave the field, nor may couples or players from one end zone seek refuge in the other.

Champion Tagging.—The players line up at one goal, 40 feet from a second one, and number off. No. 1 becomes the It first, and stands midway between the goals. At a signal, all the players run from one goal to the other. The It counts aloud as he tags players, "One," "Two," "Three," etc. After each player in rotation has been the It once, the scores are compared, and the one who tagged the most players is the champion.

MAY I?

One player is counted out to be the It. A turning line is 25 or more feet away. The other players line up in race formation before him. Each is addressed by name or number, and is assigned for his first and each subsequent move any number of steps from one to five, these steps being graded into Baby Steps, Steps, and Giant Steps. Thus, he may say, "Rose, you may take two baby steps and two giant steps," or "Three, you may take one step and three giant steps." Each player must respond "May I?" before moving; and the It must reply "Yes, you may," before the player may move. Any breach of this causes a player to return to the base, even if he has passed the turning line and is on the way home. The first player to cross the base line on the return, after making the complete course, is the winner, and is the It for the next game.

Cheesebox.—The line-up is as in May I? The turning line is 50 feet away. The It closes his eyes and counts, "One, two, three," and so on up to "nine, ten, cheesebox." At "cheesebox," he opens his eyes. The other players may move until he opens his eyes. Any one seen moving then must return to the base line; if, however, he has passed the turning line, he merely returns to it. The first player to cover the entire course and cross the base line on the return is the winner, and is the It for the next round. This is a popular variation of Steps.

DUCK-ON-THE-ROCK

A large rock or block of wood is the rock. Each player has a small stone. Indoors, beanbags and a stool are used instead. To decide who is the It, each player throws his stone from a throwing line 30 feet away. The one whose stone is farthest from the rock becomes the It.

The It places his stone, called the duck, on the rock, and stands beside it to protect it. In turn the other players throw their stones at the duck, from the throwing line, seeking to knock it off. If a player fails, he may stand back of the line and wait until some player does knock it off; or he may run out, pick up his stone, and try to get back to the throwing line before the It tags him. While beyond the line, he is safe while his foot is on his stone; but, once he has picked it up, he may not place it on the ground again for safety. If he returns in safety, he is allowed another throw.

When a player knocks the duck off, all whose stones have been thrown and lie beyond the throwing line may run out and pick up their stones, returning to the throwing line. No player may be tagged until the duck has been replaced on the rock. A player who is tagged becomes the It. If two stones touch each other, their owners may regain them without danger of being tagged.

In one variation, there is a 12-foot square around the rock, and players who have thrown may venture up to its boundaries without danger of being tagged. Tagging takes place only inside this square.

SPUD, CALL BALL

One player is counted out to start the game. He throws into the air a soft rubber ball or softball, calling out the name or number of another player. This player retrieves the ball, while the other players scatter. He calls "Halt!" as soon as he gets it. All players immediately stop. The player who retrieved the ball now throws it at one of the players. This player is allowed to dodge in any way, provided at least one foot is not moved. If he is hit, this scores one "spud" against him; if he is missed, it scores against the thrower. In the former case, the player who is hit retrieves the ball, calls "Halt!" and throws, and the game continues as above; in the latter case, where a throw is missed, the players gather around the one who missed, and the game starts as at the beginning. When a player has three "spuds" scored against him, he stands against a wall, back to the others, hands on his knees, and each other player has one free throw at him.

Buddy Spud.—This variation is played by teams of two. The player whose name is called may throw the ball after retrieving it, or may pass it once only to his partner, who must then throw it as above. "Spuds" count against the partnership; and three "spuds" require both players to line up for free throws.

ROLY POLY, NIGGER BABY

The players place their caps upon the ground in a line, with all caps touching. The player counted out to start as the It lets his hand, holding a soft rubber ball, hover over the caps, and then drops the ball in one. This player must retrieve the ball, and throw it to hit one of the other players, all of whom are fleeing as rapidly as possible in any direction each chooses. In case of a hit, the player hit has one point scored against him, and the thrower continues as the It; in case of a miss, the player missing has one point scored against him, and the one at whom he threw becomes the It. When 3 points are scored against a player, he lines up as in Spud, and the other players have a free throw apiece at him. Alternatively, all the free throws may be postponed until the end of the game, and take place then.

Ball in Cap.—The players stand 10 feet away from the caps, and the It tosses the ball at the caps until it lands in one. The owner of the cap runs, and the thrower tries to tag him. If the owner can touch his cap before he is tagged, he is safe, and becomes tosser for the next game. If he is tagged, the original thrower continues.

Hole Roly Poly.—Ten feet from a throwing line each player draws a hole 8 inches in diameter and 3 inches deep; or, indoors, a chalked circle 8 inches in diameter. The player who starts as It rolls a soft playgroundball until it enters a hole. As soon as he has secured the ball, the owner of the hole calls "Stop," and then throws as in Spud. Scoring and free throws are as in Spud. Indoors, the It walks along the holes and places the ball in one, somewhat as in Nigger Baby.

POISON CIRCLE

The players stand in as wide a circle as they can, with hands clasping those of their neighbors. A circle is drawn 4 feet inside the circle, and a soft rubber ball placed in its center. At a signal, all pull and push, endeavoring to force a player into the central Poison Circle. When a player is forced in, the others cry "Poison!" and run away. The player pushed inside gets the ball, and tries to hit one of the fleeing players. If more than one player are pushed into the circle, they scramble for the ball, and the one securing it throws. Scoring as in Spud. After each throw, the circle is formed again.

Poison Spot.—The poison circle is 3 or 4 feet in diameter. A piano stool or box of the same size is in its center. Any player stepping inside the circle or touching the stool is eliminated. The last player to remain in the game wins.

Poison Snake.—A clothesline is placed on the ground, curved irregularly to represent a snake. The players form a circle around the rope, and seek to pull and push each other into touching it. Any player touching it is eliminated. The last player to remain in the game wins.

JUMP THE SHOT

The players form a circle, with room for jumping between them. The player counted out to be the It stands in the center with a 15-foot rope, at whose end a weight is tied, and swings it in a circle until it reaches the players and is moving close to the ground. Each player must jump it as it passes. If the rope or weight touches a player, he is eliminated. The speed of the rope may be changed at will. The It may stand, sit or lie on the floor, for his swinging. The weight may be a bag of beans, an old shoe, or the like.

Variations include the players standing on one foot and hopping, only changing feet when the It so commands; or running or hopping toward the oncoming rope. Alternately, a bamboo pole may be used instead of a rope. In one variation, instead of eliminating players, the scoring is as in Spud, with free throws at the end for 3 points scored against any player.

FOX AND GEESE

Two lines are drawn on the lawn, 50 to 60 feet across. One player, who has been counted out as the Fox, stands in the center; the other players, the Geese, get behind one line. They try to steal across the open space to the other line, while the Fox tries to catch them. Any player at any time may run back to safety, or continue to try to cross over. Any Goose that is caught by a Fox becomes at once a Fox, and helps to tag the others. When none is left on the far side, the one first tagged becomes Fox for the next time. The call used in Fox in the Morning is often used in this game as well.

Pom-Pom-Pull-Away.—In this variation, the player who is the It stands in the center and calls out,

> Pom-Pom, pull away;
> Come away or I'll fetch you away!

Only then can the players try to run across. Otherwise, the game is the same.

Red Rover.—In this variation, the It is called Red Rover, and calls out, to start the run across the open space,

> Red Rover, Red Rover,
> O, won't you come over!

Players who have crossed successfully may stand on the line, holding hands with others behind them, to help pull players to safety. The call is sometimes given,

> Red Rover, come over,
> Or I'll pull you over!

Hill Dill.—This is played like Pom-Pom-Pull-Away, except that the call is:

Hill Dill, come over the hill,
Or else I'll catch you standing still.

Ham, Chicken, Bacon.—This is the same, except that the call is "Ham, ham, chicken, ham, bacon," or these words in some other order. At "bacon," all must leave the goal.

One Step Off and All the Way Across.—This is the same, with the call consisting of the name of the game.

Come Blackey.—This is the same, with the call consisting of the name of the game; and with one additional difference, that a player must be slapped three times on the back, or held for a count of 3, to be tagged.

Chinese Wall.—The same, except that the tagging area is limited to the Chinese Wall, a zone 10 feet across the center of the field. All players tagged must assist the It.

Black Tom.—The playing field is divided into three equal spaces, the It in the center. He must call "Black Tom" three times to start the run from one outer zone to the other. Any other call by him, or any call by another player, which causes a player to leave the end zone in which he is, at once is considered as having tagged the player. Thus "Black Tom, Black Tom, Blue Tom" automatically tags any player who crosses into the center. All who are caught assist the It in tagging. When all are tagged, the player first tagged becomes the It for the next game.

In some sections, the call is "Who's afraid of the Black Man?" or "Wheel away, wheel away, wheel away," the game being then named after the call.

Stingo.—The same as Pom-Pom-Pull-Away, except that the last player uncaught calls "Stingo" and runs away, seeking to remain the It as long as possible. The player tagging him becomes It.

Bears and Cattle.—Two goal lines are drawn at the two ends of the playing field, and a Bear's den off from the center. One player is counted out as Bear; the other players are the Cattle, half behind each goal. At a signal, they run across to the opposite goal.

Each one tagged becomes a Bear, and joins a line, the original Bear and the first player tagged remaining throughout the two ends of the line. Only these two may tag. If the line breaks, the Cattle may tag any members who cannot regain the den, and make them Cattle again. The last player tagged is the Bear for the next game.

Red Lion.—A Red Lion is counted out, and occupies the lion's den off from the center. The players taunt the lion:

> Red lion, red lion, come out of your den!
> Whoever you catch will help you then.

A player is tagged by being caught and held, while the Lion says "Red lion" three times. He is then carried back to the den to be another Red Lion. The other players may spank them with the open hand below the waist until they reach the den. The Red Lions must now come out with hands joined, and to tag must encircle a player with their arms while calling "Red lion" three times. Spanking is then allowed as before.

The Red Lion may now call "Doubles," in which his Lions come out in pairs; or "Cowcatcher," in which they come out in a chain, and a player is tagged when two in the chain pass their clasped hands over his head. If he calls "Tight," a player is tagged by being surrounded by the line of Lions. If players can break apart the hands of the Lions, they must return to the den, to avoid being spanked. The game ends when all players are captured. The last one caught becomes Red Lion for the next game.

OTHER TAG GAMES

Fox in the Morning.—The goals are 40 feet apart. One player is counted out to be the Fox; the rest, termed the Geese, are on one goal line. The Fox stands midway between the goals. This dialogue takes place:

> Fox: Fox in the morning.
> Geese: Goosey, goosey, gander!
> Fox: How many are you?
> Geese: More than you can handle.
> Fox: I'll see about that!

At this, the Geese run to the opposite goal, and the Fox tries to tag them. Any goose tagged becomes a Fox. The last one caught is Fox for the next game.

Dodgeball.—Divide the players into two teams. One forms a circle; the others scatter inside this circle. The circle men throw a volleyball, soccer ball, codeball, or sport ball in an effort to hit the players inside the circle, who may dodge in any way possible. The ball may be passed around the circle before being thrown at a player. Any player hit is eliminated. The last player remaining in the circle wins. The two teams then change places, and the game continues.

Soccer Dodgeball.—This is the same, except that the ball is kicked or butted, and may not be touched with the hands.

Chain Dodgeball.—This is the same, except that five players inside the circle form a horse by clasping the man in front. Only the rear man, the tail of the horse, may be hit. The head of the horse may use his hands to knock the ball back toward the circle. When the tail is hit, he enters the circle and the successful hitter becomes the head of the horse. With a large circle, two horses may be used.

New Orleans.—Two goal lines 60 feet apart are drawn. Two teams are selected, one placed behind each goal line. Team No. 1 agrees upon some trade it will represent, and approaches the other team with this dialogue:

One: Here we come.
Two: Where from?
One: New Orleans.
Two: What's your trade?
One: Lemonade.
Two: How's it made?

Team No. 1 acts out the movements of the trade selected. As soon as a member of Team No. 2 guesses it correctly and announces it, the members of the first team race for their goal, the other team trying to tag them. All tagged before reaching the goal join the other team. Then Team No. 2 selects a trade, and the game proceeds.

Black and White, Oyster Shell.—Two goal lines are drawn 30 to 40 feet apart. Midway of this space, a neutral space 3 feet wide is marked by two lines parallel to the goal lines. Two teams, the Whites and Blacks, line up beyond the neutral zone, each facing its goal and across the zone line from its goal. A disk, one side white, one black, is tossed up, to fall in the neutral zone. Whichever side comes up, the team of that color races for its goal, and the other team tries to tag as many of the fleeing team as possible, all players tagged joining the other team. A Leader may throw up the disk; or the captains of the teams may alternate tossing it. The team with the most players when the time limit is reached wins.

A lawn die may be used, 3 sides painted white, and 3 black; or an oyster shell, the dark side representing black, the light side, white.

Crows and Cranes.—Two goal lines are drawn 60 to 80 feet apart. One team is called the Crows; the other, the Cranes. The Leader calls "Forward March," and the two teams march forward. Then he calls "Cr-r-r-r-r-rows" or "Cr-r-r-r-r-ranes," holding the word until the teams are close together. Whichever is called must run for its goal, with the other team in pursuit. All players tagged join the other team. The largest team at the end of the time limit wins. The Leader may call some other word beginning with *Cr* to deceive the players, as "Crackers," "Crawfish," "Chromium."

Black and Blue.—This is the same, with the teams named Black and Blue. Such words as "Blank." "Blast," "Blubber," may be called, to deceive the players.

Storybook Cranes and Crows.—This is the same as Cranes and Crows, except that the Leader tells a story first, with the two teams lined up along the neutral zone, as in Black and White. He uses as many *Cr* words as he pleases in the story; as soon as he names either team, the chase to tag commences, as above.

Crows, Cranes and Crabs.—This is the same as Cranes and Crows, except that any player moving at "Crabs" switches to the other team at once.

SNATCH-BALL

Players are divided into two teams, and lined up 30 feet apart. They are then numbered off on each team, so that No. 1 of the first team is opposite the last number of the other team. A handkerchief, cap or softball is placed midway between the centers of the two teams. The Leader, standing midway between the teams and beyond the line joining two opposing end players, calls out any number. Immediately the two players run forward, and endeavor to snatch the object in the center and return to the team line, before being tagged. Tagging a player scores 1 point for the tagging team. The game is 10 points. The numbers should be called at random, and not in rotation.

PRISONER'S BASE

As usually played, the field is marked out according to this diagram:

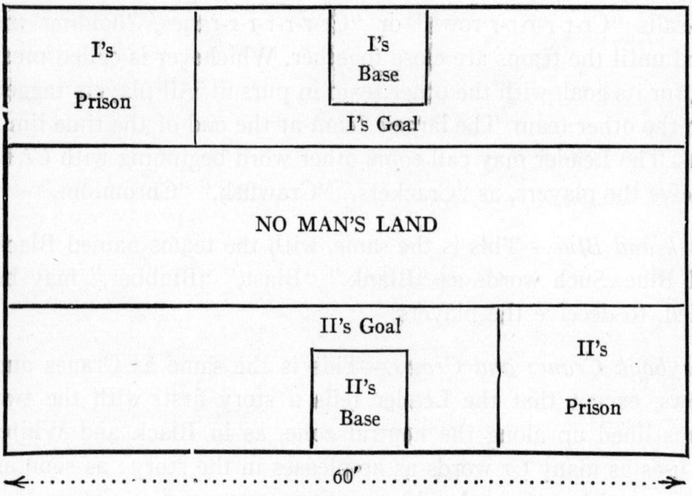

Prisoner's Base: I

Teams I and II line up behind their own goals. The play starts when a member of either team crosses into No Man's Land. At once an opponent enters in pursuit. The former player may at any time retreat to safety behind his goal line. A player may tag any opponent who left the goal territory *before* the tagging player left his. When a player is captured, his captor leads him to prison, and cannot be tagged while doing so. A captive must remain in prison until freed, by being tagged by a free member of his own team. A free member can only tag one prisoner at a time; and both are allowed to return across their goal line without being tagged. Prisoners may form a line, the first captive at the head, the others in order; this may stretch into and across No Man's Land, provided one foot of the rear captive is inside the prison. The rescuer then frees the head player in the line. The game is won when a team captures all its opponents; sends a man into the enemy's base; or has more prisoners, at the end of a fixed period of time.

Another design for the game is:

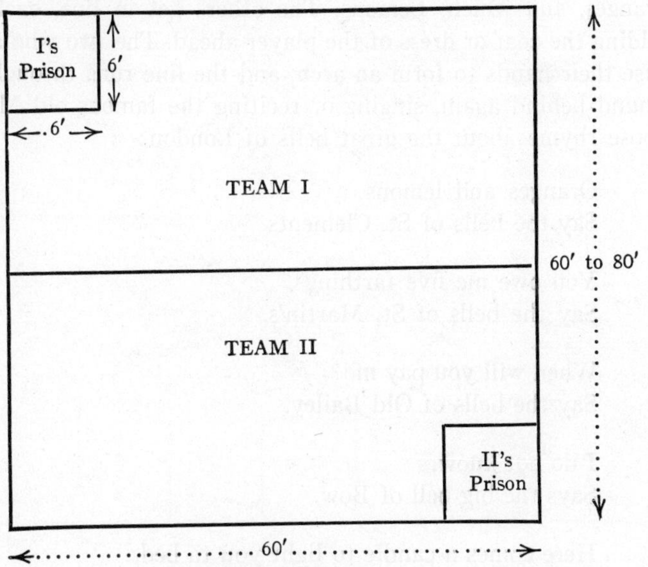

Prisoner's Base: II

Players can only be tagged in enemy territory. Rescuing is as in the first version; but rescuer and ex-captive may both be tagged while returning. A team wins as in the other game, the unoccupied prison being regarded as the team's base.

Stealing Sticks.—This follows the first version of Prisoner's Base, with the addition of 4 sticks in each base. Each team has a stick guard, who stands in front of the base, but cannot enter it until an enemy enters it. The winner is determined by the number of sticks stolen. A player cannot be tagged after he has entered the base and touched a stick, until he has returned with it to his own base.

D. SINGING AND RHYMING GAMES

ORANGES AND LEMONS

Two players are counted out to stand in the center of the room with joined hands. They agree which of them is to be called Oranges, and which, Lemons. The others get in line, each one holding the coat or dress of the player ahead. The two who are It raise their hands to form an arch, and the line runs through and around behind again, singing or reciting the famous old Mother Goose rhyme about the great bells of London:

Oranges and lemons,
Say the bells of St. Clements.

You owe me five farthings,
Say the bells of St. Martin's.

When will you pay me?
Say the bells of Old Bailey.

I do not know,
Says the big bell of Bow.

Here comes a candle to light you to bed,
And here comes a chopper to CHOP off your head!

At the word "chop," the arch made of four hands descends, imprisoning the player just passing through. Then one of the two players who are It whisper to the captive, so low that the others cannot hear, "Oranges or Lemons?" The player must choose one or the other, whispering as softly. He gets behind the It whose name he has chosen, clasping him around the waist.

This ends only when all the players are either Oranges or Lemons. The Leaders or Its call out "Hold tight!," and all clasp more tightly; then "Go!" and a tug of war results. This ends when one line pulls the other across a chalk line drawn on the floor under the arch.

As originally sung, the complete rhyme, which can be found in *Mother Goose,* was sung.

THE FARMER IN THE DELL

One player is counted out to be the Farmer, and stands in the center. The other players circle around him, singing:

Oh, the farmer in the dell,
The farmer in the dell;
Heigh-ho, the merry-oh,
The farmer in the dell.

As they sing the next verse, the Farmer bows gravely before a player of the opposite sex, chooses her as his Wife, and she enters the ring with him. Each stanza has four lines, the first, second and fourth the same, except for the "Oh" beginning the first line. The second stanza begins with this line:

Oh, the farmer takes a wife.

At the third stanza,

Oh, the wife takes a child,

the Wife chooses some player of the opposite sex for the child, and he, too, enters the ring. Successively, as similar stanzas are sung, a Nurse, a Cat, a Rat and a Cheese are chosen and enter the circle. Then all together sing the last stanza,

Oh, the cheese stands alone.

At the end of the fourth line of this, everybody tries to run away from the cheese. Whomever he catches first becomes the Farmer for the next time.

OATS, PEAS, BEANS AND BARLEY GROW

One player is counted out to be the Farmer, and stands in the center. The other players dance around him, singing:

Oats, peas, beans and barley grow,
Oats, peas, beans and barley grow,
Nor you nor I nor nobody knows
How oats, peas, beans and barley grow.

The line stands still as the second stanza is sung, each player except the Farmer acting out each line realistically:

First the farmer sows his seed,
Then he turns and takes his ease,
Stamps his foot and claps his hands,
And turns him round to view his land.

During the first two lines of the next stanza, the Farmer kneels before a player of the opposite sex. At the third line, this partner is pushed into the ring.

Waiting for a partner,
Waiting for a partner,
Open the ring and let him in,
And we will gaily welcome him.

The two within the ring now kneel, while the others dance or skip around, singing:

Now you're married you must obey,
You must be true to all you say,
You must be kind, you must be good,
And help your wife to chop the wood!

The Farmer now kisses the wife; and the Wife thereupon becomes the Farmer for the next game.

LONDON BRIDGE

Two players, who are counted out to be the Bridge, stand with their hands joined to form an arch. The other players form a line, one behind the other, and pass under the arch and round again, singing:

London bridge is falling down,
Falling down, falling down.
London Bridge is falling down,
My fair lady!

Each stanza is similarly four lines long, the first and third lines being identical, and the second line a repetition twice of the last three syllables of the first line. The other stanzas are:

You stole my watch and kept the key,
Kept the key, etc. . . .

Off to prison you must go. . . .

Take the key and lock her up. . . .

At the last word of the fourth stanza, the arch falls, and a player is captured. The two players who are the Bridge, having already agreed that one is to be represented by a Diamond Necklace and the other by a Gold Pin, take the player off to a place designated as the Prison, and whisper: "Which would you rather have, a diamond necklace or a gold pin?" Whichever is chosen, the player stands as Number Two in a line which will be prepared for a tug of war. The two players who are the Bridge return, and the game continues so, until all the other players belong to one line or the other.

The two players who are the Bridge take their places at the heads of these two lines. The tug of war is as in Oranges and Lemons. The two players who let go first become the Bridge for the next game; if none lets go, the first two who were caught become the Bridge. Instead of these words, various older forms of the song may be sung instead.

THE MULBERRY BUSH

One player is counted out to be the mulberry bush, and stands in the center of the ring, while the others dance around in a circle, singing:

Here we go round the mulberry-bush,
The mulberry-bush, the mulberry-bush;
Here we go round the mulberry-bush,
All on a summer morning.

The last line is sometimes sung as "All on a sunshiny morning." Each stanza is four lines long, patterned like the above. With each succeeding stanza down to the last, the players stand still and imitate realistically the motions about which they sing. The common stanzas are:

This is the way we wash our clothes. . . .

This is the way we dry our clothes. . . .

This is the way we make our shoes. . . .

This is the way we mend our shoes. . . .

This is the way the gentlemen walk. . . .

This is the way the ladies walk. . . .

Other stanzas may be added, dealing with mangling, smoothing, or ironing clothes, doing other housework, cleaning our rooms, and so on. To end the game, the players sing the first stanza, as at the beginning of the game. A new mulberry bush is then chosen, and the game goes on.

The Bramble Bush.—In this variation, the only difference is in the song, which commences:

Here we go round the bramble-bush,
The bramble-bush, the bramble-bush,

Here we go round the bramble-bush,
On a cold frosty morning.

Each stanza ends "On a cold frosty morning."

LOOBY LOO

The players join hands, forming a circle. As they sing the song, they march around, acting out the actions: putting the right hands inside the circle; then outside the circle; then shaking it; and, finally, turning around slowly. After each action stanza, the first or chorus stanza is sung. This, and the first action stanza, proceed:

Here we go Looby, Loo;
Here we go Looby, light;
Here we go Looby, Loo,
All on Saturday night.

I put my right hand in,
I put my right hand out;
I give my right hand a shake, shake, shake,
And turn myself about.

Other action stanzas begin: I put my left hand in; I put my right elbow in; I put my left elbow in; I put my right foot in; I put my left foot in; I put my little head in; and, I put my whole self in (in which the players jump in and out of the line of the circle).

Looby, Looby.—In this variation, the song is sung and danced with added actions to each stanza. The first stanza is:

Now we dance Looby, Looby, Looby,
Now we dance Looby, Looby, light;
Shake your right hand a little,
And turn you round about.

In subsequent stanzas, the first line of this is used, followed by the two, three, four or five action lines, and always ending "And turn you round about." These action lines, after "Shake your right hand a little," include: shaking your left hand; shaking your right foot; shaking your left foot; and, shaking your head. Thus a later stanza would be:

Now we dance Looby, Looby, Looby,
Now we dance Looby, Looby, light;
Shake your right hand a little,
Shake your left hand a little,
Shake your right foot a little,
Shake your left foot a little,
Shake your head a little,
And turn you round about.